THE LAW OF INTERNATIONAL TRADE IN AGRICULTURAL PRODUCTS

From GATT 1947 to the WTO Agreement on Agriculture

The Law of International Trade in Agricultural Products

From GATT 1947 to the WTO Agreement on Agriculture

Dr Melaku Geboye Desta
LL.B., LL.M., Ph.D.

KLUWER LAW INTERNATIONAL
THE HAGUE · LONDON · NEW YORK

Published by:
Kluwer Law International
P.O. Box 85889, 2508 CN The Hague, The Netherlands
sales@kli.wkap.nl
http://www.kluwerlaw.com

Sold and Distributed in North, Central and South America by:
Kluwer Law International
101 Philip Drive, Norwell, MA 02061, USA
kluwerlaw@wkap.com

Sold and Distributed in all other countries by:
Kluwer Law International
Distribution Centre, P.O. Box 322, 3300 AH Dordrecht, The Netherlands

Library of Congress Cataloging-in-Publication Data is available

Printed on acid-free paper

ISBN 90-411-9865-2

Kluwer Law International incorporates the imprint Martinus Nijhoff Publishers.

Typeset by BookEns Ltd, Royston, Herts

Printed and bound by Antony Rowe Ltd, Eastbourne

This book is dedicated
to the memory of my father
Geboye Desta

TABLE OF CONTENTS

ACKNOWLEDGEMENT

I feel honoured to take this opportunity to express my thanks to a number of people and institutions who have helped me in different ways in the research and writing of this book.

My first and foremost thanks go to Professor Hans van Houtte for his constant encouragement throughout the course of the research and his useful comments on earlier drafts. I am also pleased to express my thanks to Professor Marco Bronckers who has kindly written a Foreword to the book. He has also given me several useful comments and suggestions on earlier drafts.

In conducting the research, I have benefited hugely from my less than two months of stay at the Legal Affairs Division of the WTO. I am grateful to the members of the Division in general, and to Jeffrey Gertler, Joost Pauwelyn and Werner Zdouc, in particular, for the inspiring discussions I had with them.

My wife Abosent Yimer, my daughter Hanna and my son Amanuel have paid dearly throughout the course of this work. Despite my endless disappearance behind a pile of books and the computer screen for seven days a week, I have always enjoyed their unfailing understanding, love and support. This work is as much theirs as it is mine.

Finally, I would like to express my gratitude to the Katholieke Universiteit Leuven, Belgium, where the research for this book was done on a grant from the university.

Dr Melaku Geboye Desta
January 2002
CEPMLP, University of Dundee, United Kingdom

FOREWORD

It is a genuine pleasure for me to write some words of introduction to this book, and thus to be associated with its publication. With this book, Dr Melaku Geboye Desta makes a major contribution to the literature on world trade law. He deals with some of the most important and controversial issues in the WTO, which are often debated yet where the applicable rules are least understood: market access and, notably, subsidies in agricultural trade.

Dr Desta charts this highly complex territory in a rigorous and lucid way. He states the law as it stands, including its on-going interpretation in WTO dispute settlement, with welcome clarity. This is already no mean achievement. Yet happily he does not stop there. Dr Desta also gives us food for thought, by pointing out the weaknesses of some of these rules, and by offering proposals for their improvement. It is fortunate too that he has used his natural affinity with the problems encountered by developing countries to highlight on a number of occasions how such issues as agricultural subsidies continue to affect developing countries adversely, and how the present WTO rules afford them inadequate relief.

In other words, Dr Desta's book throws sunlight on the intricacies of a topic known so far to only a precious few. "Sunlight", Louis Brandeis wrote almost a century ago before he went on to become a member of the US Supreme Court, "is the best of disinfectants". He used this felicitous phrase in a book which did not deal with agriculture, but the title of which, "Other People's Money", aptly summarizes the root of the problem with undisciplined agricultural subsidies: when governments dispense these subsidies too liberally, they become a problematic expense for the taxpayers of the subsidizing country, and impose an unjustified burden on competing producers in other exporting and importing countries.

Now that Dr Desta's book has come to light, we no longer have any excuse for being vague or non-committal about agricultural trade, the rules that currently apply, and the need for their reform. Dr Desta's work forces us to become specific, to address the persistent questions raised particularly by agricultural subsidies head on. In this way, Melaku Geboye Desta achieves a goal to which all lawyers worth their salt aspire: he has made his mark not just in the legal profession but, more importantly, he has contributed to the betterment of society. For this, he is to be congratulated.

Professor Marco Bronckers
Brussels/Leiden, January 2002

CHAPTER 1

GENERAL INTRODUCTION

The development of a rules-based liberal multilateral trading system has been a long and painful process. Although the fundamental economic and philosophical tenets for a multilaterally arranged liberal trading regime had been in place since at least the early 19th century, practical steps in that direction were taken only after the world paid dearly in two devastating world wars – both of which were caused, at least in part, by the then prevailing mercantilist approach to international trade and the resulting nationalism.[1] The legal and institutional foundations of the present trading system were laid with the object as much of giving effect to the underlying economic principles as of pacifying the post-war world.

1.1 The Economic Rationale for Free Trade

At the theoretical level, there is virtually a consensus among international economists that there are net mutual gains from trade between countries. The explanation is given by the theory of *comparative advantage*. Developed in 1817 by David Ricardo and further corroborated subsequently by the theories of specialization and economies of scale, the theory of comparative advantage argues that since no two countries are identical in their natural and human resource endowments, the "differences give each country a 'comparative advantage'" over others in some products. Trade translates the individual advantages of many countries into maximum productivity for all. The differences which naturally exist between countries can be exploited to their mutual benefit by reaching arrangements enabling each to specialize in the production of what it can produce relatively well and exchange its products for what others are specializing in. Specialization in few products allows each to produce at a larger scale and more efficiently than would otherwise be the case – it enables them to achieve economies of scale in production.[2]

According to the principle of comparative advantage, it is immaterial whether a country has absolute advantage in the production of all products, or that another

---

1 A decline of 60 per cent in trade volumes in the early 1930s "is now seen as an important reason for the depth of the depression at that time and the rise of nationalism, which ultimately led to World War II." WTO, "Globalization and Trade", in *Annual Report 1998*, p. 37.

2 "In many industrial processes", writes Samuelson, "when you double *all* inputs, you may find that your output is more than doubled; this phenomenon is called '*increasing* returns to *scale*.'" P. Samuelson, *Economics* (10th ed. McGraw-Hill Auckland, 1976) p. 28 (italics in original). See also P. Krugman, and M. Obstefeld, *International Economics: Theory and Practice* (4th ed. Addison-Wesley, 1997) pp. 13–37.

country has an absolute disadvantage in the production of every product. In as long as there is a difference in their relative level of productive efficiency, which is normally the case, "there is potential from trade *for all* trading partners, regardless of how countries compare absolutely."[3] Two reasons are often given to explain why productive efficiency might differ across countries – differences in technology and in factor endowments. Since no two countries are the same in all respects, "the case for specialization through trade is a general case, applying to all countries."[4]

Stated in policy terms, the theory teaches that international trade based on the comparative advantages of countries, and not on the artificial incentives resulting from protective trade barriers (such as quotas or tariffs) or stimulants (such as export subsidies), enhances global welfare in the interest of all trading nations. In line with the laissez faire philosophy of Adam Smith,[5] the theory of comparative advantage makes a compelling case in favour of the least possible level of government intervention on the flow of international trade.[6] As summarized by Nobel Laureate Paul Samuelson, "there is essentially only one argument for free trade or freer trade, but it is an exceedingly powerful one, namely: Free trade promotes a mutually profitable division of labor, greatly enhances the potential real national product of all nations, and makes possible higher standards of living all over the globe."[7]

The theory has long been one of the most robust and widely-accepted

---

3 WTO (1998) *supra* n. 1, p. 38 (italics in original).

4 Ibid. Samuelson writes: "Whether or not one of two regions is absolutely more efficient in the production of every good than is the other, if each specializes in the products in which it has a *comparative advantage* (greatest relative efficiency), trade will be mutually profitable to both regions. Real wages of productive factors will rise in both places. ... An ill-designed prohibitive tariff or quota, far from helping the protected factor of production, will instead reduce its real wage by making imports expensive and by making the whole world less productive through eliminating the efficiency inherent in the best pattern of specialization and division of labor. This simple principle provides the unshakable basis for international trade." Samuelson (1976), *supra* n. 2, p. 673. For an interesting illustration with the help of examples as to how a country that is less efficient in absolute terms at producing everything can still have comparative advantage in some products and can potentially benefit from trade, see Krugman and Obstefeld (1997) *supra* n. 2, p. 14; and WTO, *Introduction to the WTO: Trading into the Future* (2nd rev. ed., Geneva 1999) p. 9.

5 In one of his often-quoted paragraphs, Adam Smith wrote the following: "As every individual ... endeavours as much as he can both to employ his capital in the support of domestic industry, and so to direct that industry that its produce may be of the greatest value; every individual necessarily labours to render the annual revenue of the society as great as he can. He generally, indeed, neither intends to promote the public interest, nor knows how much he is promoting it. By preferring the support of domestic to that of foreign industry, he intends only his own security; and by directing that industry in such a manner as its produce may be of the greatest value, he intends only his own gain, and he is in this, as in many other cases, led by an invisible hand to promote an end which was no part of his intention." A. Smith, *An Inquiry into the Nature and Causes of The Wealth of Nations*, (First Published in 1776; new edition by Edwin Cannan, University of Chicago Press, Chicago 1976, hereafter *Wealth of Nations*) Book IV, Chapter II, p. 477. A "full laissez faire" situation is defined by Paul Samuelson as a situation of "complete governmental noninterference with business." Samuelson (1976), *supra* n. 2, p. 41.

6 In the words of Alan Sykes, "[t]he normative economic case for free trade ... in one way or another rest[s] on the premise that government intervention into international trade flows creates economic 'inefficiency' and that inefficiency is a bad thing." A. Sykes, "Comparative Advantage and the Normative Economics of International Trade Policy" (1998) 1 *Journal of International Economic Law*, No. 1, p. 57.

7 Samuelson (1976), *supra* n. 2, p. 692.

propositions in economics.[8] However, governments were unable or unwilling to go beyond paying lip-service to these theories up until the end of World War II.[9] Describing the international situation which prevailed on the eve of the war, Clair Wilcox wrote: "Intensive economic nationalism marked the rest of the decade [the 1930s]. Exports were forced; imports were curtailed. ... Each nation wanted to sell much and buy little."[10] The mercantilist philosophy that "imports are bad, exports good"[11] still held its sway in the minds and deeds of the government policy makers of most countries. All sorts of barriers were erected on the flow of international trade. After the enactment of the notorious Smoot-Hawley Tariff Act of the US in May 1930,[12] which elevated the level of customs tariffs to their highest in the history of that country, many other countries followed suit.[13] Non-tariff measures, including subsidies, quotas and quantitative restrictions proliferated, and tension reigned in the sphere of inter-state economic relations.

1.2 Laying the Legal and Institutional Foundations for Freer Trade

The use of bilateral treaties to regulate trade between states has had a very long,[14] albeit largely unsuccessful, history. But intensive and meaningful moves in the direction of multilateral treaties of an economic nature are a thing of the inter-war and the post-war periods. Indeed, the present multilateral trade arrangements were designed as part of the overall post-war strategy for peace. On top of the economic rationale for a multilaterally-agreed discipline of free trade, they were the embodiment of the lessons learnt from those devastating World Wars – the "lessons of disaster" as Robert Hudec puts it.[15] The most important lesson was that the policy of trade restriction and discrimination has been proved wrong.[16] Multilateral

---

8 See WTO (1998) *supra* n. 1, p. 38; Krugman and Obstefeld (1997) *supra* n. 2, p. 13; and WTO (1999) *supra* n. 4, p. 9.

9 See, for example, R. Hudec, *World Trade Diplomacy and the Law of GATT* (Praeger Publishers, 1975) p. 4.

10 C. Wilcox, *A Charter for World Trade* (Arno Press, 1949) quoted in Hudec (1975) *supra* n. 9, p. 5.

11 J. H. Jackson, *Legal Problems of International Economic Relations* (West Publishing Co. 1977) p. 435. Under this theory, "the goal of nations in their economic relations was to amass gold or other treasure, so as to maximize national power... The goal therefore was 'to sell more to strangers yearly than we consume of theirs in value' ". J. H. Jackson, *The World Trading System: Law and Policy in International Economic Relations* (2nd ed. the MIT Press, 1997) p. 14.

12 Krugman and Obstefeld (1997) call it "a remarkably irresponsible tariff law". See *supra* n. 2, p. 237.

13 Canada, Cuba, France, Mexico, Italy, Spain, Australia, and New Zealand may be mentioned as examples. See Hudec (1975) *supra* n. 9, p. 5.

14 See, for instance, the treaty of commerce between England and Portugal, concluded in 1703 and reproduced in *The Wealth of Nations*, Vol. Two, Book IV, Chapter IV, *supra* n. 5, pp. 54 to 55.

15 Hudec (1975) *supra* n. 9, p. 4.

16 Ibid., pp. 5–6. International trade economists still uphold the validity of this conclusion. According to Alan Winters, "[h]istory has definitely taught us one huge lesson: closed and tightly managed economies do not prosper." A. Winters, *Trade Policy as Development Policy: Building on Fifty Years' Experience* paper prepared for the UNCTAD X High-Level Round Table on Trade and Development (Bangkok, 12 February 2000).

liberalization of the flow of trade across national frontiers was thus adopted as the leading strategy of post-war economic policy. The long-accepted economic case for free trade found strong support from the realization that international peace is very much linked with, if not dependent upon, international economic problems.[17] True to its peace mission, the principles of non-discrimination and transparency constituted the central pillars of the new system.

The process to lay the groundwork for the post-war international trading arrangement was started already before the war ended. As soon as the war was over, countries formally commenced negotiations for the establishment of an international institution in the name of the International Trade Organization (the ITO) and, on 24 March 1948, signed its Charter with a number of important objectives. The first of these objectives was to create conditions of stability and well-being which are necessary for peaceful and friendly relations among nations.[18] The ITO was designed to be one of the specialized agencies of the United Nations,[19] but the Charter never entered into force due mainly to the withdrawal of support from its original "sponsor" – the US. Interestingly enough, "United States interests and farm organisations led the opposition to the creation of an ITO."[20]

---

17 US President Truman is quoted to have said in 1947 that "trade and peace are inextricably linked." See WTO (1998) *supra* n. 1, p. 37. According to Professor Hudec, "the postwar design for international trade policy was animated by a single-minded concern to avoid repeating the disastrous errors of the 1920s and the 1930s." Hudec (1975) *supra* n. 9, p. 4.

18 *Final Act of the United Nations Conference on Trade and Employment*, (held at Havana, Cuba from 21 November 1947 to 24 march 1948) UN doc. E/Conf. 2/78 (hereafter the Havana Charter) Article 1, first paragraph. Article 1 provides the other purposes and objectives of the ITO and may be summarized as follows: to attain higher standards of living, full employment and conditions of economic and social progress and development; to assure a large and steadily growing volume of real income and effective demand, to increase the production, consumption and exchange of goods, and thus to contribute to a balanced and expanding world economy; to foster and assist industrial and general economic development, particularly of those countries which are still in the early stages of industrial development, and to encourage the international flow of capital for productive investment; to further the enjoyment by all countries, on equal terms, of access to the markets, products and productive facilities which are needed for their economic prosperity and development; to promote on a reciprocal and mutually advantageous basis the reduction of tariffs and other barriers to trade and the elimination of discriminatory treatment in international commerce; to enable countries, by increasing the opportunities for their trade and economic development, to abstain from measures which would disrupt world commerce, reduce productive employment or retard economic progress; and to facilitate through the promotion of mutual understanding, consultation and co-operation the solution of problems relating to international trade in the fields of employment, economic development, commercial policy, business practices and commodity policy.

19 See Article 86.1 of the Havana Charter; on specialized agencies in the UN system, see Article 57 of the UN Charter.

20 J. Hillman, "The US Perspective", in K. Ingersent, A. Rayner, and R. Hine (eds.) *Agriculture in the Uruguay Round* (St. Martin's press, New York 1994) p. 29. Further back in history, opposition from US agricultural interests had served as one of the main causes for US cancellation in 1865 of what is known as the "Reciprocity Treaty" of 1854 between Canada and the US. See M. Trebilcock and R. Howse, *The Regulation of International Trade* (2nd ed. Routeledge, New York 1999) p. 38.

As a result of this failure of the ITO project, the General Agreement on Tariffs and Trade (the GATT), which had initially been negotiated to serve as an interim arrangement pending the entry into force of the ITO Charter, was made operational on a "provisional" basis.[21] The chapter of the draft ITO Charter on commercial policy was incorporated into the GATT with only little modification, opened for signature on 30 October 1947 and entered into force on 1 January 1948. In general, the theory of comparative advantage, backed by the operational principles of reciprocity and most-favoured-nation treatment, found its expression in the letter and spirit of the General Agreement.[22]

1.3 Agriculture in the Multilateral Trading System

However, absolute free trade is still easier preached than practised. It could only be set as an ultimate target – and an elusive one at that. Neither the still-born ITO nor its "provisional" substitute the GATT was intended to create a completely free trading environment. However compelling the case may be for free trade, in the real world, trade policies are usually dictated by interest group politics rather than pure cost-benefit economic analysis. More than half-a-century after the entry into force of the General Agreement, trade is definitely freer, but not yet totally free, from government intervention. All governments interfere with trade by, *inter alia,* erecting different forms of barriers to imports and at times even to exports, and by providing artificial inducement to exports in the form of subsidies.

The degree of interference varies from sector to sector. The theme of this book is about a category of products for the trade of which the economic as well as political cases for liberal trade have not been learnt for long, or learnt only to mean the opposite of what they said.[23] Indeed, there are evidences that Ricardo himself had implied in his works that "'agriculture is different' and must be

---

[21] Note that the General Agreement entered into force on the basis of a document entitled "Protocol of Provisional Application of the General Agreement on Tariffs and Trade" according to which contracting parties undertook to apply "provisionally on and after 1 January 1948" Parts I and III of the GATT, and "Part II of that Agreement *to the fullest extent not inconsistent with existing legislation.*" PPA (Geneva, 30 October 1947) paras. 1(a) and (b) (italics added).

[22] As Jackson observes, "the trend toward wide use of the MFN clause necessarily coincided with the decline of mercantilism. The mercantilist view that in any commercial exchange one nation wins and the other loses does not mix with the concept of reciprocal arrangements implicit in the MFN principle." 435. Jackson (1977) supra n. 11, p. 435.

[23] Agriculture is the "long-neglected" (See Arthur Dunkel, as quoted in *GATT Focus News Letter* No. 41, October 1986, p. 8) and the most heavily protected sector of international trade. Schaffer *et al* observed that "virtually all nations provide protection to domestic agricultural interests unconstrained by the GATT." R. Schaffer, B. Earle, and F. Augusti, *International Business Law and Its Environment* (3rd ed. West Publishing Co. 1996) p. 292. Johnson wrote that "[f]ew countries – perhaps none – are willing to engage in negotiations about their domestic agricultural programs. And most countries consider their non-tariff barriers quite direct extensions of their domestic programs." D. G. Johnson, in the "Foreword" to J. Hillman, *Non-tariff Agricultural Barriers* (University of Nebraska Press, 1978) p. X. See also OECD, *The Uruguay Round: A Preliminary Evaluation of the Agreement on Agriculture in the OECD Countries* (Paris 1995).

treated differently."[24] And when governments got together to negotiate for the multilateral liberalization of international trade, agricultural products were considered as a special case befitting the status of an exception rather than the rule. This was reflected in the content of the first drafts as well as the final versions of both the Havana Charter[25] as well as the General Agreement. Two particularly important trade-restrictive and protective measures generally outlawed by the General Agreement were explicitly, albeit conditionally, permitted for agricultural products. They concern the use of quantitative restrictions and export subsidies – the two traditional weapons used by governments to protect domestic producers from foreign competition in the domestic market and to artificially enhance the competitive advantage of their producers in foreign markets, respectively.[26] What is more, even in areas where no such express exceptions were provided, countries often ignored the rules more in the area of agriculture than elsewhere.

It is interesting to observe that the special treatment of agricultural products in respect of both market access as well as export subsidies has a long history. In his famous treatise entitled *The Wealth of Nations,* Adam Smith wrote the following in 1776:

> "The law of England ... favours agriculture not only indirectly by the protection of commerce, but by several direct encouragements. Except in times of scarcity, the exportation of corn is not only free, but encouraged by a bounty. In times of moderate plenty, the importation of foreign corn is loaded with duties that amount to a prohibition. The importation of live cattle, except from Ireland, is prohibited at all times, and it is but of late that it was permitted from thence. Those who cultivate the land, therefore, have a monopoly against their countrymen for the two greatest and most important articles of land produce, bread and butcher's meat."[27]

Exactly two hundred years later, Paul Samuelson wrote that "[a]griculture may be

---

[24] Hillman (1978) supra n. 23, p. 35. According to Hillman "[o]ne may also detect in certain free-trade arguments – e.g., in Ricardo – a selective attitude in the deliberate writing off of land lords as too reactionary to make good economic agents in comparison with entrepreneurs. The implication is that 'agriculture is different' and must be treated differently." Ibid.

[25] See, *inter alia,* ITO Charter Articles 20 (on quantitative restrictions), and 27 and 28 (on export subsidies on primary products).

[26] See *inter alia* Krugman and Obstefeld (1997) *supra* n. 2, p. 5. The special treatment of agriculture in the General Agreement reflected the power and influence of the US at the end of the Second World War. As Dam observed "no treaty that impinged upon the U.S. Farm program could receive the constitutionally-required senatorial approval." See K. Dam, *The GATT: Law and International Economic Organization* (Chicago, University of Chicago Press, 1970) p. 260.

[27] *The Wealth of Nations*, Book III, Chapter IV, *supra* n. 5, p. 443. One can also learn from this book that subsidies on the exportation of corn from England, called by then "bounties", were introduced in 1688. There was an "act for ... encouraging the exportation of corn", the preamble of which states that "it hath been found by experience, that the exportation of corn and grain into foreign parts, when the price thereof is at a low rate in this kingdom, hath been a great advantage not only to the owners of land but to the trade of this kingdom in general." Ibid. Book I, Chapter XI, p. 215.

the unlucky stepchild of nature, but it is often the favoured foster child of government."[28]

In order to maintain this status of agriculture as their "favoured foster child" in the face of the rules of the General Agreement, governments have pursued a variety of strategies. Firstly, from the very beginning, they framed the important provisions of the General Agreement in such a way as to exclude agriculture from their coverage. Indeed, GATT rules on agriculture were drafted "to be consistent with the agricultural policies of the major signatories rather than vice versa."[29] As will be developed further in this book, this applies to such crucial areas as quantitative restrictions and export subsidies. Secondly, in order to avoid the little remaining discipline, some countries, notably the US, secured "country-specific derogations" in the form of waivers.[30] Finally, in cases where no such exemptions were available, countries maintained several trade-distorting practices "a large proportion [of which were] ... maintained in blatant violation of the General Agreement."[31] An observer of the evolution of the multilateral trading system has thus been quoted as saying that "GATT came into existence in the immediate aftermath of the war as a pure fruit of the industrial society, of machinery. *It largely disregarded what makes up our past – agriculture –* and what constitutes our future – services. ..."[32]

1.4 The Paradoxes of Agricultural Trade

The position of agriculture in the multilateral trading system is rich with paradoxes. While the system is able to boast a high degree of success in the liberalization of trade in industrial goods whose global average tariffs have progressively fallen from above 40 per cent down to below 4 per cent, agriculture has experienced a reverse development for most part of the lifetime of the GATT – the level of effective protection against the flow of agricultural trade has been rising.[33] The dramatic fall in the share of agriculture vis-à-vis total merchandise trade over time[34] was matched by a rising share of agricultural disputes relative to all GATT cases.[35] While

---

[28] Samuelson (1976), *supra* n. 2, p. 412.

[29] T. Stewart, *The Uruguay Round: A Negotiating History* (Kluwer Law International, 1993 in III Vols.), Vol. I, p. 134.

[30] The other notable case in this respect is Switzerland whose protocol of accession effectively exempted its agriculture from GATT disciplines.

[31] Jackson (1977) supra n. 11, p. 981.

[32] *Journal de Genève*, quoted in *GATT Focus Newsletter* No. 41, October 1986, p. 8.

[33] For example, "agricultural support in 22 industrialised countries rose from an average of about $98 billion per year during the period 1979–1986 to an estimated $ 163 billion in 1993". United States General Accounting Office, *Uruguay Round Final Act* (GAO/GGD-94-83b 1994) p. 133. See also Jackson (1977) supra n. 11, p. 981.

[34] According to WTO sources, while the share of agricultural exports fell from 47 per cent of total merchandise exports in 1970 to just 12 in 1996, the corresponding share of manufactures rose from 38 per cent to 77 per cent over the same period. See WTO (1998) *supra* n. 1, p. 34.

[35] The share of agricultural disputes in GATT for the 1950s was 23 per cent of all disputes, while its share for the following three decades (from 1960 to 1989) stood at 50 per cent. See R. Hudec, *Enforcing International Trade Law: The Evolution of the Modern GATT Legal System* (Butterworth, 1993) p. 327.

agricultural taxes are an important source of government revenue in most developing countries, agricultural subsidies are an important area of budgetary expenditure in the developed countries. According to UNCTAD, the US$350 billion paid in subsidies to OECD countries' agriculture "amount to twice the value of developing country exports."[36] In short, the position of agriculture in the multilateral trading system is so full of maze that it defies any consistent characterization. As Clayton Yeutter, former US Secretary of Agriculture and a key player in the Uruguay Round negotiations for agriculture, put it, "agricultural trade policy has long been enigmatic, often inexplicable, always exasperating, and frequently counter to the long-term best interests of a nation's own agriculturalists. For half a century, it has provided more distortions to the multilateral trading system than any other segment of the global economy. . . . Why so many nations have worked so hard over so many years to impede agricultural trade is almost beyond comprehension!"[37]

Different factors, including the uniquely excessive dependence of agriculture on the vagaries of nature, food security, culture, the environment, etc., have been invoked to justify and defend the special treatment of agricultural trade. In the latest days, a new term called "multifunctionality" has been added to the trade vocabulary as a kind of short hand expression for the so-called non-trade concerns involved in agricultural liberalization.[38] The fact that most developing countries stand to benefit from freer agricultural trade because of their comparative advantage in this sector has been accepted as one of the important reasons for developed countries' lack of will to liberalize agricultural trade. Owing to the huge subsidies provided by virtually all the developed countries, the competition has long been between (tax-paying) developing country farmers and developed country treasuries. Thanks to the subsidies, the world market share of regions with proven comparative disadvantage in agriculture has been rising dramatically,[39] while the opposite has been the case particularly for the developing countries most of which had strong comparative advantage in agriculture. In the words of former GATT Director-General Peter Sutherland, developed country subsidies "led to wasteful surpluses like the 'butter mountains' and 'wine lakes' amidst poverty, and sometimes famine, in the developing world whose farmers have been shut out of the world market by industrialized countries' subsidies".[40]

1.5 Attempts at Liberalizing Agricultural Trade

Successive attempts were made to bring agriculture into the mainstream rules of the multilateral trading system, but they were largely a failure. Over time, agricultural

---

[36] UNCTAD Press Release TAD/INF/2816, 1 September 1999.

[37] C. Yeutter, "Bringing Agriculture into the Multilateral Trading System", in J. Bhagwati, and M. Hirsch (eds.), *The Uruguay Round and Beyond: Essays in Honour of Arthur Dunkel* (Springer Verlag, Germany 1998) p. 61.

[38] Developing countries call it "a form of special and differential treatment for rich countries."

[39] The EU is a text book example of this development. See, inter alia, Krugman and Obstefeld (1997) *supra* n. 2, p. 199 (italics added).

[40] Peter Sutherland, GATT *Focus Newsletter* No. 102 (October 1993) p. 2.

trade became a subject of considerable tensions in international relations.[41] In the beginning of the 1980s, the widespread fear that the old adage – "depressions are farm-led and farm-fed"[42] – might realize for another time necessitated a prompt action. A 1982 GATT Ministerial Conference recognized not only that there was "widespread dissatisfaction with the application of GATT rules and the degree of liberalization in relation to agricultural trade",[43] but also that there was "an urgent need to find lasting solutions" to those problems.[44] The 1986 Punta del Este Declaration which launched the Uruguay Round effectively repeated the old call and stated that "there is an urgent need to bring more discipline and predictability to world agricultural trade."[45]

That these words indeed meant what they said could very easily be gleaned from the course of the negotiations of the Uruguay Round and, to some extent, even from the ongoing negotiations. Agriculture held the key to the success or failure of the entire round. Several negotiating parties, including the US and the so-called Cairns Group countries, "insisted that there would be an agreement on agriculture or no agreement at all."[46] And the result of all those developments is, at least from the legal perspective, definitely encouraging. A separate *Agreement on Agriculture* has emerged out of it. Although its practical impact might be modest in the short-run, the existence of a detailed set of legal rules governing the sector is hoped to furnish a reasonable degree of certainty, predictability, and rule of law in international relations involving the agricultural sector. The groundwork has now been laid for a rules-governed and operationally effective GATT discipline on agriculture. At the same time, this discipline is still in its infancy. Even today, agriculture is a class in itself: it still is the only area where export subsidies are explicitly permitted; three-digit tariff levels are still common only in agriculture; a number of trade-distortive agricultural domestic support measures are still shielded from the remedies of the exemplary dispute settlement system of the WTO, etc. Negotiations are already underway to push the agricultural reform process further. However, full integration of agriculture into the system still appears to be a long distance away.

---

41 It has been reported that "of the 82 disputes submitted to the dispute settlement process between 1980 and 1990, 60 per cent concerned agriculture." OECD (1995) *supra* n. 23, p. 10.

42 Hillman describes this fear as follows: "If substantial agricultural adjustment is not achieved soon and if agricultural protectionism is not reduced or checked there is a danger that, as on two occasions in the past the agriculture sector will be associated with a mass movement toward general economic protection, trade wars, and political breakdown." Hillman (1978), *supra* n. 25, p. 35.

43 GATT, *Thirty-Eighth Session at Ministerial Level: Ministerial Declaration* (L/5424, *BISD* 29S/9-22) adopted on 29 November 1982, p. 10.

44 Ibid., p. 16. See also *Statement by Mr. A. Dunkel, Director-General, to the Punta del Este Ministerial Conference* (MIN(86)/5) 15 September 1986.

45 GATT, *Ministerial Declaration on the Uruguay Round* (MIN.DEC) adopted in Punta del Este, Uruguay, on 20 September 1986, often referred to as the *Punta del Este Declaration,* reproduced in, GATT *Focus Newsletter*, No. 41, (October 1986) p. 4.

46 See United States Department of Agriculture, *Agricultural Outlook* (Dec. 1996) p.22.

1.6 Purpose and Structure of the Book

The purpose of this book is to provide an in-depth analysis of the rules and principles of the multilateral trading system as they relate to trade in agricultural products and the course of their evolution since the conclusion of GATT in 1947. The degree to which agricultural trade has been excluded from the operation of the law governing international trade in general, the real or apparent rationale behind it, and the reaction of the system in the course of its more than half-a-century of existence and evolution will be assessed. Although the primary focus of the book is on the legal aspect of agricultural trade in the GATT/WTO system, every effort has been made to shed light on the underlying policy reasons which shaped this twisted and often unfathomable legal evolution.

The book is structured along the lines of the WTO Agreement on Agriculture itself and has three parts. Part I is a general introduction to the law of international trade and highlights the most relevant principles of the General Agreement. Of the three pillars of the Agriculture Agreement, the subject of market access in general as well as its application to agricultural products is briefly discussed in this Part. The innovative approach of the tariffication of non-tariff barriers to agricultural trade and its corollary arrangements, such as the minimum and current access commitments, the special safeguard clause, as well as the problem of "dirty tariffication" and resulting tariff peaks are all addressed in this part of the book. However, the book does not treat such issues as sanitary and phytosanitary measures, technical barriers, etc. which have a significant impact on agricultural market access but fall outside the scope of the Agriculture Agreement.

Parts II and III deal with the interrelated subjects of agricultural export subsidies and domestic support, respectively. These two parts share a lot in common. Consequently, discussions made in one part are often crucial for an understanding of discussions in the other part. At the same time, the history of the multilateral trading system as well as the current make-up of the AoA show that the regimes applying to these two forms of subsidies have followed quite distinct lines of development from the early days and merit separate treatment.

Part II starts with an introduction into the concept of export subsidies and its evolution in the course of negotiations for the Charter of the ITO and the General Agreement in 1947, examines the landmark 1955 amendment to GATT Article XVI, evaluates the developments brought about by the plurilateral-type Tokyo Round Subsidies Code and analyzes the important achievements of the "multilateral" Uruguay Round Agreement on Subsidies and Countervailing Measures (the SCM Agreement). Once the general conceptual and contextual framework is set, the particular export-subsidies discipline introduced by the Agriculture Agreement is discussed at length in Part II. The analysis of pertinent provisions of the Agriculture Agreement on the subject is supplemented by a detailed study of important cases on the subject already decided by the WTO Dispute Settlement Body over the past few years, including the high-profile *FSC* dispute and the *Canada Dairy* case.

Part III also starts with a brief introduction to the concept of domestic support – a term used for the first time in the Agriculture Agreement – and discusses the problem of terminology involved, the policy underpinnings behind the practice, the incidence and the forms of domestic support, their causal role for the proliferation of market access restrictions and export subsidies, and the particular problems involved in attempting to regulate the practice. After a brief historical survey of how the regulation of domestic support measures was approached by both the draft as well as the final versions of the ITO Charter, the pertinent provisions of the General Agreement as it stood in 1947 will be closely examined. The introduction by the 1955 review session of what is often known as the doctrine of reasonable expectations, the achievements of the 1979 Subsidies Code in the area, and the relevant GATT jurisprudence which developed over the lifetime of the system are also discussed at length. This is followed by an in-depth discussion of the most fundamental improvement to the rules governing the practice of domestic subsidies in general and that of agricultural domestic support in particular which came out of the Uruguay Round. The tri-coloured categorization of all forms of agricultural domestic support measures (amber, blue and green) and the different forms of commitments for the reduction of the Aggregate Measurement of Support (AMS) on amber box measures constitutes the core of Part III.

Finally, chapter 11 looks at the ongoing agricultural negotiations at the WTO – which started in March 2000 as a sector-specific process but were later brought into the broader Development Round by the Doha Ministerial Conference – and tries to provide some perspectives into the future. Although it is still premature to speculate about the possible results of the current negotiations, an attempt is made to draw some inferences from the already known positions of leading WTO members in the process. An effort has been made to analyze the position particularly of the EU in these negotiations – a member that is traditionally associated with foot-dragging in agricultural trade negotiations – and to assess its potential role in shaping the direction of rules of the multilateral trading system in the area of agriculture.

PART I

THE LAW OF AGRICULTURAL MARKET ACCESS

CHAPTER 2

MARKET ACCESS UNDER THE GENERAL AGREEMENT

2.1 INTRODUCTION

Market access is the central problem of international trade. Countries often erect different forms of barriers against the free entry of goods and services into their territories[1] for a variety of motives – ranging from the protection of domestic producers to raising revenue for the government. The progressive liberalization of international trade through the dismantling of the plethora of barriers erected against it has always been the primary goal of the multilateral trading system since its inception in the still-born ITO and its *de facto* substitute, the GATT, down to its full-fledged successor, the WTO.

As such, we are here dealing with the issue of import barriers to international trade. This part of the book deals with GATT/WTO law on market access of goods in general and agricultural products in particular. It has two chapters. Chapter 2 gives a general introduction to the law of tariffs and non-tariff measures under the General Agreement. Such general points as GATT practice of the negotiation and binding of tariffs in Schedules of Concessions, the most-favoured nation and national treatment principles, the legal status of non-tariff barriers, and the like will be discussed in this chapter. The chapter tries to introduce the basic principles of the General Agreement, lay down the necessary conceptual background for a proper appreciation of the subsequent discussions and put agricultural market access issues in their appropriate context. This is followed by a brief discussion of the special treatment given to agricultural products in the market access provisions of GATT 1947. Although both tariffs and non-tariff measures are discussed in this section, the fact that non-tariff measures have been the main instruments of protection in use by many countries suggests that we dwell more on non-tariff barriers. The extent to which contracting parties included specific tariff bindings on agricultural products in their GATT tariff schedules, the range of non-tariff measures exceptionally allowed in the sphere of agriculture (particularly those based on Art. XI:2) and the like will be treated in this chapter. There are relatively more cases decided by GATT CONTRACTING PARTIES in the area of agricultural market access than in that of

[1] Although not as common as import barriers, countries also erect export barriers for a variety of reasons – ranging from the protection of sensitive military technology to guaranteeing food security in time of shortage. In this book we deal only with import barriers.

export subsidies (part II) and domestic support (Part III), which will be discussed at appropriate places in the present Part.

Chapter 3 deals with the market access provisions of the Uruguay Round Agreement on Agriculture together with an evaluation of the degree to which GATT 1947 loopholes in favour of agricultural protectionism have been improved thereby. The "tariffication" of non-tariff agricultural trade measures, the reduction commitments assumed by the parties on the resulting tariffs, the special safeguard provisions, and the special treatment option will be of particular emphasis in this section of the text. Finally, some concluding remarks on the trends and perspectives in the area of agricultural market access will be made in this chapter.

2.2 Forms of Import Barriers: Tariffs and Non-Tariff Measures

Import barriers are often put under either of two broad categories – tariffs and non-tariff barriers. Tariffs are a form of taxes imposed when trade items are imported. They are the oldest and the simplest form of trade policy measures.[2] Although there are several different forms of tariffs,[3] the major ones are *ad valorem*, specific, and mixed. While an *ad valorem* tariff is calculated as a percentage of the value of imported goods, specific tariffs are "levied as a fixed charge for each unit of goods imported" and are assessed on the basis of criteria other than value (e.g. weight, volume, etc.). Mixed tariffs combine these two.[4] *Ad valorem* tariffs are the most frequently used type of tariffs in GATT/WTO schedules of concessions. But, specific tariffs have also been very common especially in agricultural products.[5]

Non-tariff barriers, on the other hand, generally refer to all sorts of governmental practices, other than tariffs, that may serve the purpose of discouraging the importation of goods and services. Hillman defines them expansively as "any governmental device or practice other than a tariff which directly impedes the entry of imports into a country and which discriminates against imports – that is, does not apply with equal force on domestic production or distribution."[6] The concept of non-tariff barriers thus covers both border and non-border measures having the effect of impeding imports.

---

2 See P. Krugman, and M. Obstefeld, *International Economics: Theory and Practice* (4th ed. Addison-Wesley, 1997) p. 187.

3 Others include compound tariffs (ad valorem plus specific), technical tariffs (e.g. based on sugar, alcohol, etc. content), seasonal tariffs and alternative tariffs. See WTO Secretariat, *Market Access: Unfinished Business – Post-Uruguay Round Inventory and Issues* (Special Studies 6, Geneva 2001), p. 46; and S. Laird, *Multilateral Approaches to Market Access Negotiations*, WTO Staff Working Paper (TPRD-98-02, May 1998) p. 6.

4 For an interesting analysis of tariffs, see Krugman and Obstefeld (1997) *supra* n. 2, pp. 187–197.

5 See Laird *supra* n. 3, p. 6. As observed by Laird, not only are specific duties "very common in agriculture in all countries", they also lack both transparency and even-handedness: "The ad valorem equivalent of … specific duties … varies inversely with international prices … [Consequently,] specific rates … tend to fall more heavily on developing countries and low-cost suppliers." Ibid. p. 6.

6 J. Hillman, *Non-tariff Agricultural Barriers* (University of Nebraska Press 1978) pp. 14–15.

Non-tariff measures are of an unlimited variety and a high degree of complexity. A GATT survey in 1960 came up with a list of over 800 non-tariff barriers.[7] The list goes beyond such clear and straightforward cases as quantitative import restrictions and prohibitions applied at the border. It also includes a variety of forms of domestic programmes which play an important role as disguised barriers to the importation of competing products. Nonetheless, and despite this diversity, non-tariff measures have often been catalogued under a fair number of categories of practices, including: customs valuation, import licensing requirements, subsidies, investment performance requirements, discriminatory and restrictive government procurement policies, technical standards, health and safety regulations, labelling laws, inspection and testing requirements, and lack of intellectual property protection.[8]

Tariffs were the principal instruments of agricultural market access restriction until World War I.[9] According to Hillman, quantitative restrictions, one of the most "universally" applied forms of non-tariff barriers, were introduced in Europe in 1926, and quickly spread to the rest of the world.[10] However, it was largely after the "trade breakdown" of the 1930s that "a wide variety of non-tariff protective devices were invented and instituted by countries all over the world to bolster sagging agricultural prices."[11] These range from "sumptuary laws" requiring the mixture of a "fixed ratio of domestic and foreign grain"[12] to import licensing, quotas, veterinary and quarantine regulations, state trading and direct intervention in the production and marketing processes by the government.[13]

2.3 The Approach of the General Agreement Towards Tariffs and Non-Tariff Barriers

2.3.1 Tariffs: The Lesser of Two Evils?

Both tariffs as well as non-tariff border measures primarily serve the purpose of curtailing imports. Although the ultimate objective of the multilateral trading system is the elimination of all sorts of barriers to international trade, under prevailing conditions, this remains only an ideal goal. The real world is not yet (if it will ever be) ready for such a situation. As a result, the approach adopted for the regulation of

---

7 See J. H. Jackson, W. Davey, and A. Sykes, *Legal Problems of International Economic Relations: Cases, Materials and Text* (3rd ed., West Publishing Co. 1995), p. 377. The significance of this list has been questioned by some writers in the field. It has been said, for instance, that the list is "an arbitrary one to which no special significance should be attached." Gardner Patterson, cited in Hillman (1978), *supra* n. 6, p. 198. It remains true nonetheless that non-tariff barriers constitute a difficult and unmanageable mix of governmental measures defying any clear description or classification.

8 See Jackson *et al* (1995) *supra* n. 7, p. 378.

9 Hillman (1978) *supra* n. 6, p. 6.

10 Ibid., p. 7.

11 Ibid., p. 6.

12 Sumptuary laws such as milling regulations, were imposed on millers in Norway, France, and Germany in the period 1927–1929 and then spread throughout the world. See Ibid., p. 41.

13 See Ibid., pp. 41–42.

these two broad categories of barriers is different – GATT favours tariffs over non-tariff measures.

This is not because of any fundamental difference as such in the protectionist and trade-distortive effect of tariffs and non-tariff measures. If high enough, a tariff may be equivalent in its effect to an explicit quantitative restriction or prohibition. Rather, given the existence of a plethora of such barriers to trade in practically all countries, and the impossibility of a removal of them all at once, GATT had to approach the matter in a pragmatic way. The most that could be done under the circumstances was prioritize and choose between two evils. GATT's choice was clear – contracting parties had to abandon non-tariff barriers in favour of tariffs and that they had to enter into periodic negotiations for a stage-by-stage reduction of the latter. This is so because, inter alia, tariffs are believed to have many advantages over non-tariff measures, the most important of which is transparency.[14]

As a matter of principle, therefore, the General Agreement prohibits the use of non-tariff border measures[15] while it allows tariffs. On the basis of this general principle, the General Agreement introduced a system by which countries would negotiate and fix the maximum amount of tariffs they would impose on imports, called bindings, consolidated in special documents for each contracting party, known in GATT parlance as Schedules of Concessions. Countries do not have the obligation to reduce their tariffs; the system is designed in such a way that contracting parties would select the products of their import or export interest and negotiate on the maximum amount of tariffs to be levied upon their importation.

GATT has sponsored eight rounds of multilateral trade negotiations,[16] most of which can simply be called tariff negotiation rounds. The ninth round has been launched by the 4th WTO Ministerial Conference which was held in Doha, Qatar, from Nov. 9–14 2001 – called the Doha Development Round. In earlier rounds (from the first negotiations in Geneva in 1947 up to the Dillon Round of 1960–61), the approach took the form of traditional bilateral bargains by way of offers, counter-offers, acceptances, etc. on a product-by-product basis, just like what happens in daily transactions among private business people.[17] This is what is

---

[14] Sam Laird has summarized the major problems of NTMs as follows: they are "difficult to quantify, costly to administer, costly to consumers, costly to exporters (in terms of lost trade), inefficient ways of creating jobs, lack transparency, are inherently discriminatory, and are most intensively used against developing countries and transition economies. They also drive a wedge between world prices and domestic prices, so that domestic firms are relatively unaffected by price trends on world markets and have little incentive to adopt new technologies or modern business practices." Laird, *supra* n. 3, p. 11. See also W. Surrey and D. Wallace (eds.) *A Lawyer's Guide to International Business Transaction* (1977) quoted in J. Barton, and B. Fisher, *International Trade and Investment* (Little Brown & Co. Boston 1986) p. 146.

[15] For details, see discussion on GATT Article XI, *infra* **section 2.5.1.**

[16] The eight rounds are the following: Geneva (1947), Annecy (1949), Torquay (1951), Geneva (1956), Dillon (1960–1961), Kennedy (1964–1967), Tokyo (1973–1979), and Uruguay (1986–1994). After the failure of the 3rd Seattle Ministerial Conference in late 1999, the ninth round is now widely expected to be launched by the 4th Doha Ministerial Conference scheduled for 9–13 November 2001.

[17] For a description of the bargaining process, see Laird *supra* n. 3, pp. 8–11; J. H. Jackson, *Legal Problems of International Economic Relations* (West Publishing Co. 1977) p. 474–75, and J. Croome, *Reshaping the World Trading System: A History of the Uruguay Round* (Geneva 1995) p. 38.

known as the "request and offer" approach. In such approaches, "offer of tariff cuts (concessions) were seen as negotiating 'coin' with which to pay for the requested concession by other parties."[18] However, with growth in the number of negotiating contracting parties and in the amount of products covered, this approach proved to be rather cumbersome. It was thus changed into a formula-based, "linear-cut", approach in the Kennedy Round by which participants would agree on the overall percentage of reduction of tariffs across all product categories and then undertake a product-by-product negotiation only on those products for which they either did not want to have a binding at all, or chose to keep with tariff levels higher than those entailed by the agreed percentage cuts. The formula-based approach helped to bring a better level of tariff harmonization than the product-by-product approach of earlier rounds. It is also believed to be more favourable to the developing countries.[19] However, agricultural products were excluded from the linear-cut approach of the Kennedy Round.[20] The formula-based approach was used in the Tokyo Round as well,[21] but not as such during the Uruguay Round largely because of a US objection. Instead, the method of request and offer, supplemented by what is called the "zero for zero" approach,[22] was used in the Uruguay Round subject to an overall target of a 30 per cent average rate of reduction.[23]

2.3.2 Schedules of Concessions

The Schedules of Concessions of each contracting party are annexed to the General Agreement and are incorporated to form "an integral part of Part I of this Agreement."[24] The reference in this paragraph to *Part I* of the Agreement has been important in that those provisions of the General Agreement that fall under Parts I and III are not subject to the "grandfather clause". The "grandfather clause" is a provision included in the Protocol of Provisional Application (the PPA) which makes the obligations of GATT 1947 under Part II subordinate to inconsistent pre-existing national legislation. In its terms, contracting parties are obliged to apply "provisionally on and after 1 January 1948" Parts I and III of the General Agreement, and "Part II of that Agreement *to the fullest extent not inconsistent with existing legislation*."[25] The provisions of Part II of the General Agreement are thus obligatory only and in as much as they do not go against pre-existing legislation of

---

18 Laird *supra* n. 3, p. 8.

19 See Ibid.

20 See J. H. Jackson, *World Trade and the Law of GATT* (Bobbs-Merrill, 1969) p. 227.

21 The formula used particularly in the Tokyo Round is the so-called "Swiss Formula", which was designed such that higher tariffs would be cut deeper than the lower ones.

22 This is a reference to the case whereby a number of countries agreed to reduce their tariffs to zero in specified sectors; e.g. pharmaceuticals.

23 Laird, *supra* n. 3, p. 8.

24 Article II:7 of the General Agreement.

25 Protocol of Provisional Application of the General Agreement on Tariffs and Trade, Geneva, 30 October, 1947, paras. 1(a) and (b) (italics added).

the contracting parties.[26] The incorporation of the Schedules of Concessions into Part I of the General Agreement makes them binding on governments regardless of whether they had pre-existing inconsistent national legislation in force.

Under Article II of the General Agreement, contracting parties agreed to accord to the commerce of each other "treatment no less favourable than that provided for in the appropriate Part of the appropriate Schedule annexed to this Agreement."[27] Accordingly, products originating from contracting parties are exempt from ordinary customs duties in excess of those specified in their respective Schedules of Concessions. Countries are allowed to include in their schedules "terms, conditions or qualifications" to which those schedules are subject.[28]

The meaning and scope of this phrase has been at issue in several disputes under both GATT and the WTO. A 1981 panel said that "the words 'terms, conditions or qualifications' in para. 1(b) of Article II could not be interpreted to mean that countries could explicitly or by the manner in which a concession was administered actually limit a given concession to the products of a particular country."[29] This interpretation got its oft-quoted expression in 1989 in what is commonly referred to as the *US Sugar Headnote* case:

> "in Article II:1(b), the words 'subject to the ... qualifications set forth in that Schedule' are used in conjunction with the words 'shall ... be exempt from ordinary customs duties in excess of those set forth in [the Schedule]' ... Article II:1(b) permits contracting parties to qualify the obligation to exempt products from customs duties in excess of the levels specified in the Schedule, not however to qualify their obligations under other Articles of the General Agreement ... the title of Article II is 'Schedules of Concessions' and that the ordinary meaning of the word 'to concede' is 'to grant or yield'. This also suggests ... that *Article II permits contracting parties to incorporate into their Schedules acts yielding rights under the General Agreement but not acts diminishing obligations under that Agreement.*"[30]

---

26 The effect of this clause falls disproportionately against the interests of the weaker countries of the time, for they had no pre-existing elaborate rules on those subjects. On the other hand, if we take the US, for example, we can very easily see that almost all of the important rules of the GATT were not only preceded by their domestic counterparts, but that the former were modelled after the latter. Speaking about this historical development, Kees Jan Kuilwijk writes: "From 1934 to 1945, 32 bilateral trade agreements were negotiated and accepted by the United States. Nearly all of the clauses in GATT may be traced to one or another of the forerunner provisions contained in these agreements." K. J. Kuilwijk, *The European Court of Justice and the GATT Dilemma: Public Interest Versus Individual Rights?* (Ten Brink Meppel, 1996) pp. 49–50. Note also that the grandfather exception has been abolished by the WTO Agreement; see *infra* chapter 3.3.

27 Article II:1(a) of the General Agreement.

28 Article II:1(b) of the General Agreement.

29 *European Economic Community – Imports of Beef from Canada – Recourse to Article XXIII by Canada*, report of the panel (L/5099 *BISD* 28S/92) adopted on 10 March 1981, para. 4.5(a).

30 *United States – Restrictions on Imports of Sugar* report of the panel (L/6514, *BISD* 36S/224) adopted on 22 June 1989 (hereafter *US Sugar Headnote*), para. 5.2 (italics added). The interpretation of the *US Sugar Headnote* panel was reaffirmed in the *Bananas* case at both the panel and the Appellate Body

The products of contracting parties are also exempt from "other duties or charges of any kind[31] imposed on or in connection with importation in excess of those imposed on the date of this Agreement or those directly and mandatorily required to be imposed thereafter by legislation in force in the importing territory on that date."[32]

Once a tariff rate is fixed, the only liberty left with individual contracting parties is downwards and not upwards.[33] Normally, any act of raising bound tariff levels should follow the mechanisms specified by the General Agreement itself.[34] The principal provision in this regard is Article XXVIII on the renegotiation of commitments.[35] In any renegotiation of commitments under this and most other provisions on the subject, contracting parties are required "to endeavour to maintain a general level of reciprocal and mutually advantageous concessions not less favourable to trade than that provided for in this Agreement prior to the negotiations."[36]

Through the eight multilateral negotiation rounds it has already sponsored so far,

---

cont.

levels. See *European Communities – Regime for the Importation, Sale and Distribution of Bananas* report of the panel (WT/DS27/R/USA . . .) issued 22 May 1997, para. 7.118; and report of the Appellate Body (WT/DS27/AB/R . . .) adopted 25 September 1997, para.154. For more on the *Bananas* case, see *infra* chapter 3.3. In *Canada Dairy*, the Appellate Body observed the following: "Under Article II:1(b) of the GATT 1994, the market access concessions granted by a Member are '*subject to*' the 'terms, conditions or qualifications set forth in [its] Schedule'. In our view, the ordinary meaning of the phrase 'subject to' is that such concessions are without prejudice to and are *subordinated to*, and are, therefore, *qualified by*, any 'terms, conditions or qualifications' inscribed in a Member's Schedule." *Canada – Measures Affecting the Importation of Milk and the Exportation of Dairy Products*, report of the Appellate Body (WT/DS103/AB/R, WT/DS113/AB/R) adopted 27 October 1999, para. 134 (italics in original).

31 This is a reference to the different forms of charges including those mentioned under GATT Article VIII:4. The fundamental GATT principle regarding such fees and formalities is that they "shall be limited in amount to the approximate cost of services rendered and shall not represent an indirect protection to domestic products or a taxation of imports or exports for fiscal purposes." (GATT Article VIII:1). Despite this rule, however, there are evidences that "some countries set these as a percentage of the value of the imports not on the cost of the service . . ." See Laird, *supra* n. 3, p. 7.

32 An "Understanding on the Interpretation of Article II:1(b) of the General Agreement on Tariffs and Trade 1994" has been agreed at the end of the Uruguay Round, wherein it is provided that "In order to ensure transparency of the legal rights and obligations deriving from para. 1(b) of Article II, the nature and level of any 'other duties or charges' levied on bound tariff items, as referred to in that provision, shall be recorded in the Schedules of Concessions annexed to GATT 1994 against the tariff item to which they apply."

33 That is why the bound tariff levels are often called "ceiling bindings".

34 For details on renegotiation and modification of tariff Schedules, see Jackson (1969) *supra* n. 20, pp. 229–238.

35 Other provisions with a similar effect are Article XXVII, which allows a contracting party to withdraw or withhold any concession which was initially negotiated with a government which has not become, or has ceased to be, a contracting party; Article XXIV:6 on compensatory adjustments in case of customs unions and free trade areas; and Article XVIII:7 on the establishment by a developing country of a particular industry for whose protection the country may wish to modify or withdraw a concession. There are also exceptional cases, which involve provisional withdrawal (at least in theory) of proportional concessions. They include Article XXIII cases, anti-dumping and countervailing duties (Article VI), emergency actions (Article XIX), and waivers (XXV).

36 Article XXVIII:2 of the General Agreement.

GATT has brought about not only an extension of bindings to more product categories – a nearly all-inclusive one by now[37] – but also their significant reduction,[38] which can be called a success by any standards. The significance of the tariff negotiations may be discerned from the fact that tariffs on 44 per cent of industrial-product imports of developed countries are not just reduced, but eliminated – they are already receiving duty-free treatment.[39]

A noteworthy feature in all this for present purposes is that although this process was in principle applied to all products, at the practical level, agricultural products were always approached with more reluctance throughout the tariff negotiation rounds. A simple example would be the exemption of agricultural products from the "linear-cut" approach of the Kennedy Round.[40] By the beginning of the Uruguay Round, there were far fewer agricultural products with bound tariff levels than industrial products,[41] and that even when bindings existed, the tariffs on agricultural products were on the average much higher than their industrial counterparts.[42] Moreover, the most important barriers to agricultural trade have been non-tariff measures. Each such measure being in some ways an evasion of the results of tariff reductions, the little that existed in the form of agricultural tariff bindings has been further diminished by the widespread use of such non-tariff barriers.

2.3.3 Non-Discrimination: The MFN and National Treatment Principles

We have seen that the negotiation and binding of tariffs often took the form of bilateral and, in the later days, multilateral bargains between countries having substantial interest in the import and export of particular goods. Once bound as a result of the bilateral or multilateral negotiations of some contracting parties, however, the benefits of the concessions are immediately and unconditionally extended to all other contracting parties through the cardinal principle of Most-

---

37 The percentage of tariffs (in terms of tariff lines and not weighted according to trade volume or value) bound under the GATT at the conclusion of the Uruguay Round looks the following: 99 per cent for developed countries, 73 per cent for developing countries, and 98 per cent for transition economies. Agricultural products have all been subject to bound tariffs as a result of the tariffication process adopted by the Uruguay Round. See WTO, *Introduction to the WTO: Trading into the Future* (2nd rev. ed. Geneva 1999) p. 6; see also Laird, *supra* n. 3, pp. 1–2.

38 The average tariff rate for industrial goods has come down from above 40 per cent to less than 4 per cent. See WTO (1999), *supra* n. 37, p. 8.

39 This has just become a reality after the Uruguay Round tariff cuts of most developed countries have been phased in over the last five-year period since January 1995. See Ibid., p. 16.

40 See J. H. Jackson, "The General Agreement on Tariffs and Trade", in Surrey and Wallace (1977) *supra* n. 14, p. 144.

41 According to the OECD, "only 58 per cent of the agricultural tariffs of the developed economies were bound in the GATT, compared to 78 per cent of industrial tariffs." OECD, *The Uruguay Round: A Preliminary Evaluation of the Agreement on Agriculture in the OECD Countries* (Paris 1995) p. 10. See also D. Hathaway, and M. Ingco, *Agricultural Liberalization and the Uruguay Round*, paper presented at the World Bank Conference on "The Uruguay Round and the Developing Economies" (January 26–27, 1995) p. 2.

42 See Jackson (1977) *supra* n. 17, pp. 479 and 981–982.

Favoured-Nation Treatment (MFN). Enshrined in the very first Article of the General Agreement, this principle of non-discrimination stipulates that "any advantage, favour, privilege or immunity granted by any contracting party to any product originating in or destined for any other country shall be accorded immediately and unconditionally to the like product originating in or destined for the territories of all other contracting parties."[43]

The MFN clause thus provides every contracting party the assurance that their goods will be treated on equal basis with the like products of other contracting parties. Put differently, the MFN clause creates the obligation, on every contracting party, to treat all contracting parties in the same manner. The advantages, favours, etc. referred to here are not only those given to contracting parties, but also those granted to non-contracting parties. In other words, any advantages, favours, etc. granted by a GATT contracting party to a non-contracting party are automatically extended to all GATT contracting parties, while no such advantage given by a contracting party to another contracting party is so extended to a non-contracting party.[44] The success of the GATT in the reduction and, in many cases even elimination, of tariffs is at least in part attributed to its adoption of the MFN standard, which served the purpose of "universalizing" the most liberal of results negotiated between any two participants. The fact that it is one of two provisions falling within Part I of the General Agreement[45] safeguarded the MFN provision of GATT 1947 from the "grandfather clause" of the PPA and made it mandatory on all contracting parties regardless of pre-existing legislation on the subject.

The MFN principle does not, however, address the relationship between imported and domestically-produced products. It does not, for instance, require equality of treatment between these two groups of products. This is taken care of rather by the equally important principle of national treatment incorporated under Article III of the General Agreement. The national treatment clause prohibits the use of any internal measures for the purpose of affording protection to domestic production.[46] Article III:2 provides that "[t]he products of the territory of any contracting party imported into the territory of any other contracting party shall not be subject, directly or indirectly, to internal taxes or other internal charges of any kind in excess of those applied, directly or indirectly, to like domestic products. Moreover, no contracting party shall otherwise apply internal charges to imported or domestic products in a manner contrary to the principles set forth in paragraph 1." Unlike the

---

[43] Article I:1 of the General Agreement.

[44] Subject of course to any bilateral (or, other, as the case may be) agreement in force between the contracting party and the non-contracting parties concerned. For an interesting analysis on this subject, see Jackson (1969) *supra* n. 20, chapter 11.

[45] The other provision of the General Agreement falling under Part I is Article II on Schedules of Concessions.

[46] Para. 1 of Article III provides the principle as follows: "The contracting parties recognize that internal charges, and laws, regulations and requirements affecting the internal sale, offering for sale, purchase, transportation, distribution or use of products, and internal quantitative regulations requiring the mixture, processing or use of products in specified amounts or proportions, should not be applied to imported or domestic products so as to afford protection to domestic production."

MFN provision, Article III does not concern itself with the application of import duties; it deals only with the use of internal, domestic, measures on imported products. Import duties differ from internal taxes in that "(a) they are collected at the time of, and as a condition to, the entry of the goods into the importing country, and (b) they apply exclusively to imported products without being related in any way to similar charges collected internally on like domestic products."[47]

This principle also applies to all governmental regulatory measures, as stated under paragraph 4 of Article III: "The products of the territory of any contracting party imported into the territory of any other contracting party shall be accorded treatment no less favourable than that accorded to like products of national origin in respect of all laws, regulations and requirements affecting their internal sale, offering for sale, purchase, transportation, distribution or use." The non-discrimination obligation of contracting parties to give an identical treatment to all like products imported from all contracting parties under the MFN clause has thus been further pushed into the domestic realm by the national treatment clause which mandates treatment of imported products at least on the same level as those of domestically produced ones. This principle precludes any evasion of the liberalizing effects of tariff reductions by resorting to internal measures which discriminate against imported like products.[48]

2.4 Non-Tariff Barriers Under the General Agreement in General

Given GATT's goal of reducing trade barriers and its successful operation especially in the reduction of tariffs to their historic minimum, the use of one or another of the non-tariff barriers would obviously circumvent those beneficial results. This problem has been recognized since the very inception of the General Agreement.[49] Although full of loopholes and exceptions, GATT has had rules prohibiting or restricting the use of such non-tariff measures as quantitative restrictions (Article XI), subsidies (Article XVI), state trading enterprises (Article XVII), customs valuation (Article VII), etc. as disguised instruments of protectionism. In practice, however, these provisions did not deter countries from widely applying non-tariff measures. Some of the provisions themselves were not meant to impose any strict discipline against their use (e.g. see the original version of Article XVI on subsidies); others were either simply disregarded[50] or not applied to their letter and spirit.

---

47 Havana Reports, U.N.Doc.ICITO/1/8, p. 62, as quoted in Jackson (1969) *supra* n. 20, p. 281.

48 For more on this issue, see *infra* chapter 9 on domestic support.

49 As Jackson wrote, although GATT was "designed primarily as a tariff-reducing agreement, it was realized from the beginning that substantive obligations governing other ways in which countries could limit the inflow of goods were necessary; otherwise, the tariff reduction obligations would be meaningless. ... For this reason, GATT became a general code of conduct relating to international trade." Jackson (1977) quoted in Barton and Fisher (1986) *supra* n. 14, p. 143.

50 Several countries maintained quantitative restrictions in violation of Article XI and without any justification on the basis of any of the exceptions. See Jackson (1969) *supra* n. 20, pp. 307–308.

Furthermore, with the progressive reduction of tariffs, countries were somehow forced to resort to non-tariff barriers in order to meet domestic protectionist pressures. As rightly observed, the "removal or reduction of tariffs has an 'incitement' effect in that it gives incentive to the introduction of new, or the extension of old, non-tariff measures in order to maintain levels of domestic protection."[51] Several countries complained that "tariff concessions bought by them in earlier rounds of negotiations had been substantially impaired by non-tariff measures for the protection of agriculture applied in the importing countries."[52] Committee II of GATT, after reviewing notifications made by contracting parties regarding their agricultural policies, affirmed in its report that "the tariff is not generally the only or even the principal method; the use of a wide variety of non-tariff devices is deeply entrenched in most countries."[53] According to the Committee, despite the claims of many countries to justify their use of quantitative restrictions through the balance-of-payments outlets, "[q]uantitative restrictions appeared to be an integral part of the protective systems in force in many countries and had no longer any connexion with the balance-of-payments position of those countries."[54] This was further corroborated by the Committee's third report that "*quantitative import restrictions* (frequently in discriminatory form and sometimes amounting to complete embargoes) was found to be particularly widespread .... Of thirty-four countries examined, more than two thirds were found to apply quantitative restrictions to imports of all or some types of meat, fish, cereals, dairy products, vegetable oils and on sugar."[55]

The problem of non-tariff barriers thus turned out to be the most important challenge for the multilateral trading system mainly since the Kennedy Round (1964-1967).[56] It was observed in 1970 that:

> "If the only thing at stake were high tariffs, one's judgment could be more generous. ... Unfortunately for the prestige of the GATT, however, the most important restrictions on international trade in temperate agricultural commodities are non-tariff barriers, and a large proportion of these are maintained in blatant violation of the General Agreement. The continued violation of the terms of the General Agreement by a substantial number of

[51] Hillman (1978), *supra* n. 6, p.13. Paradoxical though it may seem, some have even speculated that the possibility to employ non-tariff barriers has played a facilitating role for the success of tariff reduction negotiations under GATT. Brian Hindley has been quoted as speculating that "the Kennedy Round success was facilitated by each government's knowledge that it could, if necessary, substitute non-tariff methods of protection for the explicit tariff protection it was giving up." Ibid. p. 29.

[52] GATT, *First Report of Committee II*, adopted (COM.II/5) on 29 May 1959, *BISD* 8S/125.

[53] GATT, *Second Report of Committee II*, adopted (L/1192) on 20 May 1960, *BISD* 9S/115.

[54] Ibid. p. 117.

[55] GATT, GATT, *Agricultural Protection: Third Report of Committee II*, (L/1461 *BISD* 10S/137), adopted on 15 November 1961.

[56] The Kennedy Round is the first ever multilateral trade negotiation round in which non-tariff barriers were identified as a problem deserving special attention and the first important agreement in the area was achieved in this round addressing the problem of anti-dumping measures.

contracting parties has become such a way of life that little embarrassment seems to be felt by national representatives and no effort is made to suggest dates on which violations might be terminated."[57]

The Tokyo Round is known largely for its breakthrough in the field of non-tariff barriers. Although of a plurilateral nature, agreements were reached in the area of subsidies and countervailing measures (the Subsidies Code), technical barriers (sometimes called the Standards Code), import licensing procedures, government procurement, customs valuation, and anti-dumping measures (replacing the Kennedy Round antidumping agreement). Under the Uruguay Round Agreements, not only are the contents of these Tokyo Round agreements improved, they were also changed in nature into multilateral agreements binding on all Members of the WTO.[58]

In all the provisions of the General Agreement, it is only at three places that we find an express or implied reference to agricultural products with a view to giving them separate treatment: Articles XI, XVI, and XX on quantitative restrictions, subsidies, and general exceptions, respectively.[59] While subsidies have been the subject of distinct parts of this book,[60] those on quantitative restrictions are treated here.[61]

2.5 Quantitative Restrictions Under GATT Article XI

Article XI: *General Elimination of Quantitative Restrictions*

1. No prohibitions or restrictions other than duties, taxes or other charges, whether made effective through quotas, import or export licences or other measures, shall be instituted or maintained by any contracting party on the importation of any product of the territory of any other contracting party or on the exportation or sale for export of any product destined for the territory of any other contracting party.
2. The provisions of paragraph 1 of this Article shall not extend to the following:
   (a) Export prohibitions or restrictions temporarily applied to prevent or relieve critical shortages of foodstuffs or other products essential to the exporting contracting party;
   (b) Import and export prohibitions or restrictions necessary to the application of standards or regulations for the classification, grading or marketing of commodities in international trade;

57 K. W. Dam, *The GATT: Law and International Organization* (University of Chicago Press, 1970), p. 257.

58 The only exception is the Agreement on Government Procurement, which still is a plurilateral agreement.

59 See specifically para. 2 of Article XI which expressly mentions agricultural products as possible exceptions to the rule on quantitative restrictions; para. 3 of Article XVI which prescribes a milder regime for the use of export subsidies on the larger category of primary products; and paragraphs (b) and (i) of Article XX which make an indirect reference to agricultural products via, respectively, the general exceptions allowed for the imposition of import restrictive measures for the protection of human, animal and plant health, and export prohibitions permitted in order to make necessary domestic materials available to a domestic processing industry during periods when the domestic price is held below the world price as part of a governmental stabilisation plan.

60 See *infra* Parts II and III on export subsidies and domestic support, respectively.

61 The general exceptions under Article XX are not, however, dealt with in this work.

(c) Import restrictions on any agricultural or fisheries product, imported in any form,* necessary to the enforcement of governmental measures which operate:
 (i) to restrict the quantities of the like domestic product permitted to be marketed or produced, or, if there is no substantial domestic production of the like product, of a domestic product for which the imported product can be directly substituted; or
 (ii) to remove a temporary surplus of the like domestic product, or, if there is no substantial domestic production of the like product, of a domestic product for which the imported product can be directly substituted, by making the surplus available to certain groups of domestic consumers free of charge or at prices below the current market level; or
 (iii) to restrict the quantities permitted to be produced of any animal product the production of which is directly dependent, wholly or mainly, on the imported commodity, if the domestic production of that commodity is relatively negligible.

Any contracting party applying restrictions on the importation of any product pursuant to sub-paragraph (*c*) of this paragraph shall give public notice of the total quantity or value of the product permitted to be imported during a specified future period and of any change in such quantity or value. Moreover, any restrictions applied under (i) above shall not be such as will reduce the total of imports relative to the total of domestic production, as compared with the proportion which might reasonably be expected to rule between the two in the absence of restrictions. In determining this proportion, the contracting party shall pay due regard to the proportion prevailing during a previous representative period and to any special factors** which may have affected or may be affecting the trade in the product concerned.

Ad Article XI
* "The term 'in any form' in this paragraph covers the same products when in an early stage of processing and still perishable, which compete directly with the fresh product and if freely imported would tend to make the restriction on the fresh product ineffective."

** "The term 'special factors' includes changes in relative productive efficiency as between domestic and foreign producers, or as between different foreign producers, but not changes artificially brought about by means not permitted under the Agreement."

Ad Article XI, XII, XIII, XIV, and XVIII
"Throughout Articles XI, XII, XIII, XIV, and XVIII, the terms 'import restrictions' or 'export restrictions' include restrictions made effective through state-trading operations."

2.5.1 General

Article XI of the General Agreement uses a sweeping language proscribing all forms of quantitative restrictions. The basic principle of the General Agreement regarding non-tariff border barriers in general and quantitative restrictions in particular is stated under Article XI.1: "No prohibitions or restrictions other than duties, taxes or other charges, whether made effective through quotas, import or export licences or other measures, shall be instituted or maintained by any contracting party on the importation of any product of the territory of any other contracting party or on the exportation or sale for export of any product destined for the territory of any other contracting party." Although with its own list of exceptions,[62] this provision prohibits all forms of trade-restrictive border measures

[62] For a discussion of the exceptions to this rule, see *infra* **section 2.5.3**

which take a form other than duties. In principle, this prohibition applies to all products – agricultural as well as industrial – regardless of whether or not they are subject to bound tariff rates.[63]

In the case of agricultural products, however, the actual picture is completely different. A number of countries have traditionally maintained different forms of quantitative restrictions – in many instances in clear violation of provisions of the General Agreement. According to a report by a GATT Group on Quantitative Restrictions, the "principal GATT provisions advanced" as justifying the maintenance of quantitative restrictions were: Article VIII, Article XI:2(c), Article XII, Article XIII:1, Article XVIII:B, Article XVIII:C, Article XIX, Article XX, Article XXI, Article XXV:5, the Protocol of Provisional Application, protocols of accession, and the Agreement on Import Licensing Procedures.[64] Of these, agriculture is given an explicit special treatment only under Article XI:2. The following discussion will first give a general overview of the rule of the General Agreement on quantitative restrictions and then concentrate on those provisions which provide for a special regime for agricultural non-tariff barriers giving a loophole for their proliferation.

2.5.2 Scope of Article XI

Although Article XI is entitled "General Elimination of Quantitative Restrictions", quantitative restrictions are in fact only one type of non-tariff measure.[65] The scope of Article XI is so wide that it covers all forms of non-tariff border measures. Indeed, the term "quantitative restrictions" as used under Article XI of the General Agreement appears to be synonymous with the term "non-tariff border barriers". It refers to all sorts of trade barriers at the border that take a form other than customs duties.[66] The extent of the restriction – whether it is a prohibition of all imports or only a mere limitation of the amount – does not matter here. Nor is the method used to effect the restrictions important.[67] It is simply provided that trade measures that are applied on the importation (or exportation) of goods that take a non-tariff form are prohibited regardless of the type of measure used – "whether they are quotas, import or export licences or other measures". As the *Japan Semi-Conductors* panel rightly pointed out, the wording of Article XI is comprehensive; it applies to "all measures instituted or maintained by a contracting party prohibiting or restricting the importation, exportation or sale for export of products other than measures that

---

63 See. Jackson *et al*, *supra* n. 7, p. 421.

64 GATT, *Report of the Group on Quantitative Restrictions and other Non-Tariff Barriers*, (L/5713 *BISD* 31S/212) adopted on 30 Nov. 1984 (hereafter GATT Group on Quantitative Restrictions), para. 20.

65 See Ibid. para. 5.

66 "Customs duties" is here used in a wider sense so as to refer to "duties, taxes or other charges" in the sense of Article XI:1.

67 For further discussion on this point, see arguments presented by the United States representative in the *Republic of Korea – Restrictions on Imports of Beef – Complaint by the United States*, report of the panel (L/6503 *BISD* 36S/268) adopted on 7 Nov. 1989, paras. 27 ff.

take the form of duties, taxes or other charges."[68] The only allowable forms of trade restriction under this principle thus consist of "duties, taxes or other charges". There is one important thing in common between these allowable forms of restrictions – they all take the form of financial levies or tariffs. All other forms of impediments, the non-tariff restrictions or prohibitions, are therefore, in principle, prohibited. This includes three categories of measures – "quotas, import or export licences or other measures" – which may be briefly discussed in turn as follows.

2.5.2.1 "Quotas"

A quota is a quantitative limit set by governments on the amount of allowable imports. A quota may be global[69] or country-specific, and its expression may be in terms of either the value or the quantity of goods to be imported.[70] Owing to the inherently trade-restrictive and distortive nature of quotas, they are expressly prohibited under Article XI of the General Agreement. Taken in relevant part, Article XI:1 provides that no restriction "made effective through quotas ... shall be ... maintained by any contracting party on the importation of any product of the territory of any other contracting party."[71] Hence, they have rightly been termed the "disfavoured device" of protection.[72]

That quotas are prohibited under the General Agreement has not as such been a subject of controversy in GATT dispute settlement history. Rather, most cases involving quotas revolved around the issue of whether they qualified for one or another of the exceptions.[73] There were also some unsuccessful attempts to justify the use of quotas on the basis of Article II:1(b) of the General Agreement.[74] This sub-paragraph provides that the products described in the Schedules of Concessions of the contracting parties "shall, on their importation into the territory to which the

68 *Japan – Trade in Semi-Conductors*, report of the panel (L/6309 *BISD* 35S/116) adopted on 4 May 1988 (hereafter *Japan Semi-Conductors*) para. 104.

69 The term "global quota" is often used "in contrast with quotas allocated on a country-specific basis", i.e. in the sense of expressing the total amount of permitted imports over a given period of time regardless of the origin of products. See *European Communities – Measures Affecting the Importation of Certain Poultry Products*, report of the Appellate Body, WT/DS69/AB/R, adopted 23 July 1998, para. 93. For further discussion of this point, see R. Schaffer, B. Earle, and F. Augusti, *International Business Law and Its Environment* (West Publishing Co. 3rd ed. 1996) p. 329; and Jackson *et al* (1995) *supra* n. 7, p. 377.

70 It can also be fixed as a percentage of the size of the domestic market for a product. On this as well as the advantages and disadvantages of quotas, see Schaffer *et al supra* n. 69, pp. 329–330.

71 See also *United States – Restrictions on Imports of Sugar* report of the panel (L/6514, *BISD* 36S/224) adopted on 22 June 1989, para. 5.1.

72 Jackson *et al* (1995), *supra* n. 7, p. 377.

73 These exceptions are discussed *infra* **section 2.5**; for a practical example of how complex a quota arrangement can become and what the legal challenges could be like, see, inter alia, *Japan – Restrictions on Imports of Certain Agricultural Products* report of the panel (L/6253 – *BISD* 36S/331) adopted on 22 March, 1988 (hereafter *Japan Agriculture*).

74 For a discussion of Article II:1(b), see *supra* **section 2.3.2**; see also *US Sugar Headnote*, *supra* n. 30; and *United States – Restrictions on the Importation of Sugar and Sugar-Containing Products Applied under the 1955 Waiver and under the Headnote to the Schedule of Tariff Concessions*, report of the panel (L6631 *BISD* 37S/228) adopted on 7 November 1990 (hereafter *US Sugar Waiver*).

Schedule relates, and *subject to the terms, conditions or qualifications set forth in that Schedule,* be exempt from ordinary customs duties in excess of those set forth and provided therein."[75] In *US Sugar Headnote,* the US argued that the challenged quotas on raw and refined sugar were maintained on the basis of a right to impose quota limitations which it had reserved in its Schedules of Concessions. Australia, on the other hand, contended that qualifications to concessions made in accordance with Article II:1(b) "cannot justify measures contrary to other provisions of the General Agreement, in particular not quantitative restrictions inconsistent with Article XI:1."[76] The panel agreed with Australia and concluded that Article II:1(b) "permits contracting parties to qualify the obligation to exempt products from customs duties in excess of the levels specified in the Schedule, *not however to qualify their obligations under other Articles of the General Agreement.*"[77] The panel pointed out, in particular, that Article II:1(b) does "not justify the maintenance of quantitative restrictions on the importation of certain sugars inconsistent with the application of Article XI:1."[78]

This is a conclusion that can also be applied to all sorts of non-tariff border barriers other than quotas. The important point thus remains to be that Article XI:1 sets a principle that cannot be overridden by any terms, conditions or qualifications inserted by countries in their Schedules of Concessions. The only permissible justifications are those provisions of the General Agreement which explicitly provide for an exception, such as Paragraph 2 of Article XI on, *inter alia,* agricultural products, and Article XX on general exceptions.

2.5.2.2 "Import Licences"

An import licence is a document issued by governmental authorities as a condition for the importation of certain products.[79] Licences may have a variety of purposes, including trade restriction and the gathering of statistical data.[80] Licences are usually used as means of administering quotas. Indeed, as the *Korea Beef* panel observed, "[t]o the extent that imports are restricted through the application of a WTO compatible import quota, a licensing system is necessary."[81] In international trade

---

[75] Article II:1(b) of the General Agreement (italics added).

[76] *US Sugar Headnote, supra* n. 30, para. 5.1.

[77] Ibid., para. 5.2 (italics added).

[78] Ibid., para. 5.7. In compliance with this ruling, the US replaced the quantitative restrictions with tariff quotas at the same levels. See R. Hudec, *Enforcing International Trade Law: The Evolution of the Modern GATT Legal System* (Butterworth, 1993) p. 569.

[79] Article 1.1 of the *Uruguay Round Agreement on Import Licensing Procedures* defines import licensing as "administrative procedures used for the operation of import licensing regimes requiring the submission of an application or other documentation (other than that required for customs purposes) to the relevant administrative body as a prior condition for importation into the customs territory of the importing Member."

[80] See *European Economic Community – Restrictions on Imports of Dessert Apples: Complaint by Chile,* report of the panel (L/6491 *BISD* 36S/93) adopted on 22 June 1989 (hereafter *Chile Dessert Apples*).

[81] *Korea – Measures Affecting Imports of Fresh, Chilled And Frozen Beef*, report of the panel (WT/DS161/R, WT/DS169/R) issued 31 July 2000, para. 589.

parlance, licensing may be automatic or discretionary. Very often, while licensing regimes intended for import-restrictive purposes are discretionary, those for non-restrictive purposes are automatic.

GATT prohibits only discretionary licensing. The reason is simple – import licensing procedures should not constitute a trade barrier in themselves. In *EC-Minimum Import Prices (MIP)*, for instance, the panel held that automatic import licences were not covered by the rule of Article XI:1.[82] It may not, however, be easy to tell whether a certain system of licensing is discretionary or automatic. In the *MIP* case, one of the issues concerned an EC Regulation prescribing a system of import certificates conditioned upon the lodging of a security to guarantee the undertaking to effect certain imports for as long as the certificate is valid, which is 75 days from issuance. Considering this and the fact that import certificates were to be issued on the fifth working day from lodging, the panel held that "this system did not depart from systems which other contracting parties claimed were justified as automatic licensing."[83] The panel further ruled that "automatic licensing did not constitute a restriction of the type meant to fall under the purview of Article XI:1."[84] The time gap between the application for licences and their issuance has also been found to be important in the determination of the automaticity or otherwise of licensing regimes. In *Japan Semi-Conductors*, the panel found that export licensing practices "leading to delays of up to three months in the issuing of licences for semi-conductors destined for contracting parties other than the United States, had been non-automatic and constituted restrictions on the exportation of such products inconsistent with Article XI."[85] More recently, the *India Quantitative Restrictions* panel followed the approach of these panels and observed that "discretionary or non-automatic licensing systems by their very nature operate as limitations on action since certain imports may not be permitted" and concluded that "a discretionary or non-automatic import licensing requirement is a restriction prohibited by Article XI:1."[86]

The Tokyo Round Agreement on Import Licensing Procedures provided for the fundamental requirement that import licensing procedures be "neutral in application and administered in a fair and equitable manner."[87] Likewise, in furtherance of the

---

[82] See *European Communities – Programme of Minimum Import Prices, Licences, and Surety Deposits for Certain Processed Fruits and Vegetable,* report of the panel (L/4687 *BISD* 25S/68) adopted on 18 October 1978 (hereafter the *MIP* case) para. 4.1.

[83] Ibid. One may, of course, question the wisdom of this conclusion. In a strict legal sense, what matters is not whether a country's practice is similar to, or different from, the practices of other countries. Rather, every governmental practice should be assessed on its merits in the light of the relevant legal obligations pertaining to the country in question. As the *Japan Agriculture* panel rightly emphasized, a country's actions "could, appropriately, be judged only against its obligations under the General Agreement and not against the practices of others." *Japan Agriculture supra* n. 73, para. 5.4.1.3.

[84] *MIP, supra* n. 82, para. 4.1.

[85] *Japan Semi-Conductors, supra* n. 68, para. 118.

[86] *India – Quantitative Restrictions on Imports of Agricultural, Textile and Industrial Products,* report of the panel (WTO/DS90/R) 6 April 1999, para. 5.129.

[87] Article 1 of the Tokyo Round Agreement on Import Licensing Procedures, *BISD* 26S/154 (1980).

basic principle that licensing procedures should not constitute trade barriers in themselves, the Uruguay Round Agreement on Import Licensing Procedures defines automatic import licensing as "import licensing where approval of the application is granted in all cases"[88] and that it is "not administered in such a manner as to have restricting effects on imports."[89] This effect is deemed to exist unless, *inter alia*:

> "(i) any person, firm or institution which fulfils the legal requirements of the importing Member for engaging in import operations involving products subject to automatic licensing is equally eligible to apply for and to obtain import licences;
> (ii) applications for licences may be submitted on any working day prior to the customs clearance of the goods;
> (iii) applications for licences when submitted in appropriate and complete form are approved immediately on receipt, to the extent administratively feasible, but within a maximum of 10 working days."[90]

It follows that to the extent import licences are used as means of restricting imports, they are prohibited under Article XI:1 of the General Agreement. Once again, therefore, any restrictive import licensing regime always needs some form of justification via the allowable exceptions to this rule.

2.5.2.3 "Other Measures"

The category of "other measures" under Article XI:1 is a residual category covering all non-tariff border measures, other than licences and quotas, that may have the effect of curtailing the amount of imports. A fairly long list of such measures has already been identified in 1984 by a GATT Group on Quantitative Restrictions and Non-Tariff Barriers.[91] The list includes, *inter alia,* government participation in trade and restrictive practices tolerated by governments, customs and administrative entry procedures, state trading, and prior import deposits.[92]

GATT case law has also identified a number of such practices. For example, the requirement of minimum import prices as a condition for importation has been found to fall under this category. In the *MIP* case, the US challenged the legality of an EC Regulation which prescribed, *inter alia,* that the importation of tomato concentrates would be subject to the production of an import certificate to be issued by Member States on condition of "the lodging of an additional security to guarantee that the free-at-frontier price of the products to be imported under cover of the certificate plus the customs duty payable thereon would together be equal to

---

88 Article 2:1 of the Uruguay Round Agreement on Import Licensing Procedures.

89 Article 2:2(a) of the Uruguay Round Agreement on Import Licensing Procedures.

90 Ibid.

91 See GATT Group on Quantitative Restrictions, *supra* n. 64.

92 Ibid., para. 59. Interestingly, most of these non-tariff barriers have been found to be concentrated mainly in the area of agricultural products. According to the Group, agriculture was one of only three product groups "severely affected by quantitative restrictions." The two other product groups are textiles, and iron and steel. Ibid., para. 12.

or more than the minimum price or the special minimum price, whichever was appropriate."[93] Both parties agreed,[94] and the panel found, that the minimum import price system, as enforced by the additional security, was a restriction "other than duties, taxes or other charges" within the meaning of Article XI:1.[95] The same position was also adopted by *Japan Semi-Conductors* in connection with export restrictions effected through minimum export price requirements.[96]

The operation of state trading enterprises which enjoy import monopolies in a manner that restricts imports has also been included in the definition of non-tariff import barriers under Article XI.[97] In reaction to a Japanese argument that Article XI:1 did not apply to import restrictions made effective through an import monopoly,[98] the *Japan Agriculture* panel observed that the wording of Article XI:1 was comprehensive and comprised restrictions made effective through an import monopoly.[99] The panel further referred to the Interpretative Note Ad to Articles XI, XII, XIII, XIV, and XVIII and stressed that "the basic purpose of this note is to extend to state-trading the rules of the General Agreement governing private trade and to ensure that the contracting parties cannot escape their obligations with respect to private trade by establishing state-trading operations. This purpose would be frustrated if import restrictions were considered to be consistent with Article XI:1 only because they were made effective through import monopolies."[100] The *Canada Alcohol* panel[101] pushed the argument one step further so as to bring non-border measures within the scope of Article XI. It ruled that limitations on the points of sale available to imported beer were restrictions within the meaning of Article XI:1.[102] The panel emphasized that the Note Ad to Articles XI, XII, XIII, XIV and XVIII "referred to 'restrictions made effective through state-trading operations' and not to 'import restrictions'."[103] According to the panel, this was a "recognition of the fact that in the case of enterprises enjoying a monopoly of both importation and

---

93 Article 4:2 of EEC Council Regulation 1927/75, as quoted in Ibid., para. 2.6.

94 See *MIP*, *supra* n. 82, para. 4.9. The only subject of contention in this respect was limited to the question of whether it qualified for exemption from the provisions of Article XI:1 provided under Article XI:2(c)(i) and (ii).

95 Ibid., para. 4.9.

96 This was stated as follows: "The panel noted that the CONTRACTING PARTIES had decided in a previous case that the import regulation allowing the import of a product in principle, but not below a minimum price level, constituted a restriction on importation within the meaning of Article XI:1 .... The panel considered that the principle applied in that case to restrictions on imports of goods below certain prices was applicable to restrictions on exports below certain prices." *Japan Semi-Conductors, supra* n. 68, para. 105.

97 See Interpretative Note Ad to Articles XI, XII, XIII, XIV, and XVIII, text reproduced *supra* **section 2.5.**

98 See *Japan Agriculture, supra* n. 73, para 5.2.2.2.

99 Ibid.

100 Ibid.

101 *Canada – Import, Distribution and Sale of Alcoholic Drinks by Canadian Provincial Marketing Agencies*, report of the panel (L/6304 *BISD* 35S/37) adopted on 22 March 1988.

102 Ibid., para. 4.24–4.25.

103 Ibid.

distribution in the domestic market, the distinction normally made in the General Agreement between restrictions affecting the importation of products and restrictions affecting imported products lost much of its significance since both types of restriction could be made effective through decision by the monopoly."[104] In its view, this was a "systematic discriminatory practice" which should be considered as a restriction made effective through "other measures" contrary to the provisions of Article XI:1.[105]

The question of whether non-binding governmental measures having import-restrictive effects are covered by the prohibition of Article XI:1 has been a subject of debate before GATT panels. In *Japan Semi-Conductors*, for instance, the EC challenged the legality of a Japanese measure by which the Government requested its producers and exporters of semi-conductors, *inter alia,* not to export those products at prices below company-specific costs. Japan argued that the measures complained of were intended "to avoid sales at dumping prices" and "were not legally binding and therefore did not fall under Article XI:1."[106] The panel rejected this argument and held that "Article XI:1, unlike other provisions of the General Agreement, did not refer to laws or regulations but more broadly to measures. This wording indicated clearly that any measure instituted or maintained by a contracting party which restricted the exportation or sale for export of products was covered by this provision, irrespective of the legal status of the measure."[107] This is the same approach as that adopted two months earlier by *Japan Agriculture* in the context of the exceptions under paragraph 2 of Article XI.[108] However, the *Japan Semi-Conductors* panel also recognized that "not all non-mandatory requests could be regarded as measures within the meaning of Article XI:1." For the Panel, the non-mandatory measure in question could be considered a governmental measure in the sense of Article XI:1 in this specific context because it satisfied two essential conditions: (1) there existed "reasonable grounds to believe that sufficient incentives or disincentives existed for non-mandatory measures to take effect", and (2) "the operation of the measures to restrict export of semi-conductors at prices below company-specific costs was essentially dependent on Government action or intervention."[109]

In sum, the principle under Article XI:1 is that all non-tariff measures having a restrictive effect on the amount of permissible imports are prohibited regardless of the form they take or their legal status. In as long as it results in having an adverse

---

[104] Ibid. This approach was recently reaffirmed by the *India Quantitative Restrictions* panel report, see *supra* n. 86, para. 5.142.

[105] *Canada Alcohol, supra* n. 101, paras. 4.24–4.25. The panel concluded that "the practices concerning listing/delisting requirements and the availability of points of sale which discriminate against imported alcoholic beverages were restrictions made effective through state-trading operations contrary to Article XI:1." Ibid. This approach was recently affirmed by the *India Quantitative Restrictions* panel report, see *supra* n. 86, para. 5.142.

[106] *Japan Semi-Conductors, supra* n. 68, para. 102.

[107] Ibid., para. 106.

[108] For further discussion of this point, see *infra* **section 2.5.3.1.1.2.**

[109] *Japan Semi-Conductors, supra* n. 68, para. 107.

effect on imports, even a non-binding governmental measure may fall within the scope of this prohibition. All forms of derogations from this principle thus need to be justified via one or another of the many exceptions to this rule.

2.5.3 Exceptions to Article XI:1

The rule against any quantitative restrictions prescribed under Article XI:1 is subject to a number of exceptions. While most are simply general exceptions applying to all sorts of products, some are agriculture-specific either by express or implied reference. The former includes such general exceptions as are prescribed under sub-paragraphs (a) and (b) of Article XI:2 on export prohibitions or restrictions in order to prevent or relieve critical shortages of essential products and import and export restrictions necessary to the application of standards or regulations for the classification, grading or marketing of commodities; under Article XII on balance-of-payments, under Article XVIII on developing countries; under Article XX on *inter alia* public morals, health and sanitary requirements, protection of exhaustible natural resources, and the like. On the other hand, the provisions of Article XI:2(c) are largely agriculture-specific exceptions to Article XI:1. Whether agriculture-specific or not, some general principles of interpretation regarding such exceptions-provisions need to be kept in mind: that the burden to demonstrate fulfilment of the requisite conditions for the exceptions lies on the party invoking them; and that exceptions need to be construed restrictively.

2.5.3.1 Article XI:2

As the length and structure of the text[110] suggests, this is one of the most complex provisions of the General Agreement. To start with, two important points of difference between the three sub-paragraphs of this paragraph need to be pointed out. Firstly, while the first two are general in their scope of application, the third one is limited to agricultural and fisheries products. And, secondly, while the exception under sub-paragraph (a) refers to cases of export prohibitions or restrictions, sub-paragraph (b) applies to both import and export prohibitions or restrictions. The third sub-paragraph, on the other hand, concerns only cases of import restrictions. Before going to the details of the agriculture-specific provisions of sub-paragraph (c), a brief look at the first exception under Article XI:2(a) appears to be in order. Sub-paragraph (b) is not, however, discussed here, for its coverage extends to all commodities and its substance appears fairly clear.

Under sub-paragraph (a), contracting parties are allowed to introduce temporary export restrictions or even prohibitions for the purpose of relieving critical shortages of foodstuffs and other essential products. Owing to the special place of most agricultural products as foodstuffs, this provision is largely a reference to the agricultural sector.[111] The rationale behind this exception needs little explanation –

---

[110] See text of the provision *supra* **section 2.5.**

[111] Note, however, that foodstuffs are supplemented by "other products essential to the exporting country".

countries cannot be expected to allow the export of products so essential as food items when they are in scarce supply within their territories. However, at least in the area of agriculture, the most important, if not the only, problem of almost all major trading nations at present is overproduction. Consequently, the export of agricultural products is not just unrestricted in these countries; it is forced in all sorts of ways.[112] The provision may thus be said to have fallen into virtual disuse at least as far as agricultural products are concerned.[113]

2.5.3.1.1 The Agriculture-Specific Exceptions of Article XI:2(c)

The origin of this provision dates back to the *Suggested Charter* for an ITO submitted by the United States in 1946, and it was tailored to reflect pertinent interests of the United States at the moment.[114] The substance of the proposal on this issue remained nearly unchanged – the only important modification being the inclusion of fisheries products.[115] The negotiating history indicates that the exemption of agricultural products from the strict prohibition of quantitative restrictions and other non-tariff barriers of Article XI:1 was necessitated by the unique features of agriculture as being heavily dependent on the unpredictable vagaries of nature and the unorganized nature of the producers.[116] As stated in the *Havana Reports,* however, the exception was not intended to provide a means of protecting domestic producers against foreign competition, but only to "permit, in appropriate cases, the enforcement of domestic governmental measures necessitated

[112] For a discussion of this particular problem and the use of export subsidies as a solution by the major trading powers as well as the resulting export subsidy wars between them, see *infra* **Part II** on agricultural export subsidies.

[113] Even in the non-agricultural sector, the use of export restrictions has not been strictly regulated under GATT. As observed by Jackson *et al*, the basic problem with GATT obligations relating to exports "stems from two facts: 1) there is no GATT obligation against the use of export taxes or fees; and 2) as to the GATT obligations restraining use of export restrictions, the GATT exceptions are so broad and vague as to almost render those obligations meaningless." Jackson *et al* (1995) *supra* n. 7, pp. 946–47.

[114] See, *inter alia,* Ibid. p. 1169. However, the US soon realized its agricultural program coming into conflict with the GATT, which ultimately brought about the 1955 US waiver for its agriculture under Article XXV. See GATT, *Waiver Granted to the United States in Connection with Import Restrictions Imposed under Section 22 of the United States Agriculture Adjustment Act (of 1993) as Amended, Decision of 5 March 1955, BISD* 3S/32. The waiver, in its relevant part, provides that "the obligations of the United States under the provisions of Articles II and XI of the General Agreement are waived to the extent necessary to prevent a conflict with such provisions of the General Agreement in the case of action required to be taken by the Government of the United States under Section 22." For an interesting analysis of the scope and effect of the US waiver, see *US Sugar Waiver, supra* n. 74.

[115] See *Japan Agriculture, supra* n. 73, para. 5.1.2. Note, however, that fisheries are not covered by this book.

[116] It was stated by the drafters of the General Agreement that "in agriculture and fisheries you have to deal with the capricious bounty of nature, which will sometimes give you a huge catch of fish or a huge crop, which knocks the bottom out of prices. You also have the phenomenon peculiar to agriculture and fisheries of a multitude of small unorganized producers that cannot organize themselves. It often happens that the Government has to step in and organize them. But if it does so, it cannot allow the results of its organization to be frustrated by uncontrolled imports." EPCT/A/PV/19, quoted in *Japan Agriculture, supra* n. 73, para. 5.1.2.

by the special problems relating to the production and marketing of agricultural ... products."[117] The *Havana reports* further warned that the exception "should not be construed as permitting the use of quantitative restrictions as a method of protecting the industrial processing of agricultural ... products."[118]

Article XI:2(c) provides that the provisions of paragraph 1 prohibiting non-tariff barriers do not extend to "import restrictions on any agricultural or fisheries product, imported in any form, necessary to the enforcement of governmental measures" which satisfy a set of additional and fairly stringent conditions.[119] Before we go to those additional conditions, however, a closer look at this introductory provision is useful. Some five important elements may be identified in this provision.

2.5.3.1.1.1 AGRICULTURAL V. NON-AGRICULTURAL PRODUCTS

The exception under sub-paragraph (c) applies only to *agricultural or fisheries products* as opposed to non-agricultural goods. GATT never had any definition for the term "agricultural product". However, some sort of a tacit consensus has developed at the level of both tariff negotiation rounds as well as dispute settlement panels that the products falling under Chapters 1 to 24 in the Customs Co-operation Council Nomenclature could in principle be regarded as agricultural products.[120] As will be developed in due course, the Uruguay Round Agreement on Agriculture has also adopted this approach with only minor modifications.[121]

2.5.3.1.1.2 IMPORT RESTRICTIONS V. IMPORT PROHIBITIONS

Unlike the first two provisions of Article XI:2, sub-paragraph (c) allows only *import restrictions* and not *prohibitions*. As observed in *US Tuna*, while sub-paragraphs (a) and (b) of paragraph 2 use the words "prohibitions and restrictions", sub-paragraph (c) mentions only "restrictions", with the result that "the provisions of Article XI:2(c)(i) could not justify the application of an import prohibition."[122] The panel in *Japan Agriculture* interpreted this requirement widely and introduced the concept of *de facto* prohibition. Accordingly, Japan's special quotas available for use only in limited places (e.g. the quota for processed cheese, evaporated milk, condensed milk,

---

117 *Havana Reports*, p. 89, quoted in *Japan Agriculture*, *supra* n. 73, para. 5.1.2.

118 Ibid.

119 See, *inter alia*, discussion *infra* **section 2.5.3.1.4.**

120 See, *inter alia*, *Japan Agriculture*, *supra* n. 73, para. 5.1.3.2; *Canada – Import Restrictions on Ice Cream and Yoghurt* report of the panel (L/6568 – *BISD* 36S/68) adopted on 5 December 1989, para. 64; the *MIP* case, *supra* n. 82, para. 12.6; *European Economic Community – Restrictions on Imports of Apples: Complaint by the United States*, report of the panel (L/6513 *BISD* 36S/135) adopted on 22 June 1989, para. 5.6; etc.

121 See *infra* chapter 3.

122 *United States – Prohibition of Imports of Tuna and Tuna Products from Canada* report of the panel (L/5198 *BISD* 29S/91) adopted on 22 February 1982, para. 4.6. In *Chile Dessert Apples*, Chile argued that measures suspending import licences for Chile "were *a prohibition, not a restriction*, of imports." *Chile Dessert Apples*, *supra* n. 80, para. 3.7. The Panel, rejecting this Chilean argument, stated that "[a]s the EEC had at no time prohibited all imports of apples, its measures therefore constituted an import restriction, rather than an import prohibition in terms of Article XI:2(c)(i)." Ibid., para. 12.5. For a closer look at the meaning of the term "restrictions", see *infra* **section 2.5.3.1.1.2.**

etc. only for use in Okinawa) or for specific purposes (e.g. for use only in international tourist hotels and international shipping vessels) were found to be a *de facto* prohibition and not a restriction of imports into the general customs tariff territory of Japan and concluded that "such prohibition was not permitted under the provisions of Article XI:2(c)(i)."[123] As will be discussed later on, not only does this rule prohibit import prohibitions, even the degree of allowable import restrictions is restricted by the rule of proportionality under the last paragraph of Article XI:2(c).[124]

2.5.3.1.1.3 "IN ANY FORM"

The restriction may be imposed on the import of agricultural products *imported in any form*. As it stands, the phrase "in any form" is so wide as to appear devoid of any meaning. Arguably, it may be taken to cover all products having an agricultural content regardless of the degree of processing they have undergone. In an effort to overcome this problem, a note to Article XI defines the phrase "in any form" as covering "the same products when in an early stage of processing and still perishable, which compete directly with the fresh product and if freely imported would tend to make the restriction on the fresh product ineffective."[125] The definition of the term "in any form" was later redrafted under the Havana Charter as follows: "imported 'in any form' means the product in the form in which it is originally sold by its producer and such processed forms of the product as are so closely related to the original product as regards utilization that their unrestricted importation would make the restriction on the original product ineffective."[126] This definition was not, however, incorporated into the General Agreement. The essential points of divergence between these two definitions pertain to the criteria of being "in an early stage of processing", and still "perishable", which form important elements of the definition adopted by the General Agreement.[127]

According to this definition, an agricultural import restriction becomes a restriction on the product *imported in any form* only if (a) it concerns the same products when in an *early stage of processing*; (b) the thus processed products are *still perishable*; and (c) they *compete directly with the fresh product* such that, if freely imported, they would tend to make the restriction on the fresh product ineffective.

(a) Early Stage of Processing: First of all, for a processed product to fall within the terms of the definition of "in any form" under Note Ad Article XI:2(c), it should be in an "early stage of processing". But, how "early" is early in this context? Being an exception to the rule, and given the concerns expressed above,[128] the concept of

---

[123] See *Japan Agriculture, supra* n. 73, at, *inter alia*, paras. 5.1.3.1, 5.3.1.2, 5.3.2.1, and 5.3.10.2.

[124] See discussion *infra* **section 2.5.3.1.4.**

[125] Note Ad Article XI:2(c).

[126] Note to Article 20 of the Havana charter as quoted in *Japan Agriculture, supra* n. 73, para. 5.1.3.4; see also WTO, *Analytical Index: Guide to GATT Law and Practice*, (Updated 6th Ed. Geneva 1995), p. 334.

[127] See *Japan Agriculture, supra* n. 73, para. 5.1.3.4.

[128] See *Havana Reports*, pp. 89–93.

"early stage of processing" should be interpreted in a restrictive manner. GATT panels that addressed the issue do not seem to have developed a consistent interpretation. For example, the panel in *Japan Agriculture* gave a prominent place to two requirements: whether a processed product was "consumer-ready",[129] and whether it was capable of being stocked.[130] The panel observed, in connection with processed cheese, for instance, that it was not in an *early stage of processing* because it was "a product not generally intended for further processing.... [and] was capable of being stocked."[131] The *Thailand Cigarettes* panel adopted this argument and held that cigarettes were not among the products eligible for import restrictions under Article XI:2(c)(i) because they could not be described as "leaf tobacco in an early stage of processing" as they had already undergone extensive processing and, moreover, they were not intended for further processing.[132]

On the other hand, the *Canada Ice Cream* panel rejected a US argument (which apparently was based on the above-mentioned "precedents") that "any consumer-ready processed product could not be considered as in an early stage of processing."[133] The panel convincingly argued that "[d]rinking milk, having been pasteurized and homogenized, was a 'processed', consumer-ready product, yet it would be difficult not to consider drinking milk to be 'in an early stage of processing'."[134] This panel also rejected a Canadian argument that products resulting from a direct continuous processing method should be considered *ipso facto* to be in an early stage of processing.[135] The panel rightly pointed out that "'continuous processing' could theoretically be continued until a highly processed product ... resulted."[136] In the end, the panel only opined that a case-by-case approach would be necessary on this subject and stopped short of making any findings on the matter.[137]

---

[129] *Japan Agriculture, supra* n. 73, paras. 5.3.2.2; 5.3.4;5.3.6; 5.3.10; and 5.3.12.

[130] *Japan Agriculture, supra* n. 73, paras. 5.3.2.2 and 5.3.11.

[131] Ibid., para. 5.3.2.2. The panel stated similar reasons for a finding of non-compliance with the conditions set under Article XI:2(c) in connection with different products. For example: such products as frozen yoghurt base, ice cream powder, prepared milk powder for infants, etc. "were *consumer ready prepared foods* as opposed to products which had undergone only initial processing" (para. 5.3.4); "starch was a stable product which was *capable of being stocked*" (para. 5.3.6.2); "the canning of pineapple enabled it *to be stocked* for a considerable length of time and therefore rendered it no longer perishable" (para. 5.3.11); "in terms of normal processing chain of tomato products, tomato juice, tomato paste and ketchup were *not normally subject to further processing but rather were consumer-ready* products" (para. 5.3.12.3); etc. (italics added).

[132] *Thailand – Restrictions on Importation of and Internal Taxes on Cigarettes* report of the panel (DS10/R *BISD* 37S/200) adopted on November 1990, para. 70. The panel cited the *Japan Agriculture* report and argued as follows: "A central requirement of the Note [defining the term 'in any form'] was that the product processed from the fresh product was still 'in early stage of processing'. It noted that a previous panel had found that agricultural products not normally intended for further processing such as ketchup could not be regarded as eligible for import restrictions under Article XI:2(c)(i)." Ibid.

[133] *Canada Ice Cream, supra* n. 120, para. 71.

[134] Ibid., para. 71.

[135] Ibid.

[136] Ibid.

[137] The panel stated that a finding with respect to the "early stage of processing" criterion would "require an examination of the processing of each type of product subject to the import restrictions. Given the

(b) Perishability: Secondly, for a processed product to be within the terms of "in any form" as defined under Note Ad Article XI:2(c), it should be "perishable". Generally speaking, perishability refers to a deterioration in the value or quality of a product over a given period of time. The problem of perishability lies at the root of the very need for a separate treatment of agricultural and fisheries products under Article XI:2. As stated in the preparatory documents of this provision, one reason agriculture and fisheries had to be separated from other product categories was because, in agriculture and fisheries, "you have to deal with the capricious bounty of nature, which will sometimes give a huge catch of fish or a huge crop, which knocks the bottom out of prices",[138] while the opposite may be the case shortly afterwards. It is mainly the problem of perishability which makes it difficult to put the excess in stock in such times of plenty for marketing in times of scarcity. Hence, the need to introduce exceptions to the basic GATT rules which respond to both aspects of the problem, i.e. import and export restriction possibilities, respectively. While the latter remains only a remote possibility for most trading nations, over-production and consequent import restrictions have been endemic in most of these countries. This is the main justification given by policy makers for their protection of agriculture against the free interplay of the market forces of supply and demand. More often than not, governments have to introduce domestic measures restricting the production or marketing of these products. And, as stated during the sessions of the Preparatory Committee, they could not allow the results of their domestic supply restriction measures "to be frustrated by uncontrolled imports."[139] Article XI:2(c) was thus "intended to enable governments to protect farmers ... who, because of the *perishability* of their produce, often could not withhold excess supplies of fresh product from the market."[140] As a result, contracting parties introduced this narrowly-coined exception saying that "what we are having in mind here is the *perishable* kind of product, not the kind which is capable of being stocked."[141]

At the theoretical level, therefore, the idea seems fairly clear – contracting parties may be allowed to introduce import restrictions on an agricultural product if the product is still fresh or, if processed, only in an early stage of processing such that it

---

cont.

variety of modern production methods and the rapid changes in technology, the panel also had doubts whether the concept 'early stage of processing' could provide much guidance as to the interpretation of Article XI:2(c)." Ibid.

[138] A statement made during the Geneva session of the Preparatory Committee, EPCT/A/PV/19, p. 42; quoted in *Japan Agriculture*, *supra* n. 73, para. 5.1.2; see also *GATT Analytical Index* (1995) *supra* n. 126, p. 328.

[139] A statement made during the Geneva session of the Preparatory Committee, EPCT/A/PV/19, at p. 42, excerpted in *GATT Analytical Index* (1995) *supra* n. 126, p. 328.

[140] *Thailand Cigarettes*, *supra* n. 132, para. 69 (italics added). The US argument in the *Japan Agriculture* dispute is also worth reproducing here: "Article XI:2(c)(i) was aimed at those products whose perishability precluded farmers from holding their production off the market until prices could stabilize." *Japan Agriculture, supra* n. 73, para. 3.2.3.

[141] A statement made during the Geneva session of the Preparatory Committee, EPCT/A/PV/19, p. 44, excerpted in *GATT Analytical Index* (1995), *supra* n. 126, p. 334 (italics added).

is not yet capable of being stocked. However, the question of what is capable of being stocked and what is not in actuality is a difficult one to resolve. The fact that technological progress is fast improving the techniques of preservation and lengthening the life of products in a "fresh" form has further complicated the problem.

In *MIP*, the US argued that "tomato concentrate, whether packed in tins or barrels, did not have characteristics of perishability in the general sense of the term as it applied to agricultural products .... With proper and normal handling and storage, tomato concentrate retained its full value for several years."[142] Against this, the EC argued that "tomato concentrates declined considerably in value the longer they were stored."[143] The panel agreed with the Community on this point and stated that "tomato concentrate was perishable because after a certain time it would decline in quality and value."[144] As will be shown later, however, this ruling was not of much practical guidance in the resolution of subsequent disputes.[145]

The *Japan Agriculture* panel found, *inter alia*, the following products as not perishable, and hence not falling within the definition of "in any form" under Article XI:2(c): prepared and preserved milk and cream, starch, processed cheese, fruit juices and fruit products entering in a canned form, "tomato juice in the canned form primarily imported into Japan",[146] tomato sauce and tomato ketchup. The "capability of being stocked" appears to have been taken as the principal test of perishability here again.[147] This is the same phrase used by the Preparatory Committee in Geneva quoted earlier.[148] However, the question about the length of time in which it is capable of being stocked and the degree of acceptable decline in the value or quality of a product, if any, are not that easy to answer. It may be plausible to say that a product is perishable "because after a certain time it would decline in quality and value."[149] But, how long is that "certain time"?

In *Canada Ice Cream*, for instance, Canada argued that ice cream, even under appropriate storage conditions, had a shelf life of only three months and was still perishable, while the US contended that the ice cream it exported could be stored for 12 months and was not perishable.[150] The final position taken by the panel was interesting for two reasons. Firstly, it rightly pointed out that "as virtually all agricultural products declined in quality and value after a certain time, the panel did not believe that this previous finding [of the *MIP* panel quoted above] provided

---

[142] The *MIP* case, *supra* n. 82, para. 3.9.

[143] Ibid., para. 3.11.

[144] Ibid., para. 4.10.

[145] See *infra* n. 151 and accompanying text.

[146] Ibid., para. 5.3.12.2. The inverted commas are used here because the panel had reached the general finding that "tomato juice was a product in an early stage of processing", while singling out that "tomato juice in the canned form primarily imported into Japan was not perishable." Ibid.

[147] See Ibid., paras. 5.3.1.4 for prepared and preserved milk, 5.3.2.2 for processed cheese, and 5.3.6.2 for starch.

[148] See *supra* n. 141.

[149] The *MIP* case, *supra* n. 82, para. 4.10.

[150] *Canada Ice Cream, supra* n. 120, paras. 32 and 33–34, respectively.

sufficient guidance for clearly distinguishing between perishable and non-perishable items."[151] Secondly, the panel underscored the element of dynamism which makes questionable the very usefulness of the concept: "rapid changes in technology since the General Agreement was drafted raised doubts as to the practicability of using the concept 'still perishable' to distinguish the items that fell within the scope of Article XI:2(c) from those that did not."[152] The panel thus desisted from making a finding on the matter. Perishability thus proved to be a concept that is too dynamic to define with any degree of precision. What is perishable at one time may be non-perishable at another time. Thus, to the extent it has to be used, it can only be interpreted on a case-by-case basis.

(c) Direct Competition: The final requirement for a product to be "in any form" as defined in Note Ad Article XI(2)(c) is that it "compete directly with the fresh product and if freely imported would tend to make the restriction on the fresh product ineffective." The key element here is that of "direct competition", and has been at issue before some important GATT cases.

In *MIP*, the US argued that there was no direct competition between tomato concentrates and fresh tomatoes,[153] while the EC contended otherwise.[154] The panel found that "tomato concentrate could compete directly with fresh tomatoes so far as a large number of end-uses were concerned."[155] In *Canada Ice Cream*, Canada argued that imported ice cream and yoghurt competed directly with raw milk in that the imports would displace domestically produced ice cream and yoghurt which would in turn result in lower demand for industrial milk.[156] The US successfully countered this argument saying that products which competed directly were those which came into rivalry in a market without any intervening step and that imported ice cream and yoghurt competed directly only with domestically produced ice cream and yoghurt and not with the fresh product – raw milk.[157] The panel supported the US view and made the point that "the essence of direct competition was that a buyer was basically indifferent if faced with the choice between one product or the other and viewed them as substitutable in terms of their use."[158] The panel further observed that "only limited competition existed between raw milk and ice cream and yoghurt", and did not qualify for direct competition in the sense of Article XI:2(c)(i) of the General Agreement.[159]

---

[151] Ibid., para. 72; see also *supra* n. 145 and accompanying text.
[152] Ibid.
[153] See the *MIP* case, *supra* n. 82, para. 3.10.
[154] See Ibid., para. 3.11.
[155] See Ibid., para. 4.10.
[156] See *Canada Ice Cream, supra* n. 120, para. 35.
[157] Ibid., para. 36. The US further argued that the language "was explicit with regard to 'compete directly with', which did not mean the same as 'compete with, compete indirectly with', or much less 'displace'. As the importation of every processed product could arguably result to some extent in a decline in demand for the commodities used as ingredients, virtually all processed food products would qualify under the displacement argument." Ibid.
[158] Ibid., para. 73.
[159] Ibid.

The London session of the Preparatory Committee had said in this context that "to take an extreme example, if a country restricted its output of apples, it could not restrict importation of bananas because they only compete with them."[160] The element of direct competition is therefore significantly more than mere substitutability. It involves some degree of sameness. Indeed, as the panel in *Canada Ice Cream* observed, the similarity should be such as to make the buyer *indifferent* as to which product he is buying. Still, a case-by-case approach is once again the best way to resolve problems involving this concept. Once the issue of direct competition between any two products is determined, the question of whether the free importation of that product may tend to make the restriction on the fresh product ineffective will be easier to resolve.

2.5.3.1.1.4 NECESSITY

The import restrictions thus introduced on an "agricultural product" imported "in any form" should be *necessary*, in this particular case, "necessary to the enforcement of governmental measures" aimed at one of three objectives under Article XI:2(c).[161] Import restrictions could be introduced only when it is absolutely unavoidable to do so. The Report of the London Session of the Preparatory Committee noted that restrictions "should not be imposed on seasonal commodities at a time when similar domestic products were not available."[162] The term *necessary* is inserted here to emphasize that countries should not resort to import restrictions on a product unless it is practically impossible for them to achieve their otherwise legitimate objectives through other, less restrictive, means.[163]

The issue has been addressed by some of the prominent GATT panels. The *Japan Agriculture* panel considered the matter in connection, *inter alia*, with dried leguminous vegetables, groundnuts, and fruit purée and paste, fruit pulp, and certain fruit juices.[164] In finding the measures on the first two products "necessary", the panel stressed the substitutability of the products (i.e. those subject to domestic supply restriction and those subject to the import restriction)[165] and the length of their marketing periods[166] as important factors. The role of these and other

---

[160] Excerpted in *GATT Analytical Index* (1995) *supra* n. 126, p. 331.

[161] For a discussion of these issues, see *infra* **section 2.5.3.1.1.5.**

[162] Report of the London session of the Preparatory Committee, quoted in *GATT Analytical Index* (1995) *supra* n. 126, p.337.

[163] As the GATT Report of the Review Session Working Party on "Quantitative Restrictions" emphasized, "the maintenance or the application of a restriction which went beyond that which would be 'necessary' to achieve the objects defined in para. 2(b) or 2(c) of Article XI would be inconsistent with the provisions of that Article." See Ibid., p. 337.

[164] *Japan Agriculture, supra* n. 73, paras. 5.3.5, 5.3.8, and 5.3.10.

[165] In connection with dried leguminous vegetables, the panel observed, "the various dried legumes were substitutable in terms of the principal form of their consumption in Japan" and therefore the restrictions "could be reasonably considered as necessary in terms of Article XI:2(c)(i)." Ibid., para. 5.3.5.2.

[166] The panel stated, in connection with groundnuts, that "Japanese groundnuts and imported groundnuts were essentially identical and perfectly substitutable in terms of their use. It further observed that the marketing period for Japanese groundnuts was not limited to a few weeks or months, but was essentially the entire year. ... The panel found, therefore, that the restrictions maintained by Japan on imports of groundnuts could be reasonably considered as 'necessary' in terms of Article XI:2(c)(i)." Ibid., para. 5.3.8.2.

considerations was authoritatively expressed by the same panel as grounds to reject the legality of Japan's import restrictions on fruit purées and pastes, prepared or preserved fruit pulp and certain fruit juices:

> "import restrictions applied under Article XI:2(c)(i) cannot exceed those 'necessary' for the operation of the domestic governmental measure concerned. Such restrictions can thus not normally be justified if applied to imports during that time of year in which domestic supplies of the product are not available.... The panel further considers that a restriction on imports of a processed product can in general not be considered as necessary if importation of more directly competitive forms of the product, i.e. the fresh product (when economically feasible) or earlier-stage products processed from the fresh product, are not restricted."[167]

The *Canada Ice Cream* panel also made the important point that "if unrestricted imports would render a government measure ineffective, it would be difficult not to conclude that some restriction of the imports was necessary."[168] The question of whether there is any practicable way of avoiding import restrictions while not affecting the effectiveness of legitimate domestic governmental measures is therefore a matter of decisive importance.

This approach also fits well with the interpretation of the term "necessary" in the context of other provisions of the General Agreement. For example, a sound "case law" interpreting this very term has already developed in the context of the general exceptions under Article XX of the General Agreement. The *US Section 337* panel observed in connection with Article XX(d) that

> "a contracting party cannot justify a measure inconsistent with other GATT provisions as 'necessary' in terms of Article XX(d) *if an alternative measure which it could reasonably be expected to employ and which is not inconsistent with other GATT provisions is available to it.* By the same token, in cases where a measure consistent with other GATT provisions is not reasonably available, a contracting party is bound to use, among the measures reasonably available to

---

[167] Ibid., para. 6.7. This interpretation may also find support from a 1955 GATT Report of the Review Session Working Party on Quantitative Restrictions, which noted *inter alia* that "if import restrictions of the type referred to in para. 2(c) were to be applied after the governmental measures referred to in that paragraph had ceased to be in force, those restrictions would no longer be necessary for the enforcement of those measures and would therefore be inconsistent with the provisions of that paragraph. It was also recognized that if restrictions of the type referred to in para. 2(c) were applied to imports during that part of the year in which domestic supplies of the product were not available, such restrictions would be regarded as consistent with the provisions of the Article only to the extent that they were necessary to enforce or to achieve the objectives of the governmental measures relating to control of the domestic product. Finally, it was recognized that it would be an abuse of intent of the provisions under para. 2(c)(i) of Article XI if contracting parties were to apply restrictions to processed products exceeding those 'necessary' to secure enforcement of the actual measure restricting production or marketing of the primary product." Report excerpted in *GATT Analytical Index* (1995) *supra* n. 126, p. 337.

[168] *Canada Ice Cream, supra* n. 120, para. 80.

it, that which entails the *least degree of inconsistency* with other GATT provisions."[169]

This interpretation has also been adopted by subsequent panel reports. The *Thailand Cigarettes* panel, which had to construe the same term as used under Article XX(b), adopted the above approach and argued that "[i]n both paragraphs the same term was used and the same objective intended: to allow contracting parties to impose trade restrictive measures inconsistent with the General Agreement to pursue overriding public policy goals to the extent that such inconsistencies were unavoidable."[170]

The reasoning in *Thailand Cigarettes* in favour of applying an interpretation given to a term in one paragraph so as to interpret the same term as used in another paragraph of the same article may reasonably be pushed one step further to apply to similar cases under other articles of the General Agreement. Both the wording as well as the object of paragraph 2(c) of Article XI appear to satisfy the basic conditions stated therein. Article XX and Article XI:2 share a lot in common. In principle all forms of non-tariff barriers are prohibited under Article XI:1. Just like the general exceptions under Article XX, it is only when exceptional situations necessitate that non-tariff import restrictions are allowed under Article XI:2(c). One of the conditions in both cases is that such measures must be *necessary*. Thus, unless the specific factual situation in a specific case dictates otherwise, it appears that the meaning given to the term *necessary* under Article XX can also be extended to cases involving Article XI:2(c). Accordingly, an import restriction becomes *necessary* in the sense of Article XI:2(c) only if there are no alternative measures consistent with the General Agreement, or less inconsistent with it, which countries could reasonably be expected to employ to achieve their policy objectives. This position may also find further support from what Schaffer calls "the principle of *least-restrictive trade*", which states that "a country, in setting otherwise valid restrictions on trade (such as those to protect public health), shall make them no more restrictive than necessary to achieve the goals for which they were imposed."[171]

2.5.3.1.1.5 GOVERNMENTAL MEASURES

The whole purpose of the import restrictions referred to under Article XI:2(c) should be to render possible the enforcement of *governmental measures* having any one of the objectives enumerated under sub-paragraphs (i) to (iii). The issue in this respect is the same as that discussed above under paragraph 1 of Article XI, i.e. whether the term *governmental measures* is limited to binding legal instruments or also covers other non-binding measures introduced by governments. Classic on this matter in

---

[169] *United States – Section 337 of the Tariff Act of 1930*, report of the panel (L/6439 *BISD* 36S/345) adopted on 7 November 1989, para. 5.26 (italics added).

[170] *Thailand Cigarettes*, *supra* n. 132, para. 74.

[171] Schaffer *et al*, *supra* n. 69, p. 399. The essence of this principle has also been expressed in a GATT Report of the Review Session Working Party on Quantitative Restrictions; see excerpts in *GATT Analytical Index* (1995) *supra* n. 126, p. 337.

the specific context of paragraph 2(c) is *Japan Agriculture*. The issue here may be contrasted with that discussed earlier in the context of Article XI:1 and *Japan Semi-Conductors*. A particular look at the apparently contradictory positions assumed by Japan on the meaning of the term "governmental measures" in these two cases clarifies this problem further.

The issue in *Japan Semi-Conductors* arose because of a contention by Japan that the measures complained of were mere encouragements to companies which were "not legally binding by any means, and there was no penalty even if the company did not comply with such encouragement."[172] The EC, on the other hand, argued that the question of whether or not the "administrative guidance" used by the Japanese authorities was legally binding was irrelevant and that what mattered was only the intended result and not the method used.[173] The panel agreed with the EC and held that "Article XI:1, unlike other provisions of the General Agreement, did not refer to laws or regulations but more broadly to measures."[174]

Also in *Japan Agriculture*, the issue remained the same, i.e. whether or not the term "governmental measures" was limited to binding legal instruments. The context was, however, different and the position of the parties reversed. Firstly, the measure in dispute for the *Semi-Conductors* panel concerned a governmental measure restricting exports in the sense of Article XI:1, while the measure in *Japan Agriculture* concerned a domestic governmental measure in the sense of Article XI:2(c) for the enforcement of which Japan had taken an import-restrictive measure in the sense of Article XI:1. The complainant, the US in this particular case, challenged that since Japan's domestic "governmental measures" were non-legally binding administrative guidance which amounted only to "an appeal for *private* measures to be taken voluntarily by private parties", the conditions for the imposition of import restrictions were not met.[175] Japan countered that "to the extent that governmental measures were 'effective' it was irrelevant whether or not the measures were mandatory and statutory."[176] The panel agreed with Japan in this case and found, with some extra caution,[177] that what mattered was the effectiveness of the measures and not the method used.

The *Chile Dessert Apples* panel also considered this issue in the context of an EC internal regime for apples, which was a hybrid of direct buying-in by Member States and withdrawals by private producer groups. The panel found that both the public and private aspects of the system qualified as *governmental measures* under Article XI:2(c)(i) for the following reasons: "the régime as a whole was established by

---

[172] *Japan Semi-Conductors, supra* n. 68, para. 50; see also para.106.

[173] Ibid., para. 51.

[174] Ibid., para.106.

[175] See *Japan Agriculture, supra* n. 73, para. 3.2.5.

[176] See Ibid., para. 3.2.6.

[177] The panel expressed its caution in this respect with the following wording: "In view of the special characteristics of Japanese society the panel wishes, however, to stress that its approach in this particular case should not be interpreted as a precedent in other cases where societies are not adapted to this form of enforcing government policies." Ibid., para. 5.4.1.4.

Community regulations which set out its structure. Its operation depended on Community decisions fixing prices, and on public financing; apples withdrawn were disposed of in ways prescribed by regulation."[178] The primary consideration for the determination of whether a measure is governmental or not is thus not the identity of the doer of the action or the method used for the purpose, but its effectiveness.

In sum, paragraph 2(c) of Article XI is a very complex provision. The five points we have been discussing so far are the important elements of only the chapeau of this sub-paragraph. The fulfilment of the conditions in this part of the provision is only a necessary, and by no means sufficient, condition for the legitimacy of any non-tariff barriers erected by governments under Article XI:2(c). The additional conditions may be divided into two categories – those stated under items (i) to (iii) pertaining to the alternative conditions required of the domestic governmental measures, and those stated under the last sub-paragraph of paragraph 2(c) pertaining to such matters as the requirements of transparency and predictability of the import-restrictive measures applied by governments and those of proportionality or even-handedness required of the impact of these measures on the relationship between imported and domestic products on the market.

2.5.3.1.2 ARTICLE XI:2(C)(I): DOMESTIC SUPPLY RESTRICTIONS

This is the most important – and the most contentious in GATT dispute settlement history – of the three provisions under Article XI:2(c). It lays down the condition that the domestic governmental measures for the enforcement of which the introduction of import restrictions has been found to be necessary should operate "to *restrict* the quantities of the *like domestic product* permitted to be marketed or produced, or, if there is no substantial domestic production of the like product, of a domestic product for which the imported product can be *directly substituted*".[179] Three important elements may be identified in this provision: (1) there should be a domestic governmental programme on the domestic production and/or marketing of an agricultural product; (2) the product subject to the programme must be a *like* (or, in certain cases, a *directly substitutable*) product to that on which an import restriction has been introduced; and (3) the domestic programme should operate to *restrict* the amount of the like or directly competitive product that can be produced or, if produced, that can be marketed.

To start with the last-mentioned element, the domestic governmental measure should operate to *restrict* the supply of the like or directly-substitutable domestic product. The Havana Reports stated that "in interpreting the term 'restrict' for the purposes of paragraph 2(c), the essential point was that the measures of domestic restriction must effectively keep output below the level which would have attained in the absence of restrictions."[180] The 1978 *MIP* panel considered the EC common

[178] *Chile Dessert Apples, supra* n. 80, para. 12.9.

[179] Article XI:2(c)(i) of the General Agreement (italics added).

[180] Havana Reports, p. 89, para. 17, as reproduced in *GATT Analytical Index, supra* n. 126, p. 340; see also the *MIP* case, *supra* n. 82, para. 3.19.

market organization for tomatoes established under Council Regulation (EEC) No. 1035/72 and ruled that the intervention system for fresh tomatoes did not qualify as a governmental measure operating to restrict the quantities of the like domestic product permitted to be produced or marketed within the meaning of Article XI:2(c) because it lacked effectiveness.[181] The 1980 *Chile Apples* panel also considered the same issue in connection with apples,[182] but reached a contrary verdict. The panel first found that the concerned Community programmes had not resulted in any significant drop in EC apple production and failed to satisfy the production-restriction requirement.[183] However, it also found that the EC "did restrict quantities of apples permitted to be marketed, through its system of intervention purchases by Member States and compensation to producer groups for withdrawing apples from the market."[184] Thus, with one of two alternative conditions satisfied in this respect, the panel in effect found that the conditions under sub-paragraph (c)(i) were met. However, as we shall see later on, the

---

[181] According to the Panel, "there was no effective Community or governmental enforcement of the withdrawals of fresh tomatoes by the Producers' organizations; these organizations were merely encouraged to make such withdrawals. The panel further considered that there was no requirement that tomato producers must create, join or market their production through such producers' organizations. In the case where member States were obligated to buy in tomatoes which had been offered to them, the panel considered that the provision allowing member States to claim an exemption from this obligation was so liberal that it would constitute a lack of effective enforcement of the intent of this Article of the Regulation [Article 19:2 of Council Regulation (EEC) No. 1035/72]. The panel further considered that, in addition, in light of the fact that the buying-in or withdrawal prices were fixed at about one half of the normal cost of production, the intervention system would not effectively restrict the marketing or production of fresh tomatoes, but simply remove any market surplus after all potential commercial markets, including processing into tomato concentrate, had been saturated. The panel further considered that, since this system was not considered to be an effective restriction on the marketing and production of fresh tomatoes, then it could not be considered to be an effective restriction on the marketing or production of tomato concentrate. Therefore, the panel concluded that ... the intervention system for fresh tomatoes did not qualify as a governmental measure which operated 'to restrict the quantities of the like domestic product permitted to be marketed or produced' ... within the meaning of Article XI:2(c)(i)." Ibid., para. 4.13.

[182] *Chile Apples* describes the essence of the Community system as follows: "The European Economic Community has a common organization for the marketing of apples which includes common quality standards, an internal price support and intervention system, and a levy system on imports. When market prices fall below a certain minimum in representative markets, for three successive marketing days, Member States are authorized to buy up at a certain price apples offered for intervention. Producer groups may also be compensated for effecting market withdrawals. Offer prices of apples from third countries are compared daily to a fixed minimum price, called a reference price which is based, *inter alia,* on EEC average costs of production. If for any origin the offer price is below the reference price, a compensatory tax is applied to apples of that origin in addition to the normal customs duty. In case there is a disruption of the Community market or threat thereof from imports, or in case of heavy EEC interventions or market withdrawals, the EC Commission is authorized under EEC regulations to suspend imports totally or partially or impose a supplementary charge on them." *EEC Restrictions on Imports of Apples from Chile* report of the panel (L/5047 *BISD* 27S/98) adopted on 10 November 1980 (hereafter *Chile Apples)* para. 2.2.

[183] Ibid., para. 4.5.

[184] Ibid., para. 4.6.

Community lost the case because the additional requirements set under the last paragraph of Article XI:2 were lacking.[185]

The 1989 *Chile Dessert Apples* panel meticulously considered this same issue and reached a well-reasoned conclusion which went contrary to what had been reached by *Chile Apples* about a decade earlier. The basic interpretative issue was whether Article XI:2(c)(i) covered only schemes which set quantitative limits on the amount producers could offer for sale, or whether it also covered schemes which could result in a reduction of products reaching the consumer through withdrawals activated by reference to a floor price without quantitative targets. The panel concluded that "the EEC measures taken under the intervention system for apples did not constitute marketing restrictions of a type which could justify import restrictions under Article XI:2(c)(i)."[186] According to the panel, measures which simply prevented consumers from buying products below certain prices "would not appear to be covered by this wording."[187] The panel stressed that if the withdrawal of a product from the market without any governmental limitation on the amount that could be sold was included within the purview of Article XI:2(c)(i), "the words 'permitted to be' would not have any function."[188] The panel further observed that "if Article XI:2(c)(i) could be used to justify import restrictions which were not the counterpart of any governmental measure capable of limiting production, the value of the General Agreement as a legal frame-work for the exchange of tariff concessions in the agricultural field would be seriously impaired."[189] Therefore, for a domestic governmental measure to satisfy the condition of being restrictive of supplies, it should not just allow withdrawal from markets but set quantitative limits on the amount that can either be produced or, after production, the amount that can reach the market.

A second and equally important element of Article XI.2(c)(i) is that the supply restriction should be on a "like product" or, in the absence of substantial production of such a product, on a product that is "directly substitutable". An import restriction under Article XI:2(c) may be allowed only if, in addition to the conditions discussed earlier, there is a domestic governmental measure that restricts the production or marketing of a product that is "like" the product whose importation is restricted. The *MIP* panel raised the question of which Community product should be considered the "like domestic product" in relation to imported tomato concentrate. The panel noted, *inter alia,* that the League of Nations had defined a "like product" to mean a product that is "practically identical with another product"[190] and concluded that only tomato concentrate produced in the Community would qualify as "the like domestic product". It was, however, "unable to decide if fresh tomatoes grown within the Community would also qualify."[191]

---

185 See Ibid.
186 *Chile Dessert Apples*, *supra* n. 80, para. 12.17.
187 Ibid., para. 12.13.
188 Ibid.
189 Ibid., para. 12.15.
190 The *MIP* case, *supra* n. 82, para. 4.12.
191 Ibid., para. 4.12.

This conclusion indicates that the degree of likeness referred to here is tantamount to some form of "sameness". Indeed, this requirement of "sameness" has sometimes been pushed to absurd extents by some contracting parties. In the 1980 *Chile Apples* dispute, for instance, Chile argued that Chilean and Community apples were neither like nor directly competitive products. In its view, "Chile Apples are of different varieties than those in surplus in the Community (Golden Delicious) and they are bought by selective consumers looking and willing to pay a premium for a fresh and high quality product."[192] The EC of course argued that an apple was always an apple[193] and the panel ruled that "Chilean Apples, although of different varieties, were 'a like product' to Community apples for the purposes of Article XI:2c."[194] Similar arguments made nearly a decade later by these same parties on *dessert apples* also ended the same way.[195] In sum, the supply control requirement of Article XI:2(c)(i) applies to domestic measures limiting the production or marketing of domestic products which are like (which in this case effectively means the *same as*) or directly competitive with the product that is subject to the import restriction in question.

2.5.3.1.3 ARTICLE XI:2(C)(II): SURPLUS REMOVAL

The second alternative requirement under Article XI:2(c) lays down the condition that the domestic governmental measures for the enforcement of which the introduction of import restrictions has been found to be necessary should operate "to remove a *temporary surplus* of the like domestic product, or, if there is no substantial domestic production of the like product, of a domestic product for which the imported product can be directly substituted, by *making the surplus available to certain groups of domestic consumers free of charge or at prices below the current market level*." The two important elements of this provision are that there must be a surplus situation which is "temporary" and that disposal of the surplus should be done in prescribed ways. Unlike import restrictions introduced under Article XI:2(c)(i), however, those which aim at the removal of a temporary surplus under Article XI:2(c)(ii) do not require any restriction on domestic output.[196]

The question of whether a given surplus situation is "temporary" has been discussed in the two cases involving Chilean apples. The finding of the *Chile Apples* panel is particularly interesting. In this case, Chile argued that high surplus levels prevailed in the EC over the years and questioned whether the situation in 1979 could be considered a "temporary surplus" in the sense of Article XI:2(c)(ii).[197] The Community argued that it was only a temporary surplus situation. The panel found that EC production statistics "indicated the EEC has constantly had a surplus of

[192] *Chile Apples, supra* n. 182, para. 3.10.

[193] The EC noted that "apples were unquestionably an agricultural product, and that an EEC apple was a like product to a Chilean or Southern Hemisphere apple." See Ibid., para. 3.15.

[194] Ibid., para. 4.4.

[195] See *Chile Dessert Apples, supra* n. 80, paras. 3.14 (for Chilean arguments) and 3.15 (for EC arguments).

[196] See Ibid., para. 4.14; and *US Apples, supra* n. 120, para. 5.14.

[197] See *Chile Apples, supra* n. 182, para. 3.12.

apples over the years" and concluded that the surplus situation "could not be considered 'temporary' as it appeared year after year." However, the panel went further and observed that the levels of stocks during 1979 were "significantly higher than normal" and concluded that the situation could be considered to be "a temporary surplus above the recurring surplus."[198]

Chile also challenged the legality of the manner of surplus disposal employed by the Community noting that apples withdrawn from the EC market "were destroyed, which was not provided for in XI:2c(ii)." The EC denied this,[199] and the panel found that "in so far as the apples withdrawn from the market during 1978/79 went into animal feed as well as were distributed freely to social organizations", the EC was "making the surplus available to certain groups of domestic consumers free of charge or at prices below the current market level". On the basis of this observation and its finding that the 1979 production situation amounted to a "temporary surplus above the recurring surplus", the panel stated in a somewhat twisted language that it "could not conclude that the EEC did not meet the conditions of XI:2c(ii)."[200]

In the 1989 *Chile Dessert Apples*, too, Chile argued that the EC could not meet the requirements of Article XI:2(c)(ii), *inter alia,* because there was no situation of "temporary surplus." Chile cited the finding of the 1980 panel on the same issue and argued that the finding of an exceptional level of surplus for 1979 above the recurring surplus of Community apples "did not imply that the EEC could be said to have had a temporary surplus above the recurring surplus every year since 1979."[201] Chile further contended that Community production in 1987/88 was substantially below that in previous years. In its reply, the EC also noted the 1980 *Chile Apples* panel finding that there could be a temporary surplus above the recurring surplus and asserted that its surplus situation in 1987/88 was "once again considerably worse than in previous years, for example in 1985/86, when production had been much the same."[202] According to the EC, this was another instance of a temporary surplus above the recurring surplus, and thus the 1980 Panel's findings were directly applicable. The new panel also noted the views of the 1980 panel on this point and underlined the fact that "that Panel's finding of a 'temporary surplus above the recurring surplus' related only to the situation in 1979."[203] The present panel considered the question of "whether the EEC's surplus at the time the import restrictions were imposed, i.e. April 1988, had been demonstrated to be temporary" by comparing the EC's apple surplus in 1988 with the situation in the previous years. It observed from the statistics that "while amounts withdrawn had varied in the

---

198 See Ibid., paras. 4.9–4.10.

199 See Ibid., para. 3.14. The EC provided the following details on the manner of disposal of the surplus apples: "apples withdrawn from the market either via public intervention purchases or by producers' groups in 1979 were utilized as follows: 3.6 per cent were distributed freely, 32.6 per cent were distilled into alcohol, 56.8 per cent went into animal feed and 7 per cent spoiled." Ibid.

200 See Ibid., para. 4.10.

201 See *Chile Dessert Apples, supra* n. 80, para. 3.27.

202 See Ibid., para. 3.28.

203 See Ibid., para. 12. 19.

years up to and including the 1987–88 marketing year, stocks had remained relatively stable at levels which indicated a substantial structural surplus. The panel thus found that the 1988 surplus could not be considered a temporary one, and that therefore the EEC did not meet the conditions for imposing import restrictions under Article XI:2(c)(ii)."[204] The *US Apples* panel, which was concerned essentially with the same subject and which was composed of the same panel members, repeated the findings of the *Chile Dessert Apples* ruling on this issue.[205]

In all three, the panels found that there existed a substantial surplus of apples in the EC for so long that it could not qualify for the terms "temporary surplus". But, while the 1980 *Chile Apples* panel found that, in the midst of the long-reigning surplus, there was an extreme case in 1979 which qualified for the terms of this provision, the 1989 panels found that there was nothing similar to the 1979 situation in the period at issue in the latter two cases. What is more, because the 1989 panels found the surplus not to be temporary, they avoided consideration of the issue of the method of surplus disposal employed by the Community.

2.5.3.1.4 LAST PARAGRAPH OF ARTICLE XI:2(C)

This provision stipulates that

> "Any contracting party applying restrictions on the importation of any product pursuant to sub-paragraph (c) of this paragraph shall give public notice of the total quantity or value of the product permitted to be imported during a specified future period and of any change in such quantity or value. Moreover, any restrictions applied under (i) above shall not be such as will reduce the total of imports relative to the total of domestic production, as compared with the proportion which might reasonably be expected to rule between the two in the absence of restrictions. In determining this proportion, the contracting party shall pay due regard to the proportion prevailing during a previous representative period and to any special factors** which may have affected or may be affecting the trade in the product concerned."

This paragraph provides for two important additional conditions for the use of quantitative restrictions. Firstly, and this applies to all three items under Article XI:2(c), a contracting party applying any import restrictions under any of these sub-paragraphs is required to give prior public notice of the total size of the quota permitted to be imported over a specified future period of time. This is another expression of the fundamental principles of transparency and predictability in trade. It was agreed already in 1955 that the public-notice requirement "should be construed as requiring the contracting party to send a copy of that notice to the CONTRACTING PARTIES ... which would circulate this information to all contracting parties concerned."[206]

---

[204] Ibid.

[205] See *US Apples*, *supra* n. 120, para. 5.19.

[206] GATT, *Report of the Review Working Party on Quantitative Restrictions* (L/332/Rev. 1 and Addenda *BISD* 3S/170) adopted on 2, 4, and 5 March 1955, para. 70.

The quotas may be expressed in quantity[207] or value[208] terms. An important objective of the multilateral trading system being the creation of a transparent and predictable trading environment, this provision requires more than mere public notification. The precise amount of allowable imports need to be specified on a product-by-product basis. As the panel in *Japan Agriculture* pointed out, the last paragraph of Article XI:2(c) implies that "only those quotas can be applied which define the particular quantity or value for each product subject to quota."[209] This panel found that a "miscellaneous quota" applied by Japan on "prepared whey" was a single quota containing "many and diverse products" and did not satisfy the requirements of Article XI:2(c).[210] Finally, the public notice requirement also applies to any subsequent changes in the quantity or value of the permissible imports. It was thus agreed in this connection that contracting parties intending to introduce restrictions pursuant to Article XI:2(c) should, whenever practicable, give "advance notice, on a confidential basis, to interested contracting parties and to the CONTRACTING PARTIES ... to give them an opportunity for consultation."[211]

Secondly, and this applies only to measures taken under Article XI:2(c)(i), the last paragraph of Article XI:2(c) prescribes the rule of proportionality as to the effect of the import restrictions on the relationship between domestic and imported products. This is another expression of the fundamental GATT principle that non-tariff barriers are in principle prohibited, and that, when they have to be permitted for exceptional and overriding public policy considerations, they should not be used as disguised forms of protecting domestic producers of competing products. Accordingly, when a contracting party introduces an import restriction for the purpose of enforcing domestic supply restriction measures, the balance between domestic and imported products which prevailed, or which would have prevailed, in the absence of the import restrictions should remain unaffected. Stated otherwise, the import restrictions should not result in a loss of market share for imported products in favour of domestically produced ones. The *Chile Dessert Apples* panel observed in this connection that imports may be restricted under Article XI:2(c)(i) only in proportion to domestic *production* "whether the government has chosen to restrict the quantities permitted to be *marketed* or those permitted to be *produced*."[212] The panel emphasized that in cases where a contracting party opts to use marketing restrictions in the sense of Article XI:2(c)(i), "imports may only be reduced to the extent that production declines."[213] Once again, this same approach is repeated by the *US Apples* panel.[214] The last paragraph of Article XI:2(c) thus prescribes the minimum amount of import quotas that contracting parties may establish in

---

207 For example, X tonnes of product Y over the next Z months.

208 For example, the equivalent of X dollars of the value of Product Y over the next Z months.

209 *Japan Agriculture, supra* n. 73, para. 5.3.1.3.

210 Ibid.

211 GATT, *Report of the Review Working Party on Quantitative Restrictions, supra* n. 164, para. 71.

212 *Chile Dessert Apples, supra* n. 80, para. 12.14.

213 Ibid.

214 See *US Apples, supra* n. 120, para. 5.14.

accordance with sub-paragraph (c)(i) of that provision. It is these quotas which must be such as not to reduce the total of imports relative to domestic production as compared with the proportion which might reasonably be expected to rule between the two in the absence of restrictions.[215]

The practical question of how to determine what the proportion of domestic production and of imports would have been during the quota period in the absence of supply and quantitative import restrictions is, however, a tricky one. The provision only stipulates that in determining the proportion, due regard need to be paid to "the proportion prevailing during a previous representative period and to any special factors which may have affected or may be affecting the trade in the product concerned." Several contentious issues have arisen from these words. To mention only a few, what does a "previous representative period" mean? Does the representative period always exist? What does the term "special factors" refer to? These issues will be briefly discussed as follows.

2.5.3.1.4.1 THE PREVIOUS REPRESENTATIVE PERIOD

In the 1980 *Chile Apples* dispute, Chile contended that EC cutbacks on apple imports were disproportionately larger than EC market withdrawals of domestic apples compared to EC production and that "the EEC had not based its restrictions on a 'representative period'."[216] Chile invoked Article XIII:2 on the administration of quantitative restrictions and challenged the EC's use of 1976–1978 as a representative period in the determination of the quotas arguing that the year 1976 "was not 'representative' as voluntary restraint agreements with the EEC were in effect at that time."[217] In Chile's view, the EC should have considered an estimate of what the supplier concerned could have exported in the absence of such restrictions for that year or taken into consideration the year immediately preceding that year.[218] The EC refuted the Chilean assertion and contended that it took into account the 1976–78 representative period which it considered was "more equitable and more in conformity with GATT practice."[219] The panel agreed in principle with the Community and stated that it conforms with normal GATT practice to consider "as a 'representative period' a three-year period previous to 1979, the year in which the EEC measures were in effect."[220] However, in line with Chile, because restrictions also existed in 1976, the panel held that that year could not be considered as representative and that the year immediately preceding 1976 should be used instead. The years 1975, 1977 and 1978 were thus chosen by the panel to be the "representative period" for the purpose. Moreover, after a comparison of the proportions between imported and domestic apples which prevailed during these three years with the levels set by the

[215] See *Japan Agriculture, supra* n. 73, para. 5.1.3.7.
[216] *Chile Apples, supra* n. 182, para. 3.11.
[217] Ibid., para. 3.21.
[218] Ibid.
[219] Ibid., para. 3.18.
[220] Ibid., para. 4.8.

EC for the year 1979, the panel found that "the EEC had not maintained this proportion."[221]

Likewise, the representative period was also at issue in the 1989 *Chile Dessert Apples* dispute between the same parties. In the determination of the amount of import quotas on apples for 1988, the EC had used the preceding three years as the representative period and argued that it was in line with the 1980 *Chile Apples* panel report on the matter.[222] Chile, too, admitted that normal GATT practice was indeed to consider the last three years as a previous representative period. But, according to Chile, this was the case only if it could not be shown for some reason that one or more of those years was not representative. Chile argued that the year 1985 was not representative because of the adverse effects caused by a severe earthquake in that year which damaged its export infrastructure. Chile argued that "the earthquake should be considered as a 'special factor' and therefore 1985 should not be considered as 'representative' nor be included in any calculation of a representative period."[223] The panel did not, however, reach a verdict on this issue as it was able to dispose of the matter on the basis of a finding that the EC system of market restriction did not satisfy the requirements of Article XI:1(c)(i).[224]

In general, there is sufficient "case law" and practice to conclude that the previous representative period is understood to mean the three years preceding the year in question in which normal production and marketing situations prevailed. However, this may not always be possible. In *Japan Agriculture*, for instance, the panel found that the import restrictions maintained by Japan had been in place for so long that there was no previous period free of restrictions in which the shares of imports and domestic supplies could "reasonably be assumed to resemble those which would prevail today."[225] What is more, the panel also used the established burden of proof rule in cases involving exceptions and ruled that Article XI:2(c)(i) "could in practice

---

[221] Ibid., para. 4.7. The figures identified by the panel look as follows: the proportion between total imports of apples from the Southern Hemisphere to total EC production had been 5.7 per cent on the average during 1975, 1977 and 1978, and would have been 4.9 per cent in 1979 based on estimated export intentions of the Southern Hemisphere countries before restraints were put into place. The levels the EC fixed during its negotiations of voluntary restraint agreements with the Southern Hemisphere countries (including Chile) totalled 313,000 m.t. which meant a proportion of imports to EC production of 4.5 per cent. Ibid. para. 4.8.

[222] See *Chile Dessert Apples*, *supra* n. 80, para. 3.32. The Community argued that "[i]n 1988, the Community had taken as the previous representative period the three years (in the form of marketing years) preceding the action, in others words 1986/87, 1985/86 and 1984/85. During this period, the proportion between gross domestic production and southern hemisphere imports came to an average of 6.4 per cent. During the marketing year 1987/88, the proportion between gross domestic production and imports from the southern hemisphere came to 7.9 per cent, or a rise of 23 per cent. Looking at the figures for net domestic production, in other words after deduction of withdrawals from marketing, the proportion came to 6.8 per cent over the past three years and 8.7 per cent in 1987/88. The Community therefore chose to go beyond the average for the last three years by substantially improving the share of imports." Ibid.

[223] Ibid., para. 4.18.

[224] See Ibid., para. 12.18.

[225] *Japan Agriculture*, *supra* n. 73, para 5.1.3.7.

not be invoked in cases in which restrictions had been maintained for such a long time that the proportion between imports and domestic supplies that would prevail in the absence of restrictions could no longer be determined on the basis of a previous representative period."[226]

2.5.3.1.4.2 SPECIAL FACTORS

The relative proportion between domestic and imported products as calculated for the representative period should respond to the effect of what are here called "special factors" upon the competitive condition between imports and domestic products. An Interpretative Note to the last paragraph of Article XI:2 defines these "special factors" to include "changes in relative productive efficiency as between domestic and foreign producers, or as between different foreign producers, but not changes artificially brought about by means not permitted under the Agreement." In line with the philosophy of the General Agreement that market shares should be the result of productive efficiency, the definition of special factors in this provision makes it mandatory that whenever countries introduce import quotas in accordance with Article XI:2(c)(i), changes in relative productive efficiency should be reflected in the size of the quotas that are determined. The impact of an import restriction should thus be as neutral and as even-handed as possible between all products regardless of their country of origin. The use of import restrictions to disturb the balance between domestic and foreign producers or between one foreign producer and another is therefore prohibited. The two *Chilean Apple* cases are once more particularly relevant to this issue.

In the 1980 *Chile Apples*, Chile claimed that the EC had not taken into account special factors, "in particular, Chile's increased export potential and its actual commercial contracts for 1979."[227] The EC replied that it did not do so because it "considered that the notion of 'productive efficiency' was difficult to take into account in allocating shares as one could not confirm whether an increase observed in exports reflected increased productivity."[228] The panel first noted that exports from Chile into the EC had been expanding rapidly,[229] and ruled that the Community should have taken into account Chile's increased export capacity in its allocation of shares.[230] According to the panel, such a consideration would be "in line with the interpretative note to the term 'special factors' as drafted in the Havana Charter, in particular with reference to 'the existence of new or additional ability to export' as between foreign producers."[231]

In the 1989 *Chile Dessert Apples*, too, Chile argued in connection with Article

[226] Ibid., para 5.1.3.7.

[227] *Chile Apples*, *supra* n. 182, para. 3.11.

[228] Ibid., para. 3.26.

[229] The panel noted that "Chile had more than doubled its share among Southern Hemisphere suppliers into the EEC market over a recent period, accounting for 5 per cent in 1974, 10 per cent in 1975, 13 per cent in 1976, 14 per cent in 1977 and 17 per cent in 1978." Ibid., para. 4.17.

[230] Ibid.

[231] Ibid., para. 4.17.

XIII:2(d) on the administration of quantitative restrictions that quotas must be allotted such that the distribution of trade in the product would approach as closely as possible the shares which the various contracting parties might be expected to obtain in the absence of such restrictions.[232] Chile cited the 1985 earth quake as a cause for the fall of its exports in that year and claimed that the earthquake should have been considered as a "special factor" in this respect. According to Chile, it was in violation of the last paragraph of Article XI:2 for the EC, in its allotment of country-specific quotas of apples for the year 1988, to have followed the normal practice of using the three preceding years as a representative period regardless of the effect of the earthquake. Chile further argued that the EC should also have considered as a "special factor" the "increase in Chilean productive efficiency vis-à-vis its southern hemisphere competitors" as provided for in the note Ad Article XI:2.[233] Chile invoked the 1980 *Chile Apples* panel report which had ruled that "Chile's increased export capacity should have been taken into account by the EEC in its allocation of shares among the southern hemisphere suppliers."[234] The EC rejected Chile's claim and contended that it had determined the traditional share as the average of the three years preceding the measure, and also taken into account special factors which could affect trade in the product and which could call for adjustment to this average figure. According to the EC, these factors included in particular new or improved export capacity of foreign suppliers.[235] It was the view of the Community, however, that the "objective assessment" it made on the situation "indicated that Chile did not have a more favourable production and export potential than the other countries."[236]

In interpreting the term "special factors", the panel recalled that an interpretative note to Article 22 of the Havana Charter (the Charter equivalent of GATT Article XIII) had defined this very term to include, *inter alia,* the following changes, as between the various foreign producers, which may have occurred since the representative period: "(1) changes in relative productive efficiency; (2) the existence of new or additional ability to export; and (3) reduced ability to export."[237] After an evaluation of the data submitted by the parties, the panel found that there was an

---

232 Article XIII:2 of the General Agreement. See Chile's argument in *Chile Dessert Apples, supra* n. 80, para. 4.18. Article XIII:2(d) provides that "the contracting party concerned shall allot to contracting parties having a substantial interest in supplying the product shares based upon the proportions, supplied by such contracting parties during a previous representative period, of the total quantity or value of imports of the product, due account being taken of any special factors which may have affected or may be affecting the trade in the product."

233 See Ibid., para. 4.19.

234 See Ibid., para. 4.19. The panel in that case felt that such a consideration was in line with the interpretative note to the term "special factors" as drafted in the Havana Charter, in particular with reference to "the existence of new or additional ability to export" as between foreign producers. See *Chile Apples, supra* n. 182, para. 4.17.

235 See *Chile Dessert Apples, supra* n. 80, para. 4.22.

236 See Ibid., para. 4.23.

237 Havana Reports, page 95, para. 52; Havana Charter Interpretative Note ad Article 22 cited in Ibid., para. 12.23.

overall trend towards an increase in Chile's relative productive efficiency and export capacity and that that trend "had not been duly taken into account, nor had the temporary reduction in export capacity caused by the 1985 earthquake."[238] The panel thus found that the account taken of special factors by the EC in allocating Chile's quota share did not meet the requirements of Article XIII:2(d).

Japan Agriculture also found that changes in relative productive efficiency are among the special factors to which due regard should be paid, "but not changes resulting from measures not permitted under the General Agreement."[239] The panel pointed out that the interpretive note specifically excludes from the definition of the term "special factors" changes artificially brought about by means not permitted under the General Agreement, but not changes artificially brought by legal means such as production subsidies or tariff protection granted within the bounds of Article II.[240]

To sum up, the "special factors" are here presented in a manner that can apply to both the past as well as the present. Their inclusion allows countries to alter the proportion dictated by the previous representative period if, during that period, some "special factors" have been at work in favour of either party. So also can the proportion derived from the representative period be modified if there is any special factor currently at work whose absence would dictate otherwise. The essential point is that when a country introduces a quantitative restriction on imports, it should apply it such that the proportion of imports could not fall below the level which would have prevailed had the quantitative restrictions not existed.

2.5.3.2 Summary of Article XI:2(c)(i)

Sub-paragraph (c)(i) of Article XI:2 is the most important provision in the area of agricultural market access under the General Agreement. It provides that contracting parties are allowed to introduce non-tariff agricultural import restrictions only if they satisfy a set of rather stringent and complex criteria. The available case law on the subject shows that panels have traditionally interpreted these already stringent conditions so strictly that no challenged agricultural import restriction has been upheld thus far.

All the important GATT cases on this issue stated, virtually in identical language, that an agricultural import restriction under Article XI:2(c)(i) needs to satisfy seven important conditions:

1. the measure must constitute an import restriction, and not a prohibition;
2. the restriction must be on an agricultural or fisheries product;

---

[238] See Ibid., para. 12.24.

[239] *Japan Agriculture, supra* n. 73, para. 5.1.3.3.

[240] Ibid., para. 5.1.3.3. The panel emphasized that "it is not necessary to restrict the level of production below the level that would exist in the absence of all government support. It also means that production which exists only because of production subsidies may be effectively restricted by imposing quantitative limits on the availability of subsidies. Other than requiring a governmental measure, Article XI:2(c)(i) does not specify how the production restriction is to be imposed." Ibid.

3. there must be a governmental measure which operates to restrict the quantities of a product permitted to be marketed or produced domestically;
4. the import restriction and the domestic supply restriction must in principle apply to "like" or directly substitutable products;
5. the import restriction must be necessary to the enforcement of the domestic supply restriction;
6. public notice must be given of the total quantity or value of the quota for each product; and
7. the restriction on imports must not reduce the total of imports relative to the total of domestic production, as compared with the proportion which might reasonably be expected to rule between the two in the absence of restrictions.[241]

These conditions are cumulative in nature – all of them must be satisfied for any import restrictive measure to be a justifiable exemption from the principle under Article XI:1. Furthermore, as conditions for an exception to a principle, it is always incumbent upon the party invoking them to carry the burden of proof and demonstrate to the satisfaction of the panel at hand that they are all satisfied. The mere showing of the existence of any of the non-tariff barriers outlawed under Article XI:1 creates the presumption in favour of a claimant that there is a GATT violation and hence a *prima facie* case of nullification or impairment. It has also been established that Article XI protects expectations on competitive conditions, not on export volumes, and that the presumption that a measure inconsistent with Article XI caused nullification or impairment could not be refuted with arguments relating to export volumes.[242]

Also worth mentioning is that even when the use of non-tariff barriers is justified via the fulfillment of all the substantive conditions summarized above, their practical application also needs to satisfy other, more of formal, requirements. They include (1) the general requirements of prompt publication of relevant laws and regulations and their uniform, impartial, and reasonable administration together with the creation of independent tribunals capable of reviewing and correcting problems in the administration of those laws[243]; and (2) the non-discriminatory administration of quantitative restrictions – application of similar prohibitions or restrictions to all supplying countries so as to bring about "distribution of trade in such product approaching as closely as possible the shares which the various contracting parties might be expected to obtain in the absence of such restrictions."[244] However, as these formal requirements do not distinguish between agricultural and non-agricultural products, they are not dealt with here at length.

---

[241] See *Japan Agriculture, supra* n. 73, para. 5.1.3.; *Canada Ice Cream, supra* n. 120, para 62; *US Apples, supra* n. 120, Para. 5.3; and *Chile Dessert Apples, supra* n. 80, para. 12.3.

[242] A 1984 panel stressed this point as follows: "the existence of a quantitative restriction should be presumed to cause nullification or impairment not only because of any effect it had on the volume of trade but also for other reasons e.g., it would lead to increased transaction costs and would create uncertainties which could affect investment plans." *Japanese Measures on Imports of Leather*, (L/5623 *BISD* 31S/94), adopted on 15/16 May 1984, para. 113.

[243] See Article X of the General Agreement.

[244] Article XIII:2 of General Agreement.

2.6 CONCLUSION

Since its very inception, the rules of the multilateral trading system approached agriculture as a sector befitting an exceptional treatment. The provisions of Article XI:2 were designed to execute that objective. However, the conditions discussed above have often been found too stringent and rigid to satisfy. Panel after panel recognized that the requirements of Article XI:2(c)(i) for invoking an exception to the general prohibition on quantitative restrictions made this provision extremely difficult to comply with in practice.[245] Panels also pointed out that "there existed widespread dissatisfaction with this provision".[246] This did not, however, deter countries from erecting non-tariff barriers against the import of agricultural products. Some contracting parties managed to get a complete waiver from the obligations of Article XI; others negotiated an exemption therefrom in their protocols of accession; a large majority simply "felt free to operate quantitative restrictions" in blatant disregard of this stringent provision.[247] The cumulative effect of all those developments expressed itself in the form of the 1982 GATT *Ministerial Declaration*[248] which laid the foundation for the initiation of the Uruguay Round.

The Declaration recognized that there was "an urgent need to find lasting solutions to the problems of trade in agricultural products", and anticipated the main Uruguay Round negotiating agenda in the area with some degree of precision. It also set up a Committee on Agriculture with a view to facilitating achievement of greater liberalization in the trade of agricultural products. In particular, the Declaration had, as one of its objectives, the examination of "trade measures affecting market access and supplies, with a view to greater liberalization in the trade of agricultural products, with respect to tariffs and non-tariff measures, on a basis of reciprocity and mutual advantage under the General Agreement."[249] The then established Committee on Agriculture examined the trading policies of the contracting parties and concluded the obvious in the following terms: "the contracting parties have all had recourse to a more or less broad range of restrictive practices, affecting both imports and exports. The perception which governments have of such restrictive measures is, broadly speaking, that their rights under the GATT permit them to take such measures."[250] The 1986 Punta del Este Declaration

---

245 See *Chile Dessert, Apples supra* n. 80, para. 12.4; *Canada Ice Cream, supra* n. 120, para. 59.

246 See *Chile Dessert Apples, supra* n. 80, para. 12.4; *Canada Ice Cream, supra* n. 120, para. 60; and *US Apples, supra* n. 120, para. 5.4. These panels also recalled, however, that it was not their function to propose changes to the provisions of the General Agreement but to make findings regarding their interpretation and application.

247 See, *inter alia,* Hillman, J. "The US Perspective", in Ingersent, K., A. Rayner, and R. Hine (eds.) *Agriculture in the Uruguay Round* (St. Martin's press, New York 1994) p. 31; Jackson (1977) *supra* n. 17, p. 981; OECD (1995) *supra* n. 41, p. 10.

248 GATT, *Thirty-Eighth Session at Ministerial Level: Ministerial Declaration,* (L/5424 *BISD* 29S/16) adopted on 29 November 1982.

249 Ibid.

250 GATT Committee on Agriculture, *Progress Report to the Council of Representatives Presented to the CONTRACTING PARTIES at their Thirty-ninth Session* (L/5563 *BISD* 30S/101). According to the Committee,

launching the Uruguay Round repeated the important concerns expressed in the 1982 Ministerial Declaration and stated, in relevant part, that the negotiations "shall aim to achieve greater liberalization of trade in agriculture and bring all measures affecting import access ... under strengthened and more operationally effective GATT rules and disciplines, taking into account the general principles governing the negotiations, by improving market access through, *inter alia*, the reduction of import barriers."[251] The ultimate result in the area of agriculture was the tariffication of all agricultural non-tariff barriers and the binding of them all with minor and only provisional exceptions. Thanks to the Uruguay Round, the exceptions provided under Article XI:2(c) for non-tariff agricultural import restrictions have lost their relevance.

---

cont.
provisions of Article XI, XVI, XVII, XX, and XXIV, "grandfather" clauses, legislation predating accession to the General Agreement or waivers have been frequently invoked to justify their action. Ibid.

[251] GATT, *Ministerial Declaration on the Uruguay Round* (MIN.DEC) adopted in Punta del Este, Uruguay, on 20 September 1986, often referred to as the *Punta del Este Declaration*, reproduced in, GATT *Focus Newsletter*, No. 41, (October 1986).

CHAPTER 3

MARKET ACCESS UNDER THE URUGUAY ROUND AGREEMENT ON AGRICULTURE

3.1 Introduction

Agriculture was one of the most sensitive subjects throughout the course of the Uruguay Round. Although not as contentious as export subsidies and domestic support, the problem of market access was at the heart of the negotiations. The rules and disciplines on market access together with the Schedules of Concessions thereon constitute one of the three pillars of the WTO Agriculture Package.

Although GATT has always favoured tariffs over non-tariff barriers, the latter have been the major obstacles to international agricultural trade. And it is only a matter of consistency with established GATT practice that the solution to the problem came in the form of the conversion of all non-tariff agricultural import barriers into their tariff equivalents and the binding of the resulting tariffs. This process is called tariffication. Given the exceptionally sensitive nature of agricultural trade, it is hardly surprising that tariffication has been praised as "one of the most significant 'systemic' achievements of the Uruguay Round",[1] the "most significant aspect of the UR Agreement on Agriculture",[2] etc. Not only are agricultural non-tariff barriers tariffied and bound, the resulting tariff levels have also been subject to binding progressive reduction commitments over a six-year implementation period.[3]

However, the result of the Uruguay Round in the area of market access has not been totally free of problems. High tariff peaks and consequent high tariff dispersion between products are two of the most notable limitations of the resulting market access discipline of the Agriculture Agreement. The minimum access and current access commitments have also resulted in the proliferation of tariff quotas whose administration in most cases necessitated a system of import licensing. As the market access discipline introduced by the Agriculture Agreement generally follows the long-established practices of the GATT over the years in the negotiation and binding of tariffs and their progressive reduction, the focus of this chapter is on these and other corollary arrangements to the tariffication process.

---

[1] OECD, *The Uruguay Round: A Preliminary Evaluation of the Agreement on Agriculture in the OECD Countries* (Paris 1995), p. 29.

[2] M. Ingco, *Agricultural Trade Liberalization in the Uruguay Round: One Step Forward, One Step Back?*, supplementary paper prepared for a World Bank Conference on "The Uruguay Round and the Developing Countries'", (Washington, D.C. 26–27 January 1995) p. 4.

[3] See Article 1(f) of the Agreement on Agriculture.

3.2 A Review of Basic Issues of Market Access Negotiated in the Uruguay Round

The first serious consideration of the issue of how to bring problems of agricultural market access barriers within a strengthened and operationally more effective multilateral discipline was made in the meetings of the GATT "Group on Quantitative Restrictions and other Non-Tariff Barriers" which was set up by the 1982 Ministerial Declaration.[4] The Group was also the first important body to consider tariffication as a potential solution to the problem. Its discussion of the concept anticipated not only the ultimate solution that was to be adopted a decade later for the problem of agricultural non-tariff barriers under the Uruguay Round Agreement on Agriculture, but also the difficulties that would be encountered in the exercise – that of "dirty tariffication", as it came to be called after the conclusion of the Uruguay Round. After weighing the pros and cons of this approach, the Group stated that "the rates of duty [thus fixed] would in many cases be very high, that this technique would in any case merely replace quantitative restrictions with another form of protection and that its use would not fulfil the Group's mandate of achieving trade liberalization."[5] The same problems were faced and, to a certain extent, the same fears have realized during and after the Uruguay Round.[6] The Group's discussion may thus well be called a precursor of the Uruguay Round negotiations on the problem of agricultural non-tariff barriers and that of tariffication.

The Punta del Este Declaration launching the Uruguay Round stated that its objectives in the area of agricultural market access were "to achieve greater liberalization of trade in agriculture and bring all measures affecting import access ... under strengthened and more operationally effective GATT rules and disciplines, taking into account the general principles governing the negotiations, by ... improving market access through, *inter alia*, the reduction of import barriers."[7] Given the widespread nature of nontariff barriers in the agricultural sector, translating these words into binding and enforceable obligations was one of the important challenges for the entire Uruguay Round.

The first proposals on agriculture in the Round were made by the US in 1987. For market access, just as for export subsidies, the US called for a complete phase out of all import barriers over a ten-year period.[8] Often known as the "zero option", this US proposal was found too sweeping for many other negotiating parties to take with any degree of seriousness. Some even felt that the US proposal was intended "primarily for domestic consumption". Real progress on this front was made

---

4 See GATT, *Report of the Group on Quantitative Restrictions and other Non-Tariff Barriers* (L/5713 *BISD* 31S/212) adopted on 30 Nov. 1984.

5 Ibid., para. 38.

6 See, for instance, the discussion on "dirty tariffication" *infra* **Section 3.3.6**.

7 GATT, *Ministerial Declaration on the Uruguay Round* (MIN.DEC) adopted in Punta del Este, Uruguay, on 20 September 1986, often referred to as the *Punta del Este Declaration,* reproduced in GATT, *Focus Newsletter*, No. 41 (October 1986).

8 See J. Croome, *Reshaping the World Trading System: A History of the Uruguay Round* (Geneva 1995) p. 114.

possible only after the negotiators agreed in the delayed Mid-Term Review on a formula of "progressive and substantial reduction in border protection and trade distorting subsidies" – thus effectively abandoning the first proposal to eliminate border measures altogether.[9]

Tariffication of all non-tariff barriers as a solution to the problem of agricultural market access was formally proposed by the US in its first detailed proposal after the Mid-Term Review.[10] Importantly, this proposal to tarrify and bind also included the typical EC system of variable levies.[11] The EC accepted that tariffication could be a useful tool, but only subject to a series of conditions, the most important one being what it called rebalancing or harmonization. As regards the variable levy, the EC in principle accepted to replace it with a "fixed tariff" but only if accompanied by what it called a "variable corrective tariff". This EC response has been termed a proposal for "partial tariffication".[12] Serious resistance to the US proposal also came from Japan.[13]

The Framework Agreement of July 1990 prepared by Aart de Zeeuw, chairman of the Negotiating Group on Agriculture – often called the "De Zeeuw Paper" – based itself on the principle of tariffication of all non-tariff border measures to be followed by a substantial reduction of the resulting tariffs and a minimum access commitment requirement.[14] The De Zeeuw Paper also envisaged the possibility to introduce special

---

[9] See A. De Zeeuw, "Implementation and Accomplishments of the WTO", paper presented at a seminar organized by the International Policy Council on Agriculture, Food and Trade, in *Proceedings of the IPC Seminar: Agriculture, the FTAA and the WTO* (Belo Horizonte, Brazil 12–13 May 1997) p. 21.

[10] See *Submission of the United States on Comprehensive Long-Term Agricultural Reform, (*GATT Doc. No. MTN.GNG/NG5/W/118, Oct. 25, 1989) pp. 3 – 5; see also T. Stewart, *The GATT Uruguay Round: A Negotiating History (1986–1992)* in III Vols. (Kluwer 1993) Vol. I, p. 173; and OECD (1995) *supra* n. 1, pp. 12–13.

[11] See Croome (1995) *supra* n. 8, p. 234.

[12] Ingersent *et al* wrote as follows: "On import access, the EC responded to the US tariffication proposal with a *partial* tariffication proposal of its own. The basis of this proposal was that border protection should consist of two elements, a fixed tariff calculated relative to an external reference price (effectively the world price expressed in domestic currency in a fixed exchange rate) and a 'corrective factor' to offset world price and exchange rate fluctuations beyond certain limits." K. Ingersent, A. Rayner, and R. Hine, "The EC Perspective", in K. Ingersent, A. Rayner, and R. Hine (eds.) *Agriculture in the Uruguay Round* (St. Martin's press, New York 1994) p. 66.

[13] Japan, which has no appreciable exports of agricultural products, "supported the prohibition of export subsidies but *vigorously opposed the abolition of quantitative import controls* for rice ...." D. Hathaway, and M. Ingco, *Agricultural Liberalization and the Uruguay Round,* paper presented at the World Bank Conference on "The Uruguay Round and the Developing Economies", (26–27 January 1995) p. 5 (italics added). It is noteworthy in this context that this Japanese opposition finally resulted in the introduction of a "special treatment" option so that countries would, under specified circumstances be able not to tarrify their non-tariff barriers. For more on this, see *infra* **Section 3.3.10.** India was also the other important negotiating party which opposed the tariffication approach. See Stewart (1993) *supra* n. 10, pp. 209–211.

[14] See De Zeeuw (1997) *supra* n. 9, p. 21. The Framework Agreement provided the parameters to be followed by countries as follows: conversion of all border measures other than normal customs duties into tariff equivalents, the binding of these tariff equivalents, maintenance of current access opportunities on terms at least equivalent to those existing through, *inter alia,* tariff quotas; and, in the absence of significant imports, establishment of minimum level of access. The modalities for the conversion of non-tariff border measures into their tariff equivalents "should be based on the existing

safeguard provisions which would enable countries to raise tariffs in cases where unexpected import surges or price slumps resulted from the reform process.[15] While the US and the Cairns Group countries generally accepted the Framework Agreement as a positive development, Japan and the EC in particular rejected it "out of hand as an insufficient basis for further negotiations."[16] All subsequent attempts to bridge the gaps before the impending Brussels Ministerial Meeting in December, 1990 – supposedly the closing meeting of the Uruguay Round – ended in failure. The failure of the Brussels Ministerial to complete the Round was thus a foregone conclusion. The EC led the rejection of the compromise plan proposed by Mats Helstrom, Swedish Agriculture Minister who chaired the ministerial negotiations on agriculture. One of the reasons for the EC to do so was because the rebalancing condition it had attached to its acceptance of the principle of tariffication was not included in the chairman's proposal.[17] Japan and Korea followed the lines of the Community claiming that their food security concerns were not properly reflected in the Helstrom text.[18]

When negotiations were resumed after the Brussels failure, the question of whether tariffication should apply to all import barriers or only to a selected few became crucial. The view that agriculture was a special case requiring the retention of "absolute barriers against some imports" was still strongly held by Japan, Korea and some other countries.[19] The EC was still pressing for a rebalancing of its tariffs. In an attempt to resolve the deadlock, on 20 December 1991, GATT Director-General Arthur Dunkel took the brave step of issuing a "Draft Final Act of the Uruguay Round".[20] Often called the Dunkel Draft, this document was prepared in line with the De Zeeuw Paper and closely approximated the final structure and content of the Uruguay Round Agreement on Agriculture. In the area of market access, Article 4:2 of the Dunkel Draft stated the principle of tariffication as follows: "participants undertake not to resort to, or revert to, any measures which have been converted into ordinary customs duties pursuant to concessions under this Agreement." Defining the scope of tariffication, Annex 3 to the draft Agreement on Agriculture, entitled *Modalities for the Establishment of Specific Binding Commitments under the Reform Programme,* provided that the policy coverage of tariffication should include all border measures other than ordinary customs duties such as: quantitative import restrictions, variable import levies, minimum import prices, discretionary import licensing, non-tariff measures maintained through state trading enterprises, voluntary export restraints and any other schemes similar to

---

cont.

gap between external and internal prices as close as possible to actual prices." See *Framework Agreement on Agriculture Reform Programme: Draft Text by the Chairman* (GATT Doc. MTN.GNG/NG5/W/170) para. 12.

15 See *Framework Agreement, supra* n. 14, para. 16.

16 See Stewart (1993) *supra* n. 10, p. 198; De Zeeuw (1997) *supra* n. 9, p. 22; Croome (1995) *supra* n. 8, p. 239.

17 See Stewart (1993) *supra* n. 10, p. 203.

18 See Ibid., p. 204.

19 See Croome (1995) *supra* n. 8, p. 295.

20 See *Draft Final Act Embodying the Results of the Uruguay Round of Multilateral Trade Negotiations* (20 December 1991, hereafter Draft Final Act) reproduced in Stewart (1993) *supra* n. 10,Vol. III, pp. 457 ff.

those listed above, whether or not the measures are maintained under country-specific derogations from the provisions of the General Agreement.[21] The resulting tariffs were to be reduced by an average of 36 per cent, with a minimum reduction of 15 per cent for every tariff line. Provisions on special safeguards, current access, as well as minimum access were also included in the Draft Final Act. Nothing was said, however, about what are called "special treatment" provisions, which were introduced in the second Blair House Accord in 1993.[22]

The Dunkel Draft also elicited mixed reactions from the major negotiating parties. The US and the Cairns Group countries accepted it, while France, Japan and Korea rejected it.[23] French opposition related largely to the draft's rules on export subsidies and its fear of attack against the CAP, while the opposition of Japan and Korea concerned the market access provisions incorporated in the Draft. The latter two particularly insisted that universal tariffication was not acceptable to them and argued that they could not give up their ban on rice imports.[24] Most outstanding issues between the US and the EU were resolved via a bilateral agreement concluded on 20 November 1992 at Blair House in Washington, D.C. – hence often called the Blair House Accord. An EC attempt to reintroduce its rebalancing proposal into the Agreement was not accepted by the US. The concerns raised by Japan and Korea against universal tariffication also remained outstanding. These and other concerns led to another round of negotiations, often called Blair House II, in which the Special Treatment provisions were introduced allowing Japan, Korea, and the Philippines to postpone tariffication of their quantitative restrictions on the import of rice, and Israel on that of cheese and sheepmeat subject to minimum access requirements.[25] The EC's insistence on rebalancing was not, however, accepted by the US and the Dunkel Draft provisions on the subject remained unaffected.

3.3 Substance of the Agriculture Agreement on Market Access: The Principle of Tariffication

3.3.1 General

The Uruguay Round is generally credited for taking the first most important step towards the full integration of agriculture into the rules-based multilateral trading system. The agreement to tariffy all non-tariff barriers to agricultural imports adopted in the specific area of market access is particularly significant. Thanks to

---

21 "Market Access: Agricultural Products Subject to Border Measures other than Ordinary Customs Duties", Annex 3 to *Modalities for the Establishment of Specific Binding Commitments under the Reform Programme*, in Draft Final Act.

22 See De Zeeuw (1997) *supra* n. 9, p. 22.

23 France in particular rejected the Draft "before it was officially published." See Hathaway and Ingco (1995) *supra* n. 13, p. 10.

24 See Ibid., p. 10.

25 See Hathaway and Ingco (1995) *supra* n. 13, p. 13; De Zeeuw (1997) *supra* n. 9, p. 22; OECD (1995) *supra* n. 1, p. 14; WTO Agriculture Division, *AG: Introduction* at 7.

tariffication, the agricultural sector now stands as the only sector in which virtually 100 per cent of the tariff lines are bound. In some (limited) sense, therefore, agriculture has now overtaken industrial goods on the road of trade liberalization.

Tariffication refers to the process by which non-tariff import barriers are converted into their tariff equivalents. The tariff equivalents are set such that the old levels of protection guaranteed by non-tariff barriers would still be guaranteed but through ordinary customs duties. Apparently, this looks like using different means to reach the same end. In as long as the tariffs resulting from the tariffication exercise can still afford the equivalent level of protection, therefore, a question may be raised as to where all the compliments for tariffication come from. There are at least two main explanations for this. Firstly, the Agriculture Agreement did not just convert the non-tariff barriers into their tariff equivalents but also introduced additional obligations to bind and reduce the resulting tariffs as well as to maintain and/or introduce current and minimum access opportunities. As the Appellate Body in the *Bananas* case observed, new market access concessions, in the form of new bindings and reductions of tariffs as well as other market access commitments, resulted from the Uruguay Round negotiations on agriculture and are included in Members' GATT 1994 Schedules.[26] Secondly and more importantly, even assuming that the new arrangement only tariffied the old nontariff barriers, the resulting tariffs have a number of advantages over their nontariff predecessors. Transparency is one of the most important benefits of tariffs. This brings with it other benefits, such as predictability and the non-discriminatory application of import-restrictive measures. Tariffs are also "easier to bind or reduce and less susceptible to corruption."[27] Indeed, it was the appreciation of such advantages by the contracting parties to GATT in 1947 that made tariffs the preferred means of protection under the rules of the multilateral trading system.[28]

3.3.2 Scope of Measures Subject to Tariffication

The Market Access part of the Agreement on Agriculture is very brief and general. Article 4 provides as follows:

"*Market Access*

1. Market access concessions contained in Schedules relate to bindings and

---

26 *European Communities–Regime for the Importation, Sale and Distribution of Bananas*, report of the Appellate Body (WT/DS27/AB/R) adopted 25 September 1997, para. 156.

27 Ingco (1995) *supra* n. 2, p. 2. Ingco also argues that tariffication further helps to indirectly control the amount of export subsidies: "even though tariffication does not deal directly with export policies, it could provide indirect control on export subsidies. Exporting countries providing export subsidies have to maintain import barriers to avoid re-importing the goods exported. Arbitrage in the market implies that in general a country cannot set an export subsidy higher than the level of the tariff plus transport costs. Hence tariffication facilitates an indirect control on the amount of export subsidies implied by removing the non-tariff barriers to reimporting." Ibid.

28 The WTO argues that there is "a solid economic rationale" for the choice of tariffs over nontariff barriers. The fact that nontariff barriers result in "quota rents" is said to make nontariff barriers more profitable to engage in lobbying activities for protection. See WTO, *Annual Report 1998*, p. 39.

reductions of tariffs, and to other market access commitments as specified therein.

2. Members shall not maintain, resort to, or revert to any measures of the kind which have been required to be converted into ordinary customs duties[1], except as otherwise provided for in Article 5 and Annex 5.

---

[1] These measures include quantitative import restrictions, variable import levies, minimum import prices, discretionary import licensing, non-tariff measures maintained through state-trading enterprises, voluntary export restraints, and similar border measures other than ordinary customs duties, whether or not the measures are maintained under country-specific derogations from the provisions of GATT 1947, but not measures maintained under balance-of-payments provisions or under other general, non-agriculture-specific provisions of GATT 1994 or of the other Multilateral Trade Agreements in Annex 1A to the WTO Agreement."

Article 4 is the only provision in the Agriculture Agreement which deals with the issue of market access in general. Indeed, Article 4.2 is the only important provision concerning market access and the fundamental principle of tariffication.[29] It proscribes the use of "any measures of the kind which have been required to be converted into *ordinary* customs duties."[30] An exception clause then follows excluding those measures that are justified under the special safeguard provisions of Article 5 and the Special Treatment provisions of Annex 5 to the Agreement. Two key questions may be asked at this juncture: (1) what measures *have been required to be converted into ordinary customs duties?* (2) what are ordinary customs duties?

The covered measures are defined in all-inclusive terms. Footnote 1 to Article 4.2 gives a non-exhaustive list of the types of measures that have to be converted into ordinary customs duties and subjected to "market access concessions". They include all quantitative import restrictions, variable import levies, minimum import prices, discretionary import licensing, non-tariff measures maintained through state-trading enterprises, voluntary export restraints, and similar border measures other than ordinary customs duties, whether or not the measures are maintained under country-specific derogations from the provisions of GATT 1947. The terms of this provision are coined such that the agriculture-specific rules of GATT Article XI:2 concerning

---

[29] The *Banana* panel stated in this connection that "Article 4.1 is not a substantive provision, but is a statement of where market access commitments can be found." See *European Communities–Regime for the Importation, Sale and Distribution of Bananas* report of the panel (WT/DS27/R/ECU, WT/DS27/R/GTM, WT/DS27/R/HND, WT/DS27/R/MEX, WT/DS27/R/USA) 22 May 1997, para. 7.124. The Appellate Body disagreed with the panel and stated that Article 4.1 "does more than merely indicate where market access concessions and commitments for agricultural products are to be found." *Bananas,* report of the Appellate Body, *supra* n. 26, para. 156. According to the Appellate Body, Article 4.1 "acknowledges that significant, new market access concessions, in the form of new bindings and reductions of tariffs as well as other market access commitments (i.e. those made as a result of the tariffication process), were made as a result of the Uruguay Round negotiations on agriculture and included in Members' GATT 1994 Schedules. These concessions are fundamental to the agricultural reform process that is a fundamental objective of the *Agreement on Agriculture.*" Ibid.

[30] Article 4.2 of the Agreement on Agriculture (italics added).

quantitative restrictions are effectively eliminated.[31] But, the tariffication requirement goes well beyond the reach of Article XI:2 and also covers such "grey area" measures as the system of variable import levies of the EC, the country-specific derogations from the General Agreement such as the 1955 US waiver, etc.

Not all these measures are non-tariff restrictions in the strict sense of the term. A variable levy is, for instance, a clear case of a duty imposed on imports, except that the rate fluctuates together with world price fluctuations.[32] Yet, the Agreement puts it as one of the border measures subject to tariffication presumably because it is not an "ordinary" customs duty. Moreover, by its own wording, the scope of Article 4.2 is not limited to the practices which may find their way into any of the measures specified in footnote 1; it extends to all other similar measures that are "of the kind" to the specified ones. The only exceptions to this universal tariffication requirement are those nontariff border barriers which are maintained under balance-of-payments provisions[33] or other general, non-agriculture-specific, provisions of the General Agreement or of the other Multilateral Trade Agreements in Annex 1A to the WTO Agreement.

It is interesting to note here that the Agriculture Agreement consistently talks in terms only of "ordinary customs duties" and not "customs duties" as such. Although no definition is given as to what "ordinary" customs duties are, it appears from the consistency of its use and its context that a distinction has effectively been introduced making certain customs duties acceptable and certain others not so. We have seen that variable levies and similar other measures are included in the tariffication process, thus indicating that taking the form of a customs duty does not necessarily immunize a measure from the requirement of tariffication. The exceptions clause of Article 4.2 also gives additional hints in that direction. Included in this exception are special safeguard measures taken in accordance with Article 5 and cases of special treatment under Annex 5 to the Agriculture Agreement. The latter refers to the few cases where countries were provisionally allowed to continue to use non-tariff barriers under strictly defined conditions and makes clear sense to be an exception from Article 4.2. In the case of special safeguard measures, however, Article 5 allows only an increase in tariffs beyond the bound levels and does not open

---

31 As the panel in the *Korea Beef* case pointed out, any measure that is inconsistent with Article XI of GATT 1994 is "necessarily inconsistent with Article 4.2 of *the Agreement on Agriculture* and its footnote …." See *Korea – Measures Affecting Imports of Fresh, Chilled And Frozen Beef*, report of the panel (WT/DS161/R, WT/DS169/R) 31 July 2000, para. 768.

32 In a system of variable levies, the amount of tariff imposed on imports is inversely related to the world market price of those imports – the rate of variable levies rises as world prices fall and vice versa.

33 A pertinent example of how these exceptions are interpreted in practice is *India Quantitative Restrictions*. In that case, the panel found that the consistency with Article 4.2 of a non-tariff import-restrictive measure maintained for balance-of-payments purposes depends on the measure's consistency with the relevant provisions of the General Agreement (Article XVIII in the case of India). Having found that India's measures were not justified under the terms of Article XVIII, the panel observed that "the question of the consistency of India's import restrictions with Article 4.2 depends on their consistency with Article XVIII:B. We therefore conclude that the Indian restrictions are not 'measures maintained under balance-of-payments provisions' within the meaning of footnote 1 to Article 4.2 of the Agreement on Agriculture." *India–Quantitative Restrictions on Imports of Agricultural, Textile and Industrial Products,* report of the panel (WT/DS90/R) 6 April 1999, para. 5.241.

any room for the introduction or re-introduction of any quantitative restrictions.[34] In as long as this is the case, special safeguard measures would normally not be inconsistent with Article 4.2 and no exceptions from this provision would be needed for the purpose. The only issue in cases involving the introduction of additional duties as special safeguard measures concerns Article II of GATT 1994 on the obligation not to impose duties in excess of bound rates. Article 5 explicitly refers to this provision and provides for derogations from it. However, despite the fact that Article 5 cannot justify the introduction of quantitative restrictions, Article 4.2 of the Agriculture Agreement also puts it as an exception to the principle of tariffication. Therefore, the key to understanding this clause, which might otherwise appear unnecessary, lies in the term "ordinary" under Article 4.2. Even if only additional duties can be justified under Article 5, those additional duties are not taken by the Agreement as "ordinary" duties. Hence the exemption from Article 4.

It is also noteworthy that, although not as consistently as the Agriculture Agreement, GATT 1994 also uses the term "ordinary customs duties".[35] In connection with the use of this terminology under Article II.1(b) thereof, the negotiating history shows that "the word 'ordinary' was used to distinguish between the rates on regular tariffs shown in the columns of the schedules and the various supplementary duties and charges."[36] This is an approach that also sheds some light for the interpretation of the term as used in the Agriculture Agreement. It is thus possible to conclude that the Agriculture Agreement created a market access regime which goes beyond a "customs-duties-only" requirement; it further requires those duties to qualify as "ordinary", whatever that may mean in particular contexts.

The Agreement has also introduced a package of additional "market access concessions". The concessions, which include all market access commitments undertaken pursuant to the Agriculture Agreement,[37] are contained in Members' Schedules. They relate to bindings and reductions of tariffs, and to other market access commitments, such as current and minimum access opportunities.[38] The market access concessions resulting from this exercise are annexed not to the Agreement on Agriculture itself but to GATT 1994.[39] The implications of this arrangement are enormous. As we shall see subsequently, solely because of this arrangement, the priority provisions of Article 21 of the Agriculture Agreement have been made inapplicable to terms and conditions on agricultural market access concessions included in Members' Schedules.[40]

---

34 This is without prejudice to safeguard measures which may be taken pursuant to Article XIX of the General Agreement and the WTO Agreement on Safeguards.

35 See Article II.1(b) and (c) of GATT 1994.

36 See WTO, *Analytical Index: Guide to GATT Law and Practice* (Updated 6th Edition, Geneva 1995) p. 78.

37 See Article 1(g) of the Agreement on Agriculture.

38 See Article 4.1 of the Agreement on Agriculture.

39 See "Marrakesh Protocol to the General Agreement on Tariffs and Trade 1994", para. 1.

40 For more on this, see *infra* **Section 3.3.8.**

3.3.3 Methods Used for Tariffication

The provisions of the Agriculture Agreement do not give any clue as to how the tariff equivalents are to be measured and for when, the form and depth of the commitments, etc. Indeed, the Agriculture Agreement does not (directly) address several of the practical details of how tariffication had to be done and how Members' schedules of concessions in this area had to be established. Uruguay Round negotiators left such details rather to a provisional document entitled *Modalities for the Establishment of Specific Binding Commitments under the Reform Programme*.[41] This document was issued for the purpose of completing draft schedules of concessions and commitments in the agricultural negotiations and for facilitating the verification process leading to the establishment of formal Schedules to be annexed to the Uruguay Round Protocol. The Modalities Agreement was, however, a transient document whose legal status ended with the conclusion of the Round. As stated by the Chairman of the Negotiating Group on Goods, the document was issued "on the understanding of participants in the Uruguay Round that these negotiating modalities shall not be used as a basis for dispute settlement proceedings under the [W]TO Agreement."[42] As such, possible inconsistencies between provisions of the Modalities and the content of Members' schedules of concessions and commitments may not be subsequently challenged on the basis of the Modalities.[43] In spite of this express statement, however, a comprehensive view of the WTO agriculture package can be obtained only if provisions of the Agriculture Agreement are discussed together with the relevant provisions of the Modalities Agreement.

The method of calculating the tariff equivalents of nontariff barriers is provided under Annex 3 to the Modalities Agreement. The basic requirement in the calculation of the tariff equivalents is that they be fixed "using the actual difference between internal and external prices in a transparent manner using data, data sources and definitions as specified in Annex 2."[44] This is what is often called the "price gap" method of establishing the tariff equivalents of nontariff barriers.[45] The assumption behind this rule is clear. Under normal circumstances, import barriers have the effect of raising the domestic price of imported goods above world market prices. Import-restrictive measures form a wedge between domestic and international market prices for a product and the price difference closely approximates the monetary equivalent of the restrictive effect of the measures at work.[46] A positive

---

41 *Modalities for the Establishment of Specific Binding Commitments under the Reform Programme* (MTN.GNG/MA/W/24) 20 Dec. 1993 hereafter "the Modalities Agreement" or simply "the Modalities".

42 See Ibid., para. 4.

43 See discussion of relevant parts of the *Banana* case on this subject, *infra* **Section 3.3.8.**

44 See Annex 3 to the Modalities Agreement, para. 2. Annex 2 provides the requirement that countries "shall submit lists of commitments and supporting material established in line with the reduction commitments and the modalities established in relation to each area of the negotiation." Ibid.

45 See Ingco (1995) *supra* n. 2, p. 15.

46 Import restrictions raise the domestic price of imported products and the price difference, "which is equal to the equivalent tariff, is referred to by economists as a 'quota price wedge'. The quota price wedge multiplied by the value of imports at world prices provides a measure of the value of the quota license." See WTO, *Annual Report 1998*, p. 39.

difference between the domestic and world market prices usually indicates the existence of import restrictions while a negative difference may show export restrictions. As reiterated, however, the chronic problem of agricultural trade (at least in the developed countries) is especially the former. In an attempt to minimize the role of transportation and other costs on this relationship, paragraph 4 of Annex 3 to the Modalities Agreement provides that the external prices should generally be the actual average c.i.f. unit values for the importing country and the internal price should generally be a representative wholesale price ruling in the domestic market.[47] Finally, the thus calculated tariff equivalents may be expressed as *ad valorem* or specific rates[48] and a look at the Uruguay Round schedules of many countries shows that several agricultural tariff rates are expressed in a combination of these two forms.[49]

3.3.4 The Base Period for Market Access Commitments

Given the high degree of price fluctuation characteristic of most agricultural products, the time period for which price data are to be used in the calculation of the tariff equivalents plays a pivotal role. The importance of the base period in the structure of the market access discipline resulting from the Agriculture Agreement may be demonstrated by the following introductory observations: (1) the maximum bound tariff levels are set on the basis of tariff equivalents calculated for that period; (2) the size of minimum and current access commitments is established as a proportion of imports to domestic consumption in the base period; (3) the application of the Special Treatment provisions depends on the proportion of imports to domestic consumption of a product during the base period; and (4) resort to the price-triggered special safeguard measures is determined on the basis of the state of current prices as compared with the prices during the base period.

In as long as the tariff equivalents were meant to set an upper limit and a benchmark from which reduction commitments were to be negotiated, countries would have a vested interest in pushing for those years in which the difference was at its highest for them. In other words, Members had the incentive to go for periods for which the highest internal prices coincided with the lowest external prices. This was fully reflected in the selection of the years 1986 to 1988 to serve as the base period for

---

47 See Annex 3 to the Modalities Agreement, paras. 4–5. The Modalities Agreement further provides that in cases where average c.i.f. unit values are not available or appropriate, "external prices shall be either: (i) appropriate average c.i.f. unit values of a near country; or (ii) estimated from average f.o.b. unit values of (an) appropriate major exporter(s) adjusted by adding an estimate of insurance, freight and other relevant costs to the importing country." See Ibid. For a discussion of the c.i.f. and f.o.b. prices, see *infra* chapter 10. The external prices, however determined, need to be converted to domestic currencies on the basis of "the annual average market exchange rate for the same period as the price data." See para. 5 of Annex 3 to the Modalities Agreement.

48 See para. 2 of Annex 3 to the Modalities Agreement; for a description of what these rates are, see *supra* chapter 2, section 2.3.1.

49 To give just one example, Uruguay Round Schedule LXXX of the EC shows that the tariff rate for "boneless meat of bovine animals" is bound at 12.8% plus 1768 ECU/T. See Schedule, p. 16212.

market access purposes.[50] After assessing the condition of the market over time, economists have found that the agreed base period was a "generous" choice in the sense that world-market prices at that time were "at their lowest level in recent decades".[51] As we shall see subsequently, the weakening effect of this choice has been exacerbated by the high level of "dirty tariffication" witnessed on the part of virtually every major trading nation.

3.3.5 Agricultural Tariff Reduction Commitments

As pointed out already, the Uruguay Round Agriculture Agreement did not just tariffy the nontariff barriers and bind them against future increase. It has also introduced a set of market access concessions, the most important being the commitment to reduce tariffs. The tariff reduction commitment applies to both old as well as new tariffs. In cases where agricultural products were already subject to ordinary customs duties only, the reduction commitments were applied to the existing tariff levels. While bound tariffs were taken as they stood, for unbound duties, the tariff rates applied as at 1 September 1986 served as the starting point.[52] In the case of products that were (also) subject to non-tariff border measures, the tariff levels resulting from tariffication served as the base level for the implementation of reduction commitments.[53] Once the tariffication of all agricultural nontariff barriers was completed, the resulting tariffs were considered on the same level as the old ones and the minimum reduction commitments applied to both categories in the same manner.[54]

The Modalities Agreement set minimum tariff reduction requirements at two levels – the level of individual tariff lines and the overall averages for all agricultural products – to be implemented over a six-year implementation period commencing in 1995.[55] Each tariff line was required to be reduced by a minimum of 15 per cent while the average minimum was 36 per cent. The corresponding figures for developing countries are two-thirds of those relating to developed countries (i.e. 24 per cent average and 10 per cent per tariff line) to be implemented over a period of up to 10

---

[50] See para. 2 of Annex 3 to the Modalities Agreement.

[51] Ingco (1995) *supra* n. 2, p. 22. See also S. Tangermann, *Implementation of the Uruguay Round Agreement on Agriculture by Major Developed Countries*, A report prepared for the United Nations Conference on Trade and Development, (Distr. GENERAL, UNCTAD /ITD/16, 3 October 1995), p. 5. According to Tangermann, this was more pronounced especially in the case of the EC and Japan because of a significant fall during the base period in the exchange rate of the US dollar from pre-base period levels. He thus concluded that base period world market prices "were particularly low if expressed in European currency units (ECU) and yen." Ibid.

[52] See Modalities Agreement, para. 3.

[53] Note that tariffs resulting from the tariffication process accounted, on average, for around one fifth of the total agricultural tariff lines of developed countries; for developing countries, this share is "considerably smaller". See WTO Secretariat, *Market Access: Unfinished Business – Post-Uruguay Round Inventory and Issues* (Special Studies 6, Geneva 2001), p. 46.

[54] Apparently, the only difference between them pertains to the use of the special safeguard measures as provided under Article 5 of the Agriculture Agreement. See *infra* **Section 3.3.9.**

[55] See Modalities Agreement, para. 5.

years. Least-Developed countries are required only to tariffy and bind their tariffs; they are not obliged to undertake reduction commitments. [56] In both cases, however, the figures refer only to a *simple* average in the sense that it takes the mean of all tariff lines considered on equal basis regardless of the amount or value of trade represented by each of those tariff lines. Put differently, the averages referred to here are not *trade-weighted* averages. This has significant practical implications, for it "opened up the possibility of spreading the reduction requirement unevenly across products" and enabled countries to continue providing particularly high protection to their "sensitive" products.[57] In line with expectations, it was later found that, in achieving the agreed 36 per cent average tariff reduction in agriculture, the developed countries in particular "reduced their low tariffs by high rates and high tariffs by low rates."[58] Although perhaps very few, there have also been cases where countries undertook less than the absolute minimum 15 per cent reduction required of them by the Modalities Agreement.[59] The high degree of tariff dispersion which thus resulted from this situation has led some writers to question whether this approach might have worsened, rather than improved, the level of distortions in agricultural trade flows.[60]

---

[56] See paras. 15 and 16 of the Modalities Agreement and Article 15.2 of the Agreement on Agriculture.

[57] Tangermann (1995) *supra* n. 51, p. 7. On the benefits of import-weighted averages, see Laird, S. *Multilateral Approaches to Market Access Negotiations,* WTO Staff Working Paper (TPRD-98-02, May 1998) p. 3.

[58] UNCTAD, *The Uruguay Round and Its Follow-up: Building a Positive Agenda for Development,* (Geneva 1997) p. 45. After a detailed analysis of the Uruguay Round tariff schedules for agriculture of the US, the EC and Japan, Tangermann found that the three countries "have exhibited a not unexpected tendency to reduce low tariffs more than high tariffs. . . . For example, the EU has reduced many low tariffs by 100 per cent, most tariffs by the required average rate of 36 per cent, and tariffs on a number of 'sensitive' products by 20 per cent." Tangermann (1995) *supra* n. 51, p. 7. A simple example given by Tangermann may further illustrate this point. He gives the example of "a country with four items subject to tariffs, three sensitive ones with 100 per cent duty rates and one with a 4 per cent duty. Reducing the three high rates to 85 per cent (a 15 per cent cut) and eliminating the 4 per cent rate (a 100 per cent cut) would give an unweighted average cut of 36.25 per cent. This would meet the requirement for an unweighted average cut of 36 per cent and minimum cuts per item of 15 per cent, but it would allow high protection on sensitive products to remain and it may increase the dispersion rates." S. Tangermann, "An Assessment of the Uruguay Round Agreement on Agriculture", paper prepared for the OECD's Agriculture Directorate, Paris (1994); see also K. Anderson, *Agriculture and the WTO into the 21st Century*, paper prepared for the Cairns Group Farm Leaders' Trade Strategy Seminar, Sydney, 2–3 April 1998, p. 3; and H. Binswanger, and E. Lutz, *Agricultural Trade Barriers, Trade Negotiations, and the Interests of Developing Countries*, paper prepared for the UNCTAD X High-Level Round Table on Trade and Development (Bangkok, 12 February 2000), p. 13.

[59] Ingco has found, for instance, that the overall EC reduction commitment for sugar throughout the implementation period was only 6 per cent of the base level. See Ingco (1995) *supra* n. 2, p. 49. What is worse, in as long as those minimum requirements were set only by the Modalities Agreement and not by the Agriculture Agreement, the possibilities of challenge were not available.

[60] See, *inter alia,* Ingco (1995) *supra* n. 2, p. 50; and Tangermann (1995) *supra* n. 51, p. 7. According to Tangermann, "economic theory and quantitative analysis suggest that uneven rates of protection among products closely related in production and/or use can distort the use of resources in world agriculture even more than a slightly higher but more uniform level of protection." S. Tangermann, *A Developed Country Perspective of the Agenda for the Next WTO Round of Agricultural Negotiations*, paper presented at the Graduate Institute of International Studies, 3 March 1997, p. 12.

Be that as it may, the tariff reduction commitments are required to be implemented on equal annual instalments over a six year implementation period (ten years in the case of developing countries). It goes to the credit of the Uruguay Round that, whether as a result of tariffication or otherwise, the importation of virtually all agricultural products into all WTO Members is now subject to bound tariffs. However, this does not necessarily guarantee, at least not in the short term, that agricultural imports are freer after the Uruguay Round than before. Indeed, due largely to what is now known as "dirty tariffication", tariffs are set at such high levels that agricultural imports in several cases are still restricted as much as, if not more than, the pre-Uruguay Round days.[61]

3.3.6 The Problem of "Dirty Tariffication"

Once the base period from which data would be used for the calculation of the internal and external prices was agreed on the negotiating table, the actual conversion of non-tariff barriers into their tariff equivalents was left to the individual countries concerned. It was at this stage that most countries used data which allowed them to bind tariffs "as high as possible." The data used for the purpose mostly exaggerated the domestic market prices and/or understated the world market prices which prevailed during the 1986 to 1988 base period.[62] This is what is often referred to as "dirty tariffication" – i.e. the resulting tariffs "contain 'dirt' in the sense that they are higher than what would have been exact equivalents of the non-tariff barriers existing in the base period."[63]

This process resulted in tariff levels rarely heard of in the history of international trade. The bound tariff peaks for agriculture in many developed countries "range from 100 per cent to nearly 500 percent."[64] Swiss tariffs for dairy products might be a good, albeit perhaps extreme, example here. According to an assessment made by Hathaway and Ingco, the estimated (genuine) base period *ad valorem* tariff equivalent in Switzerland for non-tariff restrictions on the import of dairy products would be 321 per cent while the declared base rate actually used for purposes of the market access commitments in the Uruguay Round was a staggering 795 per cent. The 474 percentage figure difference exhibited in this specific case is accounted for by the "dirt" included in the tariffs.[65] It is thus hardly surprising that the final bindings

---

61 The USDA has observed in this respect that "dirty tariffication and new ceiling bindings resulted in some cases in new bound tariffs that provided greater protection than had previously existed." United States Department of Agriculture, *Agriculture in the WTO* (December 1998) p. 8.

62 See, *inter alia,* USDA (1998) *supra* n. 61, p. 8.

63 Tangermann (1995) *supra* n. 51, p. 6; see also Hathaway and Ingco (1995) *supra* n. 13, p. 18.

64 USDA, *Agriculture Outlook* (Dec. 1996) p. 18. According to the USDA, this situation contrasts with non-agricultural tariff peaks which range from 25 to 50 percent.

65 See Hathaway and Ingco (1995), *supra* n. 13, Table 2b. As Switzerland used specific rates, the conversion to *ad valorem* equivalents was made by the analysts. Interestingly, even this figure is an average for a set of "dairy products" and hides a number of extreme cases inside itself. For instance, according to the OECD, the Swiss base tariff (*ad valorem* equivalent) for butter was 1,136 per cent and was reduced only by the 15 per cent minimum required by the Modalities. See OECD (1995) *supra* n. 1,

by the end of the implementation period in 2000 for several Members were much higher than the actual tariff equivalents for the pre-Uruguay Round days.[66]

It is of course true that many of these "megatariffs" serve only as ceiling bindings while in fact lower tariffs are applied in day-to-day business. However high they may be, ceiling bindings assure the importer at least one thing – tariffs may not exceed that level. Yet, while lower applied tariffs are more conducive to trade than higher bound tariffs, in as long as countries are willing to respond to changing market conditions by varying the level of applied tariffs within the limits of the ceiling, the important principles of transparency and predictability fall under serious threat.[67] Although within certain limits, this brings a situation very similar to the EC variable levy system which was included in the tariffication process of the Uruguay Round. To this extent at least, there is room to re-raise the question of whether such duties qualify as "ordinary customs duties".

The cumulative effect of all these developments is that no significant liberalization is expected in the short term. Indeed, Ingco has found that "relative to average protection levels in recent years and the average during the last ten to fifteen years, the post-UR base and final tariff equivalents and bindings are significantly higher in most countries."[68] In an attempt to minimize the adverse consequences of (dirty) tariffication, arrangements have been made to maintain existing access opportunities if they are already above a given threshold (current access) or to introduce minimum access opportunities (minimum access) at minimal tariff rates.[69]

3.3.7 Current Access and Minimum Access Commitments

The high tariff levels resulting from the tariffication process created the well-grounded fear that the new tariffs could turn out to be more restrictive than their non-tariff predecessors. To mitigate the impact of such possibilities, Members agreed to include current and minimum access commitments in their schedules for all

---

cont.
p. 28. Ingco has made a detailed analysis of this issue and reached the conclusion that although the extent of "dirt" included in the resulting tariffs varied between countries, the EU (with the largest differential of about 207 per cent for rice) and EFTA countries had the largest magnitude. What is more, even some developing countries which historically had "import subsidies" and "export taxes" and with negative tariff equivalents for the base period, such as Egypt, Pakistan, Zimbabwe, etc. set ceiling bindings "way above historical protection." See Ingco (1995) *supra* n. 2, p. 22–23.

66 According to recent studies, the bindings for the EU are on average "about 60 per cent above the actual tariff equivalents of the CAP in recent years, while the United States has set theirs about 45 percent above recent applied rates – and developing countries are even more involved in the practice." K. Anderson, Erwidodo and M. Ingco, *Integrating Agriculture into the WTO: The Next Phase*, paper presented to the WTO/World Bank Conference on "Developing Countries in a Millennium Round", (Geneva, 20–21 September 1999) pp. 8–9. See also K. Anderson, B. Hoekman and A. Strutt, *Agriculture and the WTO: Next Steps*, paper presented at the Second Annual Conference on Global Economic Analysis (Denmark 20–22 June 1999); and Binswanger and Lutz (2000) *supra* n. 58.

67 See, *inter alia*, USDA (1998) *supra* n. 61, p. 6.

68 Ingco (1995) *supra* n. 2, p. 52.

69 See also OECD (1995) *supra* n. 1, p. 29.

tariffied products – thus undertaking to create the conditions that would enable the importation of certain minimum amounts of imports of such products into their domestic markets. Current access commitments attempted to guarantee that historic levels of imports would remain unaffected by the tariffication process. Minimum access commitments, on the other hand, were intended to create that access from scratch in cases where those historic import levels were found to have been below a five per cent threshold.[70]

Paragraph 6 of the Modalities Agreement provides the principle that current access opportunities should be maintained and increased over the implementation period. This is done by means of creating terms and conditions of importation at least equivalent to those existing during the base period so that an amount of imports "no less than average annual import quantities for the years 1986 to 1988" would be possible in each year of the implementation period. However, most access opportunities in agriculture prior to the Uruguay Round were based on bilateral arrangements such as voluntary restraint agreements and the like. The amount of current access opportunities in such cases was defined as the quantity of product permitted to be imported in the base period under those measures regardless of whether that quantity was actually imported. Where actual imports exceeded the permissible quantity under those measures in the base period, the actual imported quantities were taken for purposes of current access commitments.[71]

However, the obligation to maintain and increase current access opportunities applied only if imports of a product already represented at least 5 per cent of corresponding domestic consumption in the base period 1986–88.[72] In cases where this threshold level had not been reached for the base period, the Agreement talks in terms of an obligation to create "minimum access opportunities" and not the maintenance of the status quo. The minimum amount for the first year of the six-year implementation period (1995) is set at 3 per cent of domestic consumption of the product for the base period, which should reach 5 per cent of that base figure by the year 2000. In an attempt to create this level of trade where there was (almost) none, the Modalities Agreement required that tariff quotas be established at a "low or minimal" rate and that the minimum access opportunities be implemented on an MFN basis.[73]

At the practical level, however, the distinction between current and minimum access was rather blurred. As many agricultural products were subject to absolute quantitative restrictions during the base period, the proportion of imports to

---

70 See Ibid., p. 22.

71 Para. 12 of Annex 3 to the Modalities Agreement. According to para. 13, "for existing non-automatic import licensing, non-tariff measures maintained through state trading enterprises and like measures, current access opportunities shall be defined as the quantity of product imported during the base period." For a discussion of the problems involved in the administration of current access commitments, see *infra* **Section 3.3.8.**

72 See para. 5 of the Modalities Agreement.

73 See para. 14 of Annex 3 to the Modalities Agreement. For more on minimum and current access commitments, see OECD (1995) *supra* n. 1, pp. 21–22.

domestic consumption was often very small or totally non-existent. Normally, this should mean that the importing country would undertake a minimum access commitment as part of the tariffication process. But, as the *Canada Dairy* dispute clearly demonstrated, this was not always the case. That dispute revealed, for example, that Canada's trade statistics for the base period showed no imports of milk and yet Canada only undertook a current access commitment. According to the US, because Canada did not want to undertake minimum access commitments, Canada "seized upon the idea of demonstrating the existence of some 'current access'" relying on unrecorded imports brought by returning Canadian shoppers.[74] The Appellate Body also found that both Canada and the US "understood that this commitment represented a continuation by Canada of 'current access' opportunities, not a commitment to provide 'minimum access' opportunities under the *Agreement on Agriculture*."[75]

This case shows, and a look at the Schedules of Concessions of many other Members affirms, that the rules of the Modalities Agreement on the form and content of actual market access commitments to be undertaken by Members were not always strictly observed. Once again, in as long as the relevant provisions are found only in the Modalities Agreement, the possibilities of challenge are out of the question.

The current and minimum access requirements included in the Uruguay Round arrangement for agriculture have their own positive and negative sides. The fact that they attempted to guarantee a certain level of market access regardless of the level of import tariffs resulting from the tariffication process is one of the notable positive aspects of the resulting system. At the same time, the introduction of these minimum levels has necessitated the institution of tariff rate quotas demanding deeper government involvement in trade in the form of licensing regimes and the like, which stands on the negative end of the scale.

3.3.8 Tariff Rate Quotas

The current and minimum access commitments of Members expressed themselves in the introduction of tariff-rate quotas whereby the designated minimum amounts (the in-quota amounts) would be imported at lower tariff levels and those above that threshold (the over-quota amounts) would be imported at the newly-bound tariff rates.[76] According to a WTO study, while fruits and vegetables, meat, cereals, dairy

---

[74] In creating a tariff-rate quota for milk as part of the required tariffication process, Canada "sought to dress up this unknown quantity of trade as 'current access' within the meaning of the modalities." *Canada–Measures Affecting the Importation of Milk and the Exportation of Dairy Products*, report of the panel (WT/DS103/R, WT/DS113/R) 17 May 1999, para. 4.499. The US further asserted that "in the absence of any official trade statistics to justify a current access concession, rather than the more onerous minimum access concession, Canada had to place in its schedule an ostensible basis for this lesser concession." Ibid.

[75] *Canada–Measures Affecting the Importation of Milk and the Exportation of Dairy Products* report of the Appellate Body (WT/DS103/AB/R) adopted 27 October 1999, para. 139.

[76] The WTO has reported that 37 Members, counting the EC as one, have bound a total of 1,367 tariff quotas in their WTO Schedules. See *WTO Annual Report 2000*, p. 39.

products and oilseeds are the sectors most affected by tariff quotas, Europe is the highest user. Norway leads with 232 quotas; Poland, Iceland and the EU follow with 109, 90, and 87 quotas respectively.[77]

The existence of a tariff quota very often means, however, that some kind of import licensing has to be used for the allocation of the in-quota imports.[78] Because the gap between the in-quota and the over-quota tariffs is often very wide, the manner of allocation of in-quota tariff rates is of crucial importance.[79] The administration of tariff quotas, in general, and the question of whether tariff rate quotas are made on a country-specific or an MFN basis, in particular, are the most important problems that resulted from this arrangement.

Those tariff rate quotas for the enforcement of current access commitments are particularly interesting. The Modalities Agreement distinguishes between quantitative access commitments maintaining existing levels, on the one hand, and those making subsequent expansions, on the other. Regarding the latter, the Modalities clearly stipulated that "[a]ny such expansion in access opportunities shall be provided on an m.f.n. basis."[80] No such explicit statement was made concerning the administration of current access opportunities that would not be so expanded. Given the unstated assumption behind current access commitments that exporting countries should not be worse off as a result of the Uruguay Round arrangements for agriculture, this omission does not appear to have been a result of mere inadvertence. Rather, as most access opportunities in agriculture prior to the Uruguay Round were based on bilateral arrangements such as voluntary restraint agreements and the like, it seems that there was some form of consensus that the obligation was meant to maintain the benefits of those countries in particular.

This approach explains as to why several current access commitments are expressed in the form of country-specific tariff quotas inconsistent with the MFN principle and (actually or potentially) in violation of the basic principles set forth under Article XIII of GATT 1994 on the administration of tariff and other quotas.[81] This view gets further support from the explicit MFN requirement included regarding the administration of "minimum access" commitments.[82] Read together

---

[77] See WTO Secretariat (2001), *supra* n. 53, p. 52.

[78] For an exceptional case where tariff rate quotas are used without any system of licensing for their administration, see *Canada Dairy,* report of the panel, *supra* n. 74.

[79] For OECD countries, the average in-quota rate for agricultural products is 36 per cent while the average out-of-quota rate is 120 per cent. See WTO Secretariat (2001), *supra* n. 53, p. 53.

[80] Para. 11 of Annex 3 to the Modalities Agreement.

[81] Note that although GATT Article XIII is entitled *Non-discriminatory Administration of Quantitative Restrictions,* thus apparently not applying to the tariffs-only system of the Agriculture Agreement, paragraph 5 provides the following: "The provisions of this Article shall apply to any *tariff quota* instituted or maintained by any contracting party, and, in so far as applicable, the principles of this Article shall also extend to export restrictions." (Italics added). Consequently, the m.f.n. principle that is prescribed under Article XIII concerning the administration of non-tariff barriers also applies to the administration of tariff quotas forming part of the new agricultural market access regime.

[82] See para. 14 of Annex 3 to the Modalities Agreement. See also Anderson, Erwidodo and Ingco (1999) *supra* n. 66, p. 12; and D. Skully, *The Economics of TRQ Administration,* IATRC Working Paper # 99–6 (St. Paul: University of Minnesota, 1999).

with the same express MFN requirement for expanding current access opportunities and its noticeable absence in the case of maintenance of existing access levels, this provision suggests that new access opportunities have to be made on an MFN basis while pre-existing access opportunities could be reserved for the beneficiaries of pre-Uruguay Round bilateral or other non-MFN arrangements.[83] Many writers on the subject have also observed that the allocation of current access opportunities by several Member states was made in a country-specific and non-MFN form.[84] According to a survey made in September 1999, of the 1,400 tariff rate quotas notified to the WTO until then, about 200 were country-specific rather than global.[85]

Non-MFN, country-specific, tariff quotas are not of course necessarily inconsistent with the multilateral trade rules. Indeed, Article XIII:2(d) of the General Agreement expressly allows quotas to be allocated among supplying countries, which in practice means the exclusion of other Members because not all Members can normally be called supplying countries. The fundamental requirement in the allocation of tariff quotas is to "aim at a distribution of trade in such product approaching as closely as possible the shares which the various [Members] might be expected to obtain in the absence of such restrictions."[86] As the *Bananas* panel

---

[83] The third-party arguments made by Colombia to the Appellate Body in the *Bananas* case are worth noting: "Colombia submits that the review of the tariff quotas scheduled by the European Communities and the United States, which entail commitments negotiated with more than fifty other participants in the Uruguay Round, shows that few, if any, of these quota allocation commitments presently conform to the requirements set out in Article XIII of the GATT 1994. Therefore, in Colombia's view, it can be safely assumed that all quota allocation commitments made pursuant to the *Agreement on Agriculture* are actually or potentially inconsistent with Article XIII of the GATT 1994." *Bananas,* report of the Appellate Body, *supra* n. 26, para. 115.

[84] Tangermann wrote, for instance, that "[m]any TRQ are, openly or silently, administered on a bilateral basis, thereby undermining the MFN principle." Tangermann (1997) *supra* n. 60, p. 13. Ingco wrote the following: "In cases where exporters enjoyed preferential market access in the past, or previously had voluntary export restraint agreements, their access opportunities were maintained under a 'current access' provision." Ingco (1995) *supra* n. 2, p. 7. The OECD also observed as follows: "Some of the minimum access commitments, as reflected in the Schedules, may incorporate pre-existing or new bilateral arrangements, which, by definition, are offered on a country-specific basis and are, therefore, not consistent with an m.f.n. principle. (Much of the current access commitments is also on a country-specific basis)." OECD (1995) *supra* n. 1, p. 22. According to Panagariya, bilateral and global quotas resulted from the whole arrangement in the area of agricultural market access. "The bilateral quotas have resulted from the provision to maintain 'current access opportunities'. These quotas are pre-allocated to traditional export suppliers on the basis of historical market shares that were achieved within the limits of pre-UR quantitative restrictions and voluntary export restraints. The global, unallocated quotas, available in principle for distribution on an MFN basis, have resulted from the provision for 'minimum access opportunities." A. Panagariya, "The Millennium Round and Developing Countries: Negotiating Strategies and Areas of Benefits", paper prepared for presentation at the *Conference on Developing Countries and the New Multilateral Round of Trade Negotiations* (Harvard University, Massachusetts, 5–6 September 1999, at 23). Finally, Hathaway and Ingco wrote that "[d]espite the MFN requirement, countries also were allowed to count special arrangements as part of their minimum access commitments and to allocate their minimum access to exporters having special arrangements." Hathaway and Ingco (1995) *supra* n. 13, p. 21.

[85] Anderson, Erwidodo and Ingco (1999) *supra* n. 66, p. 12.

[86] Article XIII:2 of GATT 1994.

pointed out, the object and purpose of Article XIII:2 is "to minimize the impact of a quota or tariff quota regime on trade flows by attempting to approximate under such measures the trade shares that would have occurred in the absence of the regime."[87]

The preferred way of allocating tariff quotas under Article XIII is to do it with the agreement of all Members having a substantial interest in supplying the product concerned; but when this is not practicable, the unilateral decision of the importing country may suffice. In the latter case, however, the importing country is required to allocate the shares "based upon the proportions, supplied by such contracting parties during a previous representative period, of the total quantity or value of imports of the product, due account being taken of any special factors which may have affected or may be affecting the trade in the product."[88] As reiterated, the problem that could arise in the case of several agricultural tariff rate quotas resulting from the Uruguay Round is that they were not made in compliance with the requirements set by this provision. To complicate matters, these tariff quotas are included in Members' Schedules of Concessions as parts of their current and/or minimum access commitments under the Agriculture Agreement. The question for present purposes is therefore as to whether the administration of tariff rate quotas introduced as part of the Uruguay Round agriculture package are also governed by the principles of non-discriminatory application of import restrictions enshrined in Article XIII.

These problems were at the heart of the famous *Bananas* dispute in the WTO. The issue arose from the following facts. The import regime for bananas in the EC introduced a system of tariff rate quotas in which one class of bananas would be permitted to enter duty-free; a second class would enter at a tariff rate of 75 ECU per tonne; and a third (out of quota) class would be imported at a tariff of 822 ECU per tonne (exceptionally 722 ECU). The important interpretive problem for our purposes arose concerning the allocation of the second class of bananas. The quota covered about 2.2 million tonnes of bananas and was to be allocated as follows: (i) 49.4 per cent to the countries that were parties to the so-called Banana Framework Agreement (BFA); (ii) 90,000 tonnes to ACP countries in respect of amounts that they did not traditionally supply to EC Member States (admitted duty-free); and (iii) the rest (46.5 per cent) to other banana exporters.[89] The EC Schedules show that the four BFA countries have the following shares: Costa Rica 23.40 %; Colombia 21.00 %; Nicaragua 3.00 %; and Venezuela; 2.00 %. All non-BFA and non-ACP suppliers are put under an "Others" category with 46.32 % for 1994 and 46.51 % for 1995.[90]

Five countries – Ecuador, Guatemala, Honduras, Mexico and the US – filed complaints against this and other aspects of the EC bananas regime claiming, in relevant part, that the EC had failed to allocate country-specific tariff quota shares to those Complainants that export bananas to the EC and that the EC's allocation of

---

87 *Bananas*, report of the panel, *supra* n. 29, para. 7.68.
88 Article XIII:2(d) of GATT 1994.
89 See *Bananas*, report of the panel, *supra* n. 29, para. 7.64.
90 See Ibid., para. 3.11.

tariff quota shares to the ACP and BFA countries was inconsistent with the requirements of the tariff quota allocation rules of Article XIII of GATT 1994.[91] The EC responded that it had complied with the requirements of Article XIII and that "its treatment of BFA and other bananas is provided pursuant to the EC's Schedule into which the BFA is incorporated."[92] More specifically, the EC argued that even if the tariff quota share allocations to the BFA countries and in respect of non-traditional ACP bananas did not satisfy the requirements of Article XIII, they were consistent with GATT rules because of their inclusion in its Schedule as a result of the Uruguay Round negotiations.[93] The Complainants invoked the *Sugar Headnote* case[94] and argued that tariff bindings in schedules "cannot justify inconsistencies with the requirements of generally applicable GATT rules."[95] The EC's response at this point was particularly interesting. It argued that the Uruguay Round Schedules "are of a different nature than past GATT tariff protocols and that, in any event, the inclusion of the BFA tariff quota shares in its Schedule overrides Article XIII *because of the priority provision of the Agreement on Agriculture*."[96]

The panel first found that the EC allocation of tariff rate quotas was inconsistent with the requirements of Article XIII. Sticking to the well-established precedent set by the *Sugar Headnote* case, the panel ruled that the "inclusion of allocations inconsistent with the requirements of Article XIII in its Schedule does not prevent them from being challenged by other Members."[97] On the more pertinent question of whether the priority provisions of the Agriculture Agreement protected the EC measures from being challenged under GATT Article XIII, the panel made the following important ruling:

> "It is clear from Article 21.1 that the provisions of the Agreement on Agriculture prevail over GATT and the other Annex 1A agreements. But there must be a provision of the Agreement on Agriculture that is relevant in order for this priority provision to apply. It is not the case that Article 21.1 of the Agreement on Agriculture means that no GATT/WTO rules apply to trade in agricultural products unless they are explicitly incorporated into the Agreement on Agriculture. There is no provision of the Agreement on Agriculture that incorporates tariff bindings related to agricultural products into the Agreement on Agriculture. While the Annexes to the Agreement are incorporated into the Agreement by Article 21.2 thereof, tariff bindings are not. Indeed, under paragraph 1 of the Marrakesh Protocol, the Uruguay Round schedules attached to that protocol, which include the agricultural tariff bindings, are explicitly made schedules to GATT."[98]

---

91 See Ibid., para. 7.65.
92 See Ibid.
93 Ibid., para. 7.112.
94 See *United States–Restrictions on Imports of Sugar*, report of the panel (L/6514, *BISD* 36S/224) adopted on 22 June 1989, paras. 5.2–5.7. For more on this, see *supra* chapter 2, section 2.3.2.
95 *Bananas*, report of the panel, *supra* n. 29, para. 7.112.
96 Ibid., para. 7.112 (italics added). This is a reference to Article 21 of the Agreement on Agriculture.
97 Ibid., para. 7.114.
98 Ibid., paras. 7.122–7.123.

The Appellate Body agreed with the panel on this point and ruled as follows:

> "[W]e do not see anything in Article 4.1 [of the Agreement on Agriculture] to suggest that market access concessions and commitments made as a result of the Uruguay Round negotiations on agriculture can be inconsistent with the provisions of Article XIII of the GATT 1994. There is nothing in Articles 4.1 or 4.2, or in any other article of the *Agreement on Agriculture*, that deals specifically with the allocation of tariff quotas on agricultural products. If the negotiators had intended to permit Members to act inconsistently with Article XIII of the GATT 1994, they would have said so explicitly. [T]he negotiators of the *Agreement on Agriculture* did not hesitate to specify such limitations elsewhere in that agreement; had they intended to do so with respect to Article XIII of the GATT 1994, they could, and presumably would, have done so. We note further that the *Agreement on Agriculture* makes no reference to the *Modalities* document or to any 'common understanding' among the negotiators of the *Agreement on Agriculture* that the market access commitments for agricultural products would not be subject to Article XIII of the GATT 1994."[99]

The significance of these interpretations can hardly be overemphasized. They represent a symbolic application of the customary rules of treaty interpretation enshrined in Article 31 of the Vienna Convention.[100] As indicated earlier, there was what might be termed sufficient evidence showing that Uruguay Round negotiators agreed to continue pre-existing access opportunities resulting from bilateral (or non-MFN) arrangements unaffected and perhaps even intended to keep country-specific tariff rate quotas despite their inconsistencies with Article XIII of the General Agreement. Furthermore, by expressly requiring MFN in the case of minimum access and expanding current access opportunities, while saying nothing as regards the maintenance of pre-existing access opportunities, the Modalities Agreement has arguably made a tacit endorsement of such situations. However, as the Appellate Body has rightly pointed out, in as long as the text of the Agriculture Agreement makes no reference to the "Modalities document or to any 'common understanding' ", the value of such documents can not be more than "supplementary" in the sense of Article 32 of the Vienna Convention.[101] The pertinent provisions of the Agriculture Agreement leave no room to import such preparatory documents in this particular case. In line with the *Sugar Headnote* case, the *Bananas* case made it clear that whatever may be included by Members in their Schedules of Concessions, the

---

[99] *Bananas*, report of the Appellate Body, *supra* n. 26, para. 157 (italics in original).

[100] *Vienna Convention on the Law of Treaties* (done at Vienna, 23 May 1969, 1155 U.N.T.S. 33). Article 31(1) of this Convention provides as follows: "A treaty shall be interpreted in good faith in accordance with the ordinary meaning to be given to the terms of the treaty in their context and in light of its object and purpose."

[101] According to this Article, recourse may be had to the preparatory work of the treaty and the circumstances of its conclusion only "to confirm the meaning resulting from application of Article 31, or to determine the meaning when the interpretation according to Article 31: (a) leaves the meaning ambiguous or obscure; or (b) leads to a result which is manifestly absurd or unreasonable."

rules and principles of other provisions remain unaffected. This interpretation has understandably made several doubtful cases vulnerable to a similar challenge.

Finally, even in cases where discriminatory administration of tariff rate quotas is not at issue, importing countries often try to set all sorts of hurdles against in-quota imports. In *Canada Dairy,* for instance, Canada had established an in-quota tariff rate of 17.5 per cent (to be reduced to 7.53 per cent by the end of the implementation period) for 64,500 tonnes of "fluid milk". The over-quota rate for the same product was 283.3 per cent, to decline to 241.3 per cent in 2001. Although the quota was expressed in global terms, both geography and economics have effectively turned it into a *de facto* US-specific quota.

The issue particularly relevant here arose from the fact that Canada had attached "terms and conditions" to its Schedule which purported to limit in-quota rates to cross-border retail purchases of C$ 20 or less, by residents of Canada for their own personal use, while applying the over-quota tariffs to "fluid milk" shipments in commercial containers or in bulk.[102] The US challenged this requirement and argued that Canada was administering its tariff-rate quota "in a manner that denies market access" against Canada's obligations under Article II:1(b) of GATT 1994. Canada defended its position by invoking a phrase in the "other terms and conditions" part of its Schedule which stated "this quantity 64,500 tonnes represents the estimated annual cross-border purchases imported by Canadian consumers." Canada claimed that this was a term, condition, or qualification in the sense of Article II:1(b) of GATT 1994 to which its bound tariffs were subject.

The panel rejected Canada's contention and ruled that "by restricting the access of the tariff-rate quota for fluid milk to (i) consumer packaged milk for personal use and (ii) entries valued at less than C$ 20, acts inconsistently with its obligations under Article II:1(b) of GATT 1994."[103] Of the two grounds of violation relied upon

---

[102] See *Canada Dairy,* report of the panel, *supra* n. 74, paras. 7.143–7.144.

[103] See Ibid., para. 8.1(b). Indeed, the panel stated that "the words 'this *quantity represents* the *estimated* annual ...' are ... introducing 'terms' related to the *quantity* of the quota – i.e., describing the way the size of the quota was determined–rather than setting out 'conditions' as to the *kind* of imports qualified to enter Canada under this quota. In particular, the ordinary meaning of the word 'represent' in this context does not, in our view, call to mind the setting out of specific restrictions or conditions." Ibid. para. 7.151. The Appellate Body disagreed with this approach. Invoking the principle of *effet utile* in treaty interpretation, the Appellate Body recalled that "the task of the treaty interpreter is to ascertain and give effect to a legally operative meaning for the terms of the treaty" and that "a treaty interpreter is not free to adopt a meaning that would reduce parts of a treaty to redundancy or inutility." *Canada Dairy,* report of the Appellate Body, *supra* n. 75, para. 133. The Appellate Body argued that the phrase "terms and conditions" under Article II is "a composite one which, in its ordinary meaning, denotes the imposition of qualifying restrictions or conditions. A strong presumption arises that the language which is inscribed in a Member's Schedule under the heading, 'Other Terms and Conditions', has some *qualifying* or *limiting* effect on the substantive content or scope of the concession or commitment. ... The net consequence of the Panel's interpretation is a failure to give the notation in Canada's Schedule *any* legal effect as a 'term and condition'. If the language is *merely* a 'description' or a 'narration' of how the quantity was arrived at, we do not see what purpose it serves in being inscribed in the Schedule. The Panel, in other words, acted upon the assumption that Canada projected no identifiably necessary or useful qualifying or limiting purpose in inscribing the notation in its Schedule. The Panel thus disregarded the principle of effectiveness in its interpretive effort." Ibid. paras. 134–135 (italics in original).

by the panel, the Appellate Body agreed only with the latter and reversed the first part of the panel's ruling.[104]

To sum up, the proliferation of tariff rate quotas as a result of the minimum and current access commitments means that governments have to remain deeply involved in agricultural trade more than in any other sector of merchandise trade. Tariff rate quotas and the systems introduced by governments to administer them have thus been another cause for concern about the liberalizing significance of the Agriculture Agreement.[105] It has indeed been found that the average fill rate for 1995 was only 66 per cent "before it slightly decreased to reach 62 per cent in 1998."[106] Different possible causes have been identified by different studies, including already prohibitive in-quota tariff rates and bad tariff-quota administration systems. One study even goes further and states that tariff quotas are allocated "deliberately to suppliers incapable of making full use of them because of their international uncompetitiveness despite the advantageous market environment."[107]

To ensure that market access opportunities are not further restricted by administrative measures, countries such as the US started expressing the need for more detailed rules on tariff-rate quota administration already before the agriculture negotiations were launched in March 2000.[108] This is also one of the most important issues being discussed in the ongoing negotiations. In order to minimize the adverse effects of such administrative measures, Tangermann has suggested the auctioning of licences as the "only neutral and economically satisfactory method" in all such cases of government intervention.[109] However, discussions during the informal session of

---

[104] The Appellate Body "reverses the Panel's finding that Canada, by restricting access to the tariff-rate quota for fluid milk in its Schedule to consumer packaged milk, imported by Canadian consumers for personal use, acts inconsistently with its obligations under Article II:1(b) of the GATT 1994; but upholds the Panel's finding that Canada, by restricting access to the tariff-rate quota for fluid milk in its Schedule to entries valued at less than C$20, acts inconsistently with its obligations under Article II:1(b) of the GATT 1994." See *Canada Dairy*, report of the Appellate Body, *supra* n. 75, para. 144(d).

[105] Tariff rate quotas have "several undesirable features: they legitimize a role for state trading agencies, they generate quota rents, and they introduce scope for discriminating between countries." Anderson, Erwidodo and Ingco (1999) *supra* n. 66, p. 9. In the words of Tangermann, tariff rate quotas have been "one of the most strongly criticized elements of the current WTO regime for agriculture." See Tangermann (1997) *supra* n. 60, p. 13.

[106] See WTO Secretariat (2001), *supra* n. 53, p. 53.

[107] See Anderson, Erwidodo and Ingco (1999) *supra* n. 66, p. 9.

[108] In one of the deliberations of the WTO Agriculture Committee in what is called the Analysis and Information Exchange (AIE) series, the US presented a paper entitled "Administration of Tariff-Rate Quotas" (AIE/46) and "the view was supported that while Article XIII of GATT 1994 and the Agreement on Import Licensing Procedures include some provisions on the administration of tariff quotas, these are not considered to be sufficient." WTO Committee on Agriculture, *Summary Report of the Meeting Held on 25–26 March 1999* (G/AG/R/18) 7 May 1999, para. 33 (viii).

[109] Tangermann (1997) *supra* n. 60, p. 14. Supporting this view of Tangermann's, Josling argues that "[t]o allocate the TRQs to the exporting country government . . . implies a deliberate attempt to influence the pattern of trade in favour of the recipient countries. This has in the past been done to target developmental aid or reward political friendship. Such non-market allocation schemes may have had their purpose. They do not, however, promote the competitive trade system that is the fundamental goal of the WTO." T. Josling, "Developing Countries and the New Round of Multilateral Trade

the Agriculture Committee on 21–23 May 2001 have shown a clear division of views on this option. Many participants argued that "the practice of auctioning import lots constituted a 'quota rent', or an illegitimate means of raising money for governments, and should be prohibited."[110]

3.3.9 Special Safeguard Provisions

As pointed out already, negotiators in the Uruguay Round agreed not only to convert their agricultural non-tariff barriers into ordinary customs duties, but also to bind the resulting tariffs and to undertake binding tariff reduction commitments. Under the general rules of the multilateral trading system, countries are not normally allowed to impose any duties in excess of those incorporated in their Schedules of Concessions.[111] This situation created the fear that their conversion of the non-tariff barriers into ordinary tariffs may have the effect of attracting the inflow of unduly low-priced products or simply a surge in imports in a manner disruptive of domestic production of competing products. The special safeguard (SSG) provisions were introduced to address those fears.

The purpose of Article 5 in the Agriculture Agreement is, therefore, comparable to the purpose of Article XIX under the General Agreement – it is intended to allow Members to deviate temporarily from their obligations under Article II in cases where certain conditions, in the form of trigger levels of quantities and/or prices, are met. It is, however, narrower than GATT Article XIX. While Article XIX allows a Member to deviate temporarily from its obligations under both GATT Articles II and XI, Article 5 of the Agreement on Agriculture allows such deviations only from the former. Moreover, Article 5 does not exclude the application to agriculture of the provisions of GATT Article XIX and the Uruguay Round Agreement on Safeguards. To the extent that the Agriculture Agreement does not provide otherwise,[112] these rules remain operational in agriculture as much as they are in other sectors. The *Korea Dairy* dispute is a good example of safeguard measures taken on an agricultural product addressed exclusively under Article XIX of GATT 1994 and the WTO Agreement on Safeguards.[113]

---

cont.

Negotiations: Background Notes on Agriculture", paper prepared for the *Workshop on Developing Countries and the New Round of Multilateral Trade Negotiations* (Center for International Development at Harvard University, Nov. 5–6, 1999).

[110] International Institute for Sustainable Development, 5 *Bridges Weekly Trade News Digest*, No. 19, 22 May, 2001. For an interesting discussion of this issue and the possible solutions, see WTO Secretariat (2001), *supra* n. 53, p. 53–57.

[111] See Article II of the General Agreement.

[112] See, for example, Article 5.8 of the Agriculture Agreement which provides as follows: "Where measures are taken in conformity with paragraphs 1 through 7 above, Members undertake not to have recourse, in respect of such measures, to the provisions of paragraphs 1(a) and 3 of Article XIX of GATT 1994 or paragraph 2 of Article 8 of the Agreement on Safeguards."

[113] See *Korea–Definitive Safeguard Measure on Imports of Certain Dairy Products,* report of the panel (WT/DS98/R) and report of the Appellate Body (WT/DS98/AB/R) adopted on 12 January 2000.

Article 5 is there only to allow countries which have converted their agricultural nontariff barriers into ordinary customs duties some flexibility so that they would be able to raise duties even when they do not satisfy the more stringent requirements of Article XIX and the Safeguards Agreement.[114] For instance, while Article XIX and the Agreement on Safeguards can be invoked only if serious injury is caused or threatened by the increased imports,[115] resort to Article 5 of the Agreement on Agriculture needs to satisfy only the requirement on quantity and/or price trigger levels regardless of injury considerations.

Moreover, the "public interest" considerations of the Safeguards Agreement[116] do not apply to special agricultural safeguards – there is no "public interest" requirement in Article 5 of the AoA. As there is no requirement of injury, the SSG measures can be activated just by the trigger price or volume levels. As the Appellate Body put it in the *Poultry* case, the safeguard mechanism in Article 5 of the *Agreement on Agriculture* "is not conditional upon a test of injury as it is the case with other safeguard provisions; it can be automatically activated when there is a certain surge in the volume of imports (Article 5.1(a)) or a certain drop in the price of the product (Article 5.1(b))."[117] This means, inter alia, that there is no any requirement for any kind of investigation as such. Naturally, the absence of an investigation, coupled with the element of automaticity enshrined in AoA Article 5, mean that there is no room for any "public interest" consideration. The absence of a requirement to investigate, and consequently to consider the "public interest", is presumably intended to allow Members to introduce special safeguards relatively more easily.

At the same time, while a Member invoking those general rules may be able to introduce non-tariff restrictions as safeguard measures, only duties above bound levels may be justified under Article 5 of the Agriculture Agreement.

The special safeguard option is not, however, available to all products that have been subjected to tariffication. There is the additional requirement that countries

---

cont.

Korea had reserved its right to have recourse to Article 5 of the Agreement on Agriculture for about 111 tariff items, falling in about 34 product groups, dairy products were not among them. See Committee on Agriculture, *Special Agricultural Safeguard: Background Paper by the Secretariat* (G/AG/NG/S/9) 6 June 2000, tables 2 and 3, pp. 5–6. As a result, although the Agriculture Agreement in general, and Article 5 in particular, would have favoured its position, Korea could not invoke those provisions. See, *inter alia,* paragraphs 4.54 and 4.282 of the *Korea Dairy* panel report.

114 For a collection of relevant GATT interpretations of Article XIX, see *GATT Analytical Index supra* n. 36, pp. 517 ff.

115 See Article XIX:1(a) of the General Agreement and Article 2 of the Safeguards Agreement.

116 See Article 3.1 of the Safeguards Agreement. Note that this provision does not require consideration of the public interest as such as a condition for the adoption of safeguard measures; it only introduces a procedure that might require the authorities at least to carefully consider submission made on issues of public interest. For more on issues of "public interest", see M. Bronckers, *A Cross-Section of WTO Law* (Cameron May, London 2000) p. 78.

117 *European Communities – Measures Affecting the Importation of Certain Poultry Products*, report of the Appellate Body (WT/DS69/AB/R) adopted 23 July 1998, para. 167.

specifically reserve a right to do so by selecting those products which they considered particularly sensitive and designating them with the symbol SSG in their Schedules. According to WTO sources, 38 Members have done this in respect of more than six thousand products in total.[118]

There are two alternative grounds for invoking the special safeguard provisions – surges in the volume of imports and falling import prices. Needless to say, not every rise in the volume or every fall in the price of imports entitles countries to resort to the special safeguard provisions. In each case, there are threshold levels set, which are often called the volume- and price-trigger levels.

The volume trigger is determined according to market access opportunities defined in terms of imports as a percentage of the corresponding domestic consumption during the three preceding years for which data are available.[119] The higher the share of imports in domestic consumption during this three year period, the lower the base trigger level. Accordingly, for cases where imports constituted less than or equal to 10 per cent of domestic consumption for the three preceding years, the base trigger amount is set at 125 per cent; where the shares are between 10 and 30 per cent, the base trigger level equals 110 per cent; and where the shares are greater than 30 per cent, the base trigger level equals 105 per cent.[120] To illustrate with the help of the first proportion, before a country invokes the special safeguards provision so as to impose additional duties in respect of a certain product whose previous share in the domestic consumption has been within the 10 per cent limit, the current volume of imports should grow to be at least 125 per cent of this traditional quantity. For example, if a country consumes an average of 100 tonnes of wheat per year for the past three years, of which only 10 tonnes is covered by imports, keeping other things constant, the special safeguards provision of Article 5 may be invoked by that country only if the amount of wheat imports for this year reaches at least 12.5 tonnes.[121] Additional duties introduced in any year on the basis of the volume-trigger are limited in two forms: their amount cannot exceed one-third of the level of the ordinary customs duties for the product in question in that year, and that they

---

[118] See G/AG/NG/S/9, *supra* n. 113, para. 3. This document also contains an exhaustive list of all the members with such reservations and all the products on which the reservations were made. Switzerland-Liechtenstein takes the lead with a reservation for 961 products, followed by Norway and the EU with 581 and 539 products, respectively. In general, according to UNCTAD, close to 80 percent of the tariffied items of the OECD countries are subject to SSGs. See UNCTAD, *Identification of New Trading Opportunities Arising from the Implementation of the Uruguay Round Agreements in Selected Sectors and Markets* (TD/B/WG.8/2), 1995.

[119] Article 4:4 of the Agreement on Agriculture.

[120] See Article 5.4(a)-(c) of the Agriculture Agreement.

[121] The last sub-paragraph of Article 5.4 of the Agriculture Agreement also opens room for consumption trends to be taken into consideration as follows: "In all cases the additional duty may be imposed in any year where the absolute volume of imports of the product concerned entering the customs territory of the Member granting the concession exceeds the sum of (*x*) the base trigger level set out above multiplied by the average quantity of imports during the three preceding years for which data are available and (*y*) the absolute volume change in domestic consumption of the product concerned in the most recent year for which data are available compared to the preceding year, provided that the trigger level shall not be less than 105 per cent of the average quantity of imports in (*x*) above."

can be maintained only until the end of the year in which they are imposed.[122] The most important problem associated with the quantity trigger has been found to be that "it is often switched on and off for very short periods and therefore creates considerable uncertainty for trade."[123]

The price trigger, on the other hand, is determined on a shipment-by-shipment basis. The special safeguard provisions may be invoked for reasons of falling import prices only if the price, as determined on the basis of the c.i.f. import price of the shipment concerned expressed in terms of its domestic currency, "falls below a trigger price equal to the average 1986 to 1988 reference price for the product concerned."[124] In *EC Poultry*, Brazil claimed that the import price referred to under Article 5.1(b) of the Agreement on Agriculture "should be the c.i.f. price plus the bound duty" and that "the EC has violated this provision because it merely measures the c.i.f. price and should that price fall below the trigger price it imposes an additional duty".[125] The EC counter-argued that "the term 'on the basis of the c.i.f. import price' in Article 5.1(b) means the c.i.f. price itself" and that, by using that threshold, it did not violate its obligations under the Agriculture Agreement.[126] An issue was thus raised as to whether it was the "c.i.f. price" alone or the "c.i.f. price *plus* ordinary customs duties" which should fall below the reference price in order for the special safeguard mechanism in Article 5.1(b) to be triggered.

The practical consequence of choosing one over the other may be significant.[127] In

---

[122] See Article 5.4 of the Agriculture Agreement.

[123] UNCTAD (1997) *supra* n. 58, p. 46.

[124] See Article 5.1(b) of the Agriculture Agreement. A footnote to this provision provides that "[t]he reference price used to invoke the provisions of this subparagraph shall, in general, be the average c.i.f. unit value of the product concerned, or otherwise shall be an appropriate price in terms of the quality of the product and its stage of processing. It shall, following its initial use, be publicly specified and available to the extent necessary to allow other Members to assess the additional duty that may be levied."

[125] See *European Communities – Measures Affecting the Importation of Certain Poultry Products*, report of the panel, WT/DS69/R, 12 March 1998, para. 277.

[126] See Ibid.

[127] The Appellate Body made the following observation in this connection: "This dispute has no practical significance if both the c.i.f. import price and the c.i.f. import price plus customs duties fall above or below the trigger price. If both prices are above the trigger price, then additional duties cannot be imposed. And, if both prices fall below the trigger price, then additional duties may be imposed regardless of which definition of the relevant import price is adopted. However, the practical significance of this dispute becomes apparent whenever the trigger price falls between the other two prices, that is, when the trigger price is greater than the c.i.f. import price but smaller than the c.i.f. import price plus customs duties. To illustrate:

c.i.f. import price plus customs duties	=	1,200
trigger price	=	1,000
c.i.f. import price	=	800

In this example, if the relevant price is defined as the c.i.f. import price plus customs duties, additional duties may not be imposed since the relevant price is well above the trigger price. If, on the other hand, it is defined as the c.i.f. import price only (that is, without customs duties), additional duties may be imposed because the relevant price is below the trigger price. Thus, to adopt one definition, rather than a rather unusual situation in GATT/WTO dispute settlement tradition, the panel could not reach a unanimous verdict on this issue. The majority stated the following:

> "The relevant price of the imports concerned is referred to in Article 5.1(b) in two ways: i.e. the text of Article 5.1(b) refers to both 'the price at which imports may enter the customs territory of the Member granting the concession' and 'the c.i.f. import price'. The ordinary meaning of the phrase 'the price at which imports may enter the customs territory of the Member granting the concession' would include the payment of applicable duties since those duties must be paid prior to entry and therefore are part of 'the price'. The term 'the c.i.f. import price' in Article 5.1(b) is qualified by the phrase 'determined on the basis of', which indicates that the market entry price is something that has to be constructed using the c.i.f. price as one of the parameters."[128]

On that basis, the majority concluded that the EC had violated the special safeguard provisions of Article 5.1(b) of the Agreement on Agriculture.[129]

One of the members of the panel found this majority view "not a convincing one" and gave his dissenting opinion. According to this member, the majority read the terms in dispute out of their proper context, and particularly of footnote 2 to paragraph 1(b) and paragraph 5 of Article 5, and concluded that "Article 5 of the Agreement on Agriculture requires an importing Member to calculate the relevant import price within the meaning of Article 5.1(b) on the basis of the c.i.f. import price only."[130]

The Appellate Body reversed the majority view of the panel and gave a ruling that affirmed (although on a more elaborate and meticulous reasoning) the minority opinion. The Appellate Body started by stressing the point that "the drafters of the *Agreement on Agriculture* chose to use as the relevant import price the entry price into the *customs territory*, rather than the entry price into the *domestic market*."[131] The Appellate Body then concluded the following:

---

cont.

another, will determine whether or not an importing Member may impose additional safeguard duties." *EC Poultry*, report of the Appellate Body, *supra* n. 117, para. 143.

Although the Appellate Body is making an important point here, its statement that "[t]his dispute has no practical significance if both the c.i.f. import price and the c.i.f. import price plus customs duties fall ... below the trigger price" appears questionable. The statement holds true only as regards the imposition or otherwise of safeguard measures. However, when it comes to the amount by which bound duties can be raised (i.e. the maximum permissible amount of the safeguard duties), the structure of Article 5.5 indicates that this is a function of the gap between the import price and the reference price. The Appellate Body itself observed that "when the difference between the c.i.f. import price of the shipment and the trigger price is not greater than 10 per cent, no additional duty shall be imposed. When the difference is greater than 10 per cent, additional duties may be imposed. The amount of the additional safeguard duties increases as the difference in the two prices increases." See para. 150 of the Appellate Body report in *EC Poultry*. The inclusion or otherwise of ordinary customs duties therefore has significant practical consequences even if both the "c.i.f. import price" and the "c.i.f. import price plus customs duties" fall below the trigger price.

128 *EC Poultry*, report of the panel *supra* n. 125, para. 278.

129 See Ibid., para. 282.

130 See Ibid. paras. 290 to 292.

131 *EC Poultry*, report of the Appellate Body, *supra* n. 117, para. 145 (italics in original).

"This suggests that they had in mind the point of time *just before* the entry of the product concerned into the customs territory, and certainly before entry into the domestic market, of the importing Member. The ordinary meaning of these terms in Article 5.1(b) supports the view that the 'price at which that product may enter the customs territory' of the importing Member should be construed to mean just that – the price at which the product may enter the *customs territory*, not the price at which the product may enter the *domestic market* of the importing Member. And that price is a price that does not include customs duties and internal charges. It is upon entry of a product into the customs territory, but before the product enters the domestic market, that the obligation to pay customs duties and internal charges accrues."[132]

The amount of permissible additional duty in price-triggered situations depends on the degree to which the actual import price falls below the trigger price. While this permissible amount is set at zero in cases where the difference between the import price and the trigger price is less than or equal to 10 per cent of the trigger price, the Agreement has introduced a complicated formula which enables the importing country to progressively increase its additional duties in proportion to the extent of price decline.[133] Since the price trigger conditions under the special safeguards provision are related to individual shipments, there have been fears that this "may introduce certain elements of discrimination."[134]

In sum, the special safeguards arrangement is part of the tariffication package which was intended to remain in force for the duration of the entire reform process. It may be invoked only for agricultural products which have been subject to tariffication and may be applied only to over-quota imports.[135] The permissible

---

[132] Ibid. para. 145.

[133] Article 5.5 provides as follows: "The additional duty imposed under subparagraph 1(b) shall be set according to the following schedule: (a) if the difference between the c.i.f. import price of the shipment expressed in terms of the domestic currency (hereinafter referred to as the "import price") and the trigger price as defined under that subparagraph is less than or equal to 10 per cent of the trigger price, no additional duty shall be imposed; (b) if the difference between the import price and the trigger price (hereinafter referred to as the "difference") is greater than 10 per cent but less than or equal to 40 per cent of the trigger price, the additional duty shall equal 30 per cent of the amount by which the difference exceeds 10 per cent; (c) if the difference is greater than 40 per cent but less than or equal to 60 per cent of the trigger price, the additional duty shall equal 50 per cent of the amount by which the difference exceeds 40 per cent, plus the additional duty allowed under (b); (d) if the difference is greater than 60 per cent but less than or equal to 75 per cent, the additional duty shall equal 70 per cent of the amount by which the difference exceeds 60 per cent of the trigger price, plus the additional duties allowed under (b) and (c); (e) if the difference is greater than 75 per cent of the trigger price, the additional duty shall equal 90 per cent of the amount by which the difference exceeds 75 per cent, plus the additional duties allowed under (b), (c) and (d)." The approach has been called "a formula which could come straight from a university seminar on the economics of price stabilization." T. Josling, S. Tangermann, and T. Warley, *Agriculture in the GATT* (MacMillan, London 1996) p. 181.

[134] See Ingco (1995) *supra* n. 2, p. 49.

[135] As provided under paragraph 2 of Article 5, imports under current and minimum access commitments "shall be counted for the purpose of determining the volume of imports required for invoking the provisions of subparagraph 1(a) and paragraph 4, but imports under such commitments shall not be

amounts of additional duties under this provision differ depending on what they are triggered by – while the maximum in volume-triggered cases is limited to one-third of the level of ordinary customs duties applicable in any year, that amount may (theoretically) go somehow higher in price-triggered cases. Although several countries (about 38) have designated hundreds of tariff lines with SSG as a symbol of reserving their right to use the special safeguards arrangement,[136] the experience so far appears that not many countries are actually exercising those rights.[137] This situation has prompted many countries to question the need for its continued existence, but others have expressed their preference to keep it stressing the fact that the Agreement foresees its duration throughout the reform process and that future market situations might make it more useful.[138]

3.3.10 Special Treatment

Annex 5 to the Agreement on Agriculture provides for one of the last-minute compromises reached in the agricultural negotiations of the Uruguay Round. Mainly due to the insistence of Japan and Korea, an exception was introduced to the universal tariffication requirement enshrined in Article 4 of the Agriculture Agreement. Entitled as "Special Treatment with Respect to Paragraph 2 of Article 4", Annex 5 stipulates that the provisions of Article 4.2 may not apply to agricultural products which satisfy a list of conditions.[139] The conditions slightly differ depending on whether they apply to a "predominant staple in the traditional diet of a developing country" or to other agricultural products.

The conditions applying generally to "any primary agricultural product and its

---

cont.

affected by any additional duty imposed under either subparagraph 1(a) and paragraph 4 or subparagraph 1(b) and paragraph 5 below."

136 See WTO Agriculture Division, *supra* n. 25, p. 7. A look at Schedule LXXX of the EC reveals that more than 500 tariff lines of agricultural products have been marked SSG.

137 As of the beginning of 2000, only eight Members had actually applied special safeguard measures. See *WTO Annual Report 2000*, p. 39. According to a later note by the WTO Secretariat, of the thirty-eight Members that have reserved in their Schedules the right to have recourse to the special agricultural safeguard in respect of certain designated products: "Four Members have notified that they have taken action under, or, in the case of the European Communities, made operational, the SSG in 1995, five in 1996, six in 1997, five in 1998, four in 1999 and one in 2000. Thirty Members have notified that no SSG action was taken in 1995, 27 in 1996, 26 in 1997, 23 in 1998 and 7 in 1999." See G/AG/NG/S/9, *supra* n. 113, para. 3 (footnotes omitted).

138 In an Agriculture Committee discussion on the subject of special safeguard provisions on the basis of a paper prepared by New Zealand as part of the AIE process, countries argued that "relatively tight market conditions in recent years did not mean that the SSG would not be used more extensively and would not continue to have an important general function in the future." See WTO Committee on Agriculture, *Summary Report of the Meeting Held on 19–20 March 1998* (G/AG/R/14) 30 April 1998, para. 30(iv). The same mixed views were entertained also in subsequent discussions of the Committee. See, for example, WTO Committee on Agriculture, *Summary Report of the Meeting Held on 17–18 November 1998* (G/AG/R/17) 25 January 1999, para. 36 (ix).

139 See paragraph 1 of Annex 5 to the Agreement on Agriculture.

worked and/or prepared products" are stated under Section A of Annex 5 and may be summarized as follows:

- imports of the product comprised less than 3 per cent of corresponding domestic consumption in the base period 1986–1988;
- no export subsidies have been provided since the beginning of the base period for the designated products;
- effective production-restricting measures are applied to the primary agricultural product;
- such products are designated with the symbol "ST-Annex 5" in Section I-B of Part I of a Member's Schedule; and
- minimum access opportunities in respect of such products correspond to 4 per cent of base period domestic consumption of the designated products from the beginning of the first year of the implementation period and, thereafter, are increased by 0.8 per cent of corresponding domestic consumption in the base period per year for the remainder of the implementation period.

The minimum access commitments prescribed in this provision (4 per cent in 1995 and 8 per cent in 2000), which are higher than what is normally required when tariffication is done (3 per cent in 1995 and 5 per cent in 2000), are a *quid pro quo* by the countries invoking the Special Treatment provisions for being allowed to delay tariffication. All conditions except this last one apply to cases involving "staple foods" for developing countries under Section B.[140]

Members may unilaterally cease to apply special treatment in respect of a designated product at the beginning of any year of the implementation period. In such cases, the Member concerned "shall maintain the minimum access opportunities already in effect at such time and increase the minimum access opportunities by 0.4 per cent of corresponding domestic consumption in the base period per year for the remainder of the implementation period."[141] Moreover, unlike the special safeguard provisions, special treatment under Annex 5 is not meant for the entire

[140] On the issue of minimum access, a developing country which desires to use this option is required to create opportunities for 1 per cent of base period domestic consumption of the products concerned from the beginning of the first year of the implementation period and are increased in equal annual instalments to 2 per cent of corresponding domestic consumption in the base period at the beginning of the fifth year of the implementation period. From the beginning of the sixth year of the implementation period, minimum access opportunities in respect of the products concerned correspond to 2 per cent of corresponding domestic consumption in the base period and are increased in equal annual instalments to 4 per cent of corresponding domestic consumption in the base period until the beginning of the 10th year. Thereafter, the level of minimum access opportunities resulting from this formula in the 10th year shall be maintained in the Schedule of the developing country Member concerned. A second additional requirement is that such a country must have provided for what are called "appropriate market access opportunities" in respect of other, non-staple products under the Agreement. See paras. 7 (a) and (b) of Annex 5 to the Agreement on Agriculture.

[141] See para. 2 of Annex 5 to the Agriculture Agreement. The level of minimum access opportunities resulting from this modification in the final year of the implementation period are required to be maintained in the Schedule of the Member concerned.

reform process and its continuation depends on future negotiations.[142] Once the special treatment ended, whether because of unilateral termination before the end of the implementation period or due to a subsequent agreement to abolish the system, the principle of tariffication under Article 4.2 of the Agriculture Agreement fully applies to these products.[143] In view of the fact that the guidelines for the calculation of the tariff equivalents were included only in the Modalities, and not in the Agriculture Agreement itself – hence no more useful for new tariffication purposes – an Attachment to Annex 5 to the Agriculture Agreement has been included which nearly reproduced the pertinent provisions of Annex 3 to the Modalities Agreement on the calculation of tariff equivalents.[144]

The Special Treatment arrangement is not, however, that important in actual practice. First of all, as the right to invoke this provision was conditioned upon a reservation made in Members' Schedules of Concessions to that effect, it was so reserved only by four countries in respect of a limited number of agricultural products: Japan, Korea, and the Philippines in respect of rice, and Israel in respect of cheese and sheepmeat.[145] Secondly, even from these few countries, Japan already decided to cease to apply Special Treatment in December 1998 and to tariffy rice as of 1 April 1999 in line with paragraph 2, Section A of Annex 5 to the Agriculture Agreement.[146] And finally, although the possibility of extending Special Treatment provisions after the end of the implementation period is not completely closed, Japan's decision to cease to use this option is an indication that the continued existence of this option is less likely.

3.3.11 Surveillance of Implementation of the Market Access Discipline

The Agriculture Agreement did not only introduce the discipline governing agricultural trade; it also established the mechanism by which the practical implementation of the Agreement would be monitored. To that end, a Committee on Agriculture has been established[147] with the task, *inter alia*, of reviewing progress in the implementation of commitments.[148] According to Article 18.2, this review is to

---

[142] See paras. 3–5 of Annex 5 to the Agreement on Agriculture.

[143] See para. 6 of Annex 5 to the Agreement on Agriculture. See also para. 10 concerning developing countries and the application of the principle of special and differential treatment in the process.

[144] For a discussion of these guidelines in the context of the Modalities Agreement, see *supra* **Section 3.3.3.**

[145] See Hathaway and Ingco (1995) *supra* n. 13, p. 13; De Zeeuw (1997) *supra* n. 9, p. 22; OECD (1995) *supra* n. 1, p. 14; WTO Agriculture Division, *supra* n. 25, p. 7.

[146] See G/AG/R/18, *supra* n. 108, para. 43. Japan had notified its intention to cease to apply special treatment on 21 December 1998 in document G/MA/TAR/RS/57. In line with the requirements set under paragraph 2 of the Agriculture Agreement, this decision by Japan entailed the abolition of the existing quantitative import restriction system, replacing it with a tariff rate quota system, and the establishment of an out-of-quota tariff rate for imports outside the minimum access quantity. Although many countries welcomed the Japanese decision, some raised concerns regarding the methodology proposed by Japan in the tariffication process. See Ibid. paras. 43–45.

[147] See Article 17 of the Agreement on Agriculture.

[148] See Article 18.1 of the Agreement on Agriculture.

be undertaken "on the basis of notifications submitted by Members in relation to such matters and at such intervals as shall be determined." At its meeting on 31 January 1995, the WTO General Council adopted the following terms of reference for the Committee on Agriculture: "The Committee shall oversee the implementation of the Agreement on Agriculture. The Committee shall afford members the opportunity of consulting on any matter relating to the implementation of the provisions of the Agreement."[149] The Committee commenced its task by adopting the requirements and formats for notifications under Article 18.2, which also covers those applying to agricultural market access, including tariff quotas and special safeguard provisions.[150]

Accordingly, all Members with market access commitments in their Schedules of Concessions are required to make a comprehensive one-off notification in 1995 on the administration of quotas which should be followed by the *ad hoc* notification of any changes in their administration. The initial notification should normally be made in advance of the opening of the quota but in any event no later than 30 days following that date.[151]

As regards special safeguard, Article 5.7 of the Agriculture Agreement prescribes that it should be carried out in a transparent manner. To that end, all Members that have reserved the right in their Schedules to use the special safeguard provisions are required to make notifications. The format and frequency of the notifications varies depending on whether the special safeguard in question is volume-triggered or price-triggered. In the former case, a notification should be made "as far in advance as may be practicable, and in any event within 10 days of the implementation of such action."[152] In the case of the "price-based" special safeguard, a notification should be submitted within 10 days of the implementation of the first such action. The notice in this case may be provided in the form of either an "up-front" notification of trigger prices or on a case-by-case basis for the first use of the price-based special safeguard for any particular product. Finally, whether volume- or price-triggered, an annual notification should be made indicating the use of the special safeguard provisions in any year no later than 30 days following the end of the calendar, fiscal, etc. year.[153]

---

[149] WTO General Council, *WTO Committee On Agriculture: Decision by the General Council on 31 January 1995* (WT/L/43) 17 February 1995.

[150] At its meeting on 8 June 1995, the Committee on Agriculture adopted a document in which it set out the requirements and formats for notifications under Article 18:2 and other relevant provisions of the Agreement on Agriculture. See WTO Committee on Agriculture, *Notification Requirements and Formats* (G/AG/2) 30 June, 1995.

[151] Notifications of changes should be made, where possible, prior to the change being implemented, but in any event not later than 30 days following the change. Furthermore, Members are also required to make annual notifications following the end of the calendar (or, marketing, fiscal, etc.) year in question showing imports under tariff and other quotas. The notification should normally be made 30 days following the year but, in any event, no later than 60 days following the year in question. G/AG/2, *supra* n. 150, p. 2.

[152] See Article 5.7 of the Agreement on Agriculture.

[153] It is also provided that where the special safeguard provisions have not been invoked in any year, a statement to this effect should be made. See G/AG/2, *supra* n. 150, p. 5.

3.4 Conclusion

The elimination of nontariff barriers to imports, which had been exceptionally tolerated by the General Agreement in agricultural trade, is what the Agreement on Agriculture achieved for the trading system. As such, the market access provisions of this Agreement deserve to be hailed as a success by any standards.[154] The fact that the immediate liberalizing impact of this process has been compromised by such (unintended, although anticipated) practices as "dirty tariffication" and the like does not diminish the value of the rules introduced in this respect.

At the same time, although sweeping changes have been made on the rules of the General Agreement governing agricultural market access, the Agriculture Agreement still recognizes, if perhaps only tacitly, that agriculture is different from other classes of goods.[155] The existence of the "special safeguard" and "special treatment" provisions as parts of the new rules of agricultural market access still distinguishes the new discipline from the general rules applying to non-agricultural products. Moreover, agriculture still stands alone as the area where three-digit tariffs are rather common; where tariff rate quotas have proliferated, thus necessitating deeper government involvement in their administration; where escalation of tariffs with the degree of processing is very high and prohibitive especially for developing country exports; where significant safeguard duties could be imposed on imports in the most unpredictable fashion regardless of injury considerations; etc. Despite those developments in the rules, therefore, we are still talking in terms of market access for agricultural and non-agricultural products as two somehow distinct areas of international trade. The success of the current and future negotiations in this respect will be measured, *inter alia,* by the degree to which the already reformed rules of agricultural market access are followed by deeper and more meaningful cuts in tariffs and expansion of in-quota import levels.

---

[154] Although the Agreement on Agriculture also addresses the issue of export restrictions imposed by exporting countries, the main problem has always been the restriction of imports by importing countries. A review of the discussions of the WTO Committee on Agriculture reveals that only a handful of cases involving export restrictions were discussed since its establishment in 1995. One of the first such issues arose at the request of Japan challenging the introduction by the Czech Republic of temporary prohibitions on wheat and flour exports. See WTO Committee on Agriculture, *Summary Report of the [Sixth Regular] Meeting Held on 24–25 September 1996* (G/AG/R/6).

[155] See, inter alia, para. 6 of the preamble to the Agreement on Agriculture.

PART II

THE LAW OF AGRICULTURAL EXPORT SUBSIDIES

CHAPTER 4

THE LAW OF EXPORT SUBSIDIES IN GENERAL

4.1 INTRODUCTION

One of the most important obstacles to market-based international agricultural trade has always been the excessive use of subsidies on the part of almost all major trading nations. If the term "trade war" has been used in connection with the GATT/WTO system so far, a substantial majority of cases must have been related to the sphere of agricultural trade in general and export subsidies in particular. Part II deals with this contentious subject under the system. In order to fully appreciate the role of this impediment, Part II starts with an introduction into the concept of export subsidies and its evolution in the course of negotiations for the Charter of the ITO and the General Agreement in 1947, examines the landmark 1955 amendment to GATT Article XVI, evaluates the developments brought about by the "plurilateral"-type Tokyo Round Subsidies Code and analyzes the important achievements of the "multilateral" Uruguay Round SCM Agreement.

Having thus discussed the principles applying to export subsidies in general, Part II goes into the specific case of agricultural export subsidies as contained in the Uruguay Round Agreement on Agriculture. Commencing with a brief recapitulation of the major sticking points during the arduous and testing negotiation process of the export subsidy part of the Agreement on Agriculture, this Part addresses such complex issues as the relationship between the different categories of export subsidies and agricultural products identified or implied by the Agreement, the methodology adopted in order to bring discipline to this largely undisciplined practice, the issue of circumvention of export subsidy commitments, the once controversial problems of "downstream flexibility" provisions, the institutional aspect of the Agreement on Agriculture, the types of remedies available to countries affected by the agricultural export subsidies of other Members, and the food security fears of Least-Developed (the LDCs) and Net Food-Importing Developing Countries (the NFIDCs).

The issue of subsidies concerns the different forms of support to selected spheres of the economy, provided or mandated by the government, for a variety of purposes. Although a very old and widespread practice, the views of governments as well as scholars regarding subsidies have always been divided. While some defend the practice of subsidies as an important instrument of domestic economic policy for development, others argue that subsidies only shield inefficient enterprises from market-driven technological adaptation and thereby perpetuate underdevelopment.[1] One thing seems to be clear beyond doubt, however – that a subsidy necessarily goes against the very economic theories on which the whole GATT/WTO system claims to have been based: the theories of comparative advantage and specialization.

According to these theories, a country exports goods which it can produce with the highest relative efficiency.[2] Countries or enterprises gain market shares on the basis of the quality of goods they bring to the market and the price they charge. However, subsidies, which may be given to exporters or simply to producers, have the effect of minimizing the cost of the recipients – thus enabling the latter to charge lower prices on the market than their unsubsidized counterparts. The natural consequence is that the market share of the subsidized competitors grows at the expense of the unsubsidized or the less subsidized ones. By the same token, domestic producers in importing countries surrender their own markets to subsidized foreign competitors. It creates a situation where even the most efficient producers could be driven out of the market in favour of inefficient but subsidized competitors. Hence the conclusion that subsidies can have as disruptive an effect on the market as that of tariffs or quantitative restrictions. As the principle of free trade requires that such market-distorting measures as tariffs and non-tariff barriers be eliminated, or at least minimized, the use of subsidies simply destroys the benefits that could otherwise accrue from such moves. That is why the practice of subsidies, just like that of dumping, is labelled as one of the so-called "unfair trade practices".

Yet, despite this almost universally agreed principle, it has always been the practice that governments subsidize different sectors of their economies in different ways, although to varying degrees. The agricultural sector is perhaps the most glaring case in point. It is the most heavily subsidized sector in almost all countries that are capable of doing so. This is not simply accidental. As will be explained later, the use of export subsidies is often an unavoidable consequence of the widespread national practices of agricultural price support and stabilization schemes which keep the domestic price of agricultural products artificially higher than world prices, thus encouraging surplus production that can only be disposed of on the international market with the help of export subsidies. The history of the law in this respect is thus a history of the diplomatic efforts undertaken with a view to curtailing this unfair and, at the same time, widespread practice.

4.2 Evolution of the Law of Subsidies in the Multilateral Trading System

4.2.1 GATT and the Charter of the ITO[3]

Subsidies were among the first issues to be considered when the legal framework of

---

1 For more on this, see *inter alia* R. Rivers, and J. Greenwald, "The Negotiation of a Code on Subsidies and Countervailing Measures: Bridging Fundamental Differences", *Law & Policy in International Business*, Vol. 11, 1447, (1979), pp. 1452 et seq.; Stewart, T. *The GATT Uruguay Round: A Negotiating History (1986–1992)* in III Vols. (Kluwer 1993), Vol. I, p. 844.

2 See *supra* chapter 1.

3 For an authoritative account of the negotiating history of the GATT, see R. Hudec, *The GATT Legal System and World Trade Diplomacy* (Praeger Publishers, 1975) pp. 3–55.

the post-war economic order was being carved out in the mid 1940s. The Suggested Charter of the International Trade Organization (the ITO),[4] which was prepared and submitted by the United States in 1946, distinguished between production subsidies and export subsidies and proposed distinct regimes for each of them.[5] Accordingly, while proposing to allow production subsidies subject only to the requirements of notification and consultation, the US suggested to prohibit export subsidies which would result in export prices below domestic prices, but with an exception permitting "such subsidies in the case of products in chronic oversupply".[6] Having been prepared by the US, it is interesting to note here that "most exports being subsidized under the US farm program were assumed to fall into the excepted category".[7] Indeed, later drafts of the ITO Charter also contained explicit provisions in favour of a "separate (and more lenient) treatment for subsidies as to primary products in certain circumstances."[8] The exclusion of agricultural products from the discipline of subsidies thus had its roots in the very first version of the *Suggested Charter*.

However, several participants opposed this aspect of the proposal. For some, the very distinction between export subsidies and domestic subsidies was artificial, arguing that "both production and export subsidies could effectively result in oversupply on the world market and unfairly restrict some countries' exports".[9] For others, it was the exceptional treatment of primary products that was a source of concern. Developing countries in particular felt that the proposal would allow the rich countries to subsidize those products in the production and marketing of which the poor countries may have a comparative advantage while prohibiting the subsidization of the non-primary products on which the rich stand in a better competitive position.

The cumulative effect of all this was that several participating countries forged a stiff resistance against the US position on the subject and, at one point, even reached an agreement to tighten the export subsidies discipline of the draft ITO Charter.[10] Stating the US reaction to this development, Hudec observed that although the United States was generally pleased with the Geneva draft of the ITO's Commercial Policy Chapter, "it was most unhappy with the vigorous export subsidy provisions of that draft."[11]

---

4 US Department of State, "Suggested Charter for an International Trade Organization of the United Nations", Washington D.C., (1946, hereafter the *Suggested Charter*) cited in WTO, *GATT Analytical Index: Guide to GATT Law and Practice* (Updated 6th Edition 1995) p. 4.

5 See J. H. Jackson, *World Trade and the Law of GATT* (Bobbs-Merrill, 1969) p. 368.

6 Jackson wrote the following in this connection: "One interesting exception included in the 1945 as well as the 1946 United States draft proposals ... provided that in the case of a 'burdensome world surplus' of a specific product, if nations cannot agree on measures to increase consumption and reduce production, then the treaty obligations regarding subsidies on that product 'shall cease to apply.'" Jackson (1969) *supra* n. 5, p. 368.

7 Hudec (1975) *supra* n. 3, p. 15.

8 Jackson (1969) *supra* n. 5, p. 369.

9 Ibid. p. 369.

10 See Hudec (1975) *supra* n. 3, p. 15.

11 Ibid. p. 49.

Not surprisingly, when the Preparatory Committee of the ITO, pending the conclusion of the Charter for its target organization, commenced a negotiation in Geneva to formulate the GATT, these contentious issues were excluded altogether from the first working draft of the General Agreement, which was once again prepared by the US delegation, and remained so in the final text of the General Agreement.[12] The result was that, rather than prohibiting export subsidies with a narrow exception, all subsidies – export or otherwise – were subject to the same regime regardless of their spheres of application. A uniform system was introduced for all of them. GATT contracting parties agreed to have only a "loose" obligation to report their subsidies,[13] with the possibility of consultations under Article XXIII or unilateral countervailing duties under Article VI.[14]

Yet, as the original purpose of the GATT was only to give provisional effect to "certain provisions" of the draft ITO Charter by negotiating "concrete arrangements for the relaxation of tariffs and trade barriers of all kinds",[15] the very nature of the ITO project necessitated some form of a lasting compromise on the subject of export subsidies. That compromise was to be found in a sectoral approach to the problem whereby export subsidies were to be generally prohibited with a conditional exception for "primary commodities".[16] In fact, the agreement finally reached was to introduce a "special set of rules for export subsidies on primary products, basically adopting the *Suggested Charter* provision".[17] Legalization of the practice of export subsidies on primary products, which covers most agricultural products, was thus able to satisfy the negotiating parties at least for the purpose of signing the Havana Charter. Yet, given that the Charter never entered into force,[18] and that its place was effectively taken over by the GATT, the focus of our attention shifts to the General Agreement.

---

12 This was rather exceptional. As summarized by the GATT Secretariat, "[a]lthough many of the articles of the General Agreement were adapted directly from the corresponding provisions in the Geneva Draft Charter, Article XVI in the 30 October 1947 text of the General Agreement was drawn only from Article 25 of the Geneva Draft Charter, and included only one paragraph, the present-day Article XVI:1. The Geneva Draft Charter Articles 26 through 29, which dealt in more detail with export subsidies, were omitted from the General Agreement". *GATT Analytical Index, supra* n. 4, p. 465.

13 Article XVI:1 of the General Agreement.

14 See GATT Article VI; the term "countervailing duty" is defined under paragraph:3 "to mean a special duty levied for the purpose of offsetting any bounty or subsidy bestowed, directly or indirectly, upon the manufacture, production, or export of any merchandise".

15 *GATT Analytical Index, supra* n. 4, p. 5.

16 Article 26(1) of the Havana Charter provides the principle as follows: "No Member shall grant, directly or indirectly, any subsidy on the export of any product, or establish or maintain any other system, which subsidy or system results in the sale of such product for export at a price lower than the comparable price charged for the like product to buyers in the domestic market ..." And Article 28(1) provides the conditional exception as follows: "Any Member granting any form of subsidy, which operates directly or indirectly to maintain or increase the export of any primary commodity from its territory, shall not apply the subsidy in such a way as to have the effect of maintaining or acquiring for that Member more than an equitable share of world trade in that commodity."

17 Hudec (1975) *supra* n. 3, p. 15.

18 It is worthy of note that US interests and farm organizations "led the opposition to the creation of the ITO." J. Hillman, "The US Perspective", in K. Ingersent, A. Rayner, and R. Hine (eds.) *Agriculture in the Uruguay Round* (St. Martin's press, New York 1994), p. 29.

4.2.2 GATT and the "Uniform" Regime of Subsidies: A Summary[19]

The ITO Charter failed to secure the minimum number of ratifications required for its entry into force. As a result, the GATT with its "loose" reporting obligation on subsidies, took its place through the "Protocol of Provisional Application" in a rather "permanent" form. Left only to a single paragraph – the current Article XVI:1 – all subsidies were subjected to the same rules irrespective of whether they applied to primary or industrial products. The sectoral approach of the Charter had to be suspended indefinitely in favour of the "uniform"[20] approach of the "temporary" arrangement. Nor was there any distinction as such in the treatment of domestic and export subsidies. Mainly because the rules applying to agricultural export subsidies were the same as those applying to others, this section is only a highlight of the overall regime of subsidies in the first version of the General Agreement.

Originally GATT did not prohibit the use of subsidies. Strictly speaking, Article XVI:1 – the only provision governing the subject of subsidies in the original GATT – imposes only two seemingly mandatory, but, from a truly legal and regulatory perspective nearly meaningless obligations on the contracting parties: the obligation to "notify" the subsidies they grant (and not all of them), and, in cases where the subsidization is determined to have caused or threatened serious prejudice to the interests of other contracting parties, the obligation to "discuss" with the other party or with the CONTRACTING PARTIES the possibility of limiting the subsidization.

The legal regime of subsidies in the 1947 GATT version suffers from a number of weaknesses. In the absence of any definition to the key term subsidies, even the two only obligations – notification and discussion – were in practice found to be too difficult to implement. Besides, even assuming these problems could be overcome one way or another, and with notification and discussion as the only obligations created by the provision, the very regulatory significance of the rules was doubtful.[21]

Although the lack of a definition might not have been a serious problem in the work of the dispute settlement panels,[22] particularly for purposes of agricultural export subsidies,[23] contracting parties later agreed on an illustrative list of export subsidies[24] which served as an authoritative guideline until the conclusion of the Uruguay Round in 1994 solved the matter completely.

---

19 As the subsidies discipline introduced by the General Agreement in 1947 did not distinguish between domestic and export subsidies, the discussions made under chapter 9.3 *infra* concerning the period between 1947 and 1955 apply to the case of export subsidies as well. This summary is included only to recapitulate some of the main features of the regime as it applied at that time.

20 See Article VI.7 on stabilization schemes.

21 For further discussions on this point, see *infra*, section 4.3.

22 See GATT Panel on Subsidies, *Operation of the Provisions of Article XVI*, (L/1442 & Add. 1-2 *BISD* 10S/203), report adopted on 21 November 1961, p. 208.

23 See T. Josling, S. Tangermann, and T. Warley, *Agriculture in the GATT* (MacMillan, London 1996) p. 119.

24 See for instance the 1960 *Illustrative List of Export Subsidies, infra* n. 35; and the list annexed to the 1979 Subsidies Code.

In sum, the original version of the GATT did not impose any significant constraint on the domestic policy-making powers of the contracting parties as regards subsidies. The notification and discussion obligations, coupled with the unilateral and multilateral ways of reacting to cases of injurious or prejudicial subsidy practices, applied to all sectors of the economy as well as to all forms of subsidies. Agricultural export subsidies were thus as lawful as were export subsidies applying to other, non-agricultural, products. However, the practical effect of such a rule was counter-productive to the very objectives of the GATT itself. It was realized from early on that the success achieved by the GATT in the reduction of tariffs would turn out to be meaningless if its practical effects could be circumvented[25] by a resort to such market distorting practices as subsidies with only the obligation to notify – itself an obligation not seriously taken on the part of many subsidizing countries in actual practice.[26] It was due to this and other shortcomings of the General Agreement that the contracting parties decided to revise the entire Agreement in 1952 and commenced the actual review in late 1954.[27] One result of the revision was the introduction of different categories of subsidies with different legal consequences.

4.3 The 1955 Amendments: A Two-Way Development?

As far as export subsidies in general and that of agricultural export subsidies in particular are concerned, the 1955 amendment may be taken as a landmark in the history of international trade regulation. Not only was a special discipline for export subsidies introduced, a separate sub-discipline was also created for what came to be known as "primary products" – agricultural products accounting for a major part of them.

The amendment added four new paragraphs, together with their own annexed interpretative notes, to the single-paragraph Article XVI of the GATT, all of them dealing with export subsidies.[28] The first of the additional provisions, framed in the form of a preamble to the following substantive obligations, provides the understanding that the contracting parties "recognize that the granting by a contracting party of a subsidy on the export of *any* product *may* have harmful effects for other contracting parties, ... *may* cause undue disturbance to their normal commercial interests and *may* hinder the achievement of the objectives of this Agreement."[29]

Two points in this formulation deserve special note. Firstly, the statement sheds some light on the meaning of the term "export subsidies" – that it refers to a

[25] For a discussion of the circumvention of tariff negotiation results via the use of subsidies see J. H. Jackson, *Legal Problems of International Economic Relations* (West Publishing Co. 1977), pp. 754–756.

[26] On the multilateral reactions towards this situation, see *BISD*, 5S/19.

[27] See Hudec (1975) *supra* n. 3, p. 63.

[28] Note also that almost all of these new additions were taken from the failed Havana Charter of the ITO. See, for example, paragraphs 1 and 4 of Article 28 of the Charter for Article XVI:3, and paragraphs 1 and 3 of Article 26 of the Charter for Article XVI:4 – the two important substantive modifications to the original text of the GATT.

[29] Article XVI:2 of the General Agreement (italics added).

"subsidy on the export of any product". Yet, in the absence of any definition for the root word "subsidy" the practical importance of this formulation was at best minimal. In an attempt to overcome the practical difficulties that would result from this lacuna, the contracting parties later agreed on a non-exhaustive list of practices that were "to be considered as subsidies in the sense of Article XVI:4" of the GATT. The list includes practices ranging from the provision by governments of direct subsidies on exports, the remission or exemption of charges or taxes on condition of exportation, down to the provision by governments of export credits or export credit guarantees at less than market costs.[30]

Secondly, the statement also makes it clear that the contracting parties were not yet ready to condemn the practice as such, for its own sake. The verb "may" is repeatedly used in this provision so as to underscore that the contracting parties could not agree that export subsidies always have those harmful consequences. This might be a contradiction in terms. As pointed out by writers, "[e]xport subsidies are granted *with the aim of affecting trade*. If an export subsidy does not distort trade, it is simply because it has not been effective."[31] Furthermore, at least as far as their international trade effects are concerned, export subsidies are virtually the same as dumping practices. Nevertheless, probably because there is some form of government involvement in the case of export subsidies, which makes the issue more sensitive than dumping by the private business person itself, the contracting parties were not able to extend to the case of export subsidies the word of condemnation they used against injurious dumping.[32]

---

30 The practices are the following: (a) Currency retention schemes or any similar practices which involve a bonus on exports or re-exports; (b) The provision by governments of direct subsidies to exporters; (c) The remission, calculated in relation to exports, of direct taxes or social welfare charges on industrial or commercial enterprises; (d) The exemption, in respect of exported goods, of charges or taxes, other than charges in connexion with importation or indirect taxes levied at one or several stages on the same goods if sold for internal consumption; or the payment, in respect of exported goods, of amounts exceeding those effectively levied at one or several stages on these goods in the form of indirect taxes or of charges in connexion with importation or in both forms; (e) In respect of deliveries by governments or governmental agencies of imported raw materials for export business on different terms than for domestic business, the charging of prices below world prices; (f) In respect of government export credit guarantees, the charging of premiums at rates which are manifestly inadequate to cover the long term operating costs and losses of the credit insurance institutions; (g) The grant by governments (or special institutions controlled by governments) of export credits at rates below those which they have to pay in order to obtain the funds so employed; (h) The government bearing all or part of the costs incurred by exporters in obtaining credit. GATT, *Working Party Report on Provisions of Article XVI:4*, adopted on 19 Nov. 1960, *BISD* 9S/186-187.

31 G. Depayre, and R. Petriccione, "Definition of Subsidy", in J. Bourgeois, (ed.) *Subsidies and International Trade: A European Lawyers Perspective*, (Kluwer 1991) p. 73 (italics added). As former US Agriculture Secretary Clayton Yeutter is quoted to have said in connection with a US proposal to the Uruguay Round in 1989, the purpose was "to level the playing field for farmers, so they compete fairly against one another instead of against governmental treasuries." J. Hillman, "The US Perspective", Ingersent *et al*, *supra* n. 18, p. 40.

32 Note that Article VI explicitly states that "dumping is to be condemned if it causes or threatens material injury to an established industry in the territory of a contracting party or materially retards the establishment of a domestic industry" – the very conditions set to allow countervailing duties against lawful subsidies are here used to condemn an action of the same nature but performed by different actors.

Yet, given the widespread nature of the practice and its political sensitivity, the explicit recognition that the granting of export subsidies on any product may have harmful consequences was an achievement in itself. However, the importance of the clause "any product" appears questionable as soon as we see the distinction created between primary and non-primary products by the following provisions.

Section B of Article XVI prescribes distinct regimes of export subsidies for these two categories of products. The two substantive paragraphs added in 1955 are the following:

> (3) "... contracting parties *should seek to avoid* the use of subsidies on the export of primary products. If, however, a contracting party grants directly or indirectly any form of subsidy which operates to increase the export of any primary product from its territory, such subsidy shall not be applied in a manner which results in that contracting party having more than an equitable share of world export trade in that product, account being taken of the shares of the contracting parties in such trade in the product during a previous representative period, and any special factors which may have affected or may be affecting such trade in the product.[33]
>
> (4) Further, as from January 1958 or the earliest practicable date thereafter, contracting parties *shall cease to grant* either directly or indirectly any form of subsidy on the export of any product other than a primary product which subsidy results in the sale of such product for export at a price lower than the comparable price charged for the like product to buyers in the domestic market. Until 31 December 1957 no contracting party shall extend the scope of any such subsidization beyond that existing on 1 January 1955 by the introduction of new, or the extension of existing, subsidies[34] (italics added).

---

[33] Ad Article XVI, Paragraph 3 provides as follows:

"1. The fact that a contracting party has not exported the product in question during the previous representative period would not in itself preclude that contracting party from establishing its right to obtain a share of the trade in the product concerned.

2. A system for the stabilization of the domestic price or of the return to domestic producers of a primary product independently of the movements of export prices, which results at times in the sale of the product for export at a price lower than the comparable price charged for the like product to buyers in the domestic market, shall be considered not to involve a subsidy on exports within the meaning of paragraph 3 if the CONTRACTING PARTIES determine that:

(a) the system has also resulted, or is so designed as to result, in the sale of the product for export at a price higher than the comparable price charged for the like product to buyers in the domestic market; and

(b) the system is so operated, or is designed so to operate, either because of the effective regulation of production or otherwise, as not to stimulate exports unduly or otherwise seriously to prejudice the interests of other contracting parties.

Notwithstanding such determination by the CONTRACTING PARTIES, operations under such a system shall be subject to the provisions of paragraph 3 where they are wholly or partly financed out of government funds in addition to the funds collected from producers in respect of the product concerned."

[34] Ad Article XVI, Paragraph 4 provides as follows: "The intention of paragraph 4 is that the contracting parties should seek before the end of 1957 to reach agreement to abolish all remaining subsidies as from 1 January 1958; or, failing this, to reach agreement to extend the application of the standstill until the earliest date thereafter by which they can expect to reach such agreement."

First of all, the obligation of the contracting parties concerning the export of primary products is *to seek to avoid* the use of export subsidies, while that in relation to non-primary products is *to cease to grant* any form of export subsidies which result in bi-level pricing. Moreover, while the mandatory obligation *to cease to grant* subsidies in paragraph 4 is expressed with the strength of "shall", the already weak obligation *to seek to avoid* the use of subsidies in paragraph 3 is further weakened by the use of the hortatory "should". It was in this form that the special treatment which had been given by the ITO Charter to export subsidies on primary commodities, and which had died with it, was reintroduced in 1955.[35] From then on it is, indeed, possible to speak of a distinct law of export subsidies applying to what now came to be termed as "primary products".[36] Developing Countries still objected to the differential treatment of primary and other goods.[37] They argued that "it is unfair for nations that export mainly primary products to bind themselves in the non-primary goods area while the developed nations continue their use of subsidies for primary goods."[38]

4.3.1 Principle: Export Subsidies on Non-Primary Products

The new provisions generally prohibit the granting of export subsidies on non-primary products which result in the sale of such product for export at lower than the comparable price charged for the like product to buyers in the domestic market,[39] often referred to as "dual pricing" or "bi-level pricing". They are, however, indirectly allowed for "primary products" with only vague limits on their application, viz. that such subsidy may not be applied in a manner which results in that contracting party having "more than an equitable share of world export trade in that product".[40] In either case, although it was recognized that export subsidies *may* be harmful, they were not outlawed *per se*. Arguably, even for non-primary products, it is perfectly legal to give export subsidies, but only in as long as this does not result in the sale of the subsidized product at prices lower than the domestic market. However, "dual pricing" being one of the natural or, to use the words of one panel report, the presumed,[41] consequences of any effective export subsidy, one may

---

[35] For a comparison of the two versions, see Jackson (1969) *supra* n. 5, p. 371.

[36] Interpretative Note Ad 2 to Section B of Article XVI in Annex I defines a primary product as "any product of farm, forest or fishery, or any mineral, in its natural form or which has undergone such processing as is customarily required to prepare it for marketing in substantial volume in international trade". This definition is the same as the definition given to the concept of a "primary commodity" in Article 56:1 of the ITO Charter. For discussion of the concept, see *infra* section 4.3.3.

[37] See Jackson (1977), *supra* n. 25, p. 756. As a result of this opposition of the developing countries, the important developments of the 1955 amendments under Article XVI:4 were accepted almost exclusively by the industrialised contracting parties of the GATT. For a list of these countries, see *infra* n. 43.

[38] Argument made by India, as referred to in Jackson (1969) *supra* n. 5, p. 399.

[39] GATT Article XVI:4.

[40] GATT Article XVI:3.

[41] The GATT panel in the notorious *DISC* case stated that "from an economic point of view, there was a presumption that an export subsidy would lead to any or a combination of the following consequences

conclude, at least in theory, that export subsidies on non-primary products are generally prohibited.

It is interesting to note, however, that the practical significance of the amendment's prohibition of subsidies on non-primary products was diminished for two main reasons. Firstly, despite the fact that the date of entry into force of the prohibition of Article XVI:4 had explicitly been stated to be "1 January 1958 or the earliest practicable date thereafter", translating those words into reality soon proved to be difficult. Not only did the first alternative fail, the "earliest practicable date" was also an elusive goal for some time to come. As a result, it was the "standstill" provision, obligating parties not to extend the scope of any subsidization beyond that existing on 1 January 1955 until the end of 1957, which set the only limit on the practice for about a decade. The "standstill" obligation was extended five times and remained in force until the end of 1967.[42] Moreover, even when it came to life after such a long delay, it was applicable only to the 17 countries that accepted it. Given the dissatisfaction of most developing countries, it is hardly surprising that virtually all of them were developed countries.[43]

Secondly, even after its delayed entry into force and for a small number of signatories, the practical impact of the prohibition of export subsidies on non-primary products was diluted because of reservations made by some countries and the resulting practice. The United States, Australia and the United Kingdom entered reservations during their acceptance of the 1960 Declaration Giving Effect to Article XVI:4. According to the US reservation, for instance, the acceptance of this instrument was made "with the understanding that this Declaration shall not prevent the United States, as part of its subsidization of exports of a primary product, from making a payment on an exported processed product (not itself a primary product),

---

cont.

in the export sector: (a) lowering of prices [which might be taken as a reference to the dual-pricing situation], (b) increase of sales efforts and (c) increase of profits per unit." GATT, *United States Tax Legislation (DISC)*, report of the panel (L/4422 *BISD* 23S/98) presented to the Council on 12 November 1976 and adopted on 8 December 1981, para. 73. Professor Jackson also agrees with this view and states that "one theoretical result of an export subsidy is 'bi-level pricing' whereby the goods which are exported are sold abroad at a price below that of the goods retained for the domestic market." Jackson (1977), *supra* n. 25, p. 616. This requirement has, however, been severely criticized by scholars. In the words of Hudec, for instance, the dual pricing requirement makes "no sense as a matter of policy". In his view the reason for barring export subsidies was that "they harmed producers in the importing country by encouraging export transactions that would not normally take place. An export subsidy could create such harmful effects whether or not it caused lower export prices simply by increasing the volume of exports". Hudec, *Enforcing International Trade Law: The Evolution of the Modern GATT Legal System* (Butterworth, 1993), p. 64. According to Hudec, "strange as it seems, the bi-level pricing requirement seems to have been put into the text of Article XVI:4 by mistake." Ibid, p. 76.

42 For additional reflections on this point, see *inter alia* the following: Jackson (1969) *supra* n. 5, pp. 371–376; J. H. Jackson, *Legal Problems of International Economic Relations*, (West Publishing Co. 1987), pp. 754–756; *GATT Analytical Index, supra* n. 4, pp. 465–467.

43 They are Austria, Belgium, Canada, Denmark, France, Federal Republic of Germany, Italy, Japan, Luxembourg, the Netherlands, New Zealand, Norway, Southern Rhodesia, Sweden, Switzerland, United Kingdom, and the United States.

which has been produced from such primary product, if such payment is essentially limited to the amount of the subsidy which would have been payable on the quantity of such primary product, if exported in primary form, consumed in the production of the processed product."[44] As Jackson noted in this connection, this looked more of an interpretation than a reservation – an interpretation that was not shared by all countries.[45]

The diluting effect of such unilateral statements was not limited to those countries that formally entered their respective reservations. The EC and Switzerland had, for instance, reported a practice consisting in subsidizing the primary agricultural input in exported processed agricultural products although they had no reservations attached to that effect.[46] In 1970 the EC notified refunds on processed products such as macaroni, spaghetti, etc. manufactured from agricultural products and explained that "to the extent necessary in order to allow export of agricultural products in the form of certain processed products on the basis of quotations or prices for the said products on the world market the difference between those quotations or prices and the prices in the EEC may be covered by an export refund. The amount of the refund

---

[44] *GATT Analytical Index, supra* n. 4, p. 457. The history of this reservation has been summarized by the unadopted *EC Pasta* Panel as follows: "At the 12th Session of the CONTRACTING PARTIES in 1957 the United States sought clarification of the scope of Article XVI and proposed that Article XVI:4 should not prevent a contracting party, in this particular case the United States, from subsidizing exports of processed products (cotton textiles) if such subsidy was essentially the payment that would have been made on the raw material (cotton) used in the production of this processed product if the raw material had been exported in its natural form. ... The US interpretation was not accepted by other contracting parties. No contracting party spoke in favour of it, while several contracting parties clearly rejected it. Some contracting parties proposed that the United States attach a reservation to its signature of the declaration extending the standstill provisions of Article XVI:4. The representative of the United States said that this proposal would be reported back to his Government (SR.12/22, pp. 192–194)." *European Economic Community – Subsidies on Export of Pasta Products,* report of the panel (SCM/43 issued on 19 May 1983, not adopted), paras. 2.13–2.14.

[45] See Jackson (1969) *supra* n. 5, p. 398. The EC representative in *EC Pasta* also argued that "various statements had been made regarding the Declaration, and in particular the United States had made clear their understanding that the meaning of the Declaration should be taken as allowing subsidization of exports of a primary product even if the latter was contained or incorporated in a non-primary product. It was on the basis of that statement by the United States – which was indeed an interpretation and not a reservation as that country was alleging today – that an interpretative practice developed of the prohibition of export subsidies on non-primary products." *EC Pasta, supra* n. 44, para. 3.12. The Panel was, however, of a different opinion: "The Panel recognized the well-established principle that the determination of whether a unilateral statement, however phrased or named, was an interpretative declaration or a reservation was dependent not on the particular label attached to the statement by the country concerned but on whether the statement intended to exclude or modify the legal effects of certain provisions of the agreement in their application to that country. The Panel was of the view that the US understanding was intended to limit the legal obligations of the United States under Article XVI:4 and had to be recognized as a reservation rather than an interpretation. This conclusion was confirmed by the history of this understanding, and in particular by the fact that it was referred to as a reservation by the Chairman of the CONTRACTING PARTIES at the 13th Session in 1958 as well as by four contracting parties and that these statements were not challenged by any other contracting party." Ibid., para. 4.6.

[46] See Ibid., para. 2.20.

is equivalent, as a general rule, to the quantity of each basic product utilized, multiplied by the rate of the refund applicable thereto."[47] This was repeated in 1972,[48] but, subsequent EC notifications did not contain a separate chapter dealing with processed products. However, even thereafter, goods processed from agricultural products have been "enumerated under 'Export Refunds'."[49] It is noteworthy that, despite the absence of any specific reservation to that effect by some of their users, the legality of such practices was never challenged before the dispute settlement system.[50] The effect of all these reservations and practices was that a substantial proportion of subsidies on the export of non-primary products could somehow be camouflaged as subsidization of the primary-product components. But, as will be seen later, this more or less established and unchallenged practice ultimately turned out to be a subject of contentious dispute in the unadopted *EC Pasta* case that was brought under the Tokyo Round Subsidies Code.[51]

4.3.2 Exception: Export Subsidies on Primary Products

In the case of primary products, not only is the use of an export subsidy allowed; it is also allowed to use it with "dual pricing" effects within certain limits – the acquisition by the subsidizing party of "not more than an equitable share of world export trade in that product". Stated differently, it is legitimate for the parties to apply export subsidies on primary products with the effect of bi-level pricing and the consequent market distortion to maintain a "not more than equitable" share of world export trade in that product. But, the crucial question is this: Is there such a thing as a market share, not to mention the equity thereof? As will be substantiated in a while, the general recognition of the potentially harmful nature of export subsidies was tempered, if not rendered meaningless, as regards primary products.

Before going to the details of the discipline governing the practice of export subsidies on primary products, however, we have to answer the question of what is meant by agricultural products in this context and whether and how far they fall within the category of primary products.

---

[47] GATT, L/3178/Add.14, as quoted in Ibid., para. 2.19.

[48] GATT, L/3655/Add.10, as quoted in Ibid., para. 2.19.

[49] Notification made in 1970 by the EEC (in L/3178/Add.14), as reproduced in Ibid., para. 2.19.

[50] This does not, of course, mean that the absence of a challenge legalizes an otherwise unlawful practice. Indeed, as *EC Pasta* rightly observed, "[a]s contracting parties were under no legal obligation to challenge the legality of export subsidies of other contracting parties, the mere abstaining from such a legal challenge could not be relied upon as acquiescence to or construed as approval of the legality of such export subsidies. In this context the Panel noted that another Panel had concluded that the fact that certain practices had been in force for some time without being the subject of complaints was not, in itself, conclusive evidence that there was a consensus that they were compatible with the General Agreement (*BISD* 23S/114, para. 79)." Ibid., para. 4.10.

[51] For further discussion on this point, see *infra* section 4.4.8.

4.3.3 Primary Products v. Agricultural Products

An interpretative note to Article XVI defines a primary product as "any product of farm, forest or fishery, or any mineral, in its natural form or which has undergone such processing as is customarily required to prepare it for marketing in substantial volume in international trade."[52] By using the words "any product of farm, forest or fishery", this definition makes a clear reference to agricultural products. This reference is nevertheless not sufficient to conclude that all agricultural products are covered by the definition of primary products. There is the added requirement of being either "in its natural form" or, in the alternative, of having undergone only such processing as would customarily be required for marketing purposes (hereinafter referred to as the "minimal processing" condition).

The literal understanding of agricultural products seems to fit in with the first criterion. In the ordinary sense of the term, "agricultural products" refer to products which are the direct result of animal husbandry and cultivation of the soil in their natural unprocessed condition.[53] As will be explained, however, the definition given by the interpretive note also allows those agricultural products which are in their minimal processing forms to be considered as primary products. For purposes of this text, therefore, and despite the fact that we sometimes talk of processed or "non-primary" agricultural products in the sense of Article XVI of the General Agreement,[54] "agricultural products" are taken to refer only to those agricultural products which satisfy the requirements of being "primary" in the sense of that provision. The question of what is meant by "primary" as employed under Section B of Article XVI is therefore important for the purpose of understanding the meaning of agricultural products as used here.

Two important requirements are set for a product to be a primary product – being either "in its natural form" or to have "undergone such processing as is customarily required to prepare it for marketing in substantial volume in international trade". It hardly needs to be said that this is too general a formulation for expeditious practical implementation. To cite a very simple example, what is the natural state of coffee: the cherries that are collected from the coffee trees? the coffee beans that are taken

---

52 Interpretative Note Ad 2 of Section B of GATT Article XVI in Annex I. This definition is taken from Article 56.1 of the 1948 Havana Charter. Article 56.2 of the Charter added the following: "The term shall also, for the purposes of this chapter, cover a group of commodities, of which one is a primary commodity as defined in paragraph 1 and the others are commodities, which are so closely related, as regards conditions of production or utilization, to the other commodities in the group, that it is appropriate to deal with them in a single agreement."

53 Adapted from *Black's Law Dictionary*, (6th ed. 1990), p. 68. See also Article 38:1 of the *Treaty of Rome Establishing the European Economic Community*, which defines agricultural products in a similar, but broader, way: "the products of the soil, of stockfarming and of fisheries and *products of first stage processing* directly related to these products" (italics added). For a discussion of how panels have interpreted an agricultural product in the context of Article XI:2 of the General Agreement, see *supra* **section 2.5.3.**

54 See *EC Pasta* in which the Panel concluded that "neither party had finally contended that pasta was a primary product. The Panel was of the opinion that pasta was not a primary product but was a processed agricultural product." *EC Pasta, supra* n. 44, para. 4.2.

out of the cherries? the dried coffee beans? the washed coffee beans? the roasted coffee beans? the ground and preserved coffee? etc. Nor is the minimal processing alternative any clearer. Although the same example on coffee might also work in this case, one may take another example on wheat and ask the question of at which stage the minimal processing requirement is exceeded in the following simple succession of exports with subsidies: when the wheat is milled into wheat flour and the flour is exported; when the flour is sold to a domestic bakery and the biscuits and loaves of bread made from it are exported; when the flour is sold to domestic food processors and the pasta made out of it is exported; etc.

Such problems are by no means merely imaginary. Similar cases have been encountered by GATT dispute settlement panels and working parties. For instance, the 1958 panel on *French Assistance to Exports of Wheat and Wheat Flour* considered wheat flour as a primary product by concluding that the French system was a subsidy "on the export of *wheat and wheat flour* within the terms of paragraph 3 of Article XVI."[55] The panel did not even mention the issue apparently because the parties did not raise such argument. Given that the regime of export subsidies on non-primary products was more stringent than that on primary products, and hence more favourable for the complainant to prove its case, one would have expected such an argument from Australia; but it did not. This might indicate that the understanding of the contracting parties was not to exclude such simple acts of processing as milling from the scope of primary products.

Nevertheless, one thing seems to be clear beyond doubt – that wheat flour is not in "its natural form". Hence the only remaining alternative ground for wheat flour to be called primary within the meaning of Article XVI:3 is what has been called the "minimal processing" situation. The key question will then be whether milling is a processing customarily required for wheat to be prepared for marketing in substantial volume in international trade. This question can only be answered by reference to the actual practice on the marketplace. And the answer seems to be in the negative. A look at the statistical figures on wheat production and trade for the preceding several years collected by the *French Wheat* panel vividly demonstrates that exporting wheat as it is is the rule, the dominant business custom so to speak, while converting it into flour is the exception.[56] Furthermore, the milling of wheat in this case does not seem to have had any other motive than adding more value for the purpose of raising profitability on the market.[57]

In the strict sense, therefore, wheat flour is a product neither in its natural form, nor in a form that has undergone such processing as is customarily required for marketing in substantial volume. Australia's failure to raise such an argument as well

---

[55] *French Assistance to Exports of Wheat and Wheat Flour*, report of the panel (L/924 *BISD* 7S/49) adopted on 21 Nov. 1958, para. 14 (italics added).

[56] Just to take an example, between January and June 1958 alone France exported 881,000 metric tons of raw wheat, while the corresponding figure for wheat flour for the same period was only 204,000 tons – the former being more than four times the size of the latter. For a full picture of the facts, see Table 1 on "French Wheat Production and Trade", in Ibid. p. 49.

[57] See Ibid. para. 23(e).

as the panel's conclusion seem to suggest only that the intended meaning of primary products is closer to the ordinary understanding of the term than what a strict interpretation of the words used to define it might lead to. This position has been maintained by later panel decisions as well. For example, in a similar case in 1983 initiated by the US under provisions of the Subsidies Code, the panel treated wheat flour as a primary product in the sense of Article 10 of the Code.[58] Although it may seem arbitrary to draw a line between the different stages in the processing of the natural wheat, the outright exclusion of pasta from the ambit of "primary products"[59] also leads to the same conclusion – that the common sense understanding of the term was given more weight than the interpretative note.

The meaning of the minimal processing condition may appear more clearly in the case of sugar. Obviously, sugar is not a primary product in the sense of being in its natural form. Depending on what it is made of, the natural form of sugar is the sugar cane, sugar beet, etc. from which the sugar is processed. However, it is customary that some degree of processing is required to prepare those raw materials of sugar "for marketing in substantial volume in international trade" in the sense of the definition of primary products under the interpretative note to Article XVI. This understanding got its proper expression in the two parallel sugar cases against the EC. In both cases, instead of trying to follow the easier course of Article XVI:4 on non-primary products, both complainants (Australia and Brazil) simply chose to pursue their cases under Sub-Article 3 on primary products, thus entailing consideration of such difficult-to-prove and otherwise unnecessary requirements as equitable share and the like.[60] Presumably, the choice to pursue this course does not indicate inadvertence; rather, it shows the consensus view among the contracting parties that sugar must be considered as a primary product for purposes of Article XVI:3. There are also other instances where such products as refined sugar, oil and processed tobacco have been considered as primary products.[61] As such, it is possible to conclude that the concept of primary products has in practice been construed more widely than what a strict interpretation of the definition would have allowed. The term "agricultural products" as used in this Part of the thesis therefore refers to

---

[58] *European Economic Community – Subsidies on Export of Wheat Flour,* report of the panel (SCM/42, issued on 21 March 1983, not adopted), para. 4.2. For further details on this point, see *infra* section 4.4.9.

[59] The panel noted that "neither party had finally contended that pasta was a primary product. The Panel was of the opinion that pasta was not a primary product but was a processed agricultural product." See *EC Pasta, supra* n. 44, para. 4.2.

[60] Australia argued that "[t]he Community market organization in the field of sugar, *which is a primary product in the terms of Article XVI:3,* involves export subsidy measures the application of which is not consistent with the provisions of Article XVI referred to above." *European Communities – Refunds on Exports of Sugar: [Complaint by Australia]* report of the panel (L/4833 *BISD* 26S/290-319) adopted on 6 November 1979, para. 2.6 (italics added). Brazil also said that the subsidies granted had allowed the Community "to obtain a more than equitable share of the world sugar trade", thus implicitly referring to the provisions of Article XVI:3. See *European Communities – Refunds on Exports of Sugar: Complaint by Brazil* Report of the panel (L/5011 *BISD* 27S/69-98) adopted on 10 November 1980, para. 2.1.

[61] See, for instance, GATT Panel on Subsidies, *Operation of the Provisions of Article XVI,* (L/1442 & Add. 1-2 *BISD* 10S/203), report adopted on 21 November 1961, pp. 201–209.

those products of farm which satisfy either of the two conditions for being a primary product as interpreted by the contracting parties in actual practice. With this understanding in mind, agricultural products and primary products are used here in an interchangeable manner.

4.3.4 Export Subsidies on Agricultural Products

Now that it has been demonstrated that agricultural products are a part of the so-called "primary products", the export subsidy regime established for the latter will be taken as fully applicable to the former and discussed accordingly in the following section. Paragraph 3 of Article XVI is devoted exclusively to the regulation of the use of export subsidies on primary products.[62] The obligations assumed by contracting parties by virtue of this provision may be split into two – the obligation to seek to avoid the use of export subsidies, and the obligation not to apply export subsidies in a manner which results in the subsidizing party having more than an equitable share of the world export trade in that product.

Looked at more closely, it is doubtful whether these obligations set any real legal constraint on the parties. Just like the obligation to discuss under paragraph 1 of Article XVI explained above, the most that can be implied from the statement that a country "should seek to avoid the use of subsidies" may not go beyond some form of a moral obligation not to rush for the use of subsidies in every case. It does not create any obligation to desist from granting subsidies; nor was it intended to do that in fact. It only requires good faith from the parties so that they would try to solve their problems through measures other than the use of export subsidies; but only to try and no more. In the strict sense of the term, therefore, this part of the provision does not create any legal obligation as such; hence it can hardly be violated by any party in any way. Stated differently, contracting parties are free to grant export subsidies on primary products. The manner of its application is, however, restricted under the second statement of Paragraph 3 by the no "more than equitable share standard". The restriction applies only in cases where the parties decide to go against the "moral" obligation discussed above and opt for the use of export subsidies. It is there to govern the manner of application of export subsidies when a decision to apply them has already been taken. Moreover, in order to determine whether a given market share is equitable or not, the provision requires that the shares of other contracting parties in a previous representative period be considered. Not only is this period required to be representative of a "normal" market situation, any "specific factors" which may have affected or may still be affecting trade in the product need to be considered. In the following sections, therefore, each of these elements will be discussed at a greater detail.

4.3.5.1 The "Equitable Share" Standard

Although a contracting party is free to grant a subsidy designed, whether directly or indirectly, to promote its export trade in primary products, it has the obligation not

[62] For the text of Article XVI:3, see *supra* section 4.2.

to do so in a manner that results in its acquisition of more than an equitable share of world export trade in that product. Thus the debate has always been revolving around the following question: what is an "equitable share of world export trade" in a product?

We have seen that the "equitable share" standard got the status of being part of the operative GATT only after the 1955 amendment. However, it is worth reminding that its history in this context dates back to the first drafts of the ITO Charter.[63] And since its arrival in the GATT text, it has been a source of some of the most difficult interpretative problems rather than solutions.

Different writers have criticized the concept from different perspectives. The Leutwiler Report, for instance, stated that "this concept is economically misconceived, since it implicitly endorses market-sharing. It is also too vague and subjective to permit clear judgment on whether a subsidy is acceptable or not ... A better test of legitimacy than that of equitable share is needed for subsidies on primary products."[64] As no such better test was coined, however, this rather obscure standard had to continue being at the centre of debate for academics as well as GATT lawyers and panellists. In the opinion of one writer, the word "equitable" in this context is interchangeable with the term "fair".[65] The point, however, is that not only is this alternative terminology not any less ambiguous, it is also such a value-laden term that "what seems fair to one primary commodity exporting country will seldom seem fair to a rival exporting country or to an importer of the same commodity".[66] Finally, Stewart wrote that "[t]o the extent that the term has any meaning, it suggests an approach whereby the world market is allocated among current participants."[67]

Not surprisingly, therefore, many contentious GATT disputes under Article

---

[63] See, *inter alia*, Hudec (1975) *supra* n. 3, p. 15. In its present form, paragraph 3 is essentially taken from Article 28(1) of the Havana Charter, which provides as follows: "Any Member granting any form of subsidy, which operates directly or indirectly to maintain or increase the export of any primary commodity from its territory, shall not apply the subsidy in such a way as to have the effect of maintaining or acquiring for that Member more than an equitable share of world trade in that commodity." The two important differences between these two versions may be stated as follows. Firstly, while GATT Article XVI:3 is concerned with subsidies which operate only *to increase* the export of any primary product, Havana Charter Article 28(1) concerned subsidies which would operate *to maintain or increase* such export. It is also noteworthy, however, that the term "increase" is also used in the first paragraph of Article XVI, which has been interpreted to "include the concept of maintaining exports at a level higher than would otherwise exist in the absence of the subsidy." (See *BISD* Vol. II/44, para. 29(a)) Secondly, while the Havana version would see the equitable share standard vis-à-vis *world trade* in that commodity in general, Article XVI:3 limits it to the particular category of *world export trade* in that product. For more on this, see Jackson (1969) *supra* n. 5, p. 371–376.

[64] GATT, *Trade Policies for a Better Future* (Geneva 1985) p. 40; see also J. McMahon, *Agricultural Trade, Protectionism and the Problems of Development: A Legal Perspective,* (Leicester University Press, London 1992) p. 218.

[65] C. Wilcox, *A Charter for World Trade* (1949) pp. 129–130, as quoted in C. Phegan, "GATT Article XVI:3: Export Subsidies and 'Equitable Shares'" in 16 *Journal of World Trade Law* (1982), p. 253.

[66] Phegan, *supra* n. 65, p. 253.

[67] Stewart (1993) Vol. I, *supra* n. 1, p. 136.

XVI:3 have been revolving around this single issue – "the most difficult interpretative problem of paragraph 3", as Jackson described it.[68] In the following section, an attempt will be made to see some of the problems surrounding the "not more than equitable share" language as interpreted by some of the GATT dispute settlement panels[69] throughout its life time.

The first GATT case where the matter appeared at the centre of controversy was the 1958 *French Wheat*,[70] where Australia complained that as a result of subsidies granted by the French Government on the export of wheat and wheat flour, inconsistently with the provisions of Article XVI:3, French exports had displaced Australian trade in these products particularly in its traditional wheat flour markets in Ceylon, Indonesia and Malaya.[71] After having determined that the French practice involved a subsidy on exports within the terms of Article XVI:3,[72] the panel considered whether the practice had also led France to obtain more than an equitable share of the world export trade in wheat and wheat flour. In this respect, the Panel first noted that "at both Havana and the Review Session when the provisions of this paragraph were discussed, it was implicitly agreed that the concept of 'equitable share' was meant to refer to share in 'world' export trade of a particular product and not to trade in that product in individual markets."[73]

On the basis of the facts and figures it had collected,[74] the panel observed that French exports of wheat and wheat flour began to rise in 1954 in absolute quantity to levels very substantially exceeding the quantities exported in any year since 1934 and had since remained considerably higher than in pre-war or early post-war years. According to the panel, this increase in the absolute quantities of wheat and of wheat flour exported by France "also represents an increase in France's share of world exports, especially as regards wheat flour."[75] On the question of whether this increase in France's share of world exports amounted to a "more than equitable share", the panel found that "while there is no statistical definition of an 'equitable' share in world exports, ... the present French share of world export trade, particularly in wheat flour, is more than equitable."[76] This is the only case in which a finding of violation of Article XVI:3 was found in GATT dispute settlement history. It is also known as a case that has given full effect to the terms of the provision in a straightforward manner.

Three things are worthy of a special mention from this report. Firstly, the Panel

---

[68] Jackson (1969) *supra* n. 5, p. 393.

[69] The "more than an equitable share of world export trade" language has been discussed in five GATT dispute settlement proceedings: *French Wheat, US Tobacco*, the two *EC Sugar* cases, and *EC Wheat Flour*. Relevant sections of these reports are discussed at appropriate places.

[70] *French Wheat, supra* n. 55, p. 53.

[71] Ibid. p. 47.

[72] For details on this aspect of the Panel determination, see discussion on stabilization schemes *infra* section 4.3.5.5.

[73] *French Wheat, supra* n. 55, p. 52, para 15.

[74] See Table 1 on French Wheat Production and Trade, in Ibid. p. 49.

[75] Ibid. p. 53, para 17.

[76] Ibid. *p*. 53, para 19.

pointed out that the "share" that is referred to under Article XVI:3 relates to a proportion of a country's export trade in a product relative to the overall amount of export trade in that product at the global level. Variations in trade shares in individual markets do not count in as long as the global share remains unaffected. This aspect of the interpretation was reaffirmed by a subsequent panel report on *EC Sugar – Complaint by Australia*.[77] The complainant in this case argued that "when looking at Community sugar export practices, Australia and other contracting parties should be concerned with the 'world free market'. This was the only export market accessible to both Australia and the European Communities and the only market accessible to all exporters on the basis of open competition and where, in consequence, the price effects of such competition occurred."[78] That was the GATT sense of "world export trade" in the view of the Australian representative. His argument was, however, rejected by the Panel. In its view, the "examination should be based not on the concept of 'free market' introduced by Australia ... but on the concept of 'world export trade' mentioned in Article XVI:3 of the General Agreement", and noted that "a consideration of shares of the free market involved methodological difficulties that would make any comparison difficult".[79]

Secondly, although any logical approach to the "equitable share" problem requires that statistical data be collected and analyzed, the *French Wheat* Panel rightly observed that "there is no statistical definition of an 'equitable' share in world exports".[80] Statistics may help to get an overall picture of what the distribution trends look like and to draw a conclusion therefrom. It remains possible, however, that the same statistical figures may lead to completely opposite conclusions as regards the equity they represent under different circumstances.

Thirdly, although the *French Wheat* Panel reached the conclusion that French share of world export trade was "more than equitable" and that the subsidy arrangements had contributed thereto, it did not give any general definition as to what is meant by "more than equitable". For instance, it is difficult, if not impossible, to draw a line of demarcation in the scale of growth of France's export trade within which it would have still been inside the equitable share limit. This means that the conclusion of the Panel on the equity issue, although reasonable and convincing, still has an element of arbitrariness in it. For example, the Panel, before concluding that the French share was more than equitable, noted that "French exports of wheat and wheat flour began to rise in 1954 in absolute quantity to levels very substantially exceeding the quantities exported in any year since 1934 and had since remained considerably higher than in pre-war or early post-war years. This increase in the absolute quantities of wheat and of wheat flour exported by France also represented an increase in France's share of world exports, especially as regards wheat flour."[81]

---

77 See *EC Sugar – Complaint by Australia, supra* n. 60.

78 Ibid., para. 2.20.

79 Ibid., para. 4.9.

80 *French Wheat, supra n. 55*, p. 53, para. 19.

81 Ibid. p. 53, para. 17.

If we look at the statistical figures on wheat flour upon which the Panel relied to arrive at this conclusion, the annual amount exported during that period, i.e. pre-war (1934–1938) as well as post-war (1948–1958), varied between 8,000 metric tons for 1948 as the minimum and 488,000 tons for 1955 as the maximum.[82] The question may then be asked as to where in this rather wide range the "equitable share" limit ends and the "more than equitable share" sphere begins: at 100,000 tons, at 200,000 tons, at 480,000 tons, or where? It thus seems fair to conclude that, however reasonable one may be in making the choice, one cannot help entertaining some degree of unexplainable discretion to fix a point in this continuum. It is this element of arbitrariness that could have been avoided if the Panel had been able to formulate some form of a definition or a set of criteria to be met before concluding that there is such a phenomenon in a certain issue.

It was, however, only in the *EC Sugar – Complaint by Australia* case that something close to such a formulation appeared. The Panel in this case was of the opinion that "the term 'more than an equitable share of world export trade' should include situations in which the effect of an export subsidy granted by a signatory was to displace the exports of another signatory, bearing in mind the developments in world markets."[83] Such an interpretation may look strange, especially when seen in light of the fact that there is no any direct reference to the requirement of "displacement" in Article XVI:3. The following two points may throw some light as to why the Panel took that perspective.

First of all, it seems reasonable to argue that this interpretation is implicit within the language of the provision itself. After all, it is always difficult to talk of a "more than equitable share" of one country without implying that there is at least one other country that is suffering from a "less than equitable share" of the same trade. In other words, in a saturated market of a limited capacity, one party's share can grow only at the expense of another's. Consequently, it may not be far-fetched to conclude that the "more than equitable share" standard has the element of "displacement" within it. This view can also be discerned in the 1958 *French Wheat* case wherein the Panel tried to evaluate the degree of injury sustained by Australia through an assessment of the extent of displacement of Australian supplies by French exports.[84]

Secondly, and perhaps more authoritatively, the timing of the decision of the Panel seems to have been decisive as to the source of that inspiration. This is because, as will be shown later, this is a definition fully identical with the interpretation of "equitable share" that ultimately came out in the 1979 Subsidies Code.[85] When Australia lodged its complaint on 25 September 1978, the Tokyo Round Subsidies Code had essentially been completed. The Subsidies Code was adopted on 12 April

[82] See Table 1 in Ibid., p. 49.

[83] *EC Sugar – Complaint by Australia, supra* n. 60, para. 4.17.

[84] See *French Wheat, supra n. 55*, p. 55, para. 23(c). The panel stated that "although it is difficult to estimate to what extent such incursions as these are *displacing* traditional exporters, it is nevertheless clear that French supplies have in fact to a large extent *displaced* Australian supplies in the three markets" Ibid. (italics added).

[85] See Article 10:2(a) of the Subsidies Code.

1979; and the panel report was adopted on 6 November 1979, i.e. after the Code was adopted but before its entry into force on 1 January, 1980. It is thus no more a mere speculation to say that, by the time, both the parties and the panel members "must have known ... that the meaning of the 'equitable share' concept had just been debated at length in the Tokyo Round Subsidies Code negotiations"[86] and that an understanding had been reached on what this controversial concept meant.[87] Furthermore, it is noteworthy that the panel did not even bother to adapt the language of the text to the context of the GATT.[88]

Be that as it may, the use of the new test of displacement did not make the application of the "equitable share" standard any easier. The final rulings of the two parallel sugar panels themselves are significant in this connection. In spite of a finding of increasing EC exports of sugar effected through the use of subsidies, the panels simply concluded, in identical language, that they were "not able to conclude that the increased share had resulted in the European Communities 'having more than an equitable share of world export trade in the product', in terms of Article XVI:3."[89] The use of the test of displacement in the Subsidies Code will be discussed in section 4.4.

4.3.5.2 The "Representative Period"

Another important element in this connection concerns the requirement that in determining the equitable share issue account be taken of the shares of the contracting parties in such trade in the product during a "previous representative period" and any special factors which may have affected or may be affecting such trade in the product. The concept of "previous representative period", for which once again GATT gives no explicit definition, has proved to be controversial.

To start with, it is natural that one cannot speak of an increase or decrease in a country's export trade share of a product without looking at the market condition over a given period of time. The qualifying word "representative", however, brings with it the added condition that the period should be chosen in such a way as to enable the parties to evaluate the effect of the subsidy under consideration upon the distribution of market shares that had prevailed between the different competitors prior to the subsidy in question. In other words, the period so chosen should reflect the condition of the market preceding the now challenged subsidization – the "normal", undisturbed, situation of the market, one may presume.

However, as statistical figures depicting market shares vary from year to year, each time favouring one party over another, the "representative period" concept is difficult to determine. In *EC Sugar – Complaint by Australia*, for instance, Australia argued that its complaint concerned the post-1975 period and that the entire period

86 Hudec (1993) *supra* n. 41, p. 132.

87 For a discussion of the Subsidies Code on the matter, see *infra* section 4.4.9.

88 For example, the panel used the term "signatory", which is a concept used only in the Code that, arguably, does not apply to the General Agreement, whose parties are simply called contracting parties.

89 *EC Sugar – Complaint by Australia, supra* n. 60, para. V(f). The same statement was made in the *EC Sugar – Complaint by Brazil, supra* n. 60, para. V(e).

1969–1975, i.e. starting from the first year of operation of the Common Agricultural Policy for sugar,[90] should be considered as the previous representative period. The EC, on the other hand, counter-argued that the years chosen should reflect, if possible, a normal market situation, and suggested to compare the averages for the years 1972–1974 with that for 1975–1977. In trying to resolve this issue, the Panel first determined that the search for a "previous representative period" should be one for "the three most recent calendar years for which market conditions could be considered as normal"[91] – another interpretation identical with the 1979 Tokyo Round Subsidies Code to be used without any explicit reference.[92]

The problem was not to end there, however. The Panel still had to resolve the more difficult question of which three of the several years proposed by the contending parties should be taken as "representative" of the normal market situation. It excluded Australia's suggestion to consider 1975 as part of the representative period because it felt that "1975 did not appear to be sufficiently representative, as world market prices were abnormally high in 1974/1975".[93] By this the Panel reaffirmed the view that the representative period should reflect, to the extent possible, the normal market situation preceding the now questioned subsidization. It also expressed doubts as to whether 1974 would qualify as a "fully representative" year, but concluded that "the years 1972 to 1974 would still be an acceptable approach."[94] Finally, it decided that "in view of the difficulties involved in selecting what could be considered to be the 'previous representative period', the Panel felt it necessary to consider various alternatives and to make a set of comparisons".[95] Accordingly, "the three most recent calendar years for which market conditions could be considered as normal were then 1971 to 1973, or with some reservations 1972 to 1974".[96]

A similar view could be found in the Panel decision on the parallel case of *European Communities-Refunds on Exports of Sugar – Complaint by Brazil*, where the Panel considered two periods, namely 1971–73 and 1972–74, to qualify as "previous representative periods" despite diverging suggestions by each of the parties.[97]

---

[90] The Common Market for sugar, which was established by Regulation (EEC) No.1009/67 and entered into force on 1 July 1968, remained applicable until the end of the 1974/75 sugar year, when it was replaced by a new basic regulation (Regulation (EEC) No. 3330/74 of the Council of 19 December 1974). Among its primary objectives are the following: "to ensure that the necessary guarantees in respect of employment and standards of living in a stable market are maintained for Community growers of sugar beet and sugar cane; and to help guarantee sugar supplies to the entire Community." See *EC Sugar – Complaint by Australia, supra* n. 60, para. 3.3.

[91] *EC Sugar – Complaint by Australia, supra* n. 60, para. 4.10.

[92] For a discussion of the Subsidies Code on this issue, see *infra* section 4.4.

[93] *EC Sugar – Complaint by Australia, supra* n. 60, para. 4.10.

[94] Ibid.

[95] Ibid.

[96] Ibid.

[97] The complainant suggested to compare shares in two periods, 1973–75 and 1976–78, while the EC proposed the two averages to be those for 1972–74 and 1975–77 and that the year 1978 be considered separately. The Panel, however, mentioned the 1976 to 1979 period referred to by the complainant and found that "whichever of the two previous representative periods is used for comparison, the outcome would be fairly similar". *EC Sugar – Complaint by Brazil, supra* n. 60, para. 4.9.

Notable in this connection is that the Panel decided to use the two periods despite Article 10:2(c) of the Subsidies Code, which had already entered into force by the time for the disputants, that this period "shall normally be the three most recent calendar years in which normal market conditions existed."[98] In *French Wheat*, too, although the "representative period" had not been at issue, it is illuminating to observe that the Panel used statistics collected for more than twenty years preceding the challenged subsidy.[99]

On the basis of all the panel interpretations reviewed on this question, it seems worthwhile to conclude that the concept of "representative period" is there not to limit the power of the contracting parties to this or that year, but rather to aid them gain an objective and clear picture of the normal market condition that prevailed before the challenged subsidy appeared on the scene and, on that basis, to draw a reasonable inference as to what the trends look like since then.

4.3.5.3 "Special Factors"

In considering market shares, Article XVI:3 also requires consideration of any "special factors which may have affected or may be affecting such trade in the product." The language of this provision indicates that consideration must be given to the role of "special factors" on trade in the product in question both in the past as well as at the time of examination of the market share. Just like the concepts of equitable share, previous representative period, etc., Article XVI of the General Agreement does not define "special factors". Unlike those other concepts, however, the term "special factors" has been defined by the General Agreement in the context of quantitative restrictions under Article XI:2. According to this latter Article, "[t]he term 'special factors' includes changes in relative productive efficiency as between domestic and foreign producers, or as between different foreign producers, but not changes artificially brought about by means not permitted under the Agreement."[100]

It is a fundamental principle of international law that terms of a treaty have to be interpreted in accordance with their ordinary meaning in their context and in the light of the object and purpose of the treaty.[101] The context for any treaty provision covers, *inter alia*, the text of the treaty itself together with its preamble and the annexes. As such, it is clear that Article XI, and for that matter all provisions of the text of the General Agreement, form part of the immediate context for the interpretation of terms used under Article XVI:3. Furthermore, in our specific case, the term "special factors" in both provisions serves a similar purpose – that of approximating market shares as

---

98 The Subsidies Code was adopted on 12 April, 1979 and entered into force on 1 January 1980, while this case was started on 10 November 1978, and decided and adopted on 10 November, 1980. See Article 10:2(c) of the Subsidies Code. The panel has also explicitly referred to the Code and mentioned the fact that it has been accepted by both parties to the dispute. See Ibid. para. 4.7. However, as the panel was established under the GATT, with its terms of reference limited to the provisions thereof, the panel could neither rely on, nor be constrained by, the terms of the new Agreement.

99 See *French Wheat*, Table 1 *supra* n. 55, p. 49 and relevant statements in paras. 6 and 17 of the report.

100 Interpretative Note Ad. Article XI, para. 2, last sub-paragraph.

101 See *Vienna Convention on the Law of Treaties* (done at Vienna, 23 May 1969, 1155 U.N.T.S. 33), Article 31(1).

close as possible to what would have prevailed in the absence of the artificial trade-distortive practices, quantitative restrictions and subsidies in this particular case.[102]

There is not much GATT "case law" on this subject. Of all the cases brought under the General Agreement which addressed Article XVI:3, it is only in the *EC Sugar* cases, and particularly in the one brought by Brazil, that we see a discussion of this element. The panel in this case particularly focused on the role of the entry into operation of export quotas under the International Sugar Agreement (ISA 1977) on the respective shares of the disputing parties as a "special factor" under Article XVI:3. The panel concluded *inter alia* that the entry into force on 1 January 1978 of ISA (1977) "apparently had a strong impact on the volume of world sugar trade in 1977 already."[103] The panel further observed that for the major sugar exporting countries members of the ISA, the result was "a substantial contraction in their exports."[104] In the panel's view, "[f]urther expansion in Brazilian exports in 1978 and 1979 was limited by Brazilian commitments under the ISA, but Brazil filled and even exceeded slightly its reduced ISA export quotas in both years."[105] And the effect of these factual observations was reflected in the final ruling of the panel as follows: "in light of all the circumstances related to the present complaint and especially taking into account the difficulties in establishing clearly the causal relationships between the increase in Community exports, the developments of Brazilian sugar exports and *other developments in the world sugar market*, the Panel found that on the basis of the evidence available to it in this particular case, it was not able to conclude that the increased share had resulted in the European Communities 'having more than an equitable share of world export trade in the product', in terms of Article XVI:3."[106]

The issue of "special factors" was discussed more thoroughly in the unadopted *EC Wheat Flour* case, which was brought under the Subsidies Code. But, as no substantive modification had been made by the Code to the "special factors" clause of Article XVI:3 of the General Agreement, a closer look at this panel's interpretation is in order here.

Basically, the issue of "special factors" in the *EC Wheat Flour* case arose out of the following inconsistent contentions by the parties to the dispute. According to the US, EC export subsidies on wheat flour had resulted in a dramatic rise in EC's share of the market in the product (from 29 to 75 percent) while the share of all other

---

[102] For more on this term in the context of Article XI, see *supra* chapter 2.5.3.1.4.2. See also W. Davey, "The Rules for Agricultural Trade in GATT", reproduced in J. H. Jackson, W. Davey, and A. Sykes, *Legal Problems of International Economic Relations: Cases, Materials and Text* (3rd ed., West Publishing Co. 1995), p. 1167.

[103] *EC Sugar – Complaint by Brazil, supra* n. 60, para. 4.16. The Panel explained that, in 1977, "total world exports of sugar exceeded 28 million tonnes, with an increase of one quarter from the previous year, the largest annual increase ever recorded. These developments were due to efforts made by exporters to ship as much sugar as possible before the entry into operation of export quotas under the ISA on 1 January 1978, and also to an expectation prevailing among refiners and importers that prices might increase with the entry into force of the ISA." Ibid.

[104] Ibid., para. 4.17.

[105] Ibid., para. V(c).

[106] Ibid. (italics added).

major exporters was marked by an equally dramatic decline. The EC defended, on the other hand, that US allegations in relation to changes in world market shares were based on an erroneous appreciation of the factors responsible for them. According to the EC, rather than the export subsidies provided by the Community, the possible factors responsible for the apparent decline of US shares include the undue exclusion of US concessional sales from the data on US exports, US market loss in some countries for its own political and diplomatic reasons, and the like.[107]

The panel devoted a special section in its report to the analysis of the role of "special factors" on the observed developments in market shares. The panel singled out political considerations, non-commercial sales, and the existence of regular shipping lines between the EC and most of the importing countries as particularly important.

By political developments, the panel was referring to such US measures as embargoes and changes in diplomatic relations which, in its view, "have played an important rôle at times in hindering US flour sales to a number of countries and in affecting relative market shares as between the EEC and the US."[108] The panel referred specifically to Angola, Cuba, Libya, Vietnam, North Korea and the then USSR. With respect to the USSR, for instance, the panel observed that after no shipments to the USSR in 1977/78 and 1978/79, the EEC exported 123,348 metric tons in 1979/80, and 702,651 metric tons in 1980/81.[109] The panel finally noted that substantial EC increases in volume terms in 1980/81 over the previous three-year average were registered in the markets of the USSR, Libya, and Angola, "where the US exports were disadvantaged on political grounds."[110]

In respect of non-commercial sales, too, the panel noted that during the period under review the levels of wheat flour "entering international trade under conditions not conforming to usual commercial practices, and the proportion of total wheat flour imports which were accounted for by such shipments, were considerable."[111] Finally, the panel pointed out that the existence of regular shipping lines from the Community to most of those countries could be "an important factor in permitting the transportation of small quantities of flour and in meeting irregular and unpredictable purchases at reasonable costs."[112]

On the basis of these and "other special factors", the panel reached the final finding that "it was unable to conclude as to whether the increased share has resulted in the EEC 'having more than an equitable share' in terms of Article 10, in light of the highly artificial levels and conditions of trade in wheat flour, the complexity of developments in the markets, *including the interplay of a number of special factors*, the relative importance of which it was impossible to assess, and, most importantly, the difficulties inherent in the concept of 'more than equitable share'."[113]

---

107 *EC Wheat Flour, supra* n. 58, para. 2.21.
108 Ibid., para. 2.18.
109 Ibid., para. 4.18.
110 Ibid., para. 4.18.
111 Ibid., para. 4.20.
112 Ibid., para. 4.22.
113 Ibid., para. 5.3 (italics added).

It is clear from the above-summarized cases that "special factors" were invoked to weaken the causal link between a country's rising market share in a product and its export subsidy scheme thereon. It is not, however, difficult to imagine cases where "special factors" might be invoked to strengthen this causal link. Given the dynamic nature of the market and the role of the actors thereof, two such cases related to the question of "special factors" drew the attention of the contracting parties from the early days, namely, the possibility that export subsidies might still have affected the picture in the period selected as "representative", and the case of new exporters that had had no exports at all during that previous representative period. The former has been taken care of through a Working Party Report adopted by the CONTRACTING PARTIES which embodied the understanding that "in determining what are equitable shares of world trade the CONTRACTING PARTIES should not lose sight of (a) the desirability of facilitating the satisfaction of world requirements of the commodity concerned in the most effective and economic manner, and (b) the fact that export subsidies in existence during the selected representative period may have influenced the share of the trade obtained by the various exporting countries."[114] This means, *inter alia*, that, firstly the market share of a contracting party should, at least in theory, be subservient to the demands of efficiency, that no one should be allowed to maintain a share at the expense of more efficient and more economic means of supplying the market. Secondly, since many countries have been engaged in subsidization for almost a century now, the point under (b) cautions that the share established for the contending parties in any period selected as representative should not necessarily be taken as truly "representative" and equitable in the sense these words are intended to have here.

Important on this point is again the 1981 *EC Wheat Flour* case brought under the Subsidies Code. The complainant, the US, argued that since the introduction of the Common Agricultural Program in the 1960s, the EC share of "commercial exports" had risen steadily from 29 per cent in the three years preceding the introduction of the CAP (1959–1960 to 1961–1962) to 75 per cent in the three most recent years (1978–1979 to 1980–1981). In response, the EC representative argued that "the United States' interpretation led to impracticable consequences since, as was here the case, it meant referring to years several decades ago, in other words to a period for which it was very difficult to determine exactly whether or not subsidies of any kind had existed. If one followed the United States interpretation to its logical conclusion, one would have to refer to an initial period in which there was no export subsidization by any of the contracting parties, and not merely to a period in which the incriminated subsidy did not exist."[115]

On the other hand, the case of the new entrants to the market, being rather

[114] GATT, *GATT Working Party Report on Other Barriers to Trade* (L/334, and Addendum, *BISD* 3S/226) adopted on 3 March 1955.

[115] *EC Wheat Flour, supra* n. 58, para. 2.18. Hudec summarized the point made by EC representative as an argument to the effect that "the US share in 1959 was itself the product of subsidies and other artificial inducements. The only data reflecting a genuinely free market . . . would be trade data for 1893." Hudec (1993) *supra* n. 41, p. 148.

export subsidies into those on primary commodities and those on non-primary products on the other. While domestic subsidies were permitted, the case of export subsidies depended on additional conditions: as a rule export subsidies resulting in bi-level pricing were prohibited; but those on primary commodities were exceptionally permitted if they were not applied in such a manner as to acquire more than an equitable share of world trade in that product.

However, the ITO Charter never entered into force. And it was the General Agreement, with its uniform discipline for all forms of subsidies, that continued to be the only regulatory instrument for some time to come. Whether domestic or export, agricultural or industrial, the General Agreement permitted all kinds of subsidies without distinction. The only obligations assumed by the contracting parties were the obligation to notify some subsidies, and, if found prejudicial to the interests of other contracting parties, the obligation to discuss the possibility of limiting the subsidization. Given the highly trade-distorting nature of subsidies in general and that of export subsidies in particular, however, the presence of such obligations could make no significant difference. It was soon realized that the rule amounted to nothing more than legalization of a practice the use of which would only circumvent the beneficial results gained from the successful tariff negotiations of the time. As a result, this regime could not survive the first serious amendment to the General Agreement in 1955.

The 1955 review session did nothing but resuscitate the old two-tier classification of the Havana Charter between domestic subsidies and export subsidies, as well as between export subsidies on primary commodities and export subsidies on non-primary products with only minor modifications. A separate paragraph in the form of Article XVI:3 was devoted to the regulation of export subsidies on primary products – the category wherein agricultural products fall. However, full of such ambiguous and controversial concepts and issues as the "equitable share" the "representative period", "special factors" and causation, this provision has been a source of tension and uncertainty throughout the history of the General Agreement.

Although it was not on the agenda of the first four rounds of GATT multilateral trade negotiations,[133] attempts to discipline agricultural trade were made during subsequent ones, but in vain. It has been observed for instance that the Dillon Round (1960–61) came to an end with the conditions of trade in agriculture being "even worse than they had been"[134] before. Neither did the Kennedy Round (1964–67) – which was in fact taken as "the first serious attempt to bring agricultural products within a liberal and disciplined multilateral trading system"[135] – bring much change.[136] The Tokyo Round of Multilateral Trade Negotiations (1973–79) was thus hoped to provide an important opportunity to overhaul the whole system.

[133] These GATT trade rounds were the following: Geneva (1947), Annecy (1949), Torquay (1951), and Geneva (1956).

[134] Josling *et al* (1996), *supra* n. 23, p. 50. For details on the Dillon Round concerning agriculture, see Ibid. pp. 42–51.

[135] Ibid. p. 70. For details on the Kennedy Round, see Ibid. pp. 52–71.

We know at least that, the Subsidies Code, which is one of the products of the Tokyo Round of multilateral trade negotiations, has had provisions addressing the practice of export subsidies in the area of primary products. The question of whether it has succeeded in meeting those expectations will be seen in the following section.

4.4 The 1979 Subsidies Code

4.4.5 Introduction

The Tokyo Round is different from the preceding six GATT rounds in that, apart from the traditional issue of tariffs, it gave a special emphasis to the non-tariff measures[137] affecting international trade. This new emphasis on non-tariff barriers was perhaps "the inevitable result of past success in reducing tariffs". It has been pointed out that the removal or reduction of tariffs has "an incitement effect in that it gives incentive to the introduction of new, or the extension of old, non-tariff measures in order to maintain previous levels of domestic protection."[138]

As one of the important forms of nontariff measures having a significant impact on the distribution of resources and distorting the patterns of international trade, the subsidies discipline also benefited from this overall shift of attention towards the nontariff barriers (often referred to as the NTBs). There was a general appreciation at the moment that "given the significance and growing government involvement in international commerce, some form of agreement establishing ground rules for such behaviour was essential in order to avoid sharp conflict over trade matters in the future."[139] The issue of subsidies was thus at the centre of the Tokyo Round from the very outset. The result was the conclusion of the Agreement on Interpretation and Application of Articles VI, XVI, and XXIII of the GATT, commonly called the

---

[136] The Kennedy Round "failed to attain its avowed objectives in agriculture – reducing the trade distortions caused by protectionist national agricultural policies and providing improved and assured access to import markets for efficient exporters". Josling *et al* (1996), *supra* n. 23, p. 70. The EC carried much of the blame for this failure. As observed by Davey, "[t]his was in part because after the formation of the EC, it was difficult to negotiate agricultural agreements in GATT because of the EC interest in preserving its common agricultural policy and because of the disparate interests and approaches to the issues by the US and the EC, especially France." W. Davey, "The Rules for Agricultural Trade in GATT", reproduced in Jackson *et al* (1995) *supra* n. 102, p. 1168.

[137] The term "nontariff barriers" or "nontariff measures" has not been defined by any legal instrument in the GATT. A look at the definition given by Hillman may aid understanding: "nontariff measures" refers to "any governmental device or practice, other than a tariff which directly impedes the entry of imports into a country and which discriminates against imports – that is, does not apply with equal force on domestic production or distribution. Generally speaking, nontariff measures include several types of policies or practices which interfere with or distort trade: (1) measures which restrict imports; (2) measures which provide assistance to domestic production in order to substitute for imports, and which, in effect, promote exports; and (3) measures which provide direct assistance to exporters." J. Hillman, *Non-tariff Agricultural Barriers* (University of Nebraska Press, 1978), pp. 14–15.

[138] Denton and O'Clairacain, quoted in Ibid., p. 13. Similar observations have been made by Stewart (1993) Vol. I, *supra* n. 1, p. 812; and Rivers and Greenwald (1979), *supra* n. 1, pp. 1447 et seq.

[139] Rivers and Greenwald (1979), *supra* n. 1, p. 1452.

"Subsidies Code".[140] Observers of the negotiation process have subsequently affirmed that "no Code was more controversial than the negotiation of an accord governing subsidies and countervailing measures".[141]

An important feature of the Codes, including the Subsidies Code, is that they are of a plurilateral character. As Article 19(4) of the Subsidies Code as well as corresponding provisions of the other Codes indicate, the Codes entered into force only as between those countries that have expressly accepted or acceded to them. Although they were negotiated under the auspices of the GATT and serviced by the GATT Secretariat, the Codes were separate legal instruments existing side by side with the General Agreement.[142] In the case of the Subsidies Code, for instance, it had only 25 signatories. Consequently, whatever we say in the following sections about the Subsidies Code should not be taken as a modification or an amendment of the GATT rules discussed so far, but as something that governs the trade relations of only few (although important) of the Contracting Parties to the General Agreement and that exists side by side with the latter. In a way, therefore, it is possible to say that the Code, by introducing another regime applying to the same case among a small group of GATT contracting parties, added an element of further complexity to the already divided and complex GATT system of subsidies.

Yet, although not applicable to all parties to the GATT, the developments brought about by the Subsidies Code on our subject of discussion merit independent scrutiny. In order to better comprehend these improvements the major issues discussed above will be revisited in the following section vis-à-vis the provisions of the Code. The discussion in this chapter is, however, limited to those aspects of the Code which are particularly related to the issue of export subsidies. The general rules on the subject, such as those dealing with notification, unilateral remedies and "multilateral" dispute settlement are covered in Part III of the text on Domestic Subsidies.[143]

4.4.5.1 *Definitional and Policy Matters*

One of the "main issues" addressed during the Tokyo Round in the field of subsidies concerned the question of a definition of the term "subsidy". However, as the then Director General of the GATT reported, "because of the range and extent of measures that might be considered subsidies, it [had] been impossible to agree on a precise definition or on the criteria to be applied."[144] All attempts to come to an agreed definition of the term "subsidy" ended once more in failure. Naturally, the failure to define subsidies in general had its own bearing on the type of regime that

---

[140] The text of the "Agreement on Interpretation and Application of Articles VI, XVI, and XXIII of the General Agreement on Tariffs and Trade' is published in *BISD* 26S/56-83.

[141] J. Barton, and B. Fisher, *International Trade and Investment* (Little Brown & Co., Boston 1986) p. 351. According to these writers, "two issues were particularly contentious in the Subsidies Code negotiations – the problem of domestic ... subsidies and subsidies on agricultural exports". Ibid.

[142] See O. Long, *Law and Its Limitations in the GATT Multilateral Trade System* (1987), p. 28.

[143] See in particular *infra* chapter 9.3.

[144] GATT, *The Tokyo Round of Multilateral Trade Negotiations: Report by the Director General of GATT* (Geneva, 1979), cited in Stewart (1993) Vol. I, *supra* n. 1, p. 820. A similar observation was also made by a representative of the EC who noted that it was difficult to define the term subsidy because "it

could be introduced for export subsidies in particular. Once again, parties had to content themselves with the old tradition of an "illustrative list of export subsidies"[145] – the content of which is largely similar to its 1960 predecessor.[146]

On matters of general policy, the Subsidies Code repeatedly declares to have recognized that while subsidies are used by governments to promote important objectives of national policy, they may also have harmful effects on trade and production.[147] The whole essence of the Code thus revolves around these two premises with the object of non-interference with the former and minimization of the latter to the extent possible. Consequently, the Code does not outlaw the use of subsidies; it simply tries to ensure that the use of subsidies does not adversely affect the interests of other parties to the Agreement, and, failing that, to create the mechanism by which those adversely affected by the subsidies would get the necessary relief.[148]

4.4.6 Export Subsidies v. Non-Export Subsidies

The foregoing being the general rule, the Code then goes a step further and reintroduces the dichotomy between export subsidies and subsidies other than export subsidies with totally different sets of obligations. While parties undertook the obligation not to use export subsidies in a manner inconsistent with this Agreement,[149] it was openly stated that they "do not intend to restrict the right of signatories to use such subsidies [other than export subsidies] to achieve ... important policy objectives."[150] As regards this latter category, parties are required only to seek to avoid causing injury to the interests of others[151] – a rule coined in a manner reminiscent of the 1955 amendment on the export subsidy regime of primary products. This distinction has far-reaching practical consequences. To cite only a procedural example, for a party to request consultations with a subsidizing party

---

cont.

covers a great and widely varying number of practices, the nature and importance of which vary, in particular, according to the manner, the degree and the extent of state or public sector intervention in the functioning of the economy and even of society." *Subsidies and Countervailing Duties, Addendum*, cited in Stewart (1993) Vol. I, *supra* n. 1, p. 819–820.

145 This is an approach that has been in use since the adoption on 19 November 1960 of the GATT Working Party Report on Provisions of Article XVI:4. For a list of these practices, see *supra* n. 30; the Report has been published in *BISD*, 9S/185-188.

146 See text of the Annex to the Subsidies Code in GATT, *BISD* 26S/81-83.

147 These two policy premises appear in both the preambular (paragraphs 3 and 4) as well as the operative (Article 8:1) parts of the Subsidies Code in identical wording. For more on this, see *infra* chapter 9.4.

148 See paragraph 6 of the preamble and Article 8, paragraphs 3 and 4, of the Subsidies Code.

149 Article 8:2 of the Subsidies Code.

150 Article 11:1 of the Subsidies Code.

151 Article 11:2 of the Subsidies Code. This is simply an extension of the general obligation stated under Article 8:3: "Signatories further agree that they shall seek to avoid causing, through the use of any subsidy (a) injury to the domestic industry of another signatory, (b) nullification or impairment of benefits accruing directly or indirectly to another signatory under the General agreement, or (c) serious prejudice to the interests of another signatory."

under the Subsidies Code, the only evidence it is required to present with its request as regards an export subsidy is for its existence and nature, while for other subsidies it is further required to present evidence of injury to its interests.[152]

4.4.7 Export Subsidies on "Certain Primary Products" v. Export Subsidies on Other Products

The Code then goes further down and subdivides the regime of export subsidies into those on certain primary products and those on other than certain primary products. Before going into the substance of the rules, it is noteworthy that the category of primary products excepted under Article XVI:3 of the General Agreement has now been narrowed down to almost nothing other than what are commonly known as agricultural products. Qualified with the adjective "certain", this category has in effect been redefined to mean "any product of farm, forest or fishery, in its natural form or which has undergone such processing as is customarily required to prepare it for marketing in substantial volume in international trade."[153]

However, the issue of drawing a clear line of demarcation in the continuum of processing between what is a "customarily required" one for marketing purposes and what is not still remains an unsolved problem. That is why problems similar to the pre-Code times involving this issue continued to appear after the entry into force of the Code as well. For example, it has already been pointed out[154] that in the 1983 *EC Wheat Flour* case, the complainant, the US, argued that "wheat flour is a processed product, not a primary product within the meaning of the Code."[155] The Panel was, however, able to avoid ruling on this issue on procedural grounds, saying that its terms of reference did not cover consideration of Article 9 of the Subsidies Code.[156] As a result, wheat flour was considered

[152] See Article 12, paras. 1–4.

[153] The excepted category of "primary products", as understood under Article XVI, covered "any product of farm, forest or fishery, or any mineral, in its natural form or which has undergone such processing as is customarily required to prepare it for marketing in substantial volume in international trade". The new Agreement qualifies this category with the word certain, and defines it to mean "the products referred to in Note Ad Article XVI of the General Agreement, Section B, paragraph 2, with the deletion of the words 'or any mineral'". The excluded category of "certain primary products" can thus be defined as "any product of farm, forest or fishery, in its natural form or which has undergone such processing as is customarily required to prepare it for marketing in substantial volume in international trade".

[154] See *supra* section 4.3.

[155] *EC Wheat Flour*, *supra* n. 58, para. 2.3.

[156] This is because of the following sequence of events. In his presentation to the Panel, and not during the earlier Subsidies Committee meeting, the US representative argued that "the EEC export subsidies on wheat flour are *prima facie* contrary to the obligations of Article 9 of the Code, since, in the US view, wheat flour is a processed product, not a primary product within the meaning of the Code." *EC Wheat Flour, supra* n. 58, para 2.3. In response, the EC representative argued that, "since the U.S. representative had not referred to Article 9 in raising the matter in the Committee, the question of whether Article 9 applied to wheat flour did not fall within the terms of reference of the panel." Ibid. *para. 2.4. The Panel ruled in favour of the EC on this point saying, "[w]ith regard to the United States' assertion in its presentation to the Panel that EEC export subsidies on wheat flour are prima facie*

only under Article 10 and treated as a primary product, and not a processed one.[157]

Article 9 of the Code establishes the principle for export subsidies with a simple and direct language: "signatories shall not grant export subsidies on products other than certain primary products".[158] This is a prohibition of export subsidies per se, without any condition whatsoever. Unlike Article XVI:4 on non-primary products, the prohibition here does not depend on the effect of "dual pricing" or any other situation.[159] It is a flat prohibition of export subsidies irrespective of their effects. This was indeed a commendable improvement over the previous regime, not least because it did away with the controversy that surrounded the highly criticized concept of bi-level pricing as well as the causation problem behind it. The second paragraph of Article 9 refers to the Illustrative List of export subsidies annexed to the Agreement.

The excepted case of certain primary products is addressed under Article 10 of the Subsidies Code. That provision not only incorporated Article XVI:3 of the General Agreement through an explicit reference to it, it almost restated the important parts of that provision with the addition only of a "definition" under paragraph 2 of some of the controversial concepts thereof, and the introduction of a "new" concept of "price under-cutting" under paragraph 3.[160] The following will thus be limited to a

---

cont.

contrary to Article 9 of the Code, the Panel was of the opinion that this question did not constitute part of the matter referred to the Panel by the Committee and therefore the Panel did not consider the substantive issue involved." Ibid., para. 4.2.

157 The report was not, however, adopted by the Committee on Subsidies and Countervailing Measures.

158 Article 9:1 of the Subsidies Code.

159 It is instructive to observe that "a proposal by the United States to do away with dual pricing expressly was rejected". Nevertheless, as rightly pointed out by Rivers and Greenwald, "by agreeing to a flat commitment not to use 'export subsidies' and by defining practices on the illustrative list as 'export subsidies' without regard to the price impact of those subsidies, the United States seems to have won its point and the dual pricing requirement has been effectively overruled for those practices." Rivers and Greenwald (1979), *supra* n. 1, pp. 1475–76.

160 Article 10 of the Subsidies Code provides as follows:

"1. In accordance with the provisions of Article XVI:3 of the General Agreement, signatories agree not to grant directly or indirectly any export subsidy on certain primary products in a manner which results in the signatory granting such subsidy having more than an equitable share of world export trade in such product, account being taken of the shares of the signatories in trade in the product concerned during a previous representative period, and any special factors which may have affected or may be affecting trade in such product.

2. For purposes of Article XVI.3 of the General Agreement and paragraph 1 above:

(a) 'more than an equitable share of world export trade' shall include any case in which the effect of an export subsidy granted by a signatory is to displace the exports of another signatory bearing in mind the developments in world markets;

(b) with regard to new markets traditional patterns of supply of the product concerned to the world market, region or country, in which the new market is situated shall be taken into account in determining 'equitable share of world export trade';

(c) 'a previous representative period' shall normally be the three most recent calendar years in which normal market conditions existed.

discussion of these "new developments" of the Subsidies Code in light of the practical problems encountered by the parties as evidenced in dispute settlement reports. And this notwithstanding the fact that the Subsidies Code compiled the "unenviable record" of having adoption blocked in several of the disputes brought under its provisions.[161]

4.4.8 Subsidization of the Primary Product Component of Processed Agricultural Products and the EC–Pasta Case

The *EC Pasta* dispute between the US and the EC, both signatories to the Subsidies Code, was the classic case involving the issue of whether countries were allowed to subsidize the primary-product components of processed products. The fundamental issue in the case may be stated in two different forms depending on which side one prefers to look at it: whether or not the prohibition of export subsidies on non-primary products under Article 9 also prohibited the subsidization of the primary-product component of a non-primary product; or, whether the right of signatories to (conditionally) grant export subsidies on certain primary products under Article 10 of the Subsidies Code also extended to the subsidization of those products when they were used as raw materials for processed (non-primary) export items.

The US argued that the rule set forth in Article 9 was "unambiguous, strictly prohibiting the grant of export subsidies on any product other than certain primary products."[162] According to the US, the EC export subsidy fitted precisely within the rule set forth in Article 9 because "[w]hile durum wheat was a product of the farm and thus a primary product within the definition cited above, pasta was not. The transformation of durum wheat into pasta involved a complex, multi-staged process."[163]

In the view of the EC, however, the refund was a refund on cereals granted in respect of durum wheat "whether it was in the unaltered state or has been combined with or processed into another product."[164] The Community emphasized that durum wheat was a primary product, that only the raw material was taken into account for the refund, and that no other component, for example the cost of processing, was

---

cont.

3. Signatories further agree not to grant export subsidies on exports of certain primary products to a particular market in a manner which results in prices materially below those of other suppliers to the same market."

161 Although the scenario had somehow changed since then, Hudec wrote that the Subsidies Code "compiled the unenviable record of having adoption blocked in five out of five disputes brought under its provisions." Hudec (1993) *supra* n. 41, p.14. The cases referred to by Hudec here were *EC Wheat Flour*; *EC Pasta*; *US Wine and Grapes*; *Canada Manufacturing Beef*; *US Countervailing Duty on Non-Rubber Footwear*. This picture improved somewhat with the delayed adoption of *US Wine and Grapes* as well as other subsequent cases, such as *Canada Grain Corn* and *Brazil Countervailing Duties on Milk Powder*.

162 *EC Pasta, supra* n. 44, para. 3.1.

163 Ibid., para. 3.1.

164 Ibid., para. 3.10.

taken into consideration. In the view of the Community, therefore, "the refund was granted not in respect of the pasta products but only on the durum wheat that had been used and the refund did not include any component by way of processing aid."[165] As such, it was the opinion of the EC that the only provision governing the issue was Article 10 on the subsidization of the export of certain primary products and not Article 9 of the Subsidies Code.[166]

The Panel could not reach a unanimous verdict on most of the controversial issues of this case. On the fundamental question of whether or not the subsidies in question were granted on the export of a primary product (durum wheat), which was incorporated in the processed product (pasta products), and therefore would fall under the provisions of Article 10 of the Code, the majority ruled that "durum wheat incorporated in pasta products could not be considered as a separate 'primary product' and that the EEC export refunds paid to exporters of pasta products could not be considered to be paid on the export of durum wheat."[167] The majority further noted that both the ordinary meaning of the terms as well as the context, object and purpose of the provisions "excluded the possibility of considering the export of a processed product in terms of the export of its constituent components, be they primary or processed products. The Panel therefore concluded that the EEC export refunds were granted on the export of pasta products and operated to increase exports of pasta products by refunding a part of the cost of these processed products."[168]

In the opinion of the dissenting member, however, the refund was a subsidy on the primary product (durum wheat) and not on the processed product (pasta), hence

---

165 Ibid.

166 According to the EC, "A large number of Signatories other than the Community subsidized exports of primary products even where those products were no longer in their natural form. Consequently as soon as it was established that Article 10 made it possible, on certain conditions, to subsidize exports of commodities or primary products, even if not in their natural form, it was clear that the EEC refund challenged by the United States fell within Article 10 and not Article 9 since it involved only a durum wheat refund. In these circumstances, to claim the applicability of Article 9 for a primary product, on the pretext that it has been processed – and without the processing itself being subsidized – was to recognize a superiority of Article 9 over Article 10, but this was not authorized by anything in the Code or the General Agreement." *EC Pasta*, para. 3.11. The US reacted as follows: "[The US] disagreed with the EEC view that a practice had developed whereby contracting parties had granted export subsidies on certain processed agricultural products without claiming that the subsidized product was a primary product so long as the subsidy was granted only on the primary product component incorporated into the exported product and since the practice had never been challenged, it had developed into a legal right. Whatever weight or relevance a general practice of parties might have as an interpretive aid if a provision were ambiguous, neither the language nor the history of Article 9 of the Code or Article XVI:4 of the GATT was ambiguous on the question at issue. A contracting party or Signatory clearly did not gain a legal right to engage in a prohibited practice under the GATT, or the Code either by the passage of time or because others might engage in the same or a similar practice." Ibid., para. 3.3

167 Ibid., para. 4.10.

168 Ibid. The Panel added that if the EC interpretation of Article 9 of the Code had become a general rule, "it would have radically altered the meaning of this Article thereby substantially reducing its scope and impact. Such an interpretation, if generally followed, would have permitted the subsidization of exports of almost all processed products within the purview of Article 9 which contained primary product components which were the product of farm, forest or fishery." Ibid., para. 4.11.

falling under Article 10 of the Subsidies Code. He noted that "as long as the refund merely equalized the differential between the world market price and the domestic price of durum wheat – the practical effect and the intent of the refund was to enable EEC pasta manufacturers to use domestic durum wheat in the production of exportable pasta products. The refund thus improved the competitive position of the EEC durum wheat producers rather than the processing industry and should consequently be considered as a subsidy on durum wheat."[169]

The divided positions taken by members of the *EC Pasta* Panel over this issue also extended to the conception of agricultural products and primary products. Although both the majority as well as the minority members agreed that pasta was a processed agricultural product, they were at variance on the legal treatment of such processed agricultural products.[170]

The preparatory history of Articles 9 and 10 of the Subsidies Code indicates that the first draft of the Code "considered a possibility that the prohibition of Article 9 would apply to non-agricultural products (instead of to products other than certain primary products) while agricultural products would be subject to what became Article 10 of the Code."[171] This was, however, dropped in all subsequent drafts. Instead, it was replaced by a dichotomy on the basis of whether the products are in their primary or non-primary form. There is no clear evidence showing as to why the negotiators chose the latter dichotomy over the former. The implications of this distinction have been interpreted differently by the members of the *EC Pasta* Panel. According to the majority ruling, the choice of the primary/non-primary distinction over the proposed agricultural/non-agricultural dichotomy had far-reaching implications on the treatment of non-primary agricultural products. The majority stated that "the drafters of the Code had clearly recognized that the terms 'primary product' and 'agricultural product' were not synonyms and that an agricultural product, if it was not a primary product as defined above, should be subjected to different obligations (Article 9) than a primary product (Article 10)."[172] In the opinion of the dissenting member, however, "the reason for replacing the term 'agricultural products' by 'certain primary products' related rather to the desire of the drafters to keep the terminology in line with the text of the General Agreement than to any other considerations. In the context of the drafting, ... there was never any mention of possible implications on the treatment of processed agricultural products."[173]

As noted already, this report was not adopted by the Committee on Subsidies and Countervailing Measures, which is the competent body for disputes brought under the Subsidies Code. Although both the majority as well as the dissenting opinions have reasons behind them, the view of the majority that the subsidy is on a non-primary product is much more convincing than the minority view that the subsidy is

[169] Ibid., para. 5.1.
[170] Ibid., para. 4.2 (majority) and para. 5.1 (dissenting).
[171] See MTN/NTM/W/168, cited in Ibid., para. 4.5.
[172] Ibid., para. 4.5.
[173] Dissenting Member's opinion in Ibid., para. 5.4.

on a primary product. Indeed, it is this latter approach, based on the explicit reservations attached by the US to its letter of acceptance of the Declaration Giving Effect to the Provisions of Article XVI:4 of the General Agreement and the consequent practice that developed thereby that contributed to the practical inapplicability of the export subsidy discipline of the GATT. As reiterated, interpreting such subsidies as subsidies on primary products not only goes contrary to the object and purpose of the multilateral trading system, it also allows practically every product containing agricultural, forest or fishery products – regardless of their degree of processing – to evade the prohibition against the use of export subsidies on non-primary products. Later developments show, however, that the Uruguay Round Agriculture Agreement somewhat endorsed the view of the minority rather than the majority.[174]

4.4.9 The "More than Equitable Share" Issue and the Standard of Displacement as Reflected in the EC Wheat Flour Case

As discussed earlier, the equitable share standard has always been the subject of endless controversies throughout the history of GATT.[175] During the negotiation of the Subsidies Code, the US came up with a simpler-looking idea as to how this elusive standard should be interpreted. It proposed that "an inequitable share of the world markets for a commodity would be found to exist whenever a country increased its share of any national market for such a commodity."[176] Although this proposal was hoped by some to have had the merit of simplifying the problems surrounding this elusive concept, it was rejected by others as too rigid a standard that "would have effectively frozen international market shares".[177] The standard that could win the final acceptance of the majority of the negotiating parties was the concept of "displacement". Yet, whether this is any different from the afore-mentioned US proposal is very much debatable.

According to the new standard, a Code signatory is taken to have got a more-than-equitable share of the world export trade in a product if the export subsidy it grants has the displacement of the exports of another signatory as its effect. "Displacement" is therefore the "newly agreed" measuring rod on the equitable share issue. In order to make its case, a complainant under this provision would need to prove three things: that an export subsidy has been granted by another party, that its exports have been displaced by the exports of that other party, and that there is a causal link between the grant of the subsidies and the displacement.

Keeping the above-mentioned US proposal in mind, a question may be raised as to whether it is possible to talk of displacement without an increase in the market share of the subsidizing party and the vice versa. In other words, is it possible that a

174 See Article 11 of the Agreement on Agriculture; for further discussion, see *infra* chapter 6.3.
175 For details, see *supra* section 4.3.
176 Rivers and Greenwald (1979) *supra* n. 1, p. 1477.
177 See Ibid.

country displaces the exports of another without increasing its own share of the market? Conversely, is it possible for a country to increase its market share without displacing the exports of another? Assuming the inevitable case of a saturated market condition, for otherwise no such problems would arise from the very outset, the answer to the above questions is clearly in the negative. Speaking as we are in terms of relative market shares, and not fixed absolute quantities, it is possible to increase the overall amount of one's sales to a market without a change in the percentage of its market share, as in the case of rising demand for the product in question. On the other hand, there is no room for the size of one's shares to rise without somebody-else's declining at the same time. The situation thus seems to lead to the conclusion that the "simplistic and rigid" formula proposed by the US to find an inequitable share whenever a country increased its share of any national market for such a commodity has, in effect, been accepted by the parties.[178] Nevertheless, dispute settlement experience on the issue seems to be completely out of tune with this understanding of the definition, to which we will return in due course.

It should also be remembered that the use of the displacement criterion is not a novel achievement of the Subsidies Code. It had already been used by preceding panels to interpret the equitable share issue, including the *French Wheat* case of 1958 as well as the two *EC Sugar* cases discussed earlier. Given the fact especially that the very words of this definition had been employed by the two GATT panels on *EC Sugar* and duly adopted by the GATT General Council acting in place of the CONTRACTING PARTIES without reference to the Subsidies Code,[179] two questions may be raised: First, is the displacement test a part of the GATT legal system, and not restricted to the Subsidies Code? Second, whatever its status, is it really an improvement over the preceding regime in terms of practical expediency? These will be discussed in turn as follows.

It is a well-recognized principle of interpretation of public international law that "any subsequent practice in the application of the treaty which establishes the agreement of the parties regarding its interpretation" must be taken into account in interpreting the terms of a treaty.[180] Although adopted panel reports do not as such constitute "subsequent practice" in the strict sense of Article 31:3(b) of the Vienna Convention on the Law of Treaties,[181] such panel reports have been, in the words of

[178] The only difference, if any, between the two versions, i.e. the US proposal and the final agreement seems to be limited to the scope of the market – the particular national markets and the world market as a whole, respectively.

[179] See *supra* section 4.3.

[180] *Vienna Convention supra* n. 101, Article 31(3)(b). The WTO Appellate Body has repeatedly stated that the general rules of interpretation in Articles 31 and 32 of the Vienna Convention have "attained the status of a rule of customary or general international law." *United States – Standards for Reformulated and Conventional Gasoline*, report of the Appellate Body (WT/DS2/AB/R), 20 May 1996, p. 17.

[181] This has, however, been a controversial issue until a recent Appellate Body decision brought it to rest. Writing in 1997, Petersmann said, "[t]he adoption by the Contracting Parties (usually acting through the GATT Council) of a dispute settlement report is regarded in GATT practice as a 'ruling' and authoritative determination of the existing GATT rights and obligations of the disputants in the instant case. Such ruling can also constitute 'subsequent practice in the application of the treaty which

the WTO Appellate Body, "an important part of the GATT *acquis*. They are often considered by subsequent panels. They create legitimate expectations among WTO Members, and, therefore, should be taken into account where they are relevant to any dispute."[182]

Seen in light of this general principle, the standing practice of the GATT as well as the final appearance of the words of the panels in the form of a provision of the

---

cont.

establishes the agreement of the parties regarding its interpretation' in terms of Article 31 of the 1969 Vienna Convention on the Law of Treaties, and have to be taken into account in the interpretation of GATT law. This is borne out by the fact that GATT dispute settlement practice often refers to interpretations adopted in earlier panel reports." E–U. Petersmann, *The GATT/WTO Dispute Settlement System: International Law, International Organizations and Dispute Settlement* (Kluwer 1997) p. 75. Similarly the panel in *Japan Alcohol* stated that "panel reports adopted by the GATT CONTRACTING PARTIES and the WTO Dispute Settlement Body constitute subsequent practice in a specific case by virtue of the decision to adopt them. Article 1(b)(iv) of GATT 1994 provides institutional recognition that adopted panel reports constitute subsequent practice. Such reports are an integral part of GATT 1994, since they constitute 'other decisions of the CONTRACTING PARTIES to GATT 1947'." *Japan – Taxes on Alcoholic Beverages*, report of the panel (WT/DS8/R, WT/DS10/R, WT/DS11/R) 11 July 1996, para. 6.10. The Appellate Body, however, disagreed and reversed this panel ruling as follows: "Adopted panel reports are an important part of the GATT *acquis*. They are often considered by subsequent panels. They create legitimate expectations among WTO Members, and, therefore, should be taken into account where they are relevant to any dispute. However, they are not binding, except with respect to resolving the particular dispute between the parties to that dispute. In short, their character and their legal status have not been changed by the coming into force of the WTO Agreement." *Japan – Taxes on Alcoholic Beverages*, report of the Appellate Body (WT/DS8/AB/R, WT/DS10/AB/R, WT/DS11/AB/R), 4 October 1996, p. 34 (footnotes omitted). Critics have observed, however, that it is "difficult to detect any practical difference resulting from the disagreement" of the Appellate Body from the Panel in this case and that, in the end, it "may have been largely semantic". D. Palmeter, and p. Mavroidis, "The WTO Legal System: Sources of Law", 92 *American Journal of International Law*, No. 3 (1998), p. 400. The arguments developed by these writers are worth quoting at length: "The Appellate Body held that a 'decision' to adopt a panel report is not a 'decision' within the meaning of Article 1(b)(iv). It did not say what adopted panel reports are if they are not 'decisions', other than to say that they are 'an important part of the GATT *acquis*.' This is somewhat confusing, both because the legal source of this *acquis* is not specified and because, in its discussion of the issue, the Appellate Body itself refers to 'a decision' and 'decisions' to adopt panel reports. The Appellate Body apparently was concerned that the panel's conclusion could be interpreted as holding adopted reports 'constitute a definitive interpretation of the relevant provisions of GATT 1947.' A 'definitive interpretation' would presumably be controlling and thus, on this theory, could amount to importation of rigid *stare decisis* into the WTO, if not amendment *sub rosa* of its very texts. If this was the concern, it seems misplaced. The panel treated adopted reports as 'subsidiary' sources of WTO law, comparable in status to judicial decisions in the World Court. It did not say that adopted reports were controlling. Rather, it said that they 'have to be taken into account by subsequent panels dealing with the same or similar issue'. It specified, however, that 'it does not necessarily have to follow their reasoning or results.' . . . In its description of adopted reports, the Appellate Body came very close to saying the same thing. . . . In the end the result seems to be that adopted reports are not binding precedent and do not control subsequent panels; neither may they 'add to or diminish the rights and obligations provided in the covered agreements.' Nevertheless, panels 'should' take them into account. Adopted reports have strong persuasive power and may be viewed as a form of non-binding precedent." Ibid. pp. 400–401 (footnotes omitted).

[182] *Japan Alcohol*, report of the Appellate Body, *supra* n. 181, page 34.

Subsidies Code, therefore, it seems reasonable to argue that the displacement standard is not as such new to the GATT and that its application might not be restricted to the signatories of the Subsidies Code alone.[183] The following discussion will, however, be limited to the practical aspect of this definition irrespective of its status in the GATT legal system.

The only important case on the equitable share issue under the Subsidies Code is the 1981 *EC Wheat Flour* dispute brought by the US. In that case, the US complained that EC wheat flour exports had been subsidized since 1962 to as much as 75 per cent of the US representative f.o.b. price;[184] and that, according to its calculations, EC wheat flour exports had increased from a mere 29 per cent of world commercial exports in 1959–1962 to 75 per cent in 1978–1981, while the US share had dropped from 25 per cent to 9 per cent over the same period.[185] The US also pointed out that, over the same period, Australia's average share dropped from 20 per cent to 2 per cent and Canada's average share from 25 per cent to 11 per cent. In the US view, it was "self-evident that, in a market divided among four suppliers, the dramatic expansion of one supplier's share, particularly when the market was not expanding, must displace the exports of other suppliers."[186] According to the US, the enormous increase in EC wheat flour exports, accompanied by the simultaneous decline in the market share of all other major suppliers indicated, by itself, the acquisition of "more than an equitable share" of world export trade.[187] As summarized by Hudec, it was the belief of the US representative that, "whatever "equitable share" meant, it had to cover this large a reversal of market position by means of trade dependent entirely on export subsidies."[188]

The EC defended, *inter alia,* that US allegations in relation to changes in world market shares were based on an erroneous appreciation of the factors responsible for them. According to the EC, rather than the export subsidies provided by the Community, the possible factors for the apparent decline of US shares include the undue exclusion of US concessional sales from the data on US exports; US market loss in some countries for its own political reasons; the introduction of local flour mills in a number of developing countries; and "chronic saturation" of US milling facilities.[189] The EC emphasized mainly on the exclusion of concessional shipments

---

[183] See also Phegan, *supra* n. 65, p. 262. This same logic applies to the case of the "representative period" concept discussed *infra* section 4.4.10.

[184] *EC Wheat Flour, supra* n. 58, para. 2.22.

[185] Ibid., para. 2.10.

[186] Ibid.

[187] Ibid.

[188] Hudec (1993) *supra* n. 41, p. 148.

[189] *EC Wheat Flour, supra* n. 58, para. 2.21. The EEC summarized the possible factors responsible for the decline in the market share of the US as follows: "first, the expansion of United States flour exports under PL 480 at the expense of its so-called commercial exports; secondly, the loss, sometimes a long time ago, of certain United States export markets for political reasons (for example: Sri Lanka, Egypt during a certain period, South Vietnam, Syria, Libya); thirdly, the introduction in certain developing countries of local crushing capacity (cases of Jamaica and Sri Lanka), resulting in the replacement of purchases of flour by those of wheat – such introduction being most often financed by United States

of the US in the calculation of their respective market shares. The issue pertains to diverging definitions of food aid in the Community and the US. As observed by the *EC Wheat Flour* panel, in the EC, food aid consists only of those special transactions which involve "outright gifts", while, in the US, food aid also covers transactions involving sales on concessional terms short of outright gifts.[190] The EC argued, and the Panel accepted, that any meaningful comparison of the change in market share should cover US concessional exports, for it is "impossible ... to compare figures based on these different criteria. The only objective comparison could be aggregate figures, "commercial" plus "concessional'."[191] For the EC representative, this was not just "a question of interpretation of the terms and content of the obligations to be observed by any contracting party. It was also a question of equity; indeed, by disregarding non-commercial sales, the United States subtracted 10.8 per cent from total Community exports, whereas from its own exports it could subtract 70 per cent."[192]

The decision of the Panel in this case was, however, an affirmation of the fact that the interpretation of the "equitable share" standard by the Subsidies Code in terms of displacement of exports made it by no means easier to implement in practice. The panel first found that "the EEC share of world exports of wheat flour has increased considerably over the period under consideration when application of EEC export subsidies was the general practice, while the share of the US and other suppliers has decreased."[193] This was then followed by the finding that "despite the considerable increase in EEC exports, market displacement in the sense of Article l0:2(a) was not evident in the seventeen markets examined by the Panel."[194] The panel, however, observed in the subsequent paragraph that on the basis of its examination of individual markets, "it could not rule out the possibility that the application of EEC export subsidies had resulted in reduced sales opportunities for the United States."[195] On the central issue, it simply reported that it was "unable to conclude as to whether

---

cont.

capital and associated with clauses for the purchase of United States wheat; and lastly, the particular structure of United States wheat flour exports, which was characterized by concentration (about 70 per cent) on three markets (Saudi Arabia, Sri Lanka, Egypt), where there were either PL 480 sales or the construction of flour mills, the remaining exports being marked by very great irregularity and influenced by PL 480 operations (which was reflected in a rapid expansion on certain particular markets such as Zaire, Sudan, or Somalia and a sporadic presence on other markets such as Nigeria and Indonesia)." Ibid., para. 2.19. For a discussion of the *EC Wheat Flour* case in relation to the "special factors" under Article XVI:3 of the General Agreement, see *supra* section 4.3.

190 Ibid., para. 3.20.

191 Ibid., para. 2.14. The Panel noted in this connection that "trade in wheat flour takes place under commercial and special (or concessional) terms. For purposes of its examination of market shares the Panel considered that it was difficult to exclude special transactions entirely from an analysis of the market, and that in this case, it was not necessary, or appropriate, to do so in reaching a determination as to equitable share." Ibid., para. 4.7.

192 Ibid., para. 2.16.

193 Ibid., para. 5.2.

194 Ibid., paras. 4.28 and 5.4.

195 Ibid., paras. 4.29.

the increased share has resulted in the EEC "having more than an equitable share" in terms of Article 10."[196] The panel attributed its inability here to what it called "the highly artificial levels and conditions of trade in wheat flour, the complexity of developments in the markets, including the interplay of a number of special factors, the relative importance of which it was impossible to assess, and, most importantly, the difficulties inherent in the concept of 'more than equitable share'."[197]

Hudec has observed in this connection that "[m]ore than an observer was heard to say 'If this case does not constitute taking more than an equitable share, then a violation was impossible to prove.' "[198] One may then raise the question of whether the problem actually lies with "difficulties inherent" in the standard of "equitable share" itself as the Panel in this last case claims,[199] or with its practical application by the panels as Hudec seems to imply. Although opinion is divided on this point, it must be pointed out that both factors are at work here – there are indeed difficulties inherent in the standard, but the reluctance of panels to give effect to the apparent legislative intent behind the very provision has aggravated the problem.[200]

4.4.10 The Previous Representative Period

The previous representative period is the other important concept under GATT Article XVI:3 interpreted by Article 10 of the Subsidies Code. According to this provision, the previous representative period "shall normally be the three most recent calendar years in which normal market conditions existed'. Once again the very words used here to define this concept had already been used by the two *EC Sugar* cases, and hence the argument regarding novelty raised above in connection with the equitable share concept might also be raised in this case.

The issue of "previous representative period" appeared in its most controversial form in *EC Wheat Flour*. In that case, the US proposed to use the three years before the introduction of the CAP, viz. 1959/1960 to 1961/1962, as the previous representative period in the sense of the Subsidies Code. The US representative referred to Article 10:2(c) and argued that the three most recent calendar years could not be used in that case because "given the distortion of trade patterns resulting from the heavy use of export subsidies by the EEC, it did not constitute a period during which 'normal market conditions existed'."[201] In support of this view, he invoked the

[196] Ibid., para. 5.3.

[197] Ibid., para. 5.3.

[198] Hudec (1993) *supra* n. 41, p. 150.

[199] This claim of the panel's received further support from a subsequent study made in 1985 by a group of seven eminent experts in the field who submitted a report called the Leutwiler Report. According to this report, the Subsidies Code provision restricting export subsidies for primary products on the condition that they do not lead to acquisition of more than an equitable share of world export trade "endorses market sharing, a result contrary to the basic trade liberalization tenets of the GATT". GATT, *Trade Policies for a Better Future: The Leutwiler Report* (Geneva 1987).

[200] As Davey stated, "real, effective control would be possible only if Article XVI and the Subsidies Code are interpreted more in line with the drafter's apparent intent". Davey, in Jackson *et al* (1995) *supra* n. 102, p. 1166.

statement made by the CONTRACTING PARTIES during the 1955 Review Session that in determining what is an equitable share of world trade, they should not lose sight of the fact that export subsidies in existence during the selected representative period may have influenced the share of the trade obtained by the various exporting countries.[202] The representative also quoted a 1960 Panel Report and argued that "an analysis of the effect of a subsidy should include statistics '. . . for a previous representative year, which where possible and meaningful, should be the latest period preceding the introduction of the subsidy or preceding the last major change in the subsidy.' "[203] In his view, all these considerations necessitated examination of the three-year period preceding the introduction of the EC system of subsidies, which meant the period between 1959/1960 to 1961/1962.[204] Furthermore, the US also requested the panel to compare this period with the most recent three year period and to examine the entire period from 1959/60 to 1980/81 so as to assess the trends in the market.[205]

The EC counter-argued that the above-summarized US approach was "contrary to the intention of the drafters of the Code and the logic of the regulatory system."[206] The EC also raised a problem of practicability in this US view. According to the EC, the US argument would lead to the impracticable option of "referring to years several decades ago, in other words to a period for which it was very difficult to determine exactly whether or not subsidies of any kind had existed. If one followed the United States interpretation to its logical conclusion, one would have to refer to an initial period in which there was no export subsidization by any of the contracting parties, and not merely to a period in which the incriminated subsidy did not exist."[207] Apparently on the basis of the time of origin of US subsidy law, Professor Hudec wrote that this Community argument in effect meant that the "only data reflecting a genuinely free market [condition] . . . would be trade data for 1893."[208]

The panel's final determination on this point was a combination of both. It stated that, "while the three most recent year period was in many ways instructive as regards important aspects of trade in wheat flour, it did not in itself provide a fully satisfactory basis for determining "equitable share". Market shares in this period, as

---

201 *EC Wheat Flour, supra* n. 58, para. 2.8.

202 GATT, *BISD*, 3S/226.

203 GATT, *Second Report of the Group of Experts on Anti-Dumping and Countervailing Duties* (L/1141 *BISD* 9S/194), adopted on 27 May 1960.

204 *EC Wheat Flour, supra* n. 58, para. 2.9.

205 Ibid., para. 2.9. In support of this argument, the US representative invoked the 1958 *French Wheat* case and the two parallel *EC Sugar* cases as valuable "precedent".

206 *EC Wheat Flour, supra* n. 58, para. 2.17. The EC pointed out that "during the Tokyo Round, one delegation (Australia) had deliberately proposed that the grant of subsidies made market functioning abnormal, so that in determining normal market shares account should not be taken of a period in which subsidies had been granted (MTN/NTM/W/217/Rev.1). A number of delegations, including the United States, had opposed that proposal, which had consequently not been included in the final text." Ibid.

207 Ibid., para. 2.18.

208 Hudec (1993) *supra* n. 41, p. 148.

indeed for virtually any period in at least the last twenty years, had been affected by the application of export subsidies and other developments in the market, the full import of which could be properly taken into account only by examining other periods as well."[209] And this, it must be said, is in line with the "case law" developed on the interpretation of Article XVI:3 of the General Agreement.[210] Once again, therefore, the concept of "previous representative period" has been interpreted with such flexibility as may best serve its purpose – to make an objective view of the normal market trends and the overall impact of a subsidy scheme thereon possible.

4.4.11 The Concept of Price Undercutting in Particular Markets

The last point under Article 10 of the Subsidies Code is what is known in the literature as "price undercutting" – the obligation undertaken by signatories not to grant subsidies on exports of certain primary products to particular markets in a manner which results in prices materially below those of other suppliers to the same market.[211] Although signatories are still allowed to grant subsidies, they are precluded from granting them in such a way as to enable the exporter to quote prices materially below those quoted by competitors from other sources. Looking merely at the word "materially" in this provision, one can readily foresee how controversial this would turn out to be in actual practice: how big should the difference be to say that the price quoted by one is materially below those quoted by other suppliers?

What is more, the history of GATT dispute settlement seems to suggest once again that in essence the price undercutting concept is also not a new development brought by the Subsidies Code. It was already in the 1958 *French Wheat* case that a finding of such a wide margin in market prices was taken to support a conclusion that the increase in exports could be attributed to the operation of subsidies. The observation of the panel in that case may aid our understanding of the concept of price undercutting the way it appears in the Subsidies Code: "French exporters have been able to quote prices for wheat flour lower than those quoted by other exporters, whether at f.o.b. or c.i.f. values. Moreover, judging from export unit values, the price charged by French exporters for wheat flour has in recent years barely exceeded that charged for wheat. . . . [while] the export price for flour charged by Australia, Canada and the United States does exceed the export price of wheat by 30 to 50 per cent".[212]

It is noteworthy that both before as well as after the Code, export subsidies on primary products resulting in price undercutting are generally allowed. In both cases, the extent of price undercutting might serve evidentiary purposes to answer the question of whether there is a causal relationship between a certain export subsidy practice and a corresponding rise in the market share of the subsidizing party. The only thing added by the Subsidies Code is therefore that signatories cannot use

---

209 *EC Wheat Flour, supra* n. 58, para. 4.11.

210 See *EC Sugar – Complaint by Australia, supra* n. 60, para. 4.10; and *EC Sugar – Complaint by Brazil, supra* n. 60, para. 4.9.

211 Article 10:3 of the Subsidies Code.

212 *French Wheat supra* n. 55, p. 53, para. 18.

export subsidies on a primary product which result in "material" price undercutting in particular markets. Needless to say, the question of when a price undercutting situation becomes "material" is something that can only be answered on a case-by-case basis.

4.5 CONCLUDING REMARKS

By way of a final note on the Subsidies Code of 1979, the following two observations may be made. Firstly, the discipline of export subsidies in general was somewhat strengthened in two senses – the prohibition of export subsidies on non-primary products was more or less flat and without conditions, and the excepted category was narrowed to nothing more than agricultural products. As the unadopted 1982 *EC Pasta* panel rightly observed, Article 9 of the Subsidies Code, compared with Article XVI:4 of the General Agreement, "imposes an increased discipline in that the scope of the prohibition has been increased by inclusion of minerals into the category of products other than certain primary products."[213] However, the changes introduced concerning export subsidies on agricultural products were nothing more than the use of new words retelling old stories. It is thus possible to conclude that the Subsidies Code has generally resulted in a tighter discipline for export subsidies on non-primary products, while it was virtually without effect on the export subsidy regime of agricultural products.

Secondly, as a matter of principle the Code was a side agreement and not an amendment to the GATT. As such, the little practical improvement it might have introduced in this area was limited only to those countries that specifically accepted, or acceded to, it.[214] In other words, its influence, if any, could not be extended to all contracting parties to the GATT. Rather, it created, or, still better, perpetuated the situation where countries would apply different rules to identical issues as between different Contracting Parties to the GATT depending on whether the other parties had specifically accepted the Code. Therefore, in this respect at least, it was a cause of further complication in the application of the law of subsidies in that it introduced an additional group of countries that were contracting parties to the GATT but that could not benefit from, or be constrained by, the new Code. Precisely because the Code was in the nature of a side agreement to the General Agreement, and not an amendment to it, the current multilateral trading system under the WTO has excluded the Subsidies Code (and other Codes of the Tokyo Round for that matter) from its coverage. The indirect contribution of the Tokyo Round Codes as an important step in the evolution of the multilateral trading system cannot, however, be doubted. As we shall see in the subsequent chapters, the export subsidy regime of the WTO was constructed on the foundations laid down by the Subsidies Code. As a

---

213 *EC Pasta, supra* n. 44, para. 2.21.

214 As of 1994, the following were the signatories to the Subsidies Code: Argentina, Australia, Austria, Brazil, Canada, Chile, Colombia, Egypt, EC, Finland, Hong Kong, India, Indonesia, Israel, Japan, Korea, New Zealand, Norway, Pakistan, Philippines, Sweden, Switzerland, Turkey, United States, and Uruguay.

matter of fact, the Punta del Este Declaration had already stated that negotiations on subsidies and countervailing measures "shall be based on a review of Articles VI and XVI and *the MTN Agreement on subsidies and countervailing measures* with the objective of improving GATT disciplines relating to all subsidies and countervailing measures that affect international trade."[215]

---

[215] GATT, *Ministerial Declaration on the Uruguay Round* (MIN.DEC) adopted in Punta del Este, Uruguay, on 20 September 1986, often referred to as the *Punta del Este Declaration,* reproduced in, GATT *Focus Newsletter*, No. 41 (October 1986) p. 5 (italics added).

Ministerial Declaration. Just as its predecessor, the Punta del Este Declaration stated, *inter alia,* that "there is an urgent need to bring more discipline and predictability to world agricultural trade".[12] One means of achieving this was identified to be "improving the competitive environment by increasing discipline on the use of all direct and indirect subsidies and other measures affecting directly or indirectly agricultural trade, including the phased reduction of their negative effects and dealing with their causes."[13]

Bringing discipline to this rather undisciplined sector of international trade was therefore one of the most daunting challenges of the Uruguay Round – a challenge it overcame more or less successfully by taking the first important steps towards the reintegration of agriculture into the GATT system. If the Tokyo Round was unique for its unprecedented breakthrough into the realm of nontariff barriers to trade, the Uruguay Round is also unique for, *inter alia*, its equally unprecedented breakthrough into the problems of agricultural trade. The nature and extent of this development in the law of agricultural trade as regards the practice of export subsidies will be discussed at length in this part of the book.

In order to fully appreciate the substance of this newly-developed regime of agricultural export subsidies and to put it in its appropriate context, an assessment of the overall discipline of export subsidies as developed by the WTO Agreement, which is embodied in the Agreement on Subsidies and Countervailing Measures (hereafter the Subsidies Agreement or simply the SCM Agreement) appears to be a necessary prerequisite. It is interesting to note that the SCM Agreement itself has brought about substantial changes to the law of subsidies in general so much so that, in the

---

[12] GATT, *Ministerial Declaration on the Uruguay Round* (MIN.DEC) adopted in Punta del Este, Uruguay, on 20 September 1986, often referred to as the *Punta del Este Declaration,* reproduced in, GATT *Focus Newsletter*, No. 41, (October 1986) p. 4. The full text of the Declaration on agriculture reads as follows:

"Contracting Parties agree that there is an urgent need to bring more discipline and predictability to world agricultural trade by correcting and preventing restrictions and distortions including those related to structural surpluses so as to reduce the uncertainty, imbalances and instability in world agricultural markets. Negotiations shall aim to achieve greater liberalization of trade in agriculture and bring all measures affecting import access and export competition under strengthened and more operationally effective GATT rules and disciplines, taking into account the general principles governing the negotiations, by:

(i) improving market access through , *inter alia*, the reduction of import barriers;

(ii) improving the competitive environment by increasing discipline on the use of all direct and indirect subsidies and other measures affecting directly or indirectly agricultural trade, including the phased reduction of their negative effects and dealing with their causes;

(iii) minimizing the adverse effects that sanitary and phytosanitary regulations and barriers can have on trade in agriculture, taking into account the relevant international agreements.

In order to achieve the above objectives, the negotiating group having primary responsibility for all aspects of agriculture will use the Recommendations adopted by the Contracting Parties at their Fortieth Session, which were developed in accordance with the GATT 1982 Ministerial Program and take account of the approaches suggested in the work of the Committee on Trade in Agriculture without prejudice to other alternatives that might achieve the objectives of the negotiations." Ibid., p. 4.

[13] *Id.*, p. 4.

The reaction of the contracting parties was not, however, limited to the over-use of the notoriously weak GATT dispute settlement mechanism of the day. They also used different fora to express their concerted reaction. It was indeed just after the entry into force of the Tokyo Round agreements that they began to express the urgency of a new round of multilateral trade negotiations in which agriculture would assume centre stage.[7] The 1982 GATT Ministerial Conference occupied a particularly important place in the effort to find a sustainable solution to this contentious problem. The Ministerial Declaration issued at the end of the 1982 Conference recognized not only that there was "widespread dissatisfaction with the application of GATT rules and the degree of liberalization in relation to agricultural trade",[8] but also that there was "an urgent need to find lasting solutions" to those problems.[9] Contracting parties used the occasion to express their resolve to "bring agriculture more fully into the multilateral trading system by improving the effectiveness of GATT rules, provisions and disciplines."[10] Furthermore, in an attempt to lay the institutional foundation for the effort to find lasting solutions, the Ministerial Declaration established the Committee on Trade in Agriculture for the purpose of examining the problems of agricultural trade and of "making recommendations with a view to achieving greater liberalization in the trade of agricultural products."[11] While the Declaration set the process for a new round of trade negotiations in motion, the recommendations subsequently made by the Committee on Trade in Agriculture served as important guidelines for the conduct of agricultural negotiations during the entire Uruguay Round.

Both the enormous tension of the early 1980s between countries as well as the growing consensus about the urgency of the need for a lasting reform found their proper expression in the 1986 Ministerial Declaration that launched the Uruguay Round at Punta del Este, Uruguay. The Punta del Este Declaration closely echoed the strong language of the 1982 Ministerial Declaration to express its objectives in the area; several of its statements were in fact taken directly from the 1982

---

7 In fact, as Croome recounted the story, the first move towards a new initiative in the GATT came in June 1981 when trade policy officials from the major trading powers met in the Consultative Group of Eighteen and agreed to hold a ministerial conference that would consider the overall condition of the trading system. See Ibid. p. 12. The first "formal reference in a GATT body to the idea of a new round" was however made only in 1984. See Ibid. p. 21; see also J. H. Jackson, *The World Trading System: Law and Policy in International Economic Relations* (The MIT Press, 2nd ed. 1997) chapter 12, pp. 305 ff.; and T. Josling, S. Tangermann, and T. Warley, *Agriculture in the GATT* (MacMillan, London 1996), p. 111.

8 GATT, *Thirty-Eighth Session at Ministerial Level: Ministerial Declaration* (L/5424, *BISD* 29S/9-22) adopted on 29 November 1982, p. 10.

9 Ibid., p. 16. In a speech he delivered to the 1986 Ministerial Conference at Punta del Este, the then Director General of GATT, Arthur Dunkel, reminded his audience that agriculture was one of the areas which had been subject to "intense and ... difficult discussions" during the Ministerial Conference preceding the adoption of the 1982 Ministerial Declaration. See *Statement by Mr. A. Dunkel, Director-General, to the Punta del Este Ministerial Conference* (MIN(86)/5), 15 September 1986.

10 The 1982 Ministerial Declaration *supra* n. 8, p. 11.

11 Ibid., p. 17.

Ministerial Declaration. Just as its predecessor, the Punta del Este Declaration stated, *inter alia,* that "there is an urgent need to bring more discipline and predictability to world agricultural trade".[12] One means of achieving this was identified to be "improving the competitive environment by increasing discipline on the use of all direct and indirect subsidies and other measures affecting directly or indirectly agricultural trade, including the phased reduction of their negative effects and dealing with their causes."[13]

Bringing discipline to this rather undisciplined sector of international trade was therefore one of the most daunting challenges of the Uruguay Round – a challenge it overcame more or less successfully by taking the first important steps towards the reintegration of agriculture into the GATT system. If the Tokyo Round was unique for its unprecedented breakthrough into the realm of nontariff barriers to trade, the Uruguay Round is also unique for, *inter alia*, its equally unprecedented breakthrough into the problems of agricultural trade. The nature and extent of this development in the law of agricultural trade as regards the practice of export subsidies will be discussed at length in this part of the book.

In order to fully appreciate the substance of this newly-developed regime of agricultural export subsidies and to put it in its appropriate context, an assessment of the overall discipline of export subsidies as developed by the WTO Agreement, which is embodied in the Agreement on Subsidies and Countervailing Measures (hereafter the Subsidies Agreement or simply the SCM Agreement) appears to be a necessary prerequisite. It is interesting to note that the SCM Agreement itself has brought about substantial changes to the law of subsidies in general so much so that, in the

[12] GATT, *Ministerial Declaration on the Uruguay Round* (MIN.DEC) adopted in Punta del Este, Uruguay, on 20 September 1986, often referred to as the *Punta del Este Declaration,* reproduced in, GATT *Focus Newsletter*, No. 41, (October 1986) p. 4. The full text of the Declaration on agriculture reads as follows:

"Contracting Parties agree that there is an urgent need to bring more discipline and predictability to world agricultural trade by correcting and preventing restrictions and distortions including those related to structural surpluses so as to reduce the uncertainty, imbalances and instability in world agricultural markets. Negotiations shall aim to achieve greater liberalization of trade in agriculture and bring all measures affecting import access and export competition under strengthened and more operationally effective GATT rules and disciplines, taking into account the general principles governing the negotiations, by:

(i) improving market access through , *inter alia*, the reduction of import barriers;

(ii) improving the competitive environment by increasing discipline on the use of all direct and indirect subsidies and other measures affecting directly or indirectly agricultural trade, including the phased reduction of their negative effects and dealing with their causes;

(iii) minimizing the adverse effects that sanitary and phytosanitary regulations and barriers can have on trade in agriculture, taking into account the relevant international agreements.

In order to achieve the above objectives, the negotiating group having primary responsibility for all aspects of agriculture will use the Recommendations adopted by the Contracting Parties at their Fortieth Session, which were developed in accordance with the GATT 1982 Ministerial Program and take account of the approaches suggested in the work of the Committee on Trade in Agriculture without prejudice to other alternatives that might achieve the objectives of the negotiations." Ibid., p. 4.

[13] *Id.*, p. 4.

words of one writer, it has "entirely eclipsed the GATT subsidy restrictions which are found in Article XVI".[14] Needless to say, this new regime concerning the general practice of subsidies affects the particular case of agricultural subsidies in different ways, of which three may be mentioned here.

Firstly, as envisaged by Article 21 of the Agreement on Agriculture, the provisions of all the Multilateral Trade Agreements in Annex 1A to the WTO Agreement, of which the SCM Agreement is an important element, apply to agricultural matters, subject to the provisions of the Agriculture Agreement.[15] It is only when there is an inconsistency between the provisions of those Agreements and the Agreement on Agriculture, and when a choice needs to be made between them, that the latter is given priority – and even then only to the extent of the inconsistency. Indeed, as the *Bananas* panel observed, "it is not the case that Article 21.1 of the Agreement on Agriculture means that no GATT/WTO rules apply to trade in agricultural products unless they are explicitly incorporated into the Agreement on Agriculture."[16] This, in the present context, means that loopholes within the subsidies provisions of the Agriculture Agreement are filled primarily by resorting to relevant provisions of the SCM Agreement. Any issue involving agricultural subsidies that is not particularly regulated by the Agriculture Agreement falls within the ambit of GATT 1994 and the SCM Agreement.[17] That is why the WTO Appellate Body stated that "with respect to subsidies on agricultural products, ... [t]he Agreement on Agriculture and the SCM Agreement reflect the latest statement of WTO Members as to their rights and obligations concerning agricultural subsidies."[18] Consequently, a study on the law of export subsidies in agricultural products under the multilateral trading system which does not cover at least the major features of the discipline governing the practice of export subsidies in general can only be incomplete.

Secondly, the SCM Agreement being the generic agreement regarding subsidies, it always forms "part of the general context"[19] for the interpretation of subsidy-related

---

[14] E. McGovern, *International Trade Regulation* (Loose-leaf 1995) pp. 11.31–1.

[15] Article 21:1 of the Agreement on Agriculture.

[16] *European Communities – Regime for the Importation, Sale and Distribution of Bananas,* report of the panel (WT/DS27/R/USA...) 22 May 1997 paras. 7.122–7.123.

[17] As we shall see, of course, several provisions from both Agreements specifically limit agricultural export subsidy matters solely to the Agreement on Agriculture; however, the Agriculture Agreement is far from self-sufficient for the regulation of these issues.

[18] *Brazil – Measures Affecting Desiccated Coconut* report of the Appellate Body (WT/DS22/AB/R), 21 February 1997, pp. 13-14.

[19] *Canada – Measures Affecting the Importation of Milk and the Exportation of Dairy Products*, report of the panel (WT/DS103/R, WT/DS113/R) 17 May 1999, para. 7.126. The context for the interpretation of any provision of a WTO Agreement in fact includes the entire WTO Agreement in its totality. See *United States – Anti-Dumping Duty on Dynamic Random Access Semiconductors (DRAMs) of One Megabit or Above from Korea*, report of the panel (WT/DS99/R, 19 March 1999), para. 6.21. And then, "the degree to which a provision is *relevant* context and the weight to be given to contextual element will differ from case to case, and may depend, *inter alia*, on the relationship between the provision being interpreted and the provision being relied upon as context." *United States – Tax Treatment for "Foreign Sales Corporations"* report of the panel (WT/DS108/R) 8 October 1999, para. 7.90.

issues in any of the instruments falling under the umbrella of the WTO Agreement. To take an obvious example, although the term "subsidies" is used in several agreements within the WTO system, a definition of this basic concept is found only in the SCM Agreement, and any specialized agreement under the WTO system addressing the problem of subsidies in specific areas will of necessity have to resort to the SCM Agreement for definition.[20] The provisions of the SCM Agreement therefore apply to agricultural matters not only to fill any loopholes that may, and do, exist within the subsidies provisions of the Agreement on Agriculture, but also as a principal contextual guide for the interpretation of the provisions of the Agriculture Agreement itself.

Finally, given the integrated nature of the dispute settlement system of the WTO, which applies to all "covered agreements" by virtue of Article 1.1 of the Dispute Settlement Understanding (DSU)[21] as well as its incorporation through an explicit reference under Article 19 of the Agreement on Agriculture,[22] all disputes under the provisions of the latter are governed by those of the former. However, the DSU also allows room for what are called "special or additional rules and procedures" on dispute settlement which are found in the covered agreements. These additional provisions are specifically tailored to address "the particularities of dispute settlement relating to obligations arising under a specific covered agreement."[23] An exhaustive list of these provisions has been included in Appendix 2 to the DSU. What is more, as an expression of the *lex specialis* principle of interpretation, the DSU provides that "[t]o the extent that there is a difference between the rules and procedures of this Understanding and the special or additional rules and procedures set forth in Appendix 2, the special or additional rules and procedures in Appendix 2 shall prevail."[24]

---

20 See, e.g., *Canada Dairy*, report of the panel, *supra* n. 19, para. 7.126 (italics added).

21 Article 1:1 of the DSU provides in relevant part as follows: "The rules and procedures of this Understanding shall apply to disputes brought pursuant to the consultation and dispute settlement provisions of the agreements listed in Appendix 1 to this Understanding (referred to in this Understanding as the 'covered agreements')." The Agreement on Agriculture is one of the Multilateral Agreements on Trade in Goods in Annex 1A to the Marrakesh Agreement Establishing the WTO, which is covered by the reference here.

22 Article 19 of the Agreement on Agriculture provides as follows: "The provisions of Articles XXII and XXIII of GATT 1994, as elaborated and applied by the Dispute Settlement Understanding, shall apply to consultations and the settlement of disputes under this Agreement."

23 *Guatemala – Anti-Dumping Investigation Regarding Portland Cement From Mexico,* report of the Appellate Body (WT/DS60/AB/R) 2 November 1998, para. 66.

24 Article 1.2 of the DSU. The following statement by the Appellate Body in *Guatemala Cement* summarizes the relationship between the special or additional rules and procedures on the one hand and the general rules and procedures of the DSU on the other: "if there is no 'difference', then the rules and procedures of the DSU apply together with the special or additional provisions of the covered agreement. . . . [I]t is only where the provisions of the DSU and the special or additional rules and procedures of a covered agreement cannot be read as complementing each other that the special or additional provisions are to prevail. A special or additional provision should only be found to prevail over a provision of the DSU in a situation where adherence to the one provision will lead to a violation of the other provision, that is, in the case of a conflict between them. An interpreter must, therefore, identify an inconsistency or a difference between a provision of the DSU and a special or additional provision of a covered agreement before concluding that the latter prevails and that the provision of the DSU does not apply." Ibid., para. 65.

Appendix 2 does not have provisions from the Agreement on Agriculture. But it contains some provisions from the SCM Agreement which are relevant to agricultural export subsidy issues.[25] Consequently, the moment one starts dealing with agricultural export subsidies, the "special or additional rules and procedures on dispute settlement" contained in the export subsidies part of the SCM Agreement might arguably be called in to play.[26] Given the accelerated procedures prescribed therein, which work to the benefit more of the complainant than the defendant in a case,[27] a complainant against the agricultural export subsidies of another Member may prefer to invoke these "special or additional rules and procedures on dispute settlement" of Article 4 of the SCM Agreement. Hence, a brief look at the basic features of this special aspect of dispute settlement under the SCM Agreement is once again crucial for a proper understanding of the regime of agricultural export subsidies under the existing multilateral trading system.

The following section will thus be devoted to a brief analysis of the salient features of the Uruguay Round Agreement on Subsidies and Countervailing Measures in light of the specific problems discussed so far in connection with the preceding regimes on agricultural export subsidies. As the primary purpose of this section is to put agricultural export subsidies in perspective, every attempt will be made to link the discussion on the SCM Agreement with corresponding provisions of the Agreement on Agriculture.

5.2 The Agreement on Subsidies and Countervailing Measures

5.2.1 Definition of Subsidies

The Subsidies Agreement, for the first time in the history of the multilateral trading system, resolved the perennial quest for a definition of the concept of subsidies. According to Article 1:1 of this Agreement, a subsidy is deemed to exist if:

> "(a)(1) there is a financial contribution by a government or any public body within the territory of a Member (referred to in this Agreement as "government"), i.e. where:
>
> (i) a government practice involves a direct transfer of funds (e.g. grants, loans, and equity infusion), potential direct transfers of funds or liabilities (e.g. loan guarantees);

---

[25] Particularly relevant on export subsidies is Article 4 of the SCM Agreement; for a discussion of its main features, see *infra* section 5.5.

[26] See for instance Article 13(c)(ii) of the Agreement on Agriculture on the conditional exemption of agricultural export subsidies from actions under Articles 3, 5 and 6 of the SCM Agreement. As the *Canada Dairy,* Panel rightly observed, the use of export subsidies "beyond ... scheduled limits is, in principle, also actionable under the prohibition in Article 3 of the SCM Agreement. However, by virtue of Article 13 (c) (i) of the Agreement on Agriculture, export subsidies that conform fully to Part V of the Agreement on Agriculture are exempt from actions based on Article 3 of the SCM Agreement for the duration of the 'implementation period'" *Canada Dairy,* report of the panel, *supra* n. 19, para. 7.21.

[27] This does not of course mean that the complainant is the sole beneficiary in such cases of accelerated procedure. As the *Canada Dairy* panel rightly observed, the "special or additional rules and procedures on dispute settlement" under Article 4 of the SCM Agreement "may benefit either party to a dispute". *Canada Dairy*, report of the panel, *supra* n. 19, para. 7.139; see also *infra* section 5.5.

(ii) government revenue that is otherwise due is foregone or not collected (e.g. fiscal incentives such as tax credits);

(iii) a government provides goods or services other than general infrastructure, or purchases goods;

(iv) a government makes payments to a funding mechanism, or entrusts or directs a private body to carry out one or more of the type of functions illustrated in (i) to (iii) above which would normally be vested in the government and the practice, in no real sense, differs from practices normally followed by governments;

or

(a)(2) there is any form of income or price support in the sense of Article XVI of GATT 1994;

and

(b) a benefit is thereby conferred."[28]

It should be noted at the outset that this is a rather complex definition full of "intriguing elements".[29] At the same time, and despite the complexity, the very fact that we now have a definition for such a notoriously elusive concept is an important development in itself. Indeed, the inclusion of this definition is "generally considered to represent one of the most important achievements of the Uruguay Round in the area of subsidy disciplines."[30] A clearer understanding of this complex definition is crucial for a proper appreciation of the developments brought about by the Uruguay Round in the field of subsidies, whether agricultural or otherwise. The structure of paragraph 1 of Article 1 is a good starting point for the purpose.[31]

Paragraph 1 has two subparagraphs, (a) and (b), which are connected by the conjunctive "and" – thus making them mandatory elements of the concept of subsidies as defined therein. Of these two elements, while sub-paragraph (a) refers to the nature of the acts concerned, sub-paragraph (b) addresses the required effect that should follow from those acts. Not only do these two constitute the mandatory elements for the existence of a subsidy, they should also be connected by some causal relationship – the "financial contribution" or other income or price support must result in the conferment of a "benefit" upon the recipient. The essence of these constituent elements will be discussed further in turn.

5.2.1.1 Article 1.1(a): "Financial Contribution" or "Any form of Income or Price Support"

The first element of the definition, as presented under sub-paragraph (a), may also be approached via its structure. Sub-paragraph (a) is sub-divided into two items – items (a)(1) and (a)(2) – which are connected by the disjunctive "or". They are either "a financial contribution by government or any public body" or "any form of income or price support in the sense of Article XVI of the GATT 1994". The two are therefore alternative conditions for the existence of what may be termed the "act" element of a subsidy. The first of the two mandatory elements of a subsidy may be

---

28 Article 1.1 of the SCM Agreement (footnote omitted).

29 For interesting reflections on some of the issues related to the definition of subsidies, see Jackson (1997) *supra* n. 7, pp. 290–303.

30 *FSC,* report of the panel, *supra* n. 19, para. 7.80.

31 See *Canada – Measures Affecting the Export of Civilian Aircraft*, report of the Appellate Body (WT/DS/70/AB/R) 2 August 1999, para. 156.

satisfied if either of these two alternatives – i.e., items (a)(1) or (a)(2) – is present. What is necessary for the existence of a subsidy is thus either a governmental "financial contribution" or "any form of income or price support" which results in a "benefit" being conferred on the recipient. We shall discuss these alternative conditions in Article 1.1(a) of the definition in reverse order.

5.2.1.1.1 Article 1.1(a)(2): "Any Form of Income or Price Support in the Sense of Article XVI of the GATT 1994"

The substantive elements of Article XVI of the General Agreement have already been discussed in the preceding chapter.[32] As will be seen at a later stage, however, the Uruguay Round SCM Agreement is so comprehensive that the question of how far that system still continues to have a place in the new context merits a serious scrutiny. The present analysis is, however, limited to the definitional aspect of the matter as reflected in the incorporation of Article XVI into the SCM Agreement via the explicit reference to it of Article 1 of the latter.

At the academic level, there is a growing consensus that the SCM Agreement does not leave much space any more for the entire system built around Article XVI of GATT 1994 to apply. According to McGovern, for instance, "[t]he regime established by the Subsidies Agreement is of such width and complexity that it leaves little if any room for the operation of the scheme established by GATT Article XVI."[33] Jackson also agrees with this assessment, albeit with some added caution: "The Uruguay Round subsidies text ... is sufficiently extensive and detailed that for most purposes it seems to supersede the text of GATT Articles VI and XVI, although there may still be a few concepts that would remain embedded in those Articles of GATT 1994."[34] The question will then be the following: has Article 1.1(a)(2) of the SCM Agreement become simply redundant?

WTO "case law" so far does not give much useful or definitive guidance on this issue. Article 1.1(a)(2) has been mentioned, for instance, in only few of the relevant cases decided to date. The definition of a "subsidy", somehow involving the provision of Article 1.1(a)(2), was "a critical issue" addressed by the *Canada Aircraft* panel.[35] The important point of contention in this case was of course related to the interpretation of the "benefit" element of the definition, and not to the "act" element as such. Nevertheless, the panel stated that "*[l]eaving aside the issue of 'income or price supports' (Article 1.1(a)(2))*, a 'subsidy' exists when there is a 'financial contribution' by a 'government or any public body within the territory of a Member'

[32] See also GATT, *Report on the Review Pursuant to Article XVI:5*, (L/1160 *BISD* 9S/188) adopted on 24 May, 1960, p. 192.

[33] McGovern (1995) *supra* n. 14, p. 11.38–1.

[34] Jackson (1997) *supra* n. 7, p. 290.

[35] The provision was in fact mentioned before that in the panel report on *Brazil Aircraft*, but only to say that "Brazil does not contest that actual PROEX [the challenged scheme here] payments confer a benefit within the meaning of Article 1.1(a)(2) of the SCM Agreement." *Brazil – Export Financing Programme for Aircraft* report of the panel, (WTO/DS46/R) 14 April 1999, para. 4.45. Apparently, even this must be by mistake as the issue of benefit is dealt with under Article 1.1(b) and not under 1.1(a)(2).

(Article 1.1(a)(1)) that confers a 'benefit' (Article 1.1(b))."[36] The Appellate Body in this case followed exactly the same approach as the panel, except that the latter expressly left aside the issue of income or price supports under Article 1.1(a)(2), while the former did it only silently. The Appellate Body stated that the definition of a "subsidy" in Article 1.1 has "two discrete elements: 'a financial contribution by a government or any public body' and 'a benefit is thereby conferred'. The first element of this definition is concerned with whether the government made a 'financial contribution', as that term is defined in Article 1.1(a). The focus of the first element is on the action of the government in making the 'financial contribution' ".[37] This approach was repeated in later reports on *UK Steel*, where both the panel and the Appellate Body simply ignored the "income or price support" element of the definition.[38] It is worthy of a special note that neither the panels nor the Appellate Body gave any reasons for this exclusion of an otherwise clearly stated alternative element of the definition of subsidies.

More directly, the specific issue of the "act" element of a subsidy in the sense of Article 1.1(a)(2) was highly debated between Canada and New Zealand in the *Canada Dairy* case. New Zealand argued that the Canadian scheme in question was a subsidy within the meaning of Article 1 of the SCM Agreement, *inter alia*, because "it constituted a form of income or price support within the meaning of GATT Article XVI, under Article 1.1(a)(2)."[39] Canada denied this, arguing, among others, that the system in question was operating under the control of market forces.[40] The panel did not, however, consider the issue apparently because it was able to avoid ruling over the very question of whether there was a subsidy in that case.[41] Interestingly enough, even

---

36 *Canada – Measures Affecting the Export of Civilian Aircraft*, report of the panel, (WT/DS70/R) 14 April 1999, para. 9.96 (italics added). The panel repeats this language, almost verbatim, in para. 9.120. For Canada's argument, (which incidentally is the only one that refers to income or price support as an element of the definition of subsidies), see para. 5.25, and for Brazil's argument, see *inter alia*, para. 5.39.

37 See *Canada Aircraft*, report of the Appellate Body, *supra* n. 31, para. 156.

38 The panel stated the following: "In short, Article 1.1 of the SCM Agreement provides that a subsidy exists if a 'financial contribution' by a government or public body confers a 'benefit'." *United States – Imposition of Countervailing Duties on Certain Hot-Rolled Lead and Bismuth Carbon Steel Products Originating in the United Kingdom*, report of the panel (WT/DS138/R) 23 December 1999, para. 6.58. The Appellate Body also followed exactly the same line and observed that Article 1.1 of the SCM Agreement "defines a 'subsidy' as follows: For the purpose of this Agreement, a subsidy shall be deemed to exist if: (a)(1) there is a financial contribution by a government or any public body within the territory of a Member ... and (b) a benefit is thereby conferred." *United States – Imposition of Countervailing Duties on Certain Hot-Rolled Lead and Bismuth Carbon Steel Products Originating in the United Kingdom*, report of the Appellate Body (WT/DS138/AB/R) 10 May 2000, para. 55.

39 *Canada Dairy*, report of the panel, *supra* n. 19, para. 4.301; for further arguments by New Zealand, see also, *inter alia*, paras. 4.302, 4.349, 4.350, 4.352 and 4.358.

40 See *Canada Dairy*, report of the panel, *supra* n. 19, para. 4.344; see also, *inter alia*, paras. 4.306, 4.348, 4.361, and 4.363-365.

41 See, for instance, the approach of the panel on the issue of "direct subsidies": "The plain language of Article 9.1(a) makes clear that 'payments-in-kind' are a form of direct subsidy. Hence, a determination in the instant matter that 'payments-in-kind' exist would also be a determination of the existence of a direct subsidy." *Canada Dairy*, report of the panel, *supra* n. 19, para. 7.43. This approach of the panel's was criticized by the Appellate Body as follows: "At no point did the Panel examine whether the

the Appellate Body, which in this case criticized and reversed the panel's interpretative approach on this particular point, did not bother to mention the element of "income or price support in the sense of Article XVI of GATT 1994" specified under Article 1.1(a)(2) of the SCM Agreement. True to its "tradition" on this subject, it simply reminded itself of its own previous finding on *Canada Aircraft* and ruled that "a 'subsidy', within the meaning of Article 1.1 of the SCM Agreement, arises where the grantor makes *a 'financial contribution' which confers a 'benefit'* on the recipient, as compared with what would have been otherwise available to the recipient in the marketplace."[42] Once again, given that "financial contribution" is only one of two alternative forms of action required of the government under Article 1.1 of the SCM Agreement, it is not clear as to why the Appellate Body chose to follow this line.

Finally, the issue was also addressed by the *FSC* panel. Just like its predecessors, this panel also stated as follows: "It is evident from Article 1 that two elements must be met in order for a subsidy to exist within the meaning of that Article. First, there must be a financial contribution by a government. Second, a benefit must thereby be conferred."[43] Unlike the previous panels, however, this panel was confronted with a specific problem involving the weight to be given to provisions of Article XVI of GATT 1994 in the interpretation of the provisions of the SCM Agreement.[44] Forced to address this specific problem in a specific manner, the panel noted that the provisions of the SCM Agreement "differ dramatically from those of Article XVI:4 of GATT 1947"[45] and concluded that "it would ... be inappropriate to place any

---

cont.

'payments-in-kind' that it found to exist were 'subsidies', let alone 'direct subsidies'. To the contrary, the Panel's finding under Article 9.1(a) resulted from its conclusion that the provision of reduced priced milk to processors for export under Special Classes 5(d) and (e) constitutes 'payments-in-kind' provided by Canada's 'governments or their agencies'. In making this finding, the Panel did not make any reference to the measures being 'direct subsidies'. It assumed that because the measures were 'payments-in-kind' they were, therefore, also 'direct subsidies'". *Canada – Measures Affecting the Importation of Milk and the Exportation of Dairy Products* report of the Appellate Body (WT/DS103/AB/R) 13 October 1999, para. 86 (footnotes omitted). As a matter of fact, the panel mentions the phrase "any form of income or price support in the sense of Article XVI of GATT 1994" as used in Article 1.1(a)(2) just once, and even then only as part of a general contextual guide for its interpretation of the scope of export subsidies falling under Article 10.1 of the Agreement on Agriculture. See *Canada Dairy,* report of the panel, *supra* n. 19, para. 7.126.

42 *Canada Dairy,* report of the Appellate Body, *supra* n. 41, para. 87 (italics added).

43 *FSC,* report of the panel, *supra* n. 19, para. 7.40.

44 In this case, the United States had argued, for instance, that the 1981 *Tax Legislation* panel reports "are relevant to the interpretation of the SCM Agreement because *the SCM Agreement is an 'interpretation' of Article XVI:4, and because an examination of the text of the SCM Agreement makes clear that the SCM Agreement and Article XVI are not to be construed in isolation from each other.*" Ibid., para. 7.79 (italics added).

45 Ibid., para. 7.80 (italics added). The Appellate Body's extensive comment on the relationship between Article XVI.4 of GATT 1994 and the SCM Agreement merits reproduction here:

"It is clear from even a cursory examination of Article XVI:4 of the GATT 1994 that it differs very substantially from the subsidy provisions of the *SCM Agreement*, and, in particular, from the export subsidy provisions of both the *SCM Agreement* and the *Agreement on Agriculture*. First of all, the SCM Agreement contains an express definition of the term 'subsidy' which is not contained in Article XVI:4.

weight in interpreting the definition of subsidy found in Article 1 of the SCM Agreement on an understanding regarding Article XVI:4 of GATT 1947 which was adopted more than a decade ago before that definition was formulated."[46] Apprehensive of what the implications of these statements could be on the system under consideration, the panel did not stop there. Even after acknowledging the dramatically different nature of the two sets of provisions, it added that, by saying this, "[w]e do not mean to suggest that Article XVI:4 of GATT 1994 has some how ceased to be legally operative or has been simply replaced by the SCM Agreement."[47]

This statement of the panel's closely echoes the generally accepted understanding concerning the relationship between GATT 1994 and the other goods agreements in Annex 1A to the WTO Agreement. This relationship has been summarized by the Appellate Body in its report on *Brazil Coconut* as follows: "to the extent that the provisions of the other goods agreements conflict with the provisions of the GATT 1994, the provisions of the other goods agreements prevail. This does not mean, however, that the other goods agreements in Annex 1A, such as the SCM Agreement, supersede the GATT 1994."[48] When it comes to the specific case of Article 1.1(a)(2) of the SCM Agreement, however, what the *FSC* panel said above goes contrary to its deeds. If, indeed, the panel does not mean to suggest that Article XVI of GATT 1994 has some how ceased to be legally operative or has been simply replaced by the SCM Agreement, how does it explain its repeated factual avoidance of any reference to Article 1.1(a)(2) even when the situation arguably required it? The answer to this question is nowhere to be found in the reports.[49]

---

cont.

In fact, as we have observed previously, the SCM Agreement contains a broad package of new export subsidy disciplines that 'go well beyond merely applying and interpreting Articles VI, XVI and XXIII of the GATT 1947'. Next, Article XVI:4 prohibits export subsidies only when they result in the export sale of a product at a price lower than the 'comparable price charged for the like product to buyers in the domestic market.' In contrast, the *SCM Agreement* establishes a much broader prohibition against any subsidy which is 'contingent upon export performance'. To say the least, the rule contained in Article 3.1(a) of the *SCM Agreement* that all subsidies which are 'contingent upon export performance' are prohibited is significantly different from a rule that prohibits only those subsidies which result in a lower price for the exported product than the comparable price for that product when sold in the domestic market. Thus, whether or not a measure is an export subsidy under Article XVI:4 of the GATT 1947 provides no guidance in determining whether that measure is a prohibited export subsidy under Article 3.1(a) of the *SCM Agreement." United States – Tax Treatment for "Foreign Sales Corporations"*, report of the Appellate Body (WT/DS108/AB/R) 24 February 2000, para. 117 (italics in original, footnotes omitted).

46 *FSC*, report of the panel, *supra* n. 19, para. 7.80.

47 Ibid., para. 7.82. In connection with this same case, the Appellate Body noted that "under Article 1.1(a)(2) of the *SCM Agreement*, a 'subsidy' may exist if 'there is any form of income or price support in the sense of Article XVI of GATT 1994". This is a reference to Article XVI:1 and not Article XVI:4 of GATT 1994. Footnote 1 of the *SCM Agreement*, which is attached to Article 1.1(a)(1)(ii) of that Agreement, also makes reference to Article XVI of the GATT 1994 in connection with "the exemption of an exported product from duties or taxes borne by like products destined for domestic consumption ...." *FSC*, report of the Appellate Body, *supra* n. 45, footnote 135 to para. 117.

48 *Brazil Coconut*, report of the Appellate Body, *supra* n. 18, p. 16.

49 Later panel reports on *UK Steel* and *Canada Automotive* also followed this established approach. The *UK Steel* panel stated that "[t]he criteria for determining the existence of a subsidy are set forth in

On the whole, these cases may be too few to draw any viable conclusion from. However, they show that panels as well as the Appellate Body consistently prefer to exclude Article XVI from their consideration, while at the same time reserving any explicit statement as to whether there can be any room left for the application of this provision in the present scenario. From the repeated exclusion of Article 1.1(a)(2) by both panels as well as the Appellate Body in their consideration of the definitional problems under the SCM Agreement – who limit themselves to the element of "financial contribution" under Article 1.1(a)(1) – one might be tempted to deduce that they are simply assuming that whatever is said in the former is already included in the latter. The problem with this approach is, of course, clear. It makes the provision under Article 1.1(a)(2) redundant, a result that goes against what is called the principle of "effectiveness" in treaty interpretation. As observed by the Appellate Body in *US Gasoline*, "[o]ne of the corollaries of the 'general rule of interpretation' in the Vienna Convention is that interpretation must give meaning and effect to all the terms of the treaty. An interpreter is not free to adopt a reading that would result in reducing whole clauses or paragraphs of a treaty to redundancy or inutility".[50] The apparently anomalous stand taken by panels on the issue of Article XVI – i.e., their avoidance of any reference to it in practice while at the same time expressly stating that they do not mean to suggest that it has been superseded by the provisions of the SCM Agreement – appear to be a result of their deference to this principle of interpretation rather than of any real conviction that it still has a role to play.

The question of whether this strategy of the panels and the Appellate Body might ultimately end up forming a consensus view in favour of complete disuse of Article 1.1(a)(2) must await for some more time and for some more judicial practice on the subject. In the mean time, although interpreters are not free to reduce the provisions of a treaty to inutility or redundancy, in practice, there appears to be almost no room for the provisions of Article XVI of GATT 1994 to be applied. To this extent, the incorporation of Article XVI here by way of an explicit reference to that effect appears to have the object largely of reassuring continuity in the system rather than introducing anything of substance as such that goes beyond what is already stated under the "financial contribution" element of Article 1.1(a)(1).

5.2.1.1.2 Article 1.1(a)(1): "Financial Contribution"

The existence of "a financial contribution by a government or any public body" is

---

cont.

Article 1 of the SCM Agreement. In short, Article 1.1 of the SCM Agreement provides that a subsidy exists if a 'financial contribution' by a government or public body confers a 'benefit'." *UK Steel*, report of the panel, *supra* n. 38, para. 6.58. Likewise, the *Canada Automotive* panel observed that "[i]t is clear from Article 1.1 that two criteria must be met in order for a subsidy to exist within the meaning of that Article. First, there must be a financial contribution by a government. Second, a benefit must thereby be conferred." *Canada – Certain Measures Affecting the Automotive Industry*, report of the panel (WT/DS139/R, WT/DS142/R) 11 February 2000, para. 10.156.

50 *United States – Standards for Reformulated and Conventional Gasoline*, report of the Appellate Body (WT/DS2/AB/R) 20 May 1996, p. 23.

the important, if not the only, condition constituting the "act" element of a subsidy. In the words of sub-paragraph (a)(1) of Article 1.1 of the Subsidies Agreement, "financial contribution" is deemed to exist where any of the following conditions is met: (i) a government practice involves a direct transfer of funds (e.g., grants, loans, and equity infusion), or potential direct transfers of funds or liabilities (e.g., loan guarantees); (ii) government revenue that is otherwise due is foregone or not collected (e.g., fiscal incentives such as tax credits); (iii) a government provides goods or services other than general infrastructure, or purchases goods; (iv) a government makes payments to a funding mechanism, or entrusts or directs a private body to carry out one or more of the type of functions illustrated in (i) to (iii) above which would normally be vested in the government and the practice, in no real sense, differs from practices normally followed by governments.

The question of whether the list under Article 1.1(a)(1) is illustrative or exhaustive appears to be a contentious one. There are two major considerations favouring the conclusion that the list is exhaustive. Firstly, the items in the list are so widely-framed that it is difficult, in practice, to imagine a case of "financial contribution" that falls outside the list. Secondly, as Canada consistently argued in both the *Canada Dairy* as well as the *Canada Aircraft* disputes, "the use of the term 'i.e.' [in Article 1.1(a)(1)] indicated that the items that followed were intended to be an exhaustive, rather than an illustrative list."[51] Canada further argued that its view was supported by the negotiating history of the provision and noted that the Uruguay Round negotiators agreed to replace the term "such as" in the Cartland I draft of the SCM Agreement,[52] with "i.e." in the Cartland II draft,[53] "thus clearly indicating an intent to move from an illustrative definition to an exhaustive definition."[54]

However, despite the obvious plausibility of the Canadian argument and the practical difficulty that might otherwise be involved, item (iv) of Article 1.1(a)(1) uses an expression that strongly favours the opposite conclusion. This provision addresses the three preceding items in the list as "type[s] of functions *illustrated* in (i) to (iii) above."[55] The ordinary meaning of "to illustrate" is "to clarify or explain by use of examples or comparisons."[56] Had the drafters of the provision intended to have a list that is more than a set of examples, they would have used terms having that effect in their ordinary meaning. Therefore, although it may be difficult to conceive of a practice that can be called a "financial contribution" and still fall outside the listed categories, and that the contrary argument of Canada may be well-reasoned and supported by the preparatory history of the provision, the fundamental principle of treaty interpretation, as stated under Article 31 of the

---

51 *Canada Dairy*, report of the panel, *supra* n. 19, para. 4.310. The same argument has been made by Canada, almost verbatim, in *Canada Aircraft*, report of the panel, *supra* n. 36, para. 5.27.

52 Canada here refers to GATT document MTN.GNG/NG10/W/38 (18 July, 1990).

53 Canada here refers to GATT document MTN.GNG/NG10/W/39/Rev.1 (4 September 1990).

54 *Canada Dairy*, report of the panel, *supra* n. 19, para. 4.310. The same argument has been made by Canada, almost verbatim, in *Canada Aircraft*, report of the panel, *supra* n. 36, para. 5.27.

55 Article 1.1(a)(1)(iv), (italics added).

56 *Collins Paperback Dictionary: Major New Edition*, (Harper Collins Publishers, 1995).

Vienna Convention on the Law of Treaties, dictates that preference be given to the ordinary meaning of the terms used.

Turning to the substance of the listed elements, of the four categories in Article 1.1(a)(1), while the first three address the nature of the act that needs to be carried out for a subsidy to exist, the fourth category deals generally with the manner in which those acts are carried out, including the identity of the entity that carries them out and the role of the government in the process. The first three items answer the question of what the acts should be and the fourth addresses the issues of who the doer of those acts must be and how they need to be done. As such, although illustrative, a "financial contribution" consists essentially of three different forms of activities which involve: actual or potential direct transfer of funds,[57] foregone or uncollected government revenues otherwise due,[58] and purchase or provision of goods and services at other than market prices.[59] However, as sub-paragraph (iv)

---

[57] The following observation by the *Brazil Aircraft* panel might shed some light on the essence of this practice: "according to Article 1:1[(a)(1)](i) a subsidy exists if a government practice involves a direct transfer of funds or a potential direct transfer of funds and not only when a government actually effectuates such a transfer or potential transfer (otherwise the text of (i) would read: 'a government directly transfers funds ... or engages in potential direct transfers of funds or liabilities'). ... As soon as there is such a *practice,* a subsidy exists, and the question whether the practice involves a direct transfer of funds or a potential direct transfer of funds is not relevant to the existence of a subsidy. One or the other is sufficient. If subsidies were deemed to exist only once a direct or potential direct transfer of funds had actually been effectuated, the Agreement would be rendered totally ineffective and even the typical WTO remedy (i.e. the cessation of the violation) would not be possible." *Brazil Aircraft* report of the panel, *supra* n. 35, para. 7.13.

[58] The substance of what is "otherwise due" in the context of tax exemptions and deferrals has been summarized by the *FSC* panel as follows: "In accordance with its ordinary meaning, we took the term 'otherwise due' to refer to the situation that would prevail but for the measures in question. It is thus a matter of determining whether, absent such measures, there would be a higher tax liability. In our view, this means that a panel, in considering whether revenue foregone is 'otherwise due', must examine the situation that would exist but for the measure in question. Under this approach, the question presented in this dispute is whether, if the FSC scheme did not exist, revenue would be due which is foregone by reason of that scheme." Ibid., para. 7.45. Applying this test to the case at hand, the *FSC* panel considered the different aspects of the challenged scheme and concluded that "[t]aken together, it is clear that the various exemptions under the FSC scheme result in a situation where certain types of income are shielded from taxes that would be due in the absence of the FSC scheme." Ibid., para. 7.100.

The Appellate Body agreed with this panel interpretation and observed as follows: "In our view, the '*foregoing*' of revenue '*otherwise* due' implies that less revenue has been raised by the government than would have been raised in a different situation, or, that is, 'otherwise'. Moreover, the word 'foregone' suggests that the government has given up an entitlement to raise revenue that it could 'otherwise' have raised. This cannot, however, be an entitlement in the abstract, because governments, in theory, could tax all revenues. There must, therefore, be some defined, normative benchmark against which a comparison can be made between the revenue actually raised and the revenue that would have been raised 'otherwise'. We, therefore, agree with the Panel that the term 'otherwise due' implies some kind of comparison between the revenues due under the contested measure and revenues that would be due in some other situation. We also agree with the Panel that the basis of comparison must be the tax rules applied by the Member in question." *FSC,* report of the Appellate Body *supra* n. 45, para. 90 (italics in original). For the Appellate Body's appraisal of the panel's use of a "but for" test in this specific case, see para. 91.

[59] For additional guidance on the meaning of these practices, see Article 14 of the SCM Agreement on the calculation of the amount of a subsidy. As the Appellate Body observed, the "explicit textual reference

clearly states, the fourth category refers only to the manner of making the financial contribution as specified under the preceding three categories. By making payments to a funding mechanism or by entrusting or directing a private body to carry out one or more of the functions enumerated under items (i) to (iii), the government is not involving itself in a fourth category of functions.[60] The main purpose of item (iv) appears to be only to underscore that, as long as any one of the functions listed under the preceding three paragraphs (or a practice similar to them) is carried out, neither the source of the funds nor the identity of the provider of them (whether public or private) matters as to the existence of a "financial contribution by the government" in the sense of Article 1 of the Subsidies Agreement. It must be emphasized that, for a subsidy to exist as defined by this Agreement, the involvement of the government or any other public body is mandatory. The nature of this government involvement varies from case to case. It is important, however, that, when only a non-governmental actor is directly involved, the government should be the source either of the funds or of the authority, or both.

This brings to mind the traditional debate as to whether this governmental involvement should necessarily be in a manner that results in a charge to its accounts.[61] Even after the conclusion of the Uruguay Round SCM Agreement, the traditional controversy between the cost-to-government and benefit-to-the-recipient approaches to the issue of subsidies does not seem to have gone yet. Different writers still have differing views on the issue. For Zampeti, for instance, the definition of subsidy focuses "on the existence of a public financial contribution, as opposed to a wider notion encompassing any benefit-conferring government action."[62] Jackson, on the other hand, is of the opinion that "Article 1 of the Uruguay Round text provides a definition that combines elements of the cost as well as the benefit approach."[63] A closer look at the above definition in the light of available "case law' on the subject is thus useful at this point.

As reiterated already, "financial contribution by a government or any public body' is one of two alternative requirements the fulfilment of which, if accompanied

---

cont.

to Article 1.1 in Article 14 indicates ... that 'benefit' is used in the same sense in Article 14 as it is in Article 1.1." *Canada Aircraft*, report of the Appellate Body, *supra* n. 31, para. 155; see generally paras. 153-161.

60 Compare this with the following: "The definition in Article 1 of the Agreement sets out a requirement that there be a financial contribution from government in order for a subsidy to exist, and gives an exhaustive list of four basic types of government practices that constitute financial contributions. ... Perhaps the most significant aspect of Article 1 is what is not included in the definition: any government practice that does not meet one of the four criteria laid out therein cannot be considered a subsidy for the purposes of the Agreement." T. Collins-Williams, and G Salembier "International Disciplines on Subsidies: The GATT, the WTO, and the Future Agenda", in 30 *Journal of World Trade*, No. 1 (1996) p. 10.

61 For more on this issue, see the discussion on Article 9:1 of the Agriculture Agreement *infra*, chapter 6.3.2.

62 A. Zampeti, "The Uruguay Round Agreement on Subsidies: A Forward-Looking Assessment", in 29 *Journal of World Trade*, No. 6 (1995) p. 28.

63 Jackson (1997) *supra* n. 7, p. 295.

by the conferment of a benefit on the recipient, constitutes a subsidy. Leaving the "benefit" element for the next section, the question now is whether "financial contribution by a government or any public body" necessarily involves a cost to that government or public body. Seen on the surface, it may even appear rather strange to talk about a "financial contribution by a government or any public body" and, at the same time, raise the question of whether that government or public body incurs costs in making the "contribution". However, we are here dealing with a concept that has been given a special definition for a special purpose.

A closer look at the elements of Article 1 and other provisions[64] of the SCM Agreement strongly suggests that the financial contribution or other form of income or price support element does not necessarily result in budgetary costs to governments.[65] A simple example would be that, of the four elements listed under Article 1.1(a)(1) of the SCM Agreement defining a "financial contribution", while the government definitely loses a certain sum of money when it directly transfers funds to firms or foregoes revenues that are otherwise due, it does not necessarily lose any sum as such when it directs a private body to do the work in the sense of item (iv). The available "case law" on the subject so far also confirms this interpretation.

This problem was an issue, for instance, before the *Canada Aircraft* panel in connection with the interpretation of the "benefit" element of a subsidy. In response to Canada's contention that a subsidy necessarily involves a cost to the government, the panel ruled that "if 'benefit' were to include the notion of net cost to government, it could exclude from the definition of 'subsidy' situations explicitly identified in Article 1.1(a)(1) itself as constituting government financial contributions even though no cost to the government might be involved."[66] More specifically, the panel observed that

> "Article 1.1(a)(1)(iv) identifies as a 'financial contribution' the situation where a government directs a private body to make 'financial contributions' within the meaning of Article 1.1(a)(1)(i)-(iii). In such a situation, the net cost could be incurred entirely by the private body rather than the government. Canada's interpretation of 'benefit' (i.e., to include net cost to government) would render Article 1.1(a)(1)(iv) meaningless, since a form of 'financial contribution' explicitly included in Article 1.1(a) would automatically (i.e., because it would never meet the net cost to government test) be excluded by Article 1.1(b)."[67]

---

64 See e.g. SCM Agreement Article 14 and Paragraph (c) of the *Illustrative List of Export Subsidies*, Annex I to the SCM Agreement. The Appellate Body has, for instance, used Article 14 to support a conclusion that "the word 'benefit', as used in Article 1.1, is concerned with the 'benefit to the recipient' and not with the 'cost to government' ...." *Canada Aircraft,* report of the Appellate Body, *supra* n. 31, para. 155.

65 For an actual case where a panel found a subsidy under the Agreement on Agriculture without the government bearing the cost thereof, see *Canada Dairy*, report of the panel, *supra* n. 19, Para. 7.102; see also the Appellate Body report on the same case, *supra* n. 41, para. 120.

66 *Canada Aircraft,* report of the panel, *supra* n. 36, para. 9.115.

67 Ibid., para. 9.115.

The Appellate Body expressed its approval of the panel's view on the subject in nearly identical language. According to the Appellate Body, Canada's interpretation of "benefit" "would exclude from the scope of that term those situations where a 'benefit' is conferred by a private body under the direction of government. These situations cannot be excluded from the definition of 'benefit' in Article 1.1(b), given that they are specifically included in the definition of 'financial contribution' in Article 1.1(a)(iv)."[68]

One may also mention specific practices of subsidies in which the involvement of the government may not necessarily result in a charge to its accounts. This is the case for instance when it guarantees loans to firms which respect their contractual obligations, or, arguably, even when it gives certain forms of loans to such firms.[69] The same is true when the government mandates "internal transport or freight charges on export shipments on terms more favourable than for domestic shipments."[70] It follows from this that, the involvement of the government is a necessary condition for the existence of a subsidy in the sense of Article 1 of the SCM Agreement; but this involvement does not need to be in a manner that causes a charge to its accounts.

5.2.1.2 Article 1.1(b): "Benefit" to the Recipient

According to Article 1 of the SCM Agreement, a "financial contribution", regardless of the cost incurred by a government, becomes a subsidy only if "a benefit is thereby conferred". Needless to say, a benefit "does not exist in the abstract, but must be received and enjoyed by a recipient."[71] However, neither the SCM Agreement nor any other relevant agreement defines the term "benefit".

In the absence of a definition, panels as well as the Appellate Body had to give their own definitions applying the general principles of treaty interpretation.[72] The *Canada Aircraft* panel pointed out that the ordinary meaning of "benefit"

---

68 *Canada Aircraft*, report of the Appellate Body, *supra* n. 31, para. 160.

69 One writer gives a simple example to explain this possibility. Supposing that industries in a country who borrow on the financial market have to pay 10 per cent and that the government of that country can obtain the money at the rate of 5 per cent on the capital market, a governmental offer of a preferential loan at 5 per cent to a widget producer confers a net benefit on the recipient at no budgetary cost to the government. See Quick, R. "Calculation of a Subsidy", in J. Bourgeois, (ed.) *Subsidies and International Trade: A European Lawyers Perspective* (Kluwer 1991) p. 96. In this case, the government may not necessarily incur any expenses in the sense of being financially worse off than would have been the case in the absence of this transaction. However, one may also argue that the government is losing in as long as it foregoes any profit margins it would have realized by virtue of the concessional deal it itself has got from the capital market.

70 Paragraph (c) of the *Illustrative List of Export Subsidies*, Annex I to the SCM Agreement.

71 *Canada Aircraft*, report of the Appellate Body, *supra* n. 31, para. 154.

72 Articles 31 and 32 of the Vienna Convention are the main sources of guidance in this respect. Relying on the principles enshrined in these provisions, Canada argued that the word "benefit" as it was found in Article 1.1(b) of the SCM Agreement, "could only be read as meaning a competitive advantage in trade. This conclusion flowed naturally from the ordinary meaning of 'benefit', the context in which it was found and the object and purpose of the SCM Agreement read as a whole." *Canada Dairy*, report of the panel, *supra* n. 19, para 4.368.

clearly encompasses some form of advantage.[73] The Appellate Body in the same case observed that "[t]he dictionary meaning of 'benefit' is 'advantage', 'good', 'gift', 'profit', or, more generally, 'a favourable or helpful factor or circumstance'. Each of these alternative words or phrases gives flavour to the term 'benefit' and helps to convey some of the essence of that term."[74] The "benefit" requirement is thus met as soon as the "financial contribution" results in creating some form of "competitive advantage in trade" in the export market for the product concerned in favour of the recipient.[75] The *Canada Aircraft* panel summarized the essence of this requirement as follows: "In order to determine whether a financial contribution (in the sense of Article 1.1(a)(i)) confers a 'benefit', i.e., an advantage, it is necessary to determine whether the financial contribution places the recipient in a more advantageous position than would have been the case but for the financial contribution."[76] The Appellate Body in the same case invoked Article 14 of the SCM Agreement and stressed the importance of the acquisition of an advantage on the part of the recipient for the "benefit" element to be satisfied.[77]

Thus understood, a benefit "involves the concept of comparison."[78] However, one can talk of an advantage only if one has a clear benchmark against which to compare the situation. No such benchmark has been directly identified by the definition provision of the SCM Agreement. However, one can find authoritative guidance from other provisions of the SCM Agreement, notably Article 14 on the calculation of countervailing duties[79] and paragraph (d) of the Illustrative List of

---

73 *Canada Aircraft*, report of the panel, *supra* n. 36, para. 9.112.

74 *Canada Aircraft*, report of the Appellate Body, *supra* n. 31, para. 153.

75 *Canada Dairy*, report of the panel, *supra* n. 19, para 4.368.

76 *Canada Aircraft*, report of the panel, *supra* n. 36, para. 9.112. As it is talking in terms of "financial contribution" here, the reference to Article 1.1(a)(i) in this paragraph apparently is a reference to Article 1.1(a)(1). See also para. 9.120 of the same report.

77 See generally *Canada Aircraft*, report of the Appellate Body, *supra* n. 31, paras 153-161. The Appellate Body in particular observed that "[w]e find support for this reading of 'benefit' in the context of Article 1.1(b) of the SCM Agreement. Article 14 sets forth guidelines for calculating the amount of a subsidy in terms of 'the benefit to the recipient'. Although the opening words of Article 14 state that the guidelines it establishes apply '[f]or the purposes of Part V' of the SCM Agreement, which relates to 'countervailing measures', our view is that Article 14, nonetheless, constitutes relevant context for the interpretation of 'benefit' in Article 1.1(b). The guidelines set forth in Article 14 apply to the calculation of the 'benefit to the recipient conferred pursuant to paragraph 1 of Article 1'. ... This explicit textual reference to Article 1.1 in Article 14 indicates to us that 'benefit' is used in the same sense in Article 14 as it is in Article 1.1. Therefore, the reference to 'benefit to the recipient' in Article 14 also implies that the word 'benefit', as used in Article 1.1, is concerned with the 'benefit to the recipient' and not with the 'cost to government', as Canada contends." *Id.*, 155.

78 Ibid., para. 157.

79 As summarized by the Appellate Body in *Canada Aircraft*, "[t]he guidelines set forth in Article 14 relate to equity investments, loans, loan guarantees, the provision of goods or services by a government, and the purchase of goods by a government. A 'benefit' arises under each of the guidelines if the recipient has received a 'financial contribution' *on terms more favourable than those available to the recipient in the market.*" Ibid., para. 158 (italics added).

Export Subsidies,[80] both of which prescribe the market as the appropriate standard for their respective purposes. The guidance that we get from these provisions in favour of using the market as the appropriate benchmark is further strengthened by the overall object and purpose of the SCM Agreement as well as the entire multilateral trading system at large. Indeed, we are here concerned with the benefit received by the recipient only because there is the underlying consensus that subsidies affect the market. As such, to use the words of the *Canada Aircraft* panel, the market is simply "the only logical basis for determining the position the recipient would have been in absent the financial contribution". Accordingly, a financial contribution confers a "benefit' only if it is provided "on terms that are more advantageous than those that would have been available to the recipient on the market."[81] The Appellate Body, in the *Canada Dairy* case affirmed this view as follows: "a 'subsidy', within the meaning of Article 1.1 of the SCM Agreement, arises where the grantor makes a 'financial contribution' which confers a 'benefit' on the recipient, as compared with what would have been otherwise available to the recipient in the marketplace."[82] It is mandatory that the recipient get something out of the practice that is better than what is available to it in the market under the same or comparable circumstances.[83]

Finally, the co-existence of governmental "financial contribution" and a benefit-receiving enterprise do not suffice for purposes of this provision; the two should further be connected by a causal link. By stating that there is a subsidy if there is a financial contribution and "a benefit is thereby conferred", Article 1 of the SCM Agreement stipulates this causality requirement in a passive form.[84] The term

[80] Paragraph (d) of the *Illustrative List of Export Subsidies* provides that "[t]he provision by governments or their agencies either directly or indirectly through government-mandated schemes, of imported or domestic products or services for use in the production of exported goods, on terms or conditions more favourable than for provision of like or directly competitive products or services for use in the production of goods for domestic consumption, *if (in the case of products) such terms or conditions are more favourable than those commercially available on world markets to their exporters*" (italics added). A footnote to this paragraph adds that "The term 'commercially available' means that the choice between domestic and imported products is unrestricted and depends only on commercial considerations." Footnote 58 to para. (d) of the *Illustrative List of Export Subsidies*, Annex I to the SCM Agreement.

[81] *Canada Aircraft*, report of the panel, *supra* n. 36, para. 9.112.

[82] *Canada Aircraft*, report of the Appellate Body, *supra* n. 31, para 87 (emphasis added).

[83] In *UK Steel*, the panel stated its agreement with the interpretation of the term "benefit" in the *Canada Aircraft* panel and Appellate Body reports and further observed that "[i]n our view, the existence or non-existence of 'benefit' rests on whether the potential recipient or beneficiary ... has received a 'financial contribution' on terms more favourable than those available to the potential recipient or beneficiary in the market." *UK Steel*, report of the panel, *supra* n. 38, para. 6.66. For issues involving a choice between competing benchmarks, see *Canada Dairy*, report of the panel, *supra* n. 19, paras. 7.43-7.58.

[84] In *UK Steel*, the US tried to use the language of Article 1.1 of the SCM Agreement to justify its failure to make new determinations of whether an old subsidy (given by the UK Government to a state-owned firm) and the resulting benefits to the firm still continued after the privatization of the receiving firm through an arm's length deal for fair market value and consistent with commercial considerations. The US argued before the Appellate Body that the ordinary meaning of Article 1.1 of the *SCM Agreement* confirms that the benefit of a subsidy is determined as of the time of bestowal and not afterwards. According to the US, the "requisite financial contribution and benefit are described by Article 1.1 in

"thereby" is particularly relevant in this respect. As Canada argued in *Canada Dairy,* even if both a governmental "financial contribution" and a "benefit" are found together in a case, the word "thereby" in Article 1.1(b) "required that there was no 'subsidy' until a causal link was established between the two elements."[85] The EC representative also argued before the Appellate Body in the *Canada Aircraft* case (to which the EC was a third party participant) that "[t]he word 'thereby' makes clear the need for a causal link between the financial contribution and the 'benefit'."[86] These arguments by different parties also got the approval of panels and the Appellate Body in different cases. The *Canada Dairy* panel observed in passing that "Article 1.1(b) of the SCM Agreement ... only requires that there be a benefit ... and that *the benefit in fact be conferred by the measure* or arrangement which is alleged to be a subsidy."[87] The Appellate Body expressed the importance of this causal connection in an active form as follows: "a 'subsidy', within the meaning of Article 1.1 of the SCM Agreement, arises where the grantor makes a 'financial contribution' which confers a 'benefit' on the recipient."[88]

To sum up, if a government spends billions of dollars trying to support, say, its wheat producers but confers no advantages upon the intended beneficiaries of the programme compared to what would otherwise be available to them in the marketplace, there is no subsidy in the sense that term is defined here. On the other

---

cont.

the present tense. Thus, the benefit is created by the terms on which the financial contribution is made, and arises at the same time the financial contribution is made." *UK Steel* report of the Appellate Body, *supra* n. 38, para. 12. The EC on the other hand argued that "the use of the present tense in Article 1.1 of the *SCM Agreement* does not indicate that the required determinations of financial contribution and benefit should only be made as of the moment a financial contribution was made. Rather, the use of the word 'thereby' in Article 1.1 shows that the financial contribution is the cause and the benefit is the effect." Ibid. para. 22. The Appellate Body rejected the US argument and noted that Article 1.1 "does not address the *time* at which the 'financial contribution' and/or the 'benefit' must be shown to exist. We therefore consider that Article 1.1 does not provide a basis for the argument made by the United States." Ibid. para. 60. The Appellate Body thus upheld the Panel's finding that the US should have examined whether a "benefit" still accrued to the successor firms following the changes in ownership and concluded that no "benefit" was conferred any more as a result of the "financial contributions" made to the old firm. See Ibid., para. 74.

85 *Canada Dairy*, report of the panel, *supra* n. 19, para. 4.373.

86 Statement made by the representative of the EC to the Appellate Body in *Canada Aircraft,* report of the Appellate Body, *supra* n. 31, para. 96. The EC was in fact using this approach to support its view, and that of Canada's, that "cost to government" is the appropriate measure of "financial contribution", for "financial contribution" necessarily results in a cost to government and that it is only in that way that one could establish whether a "benefit" is thereby conferred (see Ibid., paras. 96-97). The Appellate Body rejected this line of reasoning saying that "we believe that Canada's argument that 'cost to government' is one way of conceiving of 'benefit' is at odds with the ordinary meaning of Article 1.1(b), which focuses on the recipient and not on the government providing the 'financial contribution'." Ibid., para. 154. The EC view on the issue of causation, however, remains valid despite the rejection of its main argument.

87 *Canada Dairy*, report of the panel, *supra* n. 19, footnote 393, para. 7.47 (italics added).

88 *Canada Aircraft*, report of the Appellate Body, *supra* n. 31, para. 87. The Appellate Body also said the following in the *Canada Aircraft* case: "the second element in Article 1.1 is concerned with *the 'benefit ... conferred' on the recipient by that governmental action.*" Ibid., para. 156 (italics added).

hand, any government program to support the sector, although it causes little or no expenses to the government, falls under the scope of the definition in as long as it results in the acquisition of a benefit, however small, on the part of the recipient. The involvement of the government in a certain form is a mandatory requirement for the existence of a subsidy; but this involvement may take various forms and need not necessarily be in a way that results in a charge to its accounts. The definition therefore settles the long-standing controversy between the cost-to-government and benefit-to-the-recipient theories behind the concept of subsidies in favour of the latter.

5.3 OVERVIEW OF THE SUBSIDIES DISCIPLINE

According to the Subsidies Agreement, establishing the existence of a subsidy is one thing, while subjecting it to rules of discipline is totally different. In order to apply the principal rules of discipline introduced by the SCM Agreement to a practice of subsidy that is found to exist according to Article 1.1 thereof, the thus established subsidy has to meet one more criterion – that of "specificity".[89] Stated in general terms, this is a requirement to the effect that access to the subsidy must be limited, either in law or in fact, to "an enterprise or industry or group of enterprises or industries."[90]

This requirement reflects the very policy premise underlying the regulation of subsidies; to wit, the understanding that any government support programme that is equally available to all spheres of the economy does not as such distort trade or the allocation of resources, and hence not as such a subject for multilateral discipline. However, as soon as such a support programme begins to be "specific", i.e. to favour an enterprise or industry or group of enterprises or industries (generally termed "certain enterprises" in the Agreement) over others, the subsidy starts to be unfair and subject to the disciplines introduced therein.[91] Specificity is a condition not for the existence of a subsidy. Rather, it is a condition for the application on a subsidy of the measures specified under Parts II, III and V of the Agreement on prohibited subsidies, actionable subsidies, and countervailing measures, respectively. The "non-specific" subsidies fall in the so-called "non-actionable" subsidies category of Part IV of the SCM Agreement. But, not all specific subsidies are necessarily subject to

[89] Article 1.2 provides that "a subsidy as defined in paragraph 1 above shall be subject to the provisions of Part II [Prohibited Subsidies] or shall be subject to the provisions of Part III [Actionable Subsidies] or V [Countervailing Measures] of this Agreement only if such a subsidy is specific in accordance with the provisions of Article 2 below".

[90] Article 2.1 of the SCM Agreement; for a set of guiding principles in order to determine the question of specificity, see Article 2 of the Agreement.

[91] It may be instructive to cite here observations made by David Palmeter concerning the "specificity" requirement in US countervailing duty law: "programs that provide financing to the entire agricultural sector are deemed not to apply to a specific industry or group of industries, and are not countervailable .... 'Agriculture ... is more than a specific industry or group of industries.' However, benefits that are made available only to specifically 'named products' are countervailable even if the list of 'named products' is broadly phrased, such as 'livestock' and 'certain grains'." D. Palmeter, "Agriculture and Trade Regulation: Selected Issues in the Application of U.S. Antidumping and Countervailing Duty Laws", 23 *Journal of World Trade (*1989*)* No. 1, pp. 62–63.

the provisions of either of the former three Parts. There are a set of specific subsidies which fall under Part IV of the Agreement on "non-actionable" subsidies.[92]

In sum, a financial contribution or any form of income or price support by a government or any public body amounts to a subsidy if a benefit is thereby conferred upon the recipient; a subsidy is subject to the rules of Parts II, III, and V of the Agreement only if it is "specific", i.e. available to a limited group of enterprises or industries; a subsidy that is not "specific" is a "non-actionable subsidy" (without prejudice to the fact that there are also specific subsidies forming part of this group) and falls under Part IV of the Agreement.

5.3.1 Categories of Subsidies

An important feature of the SCM Agreement implicit in the preceding discussion is the sort of "traffic light" approach employed to introduce a trichotomy into the field of subsidies.[93] Accordingly, a subsidy may be prohibited (red), actionable (amber), or non-actionable (green); each with a Part devoted to itself. The practice of export subsidies falls in the category of prohibited subsidies. Before going to a detailed analysis of this category, however, a brief look at the main features of the other two classes may be in order at this point.

5.3.2 Non-Actionable Subsidies

The category of "non-actionable subsidies" covers those subsidies which are generally considered to have minimal impact on the flow of international trade. They are of two types. The first covers those subsidies that are not "specific" to an enterprise or industry or group of enterprises or industries within the meaning of Article 2 of the SCM Agreement. As indicated earlier, a subsidy is subject to the provisions of Parts II (prohibited subsidies), III (actionable subsidies), or V (countervailing measures) of the Agreement only if such a subsidy is specific in the sense of Article 2 of the same Agreement. Looked at from the other side, this means that all subsidies that are "non-specific" are neither prohibited, nor actionable, nor countervailable. Hence the conclusion that all subsidies that are not specific are non-actionable subsidies. This being clear, however, the Agreement, presumably for the sake of further clarity even at the risk of possible redundancy, reaffirms under Article 8:1(a) that subsidies which are not specific within the meaning of paragraph 1 of Article 2 are considered non-actionable subsidies.

But, if all non-specific subsidies are non-actionable subsidies, what about the converse case: are all non-actionable subsidies also non-specific? In other words, are there any specific subsidies that are also non-actionable subsidies? As pointed out

---

92 For further details on this issue, see *infra*, section 5.3.2.

93 The idea of introducing this trichotomous classification was not new to the Uruguay Round; it had even been put forward, although later withdrawn, by the US during the negotiation of the Tokyo Round Subsidies Code. See Croome (1995) *supra* n. 6, p. 75.

elsewhere,[94] the presence of three classes of practices under Article 8.2(a), (b) and (c) excludes an affirmative answer to this question. These paragraphs govern the issues, respectively, of assistance for research activities, assistance to disadvantaged regions, and assistance to promote adaptation of existing facilities to new environmental requirements, each subject to its respective set of conditions. As such, a subsidy that meets the test of specificity may still be non-actionable if the enumerated conditions are also satisfied.[95] This leads to the following conclusion: all non-specific subsidies are non-actionable subsidies, while not all non-actionable subsidies are non-specific.

It is noteworthy, however, that a specific non-actionable subsidy that is consistent with the criteria laid down in paragraph 2 of Article 8 may still cause adverse effects to the domestic industry of another Member. In such cases, the fact that the practices are termed "non-actionable" does not simply mean that the affected Member remains without remedies. Rather, Article 9 of the Subsidies Agreement provides that such a Member may request consultations with the subsidizing Member, but only if one more condition is met – that the adverse effects which resulted from the non-actionable subsidy must be "serious" and "such as to cause damage which would be difficult to repair".[96]

Under such circumstances, the Agreement imposes on the subsidizing party an obligation to enter into consultations "as quickly as possible" with the object of clarifying the facts and arriving at a mutually acceptable solution.[97] Failing this, after sixty days of the request for consultations, the requesting Member has the right to refer the matter to the Committee on Subsidies and Countervailing Measures. Unlike all other cases of subsidies under the SCM Agreement, such a Member does not go to the Dispute Settlement Body for such problems. That is perhaps the reason why these subsidies are officially called "non-actionable". However, the Committee, if it determines that the alleged effects exist, has the power to recommend, within 120 days, that the subsidizing Member "modify this programme in such a way as to remove these effects".[98] Moreover, in the event that the recommendation is not followed within six months, the Committee is required to authorize the requesting Member to take appropriate countermeasures commensurate with the nature and degree of the effects determined to exist.[99] Non-actionability in this specific case does not therefore guarantee against challenge. In a way, it is only the venue of the challenge, and the degree of injury required therefor, that is different.[100] Moreover, non-actionability is also provisional – it was only for the first five years of life of the SCM Agreement that these

---

94 See *supra* section 5.3.
95 The conditions laid down by Article 8.2(a), (b) and (c) are discussed in greater detail *infra* chapter 10.
96 See Article 9.1 of the SCM Agreement.
97 See Article 9.2 of the SCM Agreement.
98 Article 9.4 of the SCM Agreement.
99 See Article 9.4 of the SCM Agreement.
100 The difference should not, however, be underestimated; it is something that can have important practical consequences. After all, as the GATT panel on *Korea Beef* rightly put it in 1989, the difference between panels and the Subsidies Committee is a difference between examination of case by "a panel of independent experts" and consideration by "a committee of government representatives." See *Republic*

subsidies were considered non-actionable. Article 31 of the Agreement made the extension of the provisions of Articles 8 and 9 conditional upon a positive decision to that effect by the Subsidies Committee. It was reported, however, that as of 31 December 1999, no consensus was reached in the Subsidies Committee on the subject and the provisions lapsed as from 1 January 2000.[101]

However, when it comes to the unilateral remedy of countervailing duties, the term "non-actionable" takes its literal meaning. Members are not allowed to take countervailing measures against a "non-actionable subsidy".[102] It is thus possible to conclude that there is only one means available to a Member affected by a non-actionable subsidy granted by another Member – the use of remedies authorized by the Subsidies Committee.

5.3.3 Actionable Subsidies

The second category of subsidies under the SCM Agreement is that of "actionable subsidies" and covers subsidies that are not prohibited per se but against which actions may be taken (be it in the form of unilateral countervailing measures or by resorting to the institutional dispute settlement system of the WTO) depending on their "trade effects". The principle appears quite clearly under Article 5: "No Member should cause, through the use of any subsidy referred to in paragraphs 1 and 2 of Article 1, adverse effects to the interests of other Members". The concept of "adverse effects" referred to under this provision encompasses three different scenarios: (a) injury to the domestic industry of another Member; (b) nullification or impairment of benefits accruing directly or indirectly to other Members under GATT 1994 in particular the benefits of concessions bound under Article II of GATT 1994; and (c) serious prejudice to the interests of another Member.[103]

This category of subsidies will be dealt with in greater detail later under chapter 10. The following few observations are included here only to make the picture more complete for present purposes. Firstly, it covers most subsidy practices that are often referred to in the literature as "domestic subsidies"[104]; secondly, these subsidies are not outlawed *per se* – they can be lawfully granted provided that no other Member suffers any adverse consequences against its interests in the sense of Articles 5 and 6

---

cont.
of Korea – Restrictions on Imports of Beef – Complaint by the United States, report of panel (L/6503 *BISD* 36S/268) adopted on 7 Nov. 1989, para 117.

[101] See *WTO Annual Report 2001*, p. 63.

[102] Footnote 36 to Article 10 provides, in relevant part, as follows: "The provisions of Parts III and V Countervailing Measures] shall not be invoked regarding measures considered non-actionable in accordance with the provisions of Part IV."

[103] Article 5(a)-(c) of the SCM Agreement. The footnotes added to these paragraphs confirm that these concepts are used in the same sense as other parts of the SCM Agreement as well as GATT 1994.

[104] What is said here about domestic subsidies should be understood to refer to domestic subsidy practices excluding the so-called "import substitution" subsidies which, by definition, may fall within domestic subsidies, but are explicitly prohibited just like export subsidies.

thereof; thirdly, all such subsidies with adverse effects to the interests of another Member are actionable at the initiation of the thus affected Member; and finally, the provisions of the SCM Agreement on actionable subsidies apply to agricultural products subject to the Agreement on Agriculture in general and Article 13 on due restraint in particular.[105]

5.3.4 *Prohibited Subsidies*

The category of "prohibited subsidies" covers two forms of practices: export subsidies, and subsidies provided on condition that the recipient uses domestic rather than imported goods. The latter are a form of "local content" requirements – often called "import substitution" subsidies. These two classes of subsidies are flatly prohibited, "except as provided in the Agreement on Agriculture."[106]

At least one common element appears clearly between these two classes of prohibited subsidies: both are directly related to the global market in the sense that a country, by doing the former, tries to ("unfairly") raise its competitive position in the world market, while in the case of the latter it tries to artificially curtail the amount of imports into its territory. As such, they are practices whose trade distortive effects can be felt on the international market rather directly. The following section looks more closely at the export subsidy discipline introduced by the SCM Agreement.

5.4 The Discipline of Export Subsidies

5.4.1 *Definition*

Article 3.1 of the SCM Agreement is the starting point for any issue involving export subsidies under the SCM Agreement. Article 3 provides as follows:

> "3.1 Except as provided in the Agreement on Agriculture, the following subsidies, within the meaning of Article 1, shall be prohibited:
> (a) subsidies contingent, in law or in fact[4], whether solely or as one of several other conditions, upon export performance, including those illustrated in Annex I[5];
> (b) subsidies contingent, whether solely or as one of several other conditions, upon the use of domestic over imported goods.
> 3.2 A Member shall neither grant nor maintain subsidies referred to in paragraph 1.

[4] This standard is met when the facts demonstrate that the granting of a subsidy, without having been made legally contingent upon export performance, is in fact tied to actual or anticipated exportation or

[105] For further discussion on this category of subsidies in relation to the provisions of the Agreement on Agriculture, see *infra* Section 10.

[106] Article 3.1 of the SCM Agreement.

export earnings. The mere fact that a subsidy is granted to enterprises which export shall not for that reason alone be considered to be an export subsidy within the meaning of this provision.

5 Measures referred to in Annex I as not constituting export subsidies shall not be prohibited under this or any other provision of this Agreement."

Strictly speaking, the SCM Agreement does not directly define the term "export subsidies". Article 3.1(a), which is the only provision in the SCM Agreement that is often taken as giving a definition of export subsidies, simply provides that "subsidies contingent, in law or in fact, whether solely or as one of several other conditions, upon export performance, including those illustrated in Annex I" shall be prohibited. Let alone defining it, this provision does not even employ the term "export subsidies" as such. As it stands, this provision only describes a class of subsidies that are prohibited. No name is given to them here other than the wider term "prohibited subsidies", which is the title of Part II of the SCM Agreement itself. It is in fact only in the footnotes (4 and 5) to Article 3.1(a) that we see the term "export subsidy" and "export subsidies" mentioned as such.

However, this situation has never created any problem in practice; at least not until now, and probably not even in the future. A number of Member countries, panels as well as the Appellate Body have already taken Article 3.1(a) of the SCM Agreement as a definition provision even without raising the matter as such.[107] An interesting example could be the report of the *FSC* panel, which simply stated that "Article 3.1(a) contains a definition of the concept of 'export subsidy'."[108] The curious side of this statement appears when one begins to see it in light of the reasons which the same panel gave in order to reject a US argument that the case should be seen under the provisions of GATT Article XVI:4. The panel stated, *inter alia*, that "[w]hile it is of course true that Article XVI:4 contained a prohibition on *what could be termed to be 'export subsidies', in fact the text of Article XVI:4 never uses the term 'export subsidy', much less defines it*."[109] Exactly the same can be said at least as far as the body text of Article 3.1(a) is concerned. One may of course argue that the two footnotes to this provision mention "export subsidies" and that they also form part of the text of Article 3.1(a).[110] That is indeed true. Yet, as we shall see in a while, the fact remains that even the footnotes only mention, and do not explicitly define, the term "export subsidies".

That said, the absence of any explicit statement on definition does not diminish

107 The following are just examples: In *Australia Leather*, the panel simply asks the question of whether the measures before it are "export subsidies *within the meaning of Article 3.1(a)* of the SCM Agreement" *Australia – Subsidies Provided to Producers and Exporters of Automotive Leather* report of the panel (WT/DS126/R) 25 May 1999, para. 9.46 (italics added); in *Canada Aircraft*, the EC argued, as a third party participant, that "Article 3.1(a) of the SCM Agreement and its footnote provide for a … *definition* of prohibited subsidies;" *Canada Aircraft*, report of the panel, *supra* n. 36, para. 7.3 (italics added); see also, *FSC*, report of the panel, *supra* n. 19, para. 7.35 for views of the EC (claimant), para. 4.661 for views of the US (defendant); and para. 5.9 for views of Canada (a third party participant).

108 *FSC*, report of the panel, *supra* n. 19, para. 7.81. Both parties as well as third party participants to this case agreed that Article 3.1(a) defines export subsidies as such.

109 Ibid., para. 7.81 (italics added).

110 As the *Australia Leather* panel rightly observed, "[t]he text of Article 3.1(a) also includes footnote 4." *Australia Leather*, report of the panel, *supra* n. 107, para. 9.55.

the definitional import of Article 3.1(a) of the SCM Agreement. Indeed, footnote 4 can at least serve as convincing proof that Article 3.1(a) is meant to be a definition provision as far as export subsidies are concerned. According to a relevant part of this footnote, "[t]he mere fact that a subsidy is granted to enterprises which export shall not for that reason alone be considered to be an *export subsidy within the meaning of this provision*."[111] This is more than an indication that Article 3.1(a) gives the meaning of export subsidies in the sense of the SCM Agreement. Furthermore, Article 3.1(a) itself also refers to, and incorporates, the text of Annex I of the SCM Agreement, which is entitled "Illustrative List of *Export Subsidies*."[112]

This view gets further support from a provision of the Agreement on Agriculture (i.e., one of the Multilateral Agreements forming part of the WTO Agreement just like that of the SCM Agreement) which defines the term using similar language. According to a pertinent part of Article 1(e) of the Agriculture Agreement, " 'export subsidies' refers to subsidies contingent upon export performance."[113] From all this, we can conclude that export subsidies indeed mean what Article 3.1(a) says: "subsidies contingent, in law or in fact, whether solely or as one of several other conditions, upon export performance."

Accordingly, an export subsidy is first and foremost a subsidy as that term is defined under Article 1 of the SCM Agreement. This, *inter alia*, means that for a measure to be an export subsidy, there must be a governmental or public financial contribution that confers a benefit on a recipient as those elements are understood in Article 1 of the SCM Agreement. What is more, once a measure is a subsidy in this sense, it becomes an export subsidy only if it is designed, in fact or in law, to promote exports. This is a broad definition. All subsidies aiming at the promotion of exports and whose provision is dependent on the recipients' contribution thereto are styled as export subsidies; they are also explicitly prohibited with one exception – export subsidies on agricultural products. The prohibition applies not only to those subsidy practices that are explicitly spelled out in law to be contingent on export performance (*de jure* contingent), but also to those that, despite a legal appearance of applicability regardless of export considerations, actually favour exports (*de facto* contingent). As the *Canada Aircraft* Panel observed, the contingency element here refers to conditionality – that the subsidy is dependent for its existence on export performance.[114] Two types of contingency are thus envisaged by Article 3.1(a) of the SCM Agreement: contingency in law and contingency in fact. On that basis, export subsidies are for present purposes divided into *de jure* and *de facto* export subsidies.

5.4.2 De jure v. De facto Export Subsidies

---

[111] Footnote 4, second sentence, to Article 3.1 of the SCM Agreement (italics added).

[112] See also footnote 5 to Article 3.1 of the SCM Agreement.

[113] Obviously, this commonality of terminology between Article 3.1(a) of the SCM Agreement and Article 1(e) of the Agreement on Agriculture can be anything but accidental.

[114] *Canada Aircraft*, report of the panel, *supra* n. 36, para. 9.331; see also *Canada Aircraft*, report of the Appellate Body, *supra* n. 31, para. 166.

A *de jure* export subsidy is one in which the granting of the subsidy is made explicitly contingent upon export performance and the conditionality element is stipulated in a legal instrument. As such, this is the easier of the two to prove because the only means of demonstrating the existence as well as the substance of such an export subsidy is through "the words of the relevant legislation, regulation or other legal instrument."[115] In *Canada Automotive*, there was an issue as to whether a *de jure* export subsidy necessarily requires an express stipulation of conditionality or whether an implied reference would suffice. Canada favoured a narrow construction and argued that a subsidy is contingent in law upon export performance "where the underlying legal instruments of that subsidy *expressly provide that the subsidy is available to enterprises only on condition of export performance*."[116] The EC, on the other hand, adopted a wider approach and contended that a subsidy is contingent in law upon export performance "where the requirement to export is stated expressly in the law *or is implicit in other requirements that are so stated in the law*".[117] The panel ruled in favour of the EC. According to the panel, export contingency in law refers to the situation where one can ascertain its existence "on the face of the law (or other relevant legal instrument) .... [A]n examination of the terms of the underlying legal instruments of the subsidy in question would suffice to determine whether or not export contingency in law exists. We do not mean by this, however, that the terms of the law must – as Canada suggests – 'expressly provide' that the subsidy is contingent upon export performance, but rather, that the existence of export contingency can be demonstrated on the basis of the law or other relevant legal instrument, without reference to external factual elements."[118] It can thus be concluded that a *de jure* export subsidy is one in which the contingency element derives from a legislative instrument regardless of whether it is express or implicit.

The conditionality element in a *de facto* export subsidy, on the other hand, does not have a legislative basis for its existence. The relevant law, if any, may appear neutral on the question of exportation – it may be framed such that all relevant enterprises are eligible for the subsidy irrespective of export performance considerations. However, this apparent legislative neutrality may not necessarily result in a factual neutrality in the actual process of administration of the subsidy. Mindful of this danger, "[t]he Uruguay Round negotiators have, through the prohibition against export subsidies that are contingent in fact upon export performance, sought to prevent circumvention of the prohibition against subsidies contingent *in law* upon export performance."[119]

This anti-circumvention objective was attained when it was agreed that "subsidies contingent ... in fact whether solely or as one of several other conditions, upon export performance" are prohibited. Cognizant of the difficulties involved in proving the *de facto* partiality of an otherwise impartial-looking legislation, footnote 4 to

---

[115] See *Canada Aircraft*, report of the Appellate Body, *supra* n. 31, para. 167.

[116] *Canada Automotive*, report of the panel *supra* n. 49, para. 10.178.

[117] Ibid.

[118] Ibid., para. 10.179.

[119] *Canada Aircraft*, report of the Appellate Body, *supra* n. 31, para. 167.

Article 3.1(a) goes a step further and provides that this standard is met "when the facts demonstrate that the granting of a subsidy, without having been made legally contingent upon export performance, is in fact tied to actual or anticipated exportation or export earnings." An important statement of caution then follows: "The mere fact that a subsidy is granted to enterprises which export shall not for that reason alone be considered to be an export subsidy within the meaning of this provision." Both elements of footnote 4 have a number of interpretative difficulties, and many have already been subject to contentious WTO disputes.

The first sentence of footnote 4 makes it clear that a *de facto* export contingency, by definition, can be demonstrated only by the assessment of facts; there is no legal instrument that can clearly, "on its face", demonstrate that the granting of the subsidy in question is dependent upon export performance. For, otherwise, it would have been a case of *de jure* contingency.[120] The question of what facts should be considered and the weight to be given to each of them is, of course, a matter to be decided on a case-by-case basis.[121] In *Australia Leather*, for instance, one of the conditions for the receiving firm to get a governmental grant was a "best endeavours" obligation to meet sales performance targets. But, because the Australian market was known to have been unable to absorb the firm's production, the Panel used it as one of the factual bases to hold that the grant was contingent on exportation. The panel thus found that "in order to expand its sales in a manner that would enable it to reach the sales performance targets ... set out in the contract, Howe [the receiving firm] would, of necessity, have to continue and probably increase exports. ... In our view, these facts effectively transform the sales performance targets into export performance targets. We thus consider that Howe's anticipated export performance was one of the conditions for the grant of the subsidies."[122]

Footnote 4 to Article 3.1 indicates that the requisite factual assessment for the determination of whether there exists a *de facto* export subsidy should be aimed at ascertaining three different "substantive elements": that a subsidy is being granted to a certain recipient; that the recipient is involved with actual or anticipated exportation or export earnings; and that a tie of conditionality exists between the two, i.e. that the existence of the former depends upon the latter.[123]

The first element requires that there be a scheme that qualifies as a subsidy in the sense that term is defined under Article 1 of the SCM Agreement. In this context, the Appellate Body has rejected an argument that a subsidy is contingent in fact upon export performance only when "the facts and circumstances are such that the recipient will reasonably know that there is a requirement to export."[124] The Appellate Body stated that what mattered was not the act or knowledge of the

[120] See, *inter alia*, Ibid., para. 167.

[121] See, *inter alia*, *Canada Aircraft*, report of the panel, *supra* n. 36, para. 9.337; and *Canada Aircraft*, report of the Appellate Body, *supra* n. 31, para. 169.

[122] *Australia Leather*, report of the panel, *supra* n. 107, para. 9.67. The panel further observed that "Given the export-dependent nature of Howe's business, and the size of the Australian market, these sales are, in our view, effectively export performance targets." Ibid., para. 9.71.

[123] See, for instance, *Canada Aircraft*, report of the Appellate Body, *supra* n. 31, para. 169.

recipient, but only that of the granting authority.[125]

According to the second element, the recipient should be involved with some form of export-related business capable of generating actual or anticipated exportation or export earnings.[126] And the relationship between the granting of the subsidy and the actual or anticipated export sales constitutes the third substantive element of footnote 4 – that the former must be "tied to" the latter. This is another way of saying that there should be a relationship of conditionality between them. In interpreting the type of relationship that is depicted by the term "tied to" in this footnote, the *Canada Aircraft* panel adopted what it called the "but for" test. According to this test, the factual evidence adduced must demonstrate that "had there been no expectation of export *sales* (i.e., '*exportation*' or '*export earnings'*) '*ensuing*' from the subsidy, the subsidy would not have been granted."[127] This, according to the panel, implies "a strong and direct link" between the grant of the subsidy and the creation or generation of export sales. The Appellate Body affirmed this interpretation and emphasized the point that "[a] subsidy may well be granted in the knowledge, or with the anticipation, that exports will result. Yet, that alone is not sufficient, because that alone is not proof that the granting of the subsidy is *tied to* the anticipation of exportation."[128]

In the words of the second sentence of footnote 4, "[t]he mere fact that a subsidy is granted to enterprises which export shall not for that reason alone be considered to be an export subsidy within the meaning of this provision."[129] An export subsidy thus needs more than a mere coincidence that the subsidy-recipients are engaged in export-related business. There should be the element of conditionality between the grant and the recipients' actual or anticipated export sales. Indeed, as the Appellate Body concisely put it, the second sentence of footnote 4 is "a specific expression of the requirement in the first sentence to demonstrate the 'tied to' requirement."[130] The export orientation of a recipient may only be taken into consideration as a "relevant fact, provided it is one of several facts which are considered and is not the only fact supporting a finding."[131] A statement made by another panel adds clarity here: the second sentence of footnote 4 of the SCM Agreement "does not preclude consideration of the fact that a company exports, or the level of its exports, in a

---

[124] Argument by Canada in Ibid., para. 170.

[125] The Appellate Body added a statement of caution as follows: "In finding that the knowledge of the recipient is not part of the legal standard of *de facto* export contingency, we do not suggest that relevant objective evidence relating to the recipient can never be considered by a panel." Ibid., footnote 100.

[126] The anticipated exportation aspect of this requirement has been interpreted to refer to "the *expectation* that exports will flow thereby." See *Canada Aircraft*, report of the panel, *supra* n. 36, para. 9.331 (italics added).

[127] *Canada Aircraft*, report of the panel, *supra* n. 36, para. 9.339 (italics in original); see also *Canada Aircraft*, report of the Appellate Body, *supra* n. 31, footnote 102.

[128] *Canada Aircraft*, report of the Appellate Body, *supra* n. 31, footnote 173 (emphasis in original).

[129] Second sentence of footnote 4 to Article 3.1(a).

[130] *Canada Aircraft*, report of the Appellate Body, *supra* n. 31, footnote 173.

[131] Ibid., footnote 173.

prohibited subsidy examination. Rather, it merely proscribes finding a prohibited export subsidy based solely upon the fact that a subsidy is granted to a company which exports."[132]

Just as the mere fact that a subsidy-recipient is involved with exportation does not qualify a subsidy as an export subsidy, neither does the mere presence of conditions (for granting it) in addition to exportation suffice to disqualify a measure from being an export subsidy. For a subsidy to become an export subsidy, export performance does not need to be the only condition for its provision; it only has to be one of those conditions. As rightly observed by the *Australia Leather* panel, Article 3.1(a) "recognizes that there may be multiple conditions for the grant or maintenance of a subsidy, and explicitly prohibits a subsidy if one of the conditions is that the subsidy is contingent ... upon export performance."[133]

To sum up, as the US convincingly argued in one case, "the distinction between the 'in law' and 'in fact' standard is that 'in law' subsidies are explicitly contingent, and 'in fact' subsidies are implicitly contingent, upon export performance."[134] The very practice of providing subsidies contingent upon export performance, regardless of any prior legislative measure to that effect, suffices for the purpose of invoking the prohibition of Article 3.1(a). To that end, as the *Australia Leather* panel rightly pointed out, "factors other than the specific legal or administrative arrangements governing the granting or maintenance of the subsidy in question must be considered in determining whether a subsidy is 'in fact' contingent upon export performance."[135]

5.5 Multilateral Remedies Available Against Prohibited Subsidies under the "Special or Additional Rules and Procedures on Dispute Settlement"

Thanks to the integrated nature of dispute settlement under the WTO Agreement, the starting point for issues regarding the settlement of disputes involving any of the "covered agreements" are Articles XXII and XXIII of GATT 1994 as elaborated and applied by the Dispute Settlement Understanding (the DSU). In principle, therefore, the general rules of dispute settlement under the system also apply to cases involving prohibited subsidies under Article 3 of the SCM Agreement.

However, the DSU being a generic agreement on dispute settlement applicable to all agreements under the WTO Agreement,[136] it also leaves some room for the particular features of the different "covered agreements" to be reflected in the dispute settlement process. This takes the form of agreement-specific complementary

---

[132] *Australia Leather,* report of the panel, *supra* n. 107, para. 9.66.

[133] Ibid., para.9.63.

[134] Ibid., para. 7.122.

[135] Ibid., para. 9.54.

[136] Article 1.1 of the Dispute Settlement Understanding, in its pertinent part, provides the following: "The rules and procedures of this Understanding shall apply to disputes brought pursuant to the consultation and dispute settlement rules and procedures of the Agreements listed in Appendix 1 to this Understanding, hereafter the 'covered agreements.'"

rules on dispute settlement, officially called the "special or additional rules and procedures". Thus, "while Article 1 of the DSU seeks to establish an integrated and comprehensive dispute settlement system for all of the covered agreements of the WTO Agreement as a whole", the special or additional provisions "are designed to deal with the particularities of dispute settlement relating to obligations arising under a specific covered agreement."[137]

Such "special or additional rules and procedures on dispute settlement" have been made for a number of covered agreements, including the SCM Agreement. An exhaustive list of these rules has been included in Appendix 2 to the Dispute Settlement Understanding. There are no any such "special or additional rules and procedures" in the Agreement on Agriculture. Apparently, this would mean that the provisions of the DSU are the sole dispute settlement rules applicable to agricultural disputes. In other words, the rules of the DSU appear to apply to agricultural matters without being complemented by any agreement-specific additional rules and procedures on dispute settlement. This is not, however, the case. There is plenty of room for the "special or additional rules and procedures" in other covered agreements, particularly those of the SCM Agreement, to be applied to agricultural trade issues. But, first, the relationship between the provisions of the DSU and those "special or additional rules and procedures" needs to be examined more closely.

The integrated dispute settlement system of the WTO, prescribed under the first paragraph of the first Article of the DSU, accommodates the agreement-specific rules and procedures of dispute settlement by providing that DSU provisions "shall apply subject to such special or additional rules and procedures on dispute settlement contained in the covered agreements."[138] Further elaborating on this point, DSU Article 1.2 states that "to the extent that there is a *difference* between the rules and procedures of this Understanding and the special or additional rules and procedures set forth in Appendix 2, the special or additional rules and procedures in Appendix 2 *shall prevail*."[139] Stated within the context of the SCM Agreement on export subsidies, this means, for instance, that in cases involving export subsidies, both the DSU as well as the provisions of Article 4 apply together. Given the integrated nature of the system, Article 4 of the SCM Agreement is not there to replace the relevant provisions of the DSU; rather it is meant to complement the DSU with rules that can reflect the particularities inherent in export subsidy disputes.[140] As the Appellate Body ruled in *Guatemala Cement*, the special or additional rules and procedures of a particular covered agreement should be seen "as fitting together with the generally applicable rules and procedures of the DSU to form a comprehensive, integrated dispute settlement system for the WTO Agreement."[141]

However, in case of *differences* between the rules of the DSU and those of the "special or additional rules and procedures", the latter prevail. The *differences* here

---

[137] *Guatemala cement*, report of the Appellate Body, *supra* n. 23, para. 66.
[138] Article 1.2 of the DSU (italics added).
[139] Article 1.2 of the DSU (italics added).
[140] See *Guatemala Cement*, report of the Appellate Body, *supra* n. 23, para. 67.
[141] Ibid., para. 66.

are not, however, referring to any differences that may exist between any two sets of provisions. Differences in such cases are simply presumed – they explain the very need for the "special or additional rules and procedures on dispute settlement" which are designed to deal with the particularities of every case. In this connection, the Appellate Body has once said, "if there is no 'difference', then the rules and procedures of the DSU apply together with the special or additional provisions of the covered agreement."[142] If this statement is taken to mean what it says on the surface, it amounts to saying that the rules and procedures of the DSU apply together with *themselves* – a logical anomaly. The important point to bear in mind here is that not all *differences* entail the making of a choice; not all *differences* necessitate the question of one prevailing over the other. It is only when that *difference* amounts to a conflict, i.e. when the application of the one necessarily results in a violation of the other, that the question of which prevailing over which arises. It is in this sense that the use of the term difference should be understood in both the DSU as well as the above-quoted Appellate Body statement. The following paragraph from the same Appellate Body report rightly summarizes the idea:

> "[I]t is only where the provisions of the DSU and the special or additional rules and procedures of a covered agreement *cannot* be read as *complementing* each other that the special or additional provisions are to *prevail*. A special or additional provision should only be found to *prevail* over a provision of the DSU in a situation where adherence to the one provision will lead to a violation of the other provision, that is, in the case of a *conflict* between them. An interpreter must, therefore, identify an *inconsistency* or a *difference* between a provision of the DSU and a special or additional provision of a covered agreement *before* concluding that the latter *prevails* and that the provision of the DSU does not apply."[143]

This intricate relationship between the provisions of the DSU and the "special or additional rules and procedures" of the covered agreements, which is primarily enshrined in Article 1.2 of the DSU, also finds its corollary in specific provisions of the specific covered agreements themselves.[144] In the case of the SCM Agreement, Article 30 provides that "[t]he provisions of Articles XXII and XXIII of the GATT 1994 as elaborated and applied by the Dispute Settlement Understanding shall apply to consultations and the settlement of disputes under this Agreement, *except as otherwise specifically provided herein*."[145] Stated differently, this means that both Agreements have specific provisions addressing the same issues; and to the extent they are compatible with one another, they shall be implemented in their

---

[142] Ibid., para. 65.

[143] Ibid. (italics in original).

[144] See for instance Article 17.1 of the Anti-Dumping Agreement; Article 19.1 of the Customs Valuation Agreement; Article 30 of the SCM Agreement; etc. The typical expression used in these provisions looks like the following, which itself is taken from the identical wording of the respective provisions of the Anti-Dumping and Customs Valuation Agreements: "Except as otherwise provided herein, the DSU is applicable to consultations and the settlement of disputes under this Agreement."

[145] Article 30 of the SCM Agreement (italics added).

togetherness. However, whenever there are *differences* which amount to inconsistencies, the dispute settlement provisions of the SCM Agreement prevail over those of the DSU.

The question now is the following: how do these overriding "special or additional rules and procedures" of the SCM Agreement apply to agricultural trade issues? In the absence of any such "special or additional rules and procedures" within the Agriculture Agreement itself, should they not be governed solely by the provisions of the DSU rather than any other specialized agreement? As stated already, the answer lies in the fact that the Agreement on Agriculture is not a self-contained or stand-alone Agreement, with relations limited just to the DSU. Indeed, the provisions of GATT 1994 as well as other Multilateral Trade Agreements in Annex 1A to the WTO Agreement also apply to agricultural trade issues. When this happens, the relationship between provisions of the DSU and those of the "special or additional rules and procedures on dispute settlement" depicted above finds its parallel in the relationship between the provisions of the other Agreements and those of the Agriculture Agreement: the former apply to agricultural trade issues, but subject to the provisions of the latter.[146] Stated in the present context, the "special or additional rules and procedures" contained in the SCM Agreement concerning export subsidies in general are, in principle, also applicable to agricultural export subsidies. Article 13 of the Agriculture Agreement on "due restraint" is the only provision that expressly limits the scope of application of the provisions of GATT 1994 and the SCM Agreement in the area of agricultural export subsidies. And even that is both conditional (applicable only if the measure fully conforms to the export subsidy provisions of the Agreement on Agriculture) and provisional (limited to a 9 year implementation period from 1995). Hence, a closer look at the salient features of the relevant "special or additional rules and procedures on dispute settlement" of the SCM Agreement is in order here.

Article 4 of the SCM Agreement is one of the "special or additional rules and procedures", and the pertinent one for present purposes here, referred to under Article 1.2 of the DSU and included in Appendix 2 thereof.[147] As enshrined in this Article, in the area of export subsidies (and, of course, the larger domain of prohibited subsidies), we have a special set of dispute settlement rules and procedures whose main features include "an expedited timetable for action by the Dispute Settlement Body" and a requirement of further specificity in the substance of recommendations made by the panels. One may find a general sense of this difference by simply looking at paragraph 12 of Article 4 of the SCM Agreement: "For purposes of disputes conducted pursuant to this Article, except for time periods specifically prescribed in this Article, time periods applicable under the DSU for the conduct of such disputes shall be half the time prescribed therein."[148] In order to have a more complete picture of this expedited procedure, we need to have a closer

[146] See Article 21.1 of the Agreement on Agriculture.

[147] Appendix 2 covers Article 4.2 through Article 4.12, i.e. excluding only the consultation provision of para.1.

look at the provisions of Article 4 of the SCM Agreement vis-à-vis the relevant provisions of the DSU.

5.5.1 Consultation

The first step in the process of dispute settlement is consultation, whose primary purpose is to avoid a dispute from arising.[149] Article 4.1 of the SCM Agreement, which incidentally is not part of the "special or additional rules and procedures on dispute settlement",[150] provides that Members may request consultations with other Members if they have reason to believe that those other Members grant a prohibited subsidy. In such cases, while it is the obligation of the requesting party to include in its request "a statement of available evidence with regard to the existence and nature of the subsidy",[151] the requested party is obliged to enter into consultations "as quickly as possible."[152]

The corresponding rights and obligations of parties in similar position under the Dispute Settlement Understanding are as follows. Article 4.4 of the DSU requires of complainants to submit their consultation requests in writing "including identification of the measures at issue and an indication of the legal basis of the complaint."[153] The requested party in turn has the obligation not only to "accord sympathetic consideration to and afford adequate opportunity for consultation",[154] but also to reply to the request within ten days after its receipt and to enter into consultations "in good faith within a period of no more than thirty days from the date of the request."[155]

There are two major points of difference here. Firstly, while a party requesting consultations under the DSU has only to identify the measures at issue and indicate the legal basis of its complaint, one who requests consultations under Article 4 of the SCM Agreement is further required to include a "statement of available evidence" showing the existence and nature of the subsidy.[156] This requirement has been interpreted by the *Australia Leather* panel to refer to an obligation on the part of the complainant to express "in words of the facts at its disposal at the time it requests consultations in support of the conclusion that it has ... 'reason to believe that a prohibited subsidy is being granted or maintained.'"[157] This interpretation has also been repeated, almost verbatim, by the *FSC* panel.[158] What is particularly interesting

---

[148] Article 4.12 of the SCM Agreement, (italics added). On the specificity required of panels in their recommendations, see Article 4.7 of the SCM Agreement.

[149] See E-U. Petersmann, *The GATT/WTO Dispute Settlement System: International Law, International Organizations and Dispute Settlement* (Kluwer 1997), p. 68.

[150] See Appendix 2 to the DSU, which identifies only paragraphs 2 to 12 of Article 4 of the SCM Agreement; it is discussed here only for the sake of completeness.

[151] Article 4.2 of the SCM Agreement.

[152] Article 4.3 of the SCM Agreement.

[153] Article 4.4 of the DSU.

[154] Article 4.2 of the DSU.

[155] Article 4.3 of the DSU.

[156] See *FSC*, report of the Appellate Body, *supra* n. 45, para. 161.

about this latter case is that the panel took the complainant's reference to the specific legal provisions which that party set out to challenge as possible "statement of available evidence." The panel stated in particular that "there may be cases where the only evidence relied on by a complainant is a statute, regulation or other legal instrument. In this case, in fact, the primary evidence on which the European Communities relies is Sections 921 through 927 of the US Internal Revenue Code and related measures. The European Communities request for consultations, in as much as it specifically refers to these materials, contains an expression in words of evidence with regard to the existence and nature of the subsidy in question."[159] The Appellate Body observed in this regard that "it is available evidence of the character of the measure as a 'subsidy' that must be indicated, and not merely evidence of the existence of the measure. We would have preferred that the Panel give less relaxed treatment to this important distinction."[160]

In any case, the requirement to include a "statement of available evidence" showing the existence and nature of a prohibited subsidy is an additional obligation imposed upon a complainant under the SCM Agreement for the sake of expediting the dispute settlement process.[161] As an obligation on the complaining party, this requirement may constitute an advantage for the defendant. Indeed, as the *Canada Dairy* panel rightly pointed out, Article 4.2 of the SCM Agreement is "a provision which may work to the advantage of the defending party."[162] However, the dispute settlement experience on the matter so far, albeit rather limited, confirms that attempts made by defending countries to exploit this advantage have been more of a failure. Two notable examples in this respect are *Australia Leather* and *FSC*, which will be briefly discussed in turn.

In *Australia Leather*, Australia argued, *inter alia*, that the panel had to terminate the proceedings entirely, or, in the alternative, disregard during the process "all facts and arguments not explicitly set out in the request for consultations."[163] These arguments were based on Australia's assertion that the US request for consultations did not comply with the requirements of Article 4.2 of the SCM Agreement, which,

---

[157] Australia Leather, report of the panel, *supra* n. 107, para. 9.19.

[158] See *FSC*, report of the panel, *supra* n. 19, para. 7.5. The panel added that, "[o]n the basis of the ordinary meaning of Article 4.2, it is evident that a complainant must identify, but need not annex, available evidence to its request for consultations." Ibid.

[159] Ibid., para. 7.6.

[160] *FSC*, report of the Appellate Body, *supra* n. 45, para. 161.

[161] The essence of this requirement appears clearer if it is seen in light of the requirements which exist under the "standard" dispute settlement process. As summarized by the *Australia Leather* panel, "in dispute settlement proceedings pursuant to a normal schedule, a complaining Member is not even required to include a statement of the facts and arguments in a request for establishment of a panel – which comes considerably later in the dispute settlement process, after a consultation request has been made and after the parties have consulted. The complaining party is required only to identify the claims concerning the matter at issue; the facts and arguments on which it relies to establish its case must be submitted only in the first and subsequent submissions of the party to the panel." *Australia Leather*, report of the panel, *supra* n. 107, para. 9.20.

[162] *Canada dairy*, report of the panel, *supra* n. 19, para. 7.139.

[163] *Australia Leather*, report of the panel, *supra* n. 107, para. 9.16.

in its view "imposes an obligation on the complainant to disclose, in its request for consultations, not only facts, but also the argumentation why such facts lead the complainant to believe there is a violation of Article 3.1."[164] The panel rejected this argument stating that "[t]he ordinary meaning of the phrase 'include a statement of available evidence' does not, on its face, require disclosure of arguments in the request for consultations. Nothing in the context or object and purpose of Article 4.2 ... suggests a different conclusion."[165] Also noteworthy is the panel's rejection of another Australian contention to limit the scope of the evidence that the panel could consider only to that which had been submitted by the complainant (the US) at the stage of the request for consultations.[166]

In *FSC*, the US requested the panel to dismiss the EC claim under Article 3 of the SCM Agreement due to the latter's alleged failure "to include in its request for consultations a statement of available evidence with regard to the existence and nature of the subsidy in question, as it was required to do by Article 4.2 of the SCM Agreement."[167] However, not only did the panel hold that the EC had satisfied the said requirement,[168] it also went further and stated the following:

> "Even assuming that the European Communities' request for consultations does not contain a statement of available evidence, ... the sole prerequisite to requesting establishment of a panel is that consultations have been held or requested to be held and that the relevant specified time-period has elapsed. We found no specific provisions either in the DSU or Article 4 of the SCM Agreement requiring a panel to dismiss a claim under Article 3 of the SCM Agreement because the complaining Member failed to respect the requirement that the request for consultations contain a statement of available evidence."[169]

The Appellate Body agreed with the conclusion of the panel on this point, but on a different reasoning. The Appellate Body relied mainly on what it saw as an unacceptable delay in the timing of the US objection as well as on the principle of good faith. It emphasized that the principle of good faith "requires that responding Members seasonably and promptly bring claimed procedural deficiencies to the attention of the complaining Member, and to the DSB or the Panel, so that corrections, if needed, can be made to resolve disputes. The procedural rules of WTO dispute settlement are designed to promote, not the development of litigation techniques, but simply the fair, prompt and effective resolution of trade disputes."[170]

---

[164] Ibid., para. 9.17.

[165] See Ibid., para. 9.18.

[166] See Ibid., para. 9.27.

[167] *FSC*, report of the panel, *supra* n. 19, para. 4.1; see also para. 7.1.

[168] The relevant part of the European Communities' request for consultations in this case stated: "The European Communities wish to convey to the United States of America a request for consultations under Article 4 of the ... [the DSU], Article XXIII:1 GATT 1994, and Article 4 of the [... SCM Agreement] with respect to Sections 921-927 of the Internal Revenue Code and related measures establishing special tax treatment for 'Foreign Sales Corporations' (FSC)." WT/DS108/1, 28 November 1997.

[169] *FSC*, report of the panel, *supra* n. 19, para. 7.7 (footnotes omitted).

While the panel's conclusion not to dismiss the case for lack of "specific provisions either in the DSU or Article 4 of the SCM Agreement" would raise the fundamental question of how the dispute settlement system could ever enforce compliance with this mandatory requirement of Article 4.2, the reasoning of the Appellate Body has the virtue of effectively prescribing the requirement to bring claimed procedural deficiencies "seasonably and promptly." In general, however, the rationale behind the "special or additional rules and procedures on dispute settlement" in the area of export subsidies is to expedite the process so that the alleged export subsidy, if found, would be withdrawn at the earliest possible opportunity. This is done primarily for the benefit of the complaining party, and, of course, ultimately for the benefit of the entire multilateral trading system. As the primary beneficiary of this "fast-track" process, it is in the interest of the complainant to comply with the minimum that is required of it under that provision. Failure to do so would simply deprive it of the benefit of the expedited process, for it might turn out to be a practical necessity due to the lack of appropriate evidence at the appropriate time. Furthermore, a requirement that responding parties bring whatever procedural deficiencies in the request for consultations at the earliest practicable moment also enhances the efficiency of the disputes process.

A second area of difference between the "special or additional rules and procedures" of Article 4 of the SCM Agreement and the provisions of the DSU lies in the length of the deadlines set for the requested party to enter into consultations.[171] This limit under Article 4 of the SCM Agreement is simply "as quickly as possible", while that under the DSU is a maximum of thirty days. Needless to say, the "as quickly as possible" deadline is a rather vague standard. However, given the fact that the purpose of the SCM Agreement on the matter is to provide for an accelerated dispute settlement procedure, one has to interpret this phrase to mean at least less than the thirty-day maximum allowed under the DSU. This purpose-oriented interpretation gets further support and more precision from two other provisions of the SCM Agreement itself.

Firstly, Article 4.12 provides that time periods not specifically prescribed therein are to be taken to mean half the corresponding time prescribed by the DSU for the same purpose. This would mean that the thirty-day maximum prescribed for entry into consultations under the DSU comes down to fifteen days for purposes of disputes involving prohibited subsidies brought under Article 4 of the SCM Agreement. A question may be raised as to whether or not the "as quickly as possible" expression represents a "time period specifically prescribed" in the sense of Article 4.12 of the SCM Agreement. The issue never appeared before panels thus far.

---

[170] *FSC*, report of the Appellate Body, *supra* n. 45, para. 166.

[171] The difference in timing applies to almost all stages of the process. Parties are, however, free to extend, by mutual agreement, any time periods set by Article 4. See footnote 6 to Article 4.4 of the SCM Agreement. One example of such an exercise is the agreement between Canada and Brazil to extend until 2 August 1999 the time-period provided in Article 4.9 of the SCM Agreement for the Appellate Body to issue its decision in the appeal. See *Canada Aircraft*, report of the Appellate Body, *supra* n. 31, para. 4.

However, analogous situations have arisen under the closely-worded "without delay" standard of Article 4.7 of the SCM Agreement. The *Australia Leather* panel considered this latter expression as a time period "specifically prescribed in this Article."[172] The analogy from this case may lead to the conclusion that the "as quickly as possible" expression under Article 4.3 also falls under "time-periods specifically prescribed in this Article" in the sense of Article 4.12 of the SCM Agreement. The *Australia Leather* panel took this position to come up with a 90-day withdrawal period, which is significantly shorter than the seven and one-half months period that would have resulted from applying the general rules of Article 4.12 of the SCM Agreement. The Appellate Body also adopted this very interpretation to affirm a similar ruling by the *Brazil Aircraft* panel for the withdrawal period to be 90 days.[173] In either case, therefore, the time limit set under Article 4.3 may not exceed fifteen days.

The second line of reasoning appears not only to confirm this view, but also to push it further down to less than fifteen days. It bases itself on Article 4.4 of the SCM Agreement, which allows the complainant to refer the matter to the DSB for the immediate establishment of a panel "if no mutually acceptable solution has been reached within thirty days of the request for consultations." Thus, what has been set by the DSU for entry into consultations[174] is set by the SCM Agreement for the conclusion of the consultations. On the basis of these two grounds, we can conclude that the "as quickly as possible" requirement for the requested party to enter into consultations cannot be interpreted to allow that party more than fifteen days from the date of the request.

5.5.2 Establishment and Composition of Panels

A complainant under Article 4 of the SCM Agreement is entitled to refer the matter to the DSB for an immediate establishment of a panel if no mutually acceptable solution has been reached within thirty days of the request for consultations.[175] The corresponding time limit for a complainant under the DSU is sixty days after the request for consultations.[176] While a complainant under the DSU may normally[177] request for the establishment of a panel only if a mutually acceptable settlement does not come within 60 days of the request, one who complains against a prohibited export subsidy has the right to do this within half the time prescribed by the former, i.e. thirty days. Another important point of difference is that while the DSB is

[172] See *Australia Leather*, report of the panel, *supra* n. 107, para. 10.6.
[173] *Brazil – Export Financing Programme for Aircraft*, report of the Appellate Body (WT/DS46/AB/R) 2 August 1999, para. 192.
[174] See DSU Article 4.3.
[175] See Article 4.4 of the SCM Agreement.
[176] Exceptionally, however, a party proceeding under the DSU may be allowed to refer a case to the DSB for the establishment of a panel if the requested Member does not respond within ten days or does not enter into consultations within a period of no more than thirty days from the date of the request. See Article 4.3 of the DSU.

obliged to establish a panel immediately after a request is made to it under Article 4 of the SCM Agreement, in case of requests made under the DSU, the DSB has the power to postpone establishment until its meeting following that at which the request appears as an item on its agenda.[178] In both cases, the DSB can refuse to establish a panel only if there is a consensus not to do so – a "negative consensus" as it is often called. Since the complaining party is also a member of the DSB, a negative consensus is virtually impossible to be reached in any given case.

According to the DSU, the thus-established panels should be composed, at the latest, within thirty days from their establishment.[179] A complainant under the DSU can have a panel established and composed within a period of about 90 days[180] from the day of its consultation request. On the other hand, Article 4 of the SCM Agreement does not directly address the issue of composition of panels. Application of the general rule of Article 4.12 leads to the conclusion that the thus-established panels have to be composed within a maximum of fifteen days of their establishment. Seen in light of the fifteen-day limit set for panels established under the "special or additional rules and procedures" of the SCM Agreement applicable to "actionable subsidies",[181] a fifteen-day limit for prohibited subsidies may appear even excessive. However, as Article 4.12 is the governing provision on the issue, it is difficult to reach a different conclusion. This therefore brings the total length of time between request for consultations and the composition of panels under the SCM Agreement to 45 days.

Another unique feature of dispute settlement under Article 4 of the SCM Agreement is that of the Permanent Group of Experts (the PGE) – an organ composed of five independent persons qualified in the field of subsidies and trade relations established by the Committee on Subsidies and Countervailing Measures

---

[177] There are of course special cases of urgency where this process may be even quicker under the DSU than that prescribed for export subsidies under the SCM Agreement. Issues involving perishable goods are a good example. Article 4.8 of the DSU provides the following: "In cases of urgency, including those which concern perishable goods, Members shall enter into consultations within a period of no more than ten days from the date of the request. If the consultations have failed to settle the dispute within a period of twenty days after the request, the complaining party may request the establishment of a panel." And Article 4.9 pushes this special treatment further and provides that, in such cases, "the parties to the dispute, panels and the appellate body shall make every effort to accelerate the proceedings to the greatest extent possible."

[178] See Article 6.1 of the DSU.

[179] This thirty-day limit is a result of the following: under Article 8.7 of the DSU, if there is no agreement on the composition of the panellists within twenty days from the establishment of the panel, the Director-General of the WTO is required to form a panel as soon as possible and the DSB Chairman should inform the Members about the composition of the panel "no later than ten days from the date he or she receives such a request."

[180] "About ninety days" because under Article 6.1 of the DSU, the DSB can postpone establishment of the panel until its next meeting. Since the thirty-day limit for the composition of the panel is counted from the establishment date, such a postponement may also postpone the limit for the composition of the panels by the same amount of time.

[181] Article 7.4 of the SCM Agreement provides the following: "The composition of the panel and its terms of reference shall be established within fifteen days from the date when it is established." Note that Article 7.2 through 7.10 is one of the "special or additional rules and procedures" identified in Appendix 2 to the DSU.

(the Subsidies Committee) that may have an unquestionable power to determine on the existence or otherwise of a prohibited subsidy.[182] Panels have the discretion to refer to the PGE questions as to whether a measure under dispute is a prohibited subsidy; but, once they have exercised their discretion in favour of making the requests, they are bound by whatever decision the PGE may take.[183] There is nothing in the DSU similar to the PGE of the SCM Agreement.

5.5.3 *Submission of Panel Report*

Article 12.8 of the DSU stipulates the general principle in this regard as follows: "the period in which the panel shall conduct its examination, from the time the composition and terms of reference of the panel have been agreed upon to the time when the final report is provided to the parties to the dispute shall, as a general rule, not exceed six months."[184] This general rule thus sets the time between establishment of the panel and the final report at a maximum of seven months, i.e. the possible thirty-day period between the establishment of the panel and its composition and the six-month period between the composition of the panel and its submission of the final report. The DSU, however, allows some room for flexibility here. Accordingly, if and when the panel considers that it cannot provide its report within the six-month limit, "it shall inform the DSB in writing of the reasons for the delay together with an estimate of the period within which it will submit its report."[185] However, this same provision adds that "in no case should the period from the establishment of the panel to the submission of the report to the Members exceed nine months." The difference in the benchmark between these two deadlines is worth noticing – the general rule of Article 12.8 counts the six-month period from the date of composition of the panel, while the exception under Article 12.9 starts its nine-month limit from the date of the establishment of the panel. Depending on the length of time it takes to compose the panels after their establishment, the additional time allowed under Article 12.9 may vary between a minimum of two months (i.e. in cases where panels are composed thirty days after their establishment) to a maximum period of three months (i.e. in cases where establishment and composition of them take place on the same day).

The corresponding time limit for prohibited subsidy cases brought under the SCM Agreement is set at ninety days from the date of composition of panels.[186] No additional time is allowed under the SCM Agreement.

5.5.4 *Adoption of Panel Report*

[182] See Article 24.3 and 24.4 on its establishment and Article 4.5 regarding the specific powers vested in it concerning prohibited subsidies. The Rules of Procedure drafted by the PGE and submitted to the Subsidies Committee remained unapproved until very recently. See *WTO Annual Report 2001*, p. 63.

[183] See Article 4.5 of the SCM Agreement.

[184] For urgent cases, this time is set at three months. See Article 12.8 of the DSU.

[185] Article 12.9 of the DSU.

[186] Article 4.6 of the SCM Agreement. For more on this, see *Canada Dairy*, report of the panel, *supra* n. 19, para. 7.139.

Once the final panel report is issued, there are two possibilities – either it will be submitted to the DSB to be considered for adoption[187] or parties may lodge an appeal to the Appellate Body.[188] If the former, the report is adopted via a near automatic procedure within a maximum of sixty days of its issuance.[189] The only condition for it not to be adopted is if the DSB achieves a negative consensus – a consensus not to adopt the report. Once again, given the fact that the parties to the dispute are also members of the DSB, at least the winning party is expected to support adoption – thus, in effect, having a veto power against non-adoption possibilities.

The corresponding time limit for the adoption of a panel report in a prohibited subsidy case under the SCM Agreement is thirty days from its day of issuance.[190] The conditions for non-adoption of a report under the SCM Agreement are the same as those under the DSU.

5.5.5 Appellate Review

It has become one of the important features of dispute settlement under the WTO, and one of its significant contributions to general international law, that parties to a dispute may appeal a panel decision for review. To that end, a standing Appellate Body has been established by virtue of Article 17.1 of the DSU. As stated under Article 17.6 of the DSU, parties may appeal only on issues of law covered in the panel report and legal interpretations developed by the report.

The Appellate Body is generally required to issue its decision within sixty days from the date a party to a dispute "formally notifies its intent to appeal."[191] In exceptional cases, this deadline may be extended to ninety days. The corresponding time limit for prohibited subsidy cases brought under the SCM Agreement is generally thirty and exceptionally sixty days on the same benchmark.[192]

5.5.6 Adoption of Appellate Report

Article 17.14 of the DSU sets the time limit for adoption by the DSB of the appellate

---

[187] See Article 16 of the DSU.

[188] See Article 17.4 of the DSU. According to this provision, the right of appeal is limited to the parties to a dispute; it is not allowed for third party participants to lodge an appeal on their own. However, once the parties to the dispute bring a case before the Appellate Body, third parties expressing interest are given the right to make their own written submissions and also have the right to be heard by the Appellate Body. Moreover, Article 17.6 restricts the appeal to "issues of law covered in the panel report and legal interpretations developed by the panel."

[189] See Article 16.4 of the DSU. A footnote to this paragraph stresses the importance of this deadline by providing that "[i]f a meeting of the DSB is not scheduled within this period at a time that enables the requirements of paragraphs 1 and 4 of Article 16 to be met, a meeting of the DSB shall be held for this purpose."

[190] See Article 4.8 of the SCM Agreement.

[191] Article 17.5 of the DSU.

[192] See Article 4.9 of the SCM Agreement.

report at thirty days from its issuance. Here again, the DSB is required to hold a meeting for the purpose in case it has not been scheduled during that period.[193] The corresponding time period for adoption by the DSB of the appellate report in a prohibited subsidy case under the SCM Agreement is twenty days of its issuance.[194] In line with the DSU, the SCM Agreement also provides that "if a meeting of the DSB is not scheduled during this period, such a meeting of the DSB shall be held for this purpose."[195]

The following table summarizes the preceding comparative survey of the dispute settlement rules of the DSU and the SCM Agreement on export subsidies.

Table 1: Summary of Time Limits for the Settlement of Disputes under the Dispute Settlement Understanding (DSU) and Article 4 of the SCM Agreement

Stages in a Dispute Settlement Process	**DSU**	**SCM Agreement**
Entry into consultations	30 days from request therefor	"as quickly as possible"
Panel establishment request	60 days from consultation request	30 days from consultation
Composition of panels	30 days from panel establishment	15 days from panel establishment[a]
Submission of panel report	Nine months from panel establishment	Ninety days from panel composition
Adoption of panel report	Sixty days from issuance of report	Thirty days from issuance of report
Submission of appellate report	Ninety days from formal notification of appeal by a party	Sixty days from formal notification of appeal by a party
Adoption of appellate report	30 days from date of issuance	20 days from date of issuance

[a] Deduced on the basis of Article 4.12 of the SCM Agreement.

5.5.7 Differences in "Objectives" and their Ramifications

So far we have seen mainly two types of differences which exist between the "standard" and the "special or additional" rules and procedures on dispute settlement under the DSU and the SCM Agreement respectively – those pertaining mainly to the timing of production of evidence and the speed of the proceedings. In this section, we shall see some differences which also exist in the short term objectives

[193] See footnote 9 to Article 17.14 of the DSU.
[194] See Article 4.9 of the SCM Agreement.
[195] See footnote 8 to Article 4.9 of the SCM Agreement.

of these two complementary systems, which are reflected in the nature of available remedies as well as the degree of discretion allowed panels in certain respects.

As implied under Article 3.7,[196] and explicitly stated under Article 19.1, of the DSU, "[w]here a panel or the Appellate Body concludes that a measure is inconsistent with a covered agreement, it *shall recommend* that the Member concerned *bring the measure into conformity with that agreement*. In addition to its recommendations, the panel or Appellate Body *may suggest ways* in which the Member concerned could implement the recommendations."[197] The text of Article 4.7 of the SCM Agreement nearly reproduces this latter provision: "If the measure in question is found to be a prohibited subsidy, the panel *shall recommend* that the subsidizing Member *withdraw the subsidy without delay*. In this regard, the panel *shall specify in its recommendation the time-period* within which the measure must be withdrawn."[198]

Both provisions stress that the primary objective in cases involving violation of any of the covered agreements is to terminate the violation. Despite the apparent similarity, however, there are three observable differences between the DSU and the SCM Agreement in this respect. Firstly, while the DSU takes withdrawal of measure as an objective "usually" followed,[199] the SCM Agreement makes it the only permissible recommendation to be made by panels. Secondly, and as a consequence of the first difference, while panels under the DSU enjoy a certain degree of discretion on the substance of the recommendation they can make, the SCM Agreement simply instructs them to recommend that the measure be withdrawn *without delay*. Furthermore, panels are also mandatorily required to "specify" the time period within which withdrawal must be effected. Finally, unlike the general provisions of the DSU, the SCM Agreement does not open room for compensation or any other alternative even as a temporary substitute.

---

196 Article 3.7 of the DSU provides as follows: "Before bringing a case, a Member shall exercise its judgement as to whether action under these procedures would be fruitful. The aim of the dispute settlement mechanism is to secure a positive solution to a dispute. A solution mutually acceptable to the parties to a dispute and consistent with the covered agreements is clearly to be preferred. In the absence of a mutually agreed solution, the first objective of the dispute settlement mechanism is *usually* to secure the withdrawal of the measures concerned if these are found to be inconsistent with the provisions of any of the covered agreements. The provision of compensation should be resorted to only if the immediate withdrawal of the measure is impracticable and as a temporary measure pending the withdrawal of the measure which is inconsistent with a covered agreement. The last resort which this Understanding provides to the Member invoking the dispute settlement procedures is the possibility of suspending the application of concessions or other obligations under the covered agreements on a discriminatory basis vis-à-vis the other Member, subject to authorization by the DSB of such measures." (Italics added).

197 Article 19.1 of the DSU (italics added and footnotes omitted).

198 Article 4.7 of the SCM Agreement (italics added).

199 See Article 3.7 of the DSU, quoted *supra* n. 94.

As alluded to earlier,[200] the meaning of the phrase "without delay" was at issue in *Australia Leather*. The issue arose as a result of an Australian argument that "since the 'normal' period of time for implementation of panel decisions under the DSU is fifteen months, and time periods in export subsidy disputes are halved pursuant to Article 4.12, a period of seven and one-half months would be appropriate."[201] The Panel rejected that argument, and set a 90-day period for the withdrawal of the export subsidy,[202] on the basis of the following reasoning:

> "In the first place, Article 4.12 specifically provides that 'except for time periods specifically prescribed in this Article' the time periods otherwise provided for in the DSU should be halved in export subsidy disputes. Article 4.7, which provides that the subsidy shall be withdrawn 'without delay', and that the panel shall specify the time-period for withdrawal of the measure in its recommendation, in our view establishes that the time-period for withdrawal is 'specifically prescribed in this Article', that is, in Article 4 of the SCM Agreement itself. Moreover, we do not, as a factual matter, believe that a period of seven and one-half months can reasonably be described as corresponding to the requirement that the measure must be withdrawn 'without delay'."[203]

The issue was also addressed by the two parallel *Aircraft* cases, both of which agreed that the "without delay" standard would be met if the losing parties could withdraw their unlawful export subsidy measures "within 90 days".[204] Moreover, the Appellate Body affirmed this interpretation in the context of both the *Brazil Aircraft* and the *Canada Aircraft* cases between Canada and Brazil.[205] The arguments raised and the statements made before the Appellate Body particularly in *Brazil Aircraft* are illuminating.

In this case, Brazil argued, just like Australia in *Australia Leather*, that "although Article 4.7 of the SCM Agreement directs a panel to specify the time-period within which a prohibited subsidy must be withdrawn, that provision does not specify a particular time-period."[206] Invoking Article 4.12 of the SCM Agreement as well as Article 21.3(c) of the DSU, Brazil further contended that "the Panel should have concluded that Brazil must withdraw its export subsidies within half of fifteen months, that is, within seven and one-half months, rather than within 90 days."[207] The Appellate Body, however, ruled that "the Panel was correct in its reasoning and

---

[200] See *supra* section 5.3.4.

[201] *Australia Leather*, report of the panel, *supra* n. 107, para. 10.6.

[202] Ibid., para. 10.7.

[203] Ibid., para. 10.6.

[204] See *Canada Aircraft*, report of the panel, *supra* n. 36, para. 10.4, and *Brazil Aircraft*, report of the panel, *supra* n. 35, para. 8.5. It is interesting to note that these two panels, which were issued on the same day, although composed of completely different people and running parallel to each other, arrived at identical conclusions expressed in nearly identical language.

[205] See *Canada Aircraft*, report of the Appellate Body, *supra* n. 31, para. 221; and *Brazil Aircraft*, report of the Appellate Body, *supra* n. 173, para. 197.

[206] *Brazil Aircraft*, report of the Appellate Body, *supra* n. 173, para. 188.

[207] Ibid., para. 188.

conclusion on this issue."[208] Interestingly, the Appellate Body affirmed the view of the *Australia Leather* panel that Article 4.7 of the SCM Agreement "*stipulates a time-period.* It states that a subsidy must be withdrawn 'without delay'. That is the recommendation the Panel made."[209] The Appellate Body also explicitly referred to, and upheld, the 90-day withdrawal period set by the panel.[210]

The brevity of the time limits set in the above three cases shows that panels and the Appellate Body have construed the "without delay" standard fairly strictly. Indeed, the uniformity of the time limits set by all of them might even create the impression that there is a growing practice in favour of interpreting the "without delay" standard to mean just 90 days. This, as the *FSC* panel ruling has shown later, is not of course always the case. The *FSC* case has shown that such a strict approach may not be possible every time. In a remarkable departure from the growing practice, the panel in this case determined a withdrawal period of about one full year as appropriate to meet the "without delay" standard in the circumstances. In arriving at this conclusion, the panel stated that it had taken into consideration such factors as practicability, the legislative measures necessary to effect the withdrawal, the time of commencement of the US fiscal year, and even the possibility of an appeal:

> "Given that implementation of the Panel's recommendation will require legislative action (a fact recognized by the European Communities), that the United States fiscal year 2000 starts on 1 October 1999, and that this Report is not scheduled for circulation to Members until September 1999 (and, if appealed, might not be adopted until as late as early spring 2000), it is not in our view a practical possibility that the United States could be in a position to take the necessary legislative action by 1 October 1999. That being so, and acting in good faith, there is no way that this could be described as a 'delay'. However, this objective timing constraint would not be present with effect from the following fiscal year (2001), which commences on 1 October 2000. As this would be the first practicable date by which the United States could implement our recommendation, it satisfies the 'without delay' standard set forth in Article 4.7. Accordingly, we specify that FSC subsidies must be withdrawn at the latest with effect from 1 October 2000."[211]

A fifth case addressing the issue – *Canada Automotive* – reflected the influence of all the preceding reports. Just like *FSC*, the *Canada Automotive* panel heavily depended on the question of whether implementation of a recommendation might need legislative as opposed to executive measures. It specifically pointed out that "in examining what time-period would represent withdrawal 'without delay' in a particular case, we consider that we may take into account the nature of the steps necessary to withdraw the prohibited subsidy."[212] Reflecting the approach of the

---

[208] Ibid., para. 192.
[209] Ibid.
[210] Ibid., para. 197.
[211] *FSC*, report of the panel, *supra* n. 19, para. 8.8.
[212] *Canada Automotive*, report of the panel, *supra* n. 49, para. 11.6.

FSC, it observed that the measures at issue were "acts of the executive, and not the legislative, branch of government" and that "the amendment or revocation of an act of the executive branch can normally be effectuated more quickly than would be the case if legislative action were required."[213] According to this panel, the phrase "without delay", in its ordinary meaning, "suggests that the Member must not put off, postpone or defer action, but must rather act as quickly as possible to withdraw the prohibited subsidy."[214] On that basis, the panel ruled that "a time-period of 90 days would be appropriate."[215] It is interesting to note here that the panel also referred to the first three cases on the subject and noted that "in those disputes involving a prohibited subsidy in which legislative action was not required, panels have specified a time-period of 90 days."[216]

We see from the preceding survey that while four of the five relevant cases decided so far have taken the 90-day period to satisfy the "without delay" requirement of Article 4.7 of the SCM Agreement, the fifth case opted for a time-limit of about one full year for the same requirement. It is difficult to set any specific standard on the issue in the abstract. Hence, a-case-by-case approach seems to be the only practicable option. That is why all the cases summarized above have taken into account the practical procedures that may be required to implement their recommendations.[217] However, it is equally difficult to interpret one and the same requirement with so much divergence and accept a gap of this magnitude – about four fold – between two equally prohibited groups of export subsidy cases. Apparently, the presence of a domestic requirement of legislative action to implement recommended measures has played a decisive role in this respect. However, one may argue that this approach may turn out to be practically troublesome, and in the long run even counterproductive. At the practical level, it will introduce an unwarranted distinction between two countries with similar export subsidy schemes but introduced through different measures – say, executive for one and legislative for the other. Under such circumstances, it will be difficult to accept a decision that requires one to withdraw its export subsidies within 90 days while giving the other as long as a full year. In the long run, this may only become an additional incentive for countries to introduce their export subsidies via legislative instruments that cannot be changed easily in their respective domestic constitutional frameworks. Moreover, in as long as Members have the obligation to bring their laws, regulations and administrative procedures into conformity with the requirements set by the rules of the multilateral agreement, caution should be exercised so that the type of domestic legal instrument needed to implement a DSB recommendation would not frustrate the very need for the accelerated time table adopted for prohibited export subsidy cases.[218] Needless to say, this obligation also includes the requirement to withdraw any

---

[213] Ibid., para. 11.6.

[214] Ibid.

[215] Ibid., para. 11.7.

[216] Ibid., footnote 910 to para. 11 7.

[217] See *Canada Aircraft*, report of the panel, *supra* n. 36, para. 10.4; *Brazil Aircraft*, report of the panel, *supra* n. 35, para. 8.5; and *Canada Automotive*, report of the panel, *supra* n. 49, para. 11.6.

[218] See Article XVI:4 of the WTO Agreement.

prohibited subsidies, regardless of the legislative form they take, "without delay" in the strict sense of that term.

To sum up, the DSU is known for its detailed and rather stringent time limits and strict procedural rules governing the settlement of disputes under the WTO Agreements. As such, it has been rightly appraised by many scholars in the field as the single most important contribution of the WTO to the wider world of general international law and international dispute settlement. It is this already stringent and strict dispute settlement mechanism of the DSU that has been complemented by the "special or additional rules and procedures on dispute settlement" of the SCM Agreement in favour of further stringency and strictness in the area of prohibited subsidies, an important part of which is constituted by export subsidies. Seen over an historical framework, the GATT regime for export subsidies which had started with obligations of mere notification and consultation has moved to the status of being a measure not only flatly prohibited, but also subjected to the most stringent of rules of dispute settlement known in the history of international dispute settlement.

5.6 Countervailing Measures

Countervailing measures constitute one of only few self-help measures allowed under the multilateral trading system.[219] Article VI:3 of GATT 1994 defines the term countervailing duties as "a special duty levied for the purpose of offsetting any bounty or subsidy bestowed, directly or indirectly, upon the manufacture, production or exports of any merchandise."[220]

Part V of the SCM Agreement provides that Members may resort to countervailing duties to counteract the effects of two of the three categories of subsidies – "prohibited" subsidies and "actionable" subsidies. Countervailing duties cannot, however, be levied against "non-actionable" subsidies.[221] For purposes of countervailing duties, therefore, all sorts of subsidies may be divided into two broad categories – countervailable subsidies and non-countervailable subsidies.[222] While "prohibited" and "actionable" subsidies belong to the former, "non-actionable" subsidies fall under the latter. Consequently, all discussion on countervailing duties in this section applies only to the countervailable subsidies. Furthermore, Members can invoke the countervailing duty provisions in parallel with the provisions of Articles 4 and 7 on authorized countermeasures against prohibited and actionable subsidies, respectively.[223] However, only one form of remedy, i.e. either a countervailing duty under Part V or an authorized countermeasure under Parts II

---

[219] Anti-dumping duties and safeguard measures are the other two such self-help measures allowed under the GATT/WTO system.

[220] And this definition has been reproduced under Footnote 36 of the SCM Agreement.

[221] Footnote 35 to the SCM Agreement provides, in its relevant part, that "the provisions of Parts III and V shall not be invoked regarding measures considered non-actionable in accordance with the provisions of Part IV of the Agreement."

[222] See, e.g., *UK Steel*, report of the panel, *supra* n. 38, footnote 64 to para. 6.50.

[223] See footnote 35 to the SCM Agreement.

or III, can be applied against the effects of any particular subsidy in the domestic market of the importing country.[224]

Article 10 of the SCM Agreement prescribes the fundamental rule that countervailing duties may only be imposed "in accordance with the provisions of this Agreement *and the Agreement on Agriculture*."[225] Part V sets detailed rules governing, *inter alia*, the initiation, investigation, and establishment of the existence of subsidies, opportunities for consultations with the Members whose products are subject to countervailing duty investigations, calculation of the amount of subsidies, injury determination, and the imposition and administration of provisional or final countervailing duties.

As will be seen more closely later, Article 13(c) of the Agreement on Agriculture conditionally exempts agricultural export subsidies from actions based on Articles 3, 5, and 6 of the SCM Agreement for the duration of a nine-year implementation period. As regards the use of countervailing duties, however, the Agriculture Agreement merely requires that agricultural export subsidies that conform fully to its relevant provisions be "subject to countervailing duties only upon a determination of injury or threat thereof based on volume, effect on prices, or consequent impact in accordance with Article VI of GATT 1994 and Part V of the Subsidies Agreement, and due restraint shall be shown in initiating any countervailing duty investigations."[226] Accordingly, agricultural export subsidies can be subject to countervailing duties if two conditions are met – the exercise of due restraint at the initiation stage, and imposition of the duties only upon a determination of injury or threat thereof. Of these two, it is only the "due restraint' obligation that is unique to countervailing duties against agricultural subsidies.[227] Moreover, the "due restraint" requirement is also such a fluid and highly subjective concept that its practical significance in constraining the use of countervailing duties is, at best, doubtful. Even then, it is also limited to the duration of the nine-year implementation period. Thus the countervailing duty provisions of the SCM Agreement are almost fully applicable to agricultural export subsidies as well. With this in mind, the salient features of the countervailing duty system may be summarized as follows.

The most fundamental obligation as regards countervailing duties is that they may be imposed only in pursuance of investigations initiated and conducted in accordance with the provisions of the SCM Agreement and the Agreement on Agriculture.[228] The first stage in the process is initiation, the "procedural action by which a Member formally commences an investigation."[229] As the primary purpose

[224] See footnote 35 to the SCM Agreement.

[225] Article 10, last sentence (italics added). As the *UK Steel* panel observed, "A Member will therefore violate Article 10 if it imposes a countervailing duty that is not 'in accordance with' Article VI of GATT 1994 or the terms of the SCM Agreement." *UK Steel*, report of the panel, *supra* n. 38, para. 6.47.

[226] Article 13(c)(i) of the Agreement on Agriculture.

[227] See Article 15.1 of the SCM Agreement.

[228] Article 10 of the SCM Agreement.

[229] Footnote 37 to the SCM Agreement.

of a countervailing duty is to protect domestic producers of like products from unfair competition, the right to request for the commencement of the investigations is vested primarily in the relevant "domestic industry." Domestic industry here refers to "the domestic producers as a whole of the like products or to those of them whose collective output of the products constitutes a major proportion of the total domestic production of those products."[230] In special circumstances, however, competent government authorities may also commence such an investigation on their own initiative, provided that they have sufficient evidence of the existence of a subsidy, injury and causal link to justify the initiation of an investigation.[231]

Taking the general case for present purposes, the domestic industry is required to make a written application including "sufficient evidence of the existence of (a) a subsidy and, if possible, its amount, (b) injury ... and (c) a causal link between the subsidized imports and the alleged injury."[232] Investigation may commence only if the authorities are satisfied that the application has been made "by or on behalf of the domestic industry",[233] and that there is sufficient evidence to justify initiating an investigation.[234] Even then, the authorities are required to reject applications as soon as they are "satisfied that there is not sufficient evidence of either subsidization or of injury to justify proceeding with the case."[235] While such a finding also requires termination of an already proceeding investigation, there are two more grounds that oblige the authorities to terminate an investigation – finding of a *de minimis* amount of subsidy, or a negligible volume of actual or potential subsidized imports or negligible injury.[236]

Investigations are normally required to be concluded within one year, and under "special circumstances", within 18 months.[237] This is a fairly long period of time. A lot of harm could be done to the domestic industry during the investigation period itself. In order to protect Members against such possibilities, the SCM Agreement allows them to introduce provisional measures applicable during the investigation

---

[230] Article 16.1 of the SCM Agreement. This definition has been qualified by the following: "when producers are related to the exporters or importers or are themselves importers of the allegedly subsidized product or a like product from other countries, the term 'domestic industry' may be interpreted as referring to the rest of the producers."

[231] Article 11.6 of the SCM Agreement.

[232] Article 11.2 of the SCM Agreement.

[233] Article 11.4 provides that "The application shall be considered to have been made 'by or on behalf of the domestic industry' if it is supported by those domestic producers whose collective output constitutes more than 50 per cent of the total production of the like product produced by that portion of the domestic industry expressing either support for or opposition to the application. However no investigation shall be initiated when domestic producers expressly supporting the application account for less than 25 per cent of total production of the like product produced by the domestic industry."

[234] See Articles 11.9 and 22.1 of the SCM Agreement.

[235] Article 11.9 of the SCM Agreement.

[236] While the term "negligible" is not defined anywhere in the SCM Agreement, a *de minimis* amount is understood to mean a subsidy less than 1 per cent *ad valorem*. See Article 11.9 of the SCM Agreement.

[237] Article 11.11 of the SCM Agreement. Once again, no guideline is given about those "special circumstances" under which members may be allowed to extend the investigation period to 18 months – hence necessitating only a case-by-case approach.

period if they believe that such measures are necessary to prevent such injury from happening.[238] These measures may take the form of "provisional countervailing duties guaranteed by cash deposits or bonds equal to the amount of the provisionally calculated amount of subsidization."[239]

Although initiated by the application of the domestic industry (and at times by governments themselves), a countervailing duty investigation always concerns the products of at least one other member country. Furthermore, there are also some foreign business firms (or state trading companies) having an interest in the trade of the specific product that is under investigation either as producers, or exporters, or both. Any national investigative process is thus prone to disregard the interests of such foreign parties. In an attempt to safeguard these interests, the SCM Agreement has introduced a series of obligations of due process and notification on the part of the investigating Member.

Firstly, already before the initiation of any investigation, it is required to invite for consultations those Members whose products may be subject to investigation.[240] Secondly, "[w]hen the authorities are satisfied that there is sufficient evidence to justify the initiation of an investigation pursuant to Article 11, the Member or Members, the products of which are subject to such investigation and other interested parties known to the investigating authorities to have an interest therein shall be notified and public notice shall be given."[241] And thirdly, once the investigation commences, Article 12 requires that interested Members and all interested parties in a countervailing duty investigation "be given notice of the information which the authorities require and ample opportunity to present in writing all evidence which they consider relevant in respect of the investigation in question."[242]

As regards members whose products are subject to the countervailing duty investigation, the SCM Agreement goes a step further than the specific notification. It requires that such Members be afforded opportunities for consultations before the commencement, and throughout the course, of the countervailing duty investigations.[243] The importance of these procedural requirements can hardly be over-

---

[238] This is, however, subject to a number of strict conditions, including a preliminary affirmative determination on the existence of a subsidy and an injury caused thereby. For the conditions, see Article 17.1 of the SCM Agreement.

[239] Article 17.2 of the SCM Agreement.

[240] Article 13.1 of the SCM Agreement. The obligation continues throughout the course of the investigation: the investigating party is required to afford "reasonable opportunity to continue consultations, with a view to clarifying the factual situation and to arriving at a mutually agreed solution." Article 13.2 of the SCM Agreement.

[241] Article 22.1 of the SCM Agreement. The use of the terms "interested Members" and "interested parties" in these provisions is intended to cover both the Member states as well as the business firms whose interests may be directly or indirectly affected by the outcome of the countervailing duty investigation. See definition of "interested parties" under Article 12.9 of the SCM Agreement.

[242] Article 12.1 of the SCM Agreement.

[243] The purpose of these consultations is to clarify the factual situation and arrive at a mutually agreed solution. See Article 13.1 and 13.2 of the SCM Agreement.

emphasized. They are there to serve the interests of due process in the administration of countervailing duty laws. Their non-observance may – as it already did in a 1994 case brought under similar provisions of the Tokyo Round Subsidies Code[244] – frustrate the validity of a countervailing duty decision which might otherwise have been based on sound substantive law grounds.

As the provisions of the SCM Agreement under discussion were taken directly from the 1979 Subsidies Code, (See Article 2, and particularly paragraph 3, of the Subsidies Code) with only little adjustments necessitated by differences in the nature of the two instruments, a look at the *Brazil Countervailing Duty* panel ruling on those provisions may illuminate our understanding of the corresponding provisions of the SCM Agreement here. In that case, Brazil had given a public notice of the initiation of a countervailing duty investigation but had not specifically notified the EC and other known interested parties about the initiation of the investigation. The Panel then held that "a signatory could not meet its obligation under Article 2:3 [of the Subsidies Code] regarding the notification to be provided to other signatories and interested importers and exporters merely by giving a public notice of the initiation of an investigation."[245] It further pointed out that, by reaching a preliminary affirmative finding of the existence of a subsidy and an injury caused thereby in the sense of Article 5:1 of the Subsidies Code "which was not the result of an investigation conducted in accordance with the requirements of Articles 2:3 and 2:5", Brazil "had acted inconsistently with Article 5:1" of the Subsidies Code.[246]

Coming back to the SCM Agreement, once all these procedural steps are passed, the authorities may impose countervailing duties provided that they have made a final determination of the existence and amount of a countervailable subsidy in respect of the imported products, and that the subsidized imports are causing injury to the relevant domestic industry.[247] The first requirement is simple – no countervailing duty may be imposed on imported products unless they have benefited from some form of a countervailable subsidy. Moreover, as the purpose of these additional duties is to restore the balance by offsetting the benefits acquired by the subsidized imports, the amount of the countervailable subsidy should also be determined.[248]

The second condition is more complicated – it should be determined that the

---

[244] See *Brazil – Imposition of Provisional and Definitive Countervailing Duties on Milk Powder and Certain Types of Milk From the European Economic Community*, Report of the panel (SCM/179) adopted by the Committee on Subsidies and Countervailing Measures on 28 April 1994.

[245] Ibid., para. 233.

[246] Ibid., para. 268.

[247] See, for example, *UK Steel*, report of the panel, *supra* n. 38, para. 6.50.

[248] The *UK Steel* panel has found that the nexus between the existence of a countervailable subsidy and a countervailing duty is clearly established in Articles 19.1, 19.4, and 21.1 of the SCM Agreement, and Article VI:3 of the GATT 1994. It thus concluded that "consistent with the object and purpose of countervailing duties envisaged by Part V of the SCM Agreement, we consider that a countervailing duty may only be imposed on an imported product if it is demonstrated that a (countervailable) subsidy was bestowed directly or indirectly on the manufacture, production or export of that merchandise." Ibid., para. 6.57 (footnotes omitted).

subsidy has caused "injury" to the domestic industry.[249] Article 15 of the SCM Agreement sets the requirements for the determination of injury. Accordingly, a determination of injury should, first and foremost, be based on "positive evidence" and involve an examination of three things: (a) the volume of the subsidized imports (i.e. whether there has been a significant increase in subsidized imports), (b) their effect on prices (i.e. whether there has been a significant price undercutting by the subsidized imports) in the domestic market for "like products",[250] and (c) the consequent impact of these imports on the domestic producers of such products.[251]

As already pointed out, since the object of countervailing duties is to offset the unfair competitive advantage acquired by the subsidized producers/exporters, the maximum amount of a countervailing duty is limited to the amount of benefit conferred on the recipients. Article VI:3 of GATT 1994 provides that "no countervailing duty shall be levied on any product ... in excess of an amount equal to the estimated bounty or subsidy determined to have been granted ...." As it stands, the "estimated bounty or subsidy determined to have been granted" lacks in precision. Given the fact that the cost of a subsidy to the granting government is often different from the amount of benefit acquired by the recipient of that same subsidy, it has not always been clear as to which amount should be taken in the calculation of a subsidy. Article 19.4 of the SCM Agreement uses a similar language and provides that no countervailing duty may be levied "in excess of the amount of the subsidy found to exist." However, the SCM Agreement resolves the problem in favour of a calculation of the amount of the subsidy in terms of the benefit to the recipient.[252]

Accordingly, Members are required to do the calculation of the benefit conferred on the recipient on the basis of methods stipulated in a national legislation or regulation and make its practical application to each particular case transparent.[253] The methods also need to be consistent with a set of general guidelines, the essence of which is that a government practice of subsidization – whether in the form of provision of equity capital, a loan, a loan guarantee, the provision of goods and services, or whatever – may be considered as conferring a benefit only if it is more

---

[249] See Article VI:6(a) of GATT 1994 and Article 19.1 of the SCM Agreement. The term "injury" has been defined to mean "material injury to a domestic industry, threat of material injury or material retardation of the establishment of such an industry." Footnote 45 to Article 15 of the SCM Agreement.

[250] The term "like products" is defined here to mean "a product which is identical in all respects to the product under consideration, or in the absence of such a product, another product which, although not alike in all respects, has characteristics closely resembling those of the product under consideration." Footnote 46 to Article 15 of the SCM Agreement.

[251] Article 15.1 of the SCM Agreement. Article 15.4 presents a detailed, albeit not exhaustive, list of economic factors that should be considered in order to determine the impact of the subsidized imports on the domestic industry. These include "actual and potential decline in output, sales, market share, profits, productivity, return on investments, or utilization of capacity; factors affecting domestic prices; actual and potential negative effects on cash flow, inventories, employment, wages, growth, ability to raise capital or investment and, *in the case of agriculture, whether there has been increased burden on Government programmes*." Article 15.4 of the SCM Agreement (italics added).

[252] See Article 14 of the SCM Agreement.

[253] Article 14 of the SCM Agreement.

favourable to the firm than what the firm would be able to secure on the prevailing market.[254] Indeed, as the EC rightly argued in the *UK Steel* case, any determination of the "amount of subsidy" "necessarily requires" a measurement of the amount of "benefit" conferred. This requires comparing the terms of the financial contribution at issue with those that would have prevailed in the marketplace absent the subsidy.[255]

The existence of a subsidy is a necessary, but not sufficient, condition for the imposition of a countervailing duty. It should be followed by an injury to the domestic industry of the country concerned. Moreover, these two elements, i.e. the subsidy and the injury, should not just happen together; they should be linked by a causal relationship. The injury should be a result of the subsidy. Stated differently, the subsidized imports should be responsible for the injury suffered by the domestic industry.

A final determination of the fulfilment of these conditions entitles a Member to impose a countervailing duty.[256] It is important, however, that Members are not obliged to introduce countervailing duties even after a positive determination as to the fulfilment of all the necessary conditions for doing so. Furthermore, in cases where they decide to impose the duties, not only is the maximum amount of the countervailing duty limited to the amount of the benefit conferred on the recipient, they are encouraged to set them at less than the amount of the subsidy if that can remove the injury to the domestic industry. Finally, a countervailing duty, if to be imposed, is required to be imposed on a non-discriminatory basis as between all subsidized imports found to be causing injury.[257]

Once imposed, the duration of a countervailing duty is also important. The general principle, adopted during the 1979 Subsidies Code[258] and repeated verbatim by the SCM Agreement, is that a countervailing duty may remain in force "only as long as and to the extent necessary to counteract subsidization which is causing injury."[259] The moment the subsidy itself or its injurious consequences, or both, cease to exist, the countervailing duty loses its justification and should be terminated. The "as long as necessary" formula obviously lacks in precision. One of the achievements of the Uruguay Round in this respect is the introduction, for the first time, of a "sunset" provision – that while the authorities may review the need for continued imposition of the duty either on their own initiative or upon request by any interested party, a countervailing duty is mandatorily required to be terminated on a date not later than five years from its imposition or from the date of the most

---

[254] See Article 14(a) - (c) of the SCM Agreement. As regards the practical application of the market as a threshold, see, *inter alia*, *Canada Dairy*, report of the panel, *supra* n. 19, paras. 7.43-7.58; and *Canada dairy*, report of the Appellate Body *supra* n. 41, para. 87.

[255] *UK Steel*, report of the panel, *supra* n. 38, para. 6.89.

[256] Article 19 of the SCM Agreement.

[257] See Article 19.3 of the SCM Agreement.

[258] See Article 4.9 of the Subsidies Code.

[259] Article 21.1 of the SCM Agreement. For an interesting discussion of this aspect of the SCM Agreement, see *UK Steel*, reports of both the panel and the Appellate Body, *supra* n. 38.

recent review.[260] This deadline may, however, be disregarded if it is determined upon review that "the expiry of the duty would be likely to lead to continuation or recurrence of subsidization and injury."[261] In view of the potential for abuse in the administration of countervailing duty laws, Article 23 imposes on Members the obligation to maintain "judicial, arbitral or administrative tribunals or procedures for the purpose, *inter alia*, of the prompt review of administrative actions relating to final determinations and review of determinations."

5.7 Conclusion

A recapitulation of all the provisions of the Subsidies Agreement on prohibited and actionable subsidies leads to the conclusion that virtually all of them apply to agriculture subject to the provisions of the Agreement on Agriculture.[262] Despite strong positions taken by many countries against what is often called an "artificial" distinction in the treatment of export subsidies between primary and non-primary products, the Uruguay Round Agreements maintained the system of separate regimes for agricultural and non-agricultural export subsidies. The provisions of the Agreement on Subsidies and Countervailing Measures firmly state that issues of agricultural subsidies are subject primarily to the Agriculture Agreement and only secondarily to the SCM Agreement.

Consequently, all subsidies, with the exception of those given to agricultural products, that are designed to promote exports or to curtail imports are subjected to the most stringent regime by the new Agreement – that of a flat prohibition. The prohibition of import-substitution and export subsidies applies irrespective of their "trade effects". Neither is it required of any complainant against such practice to have suffered any injuries from them. The mere proof of the presence of such a subsidy suffices for any member to claim its immediate termination.[263] The rigor of the remedies available against the violation of this provision, which can also be discerned from the expedited procedures and shorter deadlines set for the resolution of disputes, is an additional proof to the stringency of the regime as regards this category of subsidies. Agriculture is thus the only sector where export subsidies are not prohibited. The following chapter will be devoted to a closer look at the provisions of the Agriculture Agreement in this respect.

---

[260] Article 21.3 of the SCM Agreement. For further discussion, see T. Stewart, and A. Dwyer, *WTO Antidumping and Subsidy Agreements – A Practitioner's Guide to "Sunset" Reviews in Australia, Canada, the European Union, and the United States* (Kluwer, 1998).

[261] Article 21.3 of the SCM Agreement.

[262] Among others, the following provisions of the SCM Agreement explicitly refer to the Agriculture Agreement: Article 3.1 on Prohibited Subsidies; Articles 5.1 and 6.9 on actionable subsidies; Article 7.1 on remedies; and Article 10 on Countervailable subsidies.

[263] For example, Article 4(2) stipulates that a request for consultations under paragraph 1 "shall include a statement of available evidence with regard to the existence and nature of the subsidy in question." Compare this requirement with that prescribed under Article 7(2) on actionable subsidies: "A request for consultations under paragraph 1 shall include a statement of available evidence with regard to (a) the existence and nature of the subsidy in question, and (b) the injury caused to the domestic industry, or the nullification or impairment, or serious prejudice caused to the interests of the Member requesting consultations."

CHAPTER 6

AGRICULTURAL EXPORT SUBSIDIES UNDER THE AGREEMENT ON AGRICULTURE: AN OVERVIEW

6.1 INTRODUCTION

Having discussed the general principles applying to export subsidies in general in the preceding chapters, the remaining portion of Part II is concerned with the specific case of agricultural export subsidies and the primary focus of attention is the Uruguay Round Agreement on Agriculture. The present chapter starts with a brief recapitulation of the major sticking points during the arduous and testing negotiation process of the export subsidy part of the Agreement on Agriculture. If agriculture was the most contentious of subjects throughout the Uruguay Round negotiations, agricultural export subsidies always stood at the centre. The background note on the negotiating history of export subsidy issues is thus aimed at enhancing understanding of the pertinent provisions of the Agriculture Agreement which are discussed subsequently.

Perhaps the most basic feature of the Agriculture Agreement on export subsidies, as on other issues, is that it is an agreement with very modest ambitions. It aims only to "establish a basis for initiating a process of reform of trade in agriculture"[1] and not as such to fully integrate agriculture into the mainstream rules of the multilateral trading system which are applicable to most non-agricultural products. The preamble declares that the reform process goes "in line with the objectives of the negotiations as set out in the Punta del Este Declaration."[2]

The Punta del Este objectives themselves were formulated after protracted negotiations among several contracting parties over a number of years.[3] The agriculture part of the 1986 Declaration was a product of the process that had been initiated during the 1982 GATT Ministerial Conference and the resulting

---

1 See preamble to the Agreement on Agriculture, para. 1.

2 See preamble to the Agreement on Agriculture, para. 1.

3 It is interesting to note here what Croome said concerning the 1982 Ministerial Conference: "Both the preparatory process and the ministerial meeting itself were extremely difficult: so much so that many participants regretted that the decision to hold the meeting had ever been taken." J. Croome, *Reshaping the World Trading System: A History of the Uruguay Round* (Geneva 1995) p. 13. In the words of another observer, "[s]uch was the intensity of the conflict between the US and the EC at the time that the inclusion of agriculture in the Uruguay Round was regarded as something of a victory in itself." Watkins, K., "Changing the Rules: The GATT Farm Trade Reform and World Food Security", in European NGO Network on Agriculture and Development (RONGEAD), *GATT Briefing on Agriculture, Food Security and the Uruguay Round*, (No. 4, November 1990), p. 6.

Declaration.[4] It was also very detailed by the standards of the same Declaration on other issues.[5] The Punta del Este Declaration underscored the urgency of the need to bring more discipline and predictability to world agricultural trade by correcting and preventing restrictions and distortions. Export subsidies being one of the fundamental factors responsible for this distortion, the negotiations were aimed at achieving greater liberalization of trade in agriculture by, among others, bringing "all measures affecting ... export competition under strengthened and more operationally effective GATT rules and disciplines."[6] The means of doing this as regards subsidies was identified to be by "improving the competitive environment by increasing discipline on the use of all direct and indirect subsidies and other measures affecting directly or indirectly agricultural trade, including the phased reduction of their negative effects and dealing with their causes."[7]

The preamble to the Agreement on Agriculture also recalls the long-term objective of the reform process – i.e., the establishment of a "fair and market-oriented agricultural trading system" – which had been agreed during the Mid-Term Review of the Uruguay Round in 1989.[8] Moreover, both the Punta del Este Declaration, the Mid-Term Review, as well as the preamble of the Agreement on Agriculture identically state that one of the strategies to further those objectives would be through the establishment of "strengthened and more operationally effective GATT rules and disciplines".[9] The latter two then add that this would be supplemented by the negotiation of specific commitments on support and protection.[10]

With these objectives and strategies in mind, export competition was identified to be one of the areas on which negotiators were "*committed* to achieving specific binding commitments."[11] However, as always, translating such widely-phrased objectives, which are of necessity expressed in the abstract, into concrete and enforceable legal norms was the most difficult problem. Just like the previous 40 years, the major trading powers took diametrically opposed positions on most crucial issues of agricultural trade, and this repeatedly caused quite a number of failures to meet deadlines for the conclusion of the Uruguay Round.[12]

---

4 Indeed, "[f]or agriculture, more than for any other issue except perhaps services, the foundations for the Uruguay Round were laid by the work programme launched by ministers in 1982." Croome (1995) *supra* n. 3, p. 110.

5 See Croome (1995) *supra* n. 3, p. 111.

6 GATT, *Ministerial Declaration on the Uruguay Round* (MIN.DEC) adopted in Punta del Este, Uruguay, on 20 September 1986, often referred to as the *Punta del Este Declaration,* reproduced in, GATT *Focus Newsletter*, No. 41 (October 1986) p. 4. The agriculture part of this Declaration has been reproduced *supra* n. 12, chapter 5.

7 Ibid., p. 4.

8 For more on this point, see *infra* n. 24.

9 *Punta del Este Declaration, supra* n. 6, p. 4; *Mid-Term Meeting*, GATT Doc. MTN.TNC/11, (Special Distribution, 21 April 1989, hereafter the *Mid-Term Review*), para. 5; and preamble to the Agriculture Agreement, para. 2.

10 See preamble to the Agriculture Agreement, para. 2, and *Mid-Term Review, supra* n. 9, para. 5.

11 See preamble to the Agriculture Agreement, para. 4.

12 On the role of agriculture in the collapse of a number meetings, see, *inter alia,* Croome (1995) *supra* n. 3, p. 173.

6.2 A Review of Basic Issues of Export Subsidies Negotiated in the Uruguay Round

That agriculture has been the most controversial of all the issues addressed during the Uruguay Round has already been reiterated; perhaps the highest share of the responsibility for this exceptionally controversial nature of agriculture, however, falls on the specific issue of agricultural export subsidies. As will be developed later on, it is agricultural export subsidies which have often been singled out as the measures primarily responsible for most of the distortions in international agricultural trade. To mention only one example, just before the onset of the Uruguay Round negotiations, an influential GATT-sponsored study, called the Leutwiler Report,[13] vehemently suggested that the ultimate goal of reform in this respect should be "the total elimination of ... export subsidies, as they produce many of the major distortions in world agricultural markets".[14] Consequently, throughout the course of the Uruguay Round negotiations, reaching an agreement on the particular case of agricultural export subsidies "proved the most difficult".[15]

The two leading powers of the day – the US and the EC – continued in their tradition of complete divergence over agricultural export subsidies. Already in their first proposals in 1987, while the US called for "complete phase out over ten years of all agricultural subsidies which directly or indirectly affect trade,"[16] the EC, insisting on its lack of preparedness "to leave agriculture entirely to the play of market forces,"[17] limited itself to an ambiguous call for "progressive reduction of such subsidies"[18] without any actual timetable for the reduction. What is more, the EC

---

13 Named after the chairman of a group of seven eminent personalities in the area of trade policy constituted by then Director General Arthur Dunkel who invited them "to identify the fundamental causes of the problems afflicting the international trading system and to consider how these may be overcome during the remainder of the 1980s." Croome (1995) *supra* n. 3, p. 18.

14 GATT, *Trade Policies for a Better Future: The Leutwiler Report* (Geneva 1987), p. 44.

15 See OECD, *The Uruguay Round: A Preliminary Evaluation of the Agreement on Agriculture in the OECD Countries* (Paris 1995), p. 13.

16 Croome (1995) *supra* n. 3, p. 114. Stewart has even reported that in the specific case of export subsidies, the US called for the phase out period to be just five years. See T. Stewart, *The GATT Uruguay Round: A Negotiating History (1986–1992)* in III Vols. (Kluwer 1993) Vol. I, p. 172. Scholars later questioned whether or not this US proposal was just a bluff. Hillman wrote, for instance, that the first negotiating proposal "was an ideological trial balloon launched by the Administration." J. Hillman, "The US Perspective", in K. Ingersent, A. Rayner, and R. Hine (eds.) *Agriculture in the Uruguay Round* (St. Martin's press, New York 1994), p. 33. Hillman further cites another writer as follows: "Paarlberg proffers the persuasive argument that, for their own ulterior motives, certain protectionist interests in the United States ... supported the zero option in the secure knowledge that it would be rejected by other parties to the negotiations and that it might possibly torpedo the entire round." Ibid. pp. 33–34.

17 Croome (1995) *supra* n. 3, p. 116. Japan was somewhere in the middle of the two powers. While supporting the US proposal for the elimination of export subsidies, Japan also agreed with the EC that agriculture could not be left entirely to the play of market forces. According to Japan, "[a]griculture ... had specific characteristics which meant that it must be treated differently from other sectors. Constraints on land resources, the need for stable food supplies and demands for environmental protection required that 'the rule of market forces should be modified.'" Croome (1995) *supra* n. 3, p. 115.

18 Stewart (1993) *supra* n. 16, p. 179.

also proposed a "rebalancing" of subsidy levels so that "subsidies would be reduced on products as to which they were deemed especially high, but the reduction on one product would act as a 'credit' to be applied to another product that was subsidized at a level below the norm."[19]

Given the fact that agricultural export subsidies have been at the very core of the Common Agricultural Policy (the CAP), the latter often taken as the glue that keeps the Community together, it is hardly surprising that the EC was "reluctant to accept specific limitations" on the subject. In fact, during the Uruguay Round negotiations, there was the suspicion within the EC that the US had the "unstated aim" of destroying the CAP.[20] The divergent positions taken by the US and the EC on agricultural issues resulted in the collapse of the Mid-Term review meeting in Montreal in December 1988.[21] Croome has observed in this connection that agriculture brought the Montreal meeting to "an abrupt and premature end" because five Latin American countries, members of the Cairns Group,[22] blocked any developments in other areas by insisting that "until there was agreement on agriculture, they would accept no agreement at all."[23] It took four additional months of intensive negotiations for the overdue Mid-Term review agreement on agriculture to be reached.

The Mid-Term review agreement on agriculture stated, *inter alia*, that "the long-term objective of the agricultural negotiations is to establish a fair and market-oriented agricultural trading system and that a reform process should be initiated through the negotiation of commitments on support and protection and through the establishment of strengthened and more operationally effective GATT rules and disciplines."[24] The US then appeared to have dropped the idea of "elimination of all trade distortions"[25] as its long-term objective and accepted the more general

---

[19] Ibid. 179.

[20] K. Ingersent, A. Rayner, and R. Hine, "The EC Perspective", in Ingersent *et al* (1994) *supra* n. 16, p. 59.

[21] See Croome (1995) *supra* n. 3, p. 172–173.

[22] The Cairns Group consists of 18 (originally 14) exporting countries who described themselves as "key fair trading countries in agricultural products": Argentina, Australia, Bolivia, Brazil, Canada, Chile, Colombia, Costa Rica, Fiji, Guatemala, Indonesia, Malaysia, New Zealand, Paraguay, Philippines, South Africa, Thailand, and Uruguay. They got their name from the city where they made their first meeting in Cairns, Australia, in August 1986. The members of the group together account for about one quarter of total world exports of agricultural products. Throughout the course of the negotiations, the positions assumed by them on issues of agricultural trade closely resembled those of the US". The position of agriculture was so vital that these countries, together with the US, insisted that there would be an agreement on agriculture or no agreement at all. For details, see *inter alia*, Croome (1995) *supra* n. 3, p. 167-178; United States Department of Agriculture, *Agriculture Outlook*, (Dec. 1996), p. 22; and J. McMahon, "The Uruguay Round and Agriculture: Charting a New Direction?", in 29 *The International Lawyer*, No. 2 (Summer 1995), p. 418.

[23] Croome (1995) *supra* n. 3, p. 173.

[24] *Mid-Term Review*, *supra* n. 9, para. 5.

[25] J. Hillman, in Ingersent *et al* (1994) *supra* n. 16, p. 40. The essence of this contention has been put as follows: "Whereas the US demanded a prior commitment by all parties to the eventual elimination of support, before negotiations could begin on merely reducing it in the short-term, the EC remained implacably opposed to the zero option on any time scale." Ingersent *et al*, in Ingersent *et al*, *supra* n. 16 (1994) p. 64.

objective of "substantial progressive reductions in agricultural support and protection sustained over an agreed period of time."[26] The commitments to be negotiated were agreed to encompass export subsidies, and in particular, "direct budgetary assistance to exports, other payments on products exported and other forms of export assistance."[27]

The importance of this delayed Mid-Term Review agreement on agriculture was such that, in the words of Croome, it "served to relaunch the Uruguay Round as a whole."[28] Needless to say, both the agreement itself as well as the consequent relaunching of the negotiations were made possible because the principal negotiating parties were able to show some signs of compromise on their original positions. However, as subsequent developments confirmed, this was more apparent than real. Even after the Mid-Term Agreement, the gap between the traditional rival powers still appeared as wide as ever before. To take an example in our specific area of interest here, it was in the very first "comprehensive proposal" after the resumption of the negotiations that the US repeated its old call for a complete phase out of all export subsidies over a period of ten years.[29] Likewise, the EC continued with its former idea of rebalancing and proposed the Aggregate Measure of Support (AMS) "as a flexible means to reduce both domestic and export subsidies, with an overall target reduction to be agreed, but with each participant free to decide how this objective was reached."[30]

In an attempt to bridge this gap, Aart De Zeeuw, chairman of the negotiating group on agriculture, put forward his own proposals in 1990.[31] The De Zeeuw text summarized the prevailing state of views on export subsidies such that "although most countries wanted to see them eliminated as being *the most trade-distorting form of support*, others believed that they were necessary as long as world and internal prices continued to diverge."[32] He thus proposed that export subsidies would continue to exist but "with bigger reductions than to other forms of protection." He did not, however, propose any figures.[33]

---

26 *Mid-Term Review*, *supra* n. *9*, para. 6.

27 Ibid., para. 7.

28 Croome (1995) *supra* n. 3, p. 233.

29 See Croome (1995) *supra* n. 3, p. 234. Clayton Yeutter, then US Secretary of Agriculture, stated that this comprehensive proposal "is designed to level the playing field for farmers, so they compete fairly against one another instead of against governmental treasuries, in order to feed this growing population with a rational set of international trade rules." Yeutter, as quoted by Hillman, in Ingersent *et al* (1994) *supra* n. 16, p. 40.

30 Croome (1995) *supra* n. 3, p. 234.

31 In a recent statement about the days of agricultural negotiations during the Uruguay Round, Aart De Zeeuw wrote that, "[i]f we look back to the course of the negotiations, we must conclude that it was a very difficult job to get a deal between the US and the Cairns Group on the one hand, and Europe, Japan and Korea on the other hand." De Zeeuw, A. "Implementation and Accomplishments of the WTO" paper presented at a Seminar organized by the International Policy Council on Agriculture, Food and Trade, in *Proceedings of the IPC Seminar: Agriculture, the FTAA and the WTO* (Belo Horizonte, Brazil 12-13 May 1997) p. 21.

32 Croome (1995) *supra* n. 3, p. 239 (italics added).

33 See also Ingersent *et al,* in Ingersent *et al* (1994) *supra* n. 16, p. 68.

The De Zeeuw text was broadly accepted by most countries, but the actual proposals made by the major negotiating parties following it came nearly unchanged. Once again, the EC made specific offers in all other areas of agricultural trade except on export subsidies,[34] while the US "softened its stand only to the extent of calling for a 90% reduction" in them.[35] Needless to say, with positions so far apart from one another, the Brussels meeting of 1990, supposedly the closing meeting of the Uruguay Round, was doomed to failure. After few days of negotiations, seeing that the meeting was not in any way capable of producing agreement in the area of agriculture, the same Latin American countries which had blocked the Montreal meeting two years before "walked out of the talks and the Brussels meeting collapsed."[36]

Once again, resumption of the negotiations was possible only after the major powers were able to show some shifts in their respective positions on agriculture. The most important development here concerns the agreement reached between the parties so that "participants 'conduct negotiations to achieve specific binding commitments' on domestic support, market access, and export competition".[37] The importance of this agreement lies in the fact that it represented a big compromise on the part of the EC from its previous position of complete refusal to discuss any proposal to undertake a separate commitment in the area of export subsidies.[38] There was of course no agreement on such details as the type of agricultural export subsidies that were to be subject to the "specific binding commitments" and the percentage by which they would have to be cut. Nevertheless, agriculture being "the most politically-explosive single component of the Uruguay Round",[39] even such a general compromise was so important a development that it was soon labelled a "breakthrough".

Building on this development, several intensive and high-level negotiations were undertaken particularly between the US and the EC.[40] The proposal by Director-General Arthur Dunkel in the Draft Final Act of December 1991 (often called the Dunkel Draft) to cut export subsidies by 36 per cent in value and by 24 per cent in volume terms was subjected to mixed reactions from different corners. While the US and the Cairns Group countries (except Canada) reacted favourably, others,

---

[34] The explanation given to this by the EC was that a reduction of internal support would necessarily result in a reduction of export subsidies. See Ibid., p. 72–73.

[35] Croome (1995) *supra* n. 3, p. 240.

[36] J. Schott, *The Uruguay Round: An Assessment* (1994), p. 45; Croome (1995) *supra* n. 3, p. 278-279; and OECD (1995) *supra* n. 15, p. 13. The Brussels deadlock "centred around the so-called Hellstrom proposal which, essentially, proposed 30 per cent reductions on internal support, border protection and export subsidies over five years." Hillman, in Ingersent *et al* (1994) *supra* n. 16, p. 47.

[37] This agreement was announced by Arthur Dunkel in February, 1991. See Croome (1995) *supra* n. 3, p. 294.

[38] See, *inter alia*, Ingersent *et al*, in Ingersent *et al* (1994) *supra* n. 16, p. 78.

[39] Croome (1995) *supra* n. 3, p. 296.

[40] The meeting between then US and EC Commission presidents George Bush and Jacques Delors in November 1991 failed to bridge the gaps mainly because even US readiness to accept a 35% cut in the volume of subsidized exports was not satisfactory to the EC. See Croome (1995) *supra* n. 3, p. 295.

including the EC, Japan and Canada were negative about it.[41] The EC in particular did not like the draft provisions introducing quantitative limits to the amount of subsidized exports.[42] These differences, coupled with the bilateral dispute between the EC and the US over oilseeds, led to a series of high-level negotiations which were concluded on 20 November 1992 in what is often called the Blair House Accord.[43] In the area of export subsidies, the Blair House agreement responded to the above-mentioned EC concern in the following two ways: (1) it scaled down the volume of subsidized exports for reduction commitments from 24 per cent to 21 per cent;[44] and (2) it introduced the so-called "peace clause" by which agricultural subsidies provided in compliance with the pertinent provisions of the Agreement on Agriculture would be immune from challenge for the duration of six years.[45]

However, despite the fact that the Blair House Accord was a bilateral accord concluded between the US, on the one hand, and the EC representing its Member States, on the other, some individual Members of the latter, and particularly France, remained dissatisfied with the quantitative aspect of the export subsidy reduction commitments. This again meant that another series of high-level bilateral negotiations had to be undergone – thus further weakening the constraining power of the Dunkel Draft provisions. The resulting agreement, often called Blair House II, did two important modifications as regards export subsidies. Firstly, it extended the duration of the "peace clause" from six years to nine years; and secondly and more importantly, it introduced a so-called "front-loading" provision by which countries with higher levels of export subsidies in the post-base-period years were allowed to start their reductions from those higher levels.[46]

This brief summary of the Uruguay Round negotiations in the specific area of export subsidies demonstrates that agriculture in general, and agricultural export subsidies in particular, held the key not just to the success or failure of that Round, but to the very continued existence or otherwise of the entire multilateral trading system at large. And, as we have seen, when the "overdue" agreement was finally reached, the contents of the agricultural package reflected the series of vicissitudes and compromises it had been forced to go through. Seen in light of the ambitious proposals made by some (perhaps most) countries at the beginning of the round

---

41 See Croome (1995) *supra* n. 3, p. 328 ff; and Ingersent *et al*, in Ingersent *et al* (1994) *supra* n. 16, p. 80.

42 See Ingersent *et al*, in Ingersent *et al* (1994) *supra* n. 16, p. 80; and D. Hathaway, and M. Ingco, *Agricultural Liberalization and the Uruguay Round*, paper presented at the World Bank Conference on "The Uruguay Round and the Developing Economies", (26–27 January 1995), p. 10.

43 *European Economic Community – Payments and Subsidies Paid to Processors and Producers of Oilseeds and Related Animal-Feed Proteins*, report of the panel (L/6627 *BISD* 37S/86) adopted on 25 January 1990. For more on the role of the *EC Oilseeds* dispute in the course of the Uruguay Round, see *infra* chapter 9.

44 Being a product of EC insistence, this compromise has been described as "the most important concession" made by the US. See Croome (1995) *supra* n. 3, p. 340.

45 See Article 13 of the Agreement on Agriculture. See also, *inter alia*, Hathaway and Ingco (1995) *supra* n. 42, p. 12; Croome (1995) *supra* n. 3, pp. 328-381; and T. Josling, S. Tangermann, and T. Warley, *Agriculture in the GATT* (MacMillan, London 1996), pp. 160–161.

46 For the essence and significance of this arrangement, see *infra* chapter 7.4.1.3.

especially concerning agricultural export subsidies, those results may appear meaningless. But, seen from the opposite end of the spectrum, and especially given EC historical intransigence on matters agricultural, they could still be hailed as a great success.

Perhaps as a result of its contentious nature and the enormous attention it acquired thereby, many eminent authorities on the subject agree that the new regime introduced to govern the practice of export subsidies constitutes one of the most stringent and potentially effective disciplines in the whole package, promising "the most immediate, direct impact on markets and trade."[47] Tangermann observed, for instance, that "[a]mong all disciplines established under the AoA [Agreement on Agriculture], the constraints on subsidized exports are likely to be the most binding elements,"[48] and the new commitments on them are "the potentially most effective and hence the most important element of the Agreement on Agriculture."[49] Likewise, the United States Department of Agriculture (the USDA) praises these commitments on agricultural export subsidies as "the most meaningful aspects of the Agreement on Agriculture."[50] UNCTAD also observed that the effect on world market prices of export subsidy commitments would be more immediate than the commitments in the areas of market access and domestic support.[51] What is more, with the benefit of hindsight, we can add that it was indeed mainly in the area of export subsidies that the constraining power of the agriculture package appeared more vividly over the past few years since its entry into force.[52]

At least two important grounds lay beneath these positive remarks, viz. the dual nature of the commitments – quantitative as well as budgetary – and the relatively

---

[47] OECD (1995) *supra* n. 15, p. 46; See also, Josling *et al* (1996), *supra* n. 45, pp. 194–195. As will be explained subsequently, however, this should not unduly raise our expectations in this sphere. After all, one has to always remember that agriculture is the only sector where export subsidies are explicitly permissible. There were even fears that the exception found in the field of agriculture regarding export subsidies may have set a bad example for other sectors to follow.

[48] S. Tangermann, *Implementation of the Uruguay Round Agreement on Agriculture by Major Developed Countries*, A Report Prepared for the United Nations Conference on Trade and Development, (Distr. GENERAL, UNCTAD /ITD/16, 3 October, 1995), p. 15. See also S. Tangermann, *A Developed Country Perspective of the Agenda for the Next WTO Round of Agricultural Negotiations*, paper presented at the Graduate Institute of International Studies, 3 March 1997, p. 19; and S. Tangermann, *The European Union Perspective on Agricultural Trade Liberalization in the WTO*, paper presented at the Department of Agricultural Economics and Business, University of Guelph, Canada, February 1999, p. 10.

[49] Tangermann (1995) *supra* n. 48, p. 11.

[50] *Agriculture Outlook, supra* n. 22, p. 20.

[51] According to UNCTAD, "[t]he main impact of the export subsidy commitments should arise from the increased security arising from the fact that subsidy competition between the major subsidizing countries has been brought within limits, which should lead to increased investment in agricultural production in the more efficient countries." UNCTAD, *Identification of New Trading Opportunities Arising from the Implementation of the Uruguay Round Agreements in Selected Sectors and Markets: Report by the UNCTAD Secretariat* (Distr. General TD/B/WG.8/2, 19 June 1995), p. 5.

[52] For details, see discussion concerning the application of "downstream flexibility" provisions, *infra* chapter 7.5; and Hungary's problems in the area of agricultural export subsidies, its request for a waiver and the decision thereon, *infra* chapter 8.

greater degree of detail and precision accorded to the rules governing it. Besides, the almost complete absence of discipline that had characterized the practice in the preceding decades also provided the ideal background for the new discipline to appear revolutionary.

Yet, the fact remains that the law of agricultural export subsidies is still in its infancy. It should always be kept in mind that it is only in the field of agriculture that export subsidies are still explicitly permitted. Some even feel that, by so doing, the Agriculture Agreement has set a bad example in that it "has set in motion the legalization of export subsidies."[53] Neither are the rules of the Agriculture Agreement on this subject as clear and as precise as they may appear to be from a distance.

6.3 Definition of Agricultural Export Subsidies

6.3.1 General

As pointed out earlier, the term "export subsidies" is directly defined only under Article 1(e) of the Agriculture Agreement.[54] According to this provision, export subsidies refer to "subsidies contingent upon export performance" and include the export subsidies listed under Article 9 of the same Agreement.[55] Included in this list are such governmental acts as the provision of direct subsidies contingent upon export performance, the sale or disposal for export of non-commercial stocks of agricultural products at prices lower than on the domestic market, payments on the export of an agricultural product financed by virtue of governmental action, the provision of subsidies to reduce the costs of marketing agricultural exports, and

---

53 *Agriculture Outlook*, *supra* n. 22, p. 20

54 See *supra* section 6.3.

55 Article 9:1 of the Agriculture Agreement provides as follows:

"The following export subsidies are subject to reduction commitments under this Agreement:

(a) the provision by governments or their agencies of direct subsidies, including payments-in-kind, to a firm, to an industry, to producers of an agricultural product, to a cooperative or other association of such producers, or to a marketing board, contingent on export performance;

(b) the sale or disposal for export by governments or their agencies of non-commercial stocks of agricultural products at a price lower than the comparable price charged for the like product to buyers in the domestic market;

(c) payments on the export of an agricultural product that are financed by virtue of governmental action, whether or not a charge on the public account is involved, including payments that are financed from the proceeds of a levy imposed on the agricultural product concerned or on an agricultural product from which the exported product is derived;

(d) the provision of subsidies to reduce the costs of marketing exports of agricultural products (other than widely available export promotion and advisory services) including handling, upgrading and other processing costs, and the costs of international transport and freight;

(e) internal transport and freight charges on export shipments, provided or mandated by governments, on terms more favourable than for domestic shipments;

(f) subsidies on agricultural products contingent on their incorporation in exported products."

subsidies on agricultural production contingent on their incorporation in exported products. The definition and the list referred to therein resolve several conceptual and practical difficulties surrounding the issue of subsidies; however, they also leave a number of problems open.

6.3.2 Scope of Export Subsidies under the Agreement on Agriculture

The term "export subsidy", defined as a "subsidy contingent upon export performance", constitutes two elements – that it is a subsidy and that it is granted contingent upon export performance.[56] However, the Agreement on Agriculture does not define what a "subsidy" is. To the extent that the Agriculture Agreement does not define the root term "subsidy", the definition of an export subsidy as a "subsidy contingent upon export performance" may not serve much useful purpose.

Neither does the reference under Article 1(e) to the export subsidies listed in Article 9:1 of the Agreement help much on this point. Article 9.1 provides only an illustrative list of the type of practices that fall within the scope of agricultural export subsidies.[57] The question of what is it that should be contingent upon export performance for an export subsidy to exist begs for a solution. The text of the Agriculture Agreement, which is the immediate context for the interpretation of the term "subsidy" as used under Article 1(e) thereof, is not of much help in this respect. Under such circumstances, the customary rules of treaty interpretation, enshrined in Article 31 of the 1969 Vienna Convention, tell us that agreements should be interpreted in accordance with their "context".[58] And that "context" in the present situation covers not only the text of the Agreement on Agriculture but also other relevant multilateral agreements forming part of the WTO Agreement.[59] Of the Agreements falling within that broader context, the SCM Agreement is the most pertinent instrument for our purposes here.[60]

The SCM Agreement has, for the first time in the history of the multilateral trading system, defined the elusive and controversial concept of "subsidies". Both the Agriculture Agreement as well as the Agreement on Subsidies and Counter-

---

[56] See also *Canada – Measures Affecting the Importation of Milk and the Exportation of Dairy Products*, report of the panel (WT/DS103/R, WT/DS113/R) 17 May, 1999, para. 4.124.

[57] The list under Article 9.1 uses the term "subsidies" in paragraphs (a) in connection with "direct subsidies", (d) to refer to the "provision of subsidies" for marketing of exports, and (f) to refer to "upstream subsidies".

[58] Article 31(1) of the Vienna Convention provides that "A treaty shall be interpreted in good faith in accordance with the ordinary meaning to be given to the terms of the treaty in their context and in the light of its object and purpose." *Vienna Convention on the Law of Treaties* (done at Vienna, 23 May 1969, 1155 U.N.T.S. 33).

[59] See, for instance, *United States – Anti-Dumping Duty on Dynamic Random Access Semiconductors (DRAMs) of One Megabit or Above from Korea*, report of the panel (WT/DS99/R, 19 March 1999), para. 6.21.

[60] See *inter alia, Canada Dairy*, report of the panel, *supra* n. 56, para. 7.126, and *United States–Tax Treatment for "Foreign Sales Corporations"* report of the panel (WT/DS108/R), 8 October 1999, para. 7.150.

vailing Measures being part of the multilateral agreements annexed to the WTO Agreement, the package deal principle stated under Article XIV of the WTO Agreement mandates that an acceptance of the WTO Agreement applies to all the multilateral agreements annexed thereto as well.[61] In the present context, this means that a country that is a party to the Agriculture Agreement is also party to the Subsidies Agreement. As parts of a bigger whole, terms defined by one agreement may conveniently be used to interpret the provisions of another agreement, subject, of course, to any explicit or implicit limitations that may have been set against such an exercise. It is such a systemic approach that can give effect to the conceptual coherence expected of such a complex international treaty as the WTO Agreement.

Indeed, as the *FSC* Panel stated, "Article 1 of the SCM Agreement, which defines the term 'subsidy' for the purposes of the SCM Agreement, represents *highly relevant context for the interpretation of the word 'subsidy' within the meaning of the Agreement on Agriculture*, as it is the only article in the WTO Agreement that provides a definition of that term."[62] On that basis, one may conveniently go to Article 1 of the SCM Agreement and adapt the definition given to the term "subsidies" in order to understand the meaning of the term "export subsidies" as defined under the Agriculture Agreement. This exercise brings us to the following definition of an export subsidy as used under Article 1(e) of the Agriculture Agreement: it refers to a financial contribution by a government or any public body or any other form of income or price support in the sense of Article XVI of the GATT 1994 contingent upon export performance and conferring a benefit on the recipient.[63]

This approach is not, however, without its problems. One question is the following: Given the cautious opening phrase of Article 1.1 of the SCM Agreement that the definition of subsidies given therein is a definition "[f]or the purpose of this Agreement", is this kind of direct transposition of the definition to apply to cases involving other agreements, including that on agriculture, justified? Stated differently, should a subsidy for the purposes of the Agriculture Agreement necessarily satisfy the requirements of being a "subsidy" under the SCM Agreement? This is a difficult issue to resolve. On the one hand, the caution that is implicit in the introductory phrase of Article 1.1 of the SCM Agreement might indicate that the intention of the parties was to limit the definition to those matters falling exclusively under the SCM Agreement. On the other hand, the customary principles of treaty interpretation dictate that terms should be construed in accordance, *inter alia*, with their context, which, *in casu*, covers the SCM Agreement.

The issue has appeared in only a couple of WTO disputes so far. What is worse,

---

61 Article II:2 of the WTO Agreement provides that "The agreements and associated legal instruments included in Annex 1, 2 and 3 (hereinafter referred to as 'Multilateral Trade Agreements') are integral parts of this Agreement, binding on all Members." Article XIV:1 then pushes this package deal approach further by providing that an acceptance of the WTO Agreement "shall apply to this Agreement and the Multilateral Trade Agreements annexed hereto."

62 *FSC*, report of the panel, *supra* n. 60, para. 7.150 (emphasis added).

63 For a discussion of the elements of this definition, see *supra* chapter 5.2.

both reports took the option of safely avoiding a ruling on the matter. In *Canada Dairy*, for instance, Canada specifically referred to the definition provision of Article 1 of the SCM Agreement and argued that the scheme under attack was "not a 'subsidy' and can therefore a priori not be an 'export subsidy'".[64] The panel admitted that the SCM Agreement was "part of the general context" which could serve as a guide for the interpretation of the meaning of an "export subsidy" as used in Articles 1(e) and 10 of the Agriculture Agreement.[65] However, by giving priority to a consideration of the matter from the perspective of the specifically-listed export subsidy practices under the Agreement on Agriculture (which obviously is a logical approach), it was able to avoid the specific issue of whether a "subsidy" under the Agriculture Agreement should necessarily be a "subsidy" under the SCM Agreement.[66]

In *FSC*, where the problem was more directly at issue, the panel recognized the relevance of the definition under the SCM Agreement as a "highly relevant context" for the interpretation of a subsidy as used under the Agriculture Agreement. It added, however, that "[t]his is not ... to say that the definition of 'subsidy' in the

---

64 *Canada Dairy*, report of the panel, *supra* n. 56, para. 7.5(a).

65 Ibid., para. 7.126.

66 The panel avoided the matter as follows:

> "Since Article 9.1 sets out the explicit reduction commitments entered into by Canada, as opposed to Article 10 which deals with circumvention of those commitments, we shall first examine whether the Special Milk Classes Scheme involves an export subsidy listed in Article 9.1. ... *We prefer this sequence to Canada's approach of first examining whether the scheme is a 'subsidy' more generally with particular reference to the SCM Agreement.* What needs to be examined here in the first place is whether an 'export subsidy' is provided for quantities of exports of agricultural products in excess of the reduction commitments made by Canada under the Agreement on Agriculture. In our view, the most specific and appropriate language provided to make this determination is found in Article 9.1 of the Agreement on Agriculture – setting out specific practices as 'export subsidies' explicitly made subject to Canada's reduction commitments; not in Article 1 of the SCM Agreement pursuant to which certain practices are deemed to be a 'subsidy' for purposes of the SCM Agreement." Ibid., para. 7.31 (italics added).

At another point, the panel observes that "Article 1 of the SCM Agreement, for example, includes as a subsidy 'any form of income or price support in the sense of Article XVI of GATT 1994' whereby a benefit is conferred. However, since in this case we need to interpret the meaning of certain 'export subsidies', we consider it more appropriate, without prejudice to the scope of Article 10.1, to examine what practices are considered under the SCM Agreement to be 'export subsidies', *rather than to examine how that Agreement defines the more general concept of a 'subsidy' in its Article 1.*" Ibid., para. 7.126 (italics added).

Finally, after finding that the measures at issue were export subsidies as listed in paragraph (d) of the *Illustrative List of Export Subsidies* annexed to the SCM Agreement, the panel added that "*We do not consider it necessary in this case to decide whether the fact that a scheme involves an export subsidy under the SCM Agreement necessarily means that it also constitutes an export subsidy under Article 1(e) of the Agreement on Agriculture. We are not called upon – and do not intend here – to decide whether the scope of the concept of export subsidy under the SCM Agreement is the same as, or different than, that under the Agreement on Agriculture.* We do find, however, that in the circumstances of this case and on the grounds outlined above, Classes 5(d) and (e)–assuming, in the alternative, that they do not constitute an export subsidy as listed in either Article 9.1(a) or Article 9.1(c)–nevertheless involve an 'other' export subsidy in the sense of Article 10.1." Ibid., para. 7.132 (italics added, footnotes omitted).

SCM Agreement, which applies '[f]or the purpose of this [i.e., the SCM] Agreement', is directly applicable to the Agreement on Agriculture."[67] As will be substantiated later on, the use of the terms "directly applicable" in this sentence appears to be calculated to conceal the panel's inability to take a firm position on the subject. And this comes out more vividly in the following statements of the panel:

> "In particular, we cannot preclude *a priori* that there could be cases where relevant provisions of the Agreement on Agriculture might lead a panel to conclude that the term 'subsidy' as used in the Agreement on Agriculture has a different meaning in a particular context from that ascribed to it by Article 1 of the SCM Agreement. As a general matter, however, and subject to any provision of the Agreement on Agriculture under which the contrary is to be inferred, we consider that a measure which represents a subsidy within the meaning of the SCM Agreement will also be a subsidy within the meaning of the Agreement on Agriculture."[68]

A footnote then adds that "a measure which is listed as an export subsidy in Article 9.1 of the Agreement on Agriculture is an export subsidy for the purposes of the Agreement on Agriculture independently of the definition of subsidy in the SCM Agreement."[69]

Clearly, there are two main reasons behind this cautious approach of the panels. Firstly, and this has already been pointed out earlier, the SCM Agreement explicitly states that the definition under its Article 1 is meant only "for the purpose of this Agreement." Secondly, and more importantly, the Agriculture Agreement identifies certain specific practices as outright export subsidies for its purposes regardless of the definition given therein.

To start with the first, although the phrase "this Agreement" under Article 1 appears to mean the SCM Agreement, such a literal approach may not always govern the meaning of a term under question. It may be interesting to note, for instance, that, in trying to interpret the phrase "this Agreement" as used under Article 32.3 of the SCM Agreement, the *Brazil – Coconut* panel admitted that " 'this Agreement' in its ordinary meaning would appear to be a reference to the SCM Agreement".[70] However, the panel did not stop there; it went further and referred, *inter alia*, to the definition provision of the same Agreement and observed as follows:

> "a strict application of the term 'this Agreement' as used elsewhere in the SCM Agreement could produce manifestly unreasonable results. For example, Article 1.1 of the SCM Agreement contains a definition of 'subsidy' and Article 16.1 of the SCM Agreement contains a definition of 'domestic industry' both of which are 'for the purposes of this Agreement'. However, the terms 'subsidy'

[67] *FSC*, report of the panel, *supra* n. 60, para. 7.150.

[68] Ibid., para. 7.150.

[69] Ibid., footnote 702 to para. 7.150.

[70] *Brazil–Measures Affecting Desiccated Coconut*, report of the panel (WT/DS22/R) 17 October 1996, para. 234.

and 'domestic industry' are used both in Article VI of GATT 1994 and the SCM Agreement. If the term 'this Agreement' were interpreted *strictu sensu* to mean the SCM Agreement, then the definitions of these key terms in the SCM Agreement would be inapplicable to the same terms as used in Article VI of GATT 1994. Such a result could not have been intended."[71]

On the same issue and in the same case, the Appellate Body stated that "[e]xamination of the ordinary meaning of this provision alone could lead us to the conclusion that the term, 'this Agreement', in Article 32.3 means the SCM Agreement. However, it is necessary also to consider this provision in its context and in light of the object and purpose of the WTO Agreement."[72] Applying this latter approach, the Appellate Body then observed that "[i]f Article 32.3 is read in conjunction with Articles 10 and 32.1 of the SCM Agreement, it becomes clear that the term 'this Agreement' in Article 32.3 means 'this Agreement *and* Article VI of the GATT 1994'."[73] From all this, we can safely conclude that the phrase "this Agreement" in Article 1 of the SCM Agreement may not necessarily have to be interpreted to mean only the SCM Agreement.

Coming to the second and more important point, the Agriculture Agreement has specified two groups of practices and designated them as export subsidies irrespective of definition (hereafter termed as "specified export subsidies"). First, the definition of export subsidies under Article 1(e) of the Agriculture Agreement as "subsidies contingent upon export performance" has been qualified by the phrase "including the export subsidy practices listed in Article 9 of this Agreement" (hereafter "listed export subsidies"). The latter phrase has as its effect that, whatever the interpretation one may give to the term "subsidy" under the former phrase, one may not interpret it in such a way as to exclude the listed practices from the ambit of "export subsidies" as defined under Article 1(e) of the Agriculture Agreement. This in turn means that, at least at the theoretical level, to the extent necessitated by the inclusion of a practice in the list, the definition of the term "export subsidies" under the Agreement on Agriculture *may* be wider than that formulated on the basis of a transposition of the definition of "subsidies" under the SCM Agreement. As rightly pointed out by New Zealand in *Canada Dairy*, "if an export subsidy were to meet the terms of one of the sub-paragraphs of Article 9.1 ... but yet did not meet the definition of Article 1 of the SCM Agreement, it would nonetheless still constitute an export subsidy for the purposes of the Agreement on Agriculture."[74] Canada also argued in the same case that "the list of export subsidy practices found in Article 9.1 served two purposes in the Agreement on Agriculture. On one hand, it served as an exhaustive list of export subsidy practices that were subject to the reduction requirements set out in the Agreement. It also provided an illustrative list of export

---

71 Ibid., para. 234.

72 *Brazil–Measures Affecting Desiccated Coconut*, report of the Appellate Body (WT/DS22/AB/R), 21 February 1997, p. 17.

73 Ibid.

74 *Canada Dairy*, report of the panel, *supra* n. 56, para. 4.134.

subsidy practices to be included within the definition of 'export subsidy' in Article 1(e) of the Agreement."[75]

The second group constitutes the three practices identified by Article 10.2 of the Agriculture Agreement as export subsidy practices for the regulation of which Members have undertaken to develop an internationally agreed discipline and, once it is developed, to be governed thereby. These practices are export credits, export credit guarantees, and insurance programmes. Stated under Article 10 on the anti-circumvention of export subsidy commitments, these practices have already been characterized as export subsidies for purposes of the Agreement on Agriculture. They are examples of practices not listed under Article 9.1 but whose status as export subsidies has already been determined regardless of definition. As will be seen later on, the only thing special about them is that they are not specifically referred to under Article 1(e) of the Agriculture Agreement; they are not covered by the reduction commitments; and they can be lawfully granted subject only to the anti-circumvention requirement. Theoretically speaking, therefore, and despite the fact that there is no reference to them in the definition provision of Article 1(e), any interpretation of the term "export subsidy" as used in the Agriculture Agreement cannot be taken to exclude these practices from its ambit.

As such, whatever definition one may adopt for the interpretation of the term "subsidy" as used in the Agreement on Agriculture, the six listed practices under Article 9.1 and the three specific examples mentioned under Article 10.2 must be covered not just as subsidies, but as export subsidies. In case this may lead to some kind of inconsistency between the SCM Agreement and the Agreement on Agriculture, the provisions of the latter prevail over those of the former. Theoretically speaking, therefore, the validity of this line of reasoning is unquestionable. It is like saying that the meaning of export subsidies under the SCM Agreement cannot be interpreted to exclude those specific practices that are singled out as such in the Illustrative List of Export Subsidies of Annex I thereto.

However, this is only a theoretical possibility which does not necessarily imply that it has been given effect to in the content of the specified export subsidies under discussion. In order to answer the question of whether these specified agricultural export subsidy practices add anything that does not fall within the definition of the term "subsidy" as provided under Article 1 of the SCM Agreement and as applied to interpret Article 1(e) of the Agreement on Agriculture, a closer look at each of those practices appears necessary.

6.3.2.1 Specified Agricultural Export Subsidies: Are They of a Wider Scope than General Export Subsidies?

A look at the definition of subsidies under the SCM Agreement (together with the illustrative list of export subsidies annexed thereto) indicates that it is wide enough to cover virtually all the practices that have been specifically characterized as export

[75] Ibid., para. 4.127.

subsidies for purposes of the Agriculture Agreement.[76] The following brief comparative survey of the essence of agricultural export subsidy practices, so designated by the Agreement on Agriculture, vis-à-vis the definition of subsidies given under Article 1 of the SCM Agreement and its description of general export subsidies in Article 3 as supplemented by the illustrative list aims at showing this relationship more vividly.

It has been argued earlier that because the term "subsidy" is not defined by the text of the Agriculture Agreement, the meaning of "export subsidies" under the latter Agreement could be interpreted by using the definition given to the root term "subsidy" in the SCM Agreement. This resulted in the definition of the term "export subsidies" under Article 1(e) of the Agreement on Agriculture as a financial contribution by a government or any public body or any other form of income or price support in the sense of Article XVI of GATT 1994 contingent upon export performance and conferring a benefit on the recipient.[77] The latter part of this adapted definition makes it nearly identical with the description of "export subsidies" under Article 3.1(a) of the SCM Agreement. Indeed, as the Appellate Body in *FSC* pointed out,

> "We see no reason, and none has been pointed out to us, to read the requirement of 'contingent upon export performance' in the *Agreement on Agriculture* differently from the same requirement imposed by the *SCM Agreement*. The two Agreements use precisely the same words to define 'export subsidies'. Although there are differences between the export subsidy disciplines established under the two Agreements, those differences do not, in our view, affect the common substantive requirement relating to export contingency. Therefore, we think it appropriate to apply the interpretation of export contingency that we have adopted under the *SCM Agreement* to the interpretation of export contingency under the Agreement on Agriculture."[78]

The practices illustrated in Annex I to the SCM Agreement, if applied in the agricultural sector, are also, in principle, covered by this adapted definition. A look at the scope of the specified agricultural export subsidies indicates that they are more or less an agricultural version of the more generic concept of export subsidies as understood and illustrated under the SCM Agreement. Although there might be overlaps between the various items specified under Articles 9.1 and 10.2 of the Agriculture Agreement,[79] we now see each of them in brief.

---

[76] See discussion on the definition of subsidies under the SCM Agreement, *supra* chapter 5.

[77] See Ibid.

[78] *United States–Tax Treatment for "Foreign Sales Corporations"*, report of the Appellate Body (WT/DS108/AB/R) 24 February 2000, para. 141 (italics in original).

[79] See *Canada Dairy*, report of the panel, *supra* n. 56, para. 7.35.

6.3.2.1.1 Article 9.1(a): Direct Subsidies[80]

Article 9.1(a) of the Agreement on Agriculture stipulates that "the provision by governments or their agencies of direct subsidies, including payments-in-kind, to a firm, to an industry, to producers of an agricultural product, to a co-operative or other association of such producers, or to a marketing board, contingent on export performance" is an agricultural export subsidy in the sense of Article 1(e) thereof. There are three key elements here – "direct subsidies", provided "by governments or their agents", and "contingent on export performance". Not only are all these elements covered by the description of export subsidies under the SCM Agreement, they are coined in nearly identical terms.[81] Moreover, paragraph (a) of the Illustrative List of Export Subsidies annexed to the SCM Agreement provides that "the provision by governments of direct subsidies to a firm or an industry contingent upon export performance" is an export subsidy in the sense of the Subsidies Agreement. The only difference between them is one of detail. It thus appears possible to conclude that Article 9.1(a) does not cover anything that is not covered by the concept of export subsidies under the SCM Agreement.

6.3.2.1.2 Article 9.1(b): Sale for Export at Less than Domestic Market Price

Article 9.1(b) provides that "the sale or disposal for export by governments or their agencies of non-commercial stocks of agricultural products at a price lower than the comparable price charged for the like product to buyers in the domestic market" is an export subsidy. The government here is providing the products to exporters on terms more favourable than what is available to them on the domestic market. Once again, this is a practice that squarely fits in with the description of export subsidies under the SCM Agreement. Moreover, Article 9.1(b) of the Agreement on Agriculture simply is a very straightforward example of the type of practices that are covered by paragraph (d) of the Illustrative List of Export Subsidies in Annex I to the SCM Agreement.[82] It is apparent that, in this specific case, the practice identified under the Agriculture Agreement is even narrower than the corresponding practice identified by the illustrative list under the SCM Agreement.

6.3.2.1.3 Article 9.1(c): Payments on Agricultural Exports

According to Article 9.1(c) of the Agriculture Agreement, an export subsidy also

---

[80] For interesting details on the elements of this practice, see the reports of both the panel and the Appellate Body on the *Canada Dairy* dispute.

[81] See discussion on general export subsidies *supra* chapter 5.4.

[82] Paragraph (d) of the *Illustrative List of Export Subsidies* in Annex I to the SCM Agreement provides as follows: "The provision by governments or their agencies either directly or indirectly through government-mandated schemes, of imported or domestic products or services for use in the production of exported goods, on terms or conditions more favourable than for provision of like or directly competitive products or services for use in the production of goods for domestic consumption, if (in the case of products) such terms or conditions are more favourable than those commercially available on world markets to their exporters." A footnote adds that "[t]he term 'commercially available' means that the choice between domestic and imported products is unrestricted and depends only on commercial considerations."

includes "payments on the export of an agricultural product that are financed by virtue of governmental action, whether or not a charge on the public account is involved, including payments that are financed from the proceeds of a levy imposed on the agricultural product concerned or on an agricultural product from which the exported product is derived." In some senses, this provision merely repeats the essence of Articles 1 and 3 of the SCM Agreement, but with an agricultural flavour. The first part of the provision, referring particularly to "payments on the export of an agricultural product that are financed by virtue of governmental action" makes it clear that, just like all other forms of export subsidies, there should be some form of transfer of economic resources which is contingent upon the export of a product and whose existence depends on some form of involvement on the part of the government. The second part plays only an explanatory role on the type of government involvement concerned.[83] In line with Article 1.1(a)(1)(iv) of the SCM Agreement, this paragraph makes it clear that for an export subsidy to exist, it does not matter whether the type of governmental involvement results in a charge on the public account or not. This is only a clearer expression of Article 1.1(a)(1)(iv) of the SCM Agreement, which provides that the requirement of a governmental "financial contribution" is met even when the government merely entrusts or directs a private body to do any of the activities illustrated under items (i) to (iii) of the same provision. Moreover, this is also a practice that falls under the wide scope of paragraph (d) of the Illustrative List of Export Subsidies in the SCM Agreement. The conclusion, once again, is therefore that the scope of Article 9.1(c) does not go beyond that covered by the more general provisions of the SCM Agreement on the subject.

6.3.2.1.4 Articles 9.1(d) and (e): Subsidization of Marketing and Transportation Costs for Exports

These two related provisions stipulate that the provision of subsidies to reduce the costs of marketing exports and internal transport and freight charges on export shipments of agricultural products are also considered as export subsidies. While the practice of subsidization to reduce export marketing costs under paragraph (d) simply and clearly involves a direct transfer of funds in the sense of Article 1.1(a)(1)(ii) of the SCM Agreement, the case of transportation subsidies under paragraph (e) is even simpler and clearer. It is identical in every respect with paragraph (c) of the Illustrative List of Export Subsidies under the SCM Agreement. Needless to say, these two forms of practice are once again covered by the more general provisions of the SCM Agreement on the matter.

---

[83] As the *Canada Dairy* panel rightly observed, "the first part of Article 9.1(c) – 'payments on the export of an agricultural product that are financed by virtue of governmental action' – includes the core elements of an export subsidy as listed in that provision. The subsequent part provides further clarification – in an illustrative way – as to the meaning of these core elements." *Canada Dairy*, report of the panel, *supra* n. 56, para. 7.89.

6.3.2.1.5 Article 9.1(f): "Upstream Subsidies"

According to this paragraph, the provision of "subsidies on agricultural products contingent on their incorporation in exported products" is also an export subsidy in the sense of the definition provided under Article 1(e) of the Agreement on Agriculture. This is a reference to what are commonly referred to as upstream subsidies. A subsidy that is dependent on a product's incorporation in exported products is a subsidy contingent on exportation. If the incorporating product is not exported, no question of an export subsidy for the incorporated product would arise. As such, this is a subsidy that squarely fits within the description of export subsidies in the SCM Agreement as subsidies contingent, in law or in fact, whether solely or as one of several other conditions, upon export performance.[84]

6.3.2.1.6 Article 10.2: Export Credits, Export Credit Guarantees and Insurance Programmes

Article 10 of the Agreement on Agriculture is an anti-circumvention provision with respect to the commitments on export subsidies. After stipulating the principle that export subsidies not listed in Article 9.1 may not be applied in a circumventory manner,[85] paragraph 2 singles out three specific practices and provides the following: "Members undertake to work toward the development of internationally agreed disciplines to govern the provision of export credits, export credit guarantees or insurance programmes and, after agreement on such disciplines, to provide export credits, export credit guarantees or insurance programmes only in conformity therewith." As reiterated already, the theoretical argument that the listed practices under Article 9.1 are always covered regardless of our definition of the term "subsidy" under Article 1(e) of the Agreement on Agriculture equally applies to these three practices. For, their status as export subsidies has already been determined. Moreover, the conclusion reached earlier on the scope of the listed subsidies vis-à-vis the scope of export subsidies under the SCM Agreement applies equally well for these three practices. This flows from the provisions of paragraphs (j)[86] and (k)[87] of the Illustrative List of Export Subsidies in the SCM Agreement.

---

84 Article 3.1(a) of the SCM Agreement.

85 Article 10.1 of the Agreement on Agriculture.

86 Paragraph (j) of the *Illustrative List of Export Subsidies* provides as follows: "The provision by governments (or special institutions controlled by governments) of *export credit guarantee or insurance programmes*, of insurance or guarantee programmes against increases in the cost of exported products or of exchange risk programmes, at premium rates which are inadequate to cover the long-term operating costs and losses of the programmes." (italics added)

87 Paragraph (k) of the *Illustrative List of Export Subsidies* in relevant part provides as follows: "The grant by governments (or special institutions controlled by and/or acting under the authority of governments) of *export credits* at rates below those which they actually have to pay for the funds so employed (or would have to pay if they borrowed on international capital markets in order to obtain funds of the same maturity and other credit terms and denominated in the same currency as the export credit), or the payment by them of all or part of the costs incurred by exporters or financial institutions in obtaining credits, in so far as they are used to secure a material advantage in the field of export credit terms." (italics added).

These paragraphs specifically address all three practices and unequivocally state that they are export subsidies. Consequently, there appears to be no room to raise the issue of whether the practices specified under Article 10 of the Agreement on Agriculture may be of a different scope than those covered by the SCM Agreement.

6.3.2.1.7 Conclusion

In conclusion, this rather brief comparative survey of the scope of export subsidies in the two agreements confirms that the practices specifically designated as export subsidies by Articles 9 and 10 of the Agreement on Agriculture are not of a different nature or of a wider scope than those covered by the SCM Agreement. The former are in fact a sector-specific version of the latter. The result of this comparative survey appears to dispel the fear of the *FSC* panel which said that it "cannot preclude *a priori* that there could be cases where relevant provisions of the Agreement on Agriculture might lead a panel to conclude that the term 'subsidy' as used in the Agreement on Agriculture has a different meaning in a particular context from that ascribed to it by Article 1 of the SCM Agreement."[88] The panel stated in particular that "a measure which is listed as an export subsidy in Article 9.1 of the Agreement on Agriculture is an export subsidy for the purposes of the Agreement on Agriculture independently of the definition of subsidy in the SCM Agreement."[89] We have seen, however, that none of the six listed export subsidy practices under Article 9.1 of the Agriculture Agreement contains anything different from what is expressed or implied in the provisions of the SCM Agreement on export subsidies. The language of the SCM Agreement is so expansive that it is virtually impossible to imagine any specified agricultural export subsidy which may fall outside its scope. Rather than adding new elements to the definition of export subsidies, the specified practices only supplement and clarify the definition. It is therefore possible to conclude that, for all practical purposes, the definition of the term subsidy under the SCM Agreement applies fully and directly for the interpretation of Article 1(e) of the Agriculture Agreement on agricultural export subsidies.

6.3.3 Listed Export Subsidies as Supplementing the Definition

We have seen that Article 9 of the Agriculture Agreement enumerates a list of practices falling under the umbrella of the term export subsidies as defined under Article 1(e) of the same Agreement that are "subject to reduction commitments". The enumeration does not affect the generality of the definition given earlier. In other words, the fact that specific practices have been designated as export subsidies regardless of definition does not imply absence of practices that fit into the definition of the term but that are not covered by any of the items enumerated under Article 9.1. That is why the list of export subsidies under Article 9.1 was taken as exhaustive for purposes of reduction requirements and as illustrative for purposes of the

---

88 *FSC*, report of the panel, *supra* n. 60, para. 7.150.

89 Ibid., footnote 702 to para. 7.150.

definition of an "export subsidy" in Article 1(e) of the Agreement.[90] Moreover, as explained earlier, virtually all items in the list fall within the ambit of the concept of "export subsidies" as defined in the Agreement on Agriculture and as interpreted with the help of the definition given to the term "subsidies" by the Subsidies Agreement.[91] Moreover, we shall see that some of the practices listed under Article 9.1 actually supplement and clarify the definition provision and further illuminate our understanding of both the conception as well as the calculation of subsidies in general.

To start with the first item in the list, in line with Article 1.1(a)(1)(iii) of the SCM Agreement,[92] Article 9.1(a) of the Agriculture Agreement explicitly states that subsidies may take the form of monetary payments or payments-in-kind. A "payment in kind" is "payment" which does not take the form of money.[93] In connection with the interpretation of "payments-in-kind" as used in Article 9.1(a) of the Agreement on Agriculture, the Appellate Body in the *Canada Dairy* case stated that "the word 'payments', in the term 'payments-in-kind', denotes a transfer of economic resources, in a form other than money, from the grantor of the payment to the recipient."[94] In other words, what is important for the existence of a subsidy is that a payment, a transfer of economic resources, be made; not the form in which it is made.[95] Once made, and regardless of its form, the only important point in this respect becomes "the economic value of the transfer."[96] This is because, as the Appellate Body rightly emphasized, a "payment-in-kind", just like a payment in money, "may be made in exchange for full or partial consideration or it may be made gratuitously."[97] As discussed elsewhere, there is a subsidy only if a benefit is conferred on the recipient – a case that can take place only if the transfer is made "for less than full consideration" on a comparable commercial benchmark. Just like a monetary payment, in as long as the recipient pays the market price for whatever he receives in kind, there is no subsidy.[98] By thus explicitly including "payments in kind" as a form of direct subsidies, Article 9.1(a) has therefore contributed to the interpretation of the wider concept of a subsidy at large.

The specific reference to "payments in kind" as a form of "direct subsidies" under Article 9.1(a) has also contributed immensely to the interpretation of the term "payments" in other paragraphs of Article 9.1 itself. For instance, in connection with the price-pooling system challenged in the *Canada Dairy* case, Canada argued that payments-in-kind were covered only when they were expressly included, and

---

90 See Canada's argument in *Canada Dairy*, quoted *supra* n. 75.

91 See *supra* chapter 5.2.

92 According to this provision, one form of making a "financial contribution" in the sense of the Agreement is when "a government provides goods or services other than general infrastructure, or purchases goods" – which obviously is a reference to a non-monetary form of providing subsidies.

93 See *Canada – Measures Affecting the Importation of Milk and the Exportation of Dairy Products*, Report of the Appellate Body (WT/DS103/AB/R, WT/DS113/AB/R) 13 October, 1999, para.107.

94 Ibid., para. 87.

95 This, of course, is in addition to the fulfilment of all other necessary elements for the existence of a subsidy. For a discussion of this issue, see *supra* chapter 5.2.

96 See *Canada Dairy*, report of the Appellate Body, *supra* n. 93, para. 87.

97 Ibid., para. 87.

98 Ibid.

that, since they were not so included in Article 9.1(c), this provision could not apply to the case under consideration.[99] The panel held, however, that all export subsidies listed under Article 9.1, including sub-paragraph (c), cover payments made either in money or in kind or in both.[100] The Appellate Body affirmed the panel's ruling and stressed that the explicit reference to payments in kind in one or more of the paragraphs of Article 9.1 does not necessarily imply exclusion from others:

> "In Article 9.1(a) and in paragraph 5 of Annex 2, the term 'payments-in-kind' is used in conjunction with the words 'direct subsidies' and 'direct payments', respectively. We believe that reference is made to 'payments-in-kind' in these two provisions to counter any suggestion that the ordinary meaning of the terms 'direct subsidies' and 'direct payments' does not include 'payments-in-kind'. By contrast, since the ordinary meaning of the word 'payments' in Article 9.1(c) includes 'payments-in-kind', there was no need for 'payments-in-kind' to be expressly provided for. Moreover, if 'payments-in-kind' are included in the qualified concept of 'direct payments' under Annex 2, paragraph 5, it would be incongruous to exclude them from the broader concept of 'payments' in Article 9.1(c)."[101]

One may thus conclude that the explicit inclusion of payments in kind in Article 9.1(a) sheds more light towards a better understanding of the meaning of subsidies in a wider scale.

Moreover, by using the words "governments or their agencies" as the possible providers of these payments, Article 9.1(a) of the Agriculture Agreement also gives some more light for the interpretation of what a "government or any public body" is in the sense of Article 1.1(a)(1) of the SCM Agreement. In *Canada Dairy*, one of the most difficult issues concerned the question of what constituted a governmental agency. In particular, the status of what are called "provincial milk marketing

---

[99] See Canada's argument before the panel in *Canada Dairy*, report of the panel, *supra* n. 56, paras. 7.96-7.97; see also Canada's argument before the Appellate Body, *Canada Dairy*, report of the Appellate Body, *supra* n. 93, paras. 32-33.

[100] The panel stated its ruling as follows:

> "The idea that the export subsidies identified in Article 9.1 generally, and Article 9.1(c) in particular, also include payments-in-kind and, specifically, the provision of a good at a reduced price, is also confirmed in other sub-paragraphs of Article 9.1. Article 9.1(a) refers to 'direct subsidies, including payments-in-kind'. Article 9.1(b) mentions the sale or disposal for export of non-commercial stocks 'at a price lower than the comparable price charged for the like product to buyers in the domestic market'. Article 9.1(d) refers to a reduction in the costs of marketing exports. Finally, Article 9.1(e) is directed at reduced internal transport and freight charges on export shipments. None of the provisions under Article 9.1 – not even Article 9.1(a) which deals with 'direct subsidies' – seems to be limited to contributions in money terms only; all of them, in one way or another, explicitly or implicitly, include reference to payments-in-kind such as lower prices or a reduction in costs or charges. In our view, this consideration further confirms our interpretation that 'payment' in the sense of Article 9.1(c) includes payment in kind." *Canada Dairy*, report of the panel, *supra* n. 56, para. 7.95.

[101] *Canada Dairy*, report of the Appellate Body, *supra* n. 93, para. 111.

boards" was controversial. These boards exist in every Canadian province and have been given general authority by the federal and provincial governments in respect of the issuance and administration of quota, the pooling of returns, pricing, producer records keeping and reporting, inspection, and agreements to co-operate with other provinces and the CDC.[102] However, while their membership is "made up mostly or exclusively of dairy producers",[103] they were not formally incorporated as agencies of the governments. Canada used these facts and argued that the milk marketing boards were "producer-run", and hence did not constitute government or government agencies.[104] New Zealand and the US, on the other hand, argued that the boards were governmental agencies because, *inter alia*, they "operated under the authority of powers delegated to them by the federal and provincial governments."[105]

The panel found that neither the membership composition of the boards, nor their formal incorporation as governmental agencies, was necessary for them to be governmental agencies in the sense of Article 9.1(a). In the opinion of the panel, regardless of such formalities, the test should be what the source of the powers of these organs is, what functions they perform, and whether they actually act under some delegation of authority from the government.[106] The Appellate Body, affirming this panel interpretation, first defined a government agency as "an entity which exercises powers vested in it by a 'government' for the purpose of performing

---

[102] Canada Dairy, report of the panel, *supra* n. 56, para. 2.17. The CDC – the Canadian Dairy Corporation – is a Crown corporation established under a federal statute, funded by the Canadian Federal Government as well as by its market activities and by producers, empowered, *inter alia*, to establish national target prices for industrial milk; to buy and sell dairy products, including through importation and exportation; and to operate pools for the marketing of milk and cream. See *Canada Dairy*, report of the Appellate Body, *supra* n. 93, paras. 8-9.

[103] *Canada Dairy*, report of the panel, *supra* n. 56, para. 2.18.

[104] According to Canada, "while legislation required that the boards take into account a broader range of interests than those of the producers alone, the fact remained that the boards operated as an extension of the commercial operations of the individual dairy producers of Canada. Canada argued that if the conduct of commercial operations by private producers and processors within a regulatory framework constituted Government provision of the good or service provided through the commercial transactions, then virtually all activities in a modern economy could be so characterized. ... Canada contended that the participation of the milk marketing boards in providing milk sourced from producers to processors did not involve any 'financial contribution' from the boards. The boards acted as agents for the producers in collecting and selling milk to the processors." *Canada Dairy*, report of the panel, *supra* n. 56, paras. 4.315-4.318.

[105] *Canada Dairy*, report of the panel, *supra* n. 56, paras. 4.321. For a summary of their views, see generally paras. 4.319-321.

[106] The *Canada Dairy* panel stated its opinion as follows: "the fact that most of the provincial boards are not formally incorporated as government agencies and that all or most of them are composed, completely or partly, of individuals which are also dairy producers, does not alter our conclusion. When – and to the extent that – these boards act under explicit delegated governmental authority, they can be presumed to act as an agency of the government .... It is precisely because the boards receive the authority from governments to regulate certain areas themselves that their actions become governmental." *Canada Dairy*, report of the panel, *supra* n. 56, para. 7.78. See also the report of that Appellate Body in the same case, *supra* n. 93, para. 98.

functions of a 'governmental' character, that is, to 'regulate', 'restrain', 'supervise' or 'control' the conduct of private citizens."[107] It then stated its ruling as follows:

> "The 'governmental' character of the boards' functions, as well as the extent of their regulatory control, is underlined by the fact that their orders and regulations are enforceable in courts of law. Thus, the powers of the provincial boards are augmented by the machinery of the State itself, and the boards have at their disposal the public force to ensure that their regulatory functions and decisions are carried out. Although the provincial boards enjoy a high degree of discretion in the exercise of their powers, governments retain 'ultimate control' over them. The Panel was, therefore, correct to conclude that the provincial milk marketing boards are 'government agencies'."[108]

Article 9.1(c) is another important provision in the list with such an illuminating impact for the understanding of the wider concept of subsidies in general and export subsidies in particular. By declaring that payments, whether in money or in kind, contingent on export performance and financed by virtue of governmental action are a form of export subsidy regardless of whether the government incurs any costs, this provision clears any remaining doubts on the question of whether a subsidy necessarily involves a charge on the public account. It explicitly provides that what matters for the existence of an export subsidy and for the application of the discipline of the Agriculture Agreement thereupon is the mere presence of some form of governmental action whether or not that action involves a charge on the public account.[109]

As the *Canada Dairy* case mainly concerned subsidies fully financed by producers, the panel's ruling on the issue is once more important. According to the panel, the fact that the government does not grant funds to finance the payment "does not prevent this payment in kind from being provided by the government or its agencies in the sense of Article 9.1(a)."[110] The panel also saw this same practice vis-à-vis

---

[107] *Canada Dairy*, report of the Appellate Body, *supra* n. 93, para. 97.

[108] Ibid., para. 100 (footnotes omitted).

[109] Agriculture Agreement, Article 9.1(c).

[110] *Canada Dairy*, report of the panel, *supra* n. 56, para. 7.65. As regards the financing, the panel has noted that "It is undisputed that only the milk producers finance the sales of milk for export. For milk produced within a producer's quota and subsequently exported, the price differential between the price for export and the higher domestic price is collectively borne by all Canadian milk producers. This is so because all in-quota export revenues are pooled with all other in-quota milk returns. This pooling results in an average or pooled milk price – lower than the domestic price – which is the same for all in-quota milk produced by a given producer." Ibid., para. 7.64.

[111] In so ruling, the panel agreed with Tangermann that "where a state agency sells domestically at a price above the price charged for exports, while domestic producers are paid the average price, exports are implicitly subsidized." Explaining the reason, Tangermann continues: "To see why, it is best to compare this policy to one of producer-financed export subsidies. In the latter case, a levy is charged on the domestic sales, and the proceeds are then used to finance export subsidies. Under a price pooling regime, the same prices can result, and it is only the technical nature of financial flows which is different, but not the economic result. Hence, price pooling differs from producer-financed export subsidies only in form, not in substance. Countries should, therefore, not be allowed to escape their export subsidy commitments by using a price pooling regime." Tangermann (1997) *supra* n. 48, p. 22–23.

Article 9.1(c) and reached a similar conclusion.[111] It rightly observed in this respect that "the provision of milk at a discounted price to processors/exporters, although it is not financed directly with governmental funds, is, nevertheless, 'financed by virtue of governmental action' in the sense of Article 9.1(c)."[112] And this finding of the panel was upheld by the Appellate Body.[113]

Article 9.1(d) addresses the issue of subsidies granted in order to reduce the marketing costs of agricultural exports which have the element of "specificity" within them.[114] In *FSC*, the panel found that different mechanisms introduced by the US to shield a category of export-related operators from paying taxes on their otherwise taxable incomes were subsidies provided with respect to "marketing exports of agricultural products",[115] and concluded that "the FSC scheme involves the provision of a subsidy to reduce the costs of marketing exports of agricultural products within the meaning of Article 9.1(d) of the Agreement on Agriculture."[116]

The Appellate Body referred to the dictionary meanings relied upon by the panel and, in reversing the latter's interpretation, noted that as "dictionary meanings leave many interpretive questions open", one must look beyond them.[117] According to the Appellate Body, the approach of the panel in this respect is so broad that "if income tax liability arising from export sales can be viewed as among the 'costs of marketing exports', then so too can virtually any other cost incurred by a business engaged in exporting. This cannot be what was intended by Article 9.1(d). We, therefore, hold that income tax liability arising from export sales is not part of the 'costs of marketing' a product."[118] In the view of the Appellate Body, marketing costs are rather "specific types of costs that are incurred as *part of* and *during* the process of selling a product."[119] In sum, the provision of subsidies to reduce the costs of marketing exports of agricultural products beyond the rendering of widely available export promotion and advisory services, is designated as an export subsidy subject to reduction commitments.

Likewise, the text of Article 9.1(e), which is identical with paragraph (c) of the Illustrative List of Export Subsidies in Annex I to the SCM Agreement, provides added guidance concerning the exact form of government involvement required for

---

112 *Canada Dairy*, report of the panel, *supra* n. 56, para. 7.106.

113 See *Canada Dairy*, report of the Appellate Body, *supra* n. 93, paras. 103–114.

114 For a discussion of the concept of "specificity", see *supra* chapter 5.3.

115 *FSC*, report of the panel, *supra* n. 60, para. 7.154. In interpreting the term "marketing", the panel adopted a definition given by *Webster's Dictionary* that it refers to "an aggregate of functions involved in transferring title and in moving goods from producer to consumer including among others buying, selling, storing, transporting, standardizing, financing, risk bearing and supplying market information" and concluded that the activities at issue here "fall squarely within the ordinary meaning of the term 'marketing'." See Ibid., para. 7.154. In the words of the panel, the different forms of exemptions provided by the FSC scheme "represent a systematic effort by the United States to exempt certain types of income which would be taxable in the absence of the FSC scheme." Ibid., para. 7.100.

116 Ibid., para. 7.159.

117 *FSC*, report of the Appellate Body, *supra* n. 78, para. 129.

118 Ibid., para. 131.

119 Ibid., para. 130 (italics in original).

the existence of subsidies. It states that "internal transport and freight charges on export shipments, *provided or mandated by governments*, on terms more favourable than for domestic shipments"[120] are also subject to the reduction commitments. This means, for example, that it is sufficient for an export subsidy to exist if a government simply issues a directive that all freight transport companies maintain a fare differential of, say, $5 per a given unit between domestic and export shipments of the same volume or weight in favour of exports. The government incurs no expenses from its accounts; nor does it carry out the task of transporting freight by itself; yet, there is an export subsidy subject to the newly-introduced discipline in the same way as direct transfers of governmental funds are subjected to it.

Equally important is the solution given to the controversy surrounding the status of what are commonly referred to as "upstream subsidies" – subsidies provided to the inputs of a manufactured export product. According to Article 9.1(f) of the Agriculture Agreement, "subsidies on agricultural products contingent upon their incorporation in exported products" are also subject to the same discipline. To illustrate, a pasta manufacturing enterprise may claim as much subsidies on the wheat it uses to produce exportable pasta products as would be given on the export of the raw wheat as such. Article 11 then prescribes a rule of anti-circumvention: "In no case may the per-unit subsidy paid on an incorporated agricultural primary product exceed the per-unit subsidy that would be payable on exports of the primary product as such."[121]

To sum up, the particular practices included in the Agreement as agricultural export subsidies do not only fall within the scope of the description of export subsidies given by the SCM Agreement; they shed some useful additional light for the interpretation of the relevant provisions of the latter.

6.4 The Regulatory Significance of Categories of Export Subsidies and Products under the Agriculture Agreement

6.4.1 General

In the preceding sections, we have been talking in terms of "specified" and "non-specified" export subsidies – a dichotomy introduced in this text for conceptual and explanatory purposes. That dichotomy served the object of resolving the question of whether the designation of specific practices as agricultural export subsidies added anything to what has been envisaged by the definition under Article 1(e) of the Agreement on Agriculture. It did not, however, show the distinction between the different forms of agricultural export subsidies in terms of the discipline applying to them, to which we turn in this section. Furthermore, we will also introduce later in

---

[120] Italics added.

[121] This is an endorsement of the minority view in *EC Pasta* which was never adopted by the Tokyo Round Subsidies Committee. See *European Economic Community–Subsidies on Export of Pasta Products*, report of the panel (SCM/43) issued on 19 May 1983, not adopted. For a discussion of the case, see *supra* chapter 4.4.8.

this section a dichotomy into agricultural products on the basis of whether they are incorporated in Members' schedules of commitments or not and assess their regulatory impact.

6.4.2 Listed v. Non-Listed Agricultural Export Subsidies

On the basis of the discipline governing the different forms of export subsidies, the Agriculture Agreement has created two distinct categories – those listed under Article 9.1 as export subsidies subject to reduction commitments (hereafter referred to as listed export subsidies), and those which are export subsidies as defined under Article 1(e) but which do not fall in any of the enumerations of Article 9.1 (hereafter referred to as non-listed export subsidies), and hence apparently not subject to reduction commitments.[122] The categorization is not simply academic; it has significant practical implications. The most important implication is that there is no uniform discipline applying to all forms of agricultural export subsidies that may be found to exist under the definition of the term discussed above.

The principal obligation of Members in the area of agricultural export subsidies in general is stated under Article 8: "Each Member undertakes not to provide export subsidies otherwise than in conformity with this Agreement and with the commitments as specified in that Member's Schedule." Article 8 – the "fundamental general provision of the Agreement on Agriculture on export subsidies", as the *Canada Dairy* panel calls it[123] – makes it clear that Members are not precluded from providing export subsidies; they only need to do it in conformity with the rules of the Agreement and their respective Schedules of Commitments. Unlike export subsidies on non-agricultural products, therefore, Members are free to use agricultural export subsidies, provided that certain conditions are satisfied. It is on the basis of the nature of the conditions attached to the different forms of export subsidies that the two categories are formulated.

As pointed out earlier, Article 9.1 lists six groups of export subsidy practices and expressly states that they are "subject to reduction commitments under this Agreement". The obligation to respect the reduction commitments each Member incorporates in its Schedules constitutes the condition for the lawful use of the practices enumerated under this provision. In this connection, Article 3.3, in relevant part, stipulates that "a Member shall not provide export subsidies listed in paragraph 1 of Article 9 in respect of the agricultural products or groups of products specified in Section II of Part IV of its Schedule in excess of the budgetary outlay and quantity commitment levels specified therein."[124]

There are three important elements in this provision. Firstly, it concerns only the six listed export subsidy practices as opposed to the non-listed ones. As will be discussed later on in greater detail, the latter group of practices are *generally* allowed subject only to an anti-circumvention requirement.[125] Secondly, this part of the

---

[122] For details on this point, see *infra* section 6.4.2

[123] *Canada dairy*, report of the panel, *supra* n. 56, para. 7.27.

[124] See first limb of Article 3.3 of the Agreement on Agriculture.

[125] See discussion *infra* section 6.4.2

provision applies only to those agricultural products that are specified in Members' schedules of commitments dealing with export subsidies (hereafter referred to as "scheduled" or "specified" agricultural products). These two observations, together, mean that this part of Article 3.3 deals with the provision of a "specific" group of export subsidies (those listed in Article 9.1) to a "specific" group of agricultural products (those specified in the Schedules). Thirdly, the provision of listed export subsidies on the specified agricultural products in excess of the reduction commitment levels is prohibited. This is a prohibition which pertains to the act of providing those subsidies on those products in excess of the permissible maximum set out in the Schedules. Put differently, the provision of the listed export subsidies on the specified agricultural products is allowed, but within the limits set by the Schedules. As the Appellate Body put it, there is a *limited authorization* for Members to provide the listed export subsidies on scheduled products up to the level of the reduction commitments specified in their Schedule.[126] But, "when the specific reduction commitment levels have been reached, the *limited authorization* to provide export subsidies as listed in Article 9.1 is transformed, effectively, into a *prohibition* against the provision of those subsidies."[127]

Article 3.3 of the Agriculture Agreement also addresses the use of listed export subsidies on non-scheduled agricultural products. It stipulates that Members "shall not provide such subsidies in respect of any agricultural product not specified in that Section of its Schedule." The listed export subsidies may not be provided in respect of agricultural products that are not specified in the Schedules (hereafter referred to as "non-scheduled" or "non-specified" agricultural products).[128] The essence of Article 3.3 may thus be summed up as follows: the provision of listed export subsidies on the specified agricultural products is allowed, but within the limits set by the Schedules; and the provision of listed export subsidies on the non-specified agricultural products is prohibited.

However, the list under Article 9.1 does not cover all forms of export subsidy practices. Consequently, there are practices which satisfy the definition of an export subsidy under Article 1(e) but which fall outside the list – hence the category of non-listed export subsidies. Moreover, the question of whether these non-listed export subsidies are allowed on the specified as well as non-specified agricultural products is much more complicated.[129] The Agriculture Agreement does not unequivocally determine their legal status, and there is a divergence of opinion between scholars on the subject.

Joseph McMahon, for instance, wrote that "non-listed export subsidies will be subject to the Subsidies Agreement, which establishes three categories of subsidies: prohibited, actionable, and non-actionable."[130] He arrives at this conclusion from the premise that "[e]xport subsidies will be subject to the

[126] See *FSC*, report of the Appellate Body *supra*, n. 78, para. 151.
[127] Ibid., para. 152 (italics in original).
[128] See discussion *infra* section 6.4.
[129] For a discussion of this issue, see *infra* section 6.4.
[130] McMahon (1995), *supra* n. 22, p. 430.

discipline provided for in the Agreement in Agriculture; subsidies falling outside this discipline will be subject to the discipline provided by the Agreement on Subsidies and Countervailing Duties."[131] This latter statement rightly suggests that those export subsidy practices that are subject to the discipline of the Agriculture Agreement are governed only by that Agreement and no other. However, it appears that the non-listed export subsidy practices, too, are generally subject to a discipline created by the Agriculture Agreement[132]; only the type of discipline applying to the listed and the non-listed categories varies. While the former are subject to reduction commitments, the latter are subject only to anti-circumvention requirements.[133]

The case of non-listed export subsidies is *generally* taken care of by Article 10.1 of the Agriculture Agreement: "Export subsidies not listed in paragraph 1 of Article 9 shall not be applied in a manner which results in, or which threatens to lead to, circumvention of export subsidy commitments." Article 10.1 and Article 9.1 have a

---

131 Ibid., pp. 430–431.

132 For a discussion of the exceptional case of the use of non-listed export subsidies on non-scheduled agricultural products, see *infra* section 6.4.4.

133 The argument in support of this conclusion may be summarized as follows. Dealing as we are here with export subsidy cases, the regime created by the SCM Agreement for them is a simple and flat prohibition. If we follow McMahon's view and apply the same to the agricultural sector, this would mean that the export subsidy practices that are not listed under Article 9.1 of the Agriculture Agreement are flatly prohibited while those that are listed therein are simply subject to reduction commitments. The question, however, is that if they are prohibited, one may ask, why does the Agriculture Agreement talk of anti-circumvention? Once prohibited, they could not be used in any manner whatsoever – whether circumventory or otherwise. But, by prohibiting the circumventory use of these practices, the Agreement is implicitly endorsing their anti-circumventory use. Besides, if this were not the case, the practices of export credits, export credit guarantees and insurance programmes referred to under Article 10.2 would also be prohibited until the envisaged internationally agreed discipline is concluded in the future. Viewed from an historical perspective, the scenario surrounding this would look the following: Before the Uruguay Round Agreements, they were permitted like all other agricultural export subsidies; now they are prohibited like all non-agricultural export subsidies; and when the envisaged international discipline is reached, they will be subject to a regime short of a flat prohibition. Not only is this situation inconsistent with the rule of reason; it is also out of tune with the very spirit, purpose and direction of the multilateral trading system under the GATT/WTO. Given the distortionary nature of these practices, this would be tantamount to the anomalous case of moving away from a liberal regime into a more restrictive one. Finally, and perhaps more importantly at least at the level of legal technicalities, Article 3.1 of the Agreement on Subsidies and Countervailing Measures on prohibited subsidies explicitly excludes agricultural export subsidies from its purview. Subsidies contingent upon export performance are prohibited "except as provided in the Agreement on Agriculture". And the Agriculture Agreement has "provided" a different regime for most, if not all, forms of non-listed agricultural export subsidies. (Concerning the special case of non-listed export subsidies on non-scheduled agricultural products, see *infra* section 6.4.4.) Consequently, Article 8 of the Agriculture Agreement stipulates the following: "Each Member undertakes not to provide export subsidies otherwise than in conformity with this Agreement and with the commitments as specified in that Member's Schedule." In as long as the provision of agricultural export subsidies conforms with this Agreement, there is no possibility to challenge the legitimacy of such a practice under any other instrument. For more on this, see Melaku Geboye Desta, "Agricultural Export Subsidies under the WTO 'Agriculture Package': A Legal Analysis", (1997) 2 *Revue Belge de Droit International*, pp. 635–660.

"mutually exclusive relationship"[134] in the sense that the former applies to a residual category of export subsidies that fall outside the scope of the latter. As pointed out already, there is generally no prohibition on the use of non-listed export subsidies; it is only the manner of their use that is subject to the anti-circumvention condition, actual or potential. Paragraph 2 of Article 10 goes a step further and picks three of the potentially significant export subsidy practices that fall outside the list of Article 9.1 – export credits, export credit guarantees, and insurance programmes – and declares that Members shall undertake to work toward the development of internationally agreed disciplines governing their use, and shall abide by any such agreement when, and if, it is reached. No such agreement has yet been reached on the issues referred to under Article 10.2.[135] To the extent that no such agreement has been reached, this provision simply remains to be an agreement to maintain good faith for a planned future negotiation devoid of any substantive additional obligation for some time to come. Until then, there seems to exist no legal distinction in the treatment of these three practices and the other forms of export subsidies not listed under Article 9.1.

---

[134] *Canada Dairy*, report of the panel, *supra* n. 56, para. 7.118. The *FSC* panel has also observed the following in this respect: "The ... anti-circumvention provision in Article 10.1... deals only with export subsidies not listed in Article 9.1, whereas Article 3.3 deals only with export subsidies that are listed in Article 9.1." *FSC*, report of the panel, *supra* n. 60, para. 7.171.

[135] The only thing that can be said so far in this connection is that OECD member countries have been working toward a set of internationally acceptable disciplines to govern export credit practices since 1996. See *Agriculture Outlook*, *supra* n. 22, p. 20. In the *Marrakesh Ministerial Decision on Measures Concerning the Possible Negative Effects of the Reform Programme on Least-Developed and Net Food-Importing Developing Countries*, Ministers had agreed "to ensure that any agreement relating to agricultural export credits makes appropriate provision for differential treatment in favour of least-developed and net food-importing developing countries." See para. 4 of this Decision. The Singapore Ministerial Conference of the WTO reaffirmed this commitment and decided that the point would "be taken fully into account in the agreement to be negotiated on agricultural export credits." The Ministerial decided that "the provisions of paragraph 4 of the Marrakesh Ministerial Decision, whereby Ministers agreed to ensure that any agreement relating to agricultural export credits makes appropriate provision for differential treatment in favour of least-developed and net food-importing developing countries, be taken fully into account in the agreement to be negotiated on agricultural export credits." Committee on Agriculture, *Report by the Committee on Agriculture on the Marrakesh Ministerial Decision on Measures Concerning the Possible Negative Effects of the Reform Programme on Least-Developed and Net Food-Importing Developing Countries:* Report for the Singapore Ministerial Conference (G/L/125), adopted by the Committee on Agriculture on 24 October 1996. No such agreement has been reached so far. However, "[i]n the ongoing negotiations on an understanding regarding agricultural export credits undertaken within the framework of the OECD, consideration is being given to this matter." "Statement by the Representative of the OECD" in WTO Committee on Agriculture, *Annual Monitoring Exercise in Respect of the Follow-Up to the Ministerial Decision on Measures Concerning the Possible Negative Effects of the Reform Programme on Least-Developed and Net Food-Importing Developing Countries* (G/AG/GEN/15) December 1997, p. 8; see also WTO Committee on Agriculture, *Implementation of the Decision on Measures Concerning the Possible Negative Effects of the Reform Programme on Least-Developed and Net Food-Importing Developing Countries Note by the Secretariat* (G/AG/W/42) 10 February 1999, and G/AG/W/42/Rev.1, para. 29. For further details on this subject, see Melaku Geboye Desta, "Food Security and International Trade Law: An Appraisal of the World Trade Organization Approach" (2001) 35 *Journal of World Trade*, No. 3, pp. 449–468.

The significance of the dichotomy between listed and non-listed export subsidies may thus be summarized as follows: the provision of listed export subsidies on the specified agricultural products is allowed, but within the limits set by the Schedules; the provision of listed export subsidies on the non-specified agricultural products is prohibited; and the provision of non-listed export subsidies is *generally* allowed subject to the anti-circumvention condition. The next important dichotomy will therefore be that between scheduled and non-scheduled agricultural products.

6.4.3 Scheduled v. Non-Scheduled Agricultural Products

The foregoing discussion on the dichotomy between listed and non-listed agricultural export subsidies and the statements made thereunder must be read in light of the dichotomy between scheduled and non-scheduled agricultural products. This dichotomy is itself the result of what may be called the "product specificity" requirement adopted during the Uruguay Round negotiations on the subject. Unlike the Uruguay Round commitments on agricultural domestic support, export subsidy reduction commitments were required to be made in terms of specific products rather than aggregates. Paragraph 7 of Annex 8 of the Modalities Agreement provided this requirement as follows: "Outlay and quantity commitment levels shall be established for all products or groups of products in any case where exports of such products are subsidized through practices listed in Annex 7 paragraphs (1)(a) through (1)(e) [which corresponds to Article 9.1(a) through 9.1(e) of the Agreement on Agriculture]". It then specified a non-exhaustive list of 22 products or product groups at a somewhat broad level of aggregation. They are, wheat and wheat flour, coarse grains, rice, oilseeds, vegetable oils, oilcakes, sugar, butter and butter oil, skim milk powder, cheese, other milk products, bovine meat, pig meat, poultry meat, sheepmeat, live animals, eggs, wine, fruit, vegetables, tobacco, and cotton.[136]

What is important is that the specific details of the Schedules are required to reflect the distribution of export subsidies across products during the base period. This is a direct extension of the fundamental Uruguay Round negotiation principle that the new regime should not allow the introduction of new or the expansion of old export subsidy practices. This principle has been restated in Paragraph 12 of the Modalities: "Commitments shall include undertakings not to introduce or re-introduce subsidies on the export of agricultural products or groups of products in respect of which such subsidies were not granted during the course of the base period". This commitment does not distinguish between listed and non-listed export subsidies. The commitment of Members not to introduce or reintroduce export subsidies on agricultural products therefore applies to all forms of export subsidies whether listed or otherwise. However, when it comes to the undertaking of specific

[136] It is worthy of note at this point that, because of the principle of special and differential treatment in favour of the less developed Members, it is only "specifying", and not necessarily undertaking a reduction commitment, that is required herein. See for instance Article 15.2 (second sentence) of the Agriculture Agreement, and para. 16 of the Modalities Agreement, which provide that least developed countries shall not be required to undertake (or shall be exempt from) reduction commitments.

reduction commitments, it was mandatory to establish schedules for all these products only if they had been subsidized through the listed practices during the base period. If agricultural products were subsidized, but not through any of the listed practices, it seems that they were not required to be so scheduled.[137] Apparently, they would only be subject to a prohibition of the introduction of new export subsidy practices in the future, while being left free to continue the use of the non-listed export subsidies on condition of anti-circumvention.

The level of aggregation in this illustrative list of agricultural products has been criticized as "too broad", thus allowing countries "too much leeway" for manipulation.[138] However, the Modalities Agreement clearly states that the list does not preclude the possibility of negotiating commitments on particular products within groups of products.[139] What this provision seems to imply is rather that countries could not negotiate commitments at higher levels of aggregation than what has been specified therein. Members have largely adhered to this listing as it is in the preparation of their Schedules. In some cases, however, they have taken some "liberty" in the allocation of individual and more specific products to these groups, and at times going as far as merging different product groups in one.[140] To cite just one example, while the product specificity provision of the Modalities provides for the two separate product groups of "fruit" and "vegetables", the EC specified its commitments concerning these products by aggregating them as "fruit and vegetables, fresh" and "fruit and vegetables, preserved". In as long as the two distinct categories of "fruit" and "vegetables" are brought together, even the distinction introduced by the Community between "fresh" and "preserved" may not qualify for the requirement set by the Modalities. However, once the thus-grouped products have escaped into the final Schedules of their makers, they become binding in their own right and a challenge of their legal status becomes effectively out of the question.[141]

Be that as it may, the importance of the "product specificity" requirement for present purposes lies in the fact that the inclusion or otherwise of a product in the schedules plays a decisive role on the question of whether a subsidy can be granted on its exportation. As pointed out earlier, an agricultural product becomes eligible for the provision of listed export subsidies within the limits set by the schedules of a Member only if it is specified in that Member's schedules of commitments from the outset. An agricultural product that is not scheduled is precluded from the benefits of any of the listed export subsidies. On the other hand, Article 10.1 of the Agreement on Agriculture stipulates that non-listed export subsidies "shall not be

---

[137] See paragraph 7 of Annex 8 of the Modalities Agreement.

[138] *Agriculture Outlook, supra* n. 22, p. 21.

[139] Paragraph 8 of Annex 8 of the Modalities.

[140] See Tangermann (1995) *supra* n. 48, p. 11.

[141] Note that the text of the Modalities was issued for the purpose of completing draft schedules of concession and commitments in the agricultural negotiations "on the understanding of participants in the Uruguay Round that these negotiating modalities shall not be used as a basis for dispute settlement proceedings under the MTO Agreement." See *Note by the Chairman of the Market Access Group*, in Modalities Agreement, paras. 1-4.

applied in a manner which results in, or which threatens to lead to, circumvention of export subsidy commitments." As will be developed later, the export subsidy commitments protected by this provision clearly cover export subsidy reduction commitments on scheduled agricultural products. As such, it is possible to conclude that the provision of non-listed export subsidies on scheduled agricultural products appears to be allowed subject to the anti-circumvention condition. But, the question of whether or not the provision of non-listed export subsidies on non-scheduled agricultural products are also allowed cannot be answered that easily.

6.4.4 The Use of Non-Listed Export Subsidies on Non-Scheduled Agricultural Products

A closer look at the question of whether the use of non-listed subsidies on the export of non-scheduled agricultural products is allowed or prohibited suggests strong grounds on both sides of the argument. There are two major lines of reasoning in favour of the argument that it is allowed, each of which is grounded on the respective provisions of the Agreement on Agriculture addressing the specific category.

Firstly, the domain of Article 3.3, which is the only provision in the Agreement dealing with non-scheduled agricultural products, is limited to the use of the listed export subsidies on this category of agricultural products. As such, while the prohibition against providing listed export subsidies in excess of the commitment levels prescribed in the first part of Article 3.3 applies only to the specified agricultural products, the complete prohibition of the use of export subsidies on non-scheduled agricultural products is limited to the listed export subsidies. Consequently, the use of non-listed export subsidies on any agricultural product, whether scheduled or non-scheduled, falls outside the scope of Article 3.3.

Secondly, the domain of Article 10 on anti-circumvention, which is the only provision in the Agreement addressing the use of non-listed export subsidies, is limited to the use of these subsidies on agricultural products that are subject to "export subsidy commitments". The whole purpose of Article 10 is to prevent circumvention of the export subsidy commitments resulting from Articles 3, 8 and 9 of the Agriculture Agreement by resorting to the non-listed export subsidies.[142] As pointed out already, these commitments are of two types – the commitment not to exceed the scheduled export subsidy reduction levels with respect to specified agricultural products, and the commitment not to provide listed export subsidies on non-specified agricultural products.

The scope of the commitment not to exceed the scheduled export subsidy reduction levels is necessarily limited to scheduled agricultural products or groups of products. In such cases, one can talk of circumvention of commitments only if the non-listed export subsidies are used on a scheduled product that is subject to a commitment in respect of the listed export subsidies. To the extent that no such commitment exists in respect of a given product, it is difficult to talk of

[142] See, *inter alia*, *FSC*, report of the Appellate Body, *supra* n. 78, para. 143.

circumvention. Consequently, within these limits, non-scheduled agricultural products fall outside the scope of Article 10 of the Agreement on Agriculture.

On the other hand, the commitment not to provide listed export subsidies on non-specified agricultural products is not an obligation not to provide export subsidies in general. Rather, it is an obligation not to provide a class of export subsidy practices specifically listed under Article 9.1 of the Agriculture Agreement. As such, not every export subsidy practice can be taken to circumvent this obligation. A Member may be said to have circumvented this obligation only if it has devised a mechanism of introducing those specific export subsidies under a different cover. For this reason, one may argue that the use of a non-listed export subsidy on a non-scheduled agricultural product does not circumvent its obligation in respect of the specific category of listed export subsidies.

It thus appears possible to conclude that the use of non-listed export subsidies on non-specified agricultural products is not subject to any "export subsidy commitments" in the sense of Article 10.1, and hence it is not subject to the anti-circumvention requirement.[143] In fact, nowhere in the Agriculture Agreement can one find any specific provision addressing this group of practices on this group of products. The first thing to come to mind under such circumstances is thus to apply the general legal maxim that "whatever is not prohibited is permitted". In terms of the provisions of the Agriculture Agreement, therefore, countries are arguably free to use such subsidies on such products without any limits whatsoever. And such a practice might still be said to be "in conformity with" the Agriculture Agreement and the commitments as specified in Members' Schedules as required by Article 8 because it does not violate any provision of the Agreement.

However, the obvious weakening effect of the above line of reasoning still leaves a question mark in mind. A careful look at the above reasoning shows that the use of non-listed export subsidies on the non-scheduled agricultural products is neither permitted nor prohibited – hence the tentative conclusion that whatever is not prohibited is permitted. This may, however, hold true only as regards the Agreement on Agriculture. But the Agriculture Agreement is not the sole legal instrument in the WTO system that may apply to the issue of agricultural export subsidies. The obvious question to ask will thus be as to whether the silence of the Agreement on Agriculture on this subject also amounts to the silence of the entire WTO Agreements at large.

The answer is clearly in the negative. This is because, as reiterated in chapter 5, as a matter of principle, the discipline of the SCM Agreement, which is one of the Multilateral Agreements forming part of the WTO Agreement, applies to all issues concerning the use of subsidies. This principle holds true unless there is a specific exception included in the SCM Agreement itself or in any of the specialized

[143] Although made in a different context, the following observation by the *FSC* panel may also help in this respect: "The ... anti-circumvention provision in Article 10.1 ... deals only with export subsidies not listed in Article 9.1, whereas Article 3.3 deals only with export subsidies that are listed in Article 9.1." *FSC*, report of the panel, *supra* n. 60, para. 7.171.

agreements forming part of the WTO Agreement. The Agriculture Agreement is one such a specialized agreement that has been referred to in many provisions of the SCM Agreement as one to which the provisions of the latter would be subject. In the specific area of export subsidies, Article 3.1 of the SCM Agreement provides that all forms of export subsidies are prohibited "except as provided in the Agreement on Agriculture." The question will then be whether what we said above concerning the provisions of the Agriculture Agreement on the use of non-listed export subsidies on non-scheduled agricultural products amounts to something "provided" in that Agreement. In other words, does the silence of the Agreement on Agriculture on this subject, and the conclusion we drew that "whatever is not prohibited is permitted", qualify for the condition of being "provided in the Agreement on Agriculture"?

Admittedly, this is a difficult question demanding a very close scrutiny. The principle regarding the use of agricultural export subsidies under Article 8 of the Agreement on Agriculture should be the starting point. It stipulates that countries may "not provide export subsidies otherwise than in conformity with this Agreement." The meaning of this requirement is not as clear as it looks at first sight. It is not, for instance, equivalent to a statement that Members may "not provide export subsidies in violation of this Agreement." The latter interpretation would in fact reduce Article 8 to total redundancy because every specific provision of the Agreement speaks that language for itself. Whether stated under Article 8 or not, the meaning and force of each provision of the Agreement is a function of its own wording. One may of course conveniently say that the provision *prohibits the use of export subsidies in violation of the rules* of the Agriculture Agreement. But, that does not say all this provision says. It further prescribes a positive standard to provide export subsidies *in conformity with the Agreement.*

The question will then be the following: what about those export subsidies for the use of which there is no rule at all in the Agreement, such as the case of non-listed export subsidies on non-scheduled agricultural products? Needless to say, they do not violate the rules because there is no relevant rule in the Agreement to be violated from the very outset. At the same time, it is difficult to say they conform with the Agreement for exactly the same reason – there is no rule against which to judge the conformity. It simply appears to be a case that neither conforms with, nor violates, the Agreement. As such, while not violating any of the provisions of the Agreement, it fails to satisfy the positive prescription of being in conformity with the Agreement. This is therefore a case of an export subsidy provided "otherwise than in conformity with the Agreement" in the sense of Article 8 because the Agriculture Agreement does not provide the requisite standard against which to measure conformity.

This situation has important implications. As shown earlier, it is only where the Agreement on Agriculture provides for its own specific rules on a particular subject that the provisions of the SCM Agreement would be excluded from applying to agricultural export subsidies. We have seen that no rule is "provided in the Agreement on Agriculture", in the sense of Article 3.1 of the SCM Agreement, concerning the use of non-listed export subsidies on non-scheduled agricultural products. This is thus a case that falls outside the scope of the Agreement on Agriculture. In other words, this is one area on which the Agreement on Agriculture has not "provided" otherwise in the sense of Article 3.1 of the SCM Agreement. The provisions of the SCM Agreement are therefore the only applicable law as regards this practice. Consequently, the rule of the SCM Agreement on export subsidies being a simple and flat prohibition, the use of non-listed export subsidies on non-scheduled agricultural products is also flatly prohibited just like all other non-agricultural export subsidies. Not only does this argument base itself on the ordinary meaning of the text of the provisions read in their appropriate context, it also accords well with the objectives of the multilateral trading system at large.

6.5 Summary

The whole idea of this chapter may be summarized as follows: Members are free to use the listed export subsidies on scheduled agricultural products within the limits of their reduction commitments; they are prohibited from using the listed export subsidies on non-scheduled agricultural products; they are free to use non-listed export subsidies on scheduled agricultural products on condition that they do not use them to circumvent, actually or potentially, their obligations vis-à-vis the listed export subsidy practices; they are prohibited from using non-listed export subsidies on non-scheduled agricultural products. The inclusion or exclusion of agricultural products in the schedules of commitments thus plays a decisive role as regards the legal status of the different forms of export subsidy practices as well as the nature of other commitments applying to them. The general state of the law from this perspective may thus be summed up in the following words: *while the use of subsidies, whether listed or otherwise, on the export of scheduled agricultural products is (conditionally) permitted, the same practice is flatly prohibited regarding the export of non-scheduled agricultural products*. The extent of the obligations undertaken by Members in this area thus varies depending as much on the identity and number of products included in schedules as on the depth of specific reduction commitments undertaken. The essence of the different forms of commitments and their practical application will be discussed at length in the next chapter.

CHAPTER 7

COMMITMENTS ON AGRICULTURAL EXPORT SUBSIDIES

7.1 General

In the previous chapter, we have seen that Members' obligations in the area of agricultural export subsidies generally depend on two factors – whether or not the particular products they want to subsidize are included in their respective schedules of commitments, and whether or not the specific export subsidies they want to provide fall within the list of Article 9.1. We have seen furthermore that Members are generally prohibited from granting export subsidies on non-scheduled agricultural products – the commitment not to introduce new, or re-introduce old, export subsidies on those products – while they are conditionally allowed to provide export subsidies on scheduled agricultural products. The conditions are of two types – the condition to respect the specific reduction commitment levels in the provision of listed export subsidies, and the commitment not to use non-listed export subsidies and non-commercial transactions to circumvent export subsidy commitments. All these have been summed up under Article 8 of the Agreement on Agriculture as the obligation not to provide export subsidies otherwise than in conformity with the provisions of the Agriculture Agreement and Members' schedules of commitments.

All these different forms of commitments have already been mentioned. In this chapter, we will go deeper and look at each of them as follows: Firstly, the general methodology adopted for the establishment of the different forms of commitments will be discussed. This includes a discussion of the underlying consensus to stop the proliferation of export subsidies, the understanding to report all forms of agricultural export subsidies during an agreed period of time called the base period, and the agreement never to introduce new or reintroduce old export subsidies that are not included in the reports. Secondly, the concept of reduction commitments, its essence as well as its depth, will be discussed in detail. This includes analyses of the agreement to limit the negotiations to existing export subsidies as are reported by negotiating parties, the consensus to achieve specific binding commitments on each of the products reported as having been subsidized on exportation, and the negotiation on the nature, depth and pace of reduction commitments. Thirdly, the exceptions that have been negotiated to accommodate the special interests of countries at the stage of implementation will be analyzed. Particular attention will be paid here to the so-called "front-loading arrangement" and the "down-stream flexibility exceptions". Finally, despite these arrangements, the problems faced by some countries in the process of implementation and the measures taken unilaterally as well as at the multilateral level will also be discussed here. The emphasis in this section will be the problems faced by Hungary in the implementation of its export subsidy commitments, its decision to ask for a waiver of its obligations in this area, and the decisions taken by the WTO General Council.

7.1.1 General Methodology Adopted for Disciplining Agricultural Export Subsidies

In trying to discipline agricultural trade, the Agriculture Agreement drew on the decades-old and fruitful experiences of the GATT in the negotiation and reduction of tariffs. Learning from these historic lessons, the Uruguay Round negotiators decided that Members should negotiate amongst themselves on the three important areas of market access, domestic support, and export subsidies and undertake specific binding commitments on each of them just like what they had been doing vis-à-vis tariffs for more than four decades previously.[1] The thus negotiated commitments would then be recorded in national schedules of concessions to form an integral part of GATT 1994 by the express stipulation, *inter alia*, of Article 3.1 of the Agriculture Agreement itself.

However, unlike tariffs, it was difficult to express with precision the degree of agricultural trade protection effected through most of these three forms of practices. For example, while most agricultural market access barriers had a non-tariff form, domestic support was given through a variety of direct and indirect mechanisms of income and price support. In the area of export subsidies, too, governments used different forms of supporting the export of agricultural products, starting from direct budgetary transfers down to credit arrangements on more favourable terms and even tax exemptions on export-related incomes. The first challenge in all cases was thus to put the diverse mechanisms of agricultural trade protectionism in terms of precise numerical figures. Tariffication (the conversion of all non-tariff border measures into their tariff equivalents) was adopted for market access; AMS (the Aggregate Measurement of Support) was used to measure the amount of domestic support; and, in the case of export subsidies, a two-way track was followed – export subsidies were expressed in terms of the quantity of products benefiting from them and the amount of budgetary outlays spent for the purpose. Consequently, on agricultural export subsidies, we have two types of reduction commitments on each scheduled agricultural product or group of products – quantitative and budgetary.

However, these dual commitments do not apply to all forms of export subsidies. Nor do they cover all forms of agricultural products. As regards the former, given the variety of forms an export subsidy may take, the Uruguay Round negotiators did not attempt to have an exhaustive list of all forms of export subsidies, for that might bring about unintended consequences in the form of inadvertent exclusions of particular practices and/or inability to foresee the development of new types of

---

[1] See *Modalities for the Establishment of Specific Binding Commitments under the Reform Programme* (MTN.GNG/MA/W/24) 20 Dec. 1993 hereafter "the Modalities Agreement" or simply "the Modalities", para. 1.

export subsidies.[2] Rather, a group of six important forms of export subsidies were selected and countries were made to report the distribution of those export subsidies across products in both quantitative as well as budgetary terms over a chosen base period.[3] The negotiations on reduction commitments were thus largely limited to the reduction of the listed export subsidies on the scheduled agricultural products. As regards the use of non-listed export subsidies on scheduled agricultural products, an agreement was reached that they can be used on condition that they do not circumvent the commitments undertaken on the listed practices. Moreover, an agreement was also reached to the effect that no new export subsidies would be introduced on products that are not reported to have been subject to export subsidies during the base period.

In order to make sure that all products with such subsidies have been reported and included in the schedules of commitments, one of the provisions in the Modalities Agreement stipulated that commitments "shall be established for all products or groups of products in any case where exports of such products are subsidized"[4] through practices listed in Article 9.1 of the Agreement on Agriculture. The sanction against non-compliance with this requirement was strong – countries would simply be precluded from providing any export subsidies at all on those products that have not been reported as having been benefiting from an export subsidy scheme during the base period and which have not been included in the schedules. In other words, export subsidies on those products that are not included in the schedules of commitments would thereby be prohibited just like non-agricultural export subsidies. This is the commitment not to introduce or re-introduce subsidies on the export of agricultural products in respect of which such subsidies were not granted during the course of the base period.[5]

Therefore, to comply with the positive standard set by Article 8 of the Agreement on Agriculture in the provision of export subsidies, there are generally two forms of "commitments" that need to be respected by Members. Firstly, there is the obligation to respect the export subsidy reduction commitment levels as are specified in Members' schedules of commitments.[6] And, secondly, there is the commitment not to introduce or re-introduce subsidies on the export of agricultural products in respect of which such subsidies were not granted during the course of the base period.[7] Members' obligations in the area of agricultural export subsidies are therefore ramifications of these two principal obligations – the obligation to reduce export subsidies on all previously subsidized products and the obligation not to

---

2 See US argument in *Canada – Measures Affecting the Importation of Milk and the Exportation of Dairy Products*, report of the panel (WT/DS103/R, WT/DS113/R) 17 May, 1999 para. 4.145.

3 For a discussion of the base period and its significance, see *infra* section 7.3.

4 See paragraph 7 of Annex 8 to the Modalities Agreement.

5 See paragraph 12 of the Modalities.

6 See first part of Article 3.3 of the Agreement on Agriculture.

7 See paragraph 12 of the Modalities. For an elaborate discussion on this point, see *United States – Tax Treatment for "Foreign Sales Corporations"*, report of the Appellate Body (WT/DS108/AB/R) 24 February 2000, paras. 144–147.

introduce new or reintroduce old export subsidies on those that were not subsidized during the base period. Article 3.3 embodies these obligations as follows:

> "Subject to the provisions of paragraphs 2(b) and 4 of Article 9, a Member shall not provide export subsidies listed in paragraph 1 of Article 9 in respect of the agricultural products or groups of products specified in Section II of Part IV of its Schedule in excess of the budgetary outlay and quantity commitment levels specified therein and shall not provide such subsidies in respect of any agricultural product not specified in that Section of its Schedule."

7.2 Export Subsidy Reduction Commitments

The six forms of agricultural export subsidies listed under Article 9.1 of the Agriculture Agreement are subject to binding reduction commitments of a dual nature – budgetary and quantitative – to be implemented at two levels of duration – annually as well as over the entire implementation period. As will be seen later on, the duality of commitments represents an important innovation by the new Agreement with tremendous practical implications in favour of greater market orientation. But, before that, some remarks on the essence of a "reduction commitment" on the basis of an illuminating discussion in the *FSC* case appears useful.

The *FSC* panel did not address the issue of reduction commitments for its own sake. Rather, the main issue was the problem of burden-of-proof in the context of Article 10.3 of the Agreement on Agriculture. That issue arose because the parties disagreed on the question of which products were subject to a "reduction commitment" and thus subject to a reversal in the burden of proof under Article 10.3.[8] The US argued that "a product is subject to a reduction commitment only if it is listed in Section II, Part IV of a Member's schedule; and that unscheduled products as such are not subject to a reduction commitment."[9] The EC, on the other hand, contended that "both scheduled and unscheduled products are subject to reduction commitments; in the case of an unscheduled product, the reduction commitment level is zero."[10]

In resolving this issue, the panel remarked that "a Member which has not scheduled a given product may well have a commitment with respect to that product, in as much as it is precluded by Article 3.3 of the Agreement from providing export subsidies listed in Article 9.1 with respect to that product. We do not consider, however, that the Member has a reduction commitment with respect to an unscheduled product."[11] The panel further noted that

> "The term 'reduction commitment' in its ordinary meaning suggests that the

---

[8] See *United States – Tax Treatment for "Foreign Sales Corporations"* report of the panel (WT/DS108/R), 8 October 1999, para. 7.137.

[9] See Ibid., para. 7.137.

[10] See Ibid.

[11] See Ibid., para. 7.138.

Member was granting export subsidies with regard to the product in the relevant base period when it prepared its schedule but committed that it would reduce the quantity of the product benefiting from Article 9.1 export subsidies during the implementation period. In the case of unscheduled products, however, the Member's commitment is that it will not provide any export subsidies with respect to that product, rather than that it will reduce the quantity of the product with respect to which it provides the subsidy. Thus, the term 'reduction commitment' in its ordinary meaning would not apply to unscheduled products."[12]

Although the panel's view of Members' commitments concerning non-scheduled products appears questionable,[13] its reasoning as regards reduction commitments seems clear beyond doubt. Moreover, the Appellate Body in this same case has affirmed this latter part of the panel statement as follows:

"[T]he terms 'export subsidy commitments' and 'reduction commitments' have different meanings. '*Reduction* commitments' is a narrower term than 'export subsidy commitments' and refers only to commitments made, under the first clause of Article 3.3, with respect to *scheduled* agricultural products. It is only with respect to *scheduled* products that Members have undertaken, under Article 9.2(b)(iv) of the *Agreement on Agriculture*, to *reduce* the level of export subsidies, as listed in Article 9.1, during the implementation period of the *Agreement on Agriculture*. The term 'export subsidy commitments' has a wider reach that covers commitments and obligations relating to *both* scheduled and unscheduled agricultural products."[14]

It is thus important to keep in mind that reduction commitments are the main, but not the only, type of commitments undertaken by Members in the context of agricultural export subsidies. And this is reflected in almost all relevant provisions of the Agriculture Agreement on export subsidies.[15]

The Agriculture Agreement sets the general framework within which Members would negotiate their respective undertakings on the subject. Schedules of commitments, by their very nature, require detailed negotiations – often taking the form of offers and acceptances – between Members having stakes in specific areas and on particular products. They often take the form of bilateral, rather than multilateral, negotiations. The rules of the Agriculture Agreement in this respect are limited to setting the general guidelines regarding the conduct of these negotiations, with only the minimum required of the Members specified. The process of

---

12 See Ibid., para. 7.139.

13 The following statement of the panel in particular appears questionable: "In the case of unscheduled products, however, the Member's commitment is that it will *not provide any export subsidies* with respect to that product...." Ibid., para. 7.139. Apparently, Article 3.3, second limb, prohibits only the listed export subsidies and not *any export subsidy*. For relevant comments, see *supra* chapter 6, and *infra* section 7.4.2.

14 *FSC*, report of the Appellate Body, *supra* n. 7, para. 147 (italics in original).

15 See also *FSC*, report of the panel, *supra* n. 8, paras. 7.140–7.141.

establishing the details of the country-specific schedule commitments was governed by provisions laid down in a "separate and transitory document",[16] entitled "Modalities for the Establishment of Specific Binding Commitments under the Reform Programme".[17] In its own words, this document was issued "for the purpose of completing draft Schedules of concession and commitments in the Agricultural negotiations and for facilitating the verification process leading to the establishment of formal Schedules to be annexed to the Uruguay Round Protocol."[18] Once negotiated, Article 3 of the Agriculture Agreement requires of Members to respect the budgetary outlay and quantity commitment levels specified in their respective schedules as commitments limiting subsidization.[19]

The Modalities Agreement then lost its legal relevance as soon as the Schedules were completed and annexed to the WTO Agreement. The text of the negotiating Modalities was in fact agreed upon on the understanding that it "shall not be used as a basis for dispute settlement proceedings under the [W]TO Agreement".[20] Provisions of the Modalities Agreement cannot be a source of rights and obligations on their own. This does not, however, deprive them of their supplementary role for the interpretation of the Agreement on Agriculture and Members' schedules of commitments as part of the negotiating history.[21] What is also important for legal purposes is that once the schedules negotiated in accordance with the Modalities are finalized and annexed to the Uruguay Round Protocol, they become an integral part of the Final Act, and hence binding in their own right. In the following section, we will discuss the general rules of the Agriculture Agreement on export subsidy reduction commitments as supplemented and elaborated by the provisions of the Modalities Agreement.

The Agriculture Agreement does, *inter alia*, the following on reduction commitments: firstly, it defines the two forms of reduction commitments – quantitative and budgetary – each Member is required to make on export subsidies; secondly, it defines the base period from which to calculate the reductions; thirdly, it sets the minimum level of quantitative and outlay concessions required of each Member by the end of the implementation period; fourthly, it indirectly requires of Members to undertake both budgetary as well as quantitative commitments for each year of the implementation period and specify the same in their Schedules; and finally, it provides for some room of flexibility so as to enable countries to adjust themselves to yearly fluctuations both in the quantity and price of agricultural

16 S. Tangermann, *Implementation of the Uruguay Round Agreement on Agriculture by Major Developed Countries*, A Report Prepared for the United Nations Conference on Trade and Development, (Distr. GENERAL, UNCTAD /ITD/16, 3 October, 1995), p. 2.

17 See *supra* n. 1.

18 Ibid., "Note by the Chairman of the Market Access Group", para. 1.

19 Article 3.1 of the Agreement on Agriculture provides the following: "The domestic support and export subsidy commitments in Part IV of each Member's Schedule constitute commitments limiting subsidization and are hereby made an integral part of GATT 1994."

20 The Modalities Agreement, "Note by the Chairman of the Market Access Group", para. 4.

21 See Article 32 of the *Vienna Convention on the Law of Treaties* (done at Vienna, 23 May 1969, 1155 U.N.T.S. 33).

products. Almost all of these points have their own more detailed (albeit at times different) versions in the Modalities Agreement.

7.3 The Base Period for Export Subsidy Reduction Commitments

To speak of reductions, the existence of a certain reference point is imperative; a benchmark must be established from which to start the calculation at both the quantitative and the budgetary levels. To do that, the element of time is a necessity; i.e., a base period has to be agreed upon. Members would then be asked to report the quantity of agricultural products exported with the aid of subsidies and the amount of budgetary expenditure used for the purpose for that base period. Given the extreme yearly fluctuations in production and prices, characteristic of most agricultural products in practically every country, the choice of one base period over another was a delicate matter with enormous consequences. Naturally, each negotiating party would propose the time when its national figures at both levels were at their highest. Bridging the gap which arose from this was a serious challenge.

After a series of intensive negotiations, the base period for purposes of agricultural export subsidies was agreed to be the 1986–1990 period.[22] Each Member was then required to report its respective figures on the quantity of subsidized exports and the amount of budgetary outlays spent for the purpose for every year of the base period. This means that, as the scope of the reduction commitments covered the six categories of export subsidies listed under Article 9:1, countries were required to list both the quantity of exports with any of those subsidies and the amount of budgetary expenditures incurred in each year of the base period. The averages calculated for this period constituted the benchmark on the basis of which to negotiate the size of the subsequent reduction commitments to be undertaken by each Member. In the words of the Modalities, the annual averages for the base period of the budgetary outlays and the quantities of products benefiting from them constitute, respectively, base outlay and quantity levels for purposes of the reduction commitments.[23] However, the choice of this period was not fully satisfactory to all negotiating parties, especially to those whose export subsidies had continued to rise after the base period. To accommodate these special cases, a particular arrangement was made in the form of what is often referred to as the "front-loading" option, to which we will return later.

7.4 The Dual Commitments: Reductions in the Values and Volumes of Export Subsidies

The Agriculture Agreement establishes a basis for progressive reductions of export subsidies through the mechanism of binding commitments of a dual nature –

[22] See Article 9.2(b)(iv) of the Agreement on Agriculture, and Paragraph 11 of the Modalities. For comments on the impact of this choice, see Tangermann (1995) *supra* n. 16, p. 5–6.

[23] See Paragraph 3 of Annex 8 to the Modalities.

commitments for the reduction of the quantity of agricultural products exportable with the aid of subsidies, and commitments for the reduction of the budgetary outlays allowed for the purpose. The Agreement on Agriculture set the level of reduction commitments at 36 per cent in budgetary expenditures and 21 per cent in the quantities of subsidized exports on a base period of 1986–1990 and to be implemented over a period of six years in equal annual instalments. These figures represent the ultimate convergence points of two opposing groups of countries which had started their negotiations standing on the two opposite poles – the US demanding complete elimination of all export subsidies over ten years, and the EC refusing any limitations whatsoever on its agricultural export subsidy practices.

7.4.1 Minimum Reduction Requirements

The Agriculture Agreement sets, directly or indirectly, a minimum limit on the degree of concession required of each Member at two levels – the level of the entire implementation period, and the levels for each of the years constituting the implementation period.

7.4.1.1 Minimum Reduction Requirements for the Entire Implementation Period

The Agriculture Agreement does not directly set the minimum allowable reduction commitments to be undertaken by Members. The issue is only touched upon under Article 9.2(b)(iv) as one of the conditions for the use of the "down-stream" flexibility exceptions[24] to the annual commitments. It is provided that in any of the second through fifth years of the implementation period – the six-year period commencing in 1995[25] – a Member may provide export subsidies in a given year in excess of the corresponding annual commitment levels on condition, *inter alia*, that "the Member's budgetary outlays for export subsidies and the quantities benefiting from such subsidies, at the conclusion of the implementation period, are no greater than 64 per cent and 79 per cent of the 1986–1990 base period levels, respectively." It then provides for the differential and more favourable treatment accorded to developing countries.[26]

Unlike the Agriculture Agreement, the Modalities Agreement is more straightforward in this respect. It provides that, by the conclusion of the implementation period, each participant "shall reduce: (i) the quantities of each agricultural product or group of products specified in this Annex benefiting from export subsidies by 21

---

24 For a discussion of this exception, see *infra* section 7.5.

25 The "implementation period" for purposes of the Agriculture Agreement is defined under Article 2(f) to mean "the six-year period commencing in the year 1995, except that, for the purposes of Article 13 [on Due Restraint], it means the nine-year period commencing in 1995."

26 In line with the principle of special, differential and more favourable treatment, while the least-developed countries are exempted from any reduction commitments altogether, developing countries are granted preference at three levels: the minimum requirements have been brought down to 24 per cent on outlays and 14 per cent on quantities; the implementation period has been extended to 10 years; and they have been exempted from assuming any reduction commitments at all in respect of two forms of export subsidies listed under Article 9:1(d) and (e).

per cent from the base period level; and (ii) its budgetary outlays for export subsidies for each agricultural product or group of products specified in this Annex by 36 per cent from the base period level."[27]

Worth noting at this juncture is that these percentage figures are nothing but the minimum that each and every Member is obliged to undertake. Being only the minimum, any move by any particular Member to go beyond the threshold was always welcome. Some countries have followed that way, the most notable case in point being the elimination of agricultural export subsidies altogether by New Zealand. More specifically, of 26 Members with a section on export subsidies in their Schedules, only 1 Member completely eliminated export subsidies, 15 set their outlay commitments at 36 per cent, 1 at 37 per cent, 5 at 24 per cent, 1 at 26 per cent, 2 at 23 per cent, and 1 assumed no commitment at all.[28] Calculations made by the WTO Secretariat regarding the overall effect these agreements would bring about have shown that the total agricultural export subsidy outlays would decline from $21.3 billion to $13.7 billion by the end of the transition period.[29]

7.4.1.2 Minimum Reduction Requirements at the Annual Level

In addition to the overall limitation for the entire implementation period, Members were also required to go a step further and specify in their Schedules the annual reduction commitment levels for each year of this period. However, the Agriculture Agreement does not say much on this point. It is rather the Modalities Agreement which established the principle of equal annual instalments. According to Paragraph 5(b) of Annex 8 to this Agreement, "the reductions ... with respect to the quantities benefiting from export subsidies shall, in the first year of the implementation period, be made to a level at least 3.5 percent below the corresponding base period level and, for the remaining years of the implementation period, in equal annual instalments...; and the reductions ... with respect to budgetary outlays for export subsidies shall, in the first year of the implementation period, be made to a level at least 6 percent below the corresponding base period level and, for the remaining years of the implementation period, in equal annual instalments ...."

In sum, Members' reduction commitments, whether on outlays or quantities, are once again made at two levels; viz. those for the entire implementation period and those for each of the years within that period. The binding power of these commitments may vary depending on different economic factors at work in different countries.[30] However, compared to the commitments on market access and domestic

---

27 Paragraph 5(a) of the Modalities Agreement.

28 For specific details on these commitments, see p. Konnandreas, and J. Greenfield, "Uruguay Round Commitments on Domestic Support and Export Subsidies: Their Implications for Developing Countries", in FAO/World Bank (eds.), *Implementing the Uruguay Round Agreement in Latin America: the Case of Agriculture* (Santiago, Chile, 1997) p. 126.

29 WTO, *Focus Newsletter*, No. 1 (January–February 1995) p. 8.

30 See D. Hathaway, and M. Ingco, *Agricultural Liberalization and the Uruguay Round*, paper presented at the World Bank Conference on "The Uruguay Round and the Developing Economies", (26–27 January 1995) pp. 25–26.

support, the commitments on export subsidies have produced the most immediate constraining effect on most of the countries with such commitments. Being reduction commitments, these levels, in principle, represent the maximum allowable expenditure that can be allocated or incurred and the utmost quantity of agricultural exports that can benefit from the subsidy schemes in each of those years.[31] However, some degree of flexibility is permitted under Subparagraph (b) of Article 9.2.

7.4.1.3 The "Front-Loading" Option

Two of the "general principles governing negotiations" in the Uruguay Round were the principles of "standstill" and "rollback".[32] In general, while the former requires, *inter alia*, that Members not take any trade restrictive or distorting measures during the course of the negotiations, the latter demands that any such measures be brought into conformity within an agreed time frame and not later than by the date of the formal completion of the negotiations. Furthermore, while the standstill requires that participants may not take any trade measures in such a manner as to improve their negotiating positions, the rollback stipulates that no quid pro quo may be requested for the elimination of such measures. Moreover, participants agreed that the implementation of the standstill and rollback commitments "shall be subject to multilateral surveillance so as to ensure that these commitments are being met.[33]

Despite these obligations, however, many Members continued to use agricultural export subsidies at an ever-expanding scale even after the launching of the Uruguay Round. Both of the two major trading powers of the day – the US and the EC – took the lead by continuing to raise their export subsidies on most products in both quantitative as well as budgetary terms throughout the course of the negotiations. What is worse, rather than taking corrective measures as required under the rollback principles, they pressed for a solution that would diminish the extent of their reduction requirements during the implementation period. The solution took the form of what is often called the "front-loading" provision included in the Modalities Agreement.[34]

---

31 See Article 9.2(a) of the Agriculture Agreement.

32 The principles of standstill and rollback were elaborately included in the Punta del Este Declaration. See GATT, *Ministerial Declaration on the Uruguay Round* (MIN.DEC) adopted in Punta del Este, Uruguay, on 20 September 1986, often referred to as the *Punta del Este Declaration,* reproduced in, GATT *Focus Newsletter*, No. 41, (October 1986) p. 3.

33 See Ibid.

34 The full text of this provision is the following:

> "Reduction to the relevant level specified in subparagraph (a) [the provision setting the minimum levels of reduction commitments] may be made beginning at levels determined by averaging the corresponding 1991 and 1992 levels if:
>
> (i) the average of the 1991 and 1992 quantities of such agricultural product or group of products benefiting from a participant's export subsidies exceeds the corresponding base period average; and
>
> (ii) the criteria set forth in subparagraphs (d)(i) and (d)(ii) are not satisfied with respect to such agricultural product or group of products; and
>
> (iii) reductions are made in equal annual instalments.
>
> Reduction to the relevant level specified in subparagraph (a) may be made beginning at levels determined by averaging the corresponding average of the 1991 and 1992 levels and the corresponding base period levels if:

In order to accommodate the special interests of those Members whose subsidized exports had increased since the 1986–1990 base period level, and the rate and size of reduction of which would be more abrupt and massive than otherwise, an arrangement was made whereby they would be allowed to start the reductions, in certain circumstances, from these higher post-1990 levels, while the ultimate commitment remains that based on the 1986–1990 base period level. In general, these countries were allowed to start the reductions from the average for 1991 and 1992 levels on condition that (i) the average of the 1991 and 1992 quantities of products benefiting from a Member's export subsidy schemes exceeded the corresponding base period average, and (ii) the reductions were to be made in equal annual instalments. However, in cases where the said excess of the average of 1991 and 1992 amounted to 25 percent or more of the base level average and where 40 percent or more of the quantity in 1992 of such a product was exported from publicly-held or intervention stocks, the reductions were required to be made beginning at levels determined by averaging the corresponding average of the 1991 and 1992 levels and the corresponding base period levels. Here again, it is required that the thus fixed reductions be made in equal annual instalments.

The "front-loading" arrangement was not, however, intended to affect the level of the reduction commitments that should be achieved by the end of the implementation period. Regardless of whether a country qualified for and opted to use the front-loading arrangement, by the end of the implementation period, each participant had to reduce the base level quantities of agricultural products benefiting from export subsidies and the budgetary outlays used for the purpose by 21 percent and 36 percent, respectively. In the interest of transparency in this respect, Paragraph 6 of Annex 8 to the Modalities provides that base levels as well as commitment levels for each year of the implementation period be specified in the Schedules.

At the level of the final Schedules as well, this front-loading exception has been utilized by almost all Members satisfying its requirements. While the limited option to use the average of the 1986–1990 and the 1991–1992 averages was used only in one case – EC beef exports – all other cases satisfying the criteria for the application of the front-loading option started from the 1991–1992 levels. In other words, the 1986–1990 base levels were used only in cases where they were not exceeded by the 1991–1992 export levels.

The "front-loading" provision has enabled qualifying Members to export significantly more subsidized products than what would have been possible in its

---

cont.

(i) the average of the 1991 and 1992 quantities of such agricultural product or group of products benefiting from a participant's export subsidies exceeds the corresponding base period average by 25 percent or more; and

(ii) 40 per cent or more of the quantity in 1992 of such product or group of products benefiting from a participant's export subsidies was exported from publicly-held or intervention stocks; and

(iii) reductions are made in equal annual instalments." Annex 8 to the Modalities Agreement, paras. 5(c) and (d).

absence.[35] The EC Directorate General for Agriculture has reported, for instance, that the "front-loading" arrangement has allowed the Community to export the following additional amounts over the implementation period.

Table 1: Effect of the Front-Loading Provision on the EC

Product	**Additionality**
wheat and wheat flour	8,116,000 tonnes
Cheese	102,000 tonnes
Other dairy products (except for butter and skimmed milk powder)	44,000 tonnes
beef and veal	362,000 tonnes
Poultry	253,000 tonnes
Eggs	16,000 tonnes
Tobacco	156,000 tonnes

Source: EC Directorate General for Agriculture, "GATT and European Agriculture", CAP Working Notes-1995, Special Issue (1996) Luxembourg, p. 24.

Likewise, the "front-loading" provision has enabled the US to export the following additional amounts over the implementation period.

Table 2: Effect of the Front-Loading Provision on the US

Product	**Additionality**
Wheat	7,432,000 tonnes
Rice	673,698 tonnes
Vegetable oils	1,244,815 tonnes
Butter and butter oils	51,656 tonnes
Skim milk powder	74,753 tonnes
Cheese	382 tonnes
Other milk products	37,244 tonnes
Eggs	65,428,000 (dozens) tonnes

Source: US Uruguay Round Schedule, GATT, as reproduced in OECD (1995) P.86.

These facts show that the "front-loading" arrangement has significantly diminished the benefits that could otherwise have resulted from the choice of

[35] As illustrated by Hathaway and Ingco with the help of US export subsidies on soybean oil, the equal annual installment requirement, as included in the Dunkel Draft, would have required the US to reduce outlays on export subsidies of soybean oil by 89 per cent in the first year. Hathaway and Ingco (1995) *supra* n. 30, p. 9.

1986-1990 as the base period for the purpose.[36] At the same time, the fact that the effect of the "front-loading" provision was not extended to the final commitment levels undertaken by those Members at the end of the implementation period guarantees that these adverse consequences are only temporary.

7.4.2 Non-Listed Export Subsidies and Circumvention Concerns

According to Article 10 of the Agriculture Agreement, there are two forms of practices that have aroused fears of circumvention of export subsidy commitments on the part of the negotiators of the Agreement. The first concerns the use of non-listed export subsidies so as to evade the discipline imposed by the export subsidy commitments. The provision intended to avert this fear, in relevant part, provides that "[e]xport subsidies not listed in paragraph 1 of Article 9 shall not be applied in a manner which results in, or which threatens to lead to, circumvention of export subsidy commitments."[37] The second concerns the use of concessional transactions, such as food aid agreements, as a means of camouflaging otherwise commercial deals. On this latter point, Article 10.1 in relevant part provides: "nor shall non-commercial transactions be used to circumvent such commitments."[38]

Both are thus concerned with the protection of the export subsidy commitments from being undermined by possible evasive practices. However, each is more than a mere anti-circumvention rule. While the first in effect prescribes the conditions for the use of non-listed export subsidies, the second, together with other provisions of the Agriculture Agreement as well as the Marrakesh Decision on LDCs and the NFIDCs, prescribes rules of behaviour for the practice of concessional food aid transactions.[39]

As reiterated already, the Agreement on Agriculture distinguishes between listed and non-listed export subsidies and subjects them to different rules of discipline. The latter covers a residual category of all sorts of practices which fall within the definition of an export subsidy under Article 1(e) but which do not satisfy the requirements of any of the six export subsidy practices listed under Article 9.1. While paragraph 1 of Article 10 provides that these practices may be used on condition of anti-circumvention of export subsidy commitments, paragraph 2 singles out three of these practices and provides as follows: "Members undertake to work toward the development of internationally agreed disciplines to govern the provision of export credits, export credit guarantees or insurance programmes and, after agreement on such disciplines, to provide export credits, export credit guarantees or insurance programmes only in conformity therewith." No such agreement has been reached

---

[36] See also Agra Europe, *The GATT Uruguay Round Agreement – An Agra Europe Special Supplement* (London December 1993) p. 15.

[37] First limb of Article 10.1 of the Agreement on Agriculture.

[38] Second limb of Article 10.1 of the Agreement on Agriculture.

[39] This section deals with the first of these two; for the second, see Melaku Geboye Desta, "Food Security and International Trade Law: An Appraisal of the World Trade Organization Approach" (2001) 35 *Journal of World Trade*, No. 3, pp. 449-468.

thus far. In as long as this is the case, there is no distinction in the legal regime applying to these three and the other non-listed export subsidies. The use of any of these non-listed export subsidies on scheduled agricultural products is therefore permitted on condition that they are not used to circumvent the export subsidy commitments. Finally, in an attempt to strengthen the force of the anti-circumvention provision, paragraph 3 of Article 10 reverses the generally accepted rules of evidence on burden of proof and provides as follows: "Any Member which claims that any quantity exported in excess of a reduction commitment level is not subsidized must establish that no export subsidy, whether listed in Article 9 or not, has been granted in respect of the quantity of exports in question."

The meaning of the anti-circumvention condition is rather obscure and controversial. In certain situations, it even becomes difficult to tell whether there is any real difference in discipline between the practice of listed export subsidies and those falling outside the list. The main problem lies in the concept of circumvention itself and the implications of the provision of Article 10.3 on burden of proof. The following section tries to address this subject on the basis of the two highly relevant cases decided by the WTO dispute settlement system to date – the *FSC* case and the *Canada Dairy* case. For ease of analysis, the circumvention issue will be discussed under two sub-sections – the first dealing with it from the perspective of non-scheduled agricultural products, and the second treating it from the perspective of scheduled agricultural products. While the *FSC* case will be the main area of emphasis in the first sub-section, *Canada Dairy* will be the primary focus of attention in the second one.

7.4.2.1 Non-Scheduled Agricultural Products and Anti-Circumvention – The FSC Case

In *FSC* the EC primarily argued that the FSC scheme represented an export subsidy listed in Article 9.1(d) of the Agreement on Agriculture. However, it also argued, in the alternative, that "the FSC scheme represents an export subsidy not listed in Article 9.1 of the Agreement on Agriculture, and that by providing FSC subsidies in excess of its export subsidy commitments under the Agreement on Agriculture the United States has circumvented its export subsidy commitments in violation of Article 10.1 of that Agreement."[40] The US denied both claims. But, as the panel found the FSC scheme to be an export subsidy "to reduce the costs of marketing exports of agricultural products" under Article 9.1(d) of the Agreement on Agriculture, it declined to address the alternative claim of the EC under Article 10.1 of the Agriculture Agreement.[41]

The Appellate Body disagreed with, and reversed, the finding of the panel that the FSC measure was a listed export subsidy under Article 9.1(d) of the Agreement on Agriculture.[42] Thanks to this reversal, the Appellate Body had to consider the EC

---

[40] *FSC*, report of the panel, *supra* n. 8, para. 7.133.

[41] See Ibid., footnote 716 to para. 7.177.

[42] See *FSC* report of the Appellate Body, *supra* n. 7, para. 132.

alternative claim that the FSC measure was inconsistent with Article 10.1 as read together with Article 8 of that Agreement.[43]

Article 10.1 provides that non-listed export subsidies "shall not be applied in a manner which results in, or which threatens to lead to, circumvention of export subsidy commitments; nor shall non-commercial transactions be used to circumvent such commitments."[44] This is the only provision in the Agreement on the use of non-listed export subsidies. What is more, this provision does not distinguish between the use of this category of export subsidies on scheduled and non-scheduled agricultural products. It simply talks in terms of "export subsidy commitments" in general. The term "export subsidy commitments" thus occupies a key position in the text of this Article. A clear understanding of this term is a necessary precondition for a proper appreciation of the anti-circumvention requirement of Article 10.

As the Appellate Body pointed out, this term "refers to commitments or obligations relating to export subsidies assumed by Members under provisions of the Agreement on Agriculture, in particular, under Articles 3, 8 and 9 of that Agreement."[45] The whole purpose of Article 10 is thus to prevent circumvention of the export subsidy commitments resulting from these three provisions by resorting to the non-listed export subsidies. The extent of the export subsidy commitments protected by the anti-circumvention provision of Article 10.1 demands a closer look at the relevant features of these three provisions.

Article 3 is perhaps the most important provision for our purposes here. Two of its three paragraphs cover export subsidies. Paragraph 1 in relevant part provides that "export subsidy commitments in Part IV of each Member's Schedule constitute commitments limiting subsidization and are hereby made an integral part of GATT 1994." This is a reference to the commitments undertaken by Members to *reduce* (or to eliminate) the level of their listed agricultural export subsidies in outlay as well as in quantitative terms. Needless to say, the scope of this provision is necessarily limited to the use of the listed export subsidies on the agricultural products specified in those schedules.

Paragraph 3 of Article 3 provides that "a Member shall not provide export subsidies listed in paragraph 1 of Article 9 in respect of the agricultural products or groups of products *specified* in Section II of Part IV of its Schedule in excess of the budgetary outlay and quantity commitment levels specified therein and shall not provide *such* subsidies in respect of any agricultural product *not specified* in that Section of its Schedule."[46] Once again, it seems fairly clear that the scope of this paragraph is limited to the use of *listed* export subsidies. But, in terms of product coverage, it concerns both *scheduled* (first limb of the paragraph) as well as *non-*

[43] See Ibid., para. 133.

[44] The Appellate Body started its analysis by noting that under this Article, "it is not necessary to demonstrate actual 'circumvention' of 'export subsidy commitments'. It suffices that 'export subsidies' are 'applied in a manner which ... threatens to lead to circumvention of export subsidy commitments'." Ibid., para. 148.

[45] Ibid., para. 143.

[46] Article 3.3 of the Agreement on Agriculture, (italics added).

scheduled (second limb of the paragraph) agricultural products. The difference is that, while the commitment as regards the former is *not to exceed* the limits set in the schedules, that concerning the latter is *not to provide* the *listed* export subsidies at all. It is worth stressing that only listed export subsidies are covered in both cases. As such, paragraph 3 of Article 3 does not, for instance, prohibit the use of non-listed export subsidies on non-scheduled agricultural products.

The *FSC* panel observed the following: "In the case of unscheduled products ... the Member's commitment is that it will not *provide* any export subsidies with respect to that product ...."[47] This statement does not seem to have any support in the text of the Agreement. As clearly stated under Article 3.3, which is the only provision on non-scheduled products, it is only *such* export subsidies as are listed under Article 9.1 that are prohibited. Although the Appellate Body did not directly comment on this part of the panel statement, it agreed with the latter interpretation.[48] It observed, *inter alia*, that under the second clause of Article 3.3, "Members have committed not to provide any export subsidies, *listed in Article 9.1*, with respect to *unscheduled* agricultural products. This clause clearly also involves 'export subsidy commitments' within the meaning of Article 10.1."[49] We may thus conclude, for now, that Article 3.3 does not prohibit the use of non-listed export subsidies on non-scheduled agricultural products.

Article 9 is the second provision particularly mentioned by the Appellate Body as one of the provisions where the export subsidy commitments or obligations of Members in the sense of Article 10.1 are found. Article 9 is the only provision in the Agreement which sets the minimum budgetary and outlay levels of export subsidy reduction requirements on the scheduled agricultural products. Moreover, paragraph 1 of this Article plays a central role in that it lists specific forms of export subsidy practices with a dual effect: (1) it provides an exhaustive list of the export subsidy practices that are allowed on scheduled agricultural products subject to reduction commitments in the sense of the first limb of Article 3.3; and (2) it provides an exhaustive list of the types of export subsidy practices that are prohibited in respect of unscheduled agricultural products in the sense of the second limb of Article 3.3. The Appellate Body once again appears to agree with this approach. It stated that "Article 9.1 relates *both* to (1) the commitments made for *scheduled* agricultural products, under the first clause of Article 3.3, and to (2) the general prohibition, in the second clause of Article 3.3, against providing export subsidies listed in Article 9.1 to *unscheduled* agricultural products."[50] It is worth stressing that both the commitment *to reduce* as well as the commitment *not to provide* relate to the listed export subsidy practices. Non-listed export subsidies fall entirely outside the scope of Article 3 as well as Article 9.

---

[47] *FSC*, report of the panel, *supra* n. 8, para. 139 (italics in original).

[48] See *FSC*, report of the Appellate Body, *supra* n. 7, paras. 145-146.

[49] Ibid., para. 146 (italics in original). The Appellate Body repeated its view on this issue more directly in another paragraph: "With respect to *unscheduled* agricultural products, Members are *prohibited* under Article 3.3 from providing any export subsidies as listed in Article 9.1." Ibid., para. 150.

[50] Ibid., para. 146 (italics in original).

The last provision particularly mentioned by the Appellate Body as one of the places where the export subsidy commitments or obligations of Members in the sense of Article 10.1 are found is Article 8. This provision sets the fundamental positive principle that Members provide export subsidies only in conformity with the Agreement and their schedules of commitments. To the extent that Members have undertaken not to provide export subsidies otherwise than in conformity with the Agreement and their respective Schedules, this may indeed be taken as an export subsidy commitment in the sense of Article 10.1. Moreover, although the second part of this provision is a reference only to export subsidy reduction commitments, in as long as it also talks in terms of conformity with "this Agreement", its scope covers the use of both categories of export subsidies (listed and non-listed) on both categories of agricultural products (scheduled and non-scheduled). However, one can talk of conformity with a legal standard only if the standard exists from the outset. We have seen, however, that as regards the use of non-listed export subsidies on non-scheduled agricultural products, the Agreement on Agriculture is simply silent. What remains of Article 8 is therefore the reduction commitments on listed export subsidies and the commitment not to provide the listed export subsidies on non-scheduled agricultural products. In as long as neither Article 3 nor Article 9 sets a standard for the use of non-listed export subsidies on non-scheduled agricultural products, they remain outside the scope of Article 8.

With this background in mind, we now turn to the practical problems involving Article 10 and how they have been approached by the dispute settlement system. As we saw earlier, the Appellate Body has found that FSC subsidies are a form of non-listed export subsidy. As such, all discussion in the following section concerns the use of non-listed export subsidies to circumvent, actually or potentially, the export subsidy commitments.

The Appellate Body found that the US "has acted inconsistently with its obligations under Article 10.1 of the *Agreement on Agriculture* by applying FSC export subsidies, with respect to both scheduled and unscheduled agricultural products, in a manner that, *at the very least, threatens to circumvent* its export subsidy commitments under Article 3.3 of the *Agreement on Agriculture*."[51] In its reasoning, the Appellate Body distinguished between scheduled and unscheduled agricultural products. In both cases, the non-discretionary nature of the FSC subsidies, together with the absence of limitations on the amount of benefit that can be earned by any qualifying FSC, served as the main reasons for the Appellate Body's conclusion that there existed at least a threat of circumvention.[52]

As regards non-scheduled agricultural products, the Appellate Body observed that:

> "Members are *prohibited* under Article 3.3 from providing any export subsidies as listed in Article 9.1. Article 10.1 prevents the application of export subsidies which '*results in*, or which *threatens to lead to, circumvention*' of that

[51] Ibid., para. 154 (italics in original).

[52] See Ibid., paras. 149-151.

> prohibition. Members would certainly have 'found a way round', a way to 'evade', this prohibition if they could transfer, through tax exemptions, the very same economic resources that they are prohibited from providing in other forms under Articles 3.3 and 9.1. Thus, with respect to the *prohibition* against providing subsidies listed in Article 9.1 on *unscheduled* agricultural products, we believe that the FSC measure involves the application of export subsidies, *not* listed in Article 9.1, in a manner that, at the very least, '*threatens* to lead to circumvention' of that 'export subsidy commitment' in Article 3.3."[53]

A number of important questions may be raised concerning this ruling. For example, the Appellate Body talks in terms of transfer of "the very same economic resources that they are prohibited from providing in other forms under Articles 3.3 and 9.1." The problem with this line of reasoning appears to be a consequence of the questionable premise that the export subsidy commitments protected by the anti-circumvention provision are expressed in terms only of the economic resources to be transferred regardless of the form of the transfer. This would mean that the prohibition is concerned only with the end – the economic resource to be transferred – and not the means, i.e. the form of the export subsidy to be used. However, had this been the case, Article 3.3 would simply have stated that Members "shall not provide *any export subsidies* in respect of any agricultural product not specified in that Section of its Schedule,"[54] and we would have been talking only in terms of outright violation and not any mysterious act of evasion or circumvention. Arguably, the Agreement did not use this approach because the intention in this particular case was limited to the prohibition of the use of the listed export subsidies in a manner that is not constrained by the agreed discipline. As argued already, therefore, Article 3.3 does not prohibit every form of export subsidy, but only those that are listed under Article 9.1. It is not the subsidization as such of exports of non-scheduled agricultural products that is prohibited, but the subsidization of those exports in any one of the forms listed under Article 9.1. The transfer of economic resources contingent on export performance in respect of such products is only a necessary, but not sufficient, condition for circumvention of this obligation to take place. The form of the transfer should also be such that it is an attempt to introduce any of the listed export subsidies in a manner that tries to evade notice. The general rule as regards non-listed export subsidies is thus to leave them unconstrained unless they are used to undermine the overall discipline regarding the listed export subsidies. Hence the anti-circumvention provision. The collective commitment undertaken under Article 10.2 strengthens this argument, for it seems to be an expression of the discomfort generated by the unconstrained nature of these groups of export subsidies. In an attempt to allay this concern, Members singled out the three important forms of non-listed export subsidies and undertook a special

---

[53] Ibid., para. 150 (italics in original).

[54] In its present version, however, this part of Article 3.3 provides that Members "shall not provide *such* subsidies in respect of any agricultural product not specified in that Section of its Schedule." (italics added)

commitment to develop an internationally agreed discipline – a commitment the materialization of which has eluded them to date.

The implication of the above-quoted Appellate Body statement on non-scheduled agricultural products may emerge clearly if it is seen in connection with one of the three export subsidy practices mentioned under Article 10.2. According to the Appellate Body, Members would not be allowed to use an export credit on non-scheduled agricultural products because they could transfer *the very same economic resources that they are prohibited from providing in other forms under Articles 3.3 and 9.1*. Two things are worth pointing out here. Firstly, Members are not prohibited from transferring economic resources on the export of non-scheduled agricultural products in the form of export credits (a non-listed export subsidy). Consequently, by providing such credits, they could not be making any prohibited transfers. Secondly, if the undertaking to conclude an international agreement on export credits materializes, which will most likely fall short of a flat prohibition (for the current deadlock does not seem to paint a different picture), Members will in the future be allowed to use export credits on these agricultural products. As we said earlier, this does not appear to go in line with the logic, purpose and direction of the process of trade liberalization.

To sum up, it is true that Members are *prohibited* under Article 3.3 from providing any export subsidies as listed in Article 9.1, and that Article 10.1 prevents the application of export subsidies which "*results in*, or which *threatens to lead to, circumvention*" of that prohibition. It is also true that the export subsidies protected by Article 10.1 refer to "commitments or obligations relating to export subsidies assumed by Members under provisions of the *Agreement on Agriculture*, in particular, under Articles 3, 8 and 9 of that Agreement."[55] However, the use of non-listed export subsidies (such as the FSC subsidies which have been found to be so) on non-specified agricultural products is subject to none of these three provisions. The conclusion is therefore that the Agriculture Agreement does not provide anything concerning the use of non-listed export subsidies on non-scheduled agricultural products. In terms of Article 8 of the Agriculture Agreement, Members have the obligation "*not to provide export subsidies otherwise than in conformity with this Agreement and with the commitments as specified in that Member's Schedule.*" As argued earlier, this provision does not just mean that Members may *not provide export subsidies in violation of the Agreement and their schedules*. It goes beyond that and prescribes the positive requirement that they provide their export subsidies only in conformity with the Agreement and their schedules. Needless to say, in as long as non-conformity with a standard does not necessarily mean violation of that standard, there is a wide grey area in the middle. As regards the use of non-listed export subsidies on unscheduled agricultural products, what is lacking in the Agriculture Agreement is that very standard against which to measure the conformity. Because of this, the sole condition for the non-application of the

55 *FSC*, report of the Appellate Body, *supra* n. 7, para. 143.

SCM Agreement is missing.[56] Under these circumstances, therefore, it is the standard rules of the SCM Agreement which govern the practice in this particular situation. And that is nothing else than an outright prohibition.

7.4.2.2 Scheduled Agricultural Products and Anti-Circumvention – The Canada Dairy Case

In *Canada Dairy*, the complainants – New Zealand and the US – contended that Canada's Special Milk Classes Scheme constituted circumvention of Canada's export subsidy commitments, while Canada denied this. The US took the ordinary definition of the term "circumvention" and argued that export subsidies, other than those listed in Article 9.1, could not be used "to evade or avoid the export subsidy disciplines contained in Article 9.1."[57] According to the US, Members might introduce export subsidies of a kind not listed in Article 9.1, but subject to the same export reduction commitments as those applying to the listed ones.[58] In the view of the US, "the object and purpose of Article 10.1 required that a Member not use any export subsidies in connection with export quantities exceeding the levels to which commitments had been made in the Member's respective schedules."[59] The US also resorted to the language of Article 10.3 of the Agriculture Agreement and argued that "[t]he key operative language in this provision was that no export subsidy, *whether or not listed in Article 9*, was permitted with regard to that quantity of exports that exceeds the reduction commitments."[60]

According to New Zealand, the issue of whether a Member can use non-listed export subsidies amounted to the question of "whether it was permissible under the Agreement on Agriculture to introduce an export subsidy that had the same effect as an export subsidy for which reduction commitments have been made."[61] For New Zealand, this was clearly proscribed by Article 10.[62] In its view, "Article 10 was included in the Agreement on Agriculture because Members were concerned that the

---

[56] Note that under Article 3.1 of the SCM Agreement, export subsidies are prohibited *except as provided in the Agreement on Agriculture*.

[57] *Canada Dairy*, report of the panel, *supra* n. 2, para. 4.268.

[58] Ibid., para. 4.269.

[59] Ibid., para. 4.271.

[60] Ibid., para. 4.271 (italics in original). According to the US, "[t]he drafters of Article 9.1 knew that the export subsidy disciplines would be undermined if Members were free to substitute different export subsidies from those listed in Article 9. Article 10.1 was simply intended to preclude such substitution if the export subsidies either resulted in, or threatened, circumvention of the reduction commitments contained in a Member's schedule." Ibid., para. 4.273.

[61] Ibid., para. 4.283.

[62] New Zealand argued that the effect of the Special Milk Classes Scheme was to circumvent Canada's export subsidy commitments under the Agreement on Agriculture and tried to support its arguments with facts as follows: Canada's export subsidy commitment for butter by volume for 1995/1996 was 9,464 tonnes. Its actual exports for that year were 14,574 tonnes. For 1996/1997, its commitment in respect of butter was 8,271 tonnes. Its actual exports were 15,567 tonnes. Canada's export subsidy commitment in respect of cheese by volume for 1996/1997 was 11,773 tonnes. Its actual exports were 20,086 tonnes. Canada's export subsidy commitment for "Other Milk Products" by volume for 1996/1997 was 35,649 tonnes. Its exports of whole milk powder alone in 1996/1997 were 36,632 tonnes. Ibid., para. 4.267.

export subsidy commitments undertaken under Article 9 could be nullified by subsidies that did not fit the precise definition of Article 9 but equally had the effect of shielding exporters from the actual cost of production of goods destined for export."[63] New Zealand, too, had recourse to Article 10.3 and quoted from preparatory documents of Article 10 to support its argument.[64]

Although there were disagreements over many of the points raised above, Canada "concurred" with the complainants that where export subsidies, other than those listed in Article 9.1, had been applied to a commodity subject to subsidy reduction commitments in excess of the reduction commitment level specified in a Member's schedule for that commodity, "a presumption of circumvention pursuant to Article 10 would arise."[65] The panel cited the concurrence of the parties[66] and concluded that "granting export subsidies 'other' than those listed in Article 9.1 in excess of the relevant reduction commitment level for the subsidized product concerned, is sufficient to conclude that Article 10.1 is violated."[67] This conclusion of the panel's accords well with its earlier statement that "a Member may use export subsidies not listed in Article 9.1 *within the limits of its scheduled reduction commitments*".[68] Together, these two statements mean that, according to the panel, non-listed export subsidies may be used by Members *only* within the limits of their scheduled reduction commitments.

The ordinary meaning of the text of Article 10.3 appears to support this view. According to this provision, "[a]ny Member which claims that any quantity exported in excess of a reduction commitment level is not subsidized must establish that no export subsidy, *whether listed in Article 9 or not*, has been granted in respect of the quantity of exports in question."[69] Apparently, this provision indicates that in as long as a country has used export subsidies on a product in excess of its quantitative

---

[63] Ibid., para. 4.285.

[64] New Zealand quoted the following from the negotiating *Draft Text on Agriculture* of 12 December 1991: "a *prima facie* case of circumvention of budgetary outlay commitments shall be deemed to exist where it is established that: (a) subsidies contingent on exports which are not subject to reduction have been or are being resorted to at the national or sub-national level; and (b) the volume of subsidized exports of the product concerned exceeds the volume of exports that could have been subsidized, or which can reasonably be expected to be subsidized." Ibid., para. 4.290.

[65] Ibid., para. 4.277.

[66] The panel observed the following:

> "Reading the second element of Article 10.1 together with Article 10.3, we note that all parties to this dispute agree that one example of applying export subsidies 'in a manner which results in, or which threatens to lead to, circumvention of export subsidy commitments' is a situation where export subsidies other than Article 9.1 export subsidies are granted to a product subject to subsidy reduction commitments in excess of the reduction commitment level. We see no reason, in the circumstances of this case, to disagree with this interpretation of Article 10. In our view, Article 10.3 does, indeed, address both (i) the question of who bears the burden of proving whether or not an export subsidy is at issue in a specific instance, and (ii) the question of when certain export subsidies can be said to be applied in a manner which results in, or which threatens to lead to, circumvention of export subsidy commitments." Ibid., para. 7.122.

[67] Ibid., para. 7.123.

[68] Ibid., para. 7.29 (italics added).

[69] Article 10.3 of the Agreement on Agriculture (italics added).

commitment levels, the question of whether the subsidies used are listed or not does not make any difference. In other words, even the non-listed export subsidies can be used subject *only* to the reduction commitments. What is more, in as long as this approach goes against the provision of more export subsidies, it also finds support in the overall objectives of the Agriculture Agreement.

However, there are several reasons to question the viability of the conclusion that non-listed export subsidies may be used by Members *only* within the limits of their scheduled reduction commitments. Although supported by the two principal elements of Article 31 of the Vienna Convention on the Law of Treaties, i.e. the text of the provision and the overall objectives of the Agreement, such an interpretation appears to lead to unintended and even unreasonable consequences. Another WTO panel rightly argued that even though the text of a term is "the starting-point for any interpretation, the meaning of a term cannot be found exclusively in that text; in seeking the meaning of a term, we also have to take account of its context."[70]

To begin with, nowhere in the text of the Agreement on Agriculture is it explicitly provided that the use of non-listed export subsidies should be *within the limits of the scheduled reduction commitments*. The only condition laid down by the Agreement concerning the use of non-listed export subsidies is that they may not be used to circumvent, actually or potentially, the export subsidy commitments. Allowing them to be used in a non-circumventory way is not equivalent to allowing them to be used only within the limits of the specific commitment levels. If the negotiators had intended this to be the case, Article 10.1 would simply have stated that "export subsidies not listed in paragraph 1 of Article 9 shall not be applied in *excess of the export subsidy commitments*."[71]

Besides, this interpretation would go against the literal meaning and the intended purpose of the anti-circumvention provision. The ordinary meaning of the verb "to circumvent" is "to find a way round, to evade",[72] and the purpose of the provision is to prevent Members from using non-listed export subsidies to evade their commitments regarding listed export subsidies.[73] It is not the purpose of this provision to prescribe that non-listed export subsidies be subject to the same discipline as the listed ones. In fact, both parties to this dispute agreed that Article 9.1 provides an *exhaustive* list of those export subsidies on which Members had to

---

[70] See *Canada – Certain Measures Affecting the Automotive Industry*, report of the panel (WT/DS139/R, WT/DS142/R) 11 February 2000, para. 10.12.

[71] Compare this with the relevant part of the text of Article 10.1: "Export subsidies not listed in paragraph 1 of Article 9 shall not be applied in a manner which results in, or which threatens to lead to, circumvention of export subsidy commitments." It may, of course, be difficult to imagine how such a subsidy may be used in practice regardless of the reduction commitments and cause no circumventions. However, that alone does not suffice to equate the two and conclude that the anti-circumvention condition is equivalent to a condition to use them *only within the limits of the reduction commitments*.

[72] See the meaning of the word "circumvent" together with the meaning of "get around" in *The New International Webster's Dictionary of the English Language* (Trident Press International, 1995 edition).

[73] All parties to this dispute have agreed on this point.

undertake export subsidy reduction commitments.[74] Article 10 cannot add other practices into the discipline introduced for the listed ones. The whole purpose of the anti-circumvention provision of Article 10 is only to protect the commitments on those exhaustively listed export subsidies from being evaded by the use of non-listed subsidies.

Moreover, the very meaning of a "reduction commitment" limits its scope of application to the listed export subsidies. As the *FSC* panel rightly observed, "[t]he term 'reduction commitment' in its ordinary meaning suggests that the Member was granting export subsidies with regard to the product in the relevant base period when it prepared its schedule but *committed that it would reduce the quantity of the product benefiting from Article 9.1 export subsidies during the implementation period*."[75] Indeed, countries were not required to report their practices as regards the non-listed export subsidies during the base period, and hence they could not be expected to reduce those practices that had not been included in the threshold amount of export subsidies.[76] A statement that granting non-listed export subsidies in excess of reduction commitment levels "is sufficient to conclude that Article 10.1 is violated" extends the scope of application of the reduction commitments beyond what they had been based on and what they were intended to cover. Placing all forms of non-listed export subsidies on the same level as the listed ones does not seem to be the purpose of the anti-circumvention provision.

Article 10.3 has been invoked particularly to support of the conclusion that the non-listed export subsidies may be used only within the limits of the export subsidy reduction commitments. It may indeed be curious that this provision talks in terms of both listed and non-listed export subsidies. On the surface, the proof required of a defending Member appears to go beyond its actual obligations. As clearly stated under the first limb of Article 3.3, the obligation not to exceed the reduction commitments is an obligation that applies only to the listed export subsidies. One may thus ask the following question: what if a Member that has exported a product in excess of its quantitative export subsidy commitment levels admits that only a non-listed export subsidy was provided on the excess, but offers proof that no circumvention took place? As indicated, the ordinary meaning of the text of Article 10.3 appears to exclude the acceptability of such a defence. The only viable defence in the case of exports exceeding the quantitative limits seems to be establishing that neither a listed nor a non-listed export subsidy has been used on the excess.

However, this text of Article 10.3 also needs to be read in its context as well as in the light of the intention of the parties. Seen in context, Article 10.3 falls under a provision entitled "prevention of circumvention of export subsidy commitments" with the purpose of distributing the burden of proof. It should be kept in mind that the provision itself, and not just this aspect of it, is an exception to the general

---

[74] For the respective positions of Canada and New Zealand, see *Canada Dairy*, report of the panel, *supra* n. 2, paras. 4.127 and 4.137, respectively.

[75] *FSC*, report of the panel, *supra* n. 8, para. 7.139 (italics added).

[76] See also T. Josling, S. Tangermann, and T. Warley, *Agriculture in the GATT* (MacMillan, London 1996), p. 197.

principles of evidence under both domestic and international law, and that, for good reasons – to support the presumably weaker party, the complainant, as it may have exceptional difficulty getting the necessary facts to demonstrate that subsidies have been granted on the exports of a product in excess of a certain amount. The fact that it is an exception from the accepted principles of evidence dictates the need to construe this provision in a restrictive manner. As such, it cannot be interpreted in any sense other than putting the onus to prove absence of circumvention on the defending party; it cannot be understood as a provision intended to bring the use of non-listed export subsidies on the same level as the listed ones. Furthermore, seen in light of Article 10.2 – which certainly forms part of the immediate context for the interpretation of Article 10.3 – if the use of non-listed export subsidies were subject to the same discipline of the reduction commitments as the listed ones, it would be impossible to find any convincing explanation why the three important non-listed export subsidies are singled out under Article 10.2 for the development of internationally agreed disciplines.

Article 9.4 of the Agreement on Agriculture may also give some added guidance on the meaning of the anti-circumvention provisions of the Agreement. According to this provision, developing country Members are not required to undertake commitments in respect of export subsidies for internal transport and marketing "provided that these are not applied in a manner that would circumvent reduction commitments."[77] If the interpretation given to the anti-circumvention provision of Article 10.1 by the *Canada Dairy* panel is applied to this case, it would mean that developing countries could use marketing and internal transport subsidies on exports only within the limits of the reduction commitments they might have undertaken on the remaining four listed export subsidies – thus going contrary to the very essence of the underlying principle of special and differential treatment applied presumably for the benefit of these countries. If this special treatment has to make any sense at all, it should be interpreted to mean that qualifying countries have the right to use these two forms of export subsidies regardless of their reduction commitments on the remaining four listed export subsidies. For the duration of the implementation period, the status of these two forms of export subsidies for developing countries is the same as the non-listed export subsidies for all Members. In both cases, the anti-circumvention condition should be construed in a restrictive manner so that countries would be able to provide these export subsidies on condition that they do not use them to evade their commitments. The way it is prescribed under Article 10.3, exceeding the commitment levels should only create a rebuttable presumption of circumvention requiring the defendant to demonstrate that the non-listed export subsidies used on the excess were not applied in such a way as to evade the commitments in respect of the listed practices.

---

77 The full text of Article 9.4 provides as follows: "During the implementation period, developing country Members shall not be required to undertake commitments in respect of the export subsidies listed in subparagraphs (d) and (e) of paragraph 1 above, provided that these are not applied in a manner that would circumvent reduction commitments."

The negotiating history of Article 10.3 also supports the view that the intention of the parties was only to create a *prima facie* case of circumvention that can be refuted by the defending party.[78] A preparatory document quoted by New Zealand itself in this case stated that "a *prima facie* case of circumvention of budgetary outlay commitments shall be deemed to exist where it is established that: (a) subsidies contingent on exports which are not subject to reduction have been or are being resorted to at the national or sub-national level; and (b) the volume of subsidized exports of the product concerned exceeds the volume of exports that could have been subsidized, or which can reasonably be expected to be subsidized."[79] The preparatory work thus indicates that Article 10.3 was not intended to prescribe a rule that the payment of non-listed export subsidies on products in excess of the commitment levels would automatically result in violation of the circumvention provision. It was intended to create only a presumption that such a practice amounts to a violation unless rebutted by the defending party. It merely creates a *prima facie*, and not conclusive, case in favour of violation. That is also what Canada said when it "concurred" with the complainants that where export subsidies, other than those listed in Article 9.1, had been applied to a commodity subject to subsidy reduction commitments in excess of the reduction commitment level specified in a Member's schedule for that commodity, "a presumption of circumvention pursuant to Article 10 would arise."[80]

To interpret it otherwise would only raise a series of questions, the most obvious being the following: if Members are allowed to give non-listed export subsidies only *within the reduction commitment levels*, which is the case for the listed export subsidies, what then is the difference between these two classes of export subsidies? What purpose does the classification serve? Moreover, if the use of non-listed export subsidies is subject to the same discipline of the reduction commitments as the listed ones, why is it that the three important non-listed export subsidies are singled out under Article 10.2 for the development of internationally agreed disciplines?

The answers are fairly simple and straightforward. The categorization of export subsidies into listed and non-listed is central to the export subsidy discipline of the Agreement on Agriculture with important conceptual as well as regulatory implications. Accordingly, countries are free to use their listed export subsidies only within the limits set by their reduction commitments in their schedules; they can use non-listed export subsidies on condition that they do not use them to evade their export subsidy commitments in general as well as their specific reduction commitments; the use of listed export subsidies in excess of the reduction commitments automatically results in violation of their obligations under Articles 3 and 8; the use of non-listed export subsidies in excess of the reduction

[78] Article 32 of the Vienna Convention on the Law of Treaties allows such a preparatory work to be used as a supplementary means of interpretation for the purpose, *inter alia*, of confirming the meaning resulting from application of Article 31. For the text of Article 32, see *supra* n. 21.

[79] *Negotiating Draft Text on Agriculture of 12 December 1991*, cited in *Canada Dairy*, report of the panel, *supra* n. 2, para. 4.290.

[80] *Canada Dairy*, report of the panel, *supra* n. 2, para. 4.277.

commitments creates the presumption that they have violated their obligations under Articles 10 and 8, which turns into a conclusive violation unless proved otherwise by the defending party. Consequently, exceeding the quantitative commitment levels with the non-listed export subsidies does not necessarily violate Article 10; it is only one of the indicators to presume a *prima facie* case of circumvention.

The Appellate Body in *FSC* adopted a more cautious stance on this point. After having found that the FSC subsidies were non-listed export subsidies, the Appellate Body considered the question of whether they have been "applied in a manner which *results in,* or which *threatens to lead to, circumvention* of *export subsidy commitments*".[81] The Appellate Body gave particular emphasis to the fact that under Article 10.1, what is necessary is to demonstrate only a potential and not necessarily an actual circumvention of "export subsidy commitments".[82] On that basis, the Appellate Body found that the US "has acted inconsistently with its obligations under Article 10.1 of the *Agreement on Agriculture* by applying FSC export subsidies, with respect to both scheduled and unscheduled agricultural products, in a manner that, *at the very least, threatens to circumvent* its export subsidy commitments under Article 3.3 of the *Agreement on Agriculture.*"[83]

In the specific case of scheduled agricultural products, the Appellate Body observed that "when the specific reduction commitment levels have been reached, the *limited authorization* to provide export subsidies as listed in Article 9.1 is transformed, effectively, into a *prohibition* against the provision of those subsidies."[84] Moreover, it observed that

> "the FSC measure allows for the provision of an unlimited amount of FSC subsidies, and scheduled agricultural products may, therefore, benefit from those subsidies when the reduction commitment levels specified in the United States' Schedule for those agricultural products have been reached. In our view, Members would have found 'a way round', a way to 'evade', their commitments under Articles 3.3 and 9.1, if they could transfer, through tax exemptions, the very same economic resources that they were, *at that time,* prohibited from providing through other methods under the first clause of Article 3.3 and under 9.1."[85]

From this, it drew the conclusion that "FSC subsidies are applied in a manner that, at the very least, *threatens* to lead to, circumvention of the export subsidy commitments made by the United States, under the first clause of Article 3.3, with respect to scheduled agricultural products."[86]

The emphasis on potential, as opposed to actual, circumvention might have resolved some, but by no means all, of the problems discussed above in connection

---

81 See *FSC*, report of the Appellate Body, *supra* n. 7, para. 143.
82 Ibid., para. 148.
83 Ibid., para. 154 (italics in original).
84 Ibid., para. 152 (italics in original).
85 Ibid.
86 Ibid., para. 153 (italics in original).

with *Canada Dairy*. Suffice it to note here that, in reaching this conclusion, the Appellate Body stressed the fact that due to the unlimited nature of the FSC subsidies, scheduled agricultural products may benefit from those subsidies *when the reduction commitment levels specified in the United States' Schedule for those agricultural products have been reached.* Needless to say, behind this statement lies the assumption that non-listed export subsidies may be used *only* within the limits of the reduction commitment levels – thus bringing back all the arguments enunciated earlier in connection with the *Canada Dairy* case. However, the caution that is implicit in the special emphasis on potential, as opposed to actual, circumvention seems to make the conclusion less vulnerable than that made in *Canada Dairy*.

7.4.2.3 Conclusion

Most of the arguments enunciated in this chapter are highly complicated. In the midst of this complexity, however, a few general observations may be made. Firstly, the available jurisprudence so far construes the anti-circumvention provisions of Article 10.1 in an expansive manner. Secondly, strict legal analysis shows that this approach has some inconsistencies with the intent, text and context of the provision. Finally, regardless of its legal merits, the growing jurisprudence has the virtue of strengthening the discipline of agricultural export subsidies.

7.5 Article 9.2(b): "Downstream Flexibility" Exceptions

It has been reiterated throughout that one of the important reasons for the absence of any meaningful discipline governing the sphere of agricultural trade for so long is the special vulnerability of the sector to extreme seasonal and yearly fluctuations, due, among others, to the greater dependence of the production process on nature. The exceptions that are addressed in this section were included to open some room for adjustment to such problems.

These exceptions, often called "downstream flexibility" exceptions, are so complex that their potential to occupy a centre-stage in WTO fora was widely expected from the beginning. They appeared as a subject of acrimonious debate at WTO Agriculture Committee meetings between the EC, Poland, and Norway, on the one hand, and most other trading powers, including the United Sates, Australia, New Zealand and Argentina, on the other. First brought to the attention of the Committee at its 11th regular meeting on 26–27 June 1997, the WTO Secretariat described it as an issue that "aroused considerable amount of discussion."[87]

In general, Article 9.2(b) provides that in any of the second through the fifth years of the implementation period, a Member may grant export subsidies in a given year in excess of the corresponding annual commitment levels, provided that a set of rather complex and ambiguous conditions are satisfied. These will be briefly discussed in turn.

---

[87] WTO, *Focus Newsletter*, No. 23 (1997) p. 3.

7.5.1 Condition for Flexibility in Outlay Commitments

A Member may spend on export subsidies in a given year an amount in excess of the corresponding annual commitment levels on condition that:

> "the cumulative amounts of budgetary outlays for such subsidies, from the beginning of the implementation period through the year in question, does not exceed the cumulative amounts that would have resulted from full compliance with the relevant annual outlay commitment levels specified in the Members" Schedule by more than 3 per cent of the base period level of such budgetary outlays."[88]

Different factors may force Members to spend more than what their commitments allow them for a given year. An international slump in the price of agricultural products is perhaps the clearest example to come to mind. Countries may claim to resort to this exception under two different contexts and with two different targets in view. One is where a country that has been using its annual commitments to the full in the previous years of the implementation period is forced to spend more than its commitments for a given year – and thus wants to "borrow" from its future quotas; and the second concerns a case where a country that has not been using the whole of its commitments for previous years is forced to spend more than its annual commitment for a given year and claims a right to resort to its past, unused, quotas – its alleged "savings" so to say.

To shed some light on the practical sides of these two scenarios, let us take a couple of similar, but not identical, hypothetical cases. Suppose that Countries A and B provide base-period averages of 100 units each in budgetary outlays to subsidize their respective wheat exports. Assume also that the ultimate reduction commitment levels in both cases for the end of the implementation period are set at the allowable minimum (i.e., 64 units), with a fixed reduction commitment of 6 per cent of the base level per year. This means that, for each of the six years of the implementation period starting from 1995 until 2000, the corresponding outlays are set at 94, 88, 82, 76, 70, and 64 units respectively.

Suppose further that, for the first two years of the implementation period, 1995 and 1996, both the production and marketing conditions were so favourable that while country A was able to export its wheat using only its maximum allowable outlays for each year (i.e. 94 and 88 units, respectively), country B was able to export with only 50 units of money in export subsidies for each of the two years. However, in the third year, 1997, they faced such an unexpected slump in wheat prices on the world market that they had to use much more money in export subsidies than what their respective annual commitment levels would permit them.

The question now is this: is there any distinction in the legal treatment of these two hypothetical cases under the above quoted condition? In particular, can country B claim to resort to its unused export subsidies for the years 1995 and 1996? What is the maximum permissible amount for each of these countries for the year 1997 under

---

[88] Article 9.2(b)(i) of the Agriculture Agreement.

the first condition? Any meaningful attempt to resolve these issues necessarily requires a clear understanding of the complexities inherent in the condition quoted above.

The key to understanding this condition lies in the phrase "cumulative amounts that would have resulted from full compliance with the relevant outlay commitment levels". More specifically, what does "full compliance" mean in respect of reduction commitments? If we return to the preceding illustrations, how much should countries A and B spend in any year of the implementation period to be in "full compliance" with their respective obligations?

The answer that readily comes to mind is to say that a country complies with its obligations if it spends its annual commitment levels for the year in question and no more. This is not a wrong answer; it fits in with the letter of the Agreement very well. But, is it the only right answer? For instance, if in a given year the price of a certain product rises so much that the country does not need to grant any export subsidies at all, has that country, by failing to grant subsidies for that year, also failed to "fully comply" with its commitments for that same year? In other words, does full compliance require that a country use all its permissible budgetary outlays for any given year?

In trying to resolve this issue, one should always bear in mind that the Agriculture Agreement is here talking about reduction commitments which are nothing but maximum allowable limits, rather than mandatory spending levels. By fixing its reduction commitments for any given year, a country is obligating itself only not to exceed that limit. All expenditures below that limit are not only in "full compliance" with its obligations; in a strange way of saying, they represent "more full" a compliance than a use of the whole allowable amount – for, in this case, the practice is in line with both the letter and the spirit of the Agreement. It goes further towards the realization of the liberalization objective of the entire multilateral trading system. A Member fully complies with its obligations by spending any sum between zero and its commitment levels. Any other construction to the effect that countries comply with their obligations only when they spend the whole of their commitments would be tantamount to imposing an obligation to subsidize for the purpose of liberalization – an outright anomaly.

Accordingly, an issue involving the determination of the "cumulative amounts that would have resulted from full compliance with relevant annual outlay commitment levels specified in the Member's Schedule" is not simply a reference to a predetermined sum of the maximum allowable limits. That is only one instance – and certainly an extreme instance at that – of full compliance. All annual expenditures below that limit are also in full, if not fuller, compliance and should always be taken as they are during the calculation of the cumulative amounts that would have resulted from full compliance. The overall effect of all this is that it is only with the sum total of all actual expenses below or equal to the maximum annual limit – and not with the sum total of the maximum annual limits regardless of actual expenses – that the cumulative amounts of budgetary outlays for such subsidies from the beginning of the implementation period through the year in question should be compared. And it is the possible excess of the latter over the former that is required not to be more than 3 per cent of the base period level of the budgetary outlays.

Let us now apply this background principle to the two hypothetical questions we introduced earlier. To start with the easier of the two cases – that concerning country A – can it raise its budgetary expenditure for the year 1997? If yes, by how much? The answer to this question is straightforward; country A has the right to increase its budgetary outlays for that year within the limits set by the first condition. Applying the preceding analysis to this case, the maximum that this country may spend in addition to its bound level as per this condition may be calculated as follows. The condition is that the cumulative amounts of outlays from the beginning of the implementation period (i.e. 1995) through the year in question (i.e. 1997) – which is 94 + 88 + 82 + X = 264 + X, where x represents the additional amount that country A may be allowed to use for this year – should not exceed the cumulative amounts that would have resulted from full compliance with the relevant annual commitment levels specified in the Members' Schedule (which in this case is equivalent to the sum total of the commitment levels, 94 + 88 + 82 = 264) by more than 3 per cent of the base period level of such budgetary outlays (which is 100(3 ÷ 100) = 3 units; hence, X = 3). This means that the maximum that country A can spend in the year 1997 in addition to its bound level for the year is 3 units – thus bringing the total allowable sum for the year to 85 units.

The situation concerning country B is, however, more complex than the case of country A. To start with a recapitulation of the essential points of the rule under treatment with the help of the hypothetical illustrations already introduced, country B had used only 50 units in each of the 1995 and 1996 fiscal, etc. years. However, in 1997, the condition of the markets has forced it to use much more than the 82 units available for that year. The first question is thus as to whether it can revert to the unused export subsidies for the preceding two years, the total amount of which is 82 units, i.e. 44 (the difference from 1995) plus 38 (the difference from 1996). If yes, by how much? If no, why not?

Article 9.2(b) requires of us to first determine two things: the cumulative amounts of budgetary outlays for such subsidies from the beginning of the implementation period through the year in question (i.e. 1997) and the cumulative amounts that would have resulted from full compliance with the relevant annual outlay commitment levels specified in the Member's Schedule. The first one is straightforward once again: 50 + 50 + 82 + X = 182 + X (where X represents the maximum by which B may be allowed to exceed its annual commitment level for the year 1997). The second one is less clear. The question of whether it is the bound amounts of 94 and 88 or the actual amounts of 50 each that should be taken into account in the calculation for the years 1995 and 1996 has already been found controversial.

The practical effect of choosing one over the other is significant. If the former, then country B will be allowed to spend as much as 167 units (i.e., X will be equal to the sum total of the three ceiling amounts (94 + 88 + 82 = 264) minus the actually paid amount of 182 increased by 3 per cent of the base period level, which comes to 3 units; X = 264 – 182 + 3 = 85) in the year 1997. In the latter case, however, B will not be able to use more than 85 units in all because, even when spending 50 units each in 1995 and in 1996, B still "fully complied" with its obligations. Hence the cumulative amounts that would have resulted from full compliance with the relevant annual outlay commitment levels will be nothing else than the sum total of what had actually been spent in the years 1995 and 1996 plus the maximum allowable amount for the year 1997 (which comes to 50 + 50 + 82 = 182). It is with this figure that the now-raised amount should be compared, and it is from this sum that the new figure is required not to exceed by more than 3 per cent of the base period level. This means that the maximum B can spend for the year 1997 is once again 85 units.

Now, which of these two approaches gives the more appropriate solution to the problem? All preceding analyses strongly suggest that the Agriculture Agreement does not allow the transfer of unused export subsidies to a future date. This view is dictated by the very nature of reduction commitments. A country is said to have failed to comply with its obligations only if it breaches its commitments *vis-à-vis* other parties. Members' only obligation in this respect is a commitment not to spend on export subsidies, if they have to, more than their bound amounts. The whole purpose of the Agriculture Agreement being the progressive dismantling of the export subsidy schemes of countries, Members were very much encouraged during the Uruguay Round negotiations to commit themselves to the highest possible reductions they could afford under the circumstances. The same applies to cases where they set their commitments at one level, but actually granted a lower amount of export subsidies. In point of fact, GATT is rich with the experience of countries binding their tariff levels at a certain level (often called ceiling bindings) but actually applying lower tariffs in their day-to-day operation. This practice is not just tolerated, it has always been highly encouraged. A country that has bound its outlay reduction commitments for export subsidies at, say, 100 units for a specific year "fully complies" with its obligations by allocating any sum between zero and 100 units. The moment it raises its expenditures above 100 even by a penny, it, in principle, violates its obligations and stands in need of a clear justification. Furthermore, the principle stipulated under Article 3 of the Agriculture Agreement in this respect remains that Members' Schedules constitute commitments limiting subsidization and that they "shall not provide export subsidies ... *in excess of* the budgetary outlay ... levels specified therein". All deviations from this principle need to be justified under a clear authority.

All this leads to the inevitable conclusion that the "flexibility exceptions" of Article 9 of the Agriculture Agreement have nothing to do with "quota saving" or anything of that sort. There is no possibility to transfer one's rights for a given year and resort to them at a later stage. The exception is there only to govern cases where Members may be forced to use more than their annual commitment levels by affording some room for adjustment. The fact that a Member had not used all its budgetary outlays for a previous year indicates that the implicit conditions of strain for the application of the exception did not exist. As such, it cannot in any reasonable way alter the allowable amount for subsequent years. By not using its commitment levels to the full, it has "fully" complied with its obligations.

7.5.2 Flexibility in Quantitative Commitments

The second condition relates to quantitative commitments undertaken by the

Members. According to this condition, a Member may exceed its annual limits in this respect as well provided that,

> 'the cumulative quantities exported with the benefit of such export subsidies, from the beginning of the implementation period through the year in question, does not exceed the cumulative quantities that would have resulted from full compliance with the relevant annual quantity commitment levels specified in the Members' Schedule by more than 1.75 per cent of the base period quantities."[89]

Most of the factual, price-related market situations that lay beneath the controversial issue of whether to use past "unused" budgets in subsequent years also had their parallels in the quantitative front. For instance, the OECD reported that world agricultural markets for 1995 were characterized by tighter supplies and lower stocks so much so that the "current supply situation for cereals involves the lowest world stocks for two decades".[90] These positive market developments also continued in the year 1996. This means that, in those years, most exporting Members were in a position to export their products without resorting to subsidies, or at least at less than their annual commitment levels. However, as the condition of the market deteriorated in the year 1997 – thus necessitating the use of more export subsidies on additional quantities of products – actual cases similar to the hypothetical ones discussed in connection with the preceding condition were very much on the table before the Agriculture Committee meeting in relation to the "Second Condition".

What happened in that case was that, in 1995 and 1996, agricultural prices on world markets were relatively so high that "many countries with export subsidy reduction commitments were ... able to export without using the full amount of export subsidies that were available to them".[91] At the same time, the market condition in 1997 was such that these same countries were forced to subsidize much more than what their annual export subsidy commitments for that year would allow them to. The issue was brought to the attention of the Agriculture Committee when, at its 11th regular meeting on 26–27 June, 1997, the US raised its concerns about reports that the EC "might utilize, in the current implementation year, 'unused' export subsidy quantities for poultry meat carried over from the last implementation year."[92] The US then warned that "[g]iven the substantial unused export subsidy quantities available both in the United States and the EC, this action in the poultry meat sector could ... set a potentially dangerous precedent with respect to the effectiveness of the export subsidy disciplines"[93] – a threat that it ultimately carried out.[94]

---

[89] Article 9.2(b)(ii) of the Agriculture Agreement.

[90] OECD, "Agricultural Policies, Markets, and Trade in OECD Countries: Monitoring and Evaluation 1996: Summary and Conclusions", published in 8 *World Trade and Arbitration Materials,* No.5 (September 1996) p. 144.

[91] WTO, *Focus Newsletter*, No. 23, (1997) p. 3.

[92] WTO Committee on Agriculture, *Summary Report of the Meeting Held on 26-27 June, 1997: Note by the Secretariat* (G/AG/R/11) para. 21.

[93] Ibid., para. 21.

[94] See *infra* note 15.

The US found support for this position from, *inter alia*, Argentina, Australia, Canada and New Zealand.[95] Australia in particular "questioned the assumptions made regarding the *extent* to which any shortfall in the use of export subsidies permitted in one implementation year could be carried forward as a credit that could be used in a subsequent implementation year."[96] In the view of Australia, Article 9.2(b) of the Agreement involved a number of interpretative issues, one of which being the question of "what was meant by 'full compliance'."[97] However, it is noteworthy that the Australian reaction at this stage challenged only the extent to which the shortfall can be rolled over as a credit, and not the very legality of the practice of roll-over itself. New Zealand further strengthened the weight of this argument by pointing out the fact that it "was not foreseen that any Member would increase the level of export subsidies during the implementation period."[98]

The EC reacted by giving figures showing that its actual subsidized exports for the previous year were less than its commitment levels for that year.[99] However, the EC also contended that Article 9 provided the possibility of carrying over such unused quantities and reserved what it called "the right to utilize any carry-over from one implementation year to another."[100]

A more meaningful discussion of the issue was made during the 12th meeting of the Committee on Agriculture on 25–26 September, 1997. Australia in particular improved its earlier argument and pushed its position from challenging the extent of the allowable carry-over to questioning the very legality of the practice of carrying over unused export subsidies for later years. According to Australia, "it was neither the intention nor the negotiated outcome on export subsidy commitments that Members should be able to cumulate unutilized export subsidies for use in later years."[101] Australia also developed the key point it had raised earlier concerning the meaning to be given to the term "full compliance" under Article 9.2(b)(ii). In its own words, Australia argued that a Member "would be in full compliance even if it did not utilize fully its export subsidy limit in a particular year."[102] It was Australia's view that "the level of actual export subsidies

---

[95] For the views of these countries, see G/AG/R/11, *supra* n. 92, para. 23.

[96] Statement of Australia as cited in Ibid., para. 23 (italics added).

[97] Statement of Australia as cited in Ibid.

[98] Statement of New Zealand as cited in Ibid.

[99] The representative of the EC noted that "the EC had exported 418,000 tonnes of subsidized poultry meat in the marketing year 1996/95 against a commitment level of 434,500 tonnes in that year, leaving the 'unused' quantity of 16,400 tonnes with respect to the EC's commitment level in 1996/95." G/AG/R/11, Ibid., para. 22.

[100] Ibid.

[101] WTO Committee on Agriculture, *Summary Report of the Meeting Held on 25-26 September, 1997: Note by the Secretariat* (G/AG/R/12) para. 7. At a June 1998 meeting of the Committee, too, Australia continued to voice its opposition to the practice of carry-overs. Australia argued once more that "the commitments contained in the Agreement on Agriculture were designed to result in substantial progressive reductions in export subsidies, and that the intent of Article 9.2(b) had not been to allow for higher export subsidies in later years of the implementation period just because market conditions in earlier years had been unexpectedly positive." See WTO Committee on Agriculture, *Summary Report of the Meeting Held on 25–26 June 1998: Note by the Secretariat* (G/AG/R/15) para. 3.

[102] G/AG/R/12, *supra* n. 101, para. 8.

utilized could amount to, or be taken to mean, full compliance as long as there was no breach of the bound level." Several countries, including Argentina, Brazil, Canada, Chile, Colombia, Malaysia, Mexico, New Zealand, the Philippines, South Africa, Thailand, Uruguay, and the US endorsed this elaborate argument by Australia.

The argument of the Philippines is worth a special mention here, for it adds the element of strain which underlies the very need for the flexibility provisions of Article 9. According to the Philippines, "the original purpose of the flexibility provision in Article 9.2 was to allow some limited scope for exceeding the export subsidy commitments in individual years if Members concerned had difficulties in meeting their commitments exactly. It was not intended to allow countries to accumulate 'credit' that would be used to subsidize exports beyond commitment levels in subsequent years."[103]

The EC maintained its original position on the subject and argued that "the spirit of the Agreement notwithstanding, the European Communities had ultimately agreed to Article 9.2 as it stood, the text of which in the view of the European Communities was not ambiguous. ... The text as it was finally agreed by Members permitted cumulation and the carry-over of unused quantities: in other words, it allowed opportunities that were not exhausted in one year to be cumulated and carried forward."[104] Poland and Norway supported the EC position and expressed the view that "ultimately the textual side prevailed over the spirit of the Agreement."[105] The EC later admitted that it had made use of this "possibility to roll-over unused quantities from one year to the next."[106]

Professor Tangermann looked back at those problems and summarized the facts of the matter as follows:

> "[I]n the first year of the implementation period the EU did not have any difficulty with its new commitments on export subsidies. In the cereals sector, the extremely high world market prices in parts of 1995 and 1996 allowed the EU to export cereals without subsidies, and at times to impose an export tax. However, by the second year (crop year 1996/97 ...) the quantity of agricultural goods exported with subsidies from the European Union was above the basic EU commitment for that year in the case of four products, and in two of these cases outlays on export subsidies also exceed the basic commitment .... Of course, as the EU is always meticulously anxious to honor its GATT/WTO obligations and commitments, there was, in the eyes of the EU, a good legal reason for exceeding its export subsidy commitments in 1996/97; namely, the 'credit' resulting from the under-utilization of EU export subsidy commitments for the products concerned in 1995/96."[107]

---

[103] Ibid., para. 11.
[104] Ibid., para. 12.
[105] Ibid., para. 14.
[106] WTO Committee on Agriculture, *Summary Report of the Meeting Held on 20–21 November 1997: Note by the Secretariat* (G/AG/R/13).
[107] S. Tangermann, *The European Union Perspective on Agricultural Trade Liberalization in the WTO*, paper presented at the Department of Agricultural Economics and Business, University of Guelph, Canada, February 1999, p. 10.

What is worse, other countries, including Poland, Norway, Israel and the US followed suit in the use of "roll-overs".[108] Seeing that the discussions in the Agriculture Committee could not solve the problem, during the 15th meeting of the Committee in June 1998, South Africa "challenged all Members considering the use of unutilized export subsidies to refrain from doing so."[109] The United States expressed its readiness to take up this South African challenge and "wondered whether the European Communities was also willing to make such a commitment.[110] Expectedly, however, the EC was not willing to accept the call made by South Africa and later by the US.[111]

Be that as it may, it is unfortunate that, since the Agriculture Committee is not a dispute settlement organ, and, presumably, as Members raised the issues only for the sake of bringing them to the attention of the implementation-review body, no definitive and authoritative answer was forthcoming from the discussions of the Agriculture Committee even for the issue it addressed. What is worse, the use of the roll-over practice was exacerbated after it was discussed in the Agriculture Committee.

The division of opinion that was witnessed among Members of the Agriculture Committee is also observed among academics. For example, Thompson, supporting the roll-over practice, writes that "a country can overshoot its limits to some extent, *if a credit has been built up in earlier years* or the deficit repaid in the following year."[112] Professor Tangermann, too, is of the opinion that the legal merits of the practice of roll-over "on the surface appear rather convincing, given the wording of Article 9 in the Agreement on Agriculture."[113]

But, as already indicated under the first condition, Members do not have the right to roll over to the future any thing from their previous implementation years for the following three reasons: Firstly, the ordinary meaning of the key terms "full compliance" in respect of reduction commitments does not oblige countries to grant export subsidies at their ceiling levels. As Australia rightly observed, "a Member would be in full compliance even if it did not utilize fully its export subsidy limit in a particular year."[114] It has been argued already that such a Member in fact complies "more fully" with its obligations than the Member that utilizes the whole of its export subsidy commitment levels for a given year. Secondly, the downstream flexibility exception was negotiated with the object of allowing countries room for adjustment in case there are compelling reasons for so doing in a particular implementation year. Its utilization is thus implicitly contingent upon the existence of the need for it in that particular year. Contrary to the view of the EC, therefore,

---

[108] See New Zealand's argument in G/AG/R/15, *supra* n. 101, para. 5.

[109] Ibid., para. 4.

[110] Ibid., para. 15.

[111] See Ibid., para. 17.

[112] K. Thompson, "CAP and the WTO after the Uruguay Round Agreement on Agriculture" in 2 *European Foreign Affairs Review* (1996) p. 174 (italics added).

[113] Tangermann (1999), *supra* n. 107, p. 10.

[114] G/AG/R/12, *supra* n. 101.

this is not an opportunity to be saved and carried over to a future date at will. Rather, it is an outlet from exceptionally difficult situations whenever there is one. Finally, as an exception to the rule, the flexibility provisions should, of necessity, be construed restrictively.

7.5.3 Common Condition

The third condition pertains to both the quantitative as well as the budgetary commitments and further constrains the conditional exceptions that are allowed under the already stringent conditions discussed above. Accordingly, a Member may exercise the exceptions discussed above only on condition that,

> "the total cumulative amounts of budgetary outlays for such export subsidies and the quantities benefiting from such export subsidies over the entire implementation period are no greater than the totals that would have resulted from full compliance with the relevant annual commitment levels specified in the Member's Schedule."[115]

This condition makes it clear that the exceptions allowed to the principle of strict adherence to the reduction commitments are nothing but a mechanism of "internal" adjustment within the limits set for the entire implementation period. Given the fact that the whole purpose behind the exception is to give room for minor adjustments to unforeseen year-to-year fluctuations of different sorts, this condition simply stipulates that the limited excesses allowed by the preceding two conditions cannot be extended to the entire implementation period. In a sense, this condition makes it clear that these adjustments enable Members only to "borrow" from their "future rights" within the limits prescribed under the preceding conditions.

If we apply this to the hypothetical illustrations we used under the first condition above, the 3 units of money countries A and B used to alleviate their current problems in the year 1997 need to be "paid back" within the years of the implementation period. In no way may the total cumulative amount of expenditure for these countries for the entire implementation period go beyond what a full compliance with the annual reduction commitments would have resulted. In line with what has been said about the essence of this latter amount, this means that any amount spent or quantity exported in any given year between zero and the commitment level will be counted as it is in the calculation of the cumulative amount that would have resulted from full compliance with the annual reduction commitments. This cumulative amount may thus be as low as zero and as high as the sum total of the annual commitment levels.

To illustrate this point with the help of the hypothetical examples introduced earlier, Country A would be required to "pay back" the 3 units of additional money used in 1997 by reducing its expenses from its commitment levels for the remaining years of the implementation period by a minimum of 3 units. The same holds true for

[115] Article 9.2(b)(iii) of the Agriculture Agreement.

country B. Despite the fact that it did not make full use of its commitment levels for the years 1995 and 1996, the 3 units of additional money spent to subsidize the 1997 exports has to be "paid back" in any of the remaining years of the implementation period.

This third condition thus provides an additional constraint on the degree of flexibility allowed under the preceding conditions in favour of still greater market orientation. Under this condition, the outlets opened for countries by the preceding provisions are made to be only temporary mechanisms of adjustment. Members are thus allowed only to "borrow" from their "future rights" with the mandatory obligation to "pay back" before the end of the implementation period. It is precisely for this reason that the flexibility exceptions do not work during the final year of the implementation period, for there would be no time any more to make up for the excess.[116]

The fourth and the last condition stated under this same sub-paragraph (b) of Article 9.2 seems out of context. While the preceding three conditions pertain to the possibility of Members' exceeding their annual obligations at the implementation stage, this last one rather constrains the negotiating powers of the Members at the stage of fixing these annual commitments from the very outset. It is in fact the only provision in the Agriculture Agreement that sets the minimum that should be undertaken by any Member and that fixes the base period for purposes of agricultural export subsidies.

Paragraph 3 of Article 9 indicates that Members may also negotiate towards commitments limiting the scope of export subsidies and specify their limits in their Schedules. Such bindings may limit Members' rights to extend "the subsidization of exports of particular products to specific markets"[117] as specified in their commitments. In practice, though, no Member has assumed any such commitments in the Schedules.

7.5.4 Summary

The following general remarks may be made about reduction commitments in general and the flexibility conditions in particular: Firstly, the essence of the reduction commitments and the rules governing them should be understood as setting only an upper limit, a ceiling, on the policy-making and implementation powers of countries. Members are not only free to subsidize a lesser quantity of exports than their annual commitment levels or spend less than what is specified in

---

[116] It is also worthy of note that throughout the acrimonious debates on the issue of downstream flexibility provisions in the Agriculture Committee, no Member questioned the legality of this limitation. Indeed, during those debates, "one point was not contested: the agreement says that whatever happens in an individual year, over the full implementation period export subsidies cannot exceed the total committed for the whole of the period." WTO, *Focus Newsletter*, No. 23 (1997) p. 3.

[117] See "Modalities of Export Competition Commitments, Annex 8 to Uruguay Round Draft Final Act", December 1991, as reproduced in T. Stewart, *The GATT Uruguay Round: A Negotiating History (1986 – 1992)* in III Vols. (Kluwer 1993), Vol. III pp. 647–48.

their schedules of commitments; they are highly encouraged to do so. Secondly, although there is no degree in compliance with one's legal obligations, it may even be proper to say that a Member that spends or exports less than its annual commitments complies with both the letter and the spirit of the law more than the one that fully spends and subsidizes exports at its allowable maximum for a given year. Thirdly, the cumulative amounts of budgetary outlays and quantities benefiting from such subsidies that would have resulted from full compliance refer to nothing but a sum total of all actual annual expenditures and quantities below or equal to the commitment levels and those exceptional additions adjusted according to the preceding criteria. And finally, whatever the actual expenditure of a Member within its bound limits of export subsidies in preceding years of the implementation period, the annual maximum can be exceeded only within the limits set by the Agreement to be rebalanced by reducing one's future expenses and quantities within the duration of the implementation period.

CHAPTER 8

ENFORCEMENT OF THE EXPORT SUBSIDIES DISCIPLINE

8.1 Implementation and Surveillance of the Discipline of Export Subsidies

The Agriculture Agreement did not only introduce the discipline governing agricultural trade; it also established the mechanism by which the practical implementation of the Agreement would be monitored. Accordingly, a Committee on Agriculture has been established[1] with the task, *inter alia*, of reviewing progress in the implementation of commitments.[2] According to Article 18.2, this review is to be undertaken "on the basis of notifications submitted by Members in relation to such matters and at such intervals as shall be determined." At its meeting on 31 January 1995, the General Council adopted the following terms of reference for the WTO Committee on Agriculture: "The Committee shall oversee the implementation of the Agreement on Agriculture. The Committee shall afford members the opportunity of consulting on any matter relating to the implementation of the provisions of the Agreement."[3] The Committee commenced its task by adopting the requirements and formats for notifications under Article 18.2, which also includes those applying to agricultural export subsidies.

8.1.1 Notification of Export Subsidies

At its meeting on 8 June 1995, the Committee on Agriculture adopted a document in which it set out the requirements and formats for notifications under Article 18.2 and other relevant provisions of the Agreement on Agriculture.[4] Export subsidies are covered by the document.[5] Accordingly, all Members are required to make annual notifications concerning their export subsidy practices. The details to be included by a Member in its export subsidy notifications, however, depend on three main factors: whether or not it has included export subsidy reduction commitments in its

---

1 See Article 17 of the Agreement on Agriculture.

2 See Article 18.1 of the Agreement on Agriculture.

3 WTO General Council, *WTO Committee On Agriculture: Decision by the General Council on 31 January 1995* (WT/L/43, 17 February 1995).

4 WTO Committee on Agriculture, *Notification Requirements and Formats* (G/AG/2, 30 June, 1995).

5 For the notification formats relating to export subsidies, see Ibid., Tables ES:1 to ES:3 and Supporting Tables ES:1 and ES:2, pp. 26–30.

schedules; whether or not it is a "significant exporter" of agricultural products; and whether or not it is donor of food aid.

On that basis, all Members are put in one of four categories. In the first category fall those countries that have included base and annual commitment levels in their schedules.[6] They are required to make annual notifications of their export subsidies for every product included in their respective schedules of commitments, in both outlay as well as quantitative terms, no later than 60 days following the end of the calendar (or, marketing, fiscal, etc.) year in question. In cases where the notifications thus made are provisional, the final notifications have to be submitted no later than 120 days following the end of the year in question. Furthermore, the notifications are required to be made in a specific format.[7] For ease of comparison, the actual outlay and quantitative levels of export subsidies for every year are required to be set side by side with the scheduled commitment levels for the corresponding period.[8] Countries also have to include in their notification details on the use of downstream flexibility options where necessary.[9]

The second category covers those Members which had no base or annual commitment levels shown in their Schedules. These are countries which are not allowed to provide any export subsidies at all. Hence, the requirement that annual notifications be made no later than 30 days following the end of the year in question "in the form of a statement confirming that no export subsidies exist."[10]

The third category covers Members with scheduled commitments and Members with no scheduled commitments but which are significant exporters of any of the 22 agricultural products or groups of products that have been singled out by the Modalities Agreement for purposes of assuming the export subsidy reduction commitments.[11] A significant exporter for notification purposes has been defined to

---

6 Ibid., p. 24, para. (i).

7 For the notification formats, see Ibid., Tables ES:1 to ES:3 and Supporting Tables ES:1 and ES:2, pp. 26–30.

8 See Ibid., Table ES:1, p. 26.

9 Ibid., p. 24, para. (i).

10 Ibid., p. 24, para. (ii). Developing countries using either of the exempt export subsidies of Article 9:1(d) and (e) are also required to report the same according to a format set in Table ES:2 of this same document.

11 The pertinent paragraph on this subject provides as follows: "for all Members with base and annual commitment levels shown in Section II of Part IV of their Schedule plus all other Members which are significant exporters of the products listed hereunder, namely, those Members whose share of total world exports in any one or more of the following products or groups of products exceeds 5%, an annual notification of the total volume of exports of the product(s) concerned should be made. Notifications in respect of the first two years of implementation should be made no later than 120 days following the end of the end of the calendar (or, marketing, fiscal, etc.) year in question. Where a notification with respect to any product or group of products is provisional a final notification shall be made no later than 180 days following the end of the year in question. In respect of the third and subsequent years of implementation notifications shall be made no later than 120 days following the end of the implementation year in question. A list of Members that are significant exporters for the purposes of this notification requirement and of the products concerned shall be established by the Chairman following consultation as appropriate and shall be reviewed after two years. Notifications

mean a Member whose share of total world exports in any one or more of these products exceeds five per cent. Members falling in this category are required to make annual notifications of the total volumes of exports of the product(s) concerned. This is, therefore, a notification merely of total exports, and not of export subsidies as such. In order to facilitate the process, the Committee has established a list of Members that are "significant exporters for the purposes of this notification requirement and of the products concerned," which list is subject to review after two years. Currently, the list of "Significant Exporters"[12] looks as follows.

Table 1: List of "Significant Exporters"

Product Group	**Significant Exporters**
Wheat and wheat flour	Australia
Coarse grains	Argentina
Rice	Pakistan, Thailand
Oilseeds,	Argentina, Brazil, United States
Vegetable oils	Argentina, Indonesia, Malaysia, Philippines
Oilcakes	Argentina, United States
Sugar	Australia, Cuba, Thailand
Butter and butter oil	New Zealand
Skim milk powder	New Zealand
Cheese	New Zealand
Other milk products	New Zealand
Bovine meat	Australia, New Zealand
Pigmeat	Canada
Poultry meat	Thailand
Sheepmeat	Australia, New Zealand
Fruit	Chile, Costa Rica, Honduras, Philippines, United States
Vegetables	United States
Tobacco	United States, Zimbabwe
Cotton	Australia, Pakistan, United States

cont.

should take the form of Table ES:2 and, in the case of Members with base and annual commitment levels shown in Section II of Part IV of their Schedule, the data on total exports shall be on a basis comparable to that provided in Table ES:1." The products referred to here are the same products as those listed by the Modalities Agreement for the assumption of export subsidy reduction commitments: (i) Wheat and wheat flour; (ii) Coarse grains; (iii) Rice; (iv) Oilseeds (v)Vegetable oils; (vi) Oilcakes; (vii) Sugar; (viii) Butter and butter oil; (ix) Skim milk powder; (x) Cheese; (xi) Other milk products; (xii) Bovine Meat; (xiii) Pigmeat; (xiv) Poultry meat; (xv) Sheepmeat; (xvi) Live animals; (xvii) Eggs; (xviii) Wine; (xix) Fruit; (xx) Vegetables; (xxi) Tobacco; (xxii) Cotton. Ibid., p. 24.

12 WTO Committee on Agriculture, *List of "Significant Exporters" for the Purposes of the Notification Requirements in Respect of Export Subsidy Commitments: Addendum* (G/AG/2/Add.1) 16 October 1995.

Finally, the fourth category covers only the food donor Members of the WTO and requires them to notify the total volume of food aid they provide in every year. As this issue is discussed elsewhere, suffice it to note here that the amount of food aid provided by these countries has shown a dramatic decline over the past few years.[13]

One means of exerting pressure on countries to comply with their notification obligations envisaged by the Agreement on Agriculture is the so-called counter-notification. According to Article 18.7, any Member "may bring to the attention of the Committee on Agriculture any measure which it considers ought to have been notified by another Member." Under this procedure, therefore, any Member of the Committee "may present data in the form of a notification on the non-notifying Member's commitments to the Committee. This notification then becomes the basis for discussions relating to implementation of commitments by the non-notifying country."[14] Despite this, however, the degree of compliance with regard to the notification requirements has often been a subject of serious criticism.[15]

8.1.2 Waivers from Export Subsidy Commitments

We have seen that the export subsidy provisions of the Agriculture Agreement establish a fairly stringent discipline on the use of this highly sensitive practice. Needless to say, not all Members comply fully with their commitments. Several Members have, for instance, failed to discharge their notification obligations, thus making prompt review of compliance with the substantive obligations difficult.[16] Moreover, there have also been failures to comply with the substantive obligations of the Agreement on the subject. In such cases, while consultations and dispute settlement are the primary options available to affected Members, at least one country, Hungary, has succeeded in convincing the General Council to grant it a waiver from its obligations in respect of export subsidies under the Agreement on Agriculture. Given the infamous experience of waivers in the field of agriculture,[17] a closer look at the procedural and substantive issues of the Hungarian waiver as well as the safeguards against a potential abuse of such options appears to be in order at this point. But first, some observations on the overall issue of waivers and the rules governing them.

---

[13] G/AG/2, *supra* n. 4, p. 25.

[14] WTO Committee on Agriculture, *Compliance With Notification Obligations "Overdue Notifications": Discussion Paper by the United States* (G/AG/W/33) 11 June 1998.

[15] For a good survey of the major problems encountered during the first few years of the implementation period, see WTO Committee on Agriculture, *Issues Regarding Export Subsidy Notifications: Discussion Paper By Australia* (G/AG/W/37) 12 November 1998.

[16] See, for instance, WTO Committee on Agriculture, *WTO Room Document, Compliance with Notification Obligations* 19–20 March 1998.

[17] Noteworthy in this respect is the notorious US agricultural waiver of 1955, which was used to virtually exclude US agriculture from the multilateral trading regime for nearly four decades until the Uruguay Round put an end to it. See GATT, *Waiver Granted to the United States in Connection with Import Restrictions Imposed under Section 22 of the United States Agriculture Adjustment Act (of 1993) as Amended, Decision of 5 March 1955*, *BISD* 3S/32.

Article XXV of GATT 1994 provides that decision-making under GATT is vested in the CONTRACTING PARTIES. In such cases, each contracting party has one vote and that, unless otherwise provided, decisions of the CONTRACTING PARTIES may be taken by a simple majority of the votes cast.[18] One area where this decision-making power is subject to an exceptional qualified majority requirement is the power to waive an obligation imposed upon a contracting party by the Agreement. CONTRACTING PARTIES could take a waiver decision only by a two-thirds majority of the votes cast and such majority should comprise more than half of the contracting parties.[19] However, although this was supposed to take place only under "exceptional circumstances",[20] the practice of GATT has been rather "relaxed on this point".[21]

Since the entry into force of the WTO Agreement, the power to decide on waivers is given to the Ministerial Conference. The Ministerial Conference, composed of representatives of all Members, is the highest decision-making organ in the WTO with the responsibility to carry out the functions of the WTO and to take actions necessary to that effect. The Ministerial Conference has the authority to take decisions on all matters under any of the Multilateral Trade Agreements.[22] However, as the Ministerial conference normally meets only once every two years,[23] its functions in the intervals between those meetings are conducted by the General Council, which is also composed of representatives of all the Members, but at a lower level.[24] As this organ is required to meet "as appropriate", this means that, in practice, most powers and responsibilities given to the Ministerial Conference are actually exercised or carried out by the General Council.

The Ministerial Conference (or the General Council in appropriate cases) is required to consider a waiver request within a maximum of 90 days.[25] However, before they reach the Ministerial Conference, waiver requests concerning the Multilateral Trade Agreements in Annexes 1A or 1B or 1C and their annexes are required to be submitted first to the respective Councils (on Goods, Services or TRIPS) and the relevant Councils have to submit a report to the Ministerial

---

18 Article XXV.4 of GATT 1994.

19 Article XXV.5 of GATT 1994.

20 Article XXV.5 of GATT 1994. A 1955 GATT Secretariat document has stated the following in this connection: "The words 'in exceptional circumstances not elsewhere provided for in this Agreement' are clearly designed to limit the use of the waiver provision to individual problems to which the agreement as written does not provide an adequate solution and where an amendment would result in a modification both broader in its application and more permanent than is required." GATT Doc. L/403, 7 September, 1955, as reproduced in J. H. Jackson, *Legal Problems of International Economic Relations* (West Publishing Co. 1977) p. 413.

21 See J. H. Jackson, W. Davey, and A. Sykes, *Legal Problems of International Economic Relations: Cases, Materials and Text* (3rd ed., West Publishing Co. 1995), p. 313. For a more detailed treatment of the issue of the US agricultural waiver, see J. H. Jackson, *World Trade and the Law of GATT*, (Bobbs-Merrill, 1969) p. Chapter 22, and Jackson (1977) *supra* n. 20, pp.412–417.

22 See Article IV.1 of the WTO Agreement.

23 See Article IV.1 of the WTO Agreement.

24 See Article IV.2 of the WTO Agreement.

25 The WTO Agreement, Article IX. 3(a).

Conference. In the case of agriculture, for instance, any request for a waiver from any of the obligations of the Agreement on Agriculture should initially be submitted to the Goods Council, and then the Ministerial Conference decides on the issue with the help of the report submitted to it by the Goods Council.

A Uruguay Round Understanding on the subject provided the formal conditions for the request of a waiver. Accordingly, an applicant is required to describe the measures which it proposes to take, the specific policy objectives it seeks to pursue and the reasons which prevent the Member from achieving its policy objectives by measures consistent with its obligations under GATT 1994.[26]

The WTO Agreement "stiffens considerably" the substantive rules applying to waivers.[27] It provides that, while giving preference to continuing the traditional GATT practice of decision-making by consensus,[28] in cases where this is not possible, it prescribes a qualified majority of three fourths of all the Members.[29] What is more, as regards waivers in respect of any obligation subject to a transition period or a period for staged implementation that the requesting Member has not performed by the end of the relevant period, the requirement goes up to a consensus.[30] Apparently, the consensus requirement is a reference to such highly sensitive areas as agriculture and textiles, which are subject to staged implementation and a transition period.

Article IX.4 of the WTO Agreement provides that a waiver decision must state the exceptional circumstances justifying the decision, the terms and conditions governing the application of the waiver, as well as its termination date. Moreover, it also prescribes a mandatory annual review – with power to extend, modify or terminate the waiver – throughout the lifetime of the waiver. The practical application of all these procedural and substantive rules is clearly seen in the Hungary waiver case.

The problem with Hungary's implementation of its export subsidy commitments was first raised by concerned Members during the third meeting of the WTO Committee on Agriculture, which was held on 28–29 September 1995. While several countries challenged the practice, the US in particular stated that "according to the Hungarian schedule of concessions, only 16 products are eligible for export subsidies whereas under its current export subsidy programme some 300 products were eligible, some of which were not consolidated in the Hungarian schedule."[31] Pushing the matter further, on 27 March 1996, Argentina, Australia, Canada, New Zealand, Thailand and the United States requested for consultations with the Government of Hungary pursuant to Article 4 of the Understanding on Rules and Procedures

---

[26] See text of the *Uruguay Round Understanding in Respect of Waivers of Obligations under the General Agreement on Tariffs and Trade 1994*, reproduced in WTO, *The results of the Uruguay Round of Multilateral Trade Negotiations: the Legal Texts* (1995) pp. 34–35, para. 1.

[27] See Jackson *et al* (1995) *supra* n. 21, p. 313.

[28] According to the WTO Agreement, a consensus is deemed to exist if no Member, present at the meeting when the decision is taken, formally objects to a proposed decision.

[29] The WTO Agreement, Article IX. 3.

[30] The WTO Agreement, Article IX. 3.

[31] WTO Committee on Agriculture, *Summary Report of the Meeting Held on 28–29 September 1995 Note by the Secretariat* (G/AG/R/3) 6 November 1995, para. 15.

Governing the Settlement of Disputes and Article 19 of the Agreement on Agriculture (to the extent that it relates to Article XXII of the GATT 1994).[32]

Hungary acknowledged that its current agricultural export subsidy programme indeed encompassed more products and involved higher outlays than consolidated under its Uruguay Round export subsidy commitments.[33] However, Hungary indicated that "this inconsistency was due to a substantial error made during the Uruguay Round, the result of which being that Hungary's export subsidy commitments did not adequately reflect the factual situation with respect to export subsidies in the 1986–1990 base period."[34] Moreover, in a letter dated 8 September 1997, Hungary requested the Council for Trade in Goods for a waiver from its obligations under paragraph 3 of Article 3, Article 8 and paragraph 2 of Article 9 of the Agreement on Agriculture for the period ending on 31 December 2001.[35] Hungary justified its request by saying that, at the time when its schedules of commitments were established, "a critical error occurred. The reason for this error is related to the deep systemic changes in Hungary that coincided with the second phase of the Uruguay Round."[36] The request was said to have been made in accordance with the Guiding Principles to be followed in considering applications for waivers adopted on 1 November 1956,[37] the Understanding in Respect of Waivers of Obligations under the General Agreement on Tariffs and Trade 1994, and paragraphs 3 and 4 of Article IX of the Marrakesh Agreement Establishing the WTO.[38]

Hungary's request for a waiver was granted by the General Council. At its meeting of 22 October 1997, the Council, acting pursuant to the provisions of paragraph 3 of Article IX of the WTO Agreement, decided that

> "Subject to the terms and conditions set out hereunder, the provisions of Articles 3.3, 8 and 9.2 of the Agreement on Agriculture shall be waived until 31 December 2001 to the extent necessary to permit the Government of Hungary to provide export subsidies listed in paragraph 1 of Article 9 of the Agreement on Agriculture: (a) in respect of agricultural products specified in the Annexes to this decision, and (b) not in excess of the budgetary outlay and quantity commitment levels specified in the Annexes to this decision."[39]

---

32 WTO Dispute Settlement Body, *Hungary – Export Subsidies in Respect of Agricultural Products: Request for Consultations by Argentina, Australia, Canada, New Zealand, Thailand and the United States* (WT/DS35/1, G/L/70, G/AG/W/23) 2 April 1996.

33 G/AG/R/3, *supra* n. 31, para. 15.

34 Ibid.

35 WTO Council for Trade in Goods, *Hungary – Agricultural Export Subsidies* (G/L/183) 6 October 1997, para. 1. This document contains details of the description of the problem, the reasons for the request, the policy objectives pursued, etc.

36 Ibid., para. 4.

37 See GATT, *Guiding Principles* to be followed in considering applications for waivers adopted on 1 November 1956 (L/532) *BISD* 5S/25.

38 G/L/183, *supra* n. 35, para. 1.

39 WTO General Council, *Hungary – Agreement on Agriculture: Decision of 22 October 1997* (Adopted in accordance with the *Decision-Making Procedures Under Articles IX and XII of the WTO Agreement as Agreed by the General Council on 15 November 1995* (WT/L/93)) (WT/L/238) 29 October 1997, para. 1.

The conditions include, *inter alia*, the following: (1) Hungary may not use in the waiver period export subsidies as listed in Article 9.1 of the Agreement on Agriculture to the region of its non-traditional markets for agricultural products not covered by Part IV of its Schedule to the GATT 1994 where subsidized exports to this region did not take place in the period of 1994–1996;[40] (2) Hungary should submit annual reports, on the anniversary date of the granting of the waiver, on the use that has been made of this waiver;[41] and (3) the waiver should not affect Members' rights under the dispute settlement provisions of the covered agreements.[42] Since the waiver Decision was adopted, Hungary has given annual reports on the use that has been made of the waiver.[43]

8.1.3 Conclusion

The whole purpose of the notification obligations of the Agriculture Agreement is to create a transparent trading environment in which violations in the practical implementation of Members' commitments would be detected at the earliest possible opportunity. Once such failures to comply with obligations are detected, Members whose interests are affected thereby may exercise their rights in the forums of their choice – ranging from asking for explanations in the periodic meetings of the Committee on Agriculture under Article 18.6 of the Agreement on Agriculture, down to invoking the provisions of consultations and dispute settlement under the relevant provisions of the Agriculture Agreement, the DSU, and/or the SCM Agreement.[44] While a country that is the subject of complaints normally has the obligation "to accord sympathetic consideration to and afford adequate opportunity for consultation",[45] a request for a waiver from those obligations has also been recognized as an option that may be resorted to "in exceptional circumstances".[46]

---

[40] Ibid., para. 2.

[41] Ibid., para. 3.

[42] Ibid., para. 4(a). Paragraph 4(b) of this decision provides as follows: "Any Member considering that a benefit accruing to it under the Agreement on Agriculture is being nullified or impaired as a result of the failure of the Government of Hungary to observe the terms or conditions of this waiver may invoke the provisions of Article 19 of the Agreement on Agriculture as elaborated and applied by the Dispute Settlement Understanding. The Government of Hungary shall agree, at the request of the complaining party, that time-periods applicable under the Dispute Settlement Understanding for the conduct of such a dispute be half the time prescribed therein. If a panel request is submitted in such a dispute for consideration by the Dispute Settlement Body, then the Government of Hungary shall consent to the establishment of a panel at the Dispute Settlement Body meeting at which the request first appears as an item on the Dispute Settlement Body's agenda."

[43] WTO General Council, *Hungary – Report of the Government of Hungary under the Decision of 22 October 1997*, WT/L/290, 27 November 1998; WTO General Council, *Hungary – Report of the Government of Hungary under the Decision of 22 October 1997: Addendum*, WT/L/290/Add.1, 17 February 1999; and WTO General Council, *Hungary – Report of the Government of Hungary under the Decision of 22 October 1997*, WT/L/322, 21 October 1999.

[44] On this issue, see *infra* section 8.2.

[45] See Article 4.2 of the DSU.

[46] See Article IX.3 of the WTO Agreement.

Although the experience of the multilateral trading system in the area of agricultural waivers has been far from positive, the General Council was convinced that Hungary's case satisfied the stringent conditions set by the WTO Agreement for a waiver. This being an exceptional option, however, the next section addresses the question of what remedies are available to a Member affected by the agricultural export subsidy practice of another Member in violation of its obligations under the system.

8.2 Remedies Against Violation of the Rules on Agricultural Export Subsidies

8.2.1 General

Under the general rules of the multilateral trading system, a country adversely affected by export subsidies granted by another country has two options – seeking for relief under the multilateral dispute settlement rules of Articles XXII and XXIII as interpreted and supplemented by the DSU, or resorting to unilateral countervailing duties. These two are only alternatives; they cannot be used together to counter the effects of one and the same subsidy. Both options are available under the Agreement on Agriculture. But, there are some differences in the conditions set for their use in agricultural matters, which we shall discuss in this section. Before that, however, the question of what is meant by violation in the context of the export subsidy provisions of the Agreement on Agriculture needs to be answered.

8.2.2 What Amounts to a Violation in Agricultural Export Subsidy Cases?

In the preceding four chapters, we have seen the detailed rules of the Agriculture Agreement on the practice of export subsidies and the commitments undertaken by Members. We have also seen that Members have the obligation not to provide export subsidies otherwise than in conformity with the rules of the Agriculture Agreement and their respective schedules of commitments. Accordingly, while countries which have included specific reduction commitments in their respective schedules are required to provide the listed export subsidies within the limits of those commitments, those countries that have not so included such commitments in their schedules are barred from providing any of the export subsidies. Countries in the former category violate their obligations when they grant export subsidies in excess of their respective commitment levels, and those falling in the latter category violate theirs by the mere fact of granting export subsidies regardless of the levels thereof. In other words, while those in the former category have a positive commitment level on the scheduled products, the level for those falling in the latter category stands at zero. The question to discuss in this section is the following: for a country of either category to violate its export subsidy obligations under the Agreement, does it have to actually grant the export subsidies or does the mere enactment of a law making export subsidies available to potential recipients suffice? In other words, does availability of export subsidies *per se* amount to violation of the provisions of the Agriculture Agreement on export subsidies?

8.2.2.1 Is Availability of Export Subsidies Per Se a Violation?

The answer to this question depends again on which category of products is at issue. In the case of scheduled products, since the actual granting of a certain amount of export subsidies is generally allowed, i.e. except when the level of the commitments is set at zero, the mere availability of export subsidies cannot amount to a violation on its own. Under such circumstances, a complaining party is required only to show that a country has exported more than the allowable maximum quantity of the product in question. It is up to the defending party to bear the burden-of-proof to show that no export subsidy has been used on the export of the quantity in excess of the reduction commitment level.[47]

In the case of unscheduled products and products scheduled with a zero commitment level, however, countries are not allowed to subsidize a single unit of such product. The question now is the following: is this an obligation not to actually grant export subsidies or does it also exclude the mere availability of such a scheme? In *FSC*, the EC argued that "the simple availability of FSC subsidies with respect to any unscheduled agricultural product is in itself a violation of the Agreement on Agriculture", while the US contended otherwise.[48] The EC argued that "[g]iven the fact that there are agricultural products for which the United States has a commitment of *zero level* the mandatory availability of FSC to any agricultural product (i.e. the fact that anybody who wants to export any agricultural product is entitled to FSC subsidies) is in itself a violation of Articles 3 and 8."[49] In the view of the US, on the other hand, "the text of the Agreement makes clear that the mere availability of an export subsidy does not constitute a violation of the AA."[50]

The panel followed a cautious approach distinguishing between products that are scheduled at zero and those which are totally unscheduled. Basing itself on the fact that none of the products in dispute listed in the US schedule were set at zero, the panel declined to rule on the latter issue and limited its finding to the case of

---

47 For a discussion of the burden-of-proof issue under Article 10.3 of the Agreement on Agriculture, see *infra* section 8.2.5.

48 *United States – Tax Treatment for "Foreign Sales Corporations"* report of the panel (WT/DS108/R) 8 October 1999, para. 7.167.

49 Ibid., para. 4.1345 (underlining in original).

50 Ibid., para. 4.1347. The US invokes a number of provisions to support its position and its arguments may be summarize as follows: (1) the language of Article 3.3 of the AA, is inconsistent with the notion that the mere availability of an export subsidy violates the AA because it contemplates that a Member may provide export subsidies, and violates its obligations only if the amount of export subsidies provided exceeds that Member's commitment levels; (2) the language of Article 9.2, which refers to the "quantity ... in respect of which such export subsidies may be granted in that year", indicates that the mere availability of a subsidy is not enough; and (3) the languages of Articles 10.1 and 10.3, which employ the term "applied" and the phrase "has been granted", respectively, are also inconsistent with the notion that the mere availability of an export subsidy violates the Agriculture Agreement. See Ibid., paras. 4.1348-4.1350.

unscheduled products.[51] The panel noted that the US "has not contested that FSC subsidies are in fact available to FSCs which are engaged in the marketing for export of any agricultural product, nor does it contest that a FSC which satisfies the relevant requirements thereby has entitlement under the relevant provisions of the US Internal Revenue Code to FSC subsidies."[52] The panel rightly pointed out that the key to the solution of this problem lies in the interpretation of the term "provide" in the second limb of Article 3.3. The main question is "whether the term 'provide' is to be interpreted to mean making such export subsidies available, rather than just in the more restrictive sense of actually granting or paying such subsidies in respect of exports of unscheduled agricultural products."[53]

In pursuance of the customary principles of interpretation of international treaties as enshrined in Article 31 of the Vienna Convention on the Law of Treaties, the panel ruled that "the ordinary meaning of the term 'provide' includes the notion of making something available, as well as that of actually granting or paying that thing (in the present case export subsidies listed in Article 9.1 of the Agreement on Agriculture)."[54] The panel further observed that a restrictive interpretation of the term "provide" "would be problematic from the point of view of the enforcement of this prohibition, since other Members would not be able to assert their rights to challenge export subsidies when they were made available but only after they had been actually granted and the damage done."[55] The panel thus concluded that "the second limb of Article 3.3 of the Agreement on Agriculture prohibits making available export subsidies listed in Article 9.1 in respect of unscheduled products."[56] However, as the Appellate Body later reversed the finding of the panel under Article 9.1(d) of the Agriculture Agreement,[57] the FSC subsidies were found not to be inconsistent with Article 3.3 of that Agreement. As a result, the Appellate Body made it clear that "the Panel's interpretation of the word 'provide' in the second clause of Article 3.3 is moot and of no legal effect."[58]

Yet, although this sound panel interpretation of the term "provide" in Article 3.3 of the Agriculture Agreement subsequently lost its legal effect, its academic significance remains important. However, it is noteworthy that the panel made this reasoning in respect only of unscheduled products, and was not intended to apply to the case of agricultural products scheduled at zero. It is true that there is a significant difference as regards the use of non-listed export subsidies in that while these groups of export subsidies are in principle permitted on scheduled products within the limits of the anti-circumvention condition, they are completely prohibited as regards the

[51] See Ibid., footnote 710 to para. 7.165.
[52] Ibid., para. 7.168.
[53] *Id*, para. 7.169.
[54] Ibid., para. 7.170.
[55] Ibid., para. 7.174.
[56] Ibid., para. 7.175.
[57] See *United States – Tax Treatment for "Foreign Sales Corporations"* report of the Appellate Body (WT/DS108/AB/R) 24 February 2000, para. 131.
[58] Ibid., para. 132.

unscheduled products. Moreover, while scheduled products are subject to the first limb of Article 3.3, the case of unscheduled products falls under the second limb. Despite these differences, however, with respect to listed export subsidy practices, being scheduled at zero and being completely unscheduled mean practically one and the same – no listed export subsidies are allowed in either case. The term "provide", which was interpreted in the context of the second limb of Article 3.3 by the *FSC* panel to include the notion of making something available as well as that of actually granting or paying export subsidies, is also the key term in the first limb of Article 3.3. Given these similarities in both wording and effect, therefore, there appears no reason why making an export subsidy available amounts to a violation in one and not in the other. In as long as there is a law which entitles firms satisfying certain conditions to claim export subsidies on products, whether scheduled at zero or simply unscheduled, the very availability of the subsidies should amount to a violation. For, otherwise, this would result in damage that could be difficult to reverse. For these reasons, the mere availability of an export subsidy amounts to a violation as regards both zero-scheduled and unscheduled agricultural products.

However, the remedies available may not be the same in all cases of violations. For instance, we shall see that in order for a country to introduce countervailing measures against products of another Member country, not only should there be a subsidy; the existence of a resulting injury or threat thereof should also be proved. Obviously, this means that a countervailing duty may not be applied against imports coming from another country only because there is a legislation authorizing the payment of subsidies as in the *FSC* case. The subsidies need to be actually paid and their effect on the domestic industry of the importing country demonstrated.

8.2.3 Countervailing Duties under the Agreement on Agriculture

Article 13 is the only provision in the Agriculture Agreement that refers to the issue of countervailing duties. Article 13(c) in relevant part provides that "export subsidies that conform fully to the provisions of Part V of this Agreement, as reflected in each Member's Schedule, shall be subject to countervailing duties only upon a determination of injury or threat thereof based on volume, effect on prices, or consequent impact in accordance with Article VI of GATT 1994 and Part V of the Subsidies Agreement, and due restraint shall be shown in initiating any countervailing duty investigations."[59] Accordingly, subsidies that conform fully to those provisions of the Agreement dealing with agricultural export subsidies can be subject to countervailing duties only upon determination of injury or threat thereof in accordance with Article VI of GATT 1994 as well as that part of the SCM Agreement which deals with countervailing measures. These are the same conditions laid down for all sorts of subsidies under both Article VI of GATT 1994 and Part V of the SCM Agreement. The wording of Article 13(c)(i) in fact closely resembles Article 15.1 of the SCM Agreement, which provides the principle applying to all

[59] Article 13(c)(i) of the Agreement on Agriculture.

sorts of countervailing duties, whether agricultural or otherwise, that "determination of injury for purposes of Article VI of GATT 1994 shall be based on positive evidence and involve an objective examination of both (a) the volume of the subsidized imports and the effect of the subsidized imports on prices in the domestic market for like products and (b) the consequent impact of these imports on the domestic producers of such products."[60] The only special requirement added by the Agreement on Agriculture is thus the "due restraint" that is mandated in the initiation of countervailing duty investigations.

The obligation to show "due restraint" in the initiation of countervailing duty investigations is such a fluid and highly subjective obligation that its practical significance in constraining the use of countervailing duties is, at best, doubtful. It is only an expression of a good faith requirement in the administration of the rules on agricultural export subsidies – a rule devoid of any enforcement mechanism. What is more, the practical significance of this requirement is limited in at least two ways. Firstly, it applies only to those agricultural export subsidies that fully conform to the relevant provisions of the Agriculture Agreement. Any agricultural export subsidy that does not conform to these rules is treated, for purposes of countervailing duties, on the same level as other export subsidies – i.e. the "due restraint" requirement does not apply at the initiation stage. Secondly, it is limited to the nine-year implementation period which ends in 2003.[61] Consequently, we can conclude that almost all the provisions of the SCM Agreement on countervailing duties discussed earlier[62] apply to cases involving agricultural export subsidies.[63]

There is, however, one point of practical difference in the application of countervailing duties between agricultural export subsidies and their non-agricultural counterparts. We have seen elsewhere that, for purposes of countervailing duty laws, the SCM Agreement implicitly divides all forms of subsidies into two broad categories – countervailable and non-countervailable subsidies. To the former belong the class of prohibited subsidies (which includes export subsidies and import-substitution subsidies) and actionable subsidies, while the latter consists of the non-actionable subsidies of Part IV of the SCM Agreement. For present purposes, this means that although export subsidies are prohibited under the SCM Agreement, a Member has the choice of dealing with them unilaterally by resorting to countervailing duties or that it may have recourse to the particularly expedited dispute settlement procedure of the SCM Agreement for cases of prohibited subsidies. Moreover, footnote 35 of the SCM Agreement provides that the provisions of Part II (on prohibited subsidies) may be invoked in parallel with the provisions of Part V of the Agreement on the imposition of countervailing

---

60 Article 15.1 of the SCM Agreement, (footnotes omitted).

61 Article 1(f) of the Agreement on Agriculture.

62 For a discussion of the countervailing duty law of the WTO, see *supra* chapter 5.6.

63 Moreover, as the *Brazil Coconut* panel observed, the "due restraint" requirement can be called in to play only if the countervailing duties at issue are "covered by Article VI of GATT 1994 and Part V of the Agreement on Subsidies and Countervailing Measures." *Brazil – Measures Affecting Desiccated Coconut*, report of the panel (WT/DS22/R) 17 October 1996, para. 284.

duties.[64] However, from the perspective of the affected party, the standards of proof set by the countervailing duty law are more cumbersome than those set for an authorised countermeasure. To be more specific, while a proof only of the existence of an export subsidy suffices for such a party to get a panel report recommend the withdrawal of such a measure without delay,[65] a countervailing duty can be imposed only after proof of not only the existence of the subsidy in question, but also injury to its domestic industry caused thereby.[66] This is of course an incentive for the Members to use the multilateral fora rather than the unilateral one. Although not impossible, therefore, the use of a countervailing duty in order to counteract the effects of a general export subsidy is less likely. On the other hand, agricultural export subsidies being still permitted, a countervailing duty is a more practicable option. The possibilities for a recourse to the multilateral option for agricultural export subsidy cases is what we are going to see right away.

8.2.4 Authorized Countermeasures against Agricultural Export Subsidies

Agricultural export subsidies have always been the subject of highly contentious disputes between countries. As we saw in chapter4, GATT was not that effective in averting the export subsidy wars which were unleashed particularly between the US and the EC in the 1980s. It has also been shown that the ambiguous formulation of the rules on the subject carries much of the blame for these adverse developments. However, ambiguity is not the only one. The weak dispute settlement system of the GATT has been no less responsible for this state of affairs. Until the end of the Uruguay Round, an unfortunate combination of vaguely formulated rules backed only by an ineffective dispute resolution mechanism prevailed in the sphere of agricultural export subsidies.

As discussed elsewhere,[67] the Understanding on Rules and Procedures Governing the Settlement of Disputes is one of the most important achievements of the Uruguay Round. Article 19 of the Agreement on Agriculture provides that the provisions of the Dispute Settlement Understanding (the DSU) apply to consultations and settlement of disputes under this Agreement. But, the DSU is not the only other instrument applying to agricultural matters. As provided under Article 21.1 of the Agreement on Agriculture, "the provisions of GATT 1994 and of other Multilateral Trade Agreements shall apply subject to the provisions of this Agreement." This brings, *inter alia*, the SCM Agreement into the picture. As such, both the SCM Agreement and the DSU apply in the area of agriculture subject to the provisions of the Agriculture Agreement. Furthermore, in cases involving subsidies,

---

[64] This does not affect the rule that "with regard to the effects of a particular subsidy in the importing country, only one form of relief (either a countervailing duty, if other requirements of Part V are met, or a countermeasure under Articles 4 or 7 of this Agreement) shall be available." Footnote 33 to the SCM Agreement.

[65] See Article 4 of the SCM Agreement.

[66] See Article 11 of the SCM Agreement.

[67] For details on the dispute settlement process of the WTO, see *supra* chapter 5.5.

whether agricultural or not, the DSU applies subject to the provisions of the SCM Agreement.[68] The cumulative effect of this sequencing is that, as regards agricultural export subsidy disputes, the DSU applies subject to both the Agreement on Agriculture and the SCM Agreement.[69] Our analysis of the remedies available in agricultural export subsidy cases should thus start with the provisions of the Agriculture Agreement, proceed to those of the SCM Agreement, and conclude with the DSU for cases not addressed by the first two.

Not much is said about dispute settlement in the Agriculture Agreement. The only important provisions in this regard are Article 19, referring to Articles XXII and XXIII of GATT 1994 and the DSU,[70] and Article 13 concerning the "due restraint" requirement. As such, by providing that the generally-applicable dispute settlement provisions of the multilateral trading system are also applicable to matters arising under the Agriculture Agreement, Article 19 simply reaffirms the integrated nature of dispute settlement in the WTO.

We have seen, however, that the provisions of the DSU are supplemented by what are called "special or additional rules and procedures contained in the covered agreements". An exhaustive list of these rules has been appended to the text of the DSU.[71] No provision of the Agreement on Agriculture is included in this list. However, it includes provisions from the SCM Agreement that are relevant to agricultural export subsidy cases. As a matter of principle, the provisions of GATT 1994 and of other Multilateral Trade Agreements in Annex 1A to the WTO

---

68 See Article 30 of the SCM Agreement and paragraph 1 of the DSU.

69 Arranged in an ascending order of generality for purposes of agricultural export subsidy cases, the situation looks the following. Article 19 of the Agreement on Agriculture provides that "The provisions of Articles XXII and XXIII of GATT 1994, as elaborated and applied by the Dispute Settlement Understanding, shall apply to consultations and the settlement of disputes under this Agreement." Article 21.1 then goes a step further and provides that "The provisions of GATT 1994 and of other Multilateral Trade Agreements shall apply subject to the provisions of this Agreement." Read together, these two provisions thus indicate that both the DSU as well as the SCM Agreement apply to agricultural matters subject to the provisions of the Agreement on Agriculture. Article 30 of the SCM Agreement then provides that the DSU applies to subsidy matters "except as otherwise specifically provided herein." In other words, as one of the multilateral trade agreements annexed to the WTO Agreement, the provisions of the SCM Agreement apply to agricultural export subsidies by virtue of Article 21 of the Agreement on Agriculture; and then, when the provisions of the SCM Agreement apply, Article 30 of the SCM Agreement and paragraph 1.2 of the Dispute Settlement Understanding tell us that they prevail over provisions of the DSU. Paragraph 1.2 of the DSU provides that the rules and procedures of the Understanding "shall apply subject to such special or additional rules and procedures on dispute settlement contained in the covered agreements as are specified in Appendix 2 to this Understanding. To the extent that there is a difference between the rules and procedures of this understanding and the special or additional rules and procedures set forth in Appendix 2, the special or additional rules and procedures in Appendix 2 shall prevail." From all this, one can fairly conclude that agricultural export subsidy cases are primarily subject to the provisions of the Agreement on Agriculture, secondarily to the SCM Agreement, and only lastly to the DSU.

70 Article 19 of the Agreement on Agriculture provides as follows: "The provisions of Articles XXII and XXIII of GATT 1994, as elaborated and applied by the Dispute Settlement Understanding, shall apply to consultations and the settlement of disputes under this Agreement."

71 See Appendix 2 to the DSU.

Agreement apply to agricultural matters subject to the provisions of Agriculture Agreement.[72] It is the application of this principle that is restricted by the provisions of Article 13(c) of the Agriculture Agreement on due restraint.

According to Article 13 (c), export subsidies that conform fully to the provisions of Part V of the Agreement (which deals with agricultural export subsidies) are "exempt from actions based on Article XVI of GATT 1994 or Articles 3 [prohibited subsidies], 5 [trade effects of actionable subsidies] and 6 [serious prejudice caused by actionable subsidies] of the Subsidies Agreement." It is worth mentioning at this juncture that the SCM Agreement provisions referred to here also have their own parallels referring back to the provisions of the Agreement on Agriculture. Accordingly, while the first provision (Article 3) excludes from its purview what is provided in the Agreement on Agriculture on agricultural export subsidies,[73] the two others expressly stipulate, in identical language, that they do not apply at all to subsidies maintained on agricultural products as provided in Article 13 of the Agreement on Agriculture.[74] This is an important distinction with serious practical consequences. While the provisions of the SCM Agreement on "prohibited subsidies" permanently exclude agricultural export subsidies as provided in the Agriculture Agreement from their ambit, the provisions of the same Agreement on "actionable subsidies" are excluded only conditionally and temporarily.[75]

The conditions are that they "conform fully to the provisions of Part V of this Agreement as reflected in each Member's Schedule."[76] These conditions may indeed be said to apply also with regard to Article 3 of the SCM Agreement on "prohibited subsidies", because the latter provision is also referred to under Article 13(c) of the Agreement on Agriculture. Article 3 of the SCM Agreement does not, of course, refer to Article 13 of the Agriculture Agreement. But, to the extent that the former refers to the Agreement on Agriculture in general – with the phrase "except as provided in the Agreement on Agriculture" – any agricultural export subsidy that does not conform with the provisions of the Agriculture Agreement cannot satisfy the requirement of being "as provided in the Agreement on Agriculture" and hence will fall under the purview of Article 3 of the SCM Agreement on "prohibited subsidies." Compliance of an agricultural export subsidy practice with the provisions of the Agriculture Agreement is thus the only condition for its exclusion from the application of the rigorous discipline introduced by the SCM Agreement for the regulation of export subsidies in general.

As regards duration, too, agricultural export subsidies conforming to the rules of the Agriculture Agreement cannot be challenged under the "special or additional rules of dispute settlement" of the SCM Agreement for both prohibited as well as actionable subsidies for the nine-year implementation period. To that extent,

---

72 See Article 21.1 of the Agreement on Agriculture.

73 See Article 3.1 of the SCM Agreement.

74 See Articles 5, and 6.9 of the SCM Agreement.

75 The duration of the "peace clause" is limited to the nine-year implementation period as defined under Article 1(f) of the Agriculture Agreement.

76 Article 13(c) of the Agriculture Agreement.

therefore, and for purposes of the multilateral remedies, agricultural export subsidies fall in the category of "non-actionable subsidies". Article 9, the remedies provision of Part IV of the SCM Agreement, is thus the only multilateral option available under the Subsidies Agreement to a Member adversely affected by the agricultural export subsidies of another Member that conform to the provisions of the Agriculture Agreement. In a way, this is the subsidies version of the non-violation nullification or impairment provision of Article XXIII:1(b) of GATT 1994. As such, the standard of injury required for a Member to invoke the consultation and dispute settlement process is higher than that required for an actionable-subsidy case.[77]

So far Article 13 of the Agreement on Agriculture was invoked before the dispute settlement process only in the *Canada Dairy* case. In this case, the US convincingly argued that Article 3 of the SCM Agreement, when read in conjunction with Article 13 of the Agreement on Agriculture, provided that if a Member did not comply with the export subsidy disciplines contained in the Agreement on Agriculture, any offending export subsidy was to be subject to the terms of the SCM Agreement and its prohibition on export subsidies.[78] The panel agreed with this view and ruled as follows:

> "We have found that the Canadian scheme is inconsistent with: (i) Canada's obligations under both Article 3.3 and Article 8 (through Article 9.1(a) and Article 9.1(c)); or (ii) in the alternative, Canada's obligations under both Article 10.1 and Article 8, of the Agreement on Agriculture. Therefore, the exemption provided for in Article 13(c)(i) of the Agreement on Agriculture from actions under Article 3 of the SCM Agreement for 'export subsidies that conform fully to the provisions of Part V' of the Agreement on Agriculture, does not apply. In principle, the scheme could therefore also be subjected to an examination under Article 3 of the SCM Agreement."[79]

This is a very good example of the role of the provisions of Article 13 of the Agreement on Agriculture. They do not shield violations of the provisions of the Agriculture Agreement from being challenged before the dispute settlement system of the WTO. Rather, since export subsidies are generally known for causing injury to the interests of other competitors, and in as long as they are still allowed in the area of agriculture, the possibility of causing injury without violating the rules is very real. Given the traditional nullification or impairment rule of the multilateral trading

---

77 Article 9.1 of the SCM Agreement provides the following: "If, in the course of implementation of a programme referred to in paragraph 2 of Article 8 above [assistance for research, development of disadvantaged regions, and adaptation to new environmental standards], notwithstanding the fact that the programme is consistent with the criteria laid down in paragraph 2 of Article 8, a Member has reasons to believe that this programme has resulted in serious adverse effects to the domestic industry of that Member, such as to cause damage which would be difficult to repair, such Member may request consultations with the Member granting the subsidy."

78 Argument by the United States in *Canada – Measures Affecting the Importation of Milk and the Exportation of Dairy Products*, report of the panel (WT/DS103/R, WT/DS113/R) 17 May 1999, para. 4.208.

79 Ibid., para 7.136 (footnotes omitted).

system where the difference between a violation case and a non-violation case may in practice be little, the object of Article 13(c) is to protect countries from being challenged for the injuries they may cause by the agricultural export subsidies they provide in conformity with their obligations under the Agreement on Agriculture.

8.2.5 Burden of Proof as an Added Safety Valve

In a typical legal dispute the party that initiates the proceedings, the claimant, bears the onus to establish a *prima facie* case. Any party to a dispute which asserts a fact bears the burden to prove it.[80] This general principle has also been well recognized and applied by the GATT/WTO dispute settlement system. Perhaps the most classic expression of this principle was made by the WTO Appellate Body in *Shirts and Blouses*, which took this principle as so fundamental that "we find it difficult, indeed, to see how any system of judicial settlement could work if it incorporated the proposition that the mere assertion of a claim might amount to proof."[81] The Appellate Body thus stated that:

> "It is hardly surprising that various international tribunals, including the International Court of Justice, have generally and consistently accepted and applied the rule that the party who asserts a fact, whether the claimant or the respondent, is responsible for providing proof thereof. Also, it is a generally-accepted canon of evidence in civil law, common law and, in fact, most jurisdictions, that the burden of proof rests upon the party, whether complaining or defending, who asserts the affirmative of a particular claim or defence. If that party adduces evidence sufficient to raise a presumption that what is claimed is true, the burden then shifts to the other party, who will fail unless it adduces sufficient evidence to rebut the presumption. In the context of the GATT 1994 and the WTO Agreement, precisely how much and precisely what kind of evidence will be required to establish such a presumption will necessarily vary from measure to measure, provision to provision, and case to case."[82]

The Uruguay Round Agreement on Agriculture, however, deviates from this enduring principle as regards export subsidy reduction commitments. According to Article 10:3 of the Agreement, the party "which claims that any quantity exported in excess of a reduction commitment level is not subsidized must establish that no export subsidy, whether listed in Article 9 or not, has been granted in respect of the quantity of exports in question". Whether with the help of subsidies or not, exporting in excess of the maximum allowable quantity of subsidized exports creates

---

80 For more on issues of "burden of proof" in the WTO system, see J. Pauwelyn, "Evidence, Proof and Persuasion in WTO Dispute Settlement", in 1 *Journal of International Economic Law* (1998) pp. 227–258.

81 *United States – Measures Affecting Imports of Shirts and Blouses from India: Complaint by India*, report of the Appellate Body, (WT/DS33/AB/R) 25 April 1997 , para. 13.

82 Ibid., paras. 13–14, (footnotes omitted).

the presumption that that country has exceeded its quantitative export subsidy commitments – and hence a *prima facie* violation of its obligations.[83] This country then carries the burden to prove the negative – that the amount in excess of the commitment levels does not benefit from its subsidy scheme. In other words, a country that has exported more than the allowable maximum in a certain period has to demonstrate that a part of the exports has not benefited from its subsidy scheme and that that part is at least equal in amount to the excess.

This provision was applied in a straightforward manner in *Canada Dairy*, where both the complainants (New Zealand and the US) as well as the defendant (Canada) agreed that Article 10.3 has the effect of shifting the traditional rules on burden of proof.[84] Canada's approach in this respect was thus limited to an (unsuccessful) attempt to convince the panel that the said extra quantities of exports did not benefit from any export subsidy, *inter alia*, because the pooling system at issue in that case did not amount to an export subsidy.[85] On the burden-of-proof issue, therefore, the panel's task in this case was limited to merely pronouncing what appeared to be a consensus view among all the parties to the dispute that "Article 10.3 shifts the burden of proof from the complainant to the defendant. A defending party (i.e., the exporting country) alleging that exports in excess of a reduction commitment level are not subsidized must establish that no export subsidy in respect of this excess has been granted."[86]

---

83 New Zealand contended in *Canada Dairy*, that Article 10.3 was meant to create a stringent obligation reversing the general principles on burden of proof and argued that this view was supported by the preparatory work relating to Article 10. As quoted in New Zealand's submissions to the panel, the negotiating Draft Text on Agriculture of 12 December 1991 provided as follows: "a *prima facie* case of circumvention of budgetary outlay commitments shall be deemed to exist where it is established that: (a) subsidies contingent on exports which are not subject to reduction have been or are being resorted to at the national or sub-national level; and (b) the volume of subsidized exports of the product concerned exceeds the volume of exports that could have been subsidized, or which can reasonably be expected to be subsidized" New Zealand's submission to the panel in *Canada Dairy*, report of the panel, *supra* n. 78, para. 4.290.

84 For the view of all three parties to this case, see *Id.*, paras. 4.294-4.297.

85 The panel observed in this regard that "all parties agree that the actual exports of butter, cheese and 'other milk products' made by Canada, exceed Canada's reduction commitment levels and this for both marketing years at issue (1995/1996 and 1996/1997). Canada claims that these quantities exported in excess of its reduction commitment levels are not subsidized. It is thus for Canada to establish that the quantity of exports exceeding its commitment levels has not been made subject to 'export subsidies'. In other words, for purposes of the claims before us, it is for Canada to present evidence sufficient to establish a presumption that the Special Milk Classes Scheme does not involve an 'export subsidy, whether listed in Article 9 or not'. Once such presumption is established, it is for New Zealand and the United States to present evidence to rebut this presumption. New Zealand and the United States responded *in extenso* to the claim that the export quantities in question are not subject to export subsidies. Thus, our task is essentially to weigh the evidence and determine whether Canada has met the burden imposed by Article 10.3." Ibid., para. 7.34. And then the panel concluded that "we find that Canada provides export subsidies as listed in Article 9.1 in respect of the three dairy products at issue, and this for both marketing years in dispute, in excess of the quantity commitment levels specified in its Schedule, contrary to its obligations under Article 3.3." Ibid., para. 7.116.

86 Ibid., para. 7.33.

This aspect of the provision was also recognized by the panel as well as both parties to the *FSC*. In its own words, the panel considered it evident that "Article 10.3 has the effect of shifting from the complaining to the defending Member the burden of demonstrating that no export subsidies have been granted with respect to any quantity of an agricultural product exported in excess of the reduction commitment level of that Member, if the defending Member claims – as does the United States – that that quantity is not subsidized."[87] And the panel report particularly mentions that both parties to the dispute agree on this point.[88] On that basis, the panel pointed out that the US could fulfill this burden by either proving that the challenged measure did not amount to an export subsidy, or that even if the measure were an export subsidy, it was not provided to the excess quantity in question, or both.[89]

However, the application of the burden-of-proof provision of Article 10.3 is not always as simple and straightforward. Despite recognition of the reversal of the burden-of-proof by both parties, an interesting legal issue involving this provision was raised in *FSC*. It concerned whether this reversal applies on all subsidized products or only on those that are included in Members' schedules of commitments.

The EC claimed that the US, by introducing a system for the tax-exemption of part of the foreign-source income of the so-called Foreign Sales Corporations, subsidized its exports of wheat, maize, soya beans and cotton to the EC for the period 1995 to 1997 in excess of its commitment levels and therefore violated its obligations under Articles 3 and 8 of the Agreement on Agriculture. The EC pointed out that, of these four products, while the US had included no reduction commitments in its Schedule for maize, soya beans, and cotton – and hence no export subsidies allowed for these products – in the case of wheat, the US had included specific reduction commitments and subsequent notifications show that the quantities of wheat exported with subsidies were below those commitments.[90] In the view of the EC, even for wheat, this was so because, in reporting its subsidized exports, the US "does not take into account subsidies provided to agricultural products under the FSC scheme."[91] The EC thus argued that this FSC scheme, by reducing the tax liability arising out of foreign sales, is reducing the costs of marketing exports and thus falls within the ambit of Article 9.1(d) of the Agriculture Agreement.[92] In the alternative, the EC argued, that "[e]ven if the FSC scheme subsidy does not fall under Article 9.1(d), this does not prevent it from being contrary to Article 8 of the AA [Agriculture Agreement] which applies to all export subsidies to agricultural products, whether or not described in Article 9.1 of the AA."[93] The EC contended that US export subsidy commitment levels in the case of

---

87 See *FSC*, report of the panel, *supra* n. 48, para. 7.136.
88 See Ibid., para. 7.136.
89 See Ibid.
90 See Ibid., para. 4.1248.
91 See Ibid., para. 4.1258.
92 See Ibid., para. 4.1255.
93 See Ibid., para. 4.1260.

the three unscheduled products were zero.[94] In either case, the EC contended that, pursuant to Article 10.3 of the Agriculture Agreement, it was for the US "to prove that all the maize, soya beans and cotton and all the wheat in excess of its reduction commitments was exported without the benefit of FSC subsidies."[95]

In reply, the US generally argued that the FSC scheme did not constitute an export subsidy. In the alternative, the US contended that EC reliance on Article 10.3 of the AA was a mere "attempt to avoid its burden of proof."[96] According to the US, the reversal in the burden of proof that is contemplated by Article 10.3 of the Agreement on Agriculture is applicable only as regards products that appear in a Member's schedules of commitments. For the US, "only products listed in Section II [of Part IV of Members' Schedules] along with a specific positive quantity are subject to reduction commitments, and the scope of Article 10.3 is limited expressly to quantities of any product "exported in excess of a reduction commitment."[97] The US further argued that "if the burden of proof shifts to the United States at all under Article 10.3, it shifts only with respect to wheat, the only agricultural product identified by the European Communities for which the United States has a positive reduction commitment."[98]

Both the parties as well as the panel recognized that Article 10.3 had the effect of shifting the burden of proof.[99] But, on the more controversial question of whether that reversal applied to all products or only to those on which reduction commitments were included in the Schedules, the panel ruled in favour of the latter.[100] The panel introduced a distinction between export subsidy commitments on the one hand and export subsidy reduction commitments, on the other. It noted that while a reduction commitment refers to the specific obligation of Members to cut back on the quantity of subsidized exports of a product and the budgetary outlays spent therefor – hence necessarily restricted to products which had been subject to subsidies during the base period – a commitment is a general obligation covering reduction commitments as well as others, such as the commitment not to introduce any of the listed export subsidies on products that had not been subject to subsidies during that period. According to the panel, since Article 10.3 talks in terms of a reduction commitment, the central question on this particular point is "whether products which do not appear in a Member's schedule are subject to 'reduction

94 See Ibid., para. 4.1261.
95 See Ibid., para. 4.1262.
96 See Ibid., para. 4.1277.
97 See Ibid.
98 See Ibid.
99 See Ibid., para. 7.136.
100 See Ibid., paras. 7.138-7.143. The panel concluded that "we consider that Article 10.3 of the Agreement on Agriculture places the burden on the United States to present evidence and argument sufficient to establish that no export subsidy has been granted in respect of any quantity of a product exported in excess of the reduction commitment levels found in its Schedule for that product. In the case of unscheduled products, however, the burden remains with the European Communities to present evidence and argument sufficient to establish that export subsidies have been provided with respect to that product." Ibid., para. 7.143.

commitment' within the meaning of Article 10.3."[101] In its view, "a Member which has not scheduled a given product may well have a commitment with respect to that product, in as much as it is precluded by Article 3.3 of the Agreement from providing export subsidies listed in Article 9.1 with respect to that product. We do not consider, however, that the Member has a reduction commitment with respect to an unscheduled product."[102]

The panel also found support for its conclusion from the context,[103] as well as the purposes of Article 10.3. Rejecting the EC argument that "there is no reason why Article 10.3 should apply to scheduled but not to unscheduled products", the panel stated that it could imagine several reasons why the drafters might have made such a distinction and mentioned one point in particular. The panel found it reasonable to assume that Article 10.3 places on the defending Member the burden of proof in this respect "because of concern that a complainant will generally not have access to information necessary to make a *prima facie* case of a violation."[104] On the other hand, the panel believed that it should be "easier, in most cases, for a complainant to establish that an export subsidy had been provided with respect to exports of a particular product, irrespective of amount – as would be the case with respect to unscheduled products, for which the commitment under Article 3.3 is not to provide any export subsidies listed in Article 9.1 – than to demonstrate that an export subsidy has been provided with respect to a quantity of product in excess of some given level."[105]

These two cases on the burden-of-proof issue provide a good perspective of how the practical application of Article 10.3 looks like. In summary, therefore, we can say that this provision indeed reverses the usual practice of putting the burden to prove a claim on the shoulders of the party asserting it. As regards the violation of export

---

[101] See Ibid., para. 7.138.

[102] See Ibid. For more on this issue, see *supra* chapter 7.4.

[103] The panel observed, *inter alia*, the following:

> "Our conclusion is confirmed when the term 'reduction commitment' as used in Article 10.3 is read in its context. In this respect, we note that the title of Article 10 is 'Prevention of Circumvention of Export Subsidy Commitments'. While Article 10.3 refers to reduction commitment levels, Article 10.1, like the title of Article 10, refers more generally to circumvention of export subsidy commitments. We cannot assume that this distinction between two provisions in such close proximity within the same Article was inadvertent. Rather, it would appear that Article 10 distinguishes between 'export subsidy commitments', a broad term that refers to commitments with respect both to scheduled and unscheduled products, and 'reduction commitments', a narrower term relating specifically to scheduled products. Further, we note that Article 3 of the Agreement on Agriculture, titled 'Incorporation of Concessions and Commitments', deals with export subsidy obligations in respect of both scheduled and unscheduled products. If the term 'reduction commitments' were applicable to both scheduled and unscheduled products, the title of that Article could have been expected to refer to 'reduction commitments' rather than merely to 'commitments'. Again, this would appear to confirm that the phrase 'reduction commitment' refers to that subcategory of 'commitments' which relates to scheduled products." Ibid., para. 7.140-7.141.

[104] Ibid., para. 7.142.

[105] Ibid., para. 7.142.

subsidy reduction commitments, all a complaining party needs to do is show that the other party has exported more than the maximum allowable subsidized export of a given product. It will then be up to that other party to disprove the allegation. However, this reversal applies to products for which there exists a reduction commitment, not least because the provision talks in terms specifically of reduction commitments. And this has a convincing rationale. On top of the stringency that it adds to the force of the obligations created in the area of export subsidy reduction commitments, it also has a pragmatic element within it. Indeed, it would be rather difficult for a complaining party to prove that a third country has paid subsidies up to a given permissible quantity, say X, continued subsidizing up to another amount, say Y, and then the difference between Y and X constitutes a violation.

PART III

THE LAW OF AGRICULTURAL DOMESTIC SUPPORT

CHAPTER 9

THE LAW OF DOMESTIC SUPPORT IN GENERAL

9.1 Introduction

The subject matter of Part III is the discipline governing agricultural domestic support. Although Part III shares a lot in common with Part II, there are also important differences warranting a more or less independent and full-scale discussion of the subject on its own. The present chapter starts with a brief introduction to the concept of domestic support – a term used for the first time in the Agriculture Agreement – and discusses the problem of terminology involved, the policy underpinnings behind the practice, the incidence and the forms of domestic support, their causal role for the proliferation of market access restrictions and export subsidies, and the particular problems involved in attempting to regulate domestic support. After a brief historical survey of how the regulation of domestic support measures was approached by both the draft as well as the final versions of the ITO Charter, the pertinent provisions of the General Agreement as it stood in 1947 will be closely examined. The introduction by the 1955 review session of what is often known as the doctrine of reasonable expectations, the achievements of the 1979 Subsidies Code in the area, and the relevant GATT jurisprudence which developed over the lifetime of the system are also discussed at length. A discussion of the fundamental change to the rules governing domestic subsidies in general and agricultural domestic support in particular, which came out of the Uruguay Round, constitutes the core of Part III.

The practice of subsidies concerns a variety of forms of support to firms and industries provided or mandated by the government. Subsidies may take different forms and their recipients may be individuals or firms involved in targeted economic activities as producers (e.g. producer subsidies), consumers (e.g. consumer subsidies), or exporters (e.g. export subsidies). Subsidies are widespread in agricultural trade such that, in the words of one writer, the terms agriculture and subsidies are already "synonymous" concepts in international trade.[1] All forms of subsidies are here grouped under either of two categories – domestic subsidies and export subsidies – and treated accordingly. While export subsidies have been discussed in Part II, Part III is devoted to a treatment of domestic subsidies.

However, as the title of Part III indicates, we are here dealing with domestic support and not domestic subsidies as such. But, is there any difference between

---

[1] D. Palmeter, "Agriculture and Trade Regulation: Selected Issues in the Application of U.S. Antidumping and Countervailing Duty Laws", 23 *Journal of World Trade* (1989) No. 1, p. 59.

these two? There is a problem of terminology involved. In the literature on international trade law there are three basic terms referring to the subject of our discussion here: domestic support, domestic subsidies, and production subsidies. While the latter two are relatively more familiar concepts, "domestic support" is of a recent origin. It is in fact in the Uruguay Round Agreement on Agriculture that the concept formally appeared as a distinct legal concept in a multilateral legal instrument. Substantively speaking, the only important difference between these three, if any, is one of scope – production subsidies being a subset of domestic subsidies,[2] and domestic subsidies a subset of domestic support. They are, therefore, like three concentric circles where the inner-most one is taken by production subsidies, the middle by domestic subsidies, and the outer-most by domestic support.

However, as the scope of the term "subsidy" itself has not always been clearly defined, this distinction is not that useful in actual practice. It is rather quite common to see all these terms used to mean one and the same thing. It will be argued that the concept of "domestic support" is in no significant way different from "domestic subsidies". If we take the traditional division of subsidies into export subsidies and non-export subsidies, for instance, it is this latter category that we are here referring to under either of the above three (and sometimes even more[3]) terminologies. They refer to subsidies granted irrespective of export considerations. Professor Jackson defines them as follows: "Domestic or production subsidies ... are subsidies granted for the benefit of products regardless of whether those products are exported or not."[4] To this, we may add that domestic support is also used here in this same sense.

---

2 Reference to the distinction between production subsidies and domestic subsidies has been very rare in GATT jurisprudence. In the *Reconvened Oilseeds Panel Report,* there was an issue as to whether the system of income support on an acreage basis, introduced by the EC in implementation of the original *EC Oilseeds* ruling, amounted to a production subsidy. The EC argued that "the subsidies provided under the new support system are not subsidies for the production of oilseeds but subsidies to support producers' incomes that are paid for a particular allocation of land and are not directly linked to the production of oilseeds." The panel ruled that "the 1955 Decision refers to 'a domestic subsidy' without making any distinction as to the manner in which such subsidies are provided. Accordingly what is relevant, as regards the issue under consideration, is not whether the subsidies provided under the new support system are described as income or price support, or in some other manner, but rather whether they are product-specific production subsidies." *Follow-up on the Panel Report "European Economic Community – Payments and Subsidies Paid to Processors and Producers of Oilseeds and Related Animal-Feed Proteins", Report of the Members of the Original Oilseeds Panel* (DS28/R *BISD* 39S/91, hereafter *Reconvened Oilseeds Panel Report,* considered for adoption by the Council on 30 April 1992, but not adopted) para. 79.

3 Some writers also use the terms "internal subsidies" see, e.g. R. Rivers and J. Greenwald, "The Negotiation of a Code on Subsidies and Countervailing Measures: Bridging Fundamental Differences", 11 *Law & Policy in International Business* (1979), pp. 1462–1470; and J. Barton and B. Fisher, *International Trade and Investment*, (Little Brown & Co., Boston 1986) p. 351.

4 J. H. Jackson, *The World Trading System: Law and Policy of International Economic Relations* (The MIT Press, 2nd ed. 1997) p. 280.

9.1.1 Incidence of Domestic Subsidies

Virtually all countries that are financially capable of supporting their agricultural sectors employ one or another form of domestic subsidy. After a thorough analysis of subsidy notifications made to the GATT by about thirty-four countries, a GATT Panel on Subsidies concluded the following as early as 1961:

> "although some subsidies exist on non-primary products, the great bulk of the subsidization measures relate to primary products. Some forty groups of primary products are granted direct production subsidies or are affected by other forms of governmental financial support affecting production. The commodities which are most commonly subject to such measures are *cereals* (in approximately twenty out of thirty-four countries), *dairy products* (in approximately seventeen countries), *meat* (in some ten countries), and *sugar* and *vegetable oilseeds* and *oils* (in some nine countries). Other important primary products, including *cotton, eggs, potatoes,* and *tobacco*, are subject to similar subsidies in several countries."[5]

It is noteworthy that all the products particularly mentioned as being *most commonly subject* to such measures are not only primary products, but also primary agricultural products.[6] Furthermore, there is ample evidence that subsidies have since been growing in terms of the number of countries using them, the range of products subjected to them, as well as the amount of money spent on them.[7] Studies have shown that annual domestic support to agricultural producers during 1986-1990 averaged $92 billion for the EU, $35 billion for Japan, and $24 billion for the US.[8] In a 1997 issue, the OECD reported that the total transfers associated with agricultural policies in OECD countries for 1996 amounted to $297 billion, of which $120 billion belonged to the EU alone.[9] The why of this expensive and widespread practice is the obvious question that should follow from here.

---

[5] GATT Panel on Subsidies, *Operation of the Provisions of Article XVI*, (L/1442 & Add. 1-2 *BISD* 10S/203), report adopted on 21 November 1961, p. 203.

[6] The same panel has observed that "in contrast with the situation for primary products, an examination of the notifications indicates that non-primary products are subject to direct production subsidies or other forms of governmental financial support *in a very limited number of products and in a small number of countries*", and that "the share of these products in and the effect of the subsidy arrangements on international trade appears to be *insignificant*". Ibid. p. 204.

[7] See W. Miner and D. Hathaway, "World Agriculture in Crisis: Reforming Government Policies", in W. Miner, and D. Hathaway (eds.), *World Agricultural Trade: Building a Consensus* (The Institute for Research on Public Policy, Halifax, Canada, 1988), p. 47; and OECD, *National Policies and Agricultural Trade* (Paris 1987), p. 68.

[8] B. Hoekman, and M. Kostecki, *The Political Economy of the World Trading System: From GATT to WTO* (Oxford University Press, 1995), p. 197.

[9] See OECD, *Agricultural Policies, Markets, and Trade in OECD Countries, Monitoring and Evaluation 1997* (Paris 1997); See also T. Gylfason, "Prospects for Liberalization of Trade in Agriculture", 32 *Journal of World Trade*, No. 1 (1998), p. 32.

9.1.2 Policy Underpinnings[10]

There are different policy rationales behind this interventionist behaviour of states in their agricultural sectors.[11] Historically speaking, the most important consideration is the desire to achieve domestic self-sufficiency in food items which, obviously, has a national security aspect within it. As is often said, the fate of a nation that cannot feed its own people is at the mercy of those countries supplying its imports.[12]

However, although food security has served as the fundamental policy rationale behind the initiation of a plethora of domestic agricultural support measures in most developed countries, currently this is not the case any longer. With the possible exception of Japan, most are in fact suffering from a consistent glut in food production. The explanation for the progressive proliferation of these policies should thus be sought from elsewhere.

In 1960, Committee II of the GATT, after examining the agricultural policies of twenty-four individual countries, found the main policy objectives to be the following: "(i) to maintain or raise the general level of farm incomes, usually with a view to some relationship being maintained with incomes in other sectors of the economy, and (ii) to reduce or eliminate fluctuations in domestic farm prices and incomes."[13] This conclusion accords well with, for example, Article 39:1 of the EC Treaty, which enumerates the objectives of the Common Agricultural Policy as follows: "(a) to increase agricultural productivity by promoting technical progress and by ensuring the rational development of agricultural production and the optimum utilisation of the factors of production, in particular labour; (b) thus to ensure a fair standard of living for the agricultural community, in particular by increasing the individual earnings of persons engaged in agriculture; (c) to stabilise markets; (d) to ensure the availability of supplies; (e) to ensure that supplies reach consumers at reasonable prices."[14] Often undeclared but equally important considerations include the political influence of the agricultural communities in

---

[10] For a detailed account of the policy considerations behind this practice of subsidies, see GATT, *Agricultural Protection: Second Report of Committee II,* (L/1192 *BISD* 9S/110), adopted on 20 May 1960; GATT, *Agricultural Protection: Third Report of Committee II,* (L/1461 *BISD* 10S/135), adopted on 15 November 1961; and for a summarized discussion of the same issue, see, *inter alia,* Hoekman and Kostecki (1995) *supra* n. 8, pp. 197 – 206.

[11] According to the WTO, "Governments usually give three reasons for supporting and protecting their farmers, even if this distorts agricultural trade: to make sure that enough food is produced to meet the country's needs; to shield farmers from the effects of the weather and swings in world prices; [and] to preserve rural society." WTO, *Introduction to the WTO: Trading into the Future* (2nd ed. Geneva, 1998) p. 16.

[12] See J. H. Jackson, W. Davey, and A. Sykes, *Legal Problems of International Economic Relations: Cases, Materials and Text* (3rd ed., West Publishing Co. 1995), p. 1165. Some even go as far as advocating a separate treatment in the WTO of staple foods. See Bhagirath Lal Das, "The 'Big Bang' in Agriculture in the WTO", *Third World Economics: Trends and Analysis* No. 177 (16-31 January 1998, Penang, Malaysia) pp. 2-4.

[13] GATT, *Second Report of Committee II supra* n. 10, p. 113.

[14] Treaty Establishing the European Economic Community (signed in Rome on 25 March 1957).

different countries,[15] the highly cultural concern to keep the traditional agricultural way of life intact and to maintain a peasant class in many of these countries.[16] In the later days, the role of agricultural policies, and particularly of domestic support measures, on the environment is also gaining currency.[17]

The cumulative effect of all these policy considerations is that countries use several different forms of support in favour of their agricultural producers, often in a manner that completely shields the sector from the law of the market.

9.1.3 Forms of Domestic Support

In order to achieve these objectives, countries have long been using subsidies of a variety of forms – ranging from such overt forms of support as direct budgetary

---

[15] As Hillman observed, "the political power of agriculture seems to increase with the diminution in its relative size." J. Hillman, "The US Perspective", in K. Ingersent, A. Rayner, and R. Hine (eds.) *Agriculture in the Uruguay Round* (St. Martin's press, New York 1994), p. 40.

[16] It was said already in 1965 that in a number of industrial countries, notably Germany, Switzerland, Belgium, Holland, and the Scandinavian countries, "the peasantry represents a sociologically necessary element which serves not simply to produce essential food supplies in emergencies or to provide the towns with new blood but whose existence embodies a traditional mode of life to which many people living in town and countryside are strongly attached." G. Curzon, "Multilateral Commercial Diplomacy: The General Agreement on Tariffs and Trade and Its Impact on National Policies and Techniques" (1965), p. 206, reprinted in J. H. Jackson, *Legal Problems of International Economic Relations* (West Publishing Co. 1977), p. 980.

[17] It appears, however, that no consensus view has yet emerged on the interaction of agricultural domestic support measures and the environment. On the one hand, there is the argument that "agricultural production subsidies have increased incentives that have led ... to water and soil pollution." See J. Lankoski, *Environmental Effects of Agricultural Trade Liberalization and Domestic Agricultural Trade Reforms,* UNCTAD Discussion Paper Series, UNCTAD/OSG/DP/126 (April, 1997), p. 6. On the other hand, there is the argument that a reduction in agricultural support might result in further deterioration of the environment because of the producers' desire to raise productivity by the intensive use of chemicals regardless of environmental considerations. As summarized by Kym Anderson, concerns about the environmental effects of agricultural liberalization stem from the fact that reductions in distortions to international trade (a) increase real incomes in the countries whose exports expand and the consequent increase in spending will place greater demands on the environment; and (b) change the mix and international location of production and consumption. With respect to the latter, the environmentalists argue that "in the highly protected countries of Western Europe the rural countryside and villages will be less visually attractive and less populated as farmers respond to lower domestic food prices by 'getting bigger or getting out'." They also fear that the higher food prices in international markets will "stimulate greater net deforestation to expand the agricultural land (thereby reducing the forests' absorption of CO_2 from the atmosphere and its contribution to biodiversity) and the use of heavier doses of agricultural chemicals (which not only degrade the local environment but also cause greater chemical residues in food which the reforming countries might import)." See Anderson, K. "Agricultural Trade Reforms, Research Incentives, and the Environment" in E. Lutz, H. Binswanger, p. Hazell, and A. McCalla, (eds.) *Agriculture, Development, and Environment: Policy, Institutional, and Technical Perspectives* (Washington, D.C.: The World Bank, April 1998), pp. 2–4. Anderson, however, concludes that agricultural policy reform will "make a net improvement to the environment." Ibid. p. 15. Generally, see also OECD, *Agriculture and the Environment: Issues and Policies* (Paris, 1998); and F. Runge, "A Conceptual Framework for Agricultural Trade and the Environment: Beyond the "Green Box", in 33 *Journal of World Trade* No. 6 (1999), pp. 47–68.

transfers down to the highly disguised forms of market price support measures.[18] The number and type of measures used by countries for the purpose are simply unlimited.[19]

Despite their diversity, however, they have certain features in common: firstly, governments guarantee a certain level of income for their agricultural producers; secondly, the thus-guaranteed levels of income are implemented mainly by way of either setting minimum artificial prices on the market (which are higher than world market prices) or through direct budgetary transfers to agricultural producers; thirdly, more often than not, these schemes result in production much beyond domestic requirements; and finally, domestic support measures are almost inevitably accompanied by border measures and, in most cases, by export subsidies. With these points in mind, a highlight of the following two main, albeit by no means the only, forms of domestic support – market price support and deficiency payments – may give a practical perspective to the whole range of issues discussed in Part III.

9.1.3.1 Market Price Support

Market price support, which once took up about 70 per cent of assistance measures,[20] is perhaps the oldest[21] and the most commonly used form of agricultural domestic support. It is a means by which the government tries to implement its social, economic, or political objectives through direct intervention in the operation of the market. As a policy measure which nearly excludes the operation of market forces, market price support "involves the establishment of a differential between the price received by domestic producers and the price which prevails in international trade."[22] The essential objective of this policy measure is to keep the domestic price of agricultural products above a certain level, which necessarily is higher than world prices.[23] The EU having been the main user of this method of support for a long time, the following paragraph by Barents summarizes the essence of this policy instrument:

---

[18] See, *inter alia*, GATT, *Second Report of Committee II supra* n. 10.

[19] Indeed, "if the methods governments may devise to subsidize production or exports are limited, they are limited only by the bounds of human inventiveness, and surely have not been reached". Palmeter (1989), *supra* n. 1, p. 60.

[20] OECD (1987), *supra* n. 7, p. 123.

[21] It has been observed that "Agricultural protectionism has a long history that predates GATT ... but modern policies of income transfer to producers via the price system have their origins in the Depression of the 1930s". G. Annania, C. Carter, and A. McCalla, "Agricultural Policy Changes, GATT Negotiations, and the U.S.-E.C. Agricultural Trade Conflict", in G. Annania, C. Carter, and A. McCalla (eds.), *Agricultural Trade Conflicts and GATT: New Dimensions in U.S. – European Agricultural Trade Relations* (Westview Press, Oxford, 1994) p. 5.

[22] J. McMahon, *Agricultural Trade, Protectionism and the Problems of Development: A Legal Perspective,* (Leicester University Press, London 1992) p. 1.

[23] For, otherwise, it would not be a "price support" for the producer, but for the consumer. In 1994, for instance, "producer prices of food in the EU were 94 per cent above world market prices." Gylfason, *supra* n. 9, p. 35.

> "Under the common market organizations the main form of intervention relates to price support, the essential objective of which is to keep the market price at or above a certain minimum level. To this end, the Council annually fixes a number of common prices which indicate the levels at which the market price should be situated and at which the various supporting mechanisms (intervention buying, private stocking arrangements, and a variety of other financial instruments) are or become operative."[24]

The higher domestic prices fixed by the government, often called political prices, bring two important consequences to the world market. Firstly, by promising higher returns for the domestic producer, they are an artificial inducement to production and result in domestic supply exceeding domestic demand. Disposal of the excess production in the world market at world market prices not only requires export subsidies from government budgets, but also further depresses those world prices against the interest of several other competitors from other countries. Secondly, since the higher domestic prices naturally induce traders to try to import products into such markets – thus threatening the overall objectives of the domestic support programmes – subsidizing countries almost always resort to some form of restrictive border measures (in the form, *inter alia*, of quantitative restrictions, higher tariffs, tariff quotas, variable levies, etc.).[25] Hence the conclusion that "Price intervention and a certain degree of isolation from the world market ... go hand in hand."[26]

9.1.3.2 Deficiency Payments

The policy of deficiency payments is the other important form of agricultural domestic support. Mainly used by the US, the essence of this policy instrument may be comparatively described as follows. Just like in market price support, the government sets the "producer price" of agricultural products at a level considered fair and remunerative to the producer – the political price. Unlike in that of price support measures, however, the consumer in this case pays a price determined by the

---

24 R. Barents, *The Agricultural Law of the EC* (1994), p. 77.

25 See also GATT, *Second Report of Committee II, supra* n. 10, p. 115.

26 Barents (1994) *supra* n. 24, p. 77. The following paragraph by Barents vividly describes the system from a practical view point:

> "The classical model of the common price system as it is operated under the common agricultural policy, consists of three common price concepts: a *target price*, an *intervention price* and a *threshold price*. The target price is set at a level at which it is presumed that the producer will receive a fair remuneration for his production. At a certain distance below this price an intervention price is fixed. This price constitutes the level at which the various mechanisms for the regulation of the internal market are or (may) become operative, such as intervention buying by the intervention agencies, the granting of private storage premiums, etc. Derived from the target price is a threshold price. This price is fixed at such a level that imported products do not enter the Community at a price lower than the target price. The difference between the world market price and the threshold price is made up by an import levy. The three price model thus reflects the fact that the essential function of the common market organizations is to safeguard agricultural producer income through price supporting measures on the internal market and protection against the influence of world market prices." (italics added).

"free" interplay of market forces, while the producer receives the difference between the political price and the market price directly from the treasury of the state.[27]

The use of deficiency payments is less trade-distorting than market price support measures in that (i) it lets the market forces play a primary role in the determination of the initial income of the producer, (ii) it need not be followed by restrictive border measures,[28] and (iii) it is a much more overt and transparent form of support. However, to the extent that the amount transferred to each producer ultimately depends on the amount it brings to the market, it also stimulates production in excess of domestic demand with effects similar to price support.

9.1.4 The Need for, and the Challenges of, Regulation

Although a very old and widespread practice, the views of governments as well as scholars regarding subsidies have always been divided. While some defend the practice of subsidies as an important instrument of domestic economic policy for development, others argue that subsidies are totally inconsistent with the very objectives of the GATT and the liberalization of international trade.[29] In the field of subsidies, the standing ideological divergence over the role of the state in the economy reappears in its most refined and challenging form.

However, it is being progressively accepted over time that subsidies create artificial cost advantages in favour of their recipients and flout the laws of comparative advantage and specialization,[30] on which the entire multilateral trading system claims to be based. Subsidies "distort or subvert the market process and ... result in a misallocation of resources, encouraging inefficient production and lessening world wealth".[31] To the extent that this artificial benefit results in trade and even production distortions, the need for a set of rules of discipline multilaterally agreed is apparent. After all, "one can hardly speak of free and fair trade and competition if markets are obtained not on the basis of commercial considerations such as price and quality of goods, but depending on the relative strength of the national treasuries".[32] A policy statement issued by a group of specialists in the field of agricultural trade policy in 1988 provided the gist of the problem as follows:

---

27 See also McMahon (1992) *supra* n. 22.

28 See GATT, *Second Report of Committee II, supra* n. 10, p. 116.

29 See Rivers and Greenwald (1979) *supra* n. 3, p. 1452; T. Stewart, *The GATT Uruguay Round: A Negotiating History (1986 – 1992)* in III Vols. (Kluwer 1993), Vol. I, pp. 844–845.

30 See *supra* chapter 1; for more on this, see p. Krugman, and M. Obstefeld, *International Economics: Theory and Practice* (4th ed. 1997) pp. 14-15.

31 E. Grabitz, "Comment", in J. Bourgeois, (ed.) *Subsidies and International Trade: A European Lawyers Perspective*, (Kluwer 1991) p. 45.

32 K. Kautzor-Schroeder, "Comment", Ibid., p. 185. Former US Agriculture Secretary Clayton Yeutter has been quoted as saying, in connection with a US proposal to the Uruguay Round in 1989, that the purpose was "to level the playing field for farmers, so they compete fairly against one another instead of against governmental treasuries." Hillman in Ingersent *et al* (1994) *supra* n. 15, p. 40.

> "... the programs governments have developed to assist farmers, maintain farm income, and stabilize market prices are a major factor contributing to global problems. These programs have continued to encourage rapid increases in output in many countries at a time when the growth in world demand has slackened. The result, during the first half of the 1980s, was falling world agricultural commodity prices – to the lowest real levels since the 1930s."[33]

By providing generous subsidies to their domestic producers, countries often affect not only the conditions of competition in their domestic markets, but also distort the patterns of international trade against the national interests of several other countries,[34] both developed as well as developing. According to Professor Emmerij, President of the Development Centre of the OECD, the industrialized countries are in a "vicious circle" because the high and costly subsidies they provide result in excess production which in turn causes additional expenditure for stockpiling and selling at artificially low prices in world markets. What is more, while these countries compete for external markets, they diminish "the chances of agriculture in many developing countries".[35]

What makes domestic subsidies totally different from most other trade policy measures – and inevitably more sensitive – is that most are introduced with legitimate and purely internal policy objectives in view. Needless to say, it is inherent in the very sovereign nature of countries that they have every right to adopt domestic social and economic policies of their own free choice. At the same time, however, it is not uncommon for domestic subsidies to serve, intentionally or otherwise, protectionist purposes. Whatever countries may do in pursuance of their own domestic interests thus acquires an international dimension as soon as its adverse impact starts to be felt by other countries. A clash of interests thus becomes apparent here – the interest of countries to adopt policies that maximize their national interests comes into direct conflict with the interests of those countries that may be affected by the thus-adopted domestic policies of the subsidizing countries.[36]

The other complicating factor is that not all such domestic programmes have this kind of extra-territorial, trade-distorting, impact. In fact, domestic subsidies are the most perplexing because "they involve a vast range and number of government policies, *many of which are perfectly justifiable as exercises of sovereign activity within a country*".[37] Consequently, not all domestic support programmes need to be constrained.

These considerations seem to have led to some sort of a consensus, in principle, that countries should be left free to use whatever domestic mechanism to support

---

[33] "A Policy Statement by Twenty-Nine Professionals from Seventeen Countries", in Miner and Hathaway (1988) *supra* n. 7, p. 3.

[34] See OECD (1987), *supra* n. 7, p. 68.

[35] L. Emmerij, "On Agricultural Subsidies and the GATT Negotiations", 5 *Tijdschrift voor Europees en Economisch Recht* (May 1990) p. 268; for details, see pp. 267-274.

[36] See T. Collins-Williams, and G Salembier "International Disciplines on Subsidies: The GATT, the WTO, and the Future Agenda", in 30, *Journal of World Trade*, No. 1 (1996), p. 5; see also Jackson *et al* (1995) *supra* n. 12, pp. 757–780.

[37] Jackson (1997) *supra* n. 4, p. 280 (emphasis added).

their agricultural communities, but with one important condition – that the support should be made "in ways that do not distort production, consumption or trade".[38] This is what is nowadays often termed as "decoupling" or "delinking", i.e. that domestic support measures should be "decoupled" or "delinked" from decisions on resource allocation and trade patterns.[39]

The first step towards any multilateral regulation limiting the undesirable effects of domestic subsidies is, therefore, to identify the trade-distorting domestic programme from the trade-neutral or decoupled one.[40] Hence the need for some kind of a multilaterally agreed system of rules not only for setting limitations on the exercise of this sovereignty, but also for laying the standard by which to sift domestic programs that are trade-distorting from those that are not. This has always been the first serious challenge facing the multilateral trading system in this area – a challenge which has not yet been met that successfully even today.[41]

What is more – and this is the second challenge – even if one succeeds in resolving the problem of identification just mentioned, countries are often reluctant to accept any serious international discipline constraining their domestic policy-making powers. The fact that most domestic subsidies are aimed at legitimate, non-trade, domestic social and economic objectives makes them almost entirely a question of internal policy completely beyond the reach of multilateral regulation. Indeed, many countries believed until very recently that any "stringent international regulation of domestic subsidies would ... amount to intolerable interference in their internal policy matters."[42]

To sum up, agricultural domestic subsidies are not only widely used by most, if not all, developed and high-income developing countries, but also that they are often used in a manner disruptive of international trade. Besides, while their adverse effects on trade make some form of multilateral regulation necessary, their principal feature as instruments of internal social and economic policy makes the realization of such a goal difficult. In the following section, therefore, the position of the existing multilateral trading system of the GATT throughout its life time will be explored from a historical and case-oriented perspective.

---

38 Miner and Hathaway (1988) *supra* n. 7, p. 113.

39 The International Agricultural Trade Consortium (IATC) described "decoupling" as follows: "If neither the implementation nor the removal of a payment has any effect on production, the payment is fully decoupled." IATC, *Reinstrumentation of Agricultural Policies* 7 (1990), quoted in Stewart, *supra* n. 29, Vol. I, p. 161. For further details, see *infra* section 10.2; see also Miner and Hathaway (1988) *supra* n. 7, pp. 79-113. According to Professor Hillman, the decoupling concept is not a new arrival to the trade policy literature. He tells us that academic economists in the US "were advocating decoupled payments as early as the 1950s." Hillman, in Ingersent *et al* (1994) *supra* n. 15, p. 37.

40 For a critical view of this approach, see Runge (1999) *supra* n. 19, p. 48.

41 For further details on this point, see *infra* chapter 10; see also Jackson *et al* (1995) *supra* n. 12, pp. 757 et seq.

42 Rivers and Greenwald (1979) *supra* n. 3, pp. 1449–1470. Johnson wrote in 1978 that "Few countries – perhaps none – are willing to engage in negotiations about their domestic agricultural programs." D. Johnson, in "Foreword" to J. Hillman, *Non-tariff Agricultural Barriers* (University of Nebraska Press, 1978) p. X. See also Stewart (1993) *supra* n. 29, p. 816.

9.2 Domestic Support Measures and the Multilateral Trading System

9.2.1 The Need for an Integrated Approach

We have seen that domestic subsidies stimulate production and often result in excess supply. Since world market prices are lower than the domestic market, the excess can be disposed of only with the aid of export subsidies or given in the form of food aid to countries in need. Besides, as the higher domestic market prices naturally attract imports, such policies almost always need to be supplemented by some form of import restriction so that a re-importation of the subsidized exports themselves or the import of competing foreign products would not take place in a manner that frustrates the very object of the domestic programme. An international agreement to discipline the use of border measures without a concomitant agreement addressing important domestic policy issues cannot therefore achieve its goals.

The close relationship between domestic support measures and the other trade-restrictive policies has been recognized since the inception of the idea of a liberal and rules-based multilateral trading system in the early 1940s. In 1945 when the draft rules of the ITO were being formulated, the US Department of Agriculture (USDA) made the point that "the U.S. farm program, which supported farm prices well above world price levels, could not survive unless the domestic markets were protected against world prices by means of quantitative restrictions".[43] A stronger and more comprehensive version of this idea appeared three years later in a Congressional testimony by a representative of the USDA: "price supports for farm commodities here in the United States ... require a certain degree of protection through tariffs and other trade barriers. Without them foreign producers might flood our domestic market, with our government buying the domestic production. In addition, it tends to become difficult to export farm products without an export subsidy."[44] This is a very concise expression of the causal role of domestic support programmes behind other trade-restrictive and distortive measures.

A realization of this fear has been vividly witnessed throughout the life time of the GATT. As will be developed later, the practice of domestic support was not sufficiently constrained by the rules of the General Agreement and practically all developed countries and most high-income developing countries provided one or another form of domestic support to their agricultural communities. However, this was not the only result. Other trade-restrictive policy measures such as import quotas and quantitative restrictions, export subsidies and the like also proliferated.

A glimpse of any randomly-chosen GATT cases involving agricultural products – whether as issues of quotas, quantitative restrictions, export subsidies, mixing requirements, or whatever – shows that almost all of them are actually the results of the enormous pressure exerted upon governments by the presence of excessive stocks of products, which are themselves caused by generous domestic support

---

43 R. Hudec, *The GATT Legal System and World Trade Diplomacy* (Praeger Publishers, 1975), p. 13.

44 Quoted in J. H. Jackson, *World Trade and the Law of GATT* (Bobbs-Merrill, 1969) P 318.

programmes. The EC, with the CAP at its very core, is perhaps the most notorious one in this connection. A brief look at some of the agricultural cases the EC had to defend before the GATT shows that a substantial majority of the challenged policies were themselves some form of inevitable implementation measures for the domestic support programmes. The following summary may throw some light in this area.

According to a comprehensive database of GATT cases between 1948 and 1989 prepared by professor Robert Hudec, a total of 207 complaints containing the basic elements of an Article XXIII lawsuit were brought before the GATT during this period.[45] Of this total, 89 cases, or about 43 per cent, concerned agricultural products.[46] Again, out of the 207 complaints the EC appeared as a defendant in a total of 45 cases, of which 31, or nearly 70 per cent, were related to agricultural products.

Seen from another angle, this means that more than a third of all cases involving agricultural products were brought against the EC. It is also curious to note that while the 89 agricultural cases span over the entire period covered by the database (i.e. 1948 to 1989), all the cases against the EC were brought within only the latter half of this period, the first GATT case the EC had to defend having been brought on 28 April 1970, when Australia challenged the import restrictions imposed by the EC against its apples. The following synopsis of two groups of GATT agricultural cases, concerning import restrictions and export subsidies, in which the EC appeared as defendant, may help to further illuminate the degree to which domestic support measures lie beneath most agricultural controversies.

GATT challenges against EC regulations imposing import restrictions may well be exemplified by the following cases concerning different types of apples[47]: emergency quotas against imports of table apples from Australia,[48] quantitative restrictions on imports from Chile once on apples in general[49] and another time particularly on dessert apples,[50] quantitative restrictions on apple imports from the

---

[45] For a summary of all cases covered by the study and the entire database, see R. Hudec, *Enforcing International Trade Law: The Evolution of the Modern GATT Legal System* (Butterworth, 1993), pp. 373–608.

[46] The classification of cases into agricultural and non-agricultural is based on Hudec's own assessment of the products involved in each case.

[47] For details on quantitative restrictions, see Part I.

[48] In 1970 Australia claimed that emergency quotas imposed by the EC on imports of table apples from Australia were a violation of the General Agreement to its detriment. See *Australia* v. *European Community: Emergency Action on Table Apples,* case discussed in GATT Council meeting of 28 April 1970 as C/M/62, but withdrawn before reaching a ruling because the EC terminated the quotas after three months. Hudec describes the underlying phenomenon as follows: the restrictions were "*intended to deal with typical situation where price support program leads to excess production.*" Hudec (1993) *supra* n. 45, p. 452 (emphasis added).

[49] See *EEC Restrictions on Imports of Apples from Chile,* Report of the Panel (L/5047 *BISD* 27S/98) adopted on 10 November 1980.

[50] See *European Economic Community – Restrictions on Imports of Dessert Apples: Complaint by Chile,* report of the panel (L/6491 – *BISD* 36S/93) adopted on 22 June 1989.

US,[51] and quantitative restrictions on apple imports from New Zealand.[52] On the surface, these are all cases involving different forms of violations of GATT rules on import restrictions. But these market access restrictions were not instituted for their own sake. To a certain extent, they were simply inevitable consequences of the generous domestic support programmes behind them, and the enormous glut resulting therefrom. The observation made by Professor Hudec in relation to *Chilean Apples* (1979) reflects the essence of the situation underlying nearly all import restrictive policies of the EC and applies to all the cases referred to above: "*QRs quantitative restrictions] were an effort to liquidate excess stocks of apples due to overproduction under price support system* ... so as] *to dispose of stored domestic apples from previous year's harvest.*"[53] Most of these import restrictions are thus only designed to put into effect the domestic support policies. In a way, therefore, the life of these import restrictive measures itself largely, if not exclusively, depends on the existence of those domestic support systems.

In the contentious area of export subsidies,[54] too, the causal role of domestic support measures is no less important. Domestic support programmes and the resulting glut in agricultural products have often left countries in no other alternative than subsidizing their exports. In as long as domestic prices in the subsidizing countries are artificially kept above world prices, almost the only way to dispose of the resulting excess is through export subsidies.[55]

Although there are far fewer decided GATT cases involving agricultural export subsidies than those concerning import restrictions, the two parallel cases brought by Australia and Brazil in 1978 against EC refunds on exports of sugar[56] may sufficiently demonstrate the issue. Hudec has made the identical observation in connection with both cases that "EC price support program for sugar had greatly increased EC production for sugar, excess of which was exported via subsidies."[57] This is, therefore, a further reaffirmation of the conclusion that most of the trade-distorting measures taken in the area of international agricultural trade find their root in the widespread and generous domestic support programmes maintained by most of the high-income GATT contracting parties.

All the preceding observations and discussions lead to one inevitable conclusion: that the problems of international agricultural trade are so interrelated that any

---

[51] See *European Economic Community – Restrictions on Imports of Apples: Complaint by the United States*, report of the panel (L/6513 – *BISD* 36S/135) adopted on 22 June 1989.

[52] In April 1988 New Zealand lodged a similar complaint against the EC, but unlike the companion Chilean and US cases, New Zealand did not push the matter further and the restrictions against its products expired on 31 August 1988. For a summary of this case, see Hudec, Ibid., p. 563.

[53] Hudec (1993) *supra* n. 45, p. 477 (italics added).

[54] For details on agricultural export subsidies, see *supra* Part II.

[55] See GATT, *Second Report of Committee II, supra* n. 10.

[56] *European Communities – Refunds on Exports of Sugar: [Complaint by Australia]* report of the panel (L/4833 *BISD* 26S/290-319) adopted on 6 November 1979; and *European Communities – Refunds on Exports of Sugar: Complaint by Brazil* report of the panel (L/5011 *BISD* 27S/69-98) adopted on 10 November 1980. For a discussion of these cases, see *supra* chapter 4.

[57] Hudec (1993) *supra* n. 45, p. 473.

viable solution would come only from a comprehensive and integrated approach, and not from a policy-specific one. Most problems of international agricultural trade being results of the domestic support programmes underlying them, their solution largely lies in the solution found for these latter set of programmes.

This view has also been reflected during the Uruguay Round negotiations. As the Uruguay Round negotiations on domestic support will be discussed in detail later on, suffice it to note here that when the EC presented to the Uruguay Round its comprehensive proposal on agricultural issues in 1989, it proposed for a reduction only of "policy interventions in agriculture to be measured by means of an AMS" and did not mention any commitment on export subsidies. It did this because, in the opinion of the EC, "a reduction in global support would implicitly result in lower market distortions and reduced export subsidies."[58] In short, it was understood that issues of market access and subsidies are so closely inter-linked that an integrated approach was the only meaningful way to follow.[59] Agreement on a multilateral discipline over domestic support measures is an indispensable element for a lasting solution to the multidimensional problems of agricultural trade.

9.2.2 Domestic Subsidies: Attempts at Multilateral Regulation

We have seen that domestic agricultural subsidies have not only been widespread in themselves, but have also been causing the proliferation of other trade-distorting policy measures. The most important question to ask at this juncture should then be the following: if domestic support measures are so disruptive of international trade, what has their legal status been like under the General Agreement?

All attempts to regulate domestic subsidies should always be seen as part and parcel of the overall attempt to regulate the practice of subsidies in general. The first truly multilateral move in this direction was that made during the negotiation of the ITO Charter in the second-half of the 1940s.[60] Already before the start of the actual negotiations, the United States Department of Agriculture (the USDA) forced upon the trade experts the point that "the U.S. farm program, which supported farm prices well above world price levels, could not survive unless the domestic markets were protected against world prices by means of quantitative restrictions."[61] Consequently, when the formal negotiations of the ITO Charter began in October 1946, the US proposed, in its *Suggested Charter,* an exception for agricultural price supports and the necessary

---

58 See G. Annania, C. Carter, and A. McCalla, "Agricultural Policy Changes, GATT Negotiations, and the U.S.-E. C. Agricultural Trade Conflict", in Annania *et al, supra* n. 21, p. 26. See also K. Ingersent, A. Rayner, and R. Hine, "The EC Perspective", in Ingersent *et al, supra* n. 15, pp. 55-87; and D. Hathaway, and M. Ingco, *Agricultural Liberalization and the Uruguay Round,* paper presented at the World Bank Conference on "The Uruguay Round and the Developing Economies", (26-27 January 1995) p. 5.

59 W. Miner, and D. Hathaway, "World Agriculture in Crisis: Reforming Government Policies", in Miner and Hathaway (1988) *supra* n. 7, p. 14. See also McMahon (1992), *supra* n. 22.

60 For details, see *supra* chapter 4.

61 Ibid. p. 13. Hudec also observed that "the new U.S. position found a sympathetic audience in the British trade experts, who had found that they too had a 'farm problem'. Ibid.

quantitative restrictions to implement them – a proposal which faced not much opposition from the other countries.[62] This is in contradistinction to the Suggested Charter's proposal concerning export subsidies, against which there was a "stiff resistance".[63] By the time the GATT was negotiated, the only outstanding point of contention in the field of subsidies thus concerned export subsidies. The separate treatment of export subsidies, suggested by the US and supported by a few others,[64] was not acceptable to all the signatories of the GATT in 1947. And it was only for purposes of the "provisional" GATT that a compromise was found in a uniform treatment of all subsidies regardless of the purpose they were intended to serve (*e.g.* whether they were meant to promote exports, curtail imports, etc.), their sector of application (*e.g.* whether agricultural or otherwise) or whatever. The regime accepted earlier for domestic subsidies was thus extended to that of export subsidies as well and both were subjected to a "uniform" system of rules under the General Agreement as it stood in 1947.

The 1947 version of GATT Article XVI thus provided as follows:

> "If any contracting party grants or maintains any subsidy, including any form of income or price support, which operates directly or indirectly to increase exports of any product from, or to reduce imports of any product into, its territory, it shall notify the CONTRACTING PARTIES in writing of the extent and nature of the subsidization, of the estimated effect of the subsidization on the quantity of the affected product or products imported into or exported from its territory and of the circumstances making the subsidization necessary. In any case in which *it is determined* that serious prejudice to *the interests of any other contracting party* is caused or threatened by any such subsidization, the contracting party granting the subsidy shall, upon request, discuss with the other contracting party or parties concerned, or with the CONTRACTING PARTIES, the possibility of limiting the subsidization."[65]

When the final version of the ITO Charter arrived in 1948, even if the GATT compromise concerning export subsidies was reversed in favour of separate and more stringent regulation, that concerning domestic subsidies remained largely unchanged. Accordingly, Article 25 of the Havana Charter, which is the only important provision on domestic subsidies, provided as follows:

> "If any Member grants or maintains any subsidy, including any form of income or price support, which operates directly or indirectly to *maintain or* increase exports

---

[62] Ibid., p. 14.

[63] Ibid.

[64] *E.g.*, the United Kingdom.

[65] Article XVI of the original version of GATT 1947 (bold and italics added). Since the 1955 revision, this paragraph has become Article XVI.1. In bold are terms or phrases that differ from the corresponding Article 25 of the Havana Charter which result from the very nature of the respective Agreements (i.e. because the General Agreement was not intended to create any organization and referred only to contracting parties while the Charter was supposed to create the ITO whose parties would rightfully be called Members), while those in italics are the areas of substantive difference between the two provisions. See *infra* n. 66.

of any product from, or to reduce, *or prevent an increase in,* imports of any product into, its territory, the Member shall notify the Organization in writing of the extent and nature of the subsidization, of the estimated effect of the subsidization on the quantity of the affected product or products imported into or exported from its territory and of the circumstances making the subsidization necessary. In any case in which a Member *considers* that serious prejudice to *its* interests is caused or threatened by any such subsidization, the Member granting the subsidy shall, upon request, discuss with the other Member or Members concerned, or with the Organization, the possibility of limiting the subsidization."[66]

The latter provision shows that some changes were made to the Geneva draft of the ITO Charter (from which Article XVI of the General Agreement had been copied).[67] Leaving aside the changes necessitated by the very nature of the two agreements, such as the reference to contracting parties and Members, there are two noticeable differences between these two provisions. Firstly, while the obligation in GATT Article XVI concerns only those subsidies which operate to increase exports or decrease imports, Article 25 of the Havana Charter also covers those subsidies which serve to maintain existing levels of exports (which would otherwise have been lower) and imports (which would otherwise have been higher). This makes the Charter provision stronger than its GATT counterpart. Secondly, while a subsidizing Member's obligation to discuss the possibility of limiting the subsidization under the ITO Charter follows from another Member's mere consideration that its interests are being adversely affected, GATT Article XVI talks in terms of those adverse effects being determined before hand, but without specifying as to who has to do the determination. This makes the Charter provision much clearer than that of the General Agreement.

Apparently because of these improvements in the final text of the ITO Charter in 1948, a proposal was made to have them inserted in Article XVI of the General Agreement. It was, however, agreed that "the differences between Article XVI of the General Agreement and Article 25 of the Havana Charter are not of a substantial nature" and the text was kept unchanged.[68] In line with this statement, the above-noted improvements introduced by the final text of the Havana Charter were given effect to via subsequent interpretations of Article XVI of the General Agreement adopted by the CONTRACTING PARTIES.[69]

Be that as it may, it is noteworthy that in both cases, domestic subsidies were not to be subject to any serious restriction; they were subjected only to notification and consultation obligations. Moreover, with the failure of the ITO Charter to get the necessary number of ratifications for entry into force, it was the "provisional" GATT which continued as the only system of multilateral trade regulation for decades to come.

---

66 Article 25 of the Havana Charter (bold and italics added for the same purpose as in n. 65 *supra*).

67 For the few points of difference, see WTO, *GATT Analytical Index: Guide to GATT Law and Practice* (Updated 6th Edition 1995), p. 465.

68 Ibid. p. 466.

69 For more on this, see *infra* section 9.4.

9.3 Domestic Support Measures under the 1947 Version of the General Agreement

In its original 1947 version, the General Agreement treated all forms of subsidies in almost identical terms. Two provisions governed the issue – Articles XVI and VI. In general, while the former contained the rules of discipline governing the use of subsidies, the latter was concerned with the type of unilateral countermeasures that countries were allowed to take in response to subsidies causing or threatening material injury to their domestic industries.

Article XVI, which then had only one paragraph, prescribed two obligations – notification of subsidies and, if found prejudicial to the interests of any contracting party, discussion about the possibility of limiting the subsidization.[70]

Several deficiencies could be mentioned about this provision. First of all, the General Agreement speaks about a "subsidy", but nowhere in the General Agreement has the term "subsidy" been defined; it speaks about notification of subsidies without however giving much help as to what kinds of practices are notifiable and what are not. Secondly, even assuming that this problem can be resolved, what purpose does notification serve as such? Thirdly, it is provided that subsidizing contracting parties have the obligation to discuss in any case in which *it is determined* that serious prejudice to the interests of any other contracting party is caused or threatened by any such subsidization. But, as mentioned earlier, who has the power to determine in such cases? Does a determination by the complaining party itself suffice? Or, does it in any way imply that the CONTRACTING PARTIES have to make a determination before a contracting party invokes its right to discuss the possibility of limiting the subsidization? Finally, what does the obligation to *discuss the possibility of limiting the subsidization* mean: does it necessarily imply the obligation to actually limit the subsidization if an alleged serious injury or threat thereof is established through the discussions? Put differently, does it create any meaningful, enforceable legal obligation? These points will be discussed in turn.

9.3.1.1 Definition of Subsidies

Definition of the concept of subsidies is as crucial as it has always been elusive.[71] According to Jackson, "there is no term in GATT which combines ambiguity and importance to international trade policy to a degree greater than the term subsidy".[72] Article XVI simply states that a subsidy may include "any form of income or price support". It does not offer any help in the attempt to draw a boundary between such

---

[70] For the text of the provision, see *supra* n. 65.

[71] McGovern's illuminating formulation may be useful here: "a subsidy is a measurable economic advantage afforded to an enterprise by or at the direction of the government, without adequate recompense, and in a way which discriminates against other enterprises or economic activities in the country." E. McGovern, *International Trade Regulation* (1986), p. 312.

[72] J. H. Jackson, "The jurisprudence of International Trade: the DISC Case in GATT" 72 *American Journal of International Law* (1978) p. 65.

legitimate and traditional activities of the state as, for example, the building of bridges and dams, the provision of training or other educational and infrastructure-development services[73] and the probably unfair, trade-distorting, and injurious support practices. As the current movement to include labour and environment issues into the WTO system shows, this is in fact a problem with the potential to be stretched to absurd limits.[74]

Neither is subsequent GATT case law of much help in this respect. In a somewhat encouraging sort of beginning, the Working Party on the *Australian Ammonium Sulphate* case, having observed that Article XVI was "drafted in very general terms", observed that "the type of subsidy which it was intended to cover was the financial aid given by a government to support its domestic production and to improve its competitive position either on the domestic market or on foreign markets".[75] In another report, a 1960 *Review Panel* discussed the circumstances under which a system which fixes domestic prices to producers at above the world price level might be considered a subsidy within the meaning of Article XVI and concluded as follows: "it was generally agreed that a system under which a government, by direct or indirect methods, maintains such a price by purchases and resale at a loss is a subsidy."[76]

This is a clear reference to some of the types of domestic subsidies which we are dealing with here. In the view of the *Review Panel,* a subsidy exists only if the government has incurred a loss to its accounts for the purpose. This approach to the problem of definition of subsidies has of course been changed by the Uruguay Round SCM Agreement, according to which a subsidy can be found to exist regardless of any cost to the government.[77]

But, while such discussions and attempts at definition were a move in the direction of further clarity in the conception of subsidies, subsequent developments reconfirmed the old view that the issue of subsidies was too difficult to define in any meaningful way. A GATT *Panel on Subsidies*, which was set up for the purpose, *inter*

---

73 To use the example given by Wilcox, the "paradigm case is that of public roads paid for by the government. These roads will make it less expensive for virtually every industry to produce virtually any good; this could be considered a subsidy if an expansive definition were adopted. However, it is clear that if governments were allowed to use countervailing duties against every such subsidy the result would be 'absurd' and the benefits of the GATT would soon be lost." W. Wilcox, "GATT-Based Protectionism and the Definition of a Subsidy", 16 *Boston University International Law Journal* (1998) pp. 138–39.

74 There are arguments, for instance, that preventing workers from organizing in a country reduces producers' costs and such practices "can be considered subsidies". H. Wachtel, "Labor's Stake in the WTO", *The American Prospect* 37 (1998) cited in p. Evans, *Economic Governance Institutions in a Global Political Economy: Implications for Developing Countries* paper prepared for the UNCTAD X High-Level Round Table on Trade and Development (Bangkok, 12 February 2000) p. 11.

75 GATT, *The Australian Subsidy on Ammonium Sulphate,* report of the Working Party (GATT/Cp.4/39 *BISD, Vol.* II) adopted on 14 March 1950, pp. 188-196.

76 GATT, *Report on the Review Pursuant to Article XVI:5* (L/1160 *BISD* 9S/188) adopted on 24 May 1960, p. 191. According to this panel, "such purchases would need only to cover part of the production to involve a subsidy and, in determining loss on resale, such expenses as holding stocks should be taken into account." Ibid.

77 See *supra* chapter 5, and *infra* chapter 10.

alia, of examining the range and extent of subsidies maintained by contracting parties, considered the definition issue and concluded that "it was neither necessary nor feasible to seek an agreed interpretation of what constituted a subsidy."[78] In the opinion of this panel, "it would probably be impossible to arrive at a definition which would at the same time include all measures that fall within the intended meaning of the term in Article XVI without including others not so intended."[79] The issue remained unresolved until the Uruguay Round Agreement on Subsidies and Countervailing Measures was successfully concluded in 1994.

9.3.1.2 Notification of Subsidies

Article XVI creates only two obligations – the obligation to notify and the obligation to discuss. Notification serves the important purpose of creating a transparent international trading environment where every state becomes fully aware of what every other state is doing within their territory which would affect the national interests of others. It should be stressed, however, that neither notification nor transparency is an end in itself; they are only a means to another end. That end is the further liberalization of international trade through the elimination, or at least reduction, of the causes of distortion, one of which is the practice of subsidies.[80] Subsidies are thus subjected to notification not just for the sake of recording them, but so that the extent of their use may be properly understood, their trade impact appreciated, and appropriate liberalizing measures introduced accordingly.

However, even for purposes of transparency, the notification obligation does not apply to all subsidies granted or maintained by parties. It extends only to those subsidies which operate, directly or indirectly, to increase exports of any product from, or to reduce imports of any product into the territory of the subsidizing country. In other words, Article XVI implicitly distinguishes between notifiable subsidies and non-notifiable subsidies. Needless to say, if definition of subsidies is difficult, common sense dictates that sifting between what has to be notified and what need not is next to impossible.

Yet, as a mandatory obligation requiring a practical response on the part of each of the contracting parties, the notification issue had to be handled in a pragmatic way.[81] The question thus comes down to an interpretation of the conditions set for notification – that the subsidy, whatever it may mean, operate directly or indirectly to increase exports of any product from or to reduce imports of any product into a contracting party. The key issue demanding treatment in this case would thus be the

---

78 GATT Panel on Subsidies, *supra* n. 5, p.201, para. 22. The report further noted that "the lack of a precise definition had not, in practice, interfered with the operation of Article XVI."

79 Ibid. para. 22.

80 Strictly speaking, of course, it is a means to a higher end – which end is development in all its dimensions.

81 In order to facilitate compliance with this notification obligation, arrangements have been made by the CONTRACTING PARTIES since 1950 for the reporting of existing subsidies as well as modified or newly-introduced measures of subsidization. See *GATT Analytical Index*, *supra* n. 67, p. 449. A standard format for the purpose of reporting of subsidies has been adopted by the CONTRACTING PARTIES on 3 March 1955 and slightly modified a few times; See *BISD* 3S/225, 9S/193-94, 11S/58, and 33S/199.

following: What do the words "increase exports" or "reduce imports" mean? Is any rise in the amount exported, or any fall in the amount imported, over a certain period of time sufficient to satisfy this requirement?

This problem has been discussed by the GATT *Panel on Subsidies* mentioned earlier, which opined that "it is not sufficient to consider increased exports or reduced imports only in an historical sense" and reminded an earlier interpretation by the CONTRACTING PARTIES that "the phrase 'increased exports' in line 3 of Article XVI of the General Agreement was intended to include the concept of maintaining exports at a level higher than would otherwise exist in the absence of the subsidy as made clear in line 3 of Article 25 of the Havana Charter."[82] The essence of this interpretation has been summarized by the *GATT Analytical Index* as follows:

> "Article 25 of the Geneva Charter, with some changes, became Article 25 of the Havana Charter. The text of Charter Article 25 reads '... which operates directly or indirectly to *maintain or* increase exports of any product from or to reduce *or prevent an increase in* imports ...', the italicised words having been added at Havana because 'it was felt that the Geneva text of the Article failed to cover subsidies which, whilst not increasing a Member's exports nor reducing its imports, might nevertheless affect a Member's share of total trade.' "[83]

The Panel then pushed this same logic to apply to the case of reduced imports and stated that the criterion is "what would happen in the absence of a subsidy" and concluded as follows: "The Panel considers it fair to assume that a subsidy which provides an incentive to increased production will, in the absence of offsetting measures, e.g., a consumption subsidy, either increase exports or reduce imports."[84] In other words, a contracting party may have to report a subsidy which it grants or maintains even if the actual size of its imports for a given year might have been higher than that for a preceding year while keeping itself below the amount that would have been possible in the absence of the subsidy. The same is true to the case of exports. What matters is not the actual size of the import or the export, but rather its relative position *vis-à-vis* the amount that could have been imported or exported in the absence of the practice.

The same Panel considered the question whether subsidies financed by a non-governmental levy were notifiable under Article XVI and concluded that "the question of notifying levy/subsidy arrangements depends upon the source of the funds" and governments should notify those "schemes affecting imports or exports which are dependent for their enforcement on some form of government action".[85] This is a conclusion that would also shed some additional light on the problem of definition discussed earlier.

This discussion shows that the conditions for notification are somewhat

---

[82] GATT, *Review Pursuant to Article XVI:5, supra* n. 76, p.188, para. 10.

[83] *GATT Analytical Index, supra* n. 67, p. 465.

[84] GATT, *Review Pursuant to Article XVI: 5, supra* n. 76, p. 188, para. 10.

[85] Ibid. para. 12.

difficult to apply in practice. One thing is fairly clear, though – for a subsidy to be notifiable, it must have some impact on the flow of international trade. Its cross-border impact must be felt by affecting the flow of imports or exports, or both. A subsidy whose impact is limited to the territory of the subsidizing party is outside the scope of the notification obligation. The specific case of domestic subsidies may be a good example here. They are notifiable only in as long as they contribute to increase exports[86] or decrease imports, which may not necessarily be the case.[87] It is not difficult to find a case which goes against the aforementioned assumption that "a subsidy which provides an incentive to increased production will, in the absence of offsetting measures, e.g. a consumption subsidy, either increase exports or reduce imports".[88] The conclusion of the GATT Panel on Subsidies in this connection is illuminating once more. Recognizing that there are cases where determination of the existence or otherwise of subsidies may be more difficult, the panel concluded that the circumstances of each case should be examined, and, "in order to permit such an examination, the CONTRACTING PARTIES should consider asking contracting parties to notify all cases of *price support*, regardless of the precise method used".[89] It is thus possible to conclude that most, albeit by no means all, domestic subsidies are notifiable under Article XVI.

9.3.1.3 The Obligation to Discuss the "Possibility of Limiting the Subsidization"

The second sentence of Article XVI provided that in any case in which "*it is determined* that serious prejudice to the interests of any other contracting party is caused or threatened by any such subsidization, the contracting party granting the subsidy shall, upon request, *discuss* with the other contracting party or parties concerned, or with the CONTRACTING PARTIES, the *possibility of limiting the subsidization.*"[90] This point concerns the very essence of the obligations created by the provision by way of constraining the practice of subsidies. But, two important questions need to be asked at this point: (1) who determines on the existence or otherwise of serious prejudice? and (2) does it create any meaningful legal obligation?

To start with the first, it appears that a determination of the existence of serious prejudice or a threat thereof suffered by a party due to the subsidy practice of another party is a necessary condition for the former to request for discussion about the possibility of limiting the subsidization. But Article XVI of the General

---

[86] Note that all subsidies which are granted regardless of the export of the products benefiting therefrom are here referred to as domestic subsidies. As such, it is possible that a subsidy may contribute to the rise of exports without it necessarily being an export subsidy.

[87] Consider cases of decoupled income support, for example.

[88] GATT, *Review Pursuant to Article XVI:5, supra* n. 76, p. 191 (italics added). Imagine a situation where increased production of a certain product, stimulated by domestic subsidies, results in a price fall. Although the low income-elasticity of demand for most agricultural products may limit its practical significance, it is natural that falling prices are often followed by increased domestic demand. In such cases, neither the imports nor the exports may be affected.

[89] Ibid. p. 188, para 11 (italics added).

[90] Article XVI, second sentence (italics added).

Agreement does not directly answer the question of determination. It simply talks, in a passive form, about determination as a condition for requesting discussion. We have also seen that the Havana Charter closed this loophole by leaving the issue of determination of injury to the discretion of the complaining party: "In any case in which *a Member considers* that serious prejudice to its interests is caused or threatened by any such subsidization, the Member granting the subsidy shall, upon request, discuss with the other Member or Members concerned, or with the Organization, the possibility of limiting the subsidization."[91]

GATT CONTRACTING PARTIES agreed, in a subsequent decision, that the difference between GATT Article XVI and Havana Charter Article 25 was not of a substantive nature.[92] At the same time, they agreed that "[t]he intent of the last sentence of Article XVI of the General Agreement is that consultation shall proceed upon the request of a contracting party *when it considers* that prejudice is caused or threatened and would not require a prior international determination."[93] This understanding thus resolves what would have been a difficult problem for the practical operation of the already weak obligations of this provision.

This takes us back to the more important question of whether there is any meaningful obligation on subsidizing parties to modify their subsidies. According to the second sentence of Article XVI, while a contracting party affected or threatened by the subsidy of another party has the right to request the subsidizing party to "discuss ... the possibility of limiting the subsidization", the latter bears the obligation to comply with the request. The problem, however, is whether this obligation to discuss the possibility of limiting the subsidization imposes on the subsidizing party the obligation to actually limit the practice. A brief look at some of the GATT cases may show the practical problems involved and the solutions adopted.

Perhaps the classic examples in this respect are the two parallel *EC Sugar* cases where a finding was reached that the Community system constituted both "serious prejudice" as well as "threat of serious prejudice" to the interests of the complainants within the terms of Article XVI:1, and the CONTRACTING PARTIES requested the EC to discuss with them the possibility of limiting the subsidization. The bone of contention then turned out to be as to what were the concrete rights and the concrete obligations of the parties to the dispute. The EC argued that its only obligation under Article XVI:1 was "to discuss the possibility of limiting the subsidization", while Australia reacted that "the intention of the final sentence of paragraph 1 of Article XVI was ... to obtain a statement from the subsidizing contracting party of what action it intended to take to remove the serious prejudice or the threat of prejudice."[94]

---

[91] Article 25 of the Havana Charter (italics added).

[92] See *GATT Analytical Index, supra* n. 67, p. 466.

[93] Ibid., p. 451 (italics added).

[94] GATT, *European Communities Refunds on Exports of Sugar: Article XVI:1 Discussions, Report to the Council*, adopted on 10 March, 1981, *BISD* 28S/ 82-83. The most pertinent part of the argument of the Australian representative was the following: "the wording of Paragraph 1 of Article XVI was essentially the same as in the United States (1945) Draft (Article 25) and in the Havana Charter. In the discussions

Although no agreement was reached over this specific point in those discussions, it is worth pointing out that while the EC was defending its position on the basis of the literal meaning of the words of the paragraph, the complainants were basing their claims on the legislative history and intent of those words. The clear text of the provision suggests the conclusion that the obligation to "discuss the possibility of limiting the subsidization" does not imply the obligation to actually limit the subsidization.[95] It is therefore perfectly lawful to grant subsidies to the prejudice of other contracting parties and then decline to take corrective measures even after the injurious nature of the practice has been determined, no matter by who.[96]

To sum up, neither the obligation to notify nor that to discuss has any substance by way of restricting the policy-making power of the contracting parties. Even when it is determined that a duly notified subsidy granted by one party has threatened or already caused serious prejudice to the interests of another party, the subsidizing party arguably satisfies its obligation by mere attendance and participation in discussions having the object of limiting the subsidization. The most that can emanate out of the phrase "possibility of limiting the subsidization" attached to this obligation may not go beyond some form of good faith requirement during the negotiations. As a matter of fact, "there is no record of any country ever having limited a subsidizing practice as a result of consultations under Article XVI, paragraph 1."[97]

---

cont.

on the wording at the First Session of the Preparatory Committee of the United Nations Conference on Trade and Employment ('London Report' October-November 1946 – EPCT/1 = 34) it is recorded that:

"(a) In general, the intention of Article 25 of the United States draft charter is to give members, whose interests are prejudiced by subsidization, the right to full international consideration of their case, to oblige subsidizing members to participate in such consideration and to provide for limiting subsidization so that its prejudicial effects may be reduced";

...

"(d) The word 'limiting' in the last sentence of paragraph (1) of the revision is used in a broad sense to indicate maintaining the subsidy at as low a level as possible, and the gradual reduction in subsidization over a period of time where this is appropriate."

Although the Australian position is based on the legislative history of the provision and supported by many other GATT contracting parties apart from Brazil, including, Cuba, the Dominican Republic, Argentina, Colombia, and Nicaragua, the wording of Article XVI:1 appears to be too clear to allow any such an interpretation as would oblige the EC to undertake any specific measures to limit the subsidization. The end result also seems to be a further confirmation of this view – despite a series of consultations to induce the EC to limit the subsidy, "after two working parties and nine Council meetings over a two-year period, the effort was abandoned with a bitter recognition that the subsidy had actually gotten worse since the complaint was filed". Hudec (1993) *supra* n. 45, p. 134. For different views on this issue, see McGovern, (1986) *supra* n. 71, pp. 331 et seq.

95 See Hudec (1993) *supra* n. 45, p. 134.

96 For more on this, see the 1961 report of the GATT Panel on Subsidies, *supra* n. 5, para. 21. This panel observed that the prevailing widespread use of subsidies "may contribute to the reluctance of certain governments to initiate consultations regarding subsidies since they themselves employ similar measures." Ibid., para. 22.

97 Rivers and Greenwald (1979), *supra* n. 3, pp. 1459–1460.

9.3.1.4 Remedies Available to Affected Parties

In the two *EC Sugar* cases just discussed, the failure of the Community to take measures limiting the subsidization so that the already suffered prejudice as well as the threat thereof might be overcome inevitably raises the question of whether the whole exercise of determination and the consequent discussion serve any understandable rationale. The issue is as to what possible remedies are available to a party prejudiced or threatened by the subsidy of another party when that other party refuses to limit the prejudicial subsidy in the future.

The General Agreement as it then stood contemplated two possible remedies – unilateral countervailing measures by the affected party under Article VI and multilateral action through the CONTRACTING PARTIES under Articles XXII and XXIII. A brief look at the dispute settlement system of the GATT as related to the specific case of domestic subsidies (and particularly of the doctrine of "*prima facie* nullification or impairment") is important at this point. This will be followed by a discussion of the unilateral alternative of countervailing duties, again to the extent they are related to cases of domestic subsidies – a not-so-effective alternative in this particular context.

9.3.1.4.1 Domestic Subsidies and the Doctrine of *prima facie* Nullification or Impairment under Article XXIII

The dispute settlement system of the General Agreement stands on two pillars – the consultation provision of Article XXII and the nullification or impairment provision of Article XXIII. While a contracting party has the right to initiate consultations under Article XXII – bilaterally or with the involvement of the CONTRACTING PARTIES – the party to whom the request for consultations has been addressed bears the corresponding obligation to "accord sympathetic consideration to" and "afford adequate opportunity for consultation".[98] The subject of the requested consultation may concern "any matter affecting the operation of this Agreement". If no satisfactory solution has been found through the bilateral consultations of paragraph 1, the dissatisfied party has the additional right to request the CONTRACTING PARTIES to consult with the other party.[99]

It is, however, Article XXIII which constitutes the bedrock of the entire disputes system of the GATT. Paragraph 1 of this Article provides that a contracting party, which considers that any benefit accruing to it "directly or indirectly" under the General Agreement is being "nullified or impaired" or that the attainment of any objective of the Agreement is being impeded, may make "written representations or proposals" to the concerned contracting party.[100] Three alternative situations have been enumerated as possible factors causing nullification or impairment, or as impeding the attainment of the objective of the Agreement: (a) failure of another contracting party to carry out its obligations under the Agreement, (leading to

---

[98] Article XXII:1 of the General Agreement.
[99] Article XXII:2 of the General Agreement.
[100] Article XXIII:1 of the General Agreement.

"violation complaints") or (b) the application by another contracting party of any measure, whether or not it conflicts with the provisions of this Agreement, (leading to "non-violation complaints") or (c) the existence of any other situation, (leading to "situation complaints").[101]

Once again, this first paragraph of Article XXIII, just like the first paragraph of Article XXII, is an option for a bilateral and friendly settlement of disputes, the only difference being that the Article XXIII:1 alternative is more formal than its counterpart in the preceding Article.[102] Although the word "consultation" is nowhere mentioned under Article XXIII:1, the essence is in no way different from this method of dispute management. Furthermore, the obligation imposed upon the other party in both cases is to "give sympathetic consideration" to the concerns of the requesting party.

The second paragraph of Article XXIII in particular is the core of the multilateral dispute settlement system of the GATT. Accordingly, a party may refer a case to the CONTRACTING PARTIES in either of two conditions: if no satisfactory adjustment is effected "within a reasonable time", or if the difficulty is caused by "the existence of any other situation" as stated under paragraph 1(c) of this same Article. This means that, while a party relying on the two situations of paragraph 1(a) and (b) has to first wait for the passage of "reasonable time" – whatever this apparently vague standard might mean – before referring the matter to the attention of the CONTRACTING PARTIES, one who relies on the third condition may do so at any time regardless of this condition.[103] In any event, the CONTRACTING PARTIES, when a case is referred to them, have the power – and, of course, the responsibility – to investigate the case and give a recommendation or ruling which they may deem appropriate under the circumstances. This power may go to the extent that, if they consider the circumstances as "serious enough to justify such action, they may authorize a contracting party or parties to suspend the application to any other contracting party or parties of such concessions or other obligations under this Agreement as they determine to be appropriate in the circumstances".[104]

Without going to the details, the following few points need to be mentioned for purposes of this section. First of all, the rules of the General Agreement on dispute resolution were not sufficiently elaborate as to create a clear guideline to follow in practice. The existing dispute settlement system of the GATT is the result rather of a case-by-case and pragmatic approach of the CONTRACTING PARTIES in the course of

---

[101] Ibid. On the designations in brackets, see, *inter alia*, E-U. Petersmann, *The GATT/WTO Dispute Settlement System: International Law, International Organizations and Dispute Settlement* (Kluwer 1997), pp. 70–74.

[102] Note, for instance, that Article XXIII:1 requires formal written representations while Article XXII does not.

[103] Note, however, that the alternative of *situation complaints* has fallen into virtual disuse. As observed, "the very rare references in GATT dispute settlement practice to Article XXIII:1 (c) have never led to a dispute settlement ruling on situation complaints". Petersmann (1997) *supra* n. 101, p. 173. Petersmann even supports the idea that it be formally deleted from the law. Ibid., p. 176.

[104] Article XXIII:2 of the General Agreement.

its more than half-a-century of operation. Secondly, unlike other areas of general public international law, the practical difference between violation of a rule of the General Agreement and its strict observance is not very clear-cut. These points deserve further elaboration here.

Theoretically speaking, it is possible for a contracting party to suffer no consequences from a clear violation of a rule of the General Agreement, while it is also equally possible that a party which is in full compliance with its GATT obligations may suffer certain "sanctions". In other words, finding of violation by a contracting party of its obligations under the General Agreement is not a sufficient condition for a complainant to get what it seeks under Article XXIII. Neither is the proof of compliance by a defending party an absolute protection against GATT sanctions. Taking the rules as they are, therefore, there is no any important difference in position between a party which has clearly failed to carry out its obligations under the General Agreement and one which has complied with its obligations thereunder. What matters is rather the question of whether the challenged act of a contracting party, regardless of its consistency with the General Agreement, results in a "nullification or impairment" of the benefits accruing to the complainant. It is on that basis that we often see in the literature a reference to "violation nullification or impairment" and "non-violation nullification or impairment".

If we take the case of domestic subsidies, for example, the fact that they have not been outlawed by the General Agreement does not as such matter as regards the Article XXIII remedies available to a party adversely affected by them. Legal or otherwise, the important question for purposes of Article XXIII would be as to whether the subsidy under dispute has "nullified or impaired" the benefits accruing to a contracting party "directly or indirectly" under the General Agreement – the case of a non-violation nullification or impairment. Theoretically speaking, therefore, the legality or otherwise of an act in terms of the General Agreement does not have much serious impact on the remedies available to a contracting party affected by it.[105]

The practice has, however, changed this scenario. It was early in its history that GATT developed what is called the doctrine of *prima facie* nullification or impairment.[106] According to this doctrine, the mere proof of the existence of certain specific circumstances by a complaining party – a very important one being violation of an obligation of the General Agreement on the part of the defendant – brings the presumption of "nullification or impairment" in favour of that complainant. This operational principle has since been growing in importance until it was formally stated in the *Agreed Description of the Customary Practice of the GATT in the Field of Dispute Settlement* annexed to the 1979 Dispute Settlement Understanding of the Tokyo Round (hereafter the Agreed Description) in the following words: "In cases where there is an infringement of the obligations assumed under the General

[105] p. 219.
[106] See Jackson (1977) *supra* n. 16, p. 428.

Agreement, the action is considered *prima facie* to constitute a case of nullification or impairment".[107]

The immediate consequence of such a presumption is reflected in the procedure to be followed in a case. The complainant, who would normally bear the onus to prove the existence of a nullification or impairment, benefits from the presumption that once a violation is demonstrated, there is a *prima facie* nullification or impairment to its interests. Consequently, the burden of proof immediately changes its form and shifts onto the defendant which, in this case, has to prove that the challenged act, although a violation of the General Agreement, does not cause any nullification or impairment to the benefits accruing to the complainant. In other words, a presumption develops that "a breach of the rules has an adverse impact on other contracting parties, and in such cases, it is up to the contracting parties against whom the complaint has been brought to rebut the charge".[108] What is more, in the words of one panel, this operational principle has "in practice operated as an irrefutable presumption".[109] The doctrine of *prima facie* nullification or impairment

---

[107] See GATT, *BISD* 26S/216; see also *GATT Analytical Index, supra* n. 67, p. 635. This doctrine has also been retained by the Dispute Settlement Understanding of the Uruguay Round, Article 3.8 of which provides as follows: "In cases where there is an infringement of the obligations assumed under a covered agreement, the action is considered *prima facie* to constitute a case of nullification or impairment. This means that there is normally a presumption that a breach of the rules has an adverse impact on other Members parties to that covered agreement, and in such cases, it shall be up to the Member against whom the complaint has been brought to rebut the charge."

[108] *Agreed Description of the Customary Practice of the GATT in the Field of Dispute Settlement (Article XXIII)*, annexed to the 1979 Dispute Settlement Understanding, *BISD* 26S/216.

[109] *United States – Taxes on Petroleum and Certain Imported Substances:* report of the panel (L/6175, *BISD* 34S/136) adopted on 17 June 1987, (often known as the *Superfund* case, a term used hereafter as well) para. 5.1.7. The question addressed by the panel in this case was whether the presumption that a measure inconsistent with the General Agreement causes a nullification or impairment of benefits accruing under that Agreement is an absolute or a rebuttable presumption and, if rebuttable, whether a demonstration that a measure inconsistent with Article III:2, first sentence, has no or insignificant effects on trade is a sufficient rebuttal. See Ibid., para. 5.1.3. The panel invoked paragraphs 4 and 5 of the Annex to the 1979 Understanding on dispute settlement to support the conclusion that "the impact of a measure inconsistent with the General Agreement is not relevant for a determination of nullification or impairment by the CONTRACTING PARTIES." See Ibid., para. 5.1.5. The panel also examined the available "precedent" on the subject and noted that "such claims had been made in a number of cases but that *there was no case in the history of the GATT in which a contracting party had successfully rebutted the presumption that a measure infringing obligations causes nullification and impairment.*" See Ibid., para. 5.1.6 (italics added). The Panel then concluded that, "while the CONTRACTING PARTIES had not explicitly decided whether the presumption that illegal measures cause nullification or impairment could be rebutted, *the presumption had in practice operated as an irrefutable presumption.*" See Ibid., para. 5.1.7 (italics added). The Panel further examined "whether – even assuming that the presumption could be regarded as rebuttable in the present case – a demonstration that the trade effects of the tax differential were insignificant would constitute a proof that the benefits accruing to Canada, the EEC and Mexico under Article III:2, first sentence, had not been nullified or impaired." See Ibid., para. 5.1.8. The conclusion was the following: "A demonstration that a measure inconsistent with Article III:2, first sentence, has no or insignificant effects would therefore in the view of the Panel not be a sufficient demonstration that the benefits accruing under that provision had not been nullified or impaired even if such a rebuttal were in principle permitted." Ibid. See also Petersmann (1997) *supra* n. 101, pp. 84 et seq.

[110] Another equally important difference pertains to the type of available remedies. Accordingly, while, in

is therefore an important development in that it introduced a meaningful distinction between violation of the General Agreement and adherence to it.[110]

It is here that the fact of the GATT-legality of the use of domestic subsidies makes an important difference, for, as a measure consistent with countries' obligations under the General Agreement, any party challenging such an act would have to prove the existence of nullification or impairment in the sense of Article XXIII. In the words of the *Agreed Description*, 'If a contracting party bringing an Article XXIII case claims that measures which do not conflict with the provisions of the General Agreement have nullified or impaired benefits accruing to it under the General Agreement, it would be called upon to provide a detailed justification."[111] However, it is noteworthy that one of the few other circumstances under which the doctrine of *prima facie* nullification or impairment has been applied concerned that of domestic subsidies.[112] The foundation for this principle was laid down by the *Australian Ammonium Sulphate* case, which was also the first GATT case containing a finding on the non-violation nullification or impairment provision of Article XXIII.1(b).[113]

9.3.1.4.1.1 THE ROLE OF THE *AUSTRALIAN AMMONIUM SULPHATE* CASE

In what may appear to be a paradoxical development, the doctrine was first used in this connection to challenge the consequences of a decision (by Australia) to discontinue subsidization of a product (nitrate of soda – a fertilizer mainly imported from Chile) while continuing the subsidies on a competing product (ammonium

---

cont.

violation cases, "the first objective of the CONTRACTING PARTIES is usually to secure the withdrawal of the measures concerned if these are found to be inconsistent with the General Agreement", in non-violation nullification or impairment cases, there is "nothing in Article XXIII which would empower the CONTRACTING PARTIES to require a contracting party to withdraw" such measures. *GATT Analytical Index supra*, n. 67, pp. 677 and 681, respectively. See also Petersmann (1997) *supra* n. 101, pp. 70–84.

111 *Agreed Description*, *supra* n. 108, para. 5.

112 See also Jackson (1977) *supra* n. 16, p. 428. The panel in *Japan – Film* noted that the remedy in Article XXIII:1(b) "should be approached with caution and should remain an exceptional remedy". (*Japan – Measures Affecting Consumer Photographic Film and Paper*, report of the panel, (WT/DS44/R) adopted on 22 April 1998, para. 10.37.) The panel pointed out that there had been only eight cases in which panels or working parties had substantively considered Article XXIII:1(b) claims. From this, the panel deduced that "both the GATT contracting parties and WTO Members have approached this remedy with caution and, indeed, have treated it as an exceptional instrument of dispute settlement .... The reason for this caution is straightforward. Members negotiate the rules that they agree to follow and only exceptionally would expect to be challenged for actions not in contravention of those rules." (Ibid. para. 10.36.) This cautious approach to the application of Article XXIII:1(b) has also been expressly endorsed by the Appellate Body in the *Asbestos* report. See *European Communities – Measures Affecting Asbestos and Asbestos-Containing Products* report of the Appellate Body (WT/DS135/AB/R) adopted on 5 April 2001, para. 186.

113 The first case in which the non-violation nullification or impairment provisions of Article XXIII.1(b) were invoked was the US complaint against "Cuban Import Restrictions on Textiles" but the first report with a finding on this provision was *Australia Ammonium Sulphate*. See *GATT Analytical Index*, *supra* n. 67, p. 657.

sulphate – which was both produced domestically as well as imported).[114] During prior GATT tariff negotiations when Australia granted a duty-free access to the importation of nitrate of soda, both types of fertilizers had been benefiting from the subsidy. Consequently, when, on 1 July 1949, Australia decided to remove the subsidy from nitrate of soda, Chile complained that the removal of the subsidy on one, while keeping the same on the other, of the two competing products resulted in a nullification or impairment of a benefit accruing to it under the General Agreement in the sense of Article XXIII.[115] The Working Party established to report on the case concluded that, although the Australian measure did not conflict with the provisions of the General Agreement,[116] there was a "*prima facie* case that the value of a concession granted to Chile had been impaired".[117] The Working Party reasoned as follows:

> "It was agreed that such impairment would exist if the action of the Australian Government which resulted in upsetting the competitive relationship between sodium nitrate and ammonium sulphate *could not reasonably have been anticipated* by the Chilean Government, taking into consideration all pertinent circumstances and the provisions of the General Agreement, at the time it negotiated for the duty-free binding on sodium nitrate. ... [T]he Government of Chile had reason to assume, during these negotiations, that the war-time fertilizer subsidy would not be removed from sodium nitrate before it was removed from ammonium sulphate."[118]

Accordingly, the removal of a subsidy on a product whose tariffs are bound, while keeping the subsidy on its competing product, which measure had the effect of increasing the competitiveness of the latter so that imports of the former would be curtailed, was taken to constitute *prima facie* nullification or impairment in the sense of Article XXIII of the General Agreement during the very first two years of GATT's existence. This shows that the problems emanating from the lax system of rules on domestic subsidies, leading to their use in a manner circumventory of the

[114] The paradox lies in the fact that while the purpose of the General Agreement is to liberalize international trade from all sorts of restrictive national measures, including the use of subsidies, this case was brought challenging a measure which removed a subsidy, which of course resulted in changing the balance of concessions between the parties to the dispute. As a show of concern to this aspect of the report, the Working Party stated that in reaching this conclusion it "considered that the removal of a subsidy, in itself, would not normally result in nullification or impairment. In the case under consideration, the inequality created and the treatment that Chile could reasonably have expected at the time of the negotiation, after taking into consideration all pertinent circumstances, including the circumstances mentioned above, and the provisions of the General Agreement, were important elements in the working party's conclusion." *Australia Ammonium Sulphate, supra* n. 75, para. 12. As indicated in the report, the "declared intention" of the subsidy was "to give financial aid ... to the producers of certain crops." Ibid., para. 15. As such, this may be taken as a case of agricultural domestic subsidy.

[115] Ibid., para. 12.

[116] Ibid., para. 11; see also para. 13.

[117] Ibid.

[118] Ibid., para 12.

benefits of tariff concessions, have been appreciated and taken care of since the early days of the GATT. In this particular case, the dispute arose as a result of a measure which, taken independently, would seem to be not only a GATT-consistent move, but one that furthers the objectives of the General Agreement – a reduction in subsidization is a step forward in the process of liberalization of international trade. The neutral position taken by the Working Party in its final recommendation to the CONTRACTING PARTIES that the Australian Government consider "means to remove any competitive inequality between nitrate of soda and sulphate of ammonia"[119] and its observation that this "would not necessarily involve the restoration of the previous method of subsidization"[120] imply that maintenance of the balance of concessions and observance of the basic principles of the system weigh more than adherence to the overall objectives of the General Agreement.[121] What is more, the analyses and conclusion of this Working Party report have also served as important precedent for subsequent panels in their interpretation and application of the non-violation nullification or impairment provision of Article XXIII of the General Agreement.

Also noteworthy is that the Working Party did not limit itself to the case at its hand; it went out of its way to introduce a related, but hypothetical, situation and arrived at a questionable conclusion, to say the least:

> "The situation in the case is different from that which would have arisen from the granting of a new subsidy on one of two competing products. In such a case, given the freedom under the General Agreement of the Australian Government to impose subsidies and to select the products on which a subsidy would be introduced, it would be more difficult to say that the Chilean Government had reasonably relied on the continuation of the same treatment for the two products."[122]

If one could "reasonably" assume that a subsidy given to its products by a foreign government, despite its trade- and production-distorting nature, would remain applicable, it is difficult to understand why one cannot assume, with the same degree of reasonableness, the continuation of the same treatment for the two competing products in the absence of subsidies. What primarily matters in both cases should be the unanticipated nature of the new measure and the resulting disturbance of the balance of concessions – or, in the words of the report, the "upsetting" of the

---

[119] Ibid., para 17. Obviously, this could be done in one of two ways: by removing the subsidy from ammonium sulphate as well (which would further the objectives of the General Agreement) or by reintroducing the subsidy for that of nitrate of soda (one which goes against the objectives of the General Agreement).

[120] Ibid., para 14 (italics added).

[121] As the *Superfund* panel rightly observed, "it is conceivable that a tax consistent with the national treatment principle (for instance, a high but non-discriminatory excise tax) has a more severe impact on the exports of other contracting parties than a tax that violates that principle (for instance a very low but discriminatory tax)." The *Superfund* panel report, *supra* n. 109, para. 5.1.9.

[122] *Australia Ammonium Sulphate*, *supra* n. 75, para. 12.

competitive relationship – regardless of whether that measure concerns the cessation of a pre-existing subsidy or an introduction of a new one on either of two competing products. Furthermore, it was exactly this hypothetical situation, raised and rejected by the Working Party as "more difficult", which was soon authoritatively established on the very principle of "reasonable anticipation" or "reasonable expectation" developed by this same case. After all, using the theories of reasonable expectation and the like to discourage further subsidization is not only less difficult and sounder, but also more reasonable and better-tuned with the general spirit of the entire multilateral trading system.

As will be discussed in greater detail later on, therefore, it was the reasoning of the *Australia Ammonium Sulphate* case which laid the ground for the use of the doctrine of reasonable expectations to discourage countries from resorting to the introduction of new or additional subsidies on competing products. The *Australia Ammonium Sulphate* case was thus only the first, but important, step in the evolution of an important interpretative understanding which was to be formally adopted by CONTRACTING PARTIES in the 1954–55 Review Session. From this, one may safely conclude that, at least for those products whose tariffs are bound under Article II of the General Agreement and for purposes of Article XXIII, the lawfulness of domestic subsidies was of little practical importance. It is also worth reminding here that this state of the law applied, in principle, to all sorts of products, whether agricultural or otherwise.

However, the practice is somewhat different once again. The doctrine of *prima facie* nullification or impairment discussed so far applies only to those products on which "a tariff-limiting commitment has been agreed to". But, as opposed to the tariff-limiting commitments on industrial products, those on agricultural products have been fewer in number and much more limited in depth.[123] This means that, as regards those agricultural products whose tariffs remained unbound, the use of domestic subsidies in a manner that circumvents the effect of tariff bindings is impossible – the existence of bound tariffs is a necessary precondition for their circumvention. This is thus the other area of practical distinction in the law of subsidies even long before the 1955 review session formally introduced distinct regimes for export subsidies in general, on the one hand, and agricultural export subsidies, on the other.

9.3.1.4.2 Countervailing Duties as Remedial Measures

Given the legitimacy of subsidies under the 1947 version of the General Agreement, it is tempting to presume that it does not provide for any form of direct sanction that may be applied against parties who employ subsidies for their own purposes – for, it logically follows that there appears to be no room for sanctions in the absence of a

[123] See, *inter alia*, Jackson (1977) *supra* n. 16, p. 982; Stewart (1993) *supra* n. 29, p. 141.

legal obligation that can be violated.[124] We have seen, however, that this logic does not work every time; at least not with the General Agreement.

Obviously, the lawfulness of a subsidy practice does not necessarily mean that its use by a party is without harm to the legitimate interests of others. Legality is a matter for the technicalities of the law while harm is a matter of fact.[125] It is in order to safeguard these interests that the General Agreement recognizes the use of unilateral countervailing duties by the affected parties in addition to the right they have under the multilateral alternative of non-violation nullification or impairment. In this way the General Agreement allows "retaliatory" measures against practices that are otherwise lawful; it allows the use of countervailing duties against a party that has exercised its lawful right to use subsidies. This is a clear case of a unilateral sanction, although indirect, applicable without breach of a legal obligation. Countervailing duties are therefore one of only few cases where the GATT legal system deviated from its object of limiting "the customary law right of unilateral reprisals"[126] in international economic relations.[127]

A countervailing duty has been defined as "a special duty levied for the purpose of offsetting any bounty or subsidy bestowed, directly or indirectly, upon the manufacture, production or export of any merchandise".[128] A countervailing duty is, therefore, first and foremost, a duty; no countervailing measures can be taken in any other form, such as a quantitative restriction, an import quota, or whatever. A proposal intended to permit the use of quantitative restrictions under certain circumstances so as to offset the adverse effects of subsidies was rejected by the GATT *Working Party on Other Barriers to Trade* during its 1954–55 review session.[129]

Secondly, a countervailing duty, being a special duty levied in addition to the

---

[124] As Petersmann writes, "[w]hile the international legal responsibility for illegal acts or omissions imputable to a State or international organization is well recognized in State practice and in international arbitral awards and judicial decisions, the notion of 'international liability for injurious consequences arising out of acts not prohibited by international law' continues to be controversial in state practice and legal doctrine ...." E-U. Petersmann, "Violation-Complaints and Non-Violation Complaints in Public International Trade Law" 34 *German Yearbook of International Law* (1991), p. 175. He then refers to an ILC draft and observes that "the ILC decided to limit its draft articles on State responsibility to the responsibility of States for internationally wrongful acts." Ibid. See also Petersmann (1997) *supra* n. 101, p. 135.

[125] Indeed, as the *Reconvened Oilseeds Panel Report* pointed out, "even if subsidies are permitted under the General Agreement they are nevertheless recognized as being capable of distorting international trade and impairing the benefits accruing to contracting parties under the General Agreement in unacceptable ways." *Reconvened Oilseeds Panel Report, supra* n. 2, para. 77.

[126] Petersmann (1997) *supra* n. 101, p. 82.

[127] Anti-dumping duties under Article VI and (to a certain extent) safeguard measures in emergency situations under the last sentence of Article XIX:2 are the other important exceptions to GATT's restriction on the use of unilateral measures as a means of dealing with problems in international economic relations.

[128] GATT Article VI:3.

[129] GATT, *GATT Working Party Report on Other Barriers to Trade* (L/334 and Addendum, *BISD* 3S/226) adopted on 3 March 1955. See also Jackson (1969) *supra* n. 44, p. 412.

already bound duty levels,[130] always stands in need of justification; for, otherwise, any such addition would violate the party's obligations under the Schedules of Concessions of Article II.[131] Besides, since the countervailing duties, by definition, are imposed on the imports only of one or a small number of countries – those giving the concerned subsidies – it would also violate the MFN principle of Article I. In order to get this legitimacy, the party taking this measure has to determine that (i) a subsidy has been granted, and (ii) the subsidy has caused or threatened material injury[132] to an established domestic industry or that it has materially retarded the establishment of a new one.[133] These are cumulative requirements that must be met in their togetherness for the additional duty to be lawful.

Once these requirements are met and a countervailing duty legalized, the provision goes a step further and sets a maximum limit on the permissible duty level so as to minimize the likelihood of its abuse at the implementation stage. Accordingly, it is mandated that no countervailing duty may be levied in excess of an amount equal to the estimated bounty or subsidy determined to have been granted by the other party. The rationale behind countervailing duties being to counterbalance the "unfair" advantage acquired by the beneficiary of the subsidy, it follows that it be limited to the amount of the benefit obtained by the beneficiary. This serves to reduce the well-founded concern that countervailing measures, if left uncapped, might serve as a convenient cover-up for hidden protectionist objectives.

Besides, it must be underlined that not only may the amount of the countervailing duty be less than the amount of the subsidy, it can also be excluded altogether; it is simply a discretion of the parties recognized by the GATT and not something that

---

130 Note that a countervailing duty makes sense only in the context of items whose tariff rates are bound under the GATT – for, otherwise, countries would be free to raise their tariffs, on a most-favoured-nation basis, at any time without undergoing the cumbersome procedural processes preceding the imposition of countervailing duties.

131 Note that Article II:2(b) provides that "nothing in this article shall prevent any contracting party from imposing at any time on the importation of any product any countervailing duty applied consistently with the provisions of Article VI".

132 The question of whether an injury is material or not is always a subjective and controversial one. What appears material to one party may very well appear insignificant, if not non-existent, to the other. In 1959 the *Group of Experts on Anti-Dumping and Countervailing Duties* interpreted the "material injury" concept using a no-less-ambiguous phrase, viz. "substantial injury", but admitted that "no precise definitions or set of rules could be given in respect of the injury concept". The Group believed that "a common standard ought to be adopted in applying this criterion and that decisions about injury should be taken by authorities at a high level." *GATT Analytical Index, supra* n. 67, p. 241. It seems however that such a high-level decision was not forthcoming for more than three decades.

133 This requirement was meant to cover cases where "an industry became economically unprofitable because of dumping". See *GATT Analytical Index, supra* n. 67, p. 243. Article 3(a) of the 1967 Anti-Dumping Code is also relevant in this respect: "In the case of retarding the development of a new industry in the country of importation, convincing evidence of the forthcoming establishment of an industry must be shown, for example that the plans for a new industry have reached a fairly advanced stage, a factory is being constructed or machinery has been ordered." See also Jackson (1969) *supra* n. 44, p. 419-420.

should always accompany the finding of a subsidy causing material injury. A countervailing duty is not a penalty for an unlawful act, but rather a remedial measure that may be employed for the purpose of offsetting the injurious consequences of what may well be a lawful practice. The finding of an injurious subsidy does not in itself make that subsidy unlawful. Rather, it simply entitles the actual or potential victim of the practice to a right of remedial action in the form of additional duties – it legalizes what would otherwise have been an illegal act.

Finally, paragraph 7 of Article VI constitutes some form of an "exception" to the "uniform" system of subsidies introduced in 1947.[134] It introduces a more relaxed rule concerning the determination of material injury within the meaning of Article VI:6 in the case of subsidies applied to primary commodities. Accordingly, a system for the stabilization of the domestic price or of the return to domestic producers of a primary commodity, independently of the movement of export prices, which results at times in the sale of the commodity for export at a price lower than the comparable price charged for the like commodity to buyers in the domestic market shall be presumed not to result in material injury within the meaning of paragraph 6 if the following two conditions are met: (1) it is determined that the system has also resulted in the sale of the commodity for export at a price higher than the comparable price charged for the like commodity to buyers in the domestic market, and (2) the system is so operated, either because of the effective regulation of production, or otherwise, as not to stimulate exports unduly or otherwise seriously prejudice the interests of other contracting parties. Given the stringency of the conditions set for such an exceptional treatment, it is hardly surprising that this provision has been "of limited practical importance"; in actual fact, "there is no record of Article VI:7 ever having been invoked in the GATT so far".[135]

But, a word of caution should be added at this point concerning domestic subsidies and the use of countervailing duties. Although what has been said so far about countervailing duties may apply to domestic subsidies just as it applies to that of export subsidies, there are some cases in which the effect of domestic subsidies may not allow the use of countervailing duties altogether. A simple example would be a case where a domestic subsidy, rather than helping to increase exports, helps to reduce imports against the interest of former suppliers – a case of "import substitution". In situations like this, the affected country cannot resort to countervailing duties because the subsidized products are not crossing into its domestic market – normally the only scenario for the imposition of the countervailing duties by the affected party. It thus follows that, although the General

---

[134] It may be remembered that the relevant provisions of GATT on subsidies have been taken to have introduced a "uniform" system because there has been no distinction in the treatment of the different forms of subsidies whether on the basis of their objectives (domestic or export), or their sector of application (industrial or agricultural).

[135] *GATT Analytical Index*, *supra* n. 67, p. 248. It has also added that this "may signify that the justification of its use by a contracting party has never been challenged during discussion with other contracting parties".

Agreement, in its 1947 version, did not as such distinguish between export and domestic subsidies, the very nature of the effect of certain domestic subsidies makes application of the rules in some cases impossible. In a similar scenario, the possibility of a waiver under paragraph 6(b) or the emergency situations of paragraph 6(c) of Article VI remain narrow exceptions for the use of countervailing duties on any imports (subsidized or otherwise) coming from a country for the purpose of offsetting "subsidization which causes or threatens material injury to an industry in the territory of another contracting party exporting the product concerned to the territory of the importing country."[136]

This said, there were important drawbacks in the countervailing duty law as it stood in 1947. Firstly, as a unilateral alternative the application of which is left to the national authorities, the chance of its abuse at the implementation stage remains a serious risk. No significant procedural restraints were set by Article VI. Secondly, because some contracting parties had countervailing duty laws well before 1947, even the few substantive conditions prescribed by Article VI, such as the injury test, were not applicable to some countries due to what is called the "grandfather clause" of the Protocol of Provisional Application (the PPA).[137] The most notorious one in this respect was the US. The absence of the injury requirement, coupled with the non-existence of any procedural hurdles on the initiation and conduct of countervailing duty investigations, enabled the US to continue as the leading user of countervailing measures against the interests of several contracting parties.

9.3.2 Domestic Subsidies and the Principle of National Treatment

The special feature of domestic subsidies as internal measures allowed for the benefit of domestic products as opposed to imported like or competing products also raises the question of whether or not they constitute a discrimination in violation of one of the most fundamental principles of the General Agreement – the principle of national treatment. The almost free hand allowed governments under Article XVI to provide support for their domestic products and producers, without extending the same to their foreign counterparts, brings the non-discrimination rules of the General Agreement in general and the principle of national treatment in particular into serious question: does this provision not frustrate the very objectives of the national treatment principle?

Article III is one of the most fundamental principles safeguarding the interests of

---

[136] Article VI.6(b) of the General Agreement.

[137] Note that according to para. 1(b) of the PPA, Governments undertook to apply "Part II of that Agreement to the fullest extent not inconsistent with existing legislation." As one of the important provisions falling under Part II of the General Agreement, the obligations of Article VI were applicable in contracting parties only to the extent that they were not predated by mandatory existing legislation. The purpose of this clause, often referred to as the "grandfather clause" is clear; it was intended "to enable, in 1947, governments to accept the obligations of Part II of the General Agreement without having to adjust their domestic legislation." *Norway – Restrictions on Imports of Apples and Pears* report of the panel (L/6474 *BISD* 36S/306) adopted on 22 June 1989, para. 5.5.

foreign competitors against discriminatory domestic policy measures, including some forms of domestic support measures. Paragraph 4 of this Article provides the essence of the national treatment requirement as related to our theme here in the following terms: "The products of the territory of any contracting party imported into the territory of any other contracting party shall be accorded treatment no less favourable than that accorded to like domestic products of national origin in respect of all laws, regulations and requirements affecting their internal sale, purchase, transportation, distribution or internal use."

Supplementing the most-favoured-nation treatment clause of Article I, the principle of national treatment is the other important safeguard against discrimination. While the former prescribes equality of treatment among imported products, the latter mandates this same requirement as between imported and domestic products. What is important in all this for present purposes is that the national treatment clause constrains countries' law-making powers even on matters that are entirely domestic in their territorial scope of application.

However, Article III specifically exempts a category of domestic producer subsidies from this limitation. In the words of Paragraph 8(b) of Article III, "[t]he provisions of this Article shall not prevent the payment of subsidies exclusively to domestic producers, including payments to domestic producers derived from the proceeds of internal taxes or charges applied consistently with the provisions of this Article and subsidies effected through governmental purchases of domestic products." Explaining on the need for this provision, the chairman of the working party which drafted the corresponding Havana Charter provision (Article 18.8(b)) has been recorded as saying that "[t]his provision had been added to the Geneva draft because it was felt that if subsidies were paid on domestic products and not on imported products, it might be construed that Members were not applying the 'national treatment' rule".[138]

Despite the central position of the national treatment requirement, therefore, countries were allowed to use different methods of domestic support involving payment of direct subsidies to their producers so as to influence the direction of their economic development. As will be seen more closely in a moment, this is a very carefully crafted exception. Its scope and substance have been a subject of controversy in several cases, some of which are discussed subsequently.

Three cases are particularly important in this regard – the 1958 *Italian Agricultural Machinery* case brought by the United Kingdom against Italy's system of preferential and more favourable loan terms to buyers of domestically produced agricultural machinery;[139] the 1988 *EC Oilseeds* case brought by the United States against the European Community's system of oilseeds producer and processor subsidies;[140] and the 1991 *US Malt Beverages* case brought by Canada against US

[138] *GATT Analytical Index*, *supra* n. 67, p. 194.

[139] *Italian Discrimination against Imported Agricultural Machinery*, report of the panel (L/833 *BISD* 7S/60) adopted on 23 October 1958.

[140] *European Economic Community – Payments and Subsidies Paid to Processors and Producers of Oilseeds and Related Animal-Feed Proteins*, report of the panel (L/6627 *BISD* 37S/86) adopted on 25 January 1990.

systems of federal and state taxation and other internal measures which operated to create advantages for domestic beer and wine over like imported products.[141] In all these cases, while the complainants argued that the challenged systems went against the national treatment obligations of Article III, the defendants countered on the grounds that their respective systems amounted to domestic or production subsidies consistent with Article XVI and excepted from the national treatment obligation under paragraph 8(b) of Article III. A closer look at the relevant aspects of these cases is in order at this point.

9.3.2.1.1 The 1958 *Italian Agricultural Machinery* Case

In 1957 the United Kingdom claimed that Italian law granting farmers special and more favourable loan terms for the purchase of domestically produced agricultural machinery violated Article III:4 and that the violation amounted to nullification and impairment under Article XXIII of the GATT.[142] Emphasizing that this Italian practice was a subsidy on purchase and not on production, the UK added that it "would not challenge the consistency with the General Agreement of subsidies which the Italian Government might wish to grant to domestic producers of tractors and other agricultural machinery in accordance with the terms of paragraph 8(b) of Article III."[143]

Italy argued, on the other hand, that the General Agreement was a trade agreement and did not apply to domestic subsidies of that kind. According to Italy, the text of paragraph 4 of Article III applied "only to such laws, regulations and requirements which were concerned with the actual conditions for sale, transportation, etc. of the commodity in question and should not be interpreted in an extensive way."[144] Moreover, Italy invoked paragraph 8(b) of Article III and argued that the intention of the drafters of the Agreement was to limit the scope of Article III to laws and regulations directly related to the conditions of sale, purchase, and the like.[145] Italy noted UK's recognition of its right to grant subsidies exclusively to domestic producers and argued that "it would not be logical to exclude this possibility in the

---

141 *United States–Measures Affecting Alcoholic and Malt Beverages*, report of the Panel (DS23/R *BISD* 39S/206) adopted on 19 June 1992.

142 See *Italian Agricultural Machinery*, *supra* n. 139, para. 1.

143 The UK argued as follows: "As the credit facilities provided under the Italian Law were not available to the purchasers of imported tractors and other agricultural machinery these products did not enjoy the equality of treatment which should be accorded to them. The fact that these credit facilities were reserved exclusively to the purchasers of Italian tractors and other agricultural machinery represented a discrimination and the operation of the Law involved an inconsistency with the provisions of Article III of the General Agreement which provides that laws, regulations and requirements affecting internal sale should not be applied to imported products so as to afford protection to domestic producers. The United Kingdom would not challenge the consistency with the General Agreement of subsidies which the Italian Government might wish to grant to domestic producers of tractors and other agricultural machinery in accordance with the terms of paragraph 8 (b) of Article III. However, in the case of the Italian Law the assistance by the State was not given to producers but to the purchasers of agricultural machinery, a case which is not covered by the provisions of paragraph 8 (b)." Ibid., para. 5.

144 Ibid., para. 6.

case of credit facilities which had a far less pronounced effect on the terms of competition."[146] Finally, it was the view of Italy that the text of Article III:4 "could not be construed in such a way as to prevent the Italian Government from taking the necessary measures to assist the economic development of the country and to improve the conditions of employment in Italy."[147]

These latter Italian arguments in particular are indicative of the political sensitivities involved when international rules of discipline try to go deeper into domestic economic and social policy matters.[148] The Panel ruled, however, that Article III:4 covered the case under discussion and that the provisions of Article III:8(b) allowing governments to grant production subsidies to domestic producers "would not be applicable to this particular case since the credit facilities provided under the Law were granted to the purchasers of agricultural machinery and could not be considered as subsidies accorded to the producers of agricultural machinery."[149]

The fact that the credit facilities were not provided directly to the producers of the machinery in question was the decisive element in this case. In sum, the exemption of production subsidies from the ambit of the national treatment principle applies only to the extent that the sole beneficiaries are the targeted producers themselves. It is worth stressing that the national treatment requirement is excluded only for direct subsidies made *exclusively for the benefit of producers* and fully applies to all other forms of support benefiting purchasers, consumers and the like.

9.3.2.1.2 The 1988 *EC Oilseeds* Case

This is one of the most contentious cases in the history of the multilateral trading system. It concerns the system of subsidies provided by the EC to processors and producers of oilseeds and related animal-feed proteins.[150] Only those aspects of the case which involve the relationship between domestic subsidies and the principle of national treatment under Article III are discussed in this section.[151]

Just like the UK in *Italian Agricultural Machinery*, the US invoked the national treatment provision of the General Agreement and complained that EC system of providing subsidies only to purchasers and processors of domestically grown oilseeds "accords oilseeds imported from the United States and other exporting countries less

---

[145] Ibid., para. 13.

[146] Ibid., para. 9.

[147] Ibid., para. 8.

[148] The panel also gave its attention to this matter and stated that "it was not the intention of the General Agreement to limit the right of a contracting party to adopt measures which appeared to it necessary to foster its economic development or to protect a domestic industry, provided that such measures were permitted by the terms of the General Agreement. The GATT offered a number of possibilities to achieve these purposes through tariff measures or otherwise." Ibid., para. 16.

[149] Ibid., para. 14.

[150] The products include rapeseed, sunflowerseed and soyabeans and related meals, peas, beans, lupines and skim milk powder. The main products in question were soyabeans, rapeseed, sunflowerseed and the meals derived from these oilseeds. See *EC Oilseeds*, *supra* n. 140, para. 7.

[151] For more on the *EC Oilseeds* dispute, see *infra* section 9.4.

favourable treatment than that accorded to like products of Community origin"[152] and thereby violated Article III:4 in particular. Likewise, the EC also followed Italy's line in the previous case and responded that those aids were to be considered as "production aids in terms of Article III:8(b) and that as such they could not constitute an infringement of Article III:4, or of Article III as a whole."[153]

Against the EC invocation of the Article III:8(b) exception, the US specifically cited the report of the panel in *Italian Agricultural Machinery* and counter-argued that that exception was not applicable in the present case "because the subsidies complained of were paid to purchasers and not to producers."[154] The US admitted that most of the economic benefits generated by the payments to processors accrued to the producers of oilseeds but also claimed that "the resulting incentive to produce oilseeds in the Community has impaired benefits it could reasonably expect to accrue to it under the tariff concessions for oilseeds."[155]

Naturally, while the US stressed the similarity of the two cases so that the present case would benefit from the "precedential" effect of the old one, the EC stressed the opposite. According to the EC, the "precedent" cited by the US was not applicable to the case at hand, *inter alia,* because "the credit facilities granted to purchasers of Italian agricultural machinery were not subsidies for the production of, or for ensuring, a certain price to producers of such machines, whereas the aim of the Community subsidies was to enable the producer to be paid a price higher than the market price by offsetting the extra cost resulting from such payments, ... [and] the real benefit of the subsidies paid went to the oilseed producer."[156] In response, the US contended that "the purchaser incentives in the Italian Tractor case and those in the present case were *identical* in terms of their effects on the market place in the sense that both incentives encouraged the purchase and consumption of domestic over imported products."[157]

The finding of the panel in this respect was also similar to the finding in *Italian Agricultural Machinery*. In both cases, the panels stressed that for a production subsidy to qualify as a subsidy exempt from the obligations under Article III, it must be granted to the producers of the products themselves.[158] While the fact that the credit facilities were not provided directly to the tractor producers played a decisive

[152] The US submitted that "such treatment was in clear violation of Article III, in particular of paragraph 4 of Article III, and that it constituted *prima facie* nullification or impairment of benefits accruing to the United States under the General Agreement." *EC Oilseeds*, *supra* n. 140, para. 36 (emphasis in original).

[153] According to the Community, "a different interpretation of Article III:8(b) would improperly limit the rights recognized by Article XVI as regards subsidies. In the view of the Community, Article III:8(b) was just one application of the general principle that the GATT disciplines with regard to subsidies, which are concerned with the effects of subsidies and not the legal beneficiaries thereof, are entirely laid down in Article XVI." Ibid., para. 37.

[154] Ibid., para. 38.

[155] See Ibid., para. 136.

[156] A third reason mentioned by the EC for the "distinguishable" nature of the *EC Oilseeds* case was that "the effects on the market in each case were very different and in no way comparable." Ibid., para. 39.

[157] Ibid., para. 38 (italics added).

[158] See *Italian Agricultural Machinery*, *supra* n. 139, para. 14, and *EC Oilseeds*, *supra* n. 140, para. 137.

role in *Italian Agricultural Machinery,* the *EC Oilseeds* panel found that "Article III:8(b) applies only to payments made *exclusively* to domestic producers and *it can reasonably be assumed that a payment not made directly to producers is not made 'exclusively' to them*".[159] The panel stressed furthermore that "if the economic benefits generated by the payments granted by the Community can at least partly be retained by the processors, [which the panel found they did[160]] ... the payments generate a benefit conditional upon the purchase of oilseeds of domestic origin inconsistently with Article III:4."[161] According to the panel, this happens in two situations: (a) the payments to the processors are based on prices determined by the Community authorities higher than the prices the processors actually pay to producers; and (b) the payments to the processors are based on import prices determined by the Community authorities lower than the prices that the processors would actually have to pay if they bought imported instead of domestic oilseeds.[162]

The Panel thus concluded that, the payments to processors of Community oilseeds are inconsistent with Article III:4[163] and that since these payments are not made exclusively to the producers, they do not qualify for the exemptions under Article III:8(b).[164] The standard panel recommendation in such GATT-violation cases, also followed in this particular case,[165] being to request the party to bring its regimes into conformity with the General Agreement, the Community abolished its old price-based system and introduced a mechanism by which producers alone would benefit from direct per hectare payments for any area of eligible land they devoted to oilseeds production.[166] Although other aspects of this contentious case continued to plague the system until the Blair House Accord laid it to rest in late 1992,[167]

---

[159] *EC Oilseeds*, *supra* n. 140, para. 137 (italics added).

[160] The Panel found in this respect that "subsidy payments made to processors can be greater than the difference between the price processors actually pay to producers and the price that processors would have to pay for imported oilseeds. Whether such over-compensation creating an incentive to purchase domestic rather than imported products takes place depends on the circumstances of the individual purchase. The Community Regulations are thus capable of giving rise to discrimination against imported products though they may not necessarily do so in the case of each individual purchase." Ibid., para. 140.

[161] Ibid., para. 137.

[162] Ibid., para. 137. In both cases, the panel found that "the Community Regulations do not ensure that the subsidy payments are based on prices that the subsidy recipients would actually have paid had they chosen to buy imported rather than domestic products. Ibid., paras. 138-139.

[163] Ibid., para. 141.

[164] Ibid., para. 137.

[165] Ibid., para. 155.

[166] See report of the *Reconvened Oilseeds Panel Report*, *supra* n. 2, para. 75. This Report was first considered by the Council at its meeting on 30 April 1992 and then, on 19 June 1992, the Council, without adopting the report, authorized the Community to enter into negotiations under Article XXIII:4 for modification of tariff concessions with respect to certain relevant tariff positions.

[167] The Blair House Accord was an agreement concluded between the US and the EC on 20 November 1992 in order to resolve some of the important differences between these two powers which held hostage the entire process of the Uruguay Round negotiations. One of those issues concerned the *EC Oilseeds* case discussed here. For more on this, see *infra* chapter 10; see also J. Croome, *Reshaping the World Trading System: A History of the Uruguay Round* (Geneva 1995) p. 340.

that concerning Article III was thus acceptably changed in the new EC regulation.[168]

9.3.2.1.3 The 1991 *US Malt Beverages* case

Like the previous two, this is a case involving a claim (primarily) of violation[169] of the national treatment provision of Article III and a defence based on the permissibility of production subsidies under Article III:8(b) of the General Agreement. The complainant, Canada, claimed that a number of taxation and other internal measures taken by the US, at both the federal as well as the state levels, operated to create advantages for domestically produced beer and wine in violation of Article III of the General Agreement. The measures challenged by Canada are wide-ranging.[170] However, a closer look at the panel's assessment of the issue involving the "Federal Excise Tax Differential on Beer" is sufficiently representative of the whole case for our purposes here.[171]

---

168 The principal differences between the system of support that was the subject of the *EC Oilseeds* (the "former system") and the new system of support have been summarized by the *Reconvened Oilseeds Panel* in para. 70 of its report, *supra* n. 2. The differences relevant to our discussion here are the following: (i) the former system was based on arrangements under which guaranteed prices were payable by EC processors to Community producers of oilseeds, with provision being made, where these prices were higher than world market prices, for payments to compensate processors for the difference between the prices guaranteed to producers and world market prices as calculated by the Commission. Under the new system these arrangements have been abolished; (ii) under the former system producers benefited from guaranteed prices per tonne for whatever quantity of oilseeds they produced. Under the new system producers benefit from direct per hectare payments for whatever area of eligible land they devote to oilseeds production; (iii) under the former system, producers' returns were in general determined by the level of guaranteed prices. Under the new system, producers' returns would be determined by two factors: the price they are able to obtain on the Community market in competition with other producers and imported oilseeds; and a direct payment linked to average yields of cereals or oilseeds assigned to the production region in which the producers' holdings planted to oilseeds are located. These direct per hectare payments are subject to adjustment (up or down) depending on the extent to which average Community market prices for oilseeds in general or for particular oilseeds, as calculated by the Commission, deviate by more than 8 per cent from the ECU 163 reference price.

169 An alternative, "subsidiary", claim of non-violation nullification or impairment by Canada was not considered by the panel because of its finding of a US violation of its obligations under Article III. See *US Malt Beverages, supra* n. 141, para. 5.28.

170 They have been summarized by the panel to be the following: taxation measures at both the federal and state levels which operate to create lower tax rates on domestic beer and wine than on like imported products; requirements in certain states that imported beer and wine be sold only through wholesalers, which requirements do not apply to in-state like products; requirements in certain states that imported beer and wine be transported only by common carrier, which requirements do not apply to in-state like products; higher licensing fees in certain states for imported beer and wine; exemptions in one state of local wine, but not like imported wine, from decisions to prohibit the sale of alcohol within local areas; policies of certain states to fix price levels for imported beer and wine on the basis of prices of those products in other states; listing and delisting policies of states which apply different requirements to imported wine than to the in-state like product; and restrictions in certain states on points of sale, distribution and labelling based on the alcohol content of beer. *US Malt Beverages, supra* n. 141, para. 5.1.

171 Indeed, the arguments made by the parties, as well as the rulings made by the panel, in most of the specific federal as well as state measures are a copy of those made in connection with the federal excise tax differential on beer. See, for instance, paras. 5.15, 5.16, 5.18, 5.20, 5.22, 5.27, etc. of the "findings"

On this subject, Canada claimed that "the application of a lower rate of federal excise tax on domestic beer from qualifying (small) United States producers, which lower rate was not available to imported beer, was inconsistent with Articles III:1 and III:2 of the General Agreement."[172] Both parties accepted that the federal excise taxes in question were internal taxes within the meaning of Article III.2 of the General Agreement and that imported beer was subject to a higher rate of federal excise tax than domestic beer from qualifying producers.[173] The practice constituted less favourable treatment to the imported products in respect of internal taxes – hence inconsistent with the national treatment provision of Article III:2, first sentence.[174] These being accepted by both parties, the dispute revolved around the affirmative defences invoked by the US to justify the GATT-legality of its system.

One of the arguments brought by the US in this respect was that "the lower federal excise tax rate was allowable as a subsidy to domestic producers under Article III:8(b)."[175] According to the US, the clear intent of the lower tax was to subsidize small beer producers and that "a tax exemption or reduction was a GATT-consistent way in which a subsidy to small producers could be made available as it did not affect the competitive conditions any differently than measures allowed by the plain language of Article III:8(b). It differed from the direct payment of a subsidy after taxes had been collected only in that it avoided the actual transfer of funds."[176] The US thus argued, in effect, that in as long as a subsidy was allowed under the General Agreement, the form in which it was provided was not important.

Canada started its argument from the fact that Article III:8(b) was an exception, an exemption, from the principle of national treatment. Applying the general maxim of legal interpretation in such cases, Canada argued that Article III:8(b) "had to be narrowly construed."[177] Basing itself on the text, context, as well as the negotiating history of the provision, Canada argued that within the terms of Article III:8(b), "a domestic producer had to pay the taxes due and owing before it received the subsidy payment."[178] In the view of Canada, regardless of the final amount to be given in the

---

cont.

section of the report in which the panel simply reminded itself of, and repeated, its previous findings on the same issue but in connection with the federal excise tax differential on beer.

172 Ibid., para. 5.2.

173 See Ibid., para. 5.4.

174 Ibid., para. 5.5.

175 Ibid., para. 5.7.

176 Ibid., para. 3.21; see also para. 5.7. Another line of defence pursued by the US was a kind of trade-effects argument. It contended that the federal tax was not discriminatory, nor protective, because it affected only less than one per cent of total domestic beer production. However, the Panel simply invoked established precedent that Article III:2 protects competitive conditions between imported and domestic products, and not expectations on export volumes, and concluded that "the fact that only approximately 1.5 per cent of domestic beer in the United States is eligible for the lower tax rate cannot justify the imposition of higher internal taxes on imported Canadian beer than on competing domestic beer. The prohibition of discriminatory taxes in Article III:2, first sentence, is not conditional on a 'trade effects test' nor is it qualified by a *de minimis* standard. ... Thus, in the view of the Panel, the fact that only approximately 1.5 per cent of domestic beer in the United States is eligible for the lower tax rate does not immunize this United States measure from the national treatment obligation of Article III." Ibid., para. 5.6.

form of a subsidy, in the case of a tax exemption or reduction, "the domestic producer neither had to set aside capital nor arrange financing to meet its tax burden, thus giving domestic products an advantage in the market not available to imports."[179]

Canada further argued that "Article III:8(b) first referred to "the payment of subsidies." This did not mean all subsidies, but those involving a payment. Secondly, the specific reference to "payments ... derived from the proceeds of internal taxes or charges applied consistently with the provisions of this Article ..." made clear that an after-tax-collection payment was foreseen, but not an exemption from the tax. This was reinforced by the further reference to "applied consistently with the provisions of this Article."[180]

Canada got added support for its position from the drafting history of the provision. Accordingly, Canada argued that Article III:8(b) is a provision drawn from the Havana Charter which had itself been "changed to insert the notion that payments to domestic producers from the proceeds of internal taxes required that these taxes must be applied consistent with the provisions of Article III."[181] According to Canada, this position was "confirmed by the rejection of a proposal by Cuba at the Havana Conference to amend the article to read: 'The provisions of this Article shall not preclude the exemption of domestic products from internal taxes as a means of indirect subsidization in the cases covered under Article 25."[182] Canada thus argued that Article III:8(b) did not permit the exemption or remission of internal taxes to domestic products,[183] and that "only direct payments of monies exclusively to the domestic producer could constitute a subsidy for the purposes of Article III:8(b)."[184]

In line with the preceding cases, the panel in this case also agreed with the complainant. According to the panel,

> "the ordinary meaning of the text of Article III:8(b), especially the use of the words 'shall not prevent' ... suggests that Article III does apply to subsidies, and that Article III:8(b) only clarifies that the *product-related* rules in paragraphs 1 through 7 of Article III 'shall not prevent the payment of subsidies exclusively to domestic *producers'*. ... The words 'payment of subsidies' refer only to direct subsidies involving a payment, not to other subsidies such as tax credits or tax reductions. The specific reference to 'payments ... derived from the proceeds of internal taxes ... applied consistently with the provisions of this Article' relates to after-tax-collection payments and also suggests that tax credits and reduced tax rates inconsistent

---

177 Ibid., para. 3.22.
178 Ibid., para. 3.24.
179 Ibid.
180 Ibid.
181 Ibid., para. 3.22.
182 Ibid.
183 Ibid.
184 Ibid., para. 3.24.

with Article III:2, which neither involve a 'payment' nor result in 'proceeds of internal taxes applied consistently with ... this Article', are not covered by Article III:8(b)."[185]

The panel thus concluded that the provision of a lower rate of federal excise tax on domestic beer from qualifying US producers, which lower rate was not available in the case of imported beer, was "inconsistent with Article III:2, first sentence, and is not covered by Article III:8(b)."[186] The same conclusion was reached in respect of about seven similar other federal and state measures involving the granting of an advantage to domestic products over imported competitors.[187]

It thus follows that the national treatment provision of the General Agreement excepts those subsidy practices that pertain to the production process and no more – production subsidies. The producers should be the sole beneficiaries of the system. All other forms of domestic subsidies, such as consumer and processor subsidies, although allowed under Article XVI, have to be granted with the national treatment requirement unaffected. This means for instance that a consumer subsidy introduced by a country on a certain product applies to all like products regardless of origin. Moreover, the types of production subsidies exempted from the national treatment rule are direct payments made straight to the producers themselves. The presence of an intermediary – such as the purchasers of the tractors in *Italian Agricultural*

---

[185] Ibid., para. 5.8 (emphasis in original). The panel added that "[a]s any fiscal burden imposed by discriminatory internal taxes on imported goods is likely to entail a trade-distorting advantage for import-competing domestic producers, the prohibition of discriminatory internal taxes in Article III:2 would be ineffective if discriminatory internal taxes on imported products could be generally justified as subsidies for competing domestic producers in terms of Article III:8(b). Article III:8(b) limits, therefore, the permissible producer subsidies to 'payments' after taxes have been collected or payments otherwise consistent with Article III. This separation of tax rules, e.g. on tax exemptions or reductions, and subsidy rules makes sense economically and politically. Even if the proceeds from non-discriminatory product taxes may be used for subsequent subsidies, the domestic producer, like his foreign competitors, must pay the product taxes due. The separation of tax and subsidy rules contributes to greater transparency. It also may render abuses of tax policies for protectionist purposes more difficult, as in the case where producer aids require additional legislative or governmental decisions in which the different interests involved can be balanced." Ibid., paras. 5.9-5.10. The precedential role of this interpretation has continued to be important ever since. For recent references, see, *inter alia*, *Canada – Certain Measures Concerning Periodicals*, report of the Appellate Body (WT/DS31/AB/R) 30 June 1997, p. 34; and *Indonesia – Certain Measures Affecting the Automobile Industry;* report of the panel (WT/DS54/R, WT/DS55/R, WT/DS59/R, WT/DS64/R) 2 July 1998, para. 14.30.

[186] *US Malt Beverages*, *supra* n. 141, para. 6.1(a).

[187] The measures are the following: federal excise tax credits on domestic wine and cider; excise tax exemptions and reductions to domestic beer and wine by the states of New York, Oregon, Rhode Island and the Commonwealth of Puerto Rico; excise tax credits to domestic breweries based on annual beer production by the states of Kentucky, Minnesota, Ohio and Wisconsin; lower excise tax rates on wine based upon its in-state or domestic origin by the states of Alabama, Georgia, Nebraska and New Mexico; the application by the state of Iowa of an excise tax at the wholesale level, which applied to all imported wine but not necessarily to all domestic wine; the provision by the states of Michigan, Ohio and Rhode Island of preferential excise tax treatment to wine produced from local ingredients; and the provision by the state of Pennsylvania of an excise tax credit on beer for the purchase of manufacturing equipment. See Ibid., paras. 6.1(b)–6.1(g) and 6.1(i).

Machinery and the processors in *EC Oilseeds* – although not necessarily a violation of Article III:8(b), may easily create doubts as to the degree of exclusivity of the payments.

9.3.3 Conclusion

The original version of the GATT did not impose any significant constraint on the domestic policy-making power of the contracting parties in the area of subsidies. The notification and discussion obligations of Article XVI, coupled with the unilateral and multilateral ways of reacting to cases of injurious or prejudicial subsidy practices, applied to all sectors of the economy as well as to all forms of subsidies. Agricultural subsidies – both domestic as well as export – were thus as lawful as were subsidies applying to other, non-agricultural products. However, the practical effect of such a rule was counterproductive to the very objectives of the GATT itself. The success achieved by the GATT in the reduction of tariffs would turn out to be meaningless if its practical effects could be circumvented by a resort to such market-distortive practices as subsidies subject only to obligations of notification and non-binding consultation.

The contracting parties reacted to these shortcomings of the General Agreement in two ways: development of the doctrine of *prima facie* nullification or impairment (or what is also called the doctrine of *reasonable expectations*) as regards domestic subsidies and the introduction of a separate section dealing exclusively with export subsidies. The former development started very early in the lifetime of the GATT and had its foundation in "case law", but was soon formally adopted by the CONTRACTING PARTIES as an authoritative interpretation of the relevant text of the General Agreement.

9.4 DOMESTIC SUBSIDIES AND THE 1955 REVIEW SESSION

We have seen that, until the 1955 review, all forms of subsidies, regardless of their purpose or sector of application, were permitted. Section B of Article XVI – the new section that was added in 1955 – is entitled "Additional Provisions on Export Subsidies", a title which clearly indicates that the new additions do not in any way concern that of domestic subsidies. All four newly-added paragraphs to Article XVI concern themselves with the issue of export subsidies: paragraph 2 generally recognizing the possible harm that may follow from the use of export subsidies; paragraph 3 setting impracticable limits on the use of subsidies on the export of primary products; paragraph 4 prescribing a conditional prohibition on the use of subsidies on the export of non-primary products; and paragraph 5 requiring the CONTRACTING PARTIES to make a periodic review of the operation of the whole Article. By introducing a special set of rules for export subsidies, the 1955 review session, in effect, prescribed the old regime for domestic subsidies – an implicit approval of the original rules of the GATT on subsidies in general (which now forms paragraph 1 of Article XVI) to govern the particular area of domestic subsidies.

Yet, in the area of domestic subsidies, too, at least one important improvement may be said to have resulted from the Review Session – what has now been termed as the doctrine of "reasonable expectations". The *prima facie* doctrine, which had been introduced by the *Australia Ammonium Sulphate* case under slightly different factual circumstances, was somewhat modified and/or extended and given a formal approval by the CONTRACTING PARTIES. The whole purpose of the interpretative agreement was to tighten the rules of the General Agreement on domestic subsidies. In the words of the Working Party on Other Barriers to Trade, consideration was given to a number of "proposals for strengthening the present provisions of the Agreement with respect to subsidies", and an agreement was reached in the area of domestic subsidies that:

> "a contracting party which has negotiated a concession under Article II may be assumed, for the purpose of Article XXIII, to have a *reasonable expectation*, failing evidence to the contrary, that the value of the concession will not be nullified or impaired by the contracting party which granted the concession by the subsequent introduction or increase of a domestic subsidy on the product concerned."[188]

In this connection, a GATT *Panel on Subsidies* noted in 1961 that "the expression 'reasonable expectation' was qualified by the words 'failing evidence to the contrary'. By this the panel understands that the presumption is that unless such pertinent facts were available at the time the tariff concession was negotiated, it was then reasonably to be expected that the concession would not be nullified or impaired by the introduction or increase of a domestic subsidy."[189]

Although not totally new as such, these are important developments to the law. The foundation had already been laid down by the *Australia Ammonium Sulphate* case in 1950, which ruled that a *prima facie* case of nullification or impairment would exist "if the action ... which resulted in upsetting the competitive relationship between [competing products ... could not reasonably have been anticipated"[190] at the time of negotiating tariff concessions. The interpretative understanding not only based itself on the *Australia Ammonium Sulphate* case; it also cleared the doubts expressed therein. Indeed, what the Working Party in the latter case had termed "difficult to say" came to be the subject of a distinct interpretative understanding.[191] In the words of the US representative to *EC Oilseeds*, this 1955 ruling "removed any uncertainty left open by the *Ammonium Sulphate* case that the subsequent introduction of subsidies could serve as a basis for nullification or impairment and it was thus clear that Article XVI was not intended to have exclusive jurisdiction over subsidies."[192]

---

188 *GATT Working Party Report on Other Barriers to Trade*, *supra* n. 129, (italics added).

189 GATT Panel on Subsidies, *supra* n. 5, p. 209.

190 *Australia Ammonium Sulphate*, *supra* n. 75, para. 12.

191 The Working Party stated that "[t]he situation in the case is different from that which would have arisen from the granting of a new subsidy on one of the two competing products. In such a case, given the freedom under the General Agreement of the Australian Government to impose subsidies and to select the products on which a subsidy would be granted, it would be *more difficult to say* that the Chilean Government had reasonably relied on the continuation of the same treatment for the two products." Ibid., para. 12 (italics added).

192 *EC Oilseeds*, *supra* n. 140, para. 70.

Besides this element of clarity, the significance of the interpretative understanding lies in the binding force that it thus acquires. While the *prima facie* doctrine was a result of dispute settlement decisions – hence binding only as between the parties thereto – the interpretative note is, in effect, an amendment to the rules and becomes binding on all contracting parties to the GATT.[193] Consequently, while future panels are (at least theoretically) free to reject previous panel reports on the same issue (although they rarely do so in practice due to the high degree of persuasive power the dispute settlement reports often have), they are bound to respect the new interpretation in any relevant case in the future.

As stated by the Working Party that formulated the interpretative addition, this is an interpretation designed to strengthen the existing rules of the discipline. With this as the only improvement, the original provisions of the General Agreement continued to govern the practice of domestic subsidies until the conclusion of the Uruguay Round in 1994. Although the doctrine itself had its roots in GATT case law, its subsequent application by dispute settlement panels was very much limited until the beginning of the 1980s.[194] Since that time, however, there have been important cases involving this issue and will be discussed in the following section more closely.

9.4.1 GATT Case Law on Domestic Subsidies and the Doctrine of "Reasonable Expectations"

The introduction of the doctrine of "reasonable expectations" addressed one of the most serious concerns which resulted from the lax system of subsidies in general and domestic subsidies in particular. Over and above the trade distortion a subsidy may cause in its own right, the use of domestic subsidies to circumvent the value of tariff bindings was a major setback to the entire multilateral trading system. It was this aspect of the problem that was resolved by this understanding. Accordingly, although the rules of the GATT on subsidies do not set any significant restraints on the power of countries to do so, the moment they bind their tariffs on a certain product, their power to introduce new subsidies or to increase the existing ones so as to impair or nullify the benefits of tariff concessions will *de facto* be curtailed.

In essence, therefore, a country that is affected by such measures benefits from the presumption that it had "reasonable expectations" for the balance of concessions not to be upset by subsequent unilateral measures even though those measures might be consistent with GATT rules, and hence giving rise to a possible case of non-violation nullification or impairment. The importance of this development is such that the "vaguely defined" non-violation complaints of Article XXIII were progressively limited, "through GATT dispute settlement practice, ... to situations where competitive benefits, which could be reasonably expected from reciprocal

---

193 On the status of adopted dispute settlement reports, see, inter alia, *GATT Analytical Index*, *supra* n. 67, p. 755; A. Chua, "The Precedential Effect of WTO Panel and Appellate Body Reports", in 11 *Leiden Journal of International Law* (1998) p. 53; and D. Palmeter, and P. Mavroidis, "The WTO Legal System: Sources of Law", 92 *American Journal of International Law*, No. 3 (1998) p. 402.

194 For a summary of earlier practice, see Rivers and Greenwald (1979) *supra* n. 3.

tariff bindings were 'nullified or impaired' notably through unforeseen subsequent production subsidies".[195]

Yet, this implicit restriction on countries' rights to grant domestic subsidies does not amount to a prohibition. Being a GATT-consistent measure, countries are still free to introduce such subsidies, and even when they are later found to have upset the previously negotiated balance of concessions, they are not required to abolish the measures. As the *Australia Ammonium Sulphate* panel had observed, there is nothing in Article XXIII which empowers the CONTRACTING PARTIES to require the withdrawal of GATT-consistent measures that are found prejudicial to the interests of another contracting party.[196] Apart from bilaterally negotiated means of settling the dispute, such as compensation, the most that the CONTRACTING PARTIES can do is exercise their power under Article XXIII.2 of the General Agreement and authorize the affected party to suspend the application of appropriate obligations or concessions under the Agreement vis-à-vis the other party.

There are two important GATT panel reports involving this interpretative understanding, which will be discussed subsequently: *EEC – Production Aids Granted to Canned Peaches, Canned Pears, Canned Fruit Cocktail and Dried Grapes*,[197] and *EEC – Payments and Subsidies Paid to Processors and Producers of Oilseeds and Related Animal Feed Proteins*.[198]

9.4.1.1 The 1982 *EC Canned Fruits* case

This case concerns EC regulations which introduced a production aid system for canned peaches, canned pears, canned fruit cocktail and dried grapes.[199] The system involved a minimum grower price for the producers of the fresh fruits and a processor aid for the processing industries. The system was implemented such that aid would be granted to the processors on condition that they bought the fresh products from growers at at least the "minimum specified grower price."[200] The purpose of the production aid was said to be "to enable the products in question to be manufactured at a price lower than that which would result from the payment of a remunerative price to producers of the fresh products."[201] According to the relevant EC legislations, the amount of processor aid was "so fixed as to make up the difference between the prices of Community products and those of products from

---

[195] Petersmann (1997) *supra* n. 101, p. 84.

[196] *Australia Ammonium Sulphate*, *supra* n. 75, para. 16.

[197] *European Economic Community – Production Aids Granted on Canned Peaches, Canned Pears, Canned Fruit Cocktail and Dried Grapes*, report of the panel (L/5778) circulated to the contracting parties on 20 February 1985, but not adopted because of EC blockage. However, it was later reported that the parties had reached a bilateral settlement on the basis of the report.

[198] *EC Oilseeds*, *supra* n. 140.

[199] For a list of relevant EC Regulations, see *EC Canned Fruits*, *supra* n. 197, paras. 7-11.

[200] Ibid., para. 7. The aid would be paid during the marketing year "upon application from the processor, who must provide proof that he has purchased the fresh product under contract at least at the minimum price." Ibid., para. 9.

[201] Ibid., para. 7.

non-member countries".[202] While the cost of producing EC products is calculated for each product as the minimum grower price paid for the fresh product adjusted by the trend in processing costs of that product, the prices for products from non-member countries are determined "taking into account duty-free import prices of the product in question into the EEC and prices obtained in international trade."[203]

The US challenged both aspects of the system, i.e. the minimum grower prices set for producers of the fresh products, as well as the aids available to the processing industry. However, as the former was touched upon only in passing[204] and since the panel also dismissed the claim rather easily,[205] the following discussion deals almost exclusively with the system of aid available to the processors.

On this issue, the US claimed that EC production aids granted on canned peaches, canned pears, canned fruit cocktail and dried grapes "had nullified or impaired tariff concessions granted by the EEC in 1962, 1967, 1973 and 1979."[206] The US did not question the GATT-legality of the said production aid systems but presented its case as a non-violation nullification and impairment complaint in the sense of Article XXIII:1(b) of the General Agreement. Relying on the doctrine of reasonable expectations, the US argued that "when it had negotiated the tariff concessions on the products in question it had believed that these concessions would carry certain advantages for US exports to the EC."[207] The US presented its challenge to the system along two lines. In the first line, invoking established legal presumptions, the US claimed that "the mere introduction of such subsidies constituted *prima facie* nullification and impairment of tariff bindings."[208] In support of this claim, the US invoked the working party report on *Australian Ammonium Sulphate,* the 1955 interpretative understanding, as well as the 1961 statement by the GATT Panel on Subsidies.[209]

In the second line, the US asserted that not only was there a *prima facie* case of nullification or impairment, there was also evidence of actual prejudice suffered by

---

202 Ibid., para. 8.

203 Ibid.

204 See Ibid., para. 23.

205 The panel noted the US argument that the minimum grower prices "necessarily implied increased production of canned product and therefore a distortion of the competitive relationship between EC and imported canned product." Ibid., para. 57. However, the panel rejected this claim as follows: "even if the minimum grower price had stimulated production of fresh product this need not upset the competitive relationship between EC and imported canned product. ... [R]egardless of the supply situation in the fresh fruit market, EC processors were still required to pay growers the minimum price. ... [A]ny adverse effects imparted its imported products by the minimum grower price would be to imported fresh product and not to imported canned product." Ibid., para. 57. The panel thus concluded that "the minimum price granted to growers of fresh peaches and pears did not adversely affect the competitive relationship between EEC and imported canned peaches, pears or fruit cocktail." Ibid., para. 80.

206 Ibid., para. 14.

207 Ibid.

208 Ibid.

209 See Ibid., para. 15-16. For a discussion of these points, see *supra* section 9.3.

its exports due to EC production aid systems.[210] According to the US, this could be seen in the loss of competitive advantage previously enjoyed by imported products from the US and consequent reduction in overall imports into the Community market.[211] In particular, the US argued that the unanticipated production aid system had upset the competitive relationship between imported and EC products in favour of the latter – thus resulting in "sharp decreases in the volume of EEC imports of the products in question."[212] The US stressed the point that the subsequent introduction of that production aid system could not reasonably have been anticipated by the US at the time the tariff concessions on the four products in question were negotiated.[213]

The EC defended, *inter alia,* that processor aids were made only to recompense processors for having had to pay the minimum price to growers.[214] According to the EC, the minimum grower prices fixed for fresh fruits had placed the EC processor at a disadvantage vis-à-vis foreign processors who could obtain their raw materials at normal world market prices. The EC thus argued that the whole purpose of the system was only to compensate the processor for the higher cost he had to incur due to the necessity of paying the minimum grower price.[215]

Based on this premise, the EC responded to the two lines of challenge in the same way. It first contended that the "mere granting of an internal subsidy did not constitute a *prima facie* nullification or impairment of a tariff concession."[216] This meant that, in the view of the EC, the existence of actual nullification or impairment resulting from the said production aids had to be demonstrated and that the burden to do so fell on the shoulders of the US.[217] In the opinion of the EC, the US failed to provide sufficient evidence showing that tariff concessions had actually been nullified or impaired.[218] The EC further argued that processor aids did not distort competitive conditions on the market and that, even if they did, "such distortion would not be prohibited by the General Agreement. According to its paragraph 8(b), Article III did not prevent the payment of subsidies exclusively to domestic producers."[219]

This being a case brought before it as a non-violation nullification or impairment case from the outset, the panel did not address the question of whether the concerned EC practices violated the General Agreement.[220] The only issue before the panel was thus as to whether the presumably GATT-consistent domestic support measures introduced by the EC had nonetheless resulted in the nullification or impairment of

---

210 See *EC Canned Fruits, supra* n. 197, para. 14.
211 See Ibid., paras. 17-23, 44.
212 Ibid., para. 21.
213 See Ibid., para. 16.
214 Ibid., para. 25.
215 Ibid.
216 Ibid., para. 24.
217 See Ibid., para. 24.
218 See Ibid., para. 27. According to the EC, since the US did not contend that any provisions of the General Agreement had been violated, it was incumbent upon the United States to clearly demonstrate the nature of the prejudice incurred. Ibid.
219 See Ibid., para. 29.
220 See Ibid., para. 48.

the value of tariff concessions it had granted on the importation of the said products.

The panel commenced its interpretive task by referring to two previous GATT cases which had ruled on non-violation complaints – the *Australian Ammonium Sulphate* and the *German Sardine* panel reports. On that basis, the panel observed that a non-violation nullification or impairment of tariff concessions would exist if the measure in question satisfied two fundamental criteria: (1) that it could not have reasonably been anticipated by the party bringing the complaint at the time of negotiation of the tariff concessions and (2) that the measure resulted in the upsetting of the competitive position of the imported products concerned.[221] These two criteria are cumulative in the sense that both of them must be satisfied in a given case.

In its analysis, the panel followed the distinction maintained by the parties between *prima facie* nullification or impairment, on the one hand, and actual nullification or impairment, on the other. However, the panel found that its ruling on actual nullification or impairment independently of any assumptions of a *prima facie* case could dispose of the matter in full.[222] Consequently, it decided "not to include" in the report its deliberations on the legal question of whether there was a *prima facie* case of nullification or impairment. It noted in passing nonetheless that GATT case law "had not precluded the possibility that an unforeseeable subsequent introduction or increase of a domestic subsidy on a product, for which a tariff concession had been previously granted, could constitute an assumption of *prima facie* nullification or impairment of the tariff concession concerned."[223]

Turning to the issue of actual nullification or impairment, the panel applied the afore-mentioned criteria and stated that there would be a nullification or impairment caused by EC system of production aid in the present case if: (1) the introduction or increase of the EC production aids could not have been reasonably anticipated by the US at the time of the negotiations for the tariff concessions on those products, and (2) the aid systems had upset the competitive position of imported canned peaches, canned pears, canned fruit cocktail and dried grapes on the EC market.[224] The panel considered each of these requirements in detail and reached varying and carefully framed conclusions.

Given that EC tariff concessions have often been subject to withdrawals and renegotiations under GATT Article XXIV.6 due to the progressive enlargement of the Community, the question of whether the introduction or increase of its production aids could have been reasonably anticipated by the US *at the time of the negotiations for the tariff concessions* on those products raises an issue of timing. As

---

[221] See Ibid., para. 51. The panel applied these criteria throughout its analysis in the present case.

[222] Ibid., para. 76.

[223] Ibid. (emphasis in original). A similar observation had been made by a 1962 panel report: "While it is not precluded that a *prima facie* case of nullification or impairment could arise even if there is no infringement of GATT provisions, it would be in such cases incumbent on the country invoking Article XXIII to demonstrate the grounds and reasons of its invocation. Detailed submissions on the part of that contracting party on these points were therefore essential for a judgment to be made under this Article." *Report of the Panel on Uruguayan Recourse to Article XXIII* (L/1923 *BISD* 11S/95) adopted on 16 November 1962, para. 15.

noted earlier, the US claimed that the aid system constituted nullification and impairment of tariff concessions it had obtained on the products in question in 1962, 1967, 1973 and 1979.[225] The EC on the other hand argued that "it had *withdrawn*, in 1973, the tariff concessions granted in 1962 and 1967 on the four product categories concerned".[226] The question would thus be as to which negotiations and which concessions are at stake here.

This would automatically raise the issue of whether the concessions granted in 1962 and 1967 were still protected. However, the panel avoided this issue by relying instead on the two most recent concessions which had been asserted by the US and not challenged by the EC. It was noted that the EC had "neither contested the existence of the tariff bindings of 1974/79 invoked by the United States nor the US submission that the EEC tariff bindings on canned peaches, canned pears, fruit mixtures and dried grapes had been given 'as a part of a balance of concessions'."[227] From this, the panel concluded that "the tariff bindings granted by the EEC in 1974/79 on the four product categories concerned had created for the United States 'benefits accruing to it directly or indirectly under this Agreement' in terms of Article XXIII:1 of the General Agreement."[228]

Once the timing issue was resolved, the chronology of events was able to answer most of the remaining questions. Accordingly, as EC production aids for canned peaches and canned pears had been introduced in 1978 and 1979, respectively, the panel found that the US could not have anticipated the introduction of any of these subsidies during the 1974 concessions.[229] However, the case of dried grapes was different because the panel found out that Greek processors had benefited from subsidies by Greek authorities already prior to 1974. Indeed the panel concluded, in respect of both the 1974 as well as the 1979 negotiations, that the US could have reasonably expected that "in the case of an accession of Greece to the EC, Greek processors would continue to benefit from no less generous a system."[230] With dried grapes, therefore, the first requirement was not met in either of the two concessions.[231]

---

[224] See *EC Canned Fruits*, *supra* n. 197, para. 51.

[225] Ibid., para. 44(a) (emphasis in original).

[226] Ibid., para. 49 (italics added).

[227] *EC Canned Fruits*, *supra* n. 197, para. 49.

[228] Ibid., para. 49.

[229] See Ibid., paras. 52 and 79.

[230] Ibid., para. 81. The panel was more cautious on this point. As the case of dried grapes was limited to Greece, which had just joined the EC, the US' anticipation was concerned only with the continuance of pre-existing Greek subsidies and not of the introduction of new, or the increase of old, ones. To make that clear, the panel made an explicit reservation: "Only to the extent that the EEC subsidy scheme for dried grapes was more than a continuation of the prior national Greek subsidy scheme and resulted in an additional upsetting of the competitive relationship between US dried grapes and Greek dried grapes on the market of the 'EEC of nine' (i.e. without Greece), could the United States not have reasonably anticipated such additional EC subsidies and competitive distortions resulting therefrom." Ibid., para. 79.

[231] The two requirements being cumulative, therefore, this would suffice to dismiss the US claim of a non-violation nullification or impairment regarding this product. However, as we shall see subsequently, neither was the second element, i.e. disturbance of the balance of concessions, satisfied in the case of dried grapes.

With respect to the concessions on canned fruits resulting from the 1979 negotiations, the panel found that the US should have been aware of the existence of the aid system for canned peaches and, indirectly, for canned fruit mixtures.[232] On the other hand, it found that the US could not have foreseen the introduction of the aid system for canned pears, for the support system in this case was introduced after the tariff concessions.[233] In general, therefore, the major determining factor in all cases was the chronology of events, i.e. whether the subsidy system for a product in question predated the granting of tariff concessions on that product.[234] On that basis, the panel found that the first condition for the existence of a non-violation nullification or impairment was satisfied for all the canned products as regards the 1974 tariff concessions and for canned pears as regards the 1979 concessions.[235]

As regards the second requirement, i.e. the upsetting of the competitive positions of EC and imported canned peaches, canned pears and canned fruit cocktail on the EC market, the panel made a series of complex calculations and observed that, despite EC insistence that subsidies were granted only to reimburse processors for having to pay higher prices for the fresh fruit than they would otherwise have to, the production aid for each fruit was actually calculated in such a way that the processors would receive a net subsidy enabling them to improve the price competitiveness of their products vis-à-vis the prices of imported products.[236] According to the panel, the subsidies "ensured that EEC product would never be any less competitive than imported product. ... [F]oreign suppliers would never be able to improve their competitive position in the EEC market even if productivity gains in their industries, or other circumstances, permitted them to lower the cost of producing their product. ... [T]he production aids had always more than compensated the difference between the EEC minimum grower prices and the 'free market' prices for fresh peaches and Williams Pears."[237] The panel thus concluded that the subsidies granted to processors had upset the competitive relationship between EC and imported canned fruits because their amounts were not limited to defraying the additional costs necessitated by the minimum grower prices for the fresh fruit.[238] Implicit in this reasoning is that the EC would be able to provide an amount of aid which only equalized the price difference of the raw materials (i.e. fresh fruits) between world and Community markets resulting from the higher minimum grower prices set by its system of support without causing distortion in the market for processed products.[239] With respect to the production aids granted to processors of dried grapes, however, the panel found that although the EC system

[232] See *EC Canned Fruits*, *supra* n. 197, paras. 52-54, and 79.
[233] Ibid., para. 79.
[234] For details on these issues, see Ibid., paras. 52-54.
[235] For the impact of this finding on the content of the final recommendations, see *infra* n. 246 and accompanying text.
[236] See *EC Canned Fruits*, *supra* n. 197, paras. 59-60 and 80.
[237] Ibid., para. 60.
[238] Ibid., para. 80.
[239] See also Hudec (1993) *supra* n. 45, p. 156.

"*might* impart some additional market distortion at some time in the future should world market prices for dried grapes increase, it was unable to conclude that, as yet, such distortion had occurred."[240]

To sum up, two important points merit a special emphasis in this panel report. Firstly, although the panel avoided a ruling on the question of whether the mere introduction of production subsidies or the increase of existing support systems amounted to *prima facie* nullification or impairment of tariff bindings, it gave the affirmative remark that previous GATT case law "had not precluded the possibility that an unforeseeable subsequent introduction or increase of a domestic subsidy on a product, for which a tariff concession had been previously granted, could constitute an assumption of *prima facie* nullification or impairment of the tariff concession concerned." Secondly, on the general question of nullification or impairment regardless of the benefit of a presumption for either party, the panel agreed with established precedent that two requirements had to be met: that the measure could not have reasonably been anticipated at the time of the tariff concessions on a product and that the unanticipated measure resulted in the upsetting of the competitive balance established between those products at the time of the concessions. In all three product categories, the panel found that the subsidies granted to processors "upset the competitive relationship between EC and imported canned peaches, canned pears and canned fruit cocktail"[241] – thus satisfying the second of the two fundamental requirements as regards these products.

The panel thus found a non-violation nullification or impairment in respect of the three canned fruits and made the final recommendation that, in line with the established dispute settlement practice in non-violation cases, the EC "consider ways and means to restore the competitive relationship between imported US and domestic EC *canned peaches, canned pears and canned fruit cocktail which derived from the tariff concessions granted in 1974 on these products and in 1979 on canned pears*."[242] A closer look at this statement of recommendation reveals that it is carefully circumscribed to apply only to those products on which the first element has also been found to exist. It applies to 1974 concessions on all three canned fruits because the panel had already found that EC production aids for canned peaches and canned pears had been introduced in 1978 and 1979, respectively, and that the US could not reasonably have expected the introduction of these subsidies at the time it had received tariff concessions on these products in 1974.[243] The panel's recommendation as regards the 1979 concessions was, however, limited to canned pears because in the two other cases, the panel had found that EC subsidies for canned peaches had been introduced prior to the conclusion of the 1979 tariff concession and that the US should have been aware of the existence of this subsidy in

[240] *EC Canned Fruits, supra* n. 197, para. 81 (emphasis in original).
[241] See Ibid., para. 80.
[242] Ibid., para. 83 (italics added).
[243] Ibid., para. 52.

the negotiation of the tariff concessions for canned peaches in 1978/79.[244] But, as regards canned pears, the panel had noted that the subsidies had been introduced subsequent to the conclusion of the 1979 tariff concessions and that the US could not reasonably have foreseen its coming at the time it negotiated these tariff concessions.[245] Finally, the exclusion of dried grapes from the recommendation also fits in with this scenario because, as pointed out already, the panel had found that neither of the two criteria was met for these products.[246]

A conclusion may thus be drawn that the *EC Canned Fruits* panel report is a report which applied the doctrine of reasonable expectations to the letter of the 1955 interpretative understanding. Adoption of this panel report was, however, blocked by the EC, which claimed that the report suffered from errors in legal interpretation.[247] But, finally, a bilateral settlement was reached between the parties in which the EC undertook to make and/or maintain agreed levels of reductions in production subsidies for the products in question and the US undertook to withdraw the panel report from the agenda without adoption.[248]

9.4.1.2 The 1988 *EC Oilseeds* Case

The same parties were involved in another and more contentious dispute involving the issue of domestic subsidies introduced by the EC to processors and producers of oilseeds and related animal-feed proteins which were alleged by the US to have upset the relative competitive position of products on which a tariff concession had already been granted. We have seen earlier that the EC defence of its subsidy system in this case on the basis of Article III:8(b) of the General Agreement was rejected by the panel, which found an EC violation of Article III:4.[249] However, as the same panel clearly stated, its finding under Article III:4 "does not relate to the benefits accruing to the Community producers under the Community subsidy schemes but only to the benefits accruing to processors."[250] In other words, the provision of production subsidies exclusively to producers of a given product is permitted under Article III:8(b) and does not violate Article III:4. However, that does not necessarily mean that such production subsidies are immune from challenge, which will be shown in the following section more clearly. After all, a claim under the nullification or impairment provision of Article XXIII need not necessarily base itself on violation of a GATT obligation. The above-discussed *EC Canned Fruits* case is just one of several cases in point.

---

[244] Ibid., para. 52. Concerning canned fruit cocktail, the panel added that since peaches are their principal component, the panel found that the US "should also have been aware of any possible effects of these production aids on the economic benefit of the tariff concessions for fruit mixtures negotiated in 1978/79." Ibid.

[245] Ibid., para. 52.

[246] See *supra* n. 235 and accompanying texts.

[247] See Hudec (1993) *supra* n. 45, p. 498.

[248] See Ibid.

[249] See *supra* section 9.3.2.

[250] *EC Oilseeds*, *supra* n. 140, para. 142.

The US complained that EC subsidies to its producers and processors of oilseeds, regardless of their consistency with rules of the General Agreement, had nullified or impaired benefits accruing to it under the Community's tariff concessions for oilseeds.[251] A separate consideration of this issue was thus found to be necessary because, as the panel put it, compliance with the finding on Article III "could, but would not necessarily, eliminate" the basis of the US complaint of nullification or impairment.[252] This is the perspective from which the case will be discussed in this section.

To give some factual background relevant to this aspect of the dispute, a zero tariff concession was given by the EC to the imports of soyabeans, rapeseed, sunflowerseed and oilcakes or meals during the 1960–61 Dillon Round of trade negotiations.[253] Although these concessions were originally negotiated and bound as concessions of the Community (EC-6), they have been "extended and applied by the Community following its successive enlargements and related negotiations under Article XXIV:6."[254] The problem arose after the EC introduced its common market organization for oils and fats in September 1966 which was designed "to supersede a diverse range of support measures applied by individual Member States."[255]

The panel has outlined what it called the "important general considerations" which led to the adoption by the EC of its oilseeds régime. Notable among them is the statement that "taking international commitments into account, provision must be made for appropriate measures to remedy the situation in which the removal of import barriers would leave the Community market in oilseeds without defence against seriously prejudicial disturbances caused either by imports or by disparities, resulting from the action of third countries, between prices for products derived from oilseeds and prices for these oilseeds."[256] Furthermore, it was stated that "because of the situation on the world market, certain sectors of agricultural and industrial production in the Community would be adversely affected *if the effects of the removal of import barriers were not offset by other measures*."[257]

The US argued that the benefits accruing to it under the tariff concessions on oilseeds and oilcakes granted by the EC "had been nullified and impaired in the sense of Article XXIII:1(b) by the subsequent introduction of and substantial increases in producer and processor subsidies on Community oilseeds and protein animal feed components".[258] It cited previous panel reports[259] as well as the 1955

[251] See Ibid., paras. 53 and 57-61.

[252] Ibid., para. 142.

[253] See Ibid., para. 9. The United States has initial negotiating rights in respect of the bindings on soybeans and, in conjunction with Canada and Uruguay, on oilcakes. See para. 11. For initial negotiating rights, see *inter alia,* Article XXVIII of the General Agreement.

[254] Ibid., para. 10.

[255] EEC Regulation 136/66. See Ibid., para. 12-13.

[256] Ibid., para. 14(ii).

[257] Ibid., para. 14(iii) (italics added).

[258] Ibid., para. 53.

[259] The cases cited by the US were *Australian Ammonium Sulphate*; *EC Canned Fruits*; and *Treatment by Germany of Imports of Sardines*, report of the panel (G/26 *BISD* 1S/53) adopted on 31 October 1952.

interpretative ruling by the CONTRACTING PARTIES on the doctrine of reasonable expectations[260] in support of its claim. In line with the reasoning of the *EC Canned Fruits* panel, the US argued that there was an already developed "precedent" that nullification or impairment of a benefit accruing to a contracting party occurred if domestic measures taken by another contracting party subsequent to the adoption of a tariff concession (i) could not reasonably have been anticipated by the party bringing the complaint at the time of the negotiation of the concession, and (ii) upset the competitive position of the imported products on the market.[261] The US further asserted that "it could not reasonably have anticipated that the value of the 1962 concessions would be nullified and impaired, and that the onus was on the Community to overcome this presumption."[262]

The range of defences raised by the EC may for present purposes be put in three categories. The first concerns the presumption of nullification or impairment claimed by the US in cases where domestic subsidies are introduced by a contracting party subsequent to the granting of a tariff concession on a product. It argued that the measures were permitted under Articles III.8(b) as well as XVI, that in the absence of any violation of specific provisions of the General Agreement there could be no presumption of nullification or impairment and that the adverse effects must be duly established by the complaining party.[263]

The second concerns the legal status of the 1962 tariff concessions. It is noteworthy that despite repeated withdrawals of the 1962 tariff concessions and replacements by new ones in the context of successive EC enlargement renegotiations under Article XXIV:6, the most recent being in 1986/87,[264] the United States based its case on expectations it claimed to have had in 1962 when the relevant concessions were first made.[265] The Community challenged this position and argued that "for the purposes of the present case the rights and expectations of the parties should be determined on the basis of the 1988 concessions currently in force."[266]

The third one concerns the question of whether or not there were sufficient grounds for the US to reasonably anticipate the introduction of such domestic subsidies on those products when the first tariff concessions were given in 1962 as well as on the implications and extent of the expectations. Accordingly, the EC argued that, even

---

cont.

While the former two have been discussed above, the relevant parts of the *German Sardines* case have been summarized by the *EC Oilseeds* panel as follows: "In the German Sardines case a similar finding was made on facts which involved the subsequent introduction of more favourable import treatment for one species of fish in circumstances where, when the tariff concessions were negotiated, the exporting country had reason to assume that all fish in the same family would be treated similarly." see *EC Oilseeds, supra* n. 140, para. 58.

[260] See *EC Oilseeds, supra* n. 140, paras. 57–61.

[261] Ibid., para. 58.

[262] Ibid., para. 80.

[263] See Ibid., para. 54.

[264] See Ibid., para. 131.

[265] Ibid., para. 143; for arguments of the US on this point, see paras. 73-74.

[266] Ibid., para. 71.

assuming that the 1962 tariff concessions were still valid, there were sufficient grounds for the US to have developed a reasonable expectation that those domestic subsidy measures were to follow. The EC specifically mentioned three considerations as important: that several Member States of the original Community had had support and protection arrangements for the production of oilseeds before; that whatever its expectations by then, the US' claims amounted to a "freezing" of the competitive relationship existing at the time of the first negotiations; and that in any case the actual size of imports of the concerned products, which has quadrupled since 1966 alone, has more than satisfied whatever expectations the United States may have had in 1962 regarding the future development of oilseed imports into the Community.[267]

The panel first examined the issue of whether the benefits accruing to the US under the tariff concessions on oilseeds then in force included the protection of expectations which had prevailed in 1962 when the tariff concessions on oilseeds were first made.[268] In the absence of a clear provision on the subject, the panel considered the issue in the light of the purpose of the provisions of Article XXIII relating to the impairment of benefits accruing under the General Agreement[269] and observed that the answer to this question "depends on whether the concessions on oilseeds resulting from the subsequent renegotiations under Article XXIV:6 were part of a new balance of concessions or whether the reinstitution of the concessions at the same rate after the successive enlargements of the Community meant that the balance of concessions originally negotiated in 1962 was to be continued."[270] In the view of the panel, the Article XXIV:6 negotiations resulted merely in the extension of the existing tariff concessions of the Community to the new member States and did not create new ones.[271] The panel thus concluded that the balance of concessions negotiated in 1962 in respect of oilseeds was "not altered in the successive Article XXIV:6 negotiations" and that the benefits accruing to the US under the oilseed tariff concessions resulting from the Article XXIV:6 negotiations of 1986/87 "include the protection of reasonable expectations the United States had when these concessions were initially negotiated in 1962."[272]

Having thus determined on the legal status of the 1962 tariff concessions, the balance they introduced as well as the expectations emanated from them, the panel made the factual point that "the production subsidy schemes of the Community protect

[267] See Ibid., paras. 81–84. The US reacted to this EC argument by saying that "while Community imports had increased appreciably since 1962, the measure of a contracting party's reasonable expectations with regard to a concession was not a particular level of sales, but rather a question of 'trading opportunities'." Ibid., para. 85.

[268] Ibid., para.144.

[269] According to the panel, the idea underlying these provisions is that "the improved competitive opportunities that can legitimately be expected from a tariff concession can be frustrated not only by measures proscribed by the General Agreement but also by measures consistent with that Agreement." Ibid., para. 144.

[270] Ibid., para. 145.

[271] Ibid., para. 145. It further observed that "the renegotiation and modification of pre-existing concessions of the Community remained exceptional." Ibid.

[272] Ibid., para. 146.

Community producers completely from the movement of prices for imports and hence prevent the lowering of import duties from having any impact on the competitive relationship between domestic and imported oilseeds."[273] The question then turned out to be whether it was reasonable for the US "to expect that the Community would not introduce subsidy schemes systematically counteracting the price effect of the tariff concessions."[274] The finding of the panel in this respect was the following:

> "At issue in the case before it are product-specific subsidies that protect producers completely from the movement of prices for imports and thereby prevent tariff concessions from having any impact on the competitive relationship between domestic and imported oilseeds. The Panel considered that the main value of a tariff concession is that it provides an assurance of better market access through improved price competition. Contracting parties negotiate tariff concessions primarily to obtain that advantage. They must therefore be assumed to base their tariff negotiations on the expectation that the price effect of the tariff concessions will not be systematically offset. If no right of redress were given to them in such a case they would be reluctant to make tariff concessions and the General Agreement would no longer be useful as a legal framework for incorporating the results of trade negotiations. . . . For these reasons the Panel found that the United States may be assumed not to have anticipated the introduction of subsidies which protect Community producers of oilseeds completely from the movement of prices for imports and thereby prevent tariff concessions from having any impact on the competitive relationship between domestic and imported oilseeds, and which have as one consequence that all domestically-produced oilseeds are disposed of in the internal market notwithstanding the availability of imports."[275]

The panel accepted the EC argument that the US was aware of the existence in 1962 of subsidies for oilseeds in some of the member States of the Community and that a common agricultural policy was in the process of being elaborated. However, the panel concluded that the evidence showed only that the US "must reasonably have expected the transformation of national producer support measures into a Community support scheme but that it could not reasonably have anticipated the introduction of subsidy schemes which protect producers *completely* from the movement of prices for imports and thereby prevent the tariff concessions from having any impact on the competitive relationship between domestic and imported oilseeds."[276]

The panel also rejected the volume-based EC claim that the subsidy schemes for oilseeds, even if they could not reasonably have been anticipated, "did not actually impair the concessions because they did not displace or impede imports."[277] In this

[273] Ibid., para. 147.
[274] Ibid.
[275] Ibid., para. 148.
[276] Ibid., para. 149 (italics added).
[277] Ibid., para. 149.

connection, the panel simply noted that there existed a well-developed precedent that the basic provisions of the General Agreement on restrictive trade measures establish only conditions of competition and do not provide for any assurances in terms of trade volumes.[278] The panel thus concluded that "benefits accruing to the United States under Article II of the General Agreement in respect of the zero tariff bindings for oilseeds in the Community Schedule of Concessions were impaired as a result of subsidy schemes which operate to protect Community producers of oilseeds completely from the movement of prices of imports and thereby prevent the oilseeds tariff concessions from having any impact on the competitive relationship between domestic and imported oilseeds."[279]

The finding of the panel in this case reaffirms that a limit on the right of countries to subsidize their bound products is a necessary element of the tariff negotiation process. Absent this crucial element, it would indeed be of little use to spend years negotiating on tariff concessions whose effect could easily be offset by other uncontrolled domestic policy measures. At the same time, however, in line with what has been said earlier, this finding of the panel does not mean that, by resorting to domestic subsidies, the EC had violated its GATT obligations. The fact remains that, even when protecting EC producers "completely" from the movement of prices, the subsidies remain GATT-legal. To that extent, the case is only a "non-violation nullification or impairment" one. As such, in line with established GATT jurisprudence on the subject, the recommendation of the panel was limited to suggesting that the Community consider "ways and means to eliminate the impairment of its tariff concessions for oilseeds."[280] In the absence of a violation, the panel could not recommend compulsory modifications to the law. And when the Community enacted a new subsidy regime for producers of oilseeds on the basis of the panel report, which was later found to have avoided the GATT-inconsistent aspect of the previous system,[281] the issue of whether or not the non-violation nullification or impairment of tariff concessions has also ceased under the new regime reappeared. This will be discussed subsequently in connection with the report of the so-called the *Reconvened Oilseeds Panel* report.

The report of the *EC Oilseeds* panel was adopted by the CONTRACTING PARTIES on 25 January 1990. In response to the recommendations made by the panel, the EC issued a new law (Council Regulation (EEC) No. 3766/91) replacing the previous system of market price support by a new system of income support for producers of oilseeds.[282] The differences between the former and the new regimes are many, but

---

278 See Ibid., paras. 149-150.

279 Ibid., para 152. The *EC Canned Fruits* panel had also found that "it was not necessary to establish statistical evidence of damage in order to make a finding of nullification and impairment under Article XXIII. ... Benefits accruing from bound tariff concessions under Article II also encompass future trading opportunities. Consequently, complaints by contracting parties regarding nullification and impairment should be admissible even if there was not yet statistical evidence of trade damage." *EC Canned Fruits, supra* n. 197, para. 77.

280 *EC Oilseeds, supra* n. 140, para. 156.

281 See *Reconvened Oilseeds Panel Report, supra* n. 2, paras. 73-75.

282 See Ibid., para. 70.

the most relevant ones for present purposes may be put as follows: (i) the formerly per-tonne payments made to the producers through the processors have been replaced by per-hectare payments made directly to the producers for whatever area of eligible land they devote to oilseeds production; and (ii) while producers' returns in the old system were generally determined by the level of guaranteed prices, there is more room under the new system for market prices, determined in competition with imports, to affect their incomes.[283]

The *Reconvened Oilseeds Panel* report was the result of a US claim that the new regime did not comply with the recommendations made by the original oilseeds panel and that its benefits continued to be impaired under the new system.[284] The EC on the other hand asserted that its new system, which in its view only supported the income of its producers without affecting the competitive position of imported products, had eliminated the impairment of concessions as found by the original oilseeds panel. One task of the *Reconvened Oilseeds Panel* was therefore to examine whether or not the impairment of the EC's tariff concessions on oilseeds had been eliminated.[285]

The *Reconvened Panel* agreed with the US argument that "there had been a change of form but not of substance in the production subsidies which impaired and continued to impair the concessions by enabling Community producers to sell their oilseeds insulated from the effects of price competition."[286] Just like this US contention, the emphasis of the panel was on the substance of the new measure rather than the appearance of it. It stressed the fact that the subsidies under the new system were still production subsidies specific to the product which was the subject of the tariff concession in question. According to the panel, the new system was designed, just like its predecessor, "to maintain producers incomes by systematically supplementing their returns in a way which would effectively protect them from dependence on movements in prices."[287] It further observed that the new support system had "retained the essential features which led the original panel to find that the former scheme gave rise to impairment of concessions".[288]

The panel, of course, noted the legality of production subsidies under the General Agreement. However, it underscored that domestic subsidies are also recognized as

---

[283] See Ibid.

[284] In reconvening the original *Oilseeds* panel, the General Council invoked its powers under paragraph I.3 of the *Improvements to the GATT Dispute Settlement Rules and Procedures* (adopted 12 April 1989 (*BISD* 36S/61)), which in relevant part provided that the Council "shall monitor the implementation of recommendations and rulings adopted under Article XXIII:2." On that basis, the Council requested the Director-General to reconvene the members of the original panel "for the purpose of examining whether the measures taken by the European Community in Council Regulation (EEC) 3766/91 of 12 December 1991, establishing a support system for producers of soya beans, rapeseed, colzaseed and sunflowerseed, comply with the recommendations and rulings, as expressed in the Conclusions (paragraphs 155-157), of the Oilseeds Panel Report as adopted on 25 January 1990." Ibid., para. 3.

[285] Ibid., para. 72.

[286] *Reconvened Oilseeds Panel Report*, *supra* n. 2, para. 78

[287] Ibid., para. 83.

[288] Ibid.

being capable of distorting international trade and impairing the benefits accruing to contracting parties under the General Agreement "in unacceptable ways".[289] Emphasizing the importance of the 1955 interpretation,[290] the panel concluded that "benefits accruing to the United States under Article II of the General Agreement in respect of the zero tariff bindings for oilseeds in the Community Schedule of Concessions continued to be impaired as a result of the production subsidy scheme provided for in Regulation 3766/91."[291]

As in previous cases, the fact that production subsidies were GATT-consistent mattered only at the stage of the final recommendations made by the panel. As a case of non-violation nullification or impairment, the panel could not recommend compulsory modification of the system but only the cessation of the impairment of the tariff concessions – which may not necessarily require a modification. Reflecting this principle, the panel stated its recommendation in terms of options: "the Community should act expeditiously to eliminate the impairment of the tariff concessions – either by modifying its new support system for oilseeds or by renegotiating its tariff concessions for oilseeds under Article XXVIII."[292]

After the unadopted *EC Canned Fruits* case, *EC Oilseeds* is the most important case decided in line with the 1955 understanding that no unexpected subsequent domestic subsidies may impair or nullify the effects of previous tariff concessions on a product. The panel underlined that the whole purpose of the law in this regard is to protect the effect of tariff concessions from being circumvented by subsequent measures regardless of their consistency with the letter of the General Agreement.

9.4.1.3 Conclusion

The 1955 understanding, together with its straightforward application in these cases, has reasonably met its declared object of strengthening the subsidies discipline of the General Agreement. The doctrine of *prima facie* nullification or impairment, introduced by the *Ammonium Sulphate* case in its interpretation of Article III and the original version of Article XVI, and modified and improved by the 1955 understanding to take the form of the doctrine of "reasonable expectations", was applied in these cases to give effect to the assumption that contracting parties base their tariff negotiations on the expectation that the price effect of the tariff concessions will not be systematically offset by the subsequent introduction of new or the increase of existing domestic subsidies on that product. The 1955 understanding, "while not making domestic subsidies actionable under the GATT per se, gave the contracting parties a right of redress in cases where a domestic subsidy operated to undercut the value of a bound tariff concession even though the use of the subsidy was itself not prohibited."[293] Just as the obligations of Article III

[289] See Ibid., para. 77.
[290] See Ibid., para. 77.
[291] Ibid., para. 85.
[292] Ibid., para. 88.
[293] Rivers and Greenwald (1979) *supra* n. 3, p. 1462.

remained unaffected by the GATT-legality of subsidies (except to the extent exempted by paragraph 8(b) of Article III), the adoption of the principle of reasonable expectations was an appropriate response for the protection of tariff bindings under Article II from being undermined by otherwise GATT-consistent subsidies.

It has been stressed that the 1955 interpretation makes a difference only if a tariff concession already exists on the product concerned. Since not all products have been subject to bound tariffs, this obviously has its own negative sides; it restricts the usefulness of the principle. What is more, given that the number and degree of tariff bindings on agricultural products were more limited than in the non-agricultural sectors, the impact of this problem falls disproportionately against agricultural products. With this final note in mind, the next section will briefly assess the role of the Tokyo Round (1973–79) Subsidies Code in respect of the regime of domestic subsidies – which, for all practical purposes, is a failure.

9.5 Domestic Subsidies under the Subsidies Code

As its official title[294] indicates, the Subsidies Code develops the provisions of the General Agreement on the subject of subsidies and countervailing duties, the most important ones being Article XVI and Article VI, respectively. Practically all the paragraphs of these two provisions find their expanded and, in most cases, strengthened counterparts in the Code. However, this does not appear to apply to paragraphs dealing with domestic subsidies. This section tries to answer the question of whether, and how far, the Subsidies Code has brought about any developments on the regime of domestic subsidies.

9.5.1 Policy Aspects

Any multilateral attempt to regulate the practice of subsidies in general, and domestic subsidies in particular, faces the hard task of reconciling two conflicting interests: governmental desire to employ subsidies for the promotion of national economic and social priorities on the one hand, and multilateral desire to avoid the adverse consequences such a practice may entail on the production and trade interests of third countries, on the other. The structure of the Subsidies Code reflects this underlying tension between these two conflicting interests.

The Code first declares, in both its preambular and operative parts, to have recognized that subsidies, whether domestic or export, are used by governments to promote important objectives of national social and economic policy.[295] Recognition of these national interests is then followed by a similar recognition of the multilateral interest at stake – that subsidies may have harmful effects on trade and production

---

[294] "Agreement on Interpretation and Application of Articles VI, XVI, and XXIII of the General Agreement on Tariffs and Trade", published in *BISD* 26S/56-85.

[295] See para. 3 of the Preamble and Article 8(1) of the Subsidies Code.

and thereby cause adverse effects to the interests of other signatories.[296] Needless to say, striking the right balance between these two interests is the most daunting challenge the multilateral trading system seems to be doomed to grapple with.

The general approach adopted here was to emphasize on the effects of subsidies,[297] rather than on the practices as such, so as to ensure that "the use of subsidies does not adversely affect or prejudice the interests of any signatory".[298] When it comes to the details, however, the Subsidies Code, in line with the 1955 Review, distinguishes between export subsidies[299] on the one hand and domestic subsidies on the other, the latter here cautiously termed as "subsidies other than export subsidies".[300] The essence of the rules therefore varies depending on whether they apply to export subsidies or "subsidies other than export subsidies". Generally speaking, while the former are prohibited,[301] the latter are permitted. In other words, while the multilateral interest was made to prevail over the national interest in the case of export subsidies, the opposite was the case as regards domestic subsidies.

This is not simply accidental; it is rather a product of the prevailing philosophy underlying the extent to which state sovereignty should yield in favour of international regulation of the more or less internal policy instrument of domestic subsidies. After all, most of the participants in the Subsidies Code negotiations were of the view that the use of domestic subsidies was "strictly a question of national or internal policy".[302]

The cumulative effect of all this is that the explicit statement of prohibition of the Code on export subsidies is matched, in the area of domestic subsidies, by an explicit statement of approval: "Signatories recognize that subsidies other than export subsidies are widely used as important instruments for the promotion of social and economic policy objectives and do not intend to restrict the right of signatories to use such subsidies to achieve these important policy objectives which they consider desirable."[303] The Code enumerates some of the policy objectives promoted by the use of domestic subsidies, which include subsidies provided for regional development, structural adjustment, employment, research and development, the economic and social development of developing countries, and the environment.[304] It further provides that these objectives "may be achieved, *inter alia*, by means of subsidies granted with the aim of giving an advantage to certain enterprises" and gives a

---

[296] See para. 4 of the Preamble and Article 8(1) of the Subsidies Code.
[297] See para. 5 of the Preamble to the Subsidies Code.
[298] See para. 6 of the Preamble to the Subsidies Code.
[299] See Articles 9, 10, 12, and 13 of the Subsidies Code.
[300] See Articles 11, 12, and 13 of the Subsidies Code.
[301] There are two exceptions to this: the use of export subsidies in general by developing countries (see Article 14, and particularly para. 2, of the Subsidies Code), and the export subsidies applying to the so-called "certain primary products".
[302] Rivers and Greenwald (1979) *supra* n. 3, p. 1449.
[303] Article 11(1) of the Subsidies Code.
[304] Ibid.

somewhat detailed enumeration of the possible forms of subsidies that are often employed to this end.[305]

But again, this recognition of the right of signatories is immediately followed by a further recognition that domestic subsidies "may cause or threaten to cause injury to a domestic industry of another signatory or serious prejudice to the interests of another signatory or may nullify or impair benefits accruing to another signatory under the General Agreement, in particular where such subsidies would adversely affect the conditions of normal competition."[306] The substantive rules of the code on this issue aimed at avoiding the harmful consequences of domestic subsidies on third countries while at the same time leaving signatories free to employ those measures.

9.5.2 The Obligation to "Seek to Avoid" Causing Adverse Effects by Means of Domestic Subsidies

The only substantive obligation on domestic subsidies is that which is provided under Article 8(3) and repeated, verbatim, in Article 11(2) of the Code. Framed in a manner reminiscent of the 1955 formulation of the obligation of contracting parties concerning export subsidies on primary products,[307] Signatories undertook to *seek to avoid* causing adverse effects to the interests of other signatories through the use of domestic subsidies.[308] As the clause "seek to avoid" indicates, this is not as such an obligation not to cause these adverse effects; much less is it a limitation on the right of signatories to use domestic subsidies. There is no requirement for contracting parties not to be harmful to others; they only have an obligation of good faith (although nearly devoid of any legal substance) to *try* not to be so. In other words, the Subsidies Code, by not obliging signatories to avoid domestic subsidies in a manner injurious to the interests of others, simply left the previous regime without any substantive improvement.

---

[305] The possible forms of subsidies enumerated which may be used in this sense are the following: Government financing of commercial enterprises, including grants, loans or guarantees; government provision or government financed provision of utility, supply distribution and other operational or support services or facilities; government financing of research and development programmes; fiscal incentives; and government subscription to, or provision of, equity capital.

[306] Article 11(2) of the Subsidies Code.

[307] According to para. 3 of Article XVI of the General Agreement, "contracting parties shall seek to avoid the use of subsidies on the export of primary products"; for a discussion of this issue, see *supra* chapter 5.

[308] Under Article 8(3), "Signatories further agree that they shall *seek to avoid* causing, through the use of any subsidy (a) injury to the domestic industry of another signatory, (b) nullification or impairment of the benefits accruing directly or indirectly to another signatory under the General Agreement, or (c) serious prejudice to the interests of another signatory." Likewise, Article 11 states that "Signatories recognize ... that subsidies other than export subsidies ... may cause or threaten to cause injury to the interests of another signatory or may nullify or impair benefits accruing to another signatory under the General Agreement, in particular where such subsidies would adversely affect the conditions of normal competition. Signatories shall therefore *seek to avoid* causing such effects through the use of subsidies." Articles 8(3) and 11(2) of the Subsidies Code (italics added).

9.6 Conclusion

The provisions of the 1947 version of the General Agreement, supplemented only by the 1955 understanding and the few interpretations made by the CONTRACTING PARTIES in the resolution of actual disputes, continued to provide the principal regime governing domestic subsidies even after the conclusion of the Tokyo Round Subsidies Code. It is noteworthy that agricultural products have been treated in the same way as non-agricultural products in almost all aspects of domestic subsidies. The only practical distinction is that which results from the indirect role of the fact that fewer agricultural products had had bound tariff commitments, which is one condition for the doctrine of reasonable expectations to apply. It thus follows that in the field of domestic subsidies – and unlike that of export subsidies, for example – the Uruguay Round had had the task of introducing a system of rules of discipline almost from scratch not only for agricultural products in particular, but for all tradable goods in general.

CHAPTER 10

DOMESTIC SUPPORT UNDER THE URUGUAY ROUND AGREEMENT ON AGRICULTURE

10.1 Background: Domestic Support under the SCM Agreement in General

As reiterated in the previous chapters, the Uruguay Round Agreement on Subsidies and Countervailing Measures (hereafter the Subsidies Agreement or the SCM Agreement) has introduced a comprehensive regime for both domestic as well as export subsidies. In what is known as the "traffic-light" approach adopted by the SCM Agreement, subsidies are either prohibited (or "red"), actionable (or "amber"), or non-actionable (or "green"). While export subsidies fall solely in the first class, domestic subsidies span over all the three categories. But, most domestic subsidies are either actionable or non-actionable, and it is only one form of domestic subsidies – the so-called import-substitution subsidies – which falls within the ambit of the prohibited subsidies. In this section, we will discuss the regime introduced by the Subsidies Agreement as it applies to the practice of domestic subsidies in general and raise the question of whether, and to what extent, the Subsidies Agreement applies to agricultural domestic support.

10.1.1 Import-Substitution Subsidies: A "Red Box"?

According to the Subsidies Agreement, there are two forms of subsidies that are subject to a flat prohibition – export subsidies and subsidies contingent upon the use of domestic over imported products. Article 3.1 provides that "[e]xcept as provided in the Agreement on Agriculture, the following subsidies, within the meaning of Article 1 above, shall be prohibited: (a) subsidies contingent, in law or in fact, whether solely or as one of several other conditions, upon export performance, including those illustrated in Annex I; (b) *subsidies contingent, whether solely or as one of several other conditions, upon the use of domestic over imported goods.*"[1] According to paragraph 2 of the same Article, Members "shall not grant nor maintain subsidies referred to in paragraph 1."[2] While the former have been dealt with in **Part II**, the latter, often called "import-substitution subsidies", fall under domestic subsidies; as such, they will be dealt with in this section.

---

1 Article 3.1 of the SCM Agreement (italics added).

2 Article 3.2 of the SCM Agreement.

Import-substitution subsidies are a form of subsidies designed to encourage the use of domestically produced inputs or other domestic products over imports. In simple terms, the government makes some form of "financial contribution" conferring a benefit on recipient enterprises on condition that they use locally-produced products rather than imported ones. The use of domestic products by the enterprises is a condition precedent for them to benefit from the financial contribution made by the government or its agencies. To take an actual example in the agricultural sector, farmers may be told to buy, say, domestically produced tractors (like what Italy did in the 1958 case) or get no subsidies from the government. As such, this type of subsidy has the role of encouraging the use of local products and discouraging imports.

Seen in the light of the fundamental principles of the General Agreement, an import-substitution subsidy is nothing but a discrimination on the basis of the origin of the goods in the market – an issue addressed by the national treatment principles of Article III of GATT 1994. According to one of the key provisions of this Article, "the products of the territory of any contracting party imported into the territory of any other contracting party shall be accorded treatment no less favourable than that accorded to the like products of national origin in respect of all laws, regulations and requirements affecting their internal sale, offering for sale, purchase, transportation, distribution or use."[3] The whole purpose of Article III is "to ensure equality of competitive conditions between imported and like domestic products".[4] A subsidy provided to enterprises contingent on their use of domestic products deprives the imports of this equality of competitive conditions; it subjects them to treatment less favourable than that applied to domestic products. Moreover, the less favourable treatment adversely affects the internal sale or use of the imported products.

As pointed out by *Italian Agricultural Machinery,* the intention of the drafters of Article III was "clearly to treat the imported products in the same way as the like domestic products once they had been cleared through customs. Otherwise indirect protection could be given."[5] Stressing on the comprehensive nature of the specific provision, the same panel stated that the "selection of the word 'affecting' would imply ... that the drafters of the Article intended to cover in paragraph 4 not only the laws and regulations which directly governed the conditions of sale or purchase but also any laws or regulations which might adversely modify the conditions of competition between the domestic and imported products on the internal market."[6] On that basis, the panel agreed with the complainant[7] that credit facilities provided under Italian law, which were "reserved exclusively to the purchasers of Italian tractors and other agricultural machinery represented a discrimination and the

---

[3] Article III.4 of the General Agreement.

[4] *Canada – Certain Measures Concerning Periodicals*, report of the Appellate Body (WT/DS31/AB/R) 30 June 1997, p. 18.

[5] *Italian Discrimination against Imported Agricultural Machinery*, report of the panel (L/833 *BISD* 7S/60) adopted on 23 October 1958, para. 11.

[6] Ibid., para. 12.

[7] Ibid., paras. 11-16; For more on this case, see *supra* Chapter 9.

operation of the Law involved an inconsistency with the provisions of Article III of the General Agreement".[8]

A similar approach was adopted in *Parts and Components*.[9] The dispute in that case was a result of an EC decision to include in its anti-dumping regulation a provision intended to prevent the circumvention of anti-dumping duties on finished products through the importation of parts or materials for use in the assembly or production of like finished products within the EC. The regulation allowed a suspension of anti-dumping proceedings "conditional on undertakings by assemblers and producers in the EEC to limit the use of imported parts and materials."[10] This, Japan argued, was a violation, *inter alia,* of Article III.4 of the General Agreement because "it entailed a treatment of parts imported from a specific country which was less favourable than the treatment of domestically produced parts."[11] The EC responded that acceptance of undertakings was not mandatory but left to the discretion of individual contracting parties and did not qualify for a "requirement" in the sense of Article III.4 of the General Agreement.[12] The panel was thus faced with a situation in which there was no formal obligation to offer or accept undertakings to limit the use of imported parts and materials but the consequence of not so doing could be "the continuation of procedures that may lead to the imposition of [what are called] ... anti-circumvention duties."[13] The panel ruled that "the comprehensive coverage of '*all* laws, regulations or requirements *affecting*' the internal sale, etc. of imported products suggests that not only requirements which an enterprise is legally bound to carry out, ... but also those which an enterprise voluntarily accepts in order to obtain an advantage from the government constitute 'requirements' within the meaning of that provision."[14]

More recently, the *Periodicals* panel observed that imported and domestic

---

8 Ibid., para. 5. In the notorious *EC Oilseeds* case, too, the panel stated the principle in the form of a premise: "if the economic benefits generated by the payments granted by the Community can at least partly be retained by the processors of Community oilseeds, the payments generate a benefit conditional upon the purchase of oilseeds of domestic origin inconsistently with Article III:4." *European Economic Community – Payments and Subsidies Paid to Processors and Producers of Oilseeds and Related Animal-Feed Proteins,* report of the panel (L/6627 *BISD* 37S/86) adopted on 25 January 1990, para. 137.

9 *EEC – Regulation on Imports of Parts and Components*, report of the panel (L/6657, *BISD* 37S/132) adopted on 16 May 1990.

10 See Ibid., para. 5.1.

11 See Ibid., paras. 3.41-3.42; see also paras. 3.46-3.47

12 See Ibid., paras. 3.49; see also para. 5.19.

13 The Panel noted that there was "no obligation under the EEC's anti-dumping Regulation to offer parts undertakings, to accept suggestions by the EEC Commission to offer such undertakings and to maintain the parts undertakings given. However, the consequence of not offering an undertaking, or of withdrawing an existing undertaking, can be the continuation of procedures that may lead to the imposition of the anti-circumvention duties. Article 10 of Regulation No. 2324/88 states that 'where an undertaking has been withdrawn or where the Commission has reason to believe that it has been violated ... it may ... apply ... antidumping ... duties forthwith on the basis of the facts established before the acceptance of the undertaking'." Ibid., para. 5.20.

14 Ibid., para. 5.21 (emphasis in original).

periodicals were like products and that Canada Post charged lower rates on domestic periodicals than imported ones.[15] The panel found from this that "Canada Post's application of the 'commercial Canadian' and 'funded' rates to Canadian periodicals, which are lower than the 'international' rates applied to imported periodicals (including the availability of additional discounts only to Canadian periodicals), is inconsistent with Article III:4 of GATT 1994."[16]

It thus appears that there is no way by which a law or regulation making the provision of subsidies contingent upon the use of locally-produced products as opposed to imports could escape the wide reach of this provision. What is more, not only is there such a well-developed jurisprudence under the General Agreement on this subject, it has also been particularly singled out as one of the trade-related investment measures (TRIMs) declared to be inconsistent with Article III.4 of GATT 1994, and hence prohibited under Article 2.1 of the Agreement on Trade-Related Investment Measures (the TRIMs Agreement).[17] We can deduce from all this that local content subsidies clearly fall within the ambit of the prohibition under Article III of the General Agreement. The question will then be as to whether the inclusion of import-substitution subsidies in Article 3 of the SCM Agreement is simply redundant.

---

15 See *Canada – Certain Measures Concerning Periodicals*, report of the panel (WT/DS31/R) 14 March 1997, para. 5.37.

16 Ibid., para. 5.39. The panel, however, ruled that the system of subsidies in this case satisfied the exceptions under Article III:8(b): "we do not find that Canada Post retains any economic benefits from the 'funded' rate scheme it applies to certain Canadian periodicals. The payment of the subsidy is made 'exclusively' to Canadian publishers that qualify for the scheme. Since Article III:8(b) explicitly recognizes that subsidies exclusively paid to domestic producers are not subject to the national treatment rules of Article III, including those under Article III:4, we find that Canada's 'funded' rate scheme on periodicals can be justified under this provision." Ibid. para. 5.44. This was, however, reversed on appeal. The Appellate Body expressed its agreement with the *US Malt Beverages* panel interpretation of Article III:8(b) that the provision limits the permissible producer subsidies to "payments" after taxes have been collected or payments otherwise consistent with Article III and concluded that "We do not see a reason to distinguish a reduction of tax rates on a product from a reduction in transportation or postal rates. Indeed, an examination of the text, context, and object and purpose of Article III:8(b) suggests that it was intended to exempt from the obligations of Article III only the payment of subsidies which involves the expenditure of revenue by a government. . . . For these reasons, we reverse the Panel's findings and conclusions that Canada's 'funded' postal rates scheme for periodicals is justified under Article III:8(b) of the GATT 1994." *Periodicals*, report of the Appellate Body, *supra* n. 4, pp. 34-35. See also *United States – Measures Affecting Alcoholic and Malt Beverages* Report of the Panel (DS23/R *BISD* 39S/206) adopted on 19 June 1992.

17 Article 2.1 of the TRIMs Agreement provides as follows: "without prejudice to other rights and obligations under GATT 1994, no Member shall apply any TRIM that is inconsistent with the provisions of Article III ... of GATT 1994." The two measures identified in the illustrative list of TRIMs as being inconsistent with the national treatment obligation of Article III.4 of GATT 1994 are those which require "(a) the purchase or use by an enterprise of products of domestic origin or from any domestic source, whether specified in terms of particular products, in terms of volume or value of products, or in terms of a proportion of volume or value of its local production or (b) that an enterprise's purchases or use of imported products be limited to an amount related to the volume or value of local products that it exports." Paragraph 1 of the Illustrative List, Annex to the Agreement on Trade-Related Investment Measures.

A related but more sweeping argument was made by the defendant in *Indonesia Automobiles*. The challenged measures in that case were different Indonesian so-called "car programmes" which involved local content requirements. Two types of benefits were attached to those requirements: tax benefits for finished motor vehicles and "National Cars" incorporating a certain percentage value of domestic products; and customs duty benefits for imported parts and components used in motor vehicles incorporating a certain percentage value of domestic products. The complainants – the EC, the US, and Japan – claimed, *inter alia,* that these local content requirements and the tax and customs duty benefits linked to them violated the provisions of Article III:4 of GATT 1994 and Article 2 of the TRIMs Agreement.[18]

In its defence, Indonesia argued that the measures at issue were subsidies governed exclusively by Article XVI of GATT 1994 and the SCM Agreement. In its view, the only applicable law to the dispute was the SCM Agreement, which "unlike many other WTO agreements, ... provides substantial special and differential treatment for developing countries like Indonesia."[19] According to Indonesia, the SCM Agreement is in a state of "general conflict" with Article III of GATT,[20] and that, being a *lex specialis* on the subject, the SCM Agreement should prevail.[21] More importantly for our purposes here, Indonesia argued that the application to the dispute of Article III of the General Agreement would "reduce the SCM Agreement to 'inutility'."[22]

On the alleged "general conflict" between Article III and the SCM Agreement, the panel made two important points: that "in public international law there is a presumption against conflict"[23] and that "for a conflict to exist between two agreements or two provisions thereof, they must cover the same substantive

---

18 *Indonesia – Certain Measures Affecting the Automobile Industry* report of the panel (WT/DS54/R, WT/DS55/R, WT/DS59/R, WT/DS64/R) 2 July 1998, paras. 14.12 and 14.13. The complainants also argued that the tax benefits of the different "car programmes" in favour of certain domestic cars and National Cars violated the provisions of Article III:2 of the General Agreement. Ibid., paras. 14.14 to 14.16.

19 Ibid., para. 5.132. Indonesia invoked Article 27 of the SCM Agreement on special and differential treatment to developing countries and argued that the subsidies under consideration "technically fall within the scope of Article 3.1(b) as 'subsidies contingent (whether solely or as one of several other conditions) upon the use of domestic over imported goods'. ... Indonesia is a developing country. Accordingly, Indonesia is within the ambit of Article 27.3 of the SCM Agreement, which provides that '[t]he prohibition of paragraph 1(b) of Article 3 shall not apply to developing country Members for a period of five years ... from the date of entry into force of the WTO Agreement [i.e., until 1 January 2000].' Instead, the provisions of Articles 5 to 7 regarding 'actionable subsidies' apply. ... No Complainant has, as required by Article 6, demonstrated by positive evidence that the Indonesian auto subsidies result in 'serious prejudice' to its interests." Ibid., para. 5.142-5.143.

20 Ibid., para. 14.27. "General conflict" is here understood to mean "a conflict between the entirety of the SCM Agreement and the entirety of Article III". Ibid.

21 Indonesia further argued that "[s]ince Article III is not applicable, the TRIMs Agreement is not applicable." Ibid., para. 14.27.

22 Ibid., para. 14.27. In the alternative, Indonesia contended that "should Article III and/or the TRIMs Agreement be considered to apply to this dispute, there are specific conflicts between some of the provisions of the SCM Agreement, on the one hand, and some provisions of Article III on which the complainants base their claims, on the other hand." Ibid.

23 Ibid., 14.28.

matter."[24] After a thorough assessment of the issues, the panel ruled that there was no general conflict between them because they "have, generally, different coverage and do not impose the same type of obligations."[25]

The panel's assessment of whether application of Article III of the General Agreement to the dispute would reduce the SCM Agreement to *inutility* is particularly relevant to the question of possible redundancy of Article 3.1(b) of the SCM Agreement raised above. The panel noted that "in most cases the subsidies regulated under the SCM Agreement will not be covered by the provisions of Article III:2 or III:4."[26] According to the panel, the only subsidies that would be affected by the provisions of Article III are "those that would involve discrimination between domestic and imported products."[27] It is noteworthy that import-substitution subsidies fall under this particular category because, by making the subsidies contingent upon the use of domestically produced products, governments are discriminating against the use of imported products. The panel acknowledged that Article III of GATT and the SCM Agreement "appear to overlap in respect of certain measures" but insisted that "the two sets of provisions have different purposes and different coverage. Indeed, they also offer different remedies, different dispute settlement time limits and different implementation requirements."[28] On that basis, the panel rejected Indonesia's sweeping argument that the application of Article III to subsidies would reduce the SCM Agreement to "inutility".

The approach of the panel in this case is sufficiently convincing because Indonesia's argument was too broad a generalization to apply in any sensible way. However, it is difficult to see how this approach of the panel may apply to the particular relationship between Article III of the General Agreement and Article 3.1(b) of the SCM Agreement. Both provisions are concerned with the competitive relationship between imported and domestic products. An import-substitution

24 Ibid., 14.29.

25 Ibid., para. 14.36. The panel held, in this respect, that "Article III of GATT 1994 and the WTO rules on subsidies remain focused on different problems. Article III continues to prohibit discrimination between domestic and imported products in respect of internal taxes and other domestic regulations, including local content requirements. It does not 'proscribe' nor does it 'prohibit' the provision of any subsidy *per se*. By contrast, the SCM Agreement prohibits subsidies which are conditional on export performance and on meeting local content requirements, provides remedies with respect to certain subsidies where they cause adverse effects to the interests of another Member and exempts certain subsidies from actionability under the SCM Agreement. In short, Article III prohibits discrimination between domestic and imported products while the SCM Agreement regulates the provision of subsidies to enterprises." Ibid., para. 14.33.

26 Ibid., para. 14.37. The panel gives examples: "Article III:2 would not cover direct transfers of funds, e.g., loans and grants to firms, as this Article is concerned only with the application of indirect taxes on products. Subsidies in these forms may be contrary to Article III:4 to the extent that they are linked to measures which affect the internal sale, purchase, use, etc. of domestic goods. The provision of raw materials by a government at a subsidized price would not be contrary to either Article III:2 or Article III:4, unless it also contained a condition that affected as such the internal sale, offering for sale, etc. of goods." Ibid.

27 Ibid., para. 14.39.

28 Ibid., para. 14.39.

subsidy necessarily violates Article III.4 of the General Agreement. That is why subsidies affecting the competitive relationship of products have been consistently held to violate the General Agreement long before the arrival of the SCM Agreement.

However, as the Appellate Body rightly emphasized in *Reformulated Gasoline*, an interpreter is "not free to adopt a reading that would result in reducing whole clauses or paragraphs of a treaty to redundancy or inutility."[29] But respecting this principle appears difficult in this particular case. Perhaps the only way out is to emphasize on the "different remedies, different dispute settlement time limits and different implementation requirements" mentioned by the panel in *Indonesia Automobiles*[30] and argue that although all internal measures discriminating between imports and like products, including import-substitution subsidies, are already prohibited by the national treatment principle, such a measure will be subject to the accelerated dispute settlement mechanism of the SCM Agreement when it takes the form of an import-substitution subsidy.

Be that as it may, and regardless of the rationale behind the provision, import-substitution subsidies are flatly prohibited by the SCM Agreement and fall under the "red" light category. They are part of domestic subsidies because their provision does not depend on export performance.[31] Under Article 2.3 of the Agreement, they are deemed to be specific. According to Article 3.2, "Members shall not grant nor maintain subsidies referred to in paragraph 1". Such a subsidy is thus addressed on the same level as any other export subsidy. As such, it also benefits from the more expedited dispute settlement provisions of Article 4 regarding prohibited subsidies.

Finally, it should be noted that although the SCM Agreement applies, in principle, to all forms of products and services covered by the Final Act of the WTO, Article 3.1 explicitly states that the provisions of Part II apply subject to the Agreement on Agriculture. Granting an import-substitution agricultural subsidy of the type referred to under Article 3.1(b) is therefore prohibited only if it is not contradicted by any provision of the Agriculture Agreement. However, as we shall see later on, the Agreement on Agriculture does not expressly "provide" anything particularly concerning the use of import-substitution subsidies. No subsidy is prohibited by the Agriculture Agreement; it talks in terms only of reduction of the Aggregate Measurement of Support (the AMS) regardless of the method of support adopted by a country. In as long as the amount of support provided by a country does not exceed the permissible maximum for a given year, the form in which it is made does not matter as such. Apparently this would mean that the prohibition by the SCM Agreement of import-substitution subsidies does not apply to agriculture. However, as argued earlier, import-substitution subsidies are already prohibited by the national treatment provision of Article III of the General Agreement, which also

---

29 *United States – Standards for Reformulated and Conventional Gasoline*, report of the Appellate Body (WT/DS2/AB/R), 20 May 1996, p. 23.

30 *Indonesia Automobiles*, report of the panel, *supra* n. 18, para. 14.39.

31 Indeed, if there had been an export performance condition for their provision, there would have been no need for a separate paragraph from the very outset.

applies to agricultural products. Consequently, the only difference between an import-substitution subsidy in the field of agriculture and that in others seems to be limited to the availability or otherwise of the accelerated dispute settlement procedure and remedies provided for prohibited subsidies under Article 4 of the SCM Agreement on special or additional rules and procedures of dispute settlement.

10.1.2 Actionable Subsidies

The approach of the Uruguay Round in the area of domestic subsidies[32] is basically a continuation of the trade-effects principle of the Tokyo Round Subsidies Code. Accordingly, Article 5 of the SCM Agreement stipulates that "[n]o Member should cause, through the use of *any* subsidy referred to in paragraphs 1 and 2 of Article 1, adverse effects to the interests of other Members".[33] As the use of the words "any subsidies" clearly shows, this provision applies to all forms of subsidies unless they benefit from some form of specific and explicit exemption. In *Indonesia Automobiles*, the EC and the US used this language to side-step Indonesia's right as a developing country to provide local content subsidies for a limited number of years under the special and differential provision of Article 27.3. They argued that the provision excluded the application only of the prohibition contained in Article 3.1(b), and "does not confer immunity against actions based on other provisions of the SCM Agreement and, in particular, against action under Part III of the SCM Agreement."[34] They contended that Article 5 applied with respect to "all specific subsidies within the meaning of paragraphs 1 and 2 of Article 1 of the SCM Agreement, including those which are prohibited by Article 3."[35] The panel ruled in favour of the complainants on this issue. It found specifically that "the complainants are not precluded by Article 27 from seeking to demonstrate, by positive evidence, that Indonesia has caused, through the effects of the subsidies at issue in this case, serious prejudice to their interests."[36]

The "adverse effects to the interests of other Members" referred to under Article 5 of the SCM Agreement are understood to include three different situations: injury to the domestic industry of another Member[37]; nullification or impairment of benefits accruing to members in the sense of Article XXIII of the GATT[38]; and serious

32 The term "domestic subsidies" under the category of actionable subsidies is used in the sense of all non-export subsidies with the exception of import-substitution subsidies.

33 Italics added.

34 *Indonesia Automobiles*, report of the panel, *supra* n. 18, para. 8.47.

35 Ibid., para. 8.49.

36 Ibid., para. 14.162.

37 Article 5.1(a) of the SCM Agreement. Footnote 11 to this provision provides that "[t]he term 'injury to the domestic industry' is used here in the same sense as it is used in Part V", which Part deals with the subject of countervailing duties. Footnote 45 to Article 15 of this Part provides the following: "Under this Agreement the term 'injury' shall, unless otherwise specified, be taken to mean material injury to a domestic industry, threat of material injury to a domestic industry or material retardation of the establishment of such an industry and shall be interpreted in accordance with the provisions of this Article."

38 Article 5.1(b) of the SCM Agreement.

prejudice to the interests of another member.[39] But again, Article 5 expressly states that it "does not apply to subsidies maintained on agricultural products as provided in Article 13 of the Agreement on Agriculture."[40]

The concept of "serious prejudice" is addressed under Article 6, which may be summarized as follows. Paragraph 1 of Article 6 lists four different situations in which serious prejudice would be presumed. They include cases of: (a) total ad valorem subsidization of a product exceeding 5 per cent; (b) subsidies to cover operating losses sustained by an *industry*; (c) subsidies to cover operating losses sustained by an *enterprise*, other than one-time measures which are non-recurrent and cannot be repeated for that enterprise and which are given merely to provide time for the development of long-term solutions and to avoid acute social problems; and (d) direct forgiveness of debt, i.e. forgiveness of government-held debt, and grants to cover debt repayment.[41] A claimant that shows the existence of any of these situations establishes a *prima facie* case that serious prejudice has been caused. However, this is a rebuttable presumption. The subsidizing Member may refute it by demonstrating that, despite the existence of those situations, none of the effects amounts to any of the forms a serious prejudice may take as enumerated under paragraph 6.3.[42]

Regardless of whether a complainant benefits from a presumption, three forms of effects are identified by paragraph 3 to amount to serious prejudice if they are caused by subsidized products: displacement or impedance of imports (into the market of the subsidizing Member) and of exports (of another Member from a third country

---

[39] Article 5.1(c) of the SCM Agreement.

[40] Article 5.1 of the SCM Agreement.

[41] Article 6.1 of the SCM Agreement (footnotes omitted). However, the general presumption that a subsidy falling within the terms of Article 6.1 causes serious prejudice to the interests of another Member is not applicable where the subsidizing country is a developing country Member. Article 27, paragraphs 8 and 9 of the SCM Agreement on special and differential treatment for developing countries provide as follows:

> "27.8 There shall be no presumption in terms of paragraph 1 of Article 6 that a subsidy granted by a developing country Member results in serious prejudice, as defined in this Agreement. Such serious prejudice, where applicable under the terms of paragraph 9, shall be demonstrated by positive evidence, in accordance with the provisions of paragraphs 3 through 8 of Article 6.
>
> "27.9 Regarding actionable subsidies granted or maintained by a developing country Member other than those referred to in paragraph 1 of Article 6, action may not be authorized or taken under Article 7 unless nullification or impairment of tariff concessions or other obligations under GATT 1994 is found to exist as a result of such a subsidy, in such a way as to displace or impede imports of a like product of another Member into the market of the subsidizing developing country Member or unless injury to a domestic industry in the market of an importing Member occurs."
>
> In such cases, therefore, while a subsidy by a developing country Member "may be subject to a serious prejudice challenge, a complainant does not benefit from a presumption of serious prejudice; rather, a complainant must demonstrate the existence of serious prejudice by positive evidence." *Indonesia Automobiles,* report of the panel, *supra* n. 18, para. 14.158.

[42] Paragraph 2 of Article 6 thus provides that "[n]otwithstanding the provisions of paragraph 1, serious prejudice shall not be found if the subsidizing Member demonstrates that the subsidy in question has not resulted in any of the effects enumerated in paragraph 3."

market),[43] significant price undercutting,[44] and increase in market share.[45] These are all concepts with a long history in the General Agreement and the Subsidies Code.[46] Loyal to its history, the effect of an increase in market share applies only in the case of primary products.[47] Moreover, in as long as the increase is to be measured "as compared to the average share it had during the previous period of three years"[48] such old concepts as the previous representative period and the like are still part of the new scenario. The scope of application of this provision is, however, limited because, firstly, it "does not apply to subsidies maintained on agricultural products as provided in Article 13 of the Agreement on Agriculture"[49] – thus excluding the single largest category of primary products from its coverage; and secondly, it does not apply if "other multilaterally agreed specific rules apply to the trade in the product or commodity in question."[50]

The exclusion of agricultural products from the purview of the Subsidies Agreement on actionable subsidies is not absolute. As will be discussed later, the so-called "green box" agricultural domestic support measures which conform fully to the relevant provisions of the Agriculture Agreement are completely immune from challenge under Part III of the SCM Agreement.[51] On the other hand, Article 13(b) of the Agriculture Agreement opens some leeway for "blue box" agricultural domestic support measures, which otherwise fully conform with other relevant provisions, to be challenged under Articles 5 and 6 of the SCM Agreement.[52]

To sum up, while the "no-adverse-effects-through-any-subsidies" principle of the Tokyo Round was elaborated and adopted during the Uruguay Round for nearly[53] all other products, agricultural domestic support measures have been largely excluded from the Subsidies Agreement and delegated to the Agreement on Agriculture.

12.2.2.1 Multilateral Remedies Available against Actionable Subsidies

As discussed in **Part II** on the remedies available against export subsidy cases, the

---

43 Article 6.3 (a) and (b) of the SCM Agreement; for further practical details on this point, see paragraph 6.4.

44 Article 6.3(c) of the SCM Agreement; see also paragraph 6.5.

45 Article 6.3(d) of the SCM Agreement.

46 See, for instance, Article XVI.4 of the General Agreement on price undercutting, and Article 10.2 of the Subsidies Code on displacement.

47 See Article XVI.3 of the General Agreement on export subsidies in the area of primary products. For a somehow related use of market share in connection with displacement and impedance, see paragraph 6.4 of the SCM Agreement.

48 Article 6.3(d) of the SCM Agreement.

49 Article 6.9 of the SCM Agreement.

50 Footnote 17 to Article 6.3(d) of the SCM Agreement.

51 See Article 13(a) of the Agreement on Agriculture.

52 The condition is that the measures should not grant support to a specific commodity in excess of that decided during the 1992 marketing year.

53 The word "nearly" is used here so as not to exclude if there are any "other multilaterally agreed specific rules" applying to the trade of specific primary products or commodities in the sense of footnote 17 to Article 6.3(d) of the SCM Agreement.

SCM Agreement has introduced special or additional rules of its own governing the settlement of disputes involving subsidies. These special rules are meant only to further strengthen or tighten the already tight rules of dispute settlement prescribed under the DSU. The difference is bigger mainly in the area of prohibited subsidies.[54] In the case of actionable subsidies, too, there are some important differences, which will be summarised below in a comparative fashion.

According to Article 7 of the SCM Agreement, while Members are allowed to request for consultations whenever they believe that they are facing injury to their domestic industry, or nullification or impairment, or serious prejudice as a result of any subsidy maintained by other Members,[55] the requested party is obliged to enter into consultations "as quickly as possible".[56] If no mutually acceptable solution results from such consultations within sixty days, either party may refer the matter to the DSB for the establishment of a panel[57] – a time limit the same as that set for all disputes brought under the DSU,[58] and twice the limit set for prohibited subsidy cases under Article 4.4 of the SCM Agreement. Once established, however, an actionable-subsidy panel is required to be composed within fifteen days of its establishment,[59] which is equal to the time set for prohibited subsidies[60] and half that set for other disputes under the DSU.[61]

On the other hand, the time limit for the panel's submission of its final report is set at 120 days from its composition[62] – a period which falls between the ninety-day limit for prohibited subsidies[63] and the nine-month limit set for other disputes in general by paragraph 12.9 of the DSU.[64] The DSB is then required to adopt the panel report within thirty days from its issuance.[65] This time limit is the same as that set for prohibited subsidy cases[66] and half the time set for other cases under the DSU.[67] The conditions for non-adoption of a panel report are the same in all three cases – the impracticable condition of a DSB consensus against adoption, or an appeal by either of the parties to the dispute.

If there is an appeal, the Appellate Body is required to submit its report within a maximum of ninety days,[68] which is the same as that fixed for general cases under the

---

54 See *supra* chapter 6.
55 Article 7.1 of the SCM Agreement.
56 Article 7.3 of the SCM Agreement.
57 Article 7.4 of the SCM Agreement.
58 Para. 4.7 of the Dispute Settlement Understanding.
59 Article 7.4 of the SCM Agreement.
60 As this issue is no where directly addressed under Article 4 of the SCM Agreement, this is only a deduction on the basis of Article 4.12.
61 Para. 8.7 of the DSU.
62 Article 7.5 of the SCM Agreement.
63 Article 4.6 of SCM Agreement.
64 Note the difference in benchmark between the two here. While the nine-month period in the latter case starts from the date of establishment of the panel, the former start from the day of composition of the panel.
65 Article 7.6 of the SCM Agreement.
66 Article 4.9 of the SCM Agreement.
67 Para. 16.4 of the DSU.
68 Article 7.7 of the SCM Agreement.

DSU,[69] and contrasts with the sixty day maximum set by the SCM Agreement for prohibited subsidies.[70] The Appellate Body report in both actionable and prohibited subsidy cases should be adopted by the DSB within twenty days of its issuance.[71] The corresponding time limit for cases brought under the DSU is thirty days.[72]

In summary, one may easily observe from the foregoing that the dispute settlement rules under Article 7 of the SCM Agreement for actionable subsidies fall somewhere in between the general rules of the DSU and the special rules of the SCM Agreement for prohibited subsidies. Although not as tight as the latter, they are tighter than the former. This is an additional proof in support of the already drawn conclusion that the Uruguay Round has brought about an enormous change in the regime for injurious domestic subsidies.

10.1.3 Non-Actionable Subsidies

Under Part IV of the Subsidies Agreement, all non-specific subsidies as well as three types of specific subsidies applied for selected purposes, which satisfy a detailed list of criteria attached to each of them, are considered non-actionable. The three types of specific subsidies covered are those provided to assist research activities conducted by firms or higher education and research establishments, to assist disadvantaged regions in the framework of regional development, and to promote adaptation of existing facilities to new environmental requirements.[73]

It is noteworthy, however, that non-actionability as understood here means what the term literally says – i.e., full immunity from challenge – only as regards the non-specific subsidies. The three specific subsidies, even though they fully satisfy their respective conditions, may still be challenged if they cause "serious adverse effects to the domestic industry of that Member, such as to cause damage which would be difficult to repair".[74] The SCM Agreement provides for rules under which action may be brought against a "non-actionable" subsidy, although the requirements of injury and the like are more stringent here than in ordinary actionable subsidy cases. The difference between an actionable subsidy and a non-actionable subsidy in this respect is thus not as significant as the opposite nature of the terms may imply. Indeed, the differences pertain only to such matters as the level of damage suffered (which has to be of an irreparable nature for the latter while any damage may do for the former), the body to take up the matter in case of failure of bilateral consultations (which is the Subsidies Committee in the case of non-actionable subsidies, while it is the DSB in the other), etc. If, ultimately, the Subsidies Committee determines that serious adverse effects exist in the sense defined here, not only may it recommend the modification of the programme, but also that, in the

[69] Para. 17.5 of the DSU.
[70] Article 4.9 of the SCM Agreement.
[71] Articles 7.7 and 4.9 of the SCM Agreement respectively.
[72] Para. 17.14 of the DSU.
[73] See Article 8 of the SCM Agreement.
[74] See Article 9 of the SCM Agreement.

event of non-compliance with the recommendation, it "shall authorize the requesting Member to take appropriate countermeasures commensurate with the nature and degree of the effects determined to exist."[75]

Part IV of the SCM Agreement on non-actionable subsidies is the only important section of this Agreement which does not explicitly delegate agricultural subsidies to the Agreement on Agriculture. And this is understandably so. Apart from the reduction commitments assumed by Members on the most trade- and production-distorting agricultural domestic support measures, a rather detailed set of measures have been explicitly permitted by the Agriculture Agreement. There are two main types of such measures: the so-called "blue" box measures which exempt direct support measures tied up with production-limiting conditions,[76] and the so-called "green" box measures, which constitute several specific measures that are deemed to have at most minimal production and trade distorting effects.[77]

The degree to which these two categories of permitted measures are non-actionable is different, however. While the exemption of the "blue" box measures follows the type of non-actionability used in Part IV of the SCM Agreement for specific subsidies – i.e. that they can still be challenged under specified conditions – the "green" box measures are non-actionable in the full sense of the term. Article 13(a) of the Agriculture Agreement provides that during the implementation period (which is nine years for purposes of Article 13[78]), notwithstanding the provisions of the Subsidies Agreement, domestic support measures that conform fully to the provisions of Annex 2 to the Agreement, which deals with the "green" box measures, are non-actionable for the purpose of countervailing duties,[79] exempt from actions under GATT Article XVI and Part III of the SCM Agreement as well as from the non-violation nullification or impairment provisions of paragraph 1(b) of Article XXIII of GATT 1994.[80] No unilateral (i.e. countervailing) or multilateral measures (i.e. authorised suspension of proportional concessions) may be taken against them even if they are clearly causing adverse consequences to the interests of other Members. It is important, however, that this immunity is limited to the nine-year implementation period. The future once again falls in the hands of the WTO Members who had already started the scheduled negotiations on agriculture in accordance with Article 20 of the Agreement on Agriculture.[81]

---

75 Article 9.4 of the SCM Agreement. For a more complete view of the difference between the remedies available in actionable and non-actionable subsidies, compare the provisions of Articles 7 and 9 of the SCM Agreement.

76 See paragraph 5 of Article 6 of the Agreement on Agriculture.

77 See Annex 2 of the Agreement on Agriculture, discussed *infra* section 10.2.8.

78 See Article 1(f) of the Agreement on Agriculture.

79 Article 13(a)(i) of the Agreement on Agriculture.

80 See paragraphs (a)(ii) and (iii) of Article 13 of the Agreement on Agriculture.

81 For more on the ongoing negotiations, see *infra* chapter 11.

10.2 The Agriculture Agreement on Domestic Support

10.2.1 Conceptual Background

We have seen that, in international trade parlance, subsidies are divided into domestic subsidies and export subsidies. However, as the scope of the very term "subsidy" itself has been contentious for decades, the meaning of its two categories has remained far from clear. Of these two, agreement on the definition of domestic subsidies has always been the more contentious. Indeed, domestic subsidies are "the most perplexing, because they involve a vast range and number of government policies, many of which are perfectly justifiable as exercises of sovereign activity within a country."[82] Perhaps because of its inherent difficulty, the term "domestic subsidy" has rarely been used in a GATT/WTO text.[83] The Agriculture Agreement chose to use the term "domestic support" in place of domestic subsidies. The question of whether this is a simple choice of one term over another or one with deeper implications is controversial.

The term "domestic support" was put to use for the first time in the history of the GATT by the Uruguay Round Agreement on Agriculture. But, the Agreement uses the term without defining it. The following is thus aimed only at giving some general idea on what domestic support measures are all about.

The Uruguay Round has introduced a detailed regime governing international trade in agricultural products addressing four important areas: market access, export subsidies, domestic support (all three in the Agreement on Agriculture) and health legislations serving as disguised forms of restrictions (in a separate instrument called the Agreement on Sanitary and Phytosanitary Measures). These areas were generally identified by the 1986 Punta del Este Declaration launching the Uruguay Round. In its relevant part, the Punta del Este Declaration provided that the negotiations aimed at achieving greater liberalization of trade in agriculture by: "(i) improving market access through, *inter alia*, the reduction of import barriers; (ii) improving the

---

[82] J. H. Jackson, *The World Trading System: Law and Policy in International Economic Relations* (2nd ed. The MIT Press, 1997) p. 280.

[83] While Article XVI of GATT 1947 speaks only about "subsidies in general", the 1955 revision introduced a second Part which specifically mentions, and governs, export subsidies. In the 1979 Subsidies Code, the division appeared more clearly but took the form of "export subsidies" (See Articles 9 and 10) on the one hand and "subsidies other than export subsidies" (see Article 11) – a cautious terminology – on the other. In the Uruguay Round SCM Agreement, the categorization took a completely different form. Adopting the so-called "traffic light approach", all forms of subsidies have been put in either the "prohibited (or red)", "actionable (or amber)" or "non-actionable (or green)" categories. What is more, the traditional division between domestic and export subsidies was not wholly maintained in the new categorization. The practices put in the "red" category can be a good example for this: both export subsidies as well as a type of domestic subsidy (the so-called import-substitution subsidies) have been put in this basket. Significantly, however, no such term as "domestic subsidies" or "domestic support" is explicitly used in the Uruguay Round SCM Agreement. In fact, the term "domestic subsidy" as such appears only in the 1955 interpretative understanding on the doctrine of reasonable expectations. The only closely resembling terminology appearing in the WTO Agreement is the concept of "domestic support", which is used in the Agreement on Agriculture.

competitive environment by increasing discipline on the use of all direct and indirect subsidies and other measures affecting directly or indirectly agricultural trade, ... and (iii) minimizing the adverse effects that sanitary and phytosanitary regulations and barriers can have on trade in agriculture ....”[84] Item (ii) of this quotation reflects the then prevailing approach that there are measures, other than subsidies, that are both closely related to the latter (hence finding their place together with subsidies) but also different from them (thus warranting the use of the words “other measures”). This was an open-ended expression probably designed to represent a compromise of diverging views concerning a wide range of measures the nature and extent of which would be left for the actual negotiations.

The Agreement on Agriculture realized these vaguely defined objectives of the Punta del Este Declaration on subsidies by dividing them into two categories: export subsidies and domestic support. The concept of export subsidies having already been enjoying a greater degree of clarity and acceptance – hence employed as such in the 1955 review of the General Agreement, the Subsidies Code, the SCM Agreement, as well as the Agreement on Agriculture – the only difficulty at the time presumably concerned the practice of “domestic subsidies”. Just as in previous GATT instruments, the drafters of the Agriculture Agreement were not comfortable enough to use the term “domestic subsidies”. The use of the term “domestic support” therefore seems to have been intended to cover two forms of measures: those which could be called subsidies but were not export subsidies; and those practices of a similar nature which did not technically fall within the scope of subsidies. If we call the former category of non-export subsidies as “domestic subsidies”, it means that “domestic support” encompasses practices of a wider range than what the term “domestic subsidies” does. In other words, “domestic support” was meant to cover “domestic subsidies” plus practices that may not be termed subsidies as such.

The question would then be the following: how far has this apparent distinction by the Punta del Este Declaration been pushed to its logical conclusion in the final Agreement on Agriculture – are there any practices actually covered by the Agreement on Agriculture that are not subsidies? Stated otherwise, have the domestic support provisions of the Agriculture Agreement gone as far as bringing non-subsidies into the multilateral discipline? Although controversial, the answer seems to be in the negative.[85] The arguments are the following.

---

84 GATT, *Ministerial Declaration on the Uruguay Round* (MIN.DEC) adopted in Punta del Este, Uruguay, on 20 September 1986, often referred to as the *Punta del Este Declaration,* reproduced in, GATT *Focus Newsletter*, No. 41, (October 1986), p. 4 (italics added).

85 For a different view, see *inter alia* S. Tangermann, *Implementation of the Uruguay Round Agreement on Agriculture by Major Developed Countries*, A report prepared for the United Nations Conference on Trade and Development, (Distr. GENERAL, UNCTAD /ITD/16, 3 October, 1995), p. 3. He writes, for instance, that “*domestic subsidies and other forms of domestic support* were large in most developed countries and were rarely challenged in the GATT.” Ibid. (italics added). See also T. Josling, S. Tangermann, and T. Warley, *Agriculture in the GATT* (MacMillan, London 1996), p. 205. They write that the AMS “measures support in the sense that it *not only includes domestic subsidies but also price support* if provided through an administered price.”

First of all, a look at the content of the relevant rules of the Agreement on Agriculture confirms that the domain of the rules of domestic support is nothing-else than domestic subsidies. Article 3 of the Agriculture Agreement, which incorporates the Schedules of Concessions and Commitments of Members to form part of GATT 1994, states that "the domestic support and export subsidy commitments ... constitute commitments limiting *subsidization*."[86] An undertaking becomes a commitment limiting *subsidization* only if it concerns subsidization from the outset. To the extent that domestic support commitments are a limitation on Members' power of providing subsidies, the use of the word "support" in place of the commonly-used term "subsidies" does not seem to bring any meaningful difference. Because export subsidies are separately addressed by the Agreement, therefore, the only area of subsidization constrained by the domestic support commitments is that of domestic subsidies. Hence, the conclusion that "domestic support" and "domestic subsidies" refer to one and the same category of practices.

Secondly, all the practices that are included in the calculation of the Aggregate Measurement of Support (the AMS) are practices that are, conceptually as well as traditionally, considered forms of domestic subsidies. Both Article 6 and the annexes use the word "subsidy" in a way that is clearly interchangeable with "support".[87] According to paragraph 1 of Annex 3 to the Agriculture Agreement, for example, the AMS is calculated on a product-specific basis for each basic agricultural product receiving "market price support, non-exempt direct payments, or *any other subsidy* not exempted from reduction commitment."[88] Not only are market price support and direct payments two of the often-used forms of domestic agricultural subsidies, but also that all other measures to be included in the calculation of the AMS are explicitly referred to as "any other subsidy".

Paragraph 2 of Annex 3 is perhaps the most straightforward expression of the fact that domestic support measures are nothing-else than domestic subsidies. This paragraph refers to all the practices mentioned under paragraph 1 – i.e. market price support, non-exempt direct payments, and other non-exempt policies – as *subsidies*. But, paragraph 2 is more than an explicit reference to the word subsidies. In line with Article 1 of the SCM Agreement on the definition of subsidies, it provides that "subsidies under paragraph 1 shall include both budgetary outlays and revenue foregone by governments or their agents." No clearer evidence can be found to show that the concept of "domestic support" introduced by the Agriculture Agreement is simply another terminology for "domestic subsidies". As if made by design to underscore this interchangeability of "subsidies" and "support", paragraph 3 provides that, in the calculation of the AMS, "*support* at both the national and sub-national level shall be included."[89]

To sum up, although the relevant paragraphs of the Punta del Este Declaration

---

[86] Article 3:1 of the Agreement on Agriculture, (italics added).

[87] Paragraph 2 of Article 6 for instance uses the term "subsidies" in two places – investment subsidies and agricultural input subsidies.

[88] Paragraph 1 of Annex 3 to the Agreement on Agriculture (italics added).

[89] Paragraph 3 of Annex 3 to the Agreement on Agriculture (italics added).

indicate Members' views that there are practices akin to, but different from, subsidies which they wanted to address in the Round, the pertinent provisions of the Agriculture Agreement make it clear that the term "domestic support" is used only to mean "domestic subsidies". The commitments on domestic support are still called commitments on "subsidization"; the particular policies covered in the calculation of domestic support are the typical policies long considered as forms of domestic subsidies; and the Agreement uses "subsidies" and "support" in clearly interchangeable ways. It thus appears that this is only a choice of one word over another. As such these two terms – domestic subsidies and domestic support – are used in this text to mean one and the same thing.

10.2.2 A Review of Basic Issues of Domestic Support Negotiated in the Uruguay Round

Having reached a consensus at Punta del Este that there was an urgent need to correct distortions in agricultural trade, the Uruguay Round negotiators aimed at achieving this goal by, *inter alia*, "increasing discipline on the use of all direct and indirect subsidies".[90] However, as always, the devil was awaiting in the detail. The general consensus expressed with such a clear wording could not easily be translated into a set of concrete enforceable legal obligations. A summary of the most basic problem areas in the field of agricultural domestic support throughout the course of the long and arduous negotiations – from the onset of the Round at Punta del Este (Uruguay) in 1986 down to its conclusion at Marrakesh (Morocco) in 1994 – will put the subsequent details in their proper conceptual and historical context.

Important issues addressed in respect of domestic support include questions of whether all or only a selected few forms of domestic support measures have to be involved in the negotiations, the technical means by which to measure the degree of support currently provided by participants, the depth of liberalization measures to be undertaken at the end of the negotiations, and the methodology to be adopted for the purpose. Although the negotiations involved more than 120 countries, the debates were more of a bilateral affair between the two leading trading powers, the EC and the US, who often took diametrically opposed positions on most agricultural issues. Most other participants often positioned themselves behind either of the parties to this "transatlantic ping-pong".

Right at the first opportunity, in 1987, the US proposed for a "complete phase out over ten years of all agricultural subsidies which directly or indirectly affect trade".[91] The US further suggested that, as a first step in this direction, all forms of internal support, with the exception of decoupled income support and bona fide food

---

90 *Punta del Este Declaration, supra* n. 84, p. 4.

91 See Josling *et al* (1996) *supra* n. 85, pp. 141 ff.; J. Croome, *Reshaping the World Trading System: A History of the Uruguay Round* (Geneva 1995) p. 112 ff.; and T. Stewart, *The GATT Uruguay Round: A Negotiating History (1986 – 1992)* in III Vols. (Kluwer 1993), Vol. I, pp. 173 ff.

aid programmes, had to be converted into an Aggregate Measure of Support (hereafter the AMS) for each country.[92] The next step would then be "to agree on policy changes that would reduce support, as measured by the AMS, to zero over ten years."[93]

Often referred to as the "zero option", this was indeed a very radical approach. As such, it is no wonder that it was not welcomed by many participants, including the EC, Japan and even some members of the Cairns Group.[94] For the EC, reductions in support had to be given a secondary place and only as a long-term goal. In the proposal it made in 1987, the EC argued that the primary problem was the imbalance between supply and demand and the immediate need was to bring production especially in the critical areas under control.[95] What is more, the Community insisted that "it was not prepared to leave agriculture to the play of market forces, without support and aid."[96]

The polarized positions between these two parties and their respective supporters in these and other agricultural issues continued intact and led to a breakdown of the Midterm Review held in Montreal in December 1988.[97] Naturally, a resumption of the suspended Uruguay Round negotiations would be possible only in the event of a relaxation in the extreme positions assumed by the EC and the US as well as their respective supporters, which happened after four months of informal consultations and negotiations. The April 1989 meeting of the Trade Negotiations Committee (the TNC) was thus able to adopt what is called the Mid-Term Review Agreement. It was agreed that the long-term objective of the agricultural negotiations should be to establish a fair and market-oriented agricultural trading system through substantial and progressive reductions in agricultural support and protection. Furthermore, this goal was to be realised *inter alia* "through the negotiation of commitments on an aggregate measurement of support."[98]

Although this was a step forward in the right direction, the important issues of

---

92 It is noteworthy, however, that even the US never proposed the elimination of all support to producers, but "only that which is tied to out-put increasing incentives." See J. Hillman, "The US Perspective", in K. Ingersent, A. Rayner, and R. Hine (eds.) *Agriculture in the Uruguay Round* (St. Martin's press, New York 1994), p. 51.

93 Croome (1995) *supra* n. 91, p. 114.

94 As observed by Croome, "almost all other countries were surprised by the sweeping nature of ... the proposals. ... Several pointed out that the US was suggesting freer trade in agriculture than had been achieved either for manufactures or services." *Id.* 114. He further noted that even the Cairns Group did not go that far.

95 These are what the Community called the "emergency measures in the areas *inter alia* of cereals, sugar and dairy products. For details, see Croome (1995) *supra* n. 91, pp. 115–117; B. Hoekman, and M. Kostecki, *The Political Economy of the World Trading System: From GATT to WTO* (Oxford University Press, 1995), pp. 202–204.

96 Croome (1995) *supra* n. 91, p. 116.

97 See Hoekman and Kostecki (1995) *supra* n. 95, p. 203, and Croome (1995) *supra* n. 91, p. 172. In the words of Croome, agriculture simply "defied solution, and brought the Montreal meeting to an abrupt and premature end."

98 *Mid-Term Meeting*, GATT Doc. MTN.TNC/11, (Special Distribution, 21 April 1989, hereafter the *Mid-Term Review*), para. 6. .

detail were still untouched. In a 1989 proposal, the US suggested a "traffic-light" approach in the area of domestic support under which one category of measures (called the most trade-distortive or "red") would be totally phased out in a matter of ten years, another group (called the less trade-distortive or "yellow" measures) would be disciplined, and a third group (called "green" measures) would be permitted.[99] While most of the participants were generally in favour of this US proposal, the EC was once more against it. It rather proposed that the AMS should be used as a means to reduce both export and domestic subsidies "with an overall target reduction to be agreed, but with each participant free to decide how this objective was reached."[100] In the opinion of the EC, because the different forms of protectionist measures in agricultural trade are "closely inter-linked", a reduction in global support would implicitly result in lower market distortions and reduced export subsidies, and that it would be difficult and unnecessary to negotiate separately.[101]

The 1990 draft "Framework Agreement" prepared by Aart de Zeeuw, Chairman of the Agricultural Negotiating Group, based itself on the "principle of accepting a separate commitment for border protection, internal support and export competition."[102] As regards domestic support measures, the Framework Agreement identified the basic problem as being "where to draw the line between those such as market price support and deficiency payments which should be subject to the full reform commitments and those which are intended to offer a permissible way for governments to pursue policies of assistance to the agricultural sector, the rural community and the environment."[103] In an attempt to resolve this problem, the De Zeeuw text called for reductions in internal support on the basis of the AMS, largely accepting the structure suggested by the US, but leaving the pace of the reductions to be negotiated.[104]

Again, although the US and the Cairns Group were largely in favour of the De Zeeuw text, the EC was not. In a delayed proposal made in November 1990, the EC suggested, *inter alia,* a 30 per cent reduction in its internal support levels from a 1986

---

[99] See Croome (1995) *supra* n. 91, p. 234; Hoekman and Kostecki (1995) *supra* n. 95, p. 203; and Josling *et al* (1996) *supra* n. 85, p. 150.

[100] Croome (1995) *supra* n. 91, p. 234.

[101] G. Annania, C. Carter, and A. McCalla, "Agricultural Policy Changes, GATT Negotiations, and the U.S.-E. C. Agricultural Trade Conflict", in G. Annania, C. Carter, and A. McCalla (eds.) *Agricultural Trade Conflicts and GATT: New Dimensions in U.S. – European Agricultural Trade Relations* (Westview Press, Oxford 1994) p. 26. See also W. Miner, and D. Hathaway, "World Agriculture in Crisis: Reforming Government Policies", in W. Miner, and D. Hathaway (eds.), *World Agricultural Trade: Building a Consensus* (The Institute for Research on Public Policy, Halifax, Canada 1988) p. 14

[102] A. De Zeeuw, "Implementation and Accomplishments of the WTO" paper presented at a Seminar organized by the International Policy Council on Agriculture, Food and Trade, in *Proceedings of the IPC Seminar: Agriculture, the FTAA and the WTO* (Belo Horizonte, Brazil 12–13 May 1997) p. 21.

[103] Croome (1995) *supra* n. 91, p. 238.

[104] See Josling *et al* (1996) *supra* n. 85, p. 153. The De Zeeuw text has been hailed as a "milestone" in the Round and as "the first version of the ultimate agreement." Ibid. For further details, see also Croome (1995) *supra* n. 91, p. 238-39; Stewart (1993) *supra* n. 91 pp. 196–203.

base level, "of which some two-thirds was already in effect because of changes since 1986".[105] The only change in the US position was the proposal to accept a 75 per cent reduction in the "red" internal support measures (i.e. down from a proposal for a complete phase out in ten years) and a 30 per cent cut in "yellow" measures as measured by a commodity-specific AMS.[106] On the other hand, sticking to its previous position, the EC favoured the use of the AMS not as a measure of the domestic support levels but as a means of measuring overall protection and support and of undertaking the reduction commitments. In its view, "the separate commitments on import access, export competition, and domestic subsidies were both unnecessary and undesirable."[107]

The stand off continued and resulted in the collapse of the 1990 deadline to conclude the Uruguay Round in Brussels.[108] And a re-launching of the negotiations was made possible only after the EC realized that the entire process would fail "unless it accepted the need to undertake separate commitments to reduce not only its domestic support but also export subsidies and border measures."[109] According to Aart De Zeeuw himself, the "real breakthrough" came in July 1991 when EC Agriculture Commissioner Ray MacSharry "proposed to change the EU agricultural policy in such a way that income support per ha and/or per head of animal should at least partly replace price guarantees for some basic products."[110] The MacSharry reform is what later came to be known as the system of compensatory payments of the EC.

The Draft Final Act of December 1991 (prepared and submitted by then GATT Director-General Arthur Dunkel and often referred to as the "Dunkel Draft") proposed a system of domestic support in which all domestic support measures except the "green" box policies would be included in the calculation of the product-specific AMS which would then be reduced in six years by 20 per cent from a 1986-1988 base period.[111] Although a mere 20 per cent cut may appear too small for such

---

[105] Croome (1995) *supra* n. 91, p. 240. This was referred to by some as "the EC trial balloon". See C. Yeutter, "Bringing Agriculture into the Multilateral Trading System", in J. Bhagwati, and M. Hirsch (eds.), *The Uruguay Round and Beyond: Essays in Honour of Arthur Dunkel* (Springer Verlag, Germany 1998) p. 71.

[106] Croome (1995) *supra* n. 91, p. 240; and Josling *et al* (1996) *supra* n. 85, p. 154.

[107] Josling *et al* (1996) *supra* n. 85, p. 154.

[108] Croome tells the Brussels story as follows: "The EC responses were encouraging at first sight, but closer analysis showed that the Community was still essentially offering agricultural reform commitments in terms only of reductions in overall support (the AMS), rather than on specific products and measures." Croome (1995) *supra* n. 91, p. 279.

[109] Croome (1995) *supra* n. 91, p. 286.

[110] De Zeeuw (1997) *supra* n. 102, p. 22.

[111] Paragraph 8 of Part B of the Draft Agreement on Agriculture (entitled "Modalities for the Establishment of Specific Binding Commitments under the Reform Programme") provided as follows: "All domestic support in favour of agricultural producers with the exception of measures exempted from reduction under Annex 4 shall be reduced, from the year 1993 to the year 1999, by 20 per cent. The base period shall be the years 1986 to 1988. Credit shall be allowed in respect of actions undertaken since the year 1986." *Draft Final Act Embodying the Results of the Uruguay Round of Multilateral Trade Negotiations*, (MTN.TNC/W/FA/, 20 December 1991, hereafter the "Draft Final Act" or simply the "Dunkel Draft") reproduced in Stewart (1993), *supra* n. 91, Vol. III, p. 634.

trade-distorting domestic support measures, it was considered significant because the scope of the measures as it then stood covered both the deficiency payments of the US and the new compensatory payments of the EC and the manner of its application was intended to be on a product-specific, rather than on a sector-wide, basis. The draft was accepted warmly by the US and the Cairns Group,[112] but the EC once more rejected it as "unbalanced".[113] This, coupled with the *Oilseeds stalemate*, once again darkened the prospects of a lasting breakthrough on agricultural problems. Indeed, as Croome succinctly put it, the Round was "held hostage by the inability of the two largest trading powers to agree on political solutions to the key problems still outstanding."[114]

A little digression of some sort is warranted here so as to appreciate the role played by the notorious *EC Oilseeds* case in this whole process. As discussed elsewhere,[115] the adoption of the *EC Oilseeds* panel report by the CONTRACTING PARTIES on 25 January 1990 – obviously with the consent of the EC – did not prevent it from re-emerging into an important stumbling block for the conclusion of the Uruguay Round itself. Upon the enactment by the EC of a changed subsidy regime for producers of oilseeds on 12 December 1991 (Council Regulation No. 3776/91), the original *EC Oilseeds* panel was reconvened at the request of the US with a task of, *inter alia*, examining whether the Community had brought the regulations examined in the original report into conformity with Article III:4 of the General Agreement and whether the impairment of the Community's tariff concessions on oilseeds had been eliminated.[116] The *Reconvened Panel*, in its findings, noted, among others, that the new regime did not provide for any subsidy payments to processors and hence did not violate Article III:4 of the General Agreement any more.[117] On the issue of nullification or impairment, however, it found that "benefits accruing to the United States ... continue to be impaired by the production subsidy provided for in Council Regulation (EEC) No. 3766/91."[118] The panel thus recommended that "the Community should act expeditiously to eliminate the impairment of the tariff concessions – either by modifying its new support system for oilseeds or by renegotiating its tariff concessions for oilseeds under Article

[112] See, *inter alia*, Josling *et al* (1996) *supra* n. 85, p. 157–158; Ingersent *et al*, in Ingersent *et al* (1994) *supra* n. 92, pp. 55–88; D. Hathaway, and M. Ingco, *Agricultural Liberalization and the Uruguay Round*, paper presented at the World Bank Conference on "The Uruguay Round and the Developing Economies", (26–27 January 1995), pp. 10–11.

[113] Croome (1995) *supra* n. 91, p. 328. The government of France in fact rejected the Draft Final Act before it was even published. See Hathaway and Ingco (1995) *supra* n. 112, p. 10.

[114] Croome (1995) *supra* n. 91, p. 331.

[115] See *supra* chapter 9.

[116] See *Follow-up on the Panel Report "European Economic Community – Payments and Subsidies Paid to Processors and Producers of Oilseeds and Related Animal-Feed Proteins", Report of the Members of the Original Oilseeds Panel* (DS28/R *BISD* 39S/91), para. 72.

[117] Ibid., paras. 74-75. According to the panel, "the payments to processors conditional on the purchase of domestic oilseeds that had given rise to the inconsistency found by the original Panel had been superseded." Ibid. para. 74.

[118] Ibid., para. 90.

XXVIII. In the event that the dispute is not resolved expeditiously in either of these ways, the CONTRACTING PARTIES should, if so requested by the United States, consider further action under Article XXIII:2 of the General Agreement."[119]

The GATT Council considered the report of the *Reconvened Panel* but could not adopt it because of an EC blockage.[120] Instead, the Council simply "authorized the Community to enter into negotiations under Article XXVIII:4 for modification of tariff concessions with respect to certain relevant tariff positions."[121] As a result, the parties to the case continued to discuss issues of compensation on a bilateral basis, but to no avail.[122] After repeated failures to come to bilaterally-agreed levels of compensation and consequent "noisy recriminations", in early November 1992, the US invoked its right under the General Agreement and requested authorization from the GATT so as to suspend trade concessions to the Community worth $1 billion.[123] And, as a kind of first installment, the US "proclaimed a discriminatory tariff of 200 per cent ad valorem on about $350 million of EC imports, to become effective in 30 days."[124] The EC soon threatened a counter-retaliation and warned that the move would only result in a "retaliatory spiral" harmful to both parties.

The deadlock, and the resulting fear of a major trade war, not only made hostage the Uruguay Round; the very foundation of the multilateral trading system itself was seriously threatened. Leading US negotiator and then Agriculture Secretary Madigan was quoted as saying that "it is not worth reforming the GATT through the Uruguay Round if the present GATT is not respected", which was taken as an "allusion" to the EC's attitude in the oilseeds dispute.[125] Similarly, Arthur Dunkel, then GATT Director General, stated his concern at the developments in the following words: "the Round remained blocked and '*unresolved and escalating trade disputes*' made the present situation even more critical: they 'put under threat even the existing multilateral trading system which is the very foundation for our ongoing efforts in the Uruguay Round.' ... 'In short, there is a deep sense of crisis, since it appears that the Uruguay Round itself is in danger of being lost.' "[126]

After a series of threats of retaliations and counter-retaliations, on November 20, 1992 the two parties concluded an agreement on both the bilateral issue of the oilseeds dispute as well as the outstanding issues of agricultural trade over which the entire Uruguay Round negotiations had stuck. Often known as the Blair-House Accord, the parties agreed on several crucial points. On the bilateral oilseeds problem, the EC agreed *inter alia* that it would reduce the size of land used for planting oilseeds (an average of 5.128 million hectares) by 10 per cent

---

[119] Ibid., para. 92.

[120] See R. Hudec, *Enforcing International Trade Law: The Evolution of the Modern GATT Legal System* (Butterworth, 1993) p. 247.

[121] *Reconvened Oilseeds Panel Report*, *supra* n. 116, footnote 1.

[122] See Stewart (1993) *supra* n. 91, p. 221.

[123] See Croome (1995) *supra* n. 91, p. 339.

[124] Hudec (1993) *supra* n. 120, p. 248.

[125] *Agence Europe*, 18 November, 1992, p. 5.

[126] Arthur Dunkel, as Quoted in Croome (1995) *supra* n. 91, p. 339 (italics added).

over three years.[127] On the outstanding agricultural issues of the Uruguay Round, the points of agreement reached between these two powers, although theoretically only bilateral in nature, were virtually an amendment to the relevant provisions of the Dunkel Draft.

In the area of domestic support, the following changes to the Draft were particularly important: firstly, some domestic subsidies paid directly to farmers under production-limiting programmes and which were not part of the Draft's "green" measures were excluded from reduction commitments;[128] secondly, the AMS reduction commitments were changed to apply on the aggregate of agricultural products rather than on a product-specific basis; and thirdly, a "peace clause" was included (first for a duration of six years but later extended to nine years) so as to shelter conforming policies from challenge under the nullification or impairment rules of the GATT.[129] With this as a background, a closer discussion of the substance of the domestic support provisions of the Agreement on Agriculture will be made in the following section.

10.2.3 Substance of the Rules

10.2.3.1 General

The domestic support discipline introduced by the Agriculture Agreement is often characterized in two apparently contradictory terms. On the one hand, because it was for the first time in the Agriculture Agreement that domestic support measures were reduced to their monetary equivalents and quantitative limits set upon them, it is often called "innovative". On the other hand, mainly because that part of the Agreement has been watered down by a number of last-minute compromises in the Uruguay Round negotiation process, it is also known as the "least binding" part of

---

[127] *Agence Europe,* 21 Nov. 1992. Sumner summarizes this aspect of the Blair-house accord as follows: "The 1992 settlement provides a GATT-bound agreement to phase down over three years the E.C. oilseed planting to 5.128 million hectares minus an amount based on the E.C. set-aside rate on arable cropland. For oilseed area that set-aside rate must be at least 10 percent. Therefore, by 1995 marketing year the EC will be allowed no more than 4.615 million hectares of oilseeds ...." D. Sumner, "Agricultural Trade Relations Between the United States and the European Community: Recent Events and Current Policy", in Annania *et al* (1994) *supra* n. 101, p. 102.

[128] Often referred to as the "blue box" category, this was intended to shield the compensatory payments of the EC and the direct payments of the US from the AMS reduction commitments in so long as these payments are made contingent on production limitation requirements, especially in the form of set-asides. This enabled the Community to compensate its farmers "for the full amount of the income lost as a result of the planned price reduction." See European Commission, *CAP Working Notes: GATT and European Agriculture,* (Special Issue, 1995) p. 19. See also Josling *et al* (1996) *supra* n. 85, p. 161–162.

[129] For further details, see Croome (1995) *supra* n. 91, p. 328–381; and Josling *et al* (1996) *supra* n. 85, pp. 160–161. In the words of Hathaway and Ingco, "there was support on both sides of the table at Blair House to back away from the strict disciplines and commodity by commodity cutbacks of domestic support levels in the Dunkel Draft. As a result, the concept of an international agreement that would force reductions in trade-distorting domestic subsidies was abandoned in the Blair House agreement." Hathaway and Ingco (1995) *supra* n. 112, p. 29.

the Agreement.[130] This section focuses on the essence of the rules, their impact on the state of international trade in agricultural products, as well as the extent to which countries have complied with their obligations.

Although agricultural domestic support measures have long been treated as areas completely beyond the reach of international regulation, the Uruguay Round has finally succeeded in taking at least the first important step towards bringing them into the framework of the multilateral trading system. An important objective of the Agreement on Agriculture in this respect is "to provide for substantial progressive reductions in agricultural support."[131] To that end, all domestic support measures have generally been put in either of three categories: those that are considered highly trade-distortive and hence subject to reduction commitments (called ""amber box" measures); those that are provided subject to production-limiting conditions and which are exempted from reduction commitments (called "blue box" measures); and those that are considered to have no or at most minimal trade-distorting effects and hence subject to no discipline at all (called "green box" measures).

Perhaps the most fundamental obligation of Members in this respect is that expressed under Article 3.2 of the Agriculture Agreement: "Subject to the provisions of Article 6, a Member shall not provide support in favour of domestic producers in excess of the commitment levels specified in Section I of Part IV of its Schedule."[132] About 30 Members have undertaken reduction commitments on domestic support in their respective schedules of commitments.[133] This means that the 30 Members with reduction commitments are constrained by the discipline of the Agreement on "amber box" measures – they are allowed to use them only in as long as they have not exceeded their commitment levels.

On the other hand, all other Members which have not undertaken any reduction commitments in their schedules are in principle not allowed to employ any of the "amber box" measures. The absence of a reduction commitment in this respect amounts to a commitment not to provide any such subsidies – a zero level commitment. However, this restriction applies only as regards those forms of support which would normally be required to be included in the calculation of the Current Total AMS had those countries included reduction commitments in their schedules. In other words, the "green box" measures of Annex 2 as well as the *de minimis,* "blue box" and developmental subsidies of Article 6 which are normally exempted from the Current Total AMS are also "exempted" in the consideration of the compliance or otherwise of Members with no reduction commitments. Indeed, Article 7.2(b) of the Agriculture Agreement stipulates that "[w]here no Total AMS commitment exists in Part IV of a Member's Schedule, the Member shall not provide

---

[130] See, *inter alia,* S. Tangermann, *A Developed Country Perspective of the Agenda for the Next WTO Round of Agricultural Negotiations*, paper presented at the Graduate Institute of International Studies, 3 March 1997, p. 27; Josling *et al* (1996) *supra* n. 85, p. 202; and Josling (1998) p. 31.

[131] Para. 3 of the Preamble to the Agreement on Agriculture.

[132] Article 3.2 of the Agriculture Agreement.

[133] See *Korea – Measures Affecting Imports of Fresh, Chilled And Frozen Beef*, report of the panel (WT/DS161/R, WT/DS169/R, 31 July 2000), footnote 421 to para. 808.

support to agricultural producers in excess of the relevant *de minimis* level set out in paragraph 4 of Article 6."

The remedies available to Members affected by the domestic subsidies of another Member depend on the type of domestic support in question. In cases involving subsidies exempted under Article 6, the possibilities of unilateral countervailing duties as well as multilateral non-violation nullification or impairment complaints are available, but on stricter grounds than in other cases. "Green box" measures, on the other hand, are completely immune from both unilateral and multilateral action.

The commitments on domestic support, together with those on export subsidies and market access, form what are often called the three pillars of the Uruguay Round Agreement on Agriculture. Just like in the two other cases, to the extent that they set an upper limit, a ceiling, to what Member countries are allowed to do, the domestic support commitments closely resemble the tariff bindings traditionally undertaken by GATT contracting parties as mechanisms for the progressive reduction of tariffs or the export subsidy commitments undertaken under the Agriculture Agreement. However, unlike both tariffs and, to a certain extent, export subsidies, the domestic support commitments are expressed in "totals" covering all agricultural products rather than following individual tariff lines or specified products. In the words of the *Korea Beef* panel, "the annual commitment levels are sector-wide commitments."[134] Moreover, unlike tariffs again, but somewhat like export subsidies, the fact that a country does not have a reduction commitment does not mean that that country is free to give any type of domestic support. On the contrary, such countries are simply precluded from providing any of the so-called "amber box" domestic support measures except within the allowable *de minimis* limits, and the so-called "development programmes" allowed under the special and differential treatment provisions for developing countries.

Domestic support reduction commitments are, of necessity, expressed in numbers. Some kind of "monetarization" of the levels of domestic support provided by countries was thus a necessary precondition for the assumption of binding reduction commitments. Different methods of measuring the level of support, including a Producer Subsidy Equivalent (PSE),[135] a Support Measurement Unit (SMU),[136] were

---

[134] Ibid. para. 808.

[135] The PSE is defined as "the annual monetary transfers to agricultural producers from domestic consumers and taxpayers as a result of agricultural policies." OECD *The Uruguay Round: A Preliminary Evaluation of the Agreement on Agriculture in the OECD Countries* (Paris 1995), p. 35.

[136] This was a measurement proposed mainly by the EC. It is a measurement "much more restricted in conception" than the PSE. According to Ingersent *et al* (1994), the SMU "excludes direct payments for supply control (such as set-aside payments) and allows credit for the effects of quotas and similar restrictions on production. Moreover, the SMU would be based not on the difference between domestic and current world prices, but the difference between the domestic price and a *fixed* external reference price at a constant exchange rate .... Where a quota is in force, the *unit* SMU is defined, *not* as the difference between the support price, P_s, and the external reference price, P_r, but as the difference between the *shadow* price, P_u, due to the quota, and P_r. Moreover, the *aggregate* SMU is defined, not as the unit SMU times actual production, but as the unit SMU times the *quota*, i.e. aggregate SMU = $(P_u - P_r)Q$, where Q is the quota quantity." K. Ingersent, A. Rayner, and R. Hine, "The EC Perspective", in Ingersent *et al* (1994) *supra* n. 92, p. 63 (italics in original).

proposed; but, finally, participants agreed on what is called the Aggregate Measure of Support (AMS). Moreover, in as long as the amount of support provided by governments varied from year to year, the selection of an agreed threshold of time, a base period, was also necessary. The years 1986 to 1988 were agreed to serve as the base period for purposes of the domestic support commitments.

10.2.3.2 The AMS: Definition

Inspired mainly by the PSE – which had already been in use before by the OECD in order to measure the overall level of support provided to agriculture in the developed countries – the AMS is defined as "the annual level of support, expressed in monetary terms, provided for an agricultural product in favour of the producers of the basic agricultural product or non-product-specific support provided in favour of agricultural producers in general."[137] This is then followed by a statement which excludes from the scope of the definition certain forms of support which are "provided under programmes that qualify as exempt from reduction under Annex 2 to this Agreement."[138]

This definition shows, and Annex 3 on the calculation of the AMS reaffirms, that the AMS is first and foremost the monetary expression of the size of annual transfers made for the benefit of agricultural producers. The transfers may take either of two forms: a product-specific support to the producers of what is called the "basic agricultural product"[139] or non-product-specific support to all agricultural producers in general. Consequently, the calculation of the AMS takes both of these elements into account.

However, as the second part of Article 1(a) provides, not all forms of domestic support are covered by the AMS. Measures which are provided under programmes that "qualify as exempt under Annex 2"[140] are not included, for instance. But there are problems as to whether or not the Annex 2 measures are the only measures excluded from the calculation of the AMS. Although the language of Article 1(a)

---

[137] Article 1(a) of the Agreement on Agriculture. A classification by Korea of its "loan interest subsidy for livestock farming" as "non-product specific support" so as to justify it under the non-product specific *de minimis* category of Article 6.4(a)(ii) has been found by a panel to be unacceptable: "given the clear language of Article 1(a), for a measure to be classified as 'non-product-specific support' for the purposes of the exemption in Article 6.4(a)(ii), it would have to constitute 'support provided in favour of agricultural producers in general', and not a particular product-specific subset of producers." *Korea Beef*, report of the panel, *supra* n. 133, para. 836.

[138] Article 1(a) of the Agreement on Agriculture. The exception covers the following: "(i) with respect to support provided during the base period, specified in the relevant tables of supporting material incorporated by reference in Part IV of a Member's Schedule; and (ii) with respect to support provided during any year of the implementation period and thereafter, calculated in accordance with the provisions of Annex 3 of this Agreement and taking into account the constituent data and methodology used in the tables of supporting material incorporated by reference in Part IV of the Member's Schedule." Ibid.

[139] A basic agricultural product has been defined as "the product as close as practicable to the point of first sale as specified in a Member's Schedule and in the related supporting material." Article 1(b) of the Agreement on Agriculture.

[140] Article 1(a) of the Agreement on Agriculture.

does not seem to allow any other interpretation, Article 6 also appears to bring its own list of exemptions. The relationship between these two provisions and its effect on the degree to which the Agriculture Agreement constrains the policy-making power of Members in the area is an important issue to consider, which will be taken up after a brief look at the calculation of the AMS.

Regardless of the scope of the exempted measures, however, it is the existence of these exemptions which distinguishes an AMS from a PSE. The similarities and differences between the AMS and the PSE, as summarized by the OECD, look the following: "The PSE is essentially a measure of transfers resulting from agricultural policies. Although the great bulk of the transfers measured relate to market price support policies, which are the most production and trade distorting, the PSE does not distinguish between different measures in the sense of attributing a weighting which relates to the degree of trade distortion. The AMS, on the other hand, by excluding certain measures from reduction commitments implicitly makes a distinction related to production and trade distortions."[141] The PSE is therefore a measure of all transfers of resources to the agricultural sector which arise from the many different instruments of agricultural policy, while the AMS is a measure of those agricultural policies whose trade impact is considered significant (or, at least, more than minimal).

10.2.3.3 The AMS: Calculation

The calculation of the AMS is a somewhat complicated technical exercise. Depending on the nature of support in question, the AMS may take into account non-product-specific support made to all agricultural producers in general or product-specific support given to the producers of each basic agricultural product – a "bottom-up" process, as the *Korea Beef* panel put it.[142] In the former case, all support given across all agricultural products is converted to its monetary equivalent and totalled in one non-product-specific AMS.[143] In the case of product-specific support, on the other hand, the AMS is calculated at the level of specific agricultural products in their most basic form. According to paragraph 1 of Annex 3, three types of support provided to specific basic agricultural products may be included in the calculation of the product-specific AMS. They are *market price support*, *non-exempt direct payments*, or any other subsidy not exempted from the reduction commitment (called *other non-exempt policies*). Included in all these are the budgetary outlays and foregone revenues of governments or their agents.[144]

10.2.3.4 Market Price Support

As discussed in chapter 9, market price support is a system by which a differential is established by a government between the price that should be received by domestic producers, which may be called the administered price, and the price that prevails in

---

[141] OECD (1995) *supra* n. 135, p. 36.
[142] *Korea Beef*, report of the panel, *supra* n. 133, para. 810.
[143] Paragraph 1 of Annex 3 to the Agreement on Agriculture.
[144] Paragraph 2 of Annex 3 to the Agreement on Agriculture.

the world market. For purposes of calculation of the AMS in a case involving market price support, paragraph 8 of Annex 3 requires identification of three important elements: a *fixed external reference price,* an *applied administered price* and the *quantity of production* eligible to receive the applied administered price.[145]

What is called the "fixed external reference price" here is the "country-specific world market price"[146] which is calculated based on the years 1986 to 1988. One of the factors determining the level of the *country-specific world market price* of a given product is whether that country is a net-exporter or a net-importer of that product. Taking the specific situation of every Member into account, the *country-specific world market price* was thus agreed to be the average f.o.b. unit value for the product concerned in a net exporting country and the average c.i.f. unit value for the product concerned in a net importing country in the base period.[147]

The acronyms "f.o.b." (free on board) and "c.i.f." (cost, insurance and freight) are two of the "oldest and most common" incoterms developed by mercantile custom and almost universally used in present day international sales transactions.[148] In a f.o.b. transaction, the seller undertakes to place the goods on board a ship at the named port of delivery with all loading costs paid (to the extent they are not included in the freight) and export clearance formalities completed. Under normal circumstances, therefore, the f.o.b. unit value for a product is supposed to closely reflect the prevailing domestic market price increased by the cost of transportation to the port of shipment, loading charges, export duties and other charges, if any. It is this price that is chosen to reflect the *country-specific world market price* of a basic agricultural product of which that country is a net-exporter.

In a c.i.f. transaction, on the other hand, the seller's responsibilities go further and include, in addition to his obligations in f.o.b., contracting the carriage and paying the freight to the named port of destination, contracting for the insurance of the goods during the carriage, paying the insurance premium as well as the loading and unloading costs (to the extent they are included in the freight).[149] Import duties and other charges upon importation, if any, are the obligations of the buyer. Under

---

[145] Paragraph 8 of Annex 3. This paragraph also provides that budgetary payments made to maintain the gap, such as buying-in or storage costs, are not included in the AMS. This means that, as the *Korea Beef* Panel pointed out, "market price support can exist even where there are no budgetary payments. Market price support gauges the effect of a government policy measure on agricultural producers of a basic product rather than the budgetary cost of that measure borne by government." See *Korea Beef,* report of the panel, *supra* n. 133, para. 827.

[146] See Josling *et al* (1996) *supra* n. 85, p. 202.

[147] Paragraph 9 of Annex 3. In cases where there existed no relevant price data, the term "*generally*" under this paragraph "has been interpreted to allow countries to use proxy prices". See *Korea Beef,* report of the panel, *supra* n. 133, footnote 436 to para. 830.

[148] For more on incoterms, see, J. Ramberg, *Guide to Incoterms 1990* (ICC Publication No. 461/90); see also H. van Houtte, *The Law of International Trade* (Sweet & Maxwell 1995) pp. 149 ff.; and C. Schmitthoff, *The Law and Practice of International Trade* (8th ed. Stevens & Sons 1986) pp. 15 ff.

[149] However, as this is a "shipping contract" and not a "destination contract", the seller is "not responsible for seeing that the goods actually reach their intended destination." J. H. Jackson, W. Davey, and A. Sykes, *Legal Problems of International Economic Relations: Cases, Materials and Text* (3rd ed., West Publishing Co. 1995) p. 54.

normal circumstances, a c.i.f. unit value is supposed to closely reflect the domestic market price of the goods in the importing country. It is this price that is chosen to reflect the *country-specific world market price* of a basic agricultural product of which that country is a net-importer. In either case, as the use of the qualifying term "fixed" indicates, the *external reference price*, once determined for the base period, remains an unchanging *reference price* against which the size of the price gap in the calculation of the Current Total AMS would be made throughout the implementation period.

Once the *country-specific world market price* is determined, the remaining elements are easier to establish. While the applied administered price may simply be found in the relevant legislation, the quantity of production eligible to receive this price may be a matter only of statistics (or of legislation once again if the amount is so fixed). The AMS for an agricultural product benefiting from a market price support will then be the difference between the *country-specific world market price* and the *applied administered price* for that product multiplied by the *amount of production* eligible to receive the administered price. The use of the terms "eligible to receive" clearly indicate that, for purposes of calculation of the market price support, it is not just the amount of production that has been purchased by the government that counts; all production which benefits from the assurance that it would ultimately benefit from the scheme is considered for the purpose. And this remains to be the case "even though the proportion of production which is actually purchased by a governmental agency may be relatively small or even nil."[150]

To illustrate this situation with the help of a simple hypothetical example, suppose that the intervention price (i.e. the price at which the various mechanisms for the regulation of the internal market become operative, such as intervention buying by the intervention agencies[151]) for wheat in a country is $20 per tonne and the fixed *country-specific world market price* of wheat for that country during the base period was $10 per tonne. Suppose furthermore that the quantity of domestic production of wheat eligible to receive the intervention price is 1 million tonnes. The AMS provided to wheat producers in the form of *market price support* in this country will then be $10 million, i.e. $10 (the gap between the two prices) multiplied by 1 million (the quantity of eligible production). Because the reference price is fixed, assuming all other things constant, while any subsequent rise in actual world market price in a given year within the implementation period narrows the gap and enables the country to easily meet its obligations, the opposite may be true in the case of a subsequent fall in the world market prices.

10.2.3.5 Non-Exempt Direct Payments

In addition to, or in lieu of, market price support, a product may be subject to other, direct, forms of payment. Paragraph 1 of Annex 3 to the Agriculture Agreement requires the inclusion of such direct payments as well as other subsidies that are not

[150] *Korea Beef*, report of the panel, *supra* n. 133, para. 827.

[151] See R. Barents, *The Agricultural Law of the EC* (1994) p. 77.

exempted from domestic support reduction commitments. A good example of direct payments are the so-called deficiency payments.[152] In a typical case of deficiency payments, the government sets the "price" that the producer should receive for his production – often called the "political price" – and whenever the actual market price of the product in question falls below the political price, the difference is covered directly from the treasury of the state. This is a case in which, in the terms of paragraph 10 of Annex 3 to the Agriculture Agreement, a non-exempt direct payment may be dependent on a *price gap*. In such cases, the AMS may be calculated simply by using the gap between the political price and the actual market price multiplied by the quantity of eligible production. What we called here the political price is what Annex 3 in this context calls the applied administered price. But, in place of the actual market price, Annex 3 uses the term "fixed reference price".

It is noteworthy that this is not the same as the "fixed external reference price" discussed in connection with market price support above. In this case, the reference price is generally required to be "the actual price used for determining the payment rates".[153] The reference price in the case of market price support, on the other hand, is a constructed external or world market price because the domestic market price in such cases is often too artificial to serve as a basis for comparison. But, in the case of deficiency payments, the market is largely left to its own rules and it is only the income of the producer that is guaranteed through direct payments from the state – hence the use of the domestic price as the benchmark for purposes of measuring the AMS.

To illustrate the situation here, we can modify the previous example as follows. Suppose the government of a country determines that the minimum that a wheat producer should receive for his product is \$20 per tonne. Suppose also that the actual domestic market price of wheat over the base period was \$10 per tonne. In this case, assuming the same quantity of eligible production as before, the AMS will be \$10 million – i.e. \$10 (the gap between what has been set by the government and what the actual market pays for the product) multiplied by 1 million tonnes (the total quantity of wheat eligible to receive the deficiency payment from the treasury of the state). The only difference between the market price support and the deficiency payment is that, in the former, the government manipulates the market in such a way as to transfer the burden onto the consumer, while in the latter, the government pays directly from its own coffers. In cases where the direct payments are not based on a price gap, the Agreement simply takes the budgetary costs into account for the calculation of the AMS. Finally, just like the "external reference price" in market price support, the "reference price" in direct payments is also qualified by the term "fixed" – hence remaining an unchanging benchmark for determining the gap throughout the entire implementation period.

---

152 Note that, as we shall see later on, deficiency payments are one of the two major forms of domestic support exempted from reduction commitments in the form of the "blue box" measures. However, that happens only if the deficiency payments are made contingent on certain production restriction conditions. Moreover, it will be argued later on that this special treatment of "blue box" measures is of no effect as regards the calculation of the base period AMS.

153 Paragraph 11 of Annex 3 to the Agriculture Agreement.

10.2.3.6 Other Non-Exempt Policies

Annex 3 of the Agriculture Agreement also addresses the calculation of what are collectively called "other non-exempt policies". Input subsidies and marketing-cost reduction measures have been mentioned only as examples.[154] According to paragraph 13, the value of such measures is measured "using government budgetary outlays or, where the use of budgetary outlays does not reflect the full extent of the subsidy concerned, the basis for calculating the subsidy shall be the gap between the price of the subsidized good or service and a representative market price for a similar good or service multiplied by the quantity of the good or service." Thus, the price gap and the budgetary outlay approaches discussed above are also applied to the calculation of the AMS provided in the form of *other non-exempt policies*.

In general, the AMS is designed to show the monetary version of the net amount of resources transferred to the agricultural sector through the non-exempt policy measures. Accordingly, in the calculation of the AMS, while members are required to include all forms of non-exempt support, including government budgetary outlays and foregone revenues at both national and sub-national levels,[155] they are allowed to deduct specific agricultural levies or fees paid by producers.[156]

In spite of the elaborate rules on its calculation, however, the AMS may not always be easy or even possible to determine. It is in an attempt to remedy this technical problem that Annex 4 is included on what is known as the Equivalent Measurement of Support. As defined under paragraph (d) of Article 1, Equivalent Measurement of Support means "the annual level of support, expressed in monetary terms, provided to producers of a basic agricultural product through the application of one or more measures, the calculation of which in accordance with the AMS methodology is impracticable ...." The equivalent measurement of support is thus calculated in respect of all basic agricultural products where market price support or any non-exempt direct payment or support exists but for which calculation of the AMS is not practicable. However, as the difference between the AMS and the Equivalent Measurement of Support is only of a technical nature, the AMS is used in the remaining part of the thesis to represent both categories.

10.2.4 The AMS: Its Variants and the Depth of Reduction Commitments

Although the AMS is calculated in a manner which takes into account the product-specific support provided to producers, the final reduction commitments were made at an aggregate level – rather than on a product-by-product or policy-by-policy basis. To this end, a *Total Aggregate Measurement of Support (Total AMS)* – defined as "the sum total of all domestic support provided in favour of agricultural producers" – had to be determined.[157] The Total AMS is calculated as the sum of all

[154] Paragraph 13 of Annex 3 to the Agriculture Agreement.
[155] Paragraph 3 of Annex 3.
[156] Paragraph 4 of Annex 3.
[157] Article 1(h) of the Agreement on Agriculture.

aggregate measurements of support for basic agricultural products, all non-product-specific aggregate measurements of support and all equivalent measurements of support to agricultural products.

The Total AMS determined by each country for the base period is called the *Base Total AMS*. The Base Total AMS is the benchmark on the basis of which to negotiate the extent of subsequent reduction commitments. Agreement was then reached to the effect that Members would cut their support by the end of the implementation period (the six-year period from 1995 to 2000) to a level 20 per cent below the base period level.[158] It was further agreed that Members would undertake binding domestic support reduction commitments in Section I of Part IV of their respective Schedules, which, in the words of Article 3 of the Agreement on Agriculture, "constitute commitments limiting subsidization".[159]

The amount of support provided by governments to their agricultural producers by the year 2000 – called the *Final Bound Commitment Level* – should be 20 per cent below the Base Total AMS. The reductions have to be made in equal annual instalments. To put it differently, countries have been made to progressively reduce their support levels by about 3.33 per cent of the Base Total AMS for every year of the implementation period. The levels set for each year of the implementation period are called *Annual Bound Commitment Levels*. The Annual Bound Commitment Level for the year 2000 is the same as the Final Bound Commitment Level for the end of the implementation period. This may be illustrated with the help of actual examples from the EC and the US.

Table 1: Part IV, Section I of Schedule LXXX of the EC

Base Total AMS (Bll. ECU)	Annual and final bound commitment levels 1995–2000 (Bll. ECU)						Supporting tables
1		2					3
	1995	1996	1997	1998	1999	2000	
73.530	71.476	69.422	67.367	65.313	63.259	61.204	AGST/EEC

Source: EC GATT Schedule

[158] See GATT, *Modalities for the Establishment of Specific Binding Commitments under the Reform Programme* (MTN.GNG/MA/W/24 20, Dec. 1993), para. 8.

[159] Article 3.1 of the Agreement on Agriculture.

Table 2: Part IV, Section I of Schedule XX of the US

Base Total AMS (Mill. Dollars)	Annual and final bound commitment levels 1995–2000 (Mill. dollars)						Supporting tables
1		2					3
	1995	1996	1997	1998	1999	2000	
23,879.112	23,083.142	22,287.173	21,491.203	20,695.243	19,899.264	19,103.294	AGST/ USA

Source: US GATT Schedule

In order to see if a country with reduction commitments respects its obligations in any given year of the implementation period, one only needs to compare the actual amount of support provided during that year – called the *Current Total AMS* – vis-à-vis the corresponding Annual Bound Commitment Levels. Article 1(h)(ii) provides that the Current Total AMS is calculated "in accordance with the provisions of this Agreement, including Article 6, and with the constituent data and methodology used in the tables of supporting material incorporated by reference in Part IV of the Member's Schedule." In line with Article 1(a)(ii) of the Agriculture Agreement, the reference to "constituent data and methodology" in Article 1(h)(ii) ensures that the calculation of support to any given product is made in subsequent years "consistently with support calculated in the base period."[160] It follows from this that a Member is considered to be in compliance with its domestic support reduction commitments in any year in which its domestic support in favour of agricultural producers expressed in Current Total AMS does not exceed the corresponding Annual or Final Bound Commitment Levels specified in Part IV of its Schedule.[161]

The following hypothetical situation may help to further clarify the essence of the Agreement here. Suppose that the Base Total AMS of Country A is 100 units. Given the equal annual instalment of reductions required by the Modalities, this country should fix its Annual Bound Commitment Levels for the six years between 1995 and 2000 roughly at 96.66, 93.33, 90, 86.66, 83.33, and 80 units, respectively. Country A thus complies with its obligations in as long as the Current Total AMS for any of these years is between zero and the corresponding Annual Commitment Levels.

However, there is one important issue to consider here. As alluded to earlier, the provisions of the Agriculture Agreement do not seem to give a clear answer particularly to the question of whether all the policies included in the calculation of the Base Total AMS and the Annual and Final Bound Commitment Levels are also included in the calculation of the Current Total AMS. Stated from a different

[160] *Korea Beef*, report of the panel, *supra* n. 133, para. 811.
[161] Article 6:3 of the Agreement on Agriculture.

perspective, are all the policies that are excluded from the calculation of the Current Total AMS also excluded from the calculation of the Base Total AMS and the subsequent commitment levels? The answer to this question matters a great deal on the degree to which WTO Members are constrained by the commitments they have made in the area of agricultural domestic support.

As mentioned earlier on the definition of the AMS, the so-called "green box" policies of Annex 2 are the only ones mentioned under Article 1 as not included in the calculation of the AMS. However, Article 6.1 on domestic support reduction commitments appears to introduce a second exception of its own: Members' reduction commitments apply to all of their agricultural domestic support measures "with the exception of domestic measures which are not subject to reduction in terms of the criteria set out *in this Article* and in Annex 2 to this Agreement."[162] The exceptions *set out in this Article* concern the preferential treatment accorded to developing countries in the field of domestic support, *de minimis* provisions, and direct payments made to producers under production-limiting programmes. The central question will thus be as to whether these latter measures are excluded from the calculation of both the Base Total AMS as well as the reduction commitments as shown in the calculation of the Current Total AMS or only from the latter as shown under Article 6.

Strong arguments seem to be available for both positions. The following arguments may be made in support of their exclusion from both variants of the AMS: First of all, according to prevailing customary law of interpretation of international agreements, terms and provisions of a treaty should be interpreted in accordance with their ordinary meaning and *in the light of their object and purpose*.[163] The main purpose of the Agriculture Agreement in this respect is "to provide for substantial progressive reductions in agricultural support and protection sustained over an agreed period of time, resulting in correcting and preventing restrictions and distortions in world agricultural markets."[164] An interpretation which includes the policies under Article 6 in the calculation of the Base Total AMS but which excludes them from the calculation of the Current Total AMS weakens the liberalizing effect of the provisions in two ways – by raising the benchmark due to their inclusion in the Base Total AMS, and by giving an artificially lower figure representing the level of actual support provided in any one year due to their exclusion from the calculation of the Current Total AMS. An interpretation in favour of excluding these policies from both variants of the AMS helps to avoid such consequences.

Secondly, the Modalities Agreement, which was introduced to serve as a guide in the preparation and establishment of the Schedules of Commitments on the basis of the agreed rules, indicates that the difference in wording between Article 1(a) on the AMS in general and Article 6 on the Current Total AMS and the reduction

[162] Article 6:1 of the Agreement on Agriculture; italics added.

[163] See *Vienna Convention on the Law of Treaties* (done at Vienna, 23 May 1969, 1155 U.N.T.S. 33) Article 31(1).

[164] Paragraph 3 of the Preamble to the Agriculture Agreement.

commitments were not meant to give different components to different versions of the AMS. According to paragraph 8 of the Modalities, all domestic support is subject to reduction commitments "with the exception of measures meeting the criteria set out in Annex IV a verbatim copy of Annex 2 of the Agriculture Agreement *or elsewhere in these modalities*."[165] Furthermore, Paragraph 9 provides that "domestic support measures that cannot be shown to satisfy the criteria set out in Annex 4 *or elsewhere in these Modalities* shall be included in the base Total AMS."[166] Apparently, therefore, under the Modalities, there are two grounds for the exclusion of measures from the Base Total AMS: compliance with the provisions of Annex 4 to the Modalities (i.e. Annex 2 to the Agriculture Agreement), and compliance with criteria set out "elsewhere in these Modalities." Paragraph 18 of the Modalities may be cited as one such a case where domestic support measures taken by developing countries, if they meet certain criteria, "shall not be included in the base Total AMS." Finally, unlike Article 6 of the Agreement on Agriculture, paragraph 10 of the Modalities affirms that such apparently exempted measures as the *de minimis* support are excluded not only from the Current Total AMS but also from the Base Total AMS.[167] These observations thus seem to lead to the conclusion that Article 6 exemptions are excluded from both the Base Total AMS as well as the Current Total AMS.[168]

However, a closer look at the provisions of the Agriculture Agreement together with subsequent experience after the entry into force of the Agreement leads to the opposite conclusion – that the Article 6 exemptions apply only in the calculation of the Current Total AMS and not in that of the Base Total AMS and the commitment levels. The role played by the Modalities in this respect seems to be minimal at best.[169]

Firstly, the overall approach of the Agreement is that all domestic support measures that are not explicitly excluded are included. As indicated already, the definition provision leaves no room to put any measure into the exceptions box other than those explicitly mentioned therein – the Annex 2 policies – while Article 6 on domestic support reduction commitments does also expressly refer to them as so-excluded.

Secondly, Article 1, the definition provision of the Agriculture Agreement,

---

165 Italics added.

166 Paragraph 9 of the Modalities, *supra* n. 158, (italics added).

167 Paragraph 10(i) of the Modalities (*supra* n. 158) goes as follows: "Participants shall not be required to include in the calculation of their base Total AMS ... product-specific domestic support which would otherwise be required to be included where such support does not exceed 5 per cent of the total value of production of a basic agricultural product." The same rule is stated under sub-paragraph (ii) for *de minimis* non-product-specific domestic support.

168 See also Josling *et al* (1996) *supra* n. 85, p. 203. They write that "support exempt from reduction commitments, and not to be included in AMS calculation, comes in three forms, *de minimis,* 'green box', and 'blue box'." While this general statement may hold true in some senses, it may not be so in others. At least, we know for sure that the "blue box" measures have been included in the calculation of the AMS for the base period, but exempted in the calculation of the Current Total AMS.

169 On the legal status of the Modalities Agreement, see *supra* chapter 4.

mentions Article 6 only once, and that is in connection with its definition of the Current Total AMS.[170] Indeed paragraph (h) of this Article defines the Total AMS in all its senses – i.e., in the sense of the Base Total AMS, the Annual and Final Bound Commitment Levels, as well as the Current Total AMS. For all these cases, the Total AMS is defined to mean "the sum of all domestic support provided in favour of agricultural producers, calculated as the sum of all aggregate measurements of support for basic agricultural products, all non-product-specific aggregate measurements of support and all equivalent measurements of support for agricultural products." It then provides that "with respect to support provided during the base period (i.e. the 'Base Total AMS') and the maximum support permitted to be provided during any year of the implementation period or thereafter (i.e. the 'Annual and Final Bound Commitment Levels'), [the Total AMS shall be] as specified in Part IV of a Member's Schedule."[171] Note that no mention is made of Article 6 here. The provision, however, continues and provides that with respect to the level of support actually provided during any year of the implementation period and thereafter (i.e. the "Current Total AMS"), the Total AMS is "calculated *in accordance with the provisions of this Agreement, including Article 6,* and with the constituent data and methodology used in the tables of supporting material incorporated by reference in Part IV of the Member's Schedule."[172] No such a distinction between two sub-paragraphs of the same Article can be inadvertent.

Thirdly, unlike the measures of Annex 2, all measures referred to in Article 6 as exceptions are stated as measures the inclusion of which may not be required of Members in the calculation of their Current Total AMS. For example, the special and differential treatment given to developing countries in this respect is expressed as follows:

> "investment subsidies which are generally available to agriculture in developing country Members and agricultural input subsidies generally available to low-income or resource-poor producers in developing country Members shall be exempt from domestic support reduction commitments that would otherwise be applicable to such measures, as shall domestic support to producers in developing country Members to encourage diversification from growing illicit narcotic crops. Domestic support meeting the criteria of this paragraph *shall not be required to be included in a Member's calculation of its Current Total AMS.*"[173]

Likewise, paragraph 4 of Article 6 states the *de minimis* provision as follows: a Member

> "*shall not be required to include in the calculation of its Current Total AMS* and shall not be required to reduce ... product-specific domestic support *which would otherwise be required to be included in a Member's calculation of its*

[170] See Article 1(h)(ii) of the Agriculture Agreement.
[171] Article 1(h)(i) of the Agriculture Agreement.
[172] Article 1(h)(ii) of the Agriculture Agreement (italics added).
[173] Article 6.2 of the Agriculture Agreement (italics added).

Current AMS where such support does not exceed 5 per cent of that Member's total value of production of a basic agricultural product during the relevant year; and ... non-product-specific domestic support *which would otherwise be required to be included in a Member's calculation of its Current AMS* where such support does not exceed 5 per cent of the value of that Member's total agricultural production."[174]

Finally, as regards the "blue box" measures, Article 6 provides that direct payments under production-limiting programmes shall not be subject to the commitment to reduce domestic support and that the exemption from the reduction commitment for direct payments "shall be reflected by *the exclusion of the value of those direct payments in a Member's calculation of its Current Total AMS*."[175]

All these provisions have the effect that the measures which have been included in the calculation of the Base Total AMS to inflate its amount – hence allowing countries to start from higher benchmarks – are not added in the calculation of the actual amount of support made in any year of the implementation period, the Current Total AMS, thus helping Members to stay within the law possibly even after granting subsidies higher than would otherwise be the case.

Finally, a look at the Schedules of Commitments of the Members confirms that, at least as regards the "blue box" measures included in Article 6, it was this line of understanding that had actually been put into effect at the end of the Uruguay Round negotiations. Tangermann has observed in this connection that "in the base period, ... no country had 'blue box' policies which it did not count in the AMS."[176] An OECD study has also noted that the value of the payments under production-limiting programmes under Article 6 is "included in the Base Total AMS on which reduction commitments have been taken but is excluded from the Current Total AMS ...."[177]

10.2.5 The AMS and the Base Period for Reduction of Support

As pointed out already, the years 1986 to 1988 were accepted to serve as the base period for purposes of the domestic support reduction commitments.[178] This would normally mean that countries calculate the annual AMS for each of the years constituting the base period and take the average to serve as the starting point for the reduction commitments. However, this was not always the case. Mainly because of an EC insistence, a statement was added to paragraph 8 of the Modalities that "credit shall be allowed in respect of actions undertaken since the year 1986." The effect was obvious – the 1986–88 base period applied only when a country's level of support had risen after 1986.

---

[174] Article 6.4(a) of the Agriculture Agreement (italics added). The *de minimis* level for developing country Members is 10 per cent. See para. 4(a).

[175] Article 6.5 of the Agriculture Agreement (italics added).

[176] Tangermann (1995) *supra* n. 85, p. 26.

[177] OECD (1995) *supra* n. 135, p. 35.

[178] See Paragraph 8 of the Modalities Agreement, *supra* n. 158.

Since the national interest represented by each of the negotiators was to secure as much freedom to grant domestic support to their respective agricultural producers as possible, a base period of the highest amount of support was what each had wanted for itself. And it is this objective that was attained by the compromise solution finally adopted, which virtually amounted to a double-base-period situation. The following table may show the practical impact of this decision on the final Schedules of Commitments of the four major trading powers.

Table 3: Impact of the Credit on the Final Schedules of Concessions of Major Members

Member	Units	Base Period Average AMS (1986–1988)	Base Total AMS Actually Used	Current Level (1993)	Final Bound Level (2000)
US	Mill. US$	22,245	23,875	14.0[a]	19,103
EC	bill. Ecu	73.53	76.505[b]	62.0	61.204
Japan	bill. Yen	4,335	4,966	<4000 (1992)	3,973
Canada	Mill. C$	4,870.4	5376.3	4,078.2	4,301

Source: Adapted from OECD (1995), at 41.

[a]An OECD estimate

[b]Note that there is a discrepancy between this figure and the figure taken from the Schedules of Commitments, *supra* at **Table 1, Section 10.2.4.** This figure is kept here for explanatory purposes only.

As this table shows, the base period average levels of the AMS for all the four WTO Members are lower than the actual Base Total AMS levels used for the calculation of the final bound reduction commitments. The difference is about 4 per cent for the EU, 10 per cent for Canada, 13.5 per cent for the USA and 15.2 per cent for Japan.[179] All of them took the "credit" allowed them by paragraph 8 of the Modalities in respect of actions undertaken since the year 1986. The 20 per cent minimum reduction requirement over the implementation period was thus calculated for these Members from the higher 1986 levels. As a result, their final commitment levels are much less than what they would be had the 1986–1988 average levels been used as the Base Total AMS.[180] Needless to say, the effect of the credit allowed in

[179] See also Tangermann (1995) *supra* n. 85, p. 11.

[180] Perhaps because of the loophole created by the "credit" system in the area of domestic support, Korea's domestic support Schedule contained two sets of annual commitment levels. After specifying a "Total Base" of 1,718.60 billion won, one column provides for figures derived from this Base Total AMS, while a second column simply sets, in brackets, a 2,182.55 billion won for 1995 and continues to decline until it reaches 1,490.00 billion won – a figure which is equal to the final bound commitment level for 2004 on the basis of the above-mentioned "Total Base". Questioned about the duality of its Schedules in an Agriculture Committee meeting, Korea responded that "the figures in brackets correspond to Korea's real annual commitment level, using the 1993 base period for rice and the 1989–

respect of actions undertaken since 1986 is one of weakening rather than strengthening the overall impact of the reduction commitments.[181]

As reiterated already, another factor that contributed to the weakening of the effect of the domestic support reduction commitments is the manner in which the "blue box" measures of Article 6 are treated by the Agriculture Agreement. Both the Base Total AMS as well as the Annual and Final Bound levels include the Article 6 exemptions. When the Current Total AMS is calculated for each year of the implementation period, however, these measures are not counted. As a result, it has been observed in connection with the above data for the US, for instance, that, of the Base Total AMS of nearly US$ 24 billion, deficiency payments "accounted for almost US$ 10 billion during the base period and have been included in the base and final bound commitment levels."[182] That they are excluded from the Current Total AMS calculation means that the US "need not contemplate any further change in policy in order to meet its AMS commitment." In fact, the level of support for the US in 1993 – two years before the start of the implementation period – was already more than US$ 9,000 million below its commitment levels for 1995, which was about US$ 23,087 million (i.e. 23,875 million reduced by 3.3 percent for the first year of the implementation period according to the equal-installment formula), and more than US$ 5,000 million below the final commitment level for the year 2000.

Likewise, mainly due to the exemption of its compensatory payments from reduction commitments, the Current Total AMS of the EC for 1995 was already below its final commitment level for 2000.[183] The final reduction commitment levels

---

cont.

1991 base period for other products, as indicated in the footnote of Korea's Schedule LX. The said calculation and annual commitment level of AMS were already reviewed and agreed upon by the Member countries in March 1994. The other set of figures corresponds to the annual commitment using the base period of 1989–1991 for all products." See *Summary Report,* G/AG/R/9 (17 January, 1997), at 18. At first sight, this sounds more like the "front-loading" exception to the minimum levels of export subsidy reduction commitments under paras. 5(c) and (d) of Annex 8 to the Modalities Agreement. There is, however, no such room as regards domestic support commitments. Indeed, the base period referred to here does not correspond to the actual base period used for domestic support purposes (which is the years 1986 to 1988). The *Korea Beef* thus concluded as follows: "Given that it would be logically impossible, as well as contrary to the general object and purpose of the *Agreement on Agriculture* on domestic support, to have two distinct Total AMS commitment levels for each of these years, the Panel considers that the set of annual figures which are not qualified by brackets must be treated as constituting Korea's commitment levels for the years in question for the purposes Article 3.2 of the Agreement on Agriculture." *Korea Beef,* report of the panel, *supra* n. 133, para. 821. This part of the panel ruling was, however, reversed on appeal on the basis mainly of a notation dubiously inserted by Korea in its schedules of concessions. See *Korea Beef*, report of the Appellate Body, adopted on 10 January 2001, paras. 97 to 102.

181 According to an equally weighty contrary argument, however, had this possibility not been foreseen, countries would have been tempted to stay with, or even increase, their pre-Punta del Este levels of support so as to maintain their bargaining powers for the end of the Round. For a discussion of the principles of "standstill" and "roll back" included in the *Punta del Este Declaration*, see *supra* chapter 7.

182 OECD (1995) *supra* n. 135, p. 40.

183 As reported by the EC Directorate General for Agriculture, "by lowering intervention prices for cereals and beef, the CAP has already brought the Community's Total Aggregate AMS below … [the 20 per

were in fact reached for many countries well before the start of the implementation period in 1995.[184]

Almost the same is true for Canada, Japan as well as many other countries not covered by the table. The value of the domestic support reduction commitments thus lies more in their role as safeguards against future "backsliding" – for the commitment levels serve as a ceiling for the level of allowable support – than as constraints on the present policies of most Members.[185] Besides, economists also emphasize the fact that these levels are set in nominal terms, which is taken as a potentially significant factor since even a modest inflation may make the commitments "more constraining" over time.[186]

10.2.6 The Current Total AMS: What Measures are Exempted?

Regardless of the controversy as to which variant of the AMS they apply, this section addresses all sorts of exemptions as are identified in both Article 6 of the Agriculture Agreement as well as Annex 2 thereof. The fundamental principle of the Uruguay Round in this respect is stated as follows: "The domestic support reduction commitments of each Member shall apply to domestic support measures in favour of agricultural producers with the exception of domestic measures which are not subject to reduction in terms of the criteria set out in this Article and Annex 2 to this Agreement."[187] The rule is thus that the AMS covers all forms of domestic support provided to the agricultural sector. Exemption is only an exception to this rule.

An exemption from reduction commitments may be made for policies if they are specifically claimed and are justified through the fulfilment of the necessary criteria thereof. In the absence of any such claim, the Agreement simply presumes that all domestic support programmes are covered in the calculation of the Current Total AMS as well as in the reduction commitments undertaken thereon. In short, whatever is not specifically excluded is presumed included. In a way, therefore, the category of measures included in the Current Total AMS is a residual category in the sense that it consists of measures that are left after specific exempted measures are excluded.

Article 6 of the Agriculture Agreement provides that the exceptions to the rule –

---

cont.

cent] target." European Commission, *CAP Working Notes: GATT and European Agriculture* (Special Issue, 1996) p. 23. According to the OECD, "the estimated level of the Total AMS in 1993, (although subject to a significant margin of error) suggests that a fall of almost Ecu 11 billion had already occurred by 1993, the first year of the implementation of the CAp. A further reduction in the region of Ecu 1 billion is needed to bring the Community to its final bound level. This reduction should be relatively easily achieved as further price reductions, already decided for cereals, take effect in 1994 and 1995." OECD (1995) *supra* n. 135, p. 40.

184 Tangermann has observed in 1995 that the US, the EC, as well as Japan "have already achieved all of the required reductions in support in one way or another." Tangermann (1995) *supra* n. 85, p. 14; see also graph 3.3.2, p. 48.

185 For similar views, see *Id.*, p. 14.

186 OECD (1995) *supra* n. 135, p. 45; and Tangermann (1995) *supra* n. 85, p. 14–15.

187 Article 6:1 of the Agreement on Agriculture.

that all domestic support measures are covered by the reduction commitments – are found at two places in the Agreement: under Article 6 itself and in Annex 2 to the Agreement. While Article 6 introduces three excepted forms of support – *de minimis* levels of support, direct payments under production-limiting programmes, and programmes by developing countries to promote their economic development – Annex 2 provides for the so-called "green" policies. Members have the obligation to ensure that all "green box" measures are maintained in conformity with the conditions set under Annex 2.[188] Any measure, whether old or new, that is not shown to satisfy the conditions for exemption under either Article 6 or Annex 2 is required to be included in the calculation of the Current Total AMS for the year in question.[189]

10.2.7 Exemptions under Article 6

The three categories of domestic support measures that are exempted from reduction commitments on the basis of Article 6 of the Agriculture Agreement may be summarized as follows.

10.2.7.1 De Minimis Levels of Support

Both the Modalities as well as Article 6 provide that domestic support, whether product-specific or not, which does not exceed 5 per cent of the value of production of either the specific product or of total agricultural production, as the case may be, is not required to be included in the calculation of the Current Total AMS.[190] This *de minimis* level is raised to 10 per cent for developing country Members.

10.2.7.2 Direct Payments under Production-Limiting Programmes: The "Blue Box" Measures

Often known as the "blue box", these payments are excluded from the calculation of the Current Total AMS, and hence from the reduction requirements, only if certain important conditions are met. First of all, the payments need to be "direct" in the sense that they should not be transferred to the agricultural producers through market manipulation devices and the like. They have to be paid straight from governmental budgets. Secondly, payment should be conditional upon some form of production-limiting measures being taken by the recipient. The payments may be made based on a fixed acreage and yields, or on 85 per cent or less of the base level production, or, in the case of livestock payments, on a fixed number of head.[191]

---

188 See Article 7.1 of the Agriculture Agreement.

189 See Article 7.2(a) of the Agriculture Agreement.

190 Article 6:4(a) goes as follows: "A Member shall not be required to include in the calculation of its Current Total AMS and shall not be required to reduce: (i) product-specific domestic support which would otherwise be required to be included in a Member's calculation of its Current AMS where such support does not exceed 5 per cent of that Member's total value of production of a basic agricultural product during the relevant year; and (ii) non-product-specific domestic support which would otherwise be required to be included in a Member's calculation of its Current AMS where such support does not exceed 5 per cent of the value of that Member's total agricultural production."

191 See Article 6:5 of the Agreement on Agriculture.

Added during the Blair House Accord in 1992, the whole purpose of this exception was to allow the EC to continue with its newly-introduced system of compensatory payments and the US with its system of deficiency payments without being required to satisfy the conditions of decoupling.[192] The absence of any additional conditions to make these payments decoupled from production or price requirements has rightly been a cause for concern for some authors:

> "The payments referred to in this provision are not limited to compensation for not producing a given share of base period production, but cover all payments made under programmes that, among others, require farmers to limit their production. Contrary to the definition of decoupled income support in Annex 2, there is not the condition that 'no production shall be required in order to receive such payments'. Not only can governments require farmers to produce in order to be eligible for these exempted payments, they can also make the size of payments directly dependent on the volume of production, so long as it is on no more than 85 per cent of the production in the base period."[193]

Users of the "blue box" measures were not willing to consider decoupling their compensatory and/or deficiency payments so as to bring them to the "green box" just like other decoupled payments because they feared that that would make the transfer of resources to the farming community too transparent, and hence more vulnerable to challenge at the political level.[194] Yet, the "blue box" has always been some kind of "an anomaly that does not fit the overall spirit of the Agreement on Agriculture",[195] and the move in the post-Uruguay Round period seems towards its ultimate abolition. Although its major users at the beginning were the US and the EC, the new US agricultural law (the FAIR Act) is believed to have changed the previously "blue box" measures to green by complete decoupling and the EU appears to be the only major user of the blue box at present.[196] Most countries are already expressing their displeasure with this category of measures and, in the ongoing agriculture negotiations, the "blue box" promises to be a bone of contention between the EC, on the one hand, and almost all others, on the other.[197]

---

[192] See Josling *et al* (1996) *supra* n. 85, p. 204.

[193] Ibid., p. 208.

[194] As Hathaway and Ingco observed, "[t]he switch to non-distorting or de-coupled policies were an anathema to the producers ... because these policies would have exposed the extent of the income transfers and the distribution of the benefits, neither of which would be politically popular." Hathaway and Ingco (1995) *supra* n. 112, p. 29.

[195] See S. Tangermann, *The European Union Perspective on Agricultural Trade Liberalization in the WTO*, paper presented at the Department of Agricultural Economics and Business, University of Guelph, Canada, February 1999, p.26. According to Tangermann, "it has never been clear whether the measures that have been allowed to find a shelter under the blue box are really 'production-limiting' as stipulated in Article 6:5(a) of the Agreement on Agriculture." *Id.*

[196] The only three other countries making use of the blue box are Iceland, Norway and Slovakia. See Ibid., p. 26.

[197] Ibid., p. 26.

10.2.7.3 Domestic Support Provided by Developing Countries: "Development Programmes"

Three specific forms of domestic support provided by developing country Members are exempted from the reduction commitments.[198] These are investment subsidies which are generally available to agriculture, agricultural input subsidies generally available to low-income or resource-poor producers, and domestic support to producers to encourage diversification from growing illicit narcotic crops.

In general, domestic support measures meeting the conditions set by Article 6 of the Agreement on Agriculture have two major features in common: (1) they are not required to be included in the calculation of the Current Total AMS of the Member in question; and (2) their exemption from the new discipline is not absolute. Unlike the "green" box policies of Annex 2, which will be discussed subsequently, the exempted domestic support measures under Article 6 are not fully protected from challenge by the so-called "peace clause" of Article 13 of the Agreement on Agriculture.[199] A Member that is capable of establishing injury or threat thereof in the sense of Article VI of GATT 1994 and Part V of the SCM Agreement (which deals with countervailing measures) has the right to impose countervailing duties in line with the requirements set by the relevant provisions of those Agreements. The only obligation such a Member has under the Agriculture Agreement is to show "due restraint" in initiating the countervailing duty investigations – an obligation of more of a moral rather than a legal nature. Furthermore, these measures may also be subject to multilateral actions based on Article XVI:1 of GATT 1994 on subsidies in general, Articles 5 and 6 of the Subsidies Agreement on actionable subsidies, and Article XXIII(1)(b) of GATT 1994 on non-violation nullification or impairment, on condition that the support given to a *specific product* in any one year of the implementation period exceeds the corresponding amount decided in the 1992 marketing year.[200] The commodity-specific nature of this latter requirement sets apart the due restraint provision of Article 13 from the overall discipline of the Agreement on domestic support which applies on a sector-wide or aggregate basis.

10.2.8 Exemptions under Annex 2: The "Green Box" Measures

Annex 2 to the Agreement on Agriculture provides for a detailed but non-exhaustive list of practices for which governments may claim exemptions – called "green box" measures. Before going to the details of the specific policies covered and the conditions attached to each of them, it is noteworthy that no country is interested in the amount of income the farming communities of other Members get as such. Such incomes become of the essence only to the extent that they are acquired in such a manner as to distort or subvert the processes of production and trade.

Reflecting this underlying rationale, the most fundamental requirement set by the

---

[198] See Article 6:2 of the Agreement on Agriculture.

[199] See Article 13(b)(i) of the Agreement on Agriculture.

[200] See Article 13(b)(ii) and (iii) of the Agreement on Agriculture.

Agreement on Agriculture is that any support for which exemptions are claimed under Annex 2 should have "no, or at most minimal, trade distortion effects or effects on trade".[201] To that end, all measures for which exemption is claimed have to meet two types of criteria: general and policy-specific. The general criteria are stated under paragraph 1 as follows: "(a) the support shall be provided through a publicly-funded government programme (including government revenue foregone) not involving transfers from consumers; and (b) the support in question shall not have the effect of providing price support to producers."

Obviously, in order for any type of support to have no distortive effects on trade and production, market forces should be allowed a free hand; they should be made to signal the producer's return from his production and the consumer should be able to pay the market price for the products. It was because of this consideration that market price support measures had long been recognised as one of the most trade-distorting measures used by countries – hence their outright exclusion from the green box. All this means that any support exempted from reduction commitments should be covered only through governmental budgetary transfers, for, *inter alia,* they always have the advantage of transparency – an important element which is lacking from transfers involving consumers. These two conditions are thus the "basic criteria" that all measures have to satisfy in addition to their respective policy-specific requirements.

The "policy-specific criteria and conditions" depend on the nature of the particular policy under consideration. Annex 2 has created some twelve categories of such more or less specific policy measures with their own respective specific criteria and conditions, which will be summarized as follows. It should always be kept in mind throughout the following discussion, however, that these policy-specific conditions and criteria are not sufficient on their own; they are there as additional requirements to the aforementioned general conditions.

10.2.8.1 General Services

Members are allowed to claim the exemption of a variety of domestic support measures collectively called "general services".[202] They encompass a wide range of policies involving government expenditures (or revenues foregone) in relation to programmes which provide some of the most basic services to agriculture and the rural community. Paragraph 2 provides for a non-exhaustive list of such measures, which includes government-funded programmes for research, pest and disease control, training, extension and advisory services, marketing and promotion services (excluding expenditure for unspecified purposes that could be used by sellers to reduce their selling price or confer a direct economic benefit to purchasers), and infrastructure services (including expenditures for electricity reticulation, roads, etc. that are directed to the provision or construction of capital works only and excluding the subsidized provision of on-farm facilities other than the reticulation of generally

[201] Paragraph 1 of Annex 2 to the Agreement on Agriculture.

[202] See paragraph 2 of Annex 2 of the Agreement on Agriculture.

available public utilities, and also excluding subsidies to inputs or operating costs, or preferential charges). No direct payments to producers or processors may be made under this category of exempted domestic support measures. Rather fundamental and widespread as most of these measures are, they are some of the areas on which not much difference of views were reflected during the negotiation process.

10.2.8.2 Public Stockholding for Food Security Purposes

Food security being one of the underlying reasons for the growth of interventionist government policies in agriculture, it is only natural that it is included in the measures exempted from reduction commitments.[203] Although it has often been misused for a very long time in the history of international trade regulation, the decisive importance of food security for the very survival of a nation can never be doubted. What the Agriculture Agreement does here is simply recognize that Members can allocate funds for the accumulation and holding of stocks of products which form an integral part of a food security programme identified as such in national legislation. It further allows aid to private storage of products in as long as that storage forms part of the food security programme.

At the same time, wary of the already established practice of invoking food security as a pretext for several forms of trade- and production-distorting government programmes, the Agriculture Agreement stipulates the following specific conditions. Firstly, the volume and accumulation of such stocks should correspond to predetermined target levels related solely to food security. Secondly, the process of stock accumulation and disposal should be financially transparent. And finally, food purchases by the government should be made at current market prices and sales from food security stocks should be made at no less than the current domestic market price for the product and quality in question. All these three conditions are aimed at avoiding the practice of trade- and production-distorting subsidies disguised as genuine food security measures. To give a simple example, governmental purchase of agricultural products without any limitation as to amount and price could easily be used as a means of price support to farmers via unlimited purchase of the products at prices artificially set by the administration. The spirit as well as the letter of this provision may be summed up in the following words – a government may take necessary precautionary measures for food security purposes, but it has to use them genuinely and solely for that purpose.

10.2.8.3 Domestic Food Aid

Food aid here refers to the provision of food supplies to the needy portion of the population either free of charge or at subsidized prices.[204] Once again, governments are free to render such services to the poor. However, the possibilities of an abusive exercise of this loophole being rather clear, the Agriculture Agreement sets certain important conditions.

---

[203] See paragraph 3 of Annex 2 of the Agreement on Agriculture.
[204] See paragraph 4 of Annex 2 of the Agreement on Agriculture.

Firstly, eligibility to receive food aid should be subject to clearly-defined criteria related to nutritional objectives. Secondly, the aid should be made in the form of direct provision of food or the provision of means to allow eligible recipients to buy food either at market or subsidized prices. And finally, food purchases by the government should be made at current market prices and the financing and administration of the aid should be transparent.

10.2.8.4 Direct Payments to Producers

The Agriculture Agreement permits an unlimited number of different forms of direct payments made to agricultural producers to be exempted from reduction commitments. Annex 2 enumerates a detailed, but non-exhaustive, list of such direct payments.[205] Whether included in the list or not, all forms of direct payments made to producers have to satisfy the general criteria set out under paragraph 1 just like any other form of support under Annex 2.[206] Furthermore, each has to satisfy additional policy-specific criteria. For the listed ones, these criteria are specified under each category, while in the case of the unnamed forms of direct payment, the specific conditions mentioned under paragraph 6 on decoupled income support are prescribed as their "policy-specific" conditions. In other words, any form of direct payment that falls outside the list is, in effect, presumed or required to be a "decoupled income support" in the sense that this concept is used under paragraph 6(b) through (e). In general, they require that the amount of income support payments should not be related to the type or volume of production, the domestic or international price of products, or the factors of production employed in any year after the base period. Furthermore, no production should be required in order for the producer to receive such payments.

But, in cases where any of the specified means of direct payments are used, Members should comply with the policy-specific requirements stipulated thereunder. These are briefly summarized as follows.

10.2.8.4.1 Decoupled Income Support

As the name itself tells, the whole purpose here is to leave Members free to support the income of their farmers on condition that no trade and production distortions are created thereby. The only concern of the Agriculture Agreement here is to outlaw the provision of such income support in a manner, and to an extent, that it distorts the market process – hence the term "decoupled".[207] To that end, important requirements are prescribed under paragraph 6.

First and foremost, the question of who is eligible for an income support should be determined by clearly-defined criteria such as income, status as a producer or

[205] See paragraphs 6 through 13 of Annex 2 of the Agreement on Agriculture.

[206] They are: (a) the support should be provided through a publicly-funded government programme (including government revenue foregone) not involving transfers from consumers; and (b) the support in question should not have the effect of providing price support to producers.

[207] There are evidences that academic economists in the US had been advocating decoupled payments as early as the 1950s. See J. Hillman, "The US Perspective", in Ingersent *et al* (1994) *supra* n. 92, p. 37.

landowner, factor use or production level in a defined and fixed base period. These criteria, once used to determine the eligibility, disappear from the scene. Secondly, the payment has to be "decoupled" from trade and production in the sense that the amount of such direct payments in any given year should not be related to the type or volume of production, the domestic or international price of products, or the employment of factors of production undertaken by the producer. Neither should production be required in order to receive such payments. If these conditions are met, Members are free to provide any form of direct payments in favour of their agricultural producers.

10.2.8.4.2 Government Financial Participation in Income Insurance and Income Safety-Net Programmes

The unavoidable dependence of agriculture on the vagaries of nature always makes farming a rather risk-prone undertaking. Government participation in income insurance and income safety-net programmes is thus a necessary corollary of this risky nature of agriculture. However, while governmental involvement helps to avert the risk of the farmer, it also creates another risk of its own for the interests of other countries – the risk that such involvement may result in the distortion of trade and production. Hence, the need for additional criteria to be met by a government that involves itself in such income insurance practices.

Firstly, eligibility for such payments should be determined by loss of agricultural income above a fixed benchmark. This benchmark has been agreed to be a loss of 30 per cent of the gross income or the equivalent in net terms (excluding any payments from the same or similar schemes) in the preceding three-year period or a three-year average based on the preceding five-year period, excluding the highest and the lowest entries. The government has thus an option between the average of the immediate three preceding years and the average of three of the preceding five years excluding the two extreme cases (years of the highest and the lowest incomes). The choice depends on the conditions of each particular case. While the lower of the two alternative amounts may better serve the interests of a producer whose loss barely reaches the 30 per cent minimum, the higher alternative serves the interests of one who has suffered a loss much more than that threshold. This is because of the maximum limits set on the amount that can be recovered.

Secondly, the compensation should cover only less than 70 per cent of the income loss suffered. The producer is thus made to suffer part of the pains from the loss so that he would take all necessary precaution to avoid the loss from the outset. The producer is in no position to recover the full amount of his loss – much less to profit out of it. For instance, if a producer's loss is calculated to be 50 per cent of his average gross income for the past three years (regardless of which three years are taken), the maximum he can get from the government programmes is just less than 70 per cent of the 50 per cent. In other words, the government may provide only about 35 per cent of the overall average income of the producer. This limitation is, however, subject to provisions of paragraph 8 on losses caused by natural disasters. Thus, in cases where the producer benefits from disaster relief as well as income insurance at the same time, the combined maximum may go as high as just below 100 per cent of the producer's total loss. This condition, while opening both avenues for a victim producer, also limits the maximum that can be recovered therefrom.

Finally, in line with the requirement of decoupling, the amount of any such payments should relate solely to income and nothing else. As such, the payment may not be related to the type or volume of production undertaken by the producer, or to the prices applying to such production, or to the factors of production employed. Needless to say, these additional requirements are designed to abolish any link between the payments and the amount of production as well as the market for it.

10.2.8.4.3 Disaster Relief

The rule of eligibility here is largely the same as in the case of income insurance payments discussed above. The only difference is that which emanates from the very nature of a disaster. For a Member to use this avenue of direct payment to its agricultural producers, the authorities should formally recognize that a disaster – natural or man-made – has occurred in its territory. An indicative list of such disasters includes disease outbreaks, pest infestations, nuclear accidents, and war. If any of these or similar other situations occur and are formally recognized by the government, and producers thereby suffer losses exceeding 30 per cent of their income, then Members are free to provide disaster relief payments. The maximum that can be paid in such cases is limited to the total cost of replacing the losses. Once again, however, as producers may benefit from the insurance schemes as well as from disaster relief payments for the same loss, the last subparagraphs of both paragraphs 7 and 8 state that the combined total of such payments should be less than 100 per cent of the producer's total loss.

10.2.8.4.4 Structural Adjustment Assistance

Three forms of structural adjustment assistance are envisaged by the Agreement on Agriculture: one provided through producer retirement programmes, a second one through resource retirement programmes, and a third one through investment aids. The first category of programmes is designed to facilitate the retirement of persons engaged in marketable agricultural production or their movement to non-agricultural activities. The payments here are conditional upon the total and permanent retirement of the recipients from marketable agricultural activities.

The second category of programmes is designed to remove land and other resources, including livestock, from marketable agricultural production. While the livestock have to be either slaughtered or definitively and permanently disposed, the land should be retired from marketable agricultural production for a minimum of three years. Finally, such payments may not be related to either the type or quantity of production or prices applying to production undertaken using the land or other resources remaining in production. These conditions are different from the conditions regarding the "blue box" measures of Article 6 in that (1) they are stricter and more definitive, and (2) they are required to be completely decoupled from production and price considerations.

The third case of structural adjustment assistance involves investment aids. The payments here are designed to assist the financial or physical restructuring of a producer's operations in response to objectively demonstrated structural disadvantages. Government programmes for the reprivatization of agricultural land may also be eligible for such types of assistance. While the basic decoupling requirements are still specifically stated, it is mandated in addition that investment aids may not exceed the amount required to compensate for the structural disadvantage and that they should be given only for the period of time necessary for the realization of the investment in respect of which they are provided.

10.2.8.4.5 Payments under Environmental Programmes

In line with the provisions of the Subsidies Agreement on environmental subsidies,[208] such subsidies are designed only to offset the extra costs incurred by the producer in his effort to comply with specific conditions set by clearly-defined governmental environmental or conservation programmes. Payment is required to depend on the fulfilment of specific conditions under the programme, including conditions related to production methods or inputs. However, while the Subsidies Agreement requires *inter alia* that such payments be a one-time non-recurring measure limited to only 20 per cent of the total extra cost of adaptation, agricultural subsidies for environmental purposes may be given up to as much as the total extra cost incurred for the purpose, and, within that limit, they may be provided for an unlimited number of times.

10.2.8.4.6 Payments under Regional Assistance Programmes

The first requirement here is that regional assistance payments should be limited to producers in disadvantaged areas. With the conditions for decoupling the payment from production and market considerations emphasized once more, Annex 2 also requires that regional development payments should be generally available to all producers within those regions.

The approach is still similar to that adopted by the Uruguay Round Subsidies Agreement on regional development subsidies, which made such government programmes non-actionable under GATT.[209] But, only some of the main conditions

[208] Article 8.2 of the SCM Agreement on non-actionable subsidies provides in its relevant part as follows: "Notwithstanding the provisions of Parts III and V of this Agreement, the following subsidies shall be non-actionable: ... (c) assistance to promote adaptation of existing facilities to new environmental requirements imposed by law and/or regulations which result in greater constraints and financial burden on firms, provided that the assistance: (i) is a one-time non-recurring measure; and (ii) is limited to 20 per cent of the cost of adaptation; and (iii) does not cover the cost of replacing and operating the assisted investment, which must be fully born by firms; and (iv) is directly linked to and proportionate to a firm's planned reduction of nuisances and pollution, and does not cover any manufacturing cost savings which may be achieved; and (v) is available to all firms which can adopt the new equipment and/or production process.'

[209] Article 8.2 of the SCM Agreement on non-actionable subsidies provides in its relevant part as follows: "Notwithstanding the provisions of Parts III and V of this Agreement, the following subsidies shall be non-actionable: ... (b) assistance to disadvantaged regions within the territory of a Member given pursuant to a general framework of regional development ... provided that: (i) each disadvantaged region must be clearly designated contiguous geographical area with a definable economic and administrative identity; (ii)the region is considered as disadvantaged on the basis of neutral and

set by the Subsidies Agreement are repeated by paragraph 13 of Annex 2 to the Agreement on Agriculture. Requirements such as the need to demonstrate that a designated contiguous geographical area with a definable economic and administrative identity is disadvantaged on the basis of objective criteria are found in both Agreements. However, while the SCM Agreement sets a 15 per cent minimum difference in the income, household income, or GDP per capita between the national average and the concerned region, the Agriculture Agreement does not set any such requirement. Consequently, unlike a general regional development subsidy, an agricultural subsidy for the same purpose may be lawfully provided to farmers in a region having an income difference of below 15 per cent. The requirement here is simply general: that the region should be "disadvantaged", although the difference may theoretically be as insignificant as anything above zero. If the difference is more than 15 per cent as required by the SCM Agreement, Members may not even need the Agriculture Agreement's loophole as such, for they can simply resort to the SCM Agreement. Another important difference between the two pertains to the extent of "non-actionability" that is involved. As stated already, while a non-actionable subsidy under the Subsidies Agreement may still be countervailed against or challenged before the WTO, an Annex 2 measure is completely immune from either of such actions. This gives a Member an additional reason to prefer reliance on the Agriculture Agreement over that of the SCM Agreement.

10.2.8.5 Summary of the "Green" Measures

By way of summary, the following observations may be made about measures of domestic support exempted from the reduction commitments. First of all, Members are, as a matter of principle, required to undertake reduction commitments on their domestic support policies. Exceptionally, however, they have the right to claim exemptions for specific policy instruments. For these policies to be exempted from the reduction commitments as claimed by Members, certain important conditions have to be satisfied. These conditions have been put under Annex 2 and may be grouped into two broad categories – general and policy-specific.

The most fundamental of these conditions is that the measures for which exemptions are claimed must have no, or at most minimal, trade distortion effects or effects on production. This requirement, although certainly important, would nonetheless be too vague to translate into concrete and enforceable obligations. As an appreciation of this fact, the Agreement on Agriculture has gone to great lengths

---

cont.

objective criteria, indicating that the region's difficulties arise out of more than temporary circumstances; such criteria must be spelled out in law, regulations, or other official document, so as to be capable of verification; (iii) the criteria shall include a measurement of economic development which shall be based on at least the following factors: – one of either per capita or household income per capita, or GDP per capita, which must not be above 85 per cent of the average for the territory concerned; – unemployment rate, which must be at least 110 per cent of the average for the territory concerned; as measured over a three-year period: such measurement, however, may be a composite one and may include other factors."

to provide a detailed and virtually exhaustive (although explicitly provided otherwise) list of measures along with the general and specific criteria they have to satisfy before they are exempted from the reduction commitments. Accordingly, the Agreement completely excludes from the exemptions market price support and all other forms of support involving transfers from consumers. Besides, while governments are allowed to take precautionary food security measures, render general services (such as research, pest control, training, infrastructure development, etc.) to producers and food aid to the needy, they are required to carry out these tasks as much as possible within the confines of market forces.

The Agriculture Agreement also provides that governments may give an unlimited amount of direct income support to their agricultural producers so long as the payments are made in a manner that is decoupled from production decisions and trade. Furthermore, Members are allowed to provide income insurance and disaster relief services to their farming communities on condition that farmers are not thereby made to profit out of such occurrences. Finally, Members can also render assistance for structural adjustment, environmental and regional development purposes. In general, while decoupled payments may be made for whatever reason and for whatever amount, those payments that take the form of income insurance, disaster relief, structural adjustment assistance, environmental or regional development programmes have to comply with the requirement that they may not be given in excess of the actual losses suffered or extra costs incurred to implement the government programme.

Another significant feature of the "green" box measures discussed above is that, under the Peace Clause of Article 13 of the Agriculture Agreement, they are completely immune from challenge under any of the provisions of the General Agreement. As such, all domestic support measures that conform with the requirements of Annex 2 may not be challenged either through the multilateral avenue of the WTO or the unilateral option of countervailing duties even if they are injurious to the interests of other Members.[210] What is more, they are also immune from challenge under the non-violation nullification or impairment provisions of paragraph 1(b) of Article XXIII.[211] Nearly all the "green" box policies may undercut the effect of any tariff or non-tariff concessions achieved during the negotiations. Bearing in mind the historical role played by the non-violation nullification or impairment provisions of Article XXIII as the only source of discipline for domestic subsidies, this is perhaps one of the strongest setbacks to the liberalizing effect of the Agriculture Agreement in this area. The effect of the peace clause is thus a significant weakening of the results of the Uruguay Round on domestic support measures.

Finally, caution should be exercised that when we say that these measures are allowed, we are not saying that all other measures that are not included herein are already prohibited. This is only the long-term dream of the law of agricultural trade; so far the only requirement concerning all domestic support measures other than

---

[210] See Article 13(a)(i) and (ii) of the Agreement on Agriculture.

[211] See Article 13(a)(iii) of the Agreement on Agriculture.

those explicitly excluded is that they have to be included in the calculation of the Current Total AMS which must be 20 per cent below the Base Total AMS at the end of the six-year implementation period.

10.3 Implementation and Surveillance of the Discipline of Domestic Support Measures

The Agriculture Agreement did not merely introduce the discipline governing the practice of agricultural domestic support; it has also established its own mechanism of review and surveillance of actual implementation of the obligations. Article 18 of the Agreement empowers the Committee on Agriculture (established under Article 17) to review progress in the implementation of commitments negotiated under the reform programme.[212] As the Committee is required to conduct its reviews on the basis of Members' notifications, it adopted in one of its earliest meetings a document in which it set out the requirements and formats for notifications under Article 18:2 and other relevant provisions of the Agreement.[213]

In the area of agricultural domestic support, Article 18 distinguishes between existing support systems and newly-introduced or modified ones. All Members, regardless of whether they have included domestic support reduction commitments in their schedules, are required to make periodic notification of the state of their agricultural domestic support schemes.[214] When it comes to the details, however, there is a difference depending on whether or not a country has undertaken domestic support reduction commitments. Accordingly, for all Members with base and annual commitment levels shown in Section I of Part IV of their Schedule, it is required that "a notification should be made no later than 90 days following the end of the calendar (or, marketing, fiscal, etc.) year in question."[215] They are also required to include a summary table (Table DS:1) and supporting tables (Supporting Tables DS:1 to DS:9) in attached formats.[216]

---

[212] See Article 18.1 of the Agriculture Agreement.

[213] WTO Committee on Agriculture, *Notification Requirements and Formats* (G/AG/2, 30 June 1995).

[214] For the notification formats, see Ibid., Table DS:1 and Supporting Tables DS:1 to DS:9, pp. 12–21.

[215] Ibid., p. 11. The document envisages the possibility of making provisional notifications. It is thus provided that "where the notification submitted within the 90 day period is provisional, the final notification should be submitted no later than 120 days following the end of the year."

[216] The tables referred to here as Tables and Supporting Tables (ST) are notification formats and may be highlighted as follows: Table DS:1: domestic support measures granted in any calendar, marketing, etc. year in the form of Current Total AMS; ST DS:1: measures exempt from the reduction commitment under Annex 2 – "Green Box"; ST DS:2: measures exempt from the reduction commitment on grounds of special and differential treatment under Article 6.2 – development programmes; ST DS:3: measures exempt from the reduction commitment for direct payments under production-limiting programmes under Article 6.5 – the "blue box"; ST DS:4: format for reporting the detailed calculation of the Current Total AMS with a description of basic products (including non-product specific AMS), product-specific AMS (from ST DS:5 to DS:7 below), product-specific measurements of support (from ST DS:8 below), and Current Total AMS (aggregate); ST DS:5: format for the reporting of product-specific AMS provided in the form of *market price support*; ST DS:6: format for reporting product-specific AMS provided in the form of *non-exempt direct payments*; ST DS:7: format for reporting

Members who had not undertaken reduction commitments, except the LDCs, are required to submit annual notifications. However, as regards developing countries, the Committee may, at their request, "set aside this requirement other than in respect of Supporting Tables DS:1 to DS:3."[217] The least-developed Members, too, are required to submit the Supporting Tables DS:1 to DS:3 every two years.[218] In case where no support exists, "a statement to this effect should be made".[219]

The notification requirement concerning newly-introduced or modified domestic support measures is provided as follows: "any new domestic support measure, or modification of an existing measure, for which exemption from reduction is claimed shall be notified promptly. This notification shall contain details of the new or modified measure and its conformity with the agreed criteria as set out either in Article 6 or in Annex 2."[220] Separate notification requirements and formats have been adopted by the Committee for this purpose.[221] Accordingly, all Members introducing a new support measure, or making modifications to an existing measure, for which an exemption from reduction is claimed, are required to make notifications under Article 18.3 of the Agriculture Agreement. The exemptions referred to here cover all three categories – the "green box" measures contained in Annex 2; the "development programmes" of developing country Members contained in Article 6:2; and the "blue box" measures contained in Article 6:5 of the Agreement.[222] These notifications are required to be submitted for each new or modified measure "as far as practicable before such measures are adopted and in any event within 30 days of adoption."[223]

As pointed out earlier, Members' annual and final bound commitments in the area of domestic support are expressed in fixed and nominal, rather than real, terms. The question of actual compliance during the implementation period is answered on the basis of the actual amount of money spent supporting agriculture in every year of the implementation period. Needless to say, while some currency deflation would allow countries to give more support in real terms without violating their obligations, a contrary development of inflation would lead them to violation although in real terms they might still be within the limits of their commitment levels. As the most likely development in practically every country is towards inflation, this is a favourable situation for the liberalization process.[224] However, in an attempt to

cont.

product-specific AMS provided in the form of *other product-specific support*; ST DS:8: format for reporting product-specific *Equivalent Measurements of Support*; ST DS:9: format for reporting non-product-specific AMS.

217 G/AG/2, *supra* n. 213, p. 11.

218 Ibid.

219 *Id.*

220 Article 18.3 of the Agriculture Agreement.

221 G/AG/2, *supra* n. 213.

222 Ibid., p. 22.

223 Ibid.

224 It has thus been rightly observed that "since the cap on spending for trade-distorting subsidies is fixed in nominal values, it will erode with inflation and increase the incentive to move to non distorting policies." Hathaway and Ingco (1995) *supra* n. 112, pp. 29–30.

dispel the fears of those countries who might be unable to meet their obligations owing to such inflationary pressures, Article 18.4 of the Agriculture Agreement provides that, in the review process, "Members shall give due consideration to the influence of excessive rates of inflation on the ability of any Member to abide by its domestic support commitments."

Finally, the review process is designed to serve as a forum in which Members would be able to raise any matter relevant to the implementation of commitments under the reform programme as set out in the Agriculture Agreement.[225] Furthermore, the domestic support notification provisions also benefit from the "counter-notification" possibility: that any Member may bring to the attention of the Committee on Agriculture any measure which it considers ought to have been notified by another Member.[226] Stressing the importance of such issues, the Committee decided in its *Organization of Work and Working Procedures* that "counter notifications, shall be considered by the Committee *at the earliest opportunity*."[227]

The experience so far indicates that Members hardly had any difficulty meeting their obligations in the area of domestic support. In fact, statistics show that most countries provided support much less than their bound ceiling levels. As computed by the USDA, the total value of the 1995 Current Total AMS for the first 24 countries who notified was $115 billion, a figure that amounted to "only about 57 percent of the AMS level in the 1986–88 base period for these countries."[228] Given that the required reduction by the end of the six-year implementation period was to bring it down only by 20 per cent of the base period level, the actual reduction of 43 per cent in the very first year of the implementation period is a big development. However, because of Article 6 exemptions, the calculation of the Current Total AMS in this case did not include the blue box payments made in 1995 although they had been included in the base total AMS. When the 1995 blue box payments were added, for purposes of comparison, to the reported Current Total AMS for that year, the total support for 1995 amounted to only "73 percent of the base."[229]

This is just as expected from the outset. Indeed, for most of these countries, the exclusion of the "blue box" measures from the reduction commitments had brought their support levels to below the final bound commitment levels already before the beginning of the implementation period itself. This does not, however, mean that the problem of agricultural domestic support in international trade has ceased to be a cause for concern. Far from it. There is evidence suggesting that countries are shifting their forms of support from "amber" to "green", and even "blue",

---

[225] See Article 18.6 of the Agriculture Agreement.

[226] See Article 18.7 of the Agriculture Agreement.

[227] WTO Committee on Agriculture, *Organization of Work and Working Procedures of the Committee on Agriculture* (G/AG/1), adopted on 28 March 1995, para. 11.

[228] United States Department of Agriculture, *Agriculture in the WTO* (December 1998) p. 16. Note that the list of countries here includes the three largest providers of amber support in absolute terms – the EC, Japan, and the US – which accounted for "about 90 percent of the total AMS for the 24 countries that reported an AMS as of June 1998." Ibid.

[229] *Id.* p. 16.

measures.[230] In itself, this is of course a commendable development. However, in as long as the possibility of trade and production distortions due to these latter forms of support is still there, the problem of agricultural domestic support is certain to be at the centre of present as well as future agricultural trade negotiations.

10.4 Conclusion

In general, the domestic support discipline introduced by the Agriculture Agreement may easily be characterized in terms of its positive and negative sides. On the positive side, suffice it to note that, this being the first ever "successful" attempt to bring the controversial field of agricultural domestic subsidies under the multilateral trading system, it can be hailed as a milestone in the history of international agricultural trade regulation. From this perspective, the domestic support provisions have rightly been praised by some writers as "the most innovative" and "the most important" element of the Uruguay Round Agreement on Agriculture.[231]

At the same time, however, Members have still been left free to exclude from their reduction commitments a long list of domestic support measures in the form *inter alia* of so-called "green" and "blue" box measures. Not only do these exempted measures always carry the risk of market distortion within them,[232] even the "amber box" policies themselves are far from being subject to any meaningful restraint. Apart from the exemption of such important forms of support as deficiency payments of the US and the compensatory payments of the EC, the "total" nature of the final AMS commitments gives them an unlimited freedom to provide an unlimited amount of support to any specific agricultural product. The only indirect restriction against the complete discretion of Members in this respect comes from the possibility of challenge under the SCM Agreement or GATT 1994 in cases where the product-specific support for a given product exceeds that for the 1992 marketing year. As a result, the support for some "politically powerful" agricultural products rose relative to that for others.[233] Besides, thanks to the selection of a base period

---

230 See, *inter alia,* Ibid., pp. 18–19.

231 See Josling *et al* (1996) *supra* n. 85, pp. 201 and 205.

232 Indeed, as observed by Josling *et al* in connection with the "green" box measures, "after all, there are very few, if any, policies that really have no effect at all on production and hence on trade, and it is therefore a subjective matter to define what a 'minimal' distortion effect is when it comes to determining whether or not a given programme is eligible for exemption." Josling *et al* (1996) *supra* n. 85, p. 207. See also B. Hoekman, and K. Anderson, *Developing Country Agriculture and the New Trade Agenda*, Policy Research Working Paper 2125, The World Bank, Development Research Group, (May 1999) p. 12.

233 In a paper presented at the High-Level Round Table on Trade and Development of the 10th Ministerial Conference of UNCTAD, two scholars specifically mentioned sugar and dairy products as such "politically powerful" agricultural products whose levels of subsidies in developed countries had "almost no progress". H. Binswanger, and E. Lutz, *Agricultural Trade Barriers, Trade Negotiations, and the Interests of Developing Countries*, paper prepared for the UNCTAD X High-Level Round Table on Trade and Development (Bangkok, 12 February 2000), p. 7.

which constituted "an historic peak for many commodities and countries",[234] the 20 per cent minimum cut in the total AMS required of Members was actually reached by many well before even the beginning of the implementation period. It is because of these and other features that we say the domestic support provisions of the Agriculture Agreement, innovative and important as they definitely are, could not become of much practical significance at least in the short term.[235]

Yet, the fact remains that the Agreement on Agriculture has put a cap, a ceiling, on the maximum amount of support that can be given to agriculture in such notoriously trade- and production-distorting ways as market price support. Together with the rules on export subsidies and market access, the domestic support provisions of the Agreement on Agriculture have thus taken the first most important step forward for the reintegration of agriculture into the market process. Once these basics have been set, it is up to the current and future negotiations to push the process and give the past developments a meaningful future. The success of these negotiations in this area will be measured *inter alia* by the number of policies that are transferred from the currently "blue", and possibly even "green", boxes into the "amber" basket and the extent to which the latter are reduced over a given period of time.

234 OECD (1995) *supra* n. 135, p. 44.

235 See M. Ingco, *Agricultural Trade Liberalization in the Uruguay Round: One Step Forward, One Step Back?*, supplementary paper prepared for a World Bank Conference on "The Uruguay Round and the Developing Countries", (Washington, D.C. 26–27 January 1995) pp. 13–14.

CHAPTER 11

TRENDS AND PERSPECTIVES IN THE LAW OF AGRICULTURAL TRADE

11.1 General

The Uruguay Round is credited for achieving a breakthrough in the area of agricultural trade. After long and testing negotiations, a distinct Agreement on Agriculture has been concluded for the first time in the history of the multilateral trading system. The Agreement has had very modest ambitions. As reiterated in its preamble, it was intended merely to initiate, to lay the foundations for, a reform process in agricultural trade. The establishment of a "fair and market-oriented agricultural trading system" is only the long-term objective of this Agreement. With its entry into force, that foundation has been put firmly in place. A system of rules governing agricultural trade, backed by detailed Schedules of Concessions and Commitments, has now been introduced,[1] and, with it, the enduring defiance of agriculture to multilateral regulation has been tempered.

The developments thus far have, however, been largely limited to a reshaping of the rules of agricultural trade in the direction of the overall discipline applying to the trade of industrial products. The treatment of agricultural products as a distinct category still forms part of the WTO architecture. The Agriculture Agreement provides for a system of rules significantly different from mainstream GATT provisions for most other products, whose provisions have been made to prevail over inconsistent GATT/WTO rules. The conclusion of this Agreement has not as such been accompanied with meaningful actual liberalization in agricultural trade. Indeed, agriculture still stands alone as the sector where export subsidies are expressly and generously – albeit selectively – permitted under WTO law; where three-digit tariffs are common and four-digit rates may not be impossible to find; where significant additional duties can be introduced in the name of "safeguard measures" regardless of injury considerations and in the most unpredictable of ways; where a proven trade-distortive and injurious domestic support programme may escape challenge under the nullification or impairment provisions of the multilateral trading system; etc. In short, agricultural trade still has a long way to go on the road to liberalization. Seen from this perspective, therefore, although the Agreement certainly represents a significant breakthrough in the history of agricultural trade, it

[1] The WTO has reported that no major delays have been witnessed in the implementation of the agricultural commitments. See *WTO Annual Report 2000*, p. 21.

is also possible to say that the same Agreement is a standing symbol of continued failure to integrate agricultural trade into the mainstream system. It represents as much of the moves in the right direction as the perpetuation of the artificial distinction between agricultural and non-agricultural products. Paradoxical though it may seem, the Agreement may therefore be seen as an embodiment of both success and failure in agricultural trade negotiations at the same time.

One of the virtues of the Agreement on Agriculture is that it has an in-built agenda for a continuation of the liberalization process so as to realize its long-term objective of bringing fundamental change in the level of protective and restrictive devices at work in the area of agriculture in many countries.[2] The best way to achieve meaningful progress in agricultural trade liberalization was (and still is) believed to be by making agriculture part of a comprehensive trade negotiation round that covers other sectors as well. As this was expected to allow the necessary trade-offs at a wider scale, there was a belief that there could be "no real progress in agriculture if the sector is not included in a total package, together with other areas . . . ."[3] This was one of the primary objectives of the third Ministerial Conference of the WTO at Seattle.[4]

Seattle proved to be a disappointing failure, and the widely-expected Millennium Round of trade negotiations was not launched.[5] But, as pointed out earlier, since agriculture was one of the areas on which a negotiation had already been mandated by the results of the Uruguay Round, the WTO General Council agreed on 7 February 2000 on the "organization of negotiations to further liberalize ... agriculture."[6] In accordance with a programme agreed on that occasion, the WTO agriculture negotiators held their first meeting on 23–24 March 2000. In the first phase of the process (which covered the period between March 2000 and March 2001), several meetings were held and dozens of proposals submitted by about 85 percent of the WTO's membership. The negotiations then entered their second phase which was expected to involve the technical details necessary for members to develop specific proposals on each of their specific areas of interest. It was at this stage of the agriculture-specific negotiations that the 4th WTO Ministerial Conference succeeded in launching a comprehensive round of trade negotiations and decided to bring within its fold the already proceeding sector-specific negotiations in agriculture and services. In agriculture, the Doha Declaration affirmed that it would build on the

---

2 See Article 20 of the Agreement on Agriculture.

3 A. De Zeeuw, "Implementation and Accomplishments of the WTO" paper presented at a Seminar organized by the International Policy Council on Agriculture, Food and Trade, in *Proceedings of the IPC Seminar: Agriculture, the FTAA and the WTO* (Belo Horizonte, Brazil 12-13 May 1997).

4 Held at Seattle, United States, from 30 November to 3 December 1999. For details on this Conference, see http://www.wto.org/wto/seattle/english/about_e/07ag_e.htm.

5 "Millennium Round" was a name perhaps first used by former EU Trade Commissioner Sir Leon Brittan. See, *inter alia*, Europe Agri, *WTO: Farm Trade Round Delayed Until Year 2000*, 29 May 1998; Agra Europe, *OECD Meeting Provides Pointer to WTO Talks*, 3 March 1998; and Agra Europe, *EU Maintains Export Subsidisation*, 27 November 1998.

6 See *WTO Services and Agriculture negotiations: meetings set for February and March*, WTO Press Release (Press/167) 7 February 2000.

work already carried out to that date. Members further declared to have committed themselves to "comprehensive negotiations aimed at: substantial improvements in market access; reductions of, with a view to phasing out, all forms of export subsidies; and substantial reductions in trade-distorting domestic support."[6a]

The negotiations are currently proceeding actively. As such, any attempt at summarizing the process in this book may not serve much useful purpose over the long-term. Indeed, both the *Information and Media Relations* and the *Agriculture and Commodities* divisions of the WTO Secretariat provide useful summaries of the negotiations which are updated periodically to reflect the progress on the ground.[7] Consequently, this section only tries to analyze the main issues of negotiation at this moment on the basis of the positions taken primarily by the EU, a member that is often blamed for dragging its feet in agricultural trade negotiations. As the positions of some of the major players will also be reviewed along side the EU's, this section is hoped to provide some useful perspectives into the direction in which rules of agricultural trading are evolving.

11.2 The Agriculture Negotiations: Does the EU Position Provide any Perspectives into the Future?

The history of multilateral trade negotiations shows that the US was largely responsible for the exclusion of agricultural products from application of some of the core rules of the trading system for long. When the original text of the General Agreement was negotiated in 1947, agriculture was subjected to an exceptional treatment in respect of quantitative restrictions (Article XI) and, during the 1955 revision, for export subsidies (Article XVI, Section B) mainly at the insistence of the United States. However, since the development of the Common Agricultural Policy (the CAP) by the European Economic Community in the 1960s, the EC has been a symbol of intransigence against any moves to extend the rules of the system to agricultural products. The Uruguay Round negotiations had been repeatedly threatened with collapse largely because of EC unwillingness to agree to any meaningful liberalization in this sector. In the ongoing negotiations, too, the EU has already begun accusing the US and the Cairns Group countries of "taking an overly aggressive position", "shadow boxing", "repeating the mistakes that have been made before the WTO meeting in Seattle", and of remaining "camped on their extreme positions".[8] Until the very last minute of the Doha Ministerial Conference, success and failure were both hanging on the wording on the wording of the draft declaration concerning agricultural export subsidies. A closer look at the position of the EU and some other major players in the ongoing negotiations is thus believed to provide some useful insight into the evolution of agricultural trade rules under the

---

[6a] See WTO Ministerial Declaration, adopted at Doha on 14 November 2001, WT/MIN(01)/DEC/1, para. 13.

[7] These summaries are available at http://www.wto.org/english/tratop_e/agric_e/negoti_e.htm.

[8] See "Fischler hits at 'Shadow Boxing' on agriculture", *Financial Times* Sept. 27, 2001, p. 12.

WTO. This will be done on the basis of positions expressed by leading WTO members in the agriculture negotiations before, but also during, the Doha Ministerial Conference.

Since the initiation of the current agricultural negotiations in March 2000, the EC has submitted separate proposals on "blue box" domestic support measures,[9] food quality,[10] animal welfare,[11] and export competition,[12] and a joint technical submission on non-trade concerns in general.[13] In December 2000, the EC submitted its "comprehensive negotiating proposal".[14]

It is noteworthy that, for the first time in the history of multilateral trade negotiations, the EC has emphasized its position as the second largest agricultural exporting Member of the WTO and attempts, albeit not consistently, to use this fact for market opening objectives.[15] But still, the fundamental philosophy of the EC in the ongoing agricultural trade negotiations is a continuation of its traditional conservative approach to agricultural trade liberalization. In the eyes of the Community, agriculture is still different from all other sectors; as such, it can not be left entirely to the free interplay of market forces. For the EU, the question is not whether, but how, agriculture should be supported. It declares its readiness to discuss the type of support to be given to agriculture; but it appears adamant that there can be no question that it should be supported. All specific proposals made thus far are but only a translation of this basic philosophy into concrete negotiating positions.

In its 15 December 2000 proposal, the EC underlined its full commitment to the continuation of the reform process enshrined in Article 20 of the Agreement on Agriculture. At the same time, the EC puts strong emphasis on Article 20's reference to the so-called non-trade concerns which, in its view, reflect important societal goals. On that basis, the "comprehensive negotiating proposal" of the Community distinguishes between trade issues (i.e. market access, export competition, and domestic support), on the one hand, and non-trade issues (i.e. sustainable development, protection of the environment, the sustained vitality of rural areas, food safety, consumer concerns, protection of the welfare of animals, and poverty alleviation) on the other, and tries to draw a balance between the two.

---

9 See *European Communities Proposal: the Blue Box and Other Support Measures to Agriculture* (G/AG/NG/W/17) 28 June 2000.

10 See *European Communities Proposal: Food Quality – Improvement Of Market Access Opportunities* (WTO doc. G/AG/NG/W/18) 28 June 2000.

11 See *European Communities Proposal: Animal Welfare And Trade In Agriculture* (G/AG/NG/W/19) 28 June 2000.

12 See *European Communities Proposal: Export Competition* (G/AG/NG/W/34) 18 September 2000.

13 See *Non-Trade Concerns* (WTO doc. G/AG/NG/W/36/Rev.1) 9 November 2000; see also *Fourth Special Session of the Committee on Agriculture 15-17 November 2000: Statements by the European Communities* (WTO doc. G/AG/NG/W/66) 29 November 2000.

14 See *EC Comprehensive Negotiating Proposal,* WTO doc. G/AG/NG/W/90, 15 December 2000.

15 See W. Miner, "An Overview of the Issues and Positions of the Major Countries in the WTO Negotiations"' (2001) 2 *The Estey Centre Journal of International Law and Trade Policy*, No. 1, p. 20.

11.2.1 Trade Issues

On trade issues, and despite its apparent emphasis on its interests as an important agricultural exporting Member, the EC still appears to retain its traditional conservative approach with a conciliatory tone. The comprehensive proposal covers all the three pillars of the Agreement on Agriculture – market access, export competition and domestic support. These will be analyzed in turn.

(a) Market Access

This is where the position of the EC as the second largest exporter of agricultural products should matter most. The Uruguay Round has brought important developments in the areas of agricultural market access, the most notable being the conversion of all pre-existing non-tariff barriers (NTBs), including the typical EC system of variable import levies, into their tariff equivalents via the innovative approach of tariffication. Furthermore, not only are the resulting tariffs bound against any future increase, they have also been subject to a 36% minimum reduction commitment on the average tariff levels (and a 15% minimum per tariff line) over a six year implementation period (for developing countries, the reduction rate is two-thirds of the above percentages over a ten-year implementation period). But, the tariffication process resulted in very high tariffs (sometimes even higher than their NTB equivalents due to the problem of "dirty tariffication") and specific minimum and/or current access commitments have been undertaken to allay fears of more restrictive tariff levels. At the same time, to accommodate fears of excessive or low-priced imports into the newly-opened markets, a special arrangement was made to allow the introduction of special safeguard (SSG) measures under less stringent conditions than those required by GATT Article XIX and the Safeguards Agreement.

General Methodology: In the current negotiations, the EC proposes to follow the practice of the Uruguay Round so that there would be a commitment as to the overall average reduction of bound tariffs and a minimum reduction per tariff line. The EC is of the view that this approach is a well-known and well-tested way of achieving across-the-board tariff reductions which corresponds perfectly to the engagement taken in Article 20 of progressive reduction in protection which applies to all Members, while at the same time allowing for sufficient flexibility in lowering tariffs and enabling Members to take into account the particular situation of specific sectors.

Tariff Rate Quotas (TRQs): As regards TRQs, which have been introduced mainly to respond to the minimum and/or current access commitments of the Agreement on Agriculture, the EC sees only their positive role as contributing to increased market access and its only problem pertains to their administration. Consequently, rather than questioning the very need for TRQs, the EC only proposes mechanisms by which those administrative shortcomings could be resolved and the rules for their allocation clarified so that the concessions already granted would be fully realised. The EC thus believes that transparency, predictability and security of management are the main cures as regards TRQs.

Geographical Indications: The EC also wants to use the current negotiations to introduce some form of "competition rules" into the Agreement on Agriculture which would particularly aim at the protection of geographical indications[16] for agricultural products in general. The declared purpose of this EC proposal is the protection of both producers and consumers from misleading labelling as a result of which high quality food, typical of particular regions, are confused with imitation products bearing the same name. In EC view, geographical indications are needed to ensure fair competition opportunities for those products whose quality and reputation are linked to their geographical origin and traditional know-how. The TRIPS Agreement already provides for the possibility of preventing the use of a geographical indication for wines and spirits not originating in the place indicated by the geographical indication.[17] The EC wants to incorporate into the Agreement on Agriculture a strengthened form of that aspect of the TRIPS Agreement applying to the food and beverages sectors in general.[18]

Among the proposals of the Community in this respect are provisions (a) to guarantee effective protection against usurpation of names for agricultural products and foodstuffs; (b) to protect the right to use geographical indications or designations of origin; and (c) to guarantee consumer protection and fair competition through regulation of labelling. The Community thinks that there is a need for the establishment of a "multilateral register" of geographical indications which would serve as a reliable and lasting source of information on this matter. This is only an attempt at widening the scope of the Community's positions in the mandated negotiations of the TRIPS Council on the establishment of a multilateral system of notification and registration of geographical indications for wines and spirits as envisaged by Article 23.4 of the TRIPS Agreement.

Special Safeguard (SSG): A look at EC agricultural tariff schedules shows that they are cluttered with the SSG symbol by which the Community has reserved its rights to resort to the special safeguard mechanisms of Article 5 of the Agreement on Agriculture. Unlike the US and the Cairns Group (CG) countries, the EC still believes that the SSG provision is a useful adjunct to the process of tariffication providing some reassurance that this would not lead to sudden or unpredictable surges in imports or sharp reductions in import prices and proposes that a similar instrument be maintained in the Agreement.[19]

---

16 Article 22.1 of the TRIPs Agreement defines "geographical indications" to mean "indications which identify a good as originating in the territory of a Member, or a region or locality in that territory, where a given quality, reputation or other characteristic of the good is essentially attributable to its geographical origin."

17 See *Implementation of Article 23.4 of the TRIPS Agreement Relating to the Establishment of a Multilateral System of Notification and Registration of Geographical Indications: Communication from the European Communities and Their Member States, Revision* (WTO doc. IP/C/W/107/Rev.1), 22 June 2000.

18 See WTO doc. G/AG/NG/W/18, *supra* n. 10.

19 This position of the EC's is also supported by Japan. Indeed, the latter goes further and proposes the introduction of a new safeguard mechanism to apply with respect to seasonal and perishable agricultural products. See *Negotiating Proposal by Japan on WTO Agricultural Negotiations* (WTO doc. G/AG/NG/W/91) 21 December 2000, Para. 14.

(b) Export Competition

The Agreement on Agriculture introduced special rules for the use of subsidies on the export of agricultural products. There is no uniform discipline applying to all forms of export subsidies. The Agreement on Agriculture has created two distinct categories of export subsidies – listed and non-listed – each subject to distinct obligations. Listed agricultural export subsidies have generally been subject to reduction commitments of a dual nature – quantitative (by 21%) and budgetary (by 36%) – on a 1986-1990 base period and over a six-year implementation period. Developing countries undertook only two-thirds of these obligations to be implemented over a period of ten years. As regards non-listed export subsidies, the only limitation is that they cannot be used in a manner which results in, or which threatens to lead to, circumvention of export subsidy commitments (Article 10.1 Agreement on Agriculture). Article 10.2 goes a step further and picks three forms of non-listed export support practices, including export credit schemes, and declares that Members shall undertake to work toward the development of internationally agreed disciplines governing their use. To the disappointment of the EC, however, no such agreement has been reached so far due largely to a US opposition.

Different Priorities: In the area of export competition, while most agricultural exporting Members of the WTO, such as the US and the Cairns Group, are worried about the weakness of the discipline governing agricultural export subsidy practices, the EC's primary concern is the "discriminatory" nature of this otherwise weak export subsidy discipline in the sense of not applying the same discipline to similar measures of export support, particularly export credit schemes, state-trading enterprises and "abuse" of food aid. With this as its point of departure, the EC declares that there is an urgent need for a more level playing field in export competition, since the current provisions fully cover only one of the instruments – export subsidies. The same urgency is being strongly echoed by several countries, particularly those in the Cairns Group and developing countries, but in a totally different sense. While the EC makes the call so as to bring export credit schemes and other forms of export support into the present system of rules for agricultural export subsidies, the Cairns Group and other pro-liberalization forces make the same call of urgency for the prohibition of agricultural export subsidies as such, most (the US being a notable exception) including officially supported export credit schemes. The EC invokes the failure to implement the understanding of Article 10.2 of the Agreement on Agriculture, which is blamed on US intransigence in OECD negotiations. Indeed, the EC accuses the US of being pretentious in its current push for the elimination of export subsidies altogether. The EC has noted that the US proposal on the subject is that "the kinds of export subsidy in which the US has less interest should be eliminated, but that nothing, or less drastic action, should be taken on export assistance given through mechanisms which the US does use, in particular export credit and loan deficiency payments."[20] The EC thus appears to be

[20] *Statement by the European Community to the Second Special Session of the Committee on Agriculture* on 29-30 June 2000 (WTO doc. G/AG/NG/W/24).

committed to bring export credits and other unregulated mechanisms of export support under the general provisions of the Agreement on Agriculture on agricultural export subsidies.

Abuse of Food Aid: The EC uses strong language regarding the (mis)use of food aid as a means of circumventing Members' export subsidy commitments. The EC charges that some Members are subsidizing their agricultural exports disguising them as concessional food aid transactions. Relying on data concerning the relationship between the world market price for food items and food aid availabilities, which incidentally shows an inverse relationship, the EC argues that it is "a disgrace that food aid availability should increase when prices are low and be curtailed when it is most needed against a background of high commodity prices."[21] On that basis, the EC advocates the establishment of a genuine food aid system which adequately responds to the real food aid needs of countries and not to the presence or absence of surplus production in the donor countries.

Expressing its support to the approach of the new Food Aid Convention (FAC 1999), the EC proposes that food aid should be given in fully grant form and that it should not be used as a tool of market penetration to displace commercial transactions and local production. It is noteworthy that, despite the strong language of its proposal on the subject, the EC proposal fell short of suggesting to bring food aid fully into the WTO so that it would be a WTO right for the needy Members to get food aid from the donors as a matter of the latter's binding WTO obligation. It only proposes that the food aid provisions of Article 10 of the Agreement on Agriculture should be revised and strengthened and that food aid should be given in fully grant form.[22]

State-Trading Enterprises (STEs) and the Export Subsidy Discipline: The EC maintains that STEs, and particularly the so-called "single desk exporters" (i.e. enterprises with responsibility for domestic and export sales) are being widely used by several Members to circumvent their export subsidy commitments through, inter alia, cross-subsidisation, price-discrimination and price-pooling arrangements. (The *Canada Dairy* dispute is a very good example of how these things actually operate.[23]) The EC thus wants to write further disciplines into the Agreement on Agriculture for the transparent use of STEs with strict notification requirements regarding acquisition costs and export pricing which would result in indirect subsidisation of exports.

To sum up, there is every reason – logical, historical, as well as economic – to expect that bringing these other forms of export support to the same level as conventional forms of agricultural export subsidies will be one of the most

---

21 See WTO doc. G/AG/NG/W/34, *supra* n. 12, para. 11.

22 For more on this subject, see Melaku Geboye Desta, "Food Security and International Trade Law: An Appraisal of the World Trade Organization Approach" (2001) 35 *Journal of World Trade*, No. 3, pp. 449-468.

23 See *Canada – Measures Affecting the Importation of Milk and the Exportation of Dairy Products*, reports of the panel (WTO docs. WT/DS103/R, WT/DS113/R) and the Appellate Body (WTO docs. WT/DS103/AB/R, WT/DS113/AB/R) adopted on 27 October 1999.

fundamental targets of the EC in this negotiation. The un-adopted report of the 1981 *EEC Wheat Flour*[24] panel in the dispute between the EC and the US clearly shows that most export support measures identified by the Community for the current negotiations are old, deep-rooted, anomalous, and in need of urgent change. On that basis, the EC openly declares that it will negotiate further reductions in export subsidies only on condition that all forms of export subsidisation are treated on an equal basis. This is thus a delicate situation. Its major negotiating partners, including the US, CG, as well as several developing countries, are pressing for nothing less than the immediate prohibition of agricultural export subsidies. The EC, on the other hand, is ready only for further reductions in export subsidies, and even that conditionally. This is one area where real change is widely expected from the ongoing negotiations. The Doha commitment to work for "reductions of, with a view to phasing out, all forms of export subsidies" was achieved only after a series of recriminations between the EC (and France in particular), on the one hand, and most other WTO Members on the other.[24a] The degree of sensitivity with which this issue was handled by the Doha Ministerial is already an indication of how acrimonious it could become in the actual negotiations.

(c) Domestic Support

The fundamental principle of the Agreement on Agriculture in respect of domestic support measures was the decoupling or delinking of support to the farming sector from production decisions. But the Agreement on Agriculture did not prohibit market price support and other trade-distortive forms of support. It only put all forms of domestic support measures into three different "boxes" according to their trade-distortive impact and their relation to production decisions. Measures with no or minimal trade-distorting impact, such as direct income support, have been expressly permitted without limit and fall in the "green box"; those which are provided in a manner that distorts trade, such as market price support, are permitted subject to binding reduction commitments and fall in the "amber box"; and support given to farmers on condition of production limitation have been permitted and fall in the "blue box". The system got this tri-color (and not a traffic light) set up due to the last-minute addition of the "blue box" as part of the Blair House accord between the US and the EC for the benefit of both parties. In a unilateral move which complements this multilateral development, the EC has since pushed the liberalization process further as part of its "Agenda 2000" package which ended in 1999 with the enactment of several agricultural legislations. In many cases, these laws have converted "amber box" price support measures into direct income support – thus putting them into the "green box". The sticking points for the ongoing negotiations regarding domestic support appear likely to revolve around the following issues: (1)

[24] See *European Economic Community - Subsidies on Export of Wheat Flour Report of the Panel* (GATT doc. SCM/42) 21 March 1983 (not adopted).

[24a] See "Trade talks falter as France blocks farm subsidy deal" *Financial Times* 14 Nov. 2001, p. 14.

whether the "blue box" should be retained; (2) whether the criteria for "green box" exemptions should be tightened; and (3) how far to push the liberalization process in respect of the "amber box" measures – should they be eliminated or just reduced? If the latter, by how much?

Although the latter two also promise to be contentious, the major preoccupation of the EC in the ongoing negotiations on domestic support is the maintenance of the "blue box". The "blue box" still plays an important role in the EC, which is no longer the case for the US as a result of the 1996 FAIR Act which moved most "blue box" measures in the direction of the "green box". As a result, the EC appears to be rather isolated in its use of the "blue box". The only other countries known to have made use of this category of support are Iceland, Norway, and Slovakia. Despite its virtual loneliness, however, the EC appears fully prepared to defend the continued existence of the "blue box". The EC believes that the present tri-coloured arrangements under the Agreement on Agriculture constitute "globally the right framework for addressing domestic support issues."[25] Indeed, the EC has made it clear that it is ready to negotiate about the reduction of "amber box" support as well as the possible tightening of the criteria for the "green box" only if the current tri-color setting is maintained. The EC's submission of a separate proposal on "blue box" support measures is further indication of the level of determination with which it is prepared to pursue this matter. The EC has also shown its distaste for an ASEAN proposal to disaggregate the AMS commitments of developed countries so that specific commitments would be undertaken by them on a product-by-product and/or policy-by-policy basis.[26] The EC position on domestic support has received strong backing from, inter alia, Japan.[27]

11.2.2 Non-Trade Concerns (NTCs)

NTCs have been given a prominent place in the EC comprehensive negotiating proposal – hardly surprising when viewed in light of its history and the public pressure the Community is under these days. The tone of its presentations so far suggest that the EC will leave no stones unturned to get its views on NTCs accommodated in the final outcome of the negotiations. The Community has repeatedly stated that NTCs are a key element in the Article 20 (Agreement on Agriculture) negotiations in the sense of "an instrument for opening a door".[28] The EC argues that agriculture plays a specific role as a provider of public goods and demands that this multifunctional nature of the sector should be recognised. For the EC, NTCs should not be seen as an obstacle to trade liberalization, but rather as

---

[25] See G/AG/NG/W/90, *supra* n. 14.

[26] See G/AG/NG/W/66, *supra* n. 13.

[27] See G/AG/NG/W/91, *supra* n. 19, Para. 18.

[28] Aware of the possible suspicion of its negotiating partners that this might be another EC ploy to legalise otherwise unlawful import restrictive measures, the EC hastens to add that it does "not regard it as a means of locking the door on the other planks of the negotiation." See G/AG/NG/W/66, *supra* n. 13.

legitimate concerns for which appropriate mechanisms of accommodation need to be designed.[29] The EC has included specific negotiating proposals on a number of such non-trade issues, the protection of the environment, poverty alleviation and the sustainable vitality of rural areas, food safety and consumer concerns, and animal welfare. The proposals of the EC on most of these NTCs are still lacking in detail, but its resolve to their accommodation by the ongoing negotiations is manifest.

(a) Environment

The EC strongly argues that farming and conservation of the natural environment are inextricably linked and that, in order to protect the environment, countries often need to implement specific and targeted policies. According to the EC, the provision of such environmental services as the maintenance of valued landscapes, conservation of biodiversity and the protection of historical features is unlikely to be assured by market forces alone. On that premise, the EC argues that the new agricultural trading regime should be designed in such a way as to contribute to the maintenance of the visual amenities of the countryside through the use of environment-friendly production methods. The EC thus proposes that the Agreement on Agriculture should accommodate transparent measures targeting these objectives, and implemented in no more than minimally-trade-distorting ways. During the Doha Conference, the EC adamantly argued that progress in agricultural negotiations would be possible only if environmental issues were to be included in the agenda for the new negotiations. However, the Doha negotiation agenda in this respect (para. 31 of the Doha Declaration) was limited to the relationship between existing WTO rules and specific trade obligations set out in multilateral environmental agreements (MEAs) and only as regards the applicability of such existing WTO rules as among parties to the MEA in question.

(b) Poverty Alleviation and the Sustainable Vitality of Rural Areas

The EC argues that, in many developing countries, farming is too vital an economic activity to be exposed to sudden and profound changes as that could have severe consequences in terms of their social and political stability. In developed countries as well, agriculture still plays an important part in rural development in terms, inter alia, of land use, supporting employment, ancillary businesses, and environmental services. The EC thus proposes that the Agreement on Agriculture should allow "sufficient flexibility" to enable countries to promote rural development. The measures should be, once again, implemented in no more than minimally trade-distorting ways.

---

[29] See the statement made by the EC at the Seventh Special Session of the Committee on Agriculture 26-28 March 2001 (WTO doc. G/AG/NG/W/150).

(c) Food Safety

In the wake of recurring high profile stories about the outbreak of several foodborne diseases, ranging from mad cow disease to African swine fever to salmonella in eggs, old questions have reappeared on the extent to which the present international trading regime accommodates such vital societal concerns as food safety requirements without at the same time enabling countries to use such loopholes for protectionist motives. The SPS Agreement, which particularly addresses concerns of this nature in the WTO, recognizes the right of countries to adopt all measures necessary to protect human, animal or plant life or health. At the same time, in order to ensure that this right is not misused for purely protectionist motives, the SPS Agreement also requires that such measures must base themselves on sufficient scientific evidence. But, in recognition of the prevalence of scientific uncertainties in several areas, in cases where the possibility of harmful effects on human, animal or plant life or health has been identified and preliminary scientific evaluation proves inconclusive for assessing the level of risk, the SPS Agreement gives some recognition to the precautionary principle and allows countries to introduce provisional pre-emptive measures pending further scientific inquiry.[30]

The EC wants to see the application of this principle clarified and extended so as to give some place for subjective consumer concerns about the safety of the food on the market, apparently even including such contentious issues as genetically modified organisms.[31] To that end, the Community refers to its own internal laws (e.g. Article 174(2) of the EC Treaty) as well as other truly international treaty texts (e.g. the 1992 Convention on Climate Change, the 1992 Convention on Biological Diversity, the 2000 Protocol on Biosafety) and maintains that full recognition should be given to the precautionary principle which has become “a full-fledged and general principle of international law”.[32] The EC stresses that there is a public concern that the WTO could be used to force onto the markets products about whose safety there are legitimate concerns. Referring to Article 5:7 of the SPS Agreement on the precautionary principle,[33] the EC proposes that the practical application of this principle should be clarified by the current agricultural negotiations.

The agriculture negotiations have been brought within a wider round and it is certain that the EC will not have an easy ride on the issue. The US is already fiercely

---

30 The World Bank notes that the modern approach to food safety is to rely on “prevention at every stage of the food chain from farm to table.” See Rural Development Department of the World bank, *Agriculture Technology Notes* (August 2000).

31 For an elaborate presentation of the EC position on the precautionary principle, see *Communication from the European Commission on the Precautionary Principle: Submission by the European Communities* (WTO docs. WT/CTE/W/147, G/TBT/W/137) 27 June 2000.

32 See, inter alia, *Id.* para. 26; and *European Council Resolution on the Precautionary Principle, Submission by the European Communities*, (WTO docs. G/SPS/GEN/225, G/TBT/W/154, WT/CTE/W/181) 2 February 2001.

33 On the status of this principle under the WTO, see *European Communities - Measures Affecting Meat and Meat Products* (WTO docs. WT/DS26/AB/R/USA, WT/DS48/AB/R/CAN) adopted 13 February 1998, para. 124.

opposed to this EC attempt on the precautionary principle. Talks at the sixteenth session of the UN Food and Agriculture Organization's Codex Committee on General Principles (23–27 April), which aimed, inter alia, at defining the application of precaution in risk management relating to food and human health, "broke down when a number of delegates insisted on the removal of all references to the precautionary principle."[34] This was directly targeted at EU requests to clearly define and enshrine the principle in international food legislation. It has been observed that "Codex seemed to have become the latest battleground for trade negotiators, rather than health practitioners. The US has long opposed the use of the precautionary principle as unscientific and arbitrary, in particular when used by the EU in the context of its ban on US hormone-treated beef and of approvals of GM products for sale in the EU."[35] This is a sign that agricultural negotiating issues are already overflowing into other, albeit relevant, fora.

(d) Animal Welfare

This is one of the latest arrivals to the agricultural negotiating table. The EC argues that the ongoing negotiations should ensure that animal production takes place under reasonable conditions and avoid what they call "factory farming" practices.[36] The EC argues that consumers are becoming increasingly concerned about the effects that breeding and farming techniques (e.g. how farm animals are kept, transported and slaughtered) may have on animals, on their health and welfare as well as the environment.[37] The EC has shown special concern regarding highly-intensive and industrialised production methods for certain species, such as poultry and pigs. To address those concerns, the EC proposes a number of possible actions, including (i) the development of multilateral agreements dealing with the protection of animal welfare; (ii) appropriate labelling rules so as to allow consumers to make an informed choice as regards food products; and (iii) to exempt compensation of additional costs to meet animal welfare standards from reduction commitments where it can be clearly shown that these costs stem directly from the adoption of higher standards and thus are not, or at most minimally, trade distorting.[38]

To sum up, the EC has shown its strong stance for the incorporation of NTCs in the ongoing agricultural negotiations. Although it is certain to get the backing of several influential trading partners on these issues, including Japan in many cases, several others have already aired their suspicion that the NTCs are being pushed hard by the EC only to replace traditional import barriers.

---

[34] See International Centre for Trade and Sustainable Development (ICTSD), *Bridges Weekly Trade News Digest*, Vol. 5, No. 16 (1 May 2001); see also http://www.codexalimentarius.net/ccgp16/GP01_01e.htm.

[35] See ICTSD, *Bridges Weekly Trade News Digest*, Vol. 5, No. 16 (1 May 2001).

[36] See G/AG/NG/W/24, *supra* n. 20.

[37] See G/AG/NG/W/19, *supra* n. 11.

[38] See G/AG/NG/W/90, *supra* n. 14.

11.2.3 Special and Differential Treatment

The EC also devotes an important part of its comprehensive proposal to the cause of special and differential treatment for developing countries. Claiming to be "by far the largest market for the exports of agricultural products from developing countries", the EC has challenged other developed and high-income developing countries that opportunities should be created for increased market access for developing countries, while accepting the possible need for the most fragile developing countries to maintain protection in order to have adequate time for adaptation. The EC stressed its pledge to provide duty-free access to essentially all products from the least-developed countries and proposed that others should follow suit. Stressing the "need to give real meaning to special and differential treatment", the EC identifies at least three possible mechanisms that should be considered to accommodate the interests of developing countries – preferences, special access provisions, and longer time periods for tariff reductions. In some cases, the EC also appears to use developing countries to oppose proposals for drastic market access commitments arguing that such a move would only limit the scope of special and differential treatment.[39] At the same time, the credibility of the EC position on special and differential treatment stands on a more solid ground as a result of the adoption of the "Everything-but-Arms" legislation allowing duty free access to almost all products originating from least-developed countries.[40]

11.2.4 The Peace Clause

The "peace clause" refers to the last-minute arrangement of the Blair House Accord by which the EC and the US agreed that agricultural subsidies provided in compliance with the pertinent provisions of the Agreement on Agriculture would be immune from challenge for the duration of nine years (Article 13 Agreement on Agriculture). Although this clause is set to expire in 2003, the EC has already made its position clear that it should continue to be part of the new agricultural arrangement. In its view, this is only "the logical corollary of the specific nature of the Agreement on Agriculture."

This EC desire to maintain the "peace clause" has led analysts to expect that the EC would try its best for the conclusion of the current negotiations prior to its expiry date in 1993.[41] The US had also proposed that an agreement be reached by the end of 2002. But, the developments of Doha have already changed the situation. According to the Doha Declaration (see para. 14), agricultural negotiating modalities are to be established "no later than 31 March 2003" and participants are required to submit their comprehensive draft Schedules based on these modalities "no later than the date of the Fifth Session of the Ministerial Conference", which is expected to take

---

39 See G/AG/NG/W/66, *supra* n. 13.

40 See press release by DG Trade entitled *EU approves "Everything But Arms" trade access for least developed countries*, Brussels, 26 February 2001.

41 See Miner (2001), *supra* n. 15, p. 14.

place before the end of 2003. Moreover, the inclusion of agriculture in the broader Doha negotiation agenda also means that agricultural negotiations will not be completed before the (ambitious-sounding) target date for the conclusion of the round itself, which is "not later than 1 January 2005" (para. 45 of Doha Declaration). The single undertaking approach adopted by the Declaration of course allows room for the early entry into force of agreements reached at an early stage. But, if history is any guide, not only are agricultural issues often the most difficult to settle by themselves, they are often the causes of protracted delay for the entry into force of agreements already reached in most non-agricultural areas.

11.3 Conclusion

International agricultural trade is slowly coming back to the rules of the multilateral trade system. Within the EU as well, the days of the CAP as a system totally unresponsive to multilateral developments appear to be over. Instead of closing its doors for agricultural negotiations, the EC is now trying to use the multilateral forums to multilateralize its internal policy priorities starting from food safety to animal welfare and the environment. Indeed, realising its position as the largest importer and the second largest exporter of agricultural products, the EC appears to be more willing than ever before to play a proactive role in the ongoing process towards further liberalization in agricultural trade. Yet, several of the proposals still suggest that the CAP has not (yet) lost its traditional value as the glue that keeps the EC together. Agriculture thus still appears to promise endless controversies in the ongoing negotiations.

At the same time, most trade policy experts agree that the Agriculture Agreement needs significant improvements in several areas. There is virtually a consensus in academic circles that the current round of negotiations should bring about, *inter alia,* substantial reductions in the "stratospheric" tariffs in market access, elimination or substantial reduction of export subsidies, elimination of the "blue box" and substantial reduction of the "amber box" domestic support measures, and termination of the "due restraint" provision of Article 13 by the year 2003.[42]

---

[42] See, *inter alia,* S. Tangermann, *Implementation of the Uruguay Round Agreement on Agriculture by Major Developed Countries*, A Report Prepared for the United Nations Conference on Trade and Development, (Distr. GENERAL, UNCTAD /ITD/16, 3 October, 1995); H. Binswanger, and E. Lutz, *Agricultural Trade Barriers, Trade Negotiations, and the Interests of Developing Countries*, paper prepared for the UNCTAD X High-Level Round Table on Trade and Development (Bangkok, 12 February 2000); C. Yeutter, "Brining Agriculture into the Multilateral Trading System"', in J. Bhagwati, and M. Hirsch (eds.), *The Uruguay Round and Beyond: Essays in Honour of Arthur Dunkel* (Springer Verlag, Germany 1998); De Zeeuw (1997) *supra* n. 3; S. Tangermann, *The European Union Perspective on Agricultural Trade Liberalization in the WTO*, paper presented at the Department of Agricultural Economics and Business, University of Guelph, Canada (February 1999); S. Tangermann, *A Developed Country Perspective of the Agenda for the Next WTO Round of Agricultural Negotiations*, paper presented at the Graduate Institute of International Studies (3 March 1997); and D. Hathaway, and M. Ingco, *Agricultural Liberalization and the Uruguay Round,* paper presented at the World Bank Conference on "The Uruguay Round and the Developing Economies", (26-27 January 1995).

Despite this growing consensus, however, the history of GATT negotiations on agriculture teaches that the sector is not amenable to any realistic speculations. The most difficult challenge in the reform process has already been successfully overcome via the conclusion of the Uruguay Round Agreement on Agriculture. While a full integration of agriculture into the general rules applying to all other goods appears to be a long way off, significant reductions in tariff dispersions through some tariff-harmonization methods, substantial reductions in export subsidies and amber box domestic support measures, and elimination or further tightening of the blue box measures are widely expected to follow from the current negotiations. Depending on the pace of progress in current and future negotiations, it may not take very long before we see the past developments exerting meaningful constraints on the actual policy-making powers of countries in the area of agricultural trade.

In sum, the Agreement on Agriculture lays a solid foundation for the liberalization of agricultural trade; the success of this Agreement is measured by the degree to which it is closer to its own disappearance altogether. A successful conclusion of the reform process initiated by the Agreement on Agriculture means nothing else than the deletion of the Agreement itself from the list of legal instruments under the WTO.

BIBLIOGRAPHY

Books and Articles

Anderson, K. *Agriculture and the WTO into the 21st Century*, paper prepared for the Cairns Group Farm Leaders' Trade Strategy Seminar (Sydney, Australia 2-3 April 1998).

Anderson, K., B. Hoekman and A. Strutt, *Agriculture and the WTO: Next Steps,* paper presented at the Second Annual Conference on Global Economic Analysis (Denmark, 20–22 June 1999).

Anderson, K., Erwidodo and M. Ingco, *Integrating Agriculture into the WTO: The Next Phase*, paper presented to the WTO/World Bank Conference on Developing Countries in a Millennium Round (Geneva, 20–21 September 1999).

Annania, G., C. Carter, and A. McCalla (eds.) *Agricultural Trade Conflicts and GATT: New Dimensions in U.S. – European Agricultural Trade Relations* (Westview Press, Oxford 1994).

Barents, R. *The Agricultural Law of the EC* (1994).

Barton, J. and B. Fisher, *International Trade and Investment* (Little Brown & Co., Boston 1986).

Bhagirath Lal Das, "The 'Big Bang' in Agriculture in the WTO", *Third World Economics: Trends and Analysis,* No. 177 (Penang, Malaysia 16–31 January 1998).

Binswanger, H. and E. Lutz, *Agricultural Trade Barriers, Trade Negotiations, and the Interests of Developing Countries*, paper prepared for the UNCTAD X High-Level Round Table on Trade and Development (Bangkok, 12 February 2000).

Bourgeois, J. (ed.) *Subsidies and International Trade: A European Lawyers' Perspective* (Kluwer 1991).

Chua, A. "The Precedential Effect of WTO Panel and Appellate Body Reports", 11 *Leiden Journal of International Law* (1998).

Collins-Williams, T. and G. Salembier, "International Disciplines on Subsidies: the GATT, the WTO, and the Future Agenda", 30 *Journal of World Trade* (1996) No. 1

Croome, J. *Reshaping the World Trading System: A History of the Uruguay Round* (Geneva 1995).

Curzon, G. *Multilateral Commercial Diplomacy: The General Agreement on Tariffs and Trade and Its Impact on National Policies and Techniques* (1965).

Dam, K. *The GATT: Law and International Organization* (1970).

De Zeeuw, A. "Implementation and Accomplishments of the WTO" paper presented at a Seminar organized by the International Policy Council on

Agriculture, Food and Trade, in *Proceedings of the IPC Seminar: Agriculture, the FTAA and the WTO* (Belo Horizonte, Brazil 12-13 May 1997).

Emmerij, L. "On Agricultural Subsidies and the GATT Negotiations" 5 *Tijdschrift voor Europees en economisch recht* (May 1990).

Evans, P. *Economic Governance Institutions in a Global Political Economy: Implications for Developing Countries,* paper prepared for the UNCTAD X High-Level Round Table on Trade and Development (Bangkok, 12 February 2000).

FAO, *FAO Principles of Surplus Disposal and Consultative Obligations of Member Nations* (3rd ed., Rome 1992).

GATT *Focus Newsletter* (various issues).

Greenfield J., M. de Nigris, and P. Konnandreas, "The Uruguay Round Agreement on Agriculture: Food Security Implications for Developing Countries", 21 *Food Policy* No. 4/5 (1996).

Gylfason, T. "Prospects for Liberalization of Trade in Agriculture", 32 *Journal of World Trade*, No. 1 (1998).

Hathaway, D. and M. Ingco, *Agricultural Liberalization and the Uruguay Round,* paper presented at the World Bank Conference on "The Uruguay Round and the Developing Economies" (26-27 January 1995).

Hillman, J. *Nontariff Agricultural Barriers* (University of Nebraska Press, 1978).

Hoekman, B. and K. Anderson, *Developing Country Agriculture and the New Trade Agenda,* World Bank Policy Research Working Paper 2125 (May 1999).

Hoekman, B. and M. Kostecki, *The Political Economy of the World Trading System: From GATT to WTO* (Oxford University Press, 1995).

Horlick, G., R. Quick and E. Vermulst, "Government Actions against Government Domestic Subsidies: An Analysis of International Rules and an Introduction to United States" Practice", 1 *Legal Issues of European Integration* (1986).

Hudec, R. *Enforcing International Trade Law: The Evolution of the Modern GATT Legal System* (Butterworth, 1993).

Hudec, R. *The GATT Legal System and World Trade Diplomacy* (Praeger Publishers, 1975)

Ingco, M. *Agricultural Trade Liberalization in the Uruguay Round: One Step Forward, One Step Back?* supplementary paper prepared for a World Bank Conference on "The Uruguay Round and the Developing Countries" (Washington, D.C., 26–27 January 1995).

Ingco, M. *The Uruguay Round and the Least-Developed Low-Income Food-Deficit Countries,* paper presented to the Inter-Agency Meeting of the World Food Situation and Net Food-Importing Countries, the World Bank (Washington, D.C., 18–19 December 1996).

Ingersent, K., A. Rayner, and R. Hine (eds.) *Agriculture in the Uruguay Round* (St. Martin's press, New York 1994).

Jackson, J. "The Jurisprudence of International Trade: The DISC Case in GATT", 72 *American Journal of International Law* (1978).

Jackson, J. *Legal Problems of International Economic Relations* (West Publishing Co. 1977).

Jackson, J. *The World Trading System: Law and Policy in International Economic Relations* (The MIT Press, 2nd ed. 1997).

Jackson, J. *World Trade and the Law of GATT* (Bobbs-Merrill, 1969).

Jackson, J., W. Davey and A. Sykes, *Legal Problems of International Economic Relations: Cases, Materials and Text* (3rd ed., West Publishing Co., 1995).

Josling, T., S. Tangermann and T. Warley, *Agriculture in the GATT* (MacMillan Press, London 1996).

Josling, T. "Developing Countries and the New Round of Multilateral Trade Negotiations: Background Notes on Agriculture", paper prepared for the *Workshop on Developing Countries and the New Round of Multilateral Trade Negotiations* (Center for International Development, Harvard University, Cambridge, Massachusetts, 5–6 November 1999).

Konnandreas, P. and J. Greenfield, "Uruguay Round Commitments on Domestic Support and Export Subsidies: Their Implications for Developing Countries", in FAO/World Bank (eds.) *Implementing the Uruguay Round Agreement in Latin America: the Case of Agriculture* (Santiago, 1997).

Krugman, P. and M. Obstefeld, *International Economics: Theory and Practice* (4th ed. Addison-Wesley, 1997)

Laird, S. *Multilateral Approaches to Market Access Negotiations,* WTO Staff Working Paper TPRD-98-02 (May 1998).

Lankoski, J. *Environmental Effects of Agricultural Trade Liberalization and Domestic Agricultural Trade Reforms,* UNCTAD Discussion Paper Series, UNCTAD/OSG/DP/126 (April 1997).

Long, O. *Law and Its Limitations in the GATT Multilateral Trade System* (1987).

Lutz. E, H. Binswanger, P. Hazell, and A. McCalla (eds.) *Agriculture, Development, and Environment: Policy, Institutional, and Technical Perspectives* (Washington, D.C., April 1998).

McGovern, E. *International Trade Regulation* (1986).

McGovern, E. *International Trade Regulation* (Loose-leaf, 1995).

McMahon, J. "The Uruguay Round and Agriculture: Charting a New Direction?", in 29 *The International Lawyer*, No. 2 (Summer 1995).

McMahon, J. *Agricultural Trade, Protectionism and the Problems of Development: a Legal Perspective* (Leicester University Press, London 1992).

Melaku Geboye Desta, "Agricultural Export Subsidies under the WTO 'Agriculture Package': A Legal Analysis", *Revue Belge de Droit International* No. 2 (1997).

Melaku Geboye Desta, "Food Security and International Trade Law: An Appraisal of the World Trade Organization Approach", 35 *Journal of World Trade*, No. 3 (2001) pp. 449–468.

Miner, W. and D. Hathaway, *World Agricultural Trade: Building a Consensus* (The Institute for Research on Public Policy, Halifax, Canada, 1988).

OECD, "Agricultural Policies, Markets, and Trade in OECD Countries: Monitoring and Evaluation 1996: Summary and Conclusions", republished in 8 *World Trade and Arbitration Materials,* No.5 (September 1996).

OECD, *Agricultural Policies, Markets and Trade: Monitoring and Outlook* (Paris, 1994).

OECD, *Agricultural Policies, Markets, and Trade in OECD Countries, Monitoring and Evaluation* (Paris 1997).

OECD, *Agriculture and the Environment: Issues and Policies* (Paris 1998).

OECD, *National Policies and Agricultural Trade* (Paris 1987).

OECD, *The Uruguay Round: A Preliminary Evaluation of the Agreement on Agriculture in the OECD Countries* (Paris 1995).

Palmeter, D. "Agriculture and Trade Regulation: Selected Issues in the Application of U.S. Antidumping and Countervailing Duty Laws", 23 *Journal of World Trade* No. 1 (1989).

Palmeter, D. and P. Mavroidis, "The WTO Legal System: Sources of Law", 92 *American Journal of International Law* No. 3 (1998).

Panagariya, A. "The Millennium Round and Developing Countries: Negotiating Strategies and Areas of Benefits", paper prepared for presentation at the *Conference on Developing Countries and the New Multilateral Round of Trade Negotiations* (Harvard University, Massachusetts,5-6 September 1999, at 23).

Pauwelyn, J. "Evidence, Proof and Persuasion in WTO Dispute Settlement", 1 *Journal of International Economic Law* (1998).

Petersmann, E-U., "Violation-Complaints and Non-Violation Complaints in Public International Trade Law" 34 *German Yearbook of International Law* (1991).

Petersmann, E-U., *The GATT/WTO Dispute Settlement System: International Law, International Organizations and Dispute Settlement* (Kluwer 1997).

Phegan, C. "GATT Article XVI:3: Export Subsidies and "Equitable Shares" 16 *Journal of World Trade Law* (1982).

Raffer, K. "Helping Southern Net Food Importers after the Uruguay Round: A Proposal", 25 *World Development*, No. 11 (1997).

Ramberg, J. *Guide to Incoterms 1990* (ICC Publication No. 461/90, Paris 1990).

Rivers, R. and J. Greenwald, "The Negotiation of a Code on Subsidies and Countervailing Measures: Bridging Fundamental Differences", 11 *Law & Policy in International Business* (1979).

Runge, F. "A Conceptual Framework for Agricultural Trade and the Environment: Beyond the "Green Box", 33 *Journal of World Trade* No. 6 (1999).

Schaffer, R., B. Earle, and F. Augusti, *International Business Law and Its Environment* (3rd. ed., West Publishing Co. 1996).

Schmitthoff, C. *The Law and Practice of International Trade* (Stevens & Sons, 8th ed. 1986).

Schott, J. *The Uruguay Round: An Assessment* (1994).

Shaw, D. and H. Singer "A Future Food Aid Regime: Implications of the Final Act of the Uruguay Round", 21 *Food Policy* No. 4/5 (1996).

Skully, D. *The Economics of TRQ Administration,* IATRC Working Paper # 99-6 (St. Paul: University of Minnesota, May 1999).

Smith, A. *An Inquiry into the Nature and Causes of The Wealth of Nations*, First Published in 1776 (new edition by Edwin Cannan, 1976).

Stewart, T. (ed.) *The GATT Uruguay Round: A Negotiating History (1986-1992),* in III Vols. (Kluwer 1993).

Stewart, T. and A. Dwyer, *WTO Antidumping and Subsidy Agreements – A*

Practitioner's Guide to "Sunset" Reviews in Australia, Canada, the European Union, and the United States (Kluwer 1998).

Sykes, A. "Comparative Advantage and the Normative Economics of International Trade Policy" 1 *Journal of International Economic Law* No. 1 (1998).

Tangermann, S. *A Developed Country Perspective of the Agenda for the Next WTO Round of Agricultural Negotiations*, paper presented at the Graduate Institute of International Studies (Geneva 3 March 1997).

Tangermann, S. *An Assessment of the Uruguay Round Agreement on Agriculture*, paper prepared for the OECD's Agriculture Directorate (Paris 1994).

Tangermann, S. *Implementation of the Uruguay Round Agreement on Agriculture by Major Developed Countries*, A Report Prepared for the United Nations Conference on Trade and Development, Distr. GENERAL, UNCTAD /ITD/ 16 (Geneva 3 October 1995).

Tangermann, S., *The European Union Perspective on Agricultural Trade Liberalization in the WTO*, paper presented at the Department of Agricultural Economics and Business, University of Guelph, Ontario, Canada (February 1999).

Thompson, K. "CAP and the WTO after the Uruguay Round Agreement on Agriculture" 2 *European Foreign Affairs Review* (1996).

M. Trebilcock and R. Howse, *The Regulation of International Trade* (2nd ed. Routeledge, New York 1999)

UNCTAD, *The Uruguay Round and Its Follow-up: Building a Positive Agenda for Development* (Geneva 1997).

United States Department of Agriculture, *Agriculture in the WTO*, WRS-98-4 (Washington D.C., Dec. 1998).

United States Department of Agriculture, *Agriculture Outlook* (Washington D.C., Dec. 1996).

United States Department of State, *Suggested Charter for an International Trade Organization of the United Nations* (Washington D.C., 1946).

United States General Accounting Office, *Uruguay Round Final Act*, GAO/GGD - 94-83b (Washington D.C., 1994).

Van Houtte, H. *The Law of International Trade* (Sweet & Maxwell 1995).

Wachtel, H. "Labor's Stake in the WTO", 37 *The American Prospect* (1998).

Wilcox, C., *A Charter for World Trade* (Arno Press, New York 1949).

Wilcox, W. "GATT-Based Protectionism and the Definition of a Subsidy", 16 *Boston University International Law Journal* (1998).

Wolfensohn, J. *Remarks at the Tenth Ministerial Meeting of UNCTAD: Development – Challenges and Opportunities* (Bangkok, 16 February 2000).

WTO, *Annual Report 1998* (Geneva, 1998).

WTO, *Annual Report 2000* (Geneva, 2000).

WTO, *Focus Newsletter* (various issues).

WTO, *GATT Analytical Index: Guide to GATT Law and Practice* (Updated 6th ed., Geneva, 1995).

WTO, *Introduction to the WTO: Trading into the Future* (2nd rev. ed. Geneva 1999).

WTO Secretariat, *Market Access: Unfinished Business – Post-Uruguay Round Inventory and Issues* (Special Studies 6, Geneva 2001)

WTO, *The results of the Uruguay Round of Multilateral Trade Negotiations: the Legal Texts* (1995).
Yeutter, C. "Bringing Agriculture into the Multilateral Trading System", in Bhagwati, J. and M. Hirsch (eds.) *The Uruguay Round and Beyond: Essays in Honour of Arthur Dunkel* (Springer Verlag, Germany 1998).
Zampeti, A. "The Uruguay Round Agreement on Subsidies: A Forward-Looking Assessment", 29 *Journal of World Trade* No. 6 (1995).

GATT CASES

Australia v. EC: *European Communities – Refunds on Exports of Sugar* report of the panel (L/4833 *BISD* 26S/290) adopted on 6 November 1979.
Australia v. France: *French Assistance to Exports of Wheat and Wheat Flour*, report of the panel (L/924 *BISD* 7S/49) adopted on 21 Nov. 1958.
Australia v. United States: *United States - Restrictions On Imports Of Sugar:* report of the panel (L/6514 *BISD* 36S/331) adopted on 22 June 1989.
Brazil v. EC: *European Communities – Refunds on Exports of Sugar: Complaint by Brazil* report of the panel (L/5011 *BISD* 27S/69) adopted on 10 November 1980.
Canada v. EC: *European Economic Community – Imports of Beef from Canada: Recourse to Article XXIII by Canada,* report of the panel (L/5099 *BISD* 28S/92) adopted on 10 March 1981.
Canada v. United States: *United States - Measures Affecting Alcoholic and Malt Beverages,* report of the Panel (DS23/R *BISD* 39S/206) adopted on 19 June 1992.
Canada v. United States: *United States – Prohibition of Imports of Tuna and Tuna Products from Canada* report of the panel (L/5198 *BISD* 29S/91) adopted on 22 February 1982.
Chile v. Australia: *The Australian Subsidy on Ammonium Sulphate,* report of the Working Party (GATT/CP.4/39 *BISD,* Vol. II) adopted on 14 March 1950.
Chile v. EC: *European Economic Community – Restrictions on Imports of Dessert Apples - Complaint by Chile,* report of the panel (L/6491 *BISD* 36S/93) adopted on 22 June 1989.
Chile v. EC: *EEC Restriction on Imports of Apples from Chile,* report of the panel (L/5047, *BISD* 27S/98) adopted on 10 Nov. 1980.
EC v. Brazil: *Brazil – Imposition of Provisional and Definitive Countervailing Duties on Milk Powder and Certain Types of Milk from the European Economic Community,* Report of the panel (SCM/179) adopted by the Committee on Subsidies and Countervailing Measures on 28 April 1994.
EC v. Canada: *Canada – Import, Distribution and Sale of Alcoholic Drinks by Canadian Provincial Marketing Agencies,* report of the Panel (L/6304 *BISD* 35S/37) adopted on 22 March 1988.
EC v. Canada: *Canada – Imposition of Countervailing Duties on Imports of Manufacturing Beef from the EEC,* report by the Panel (SCM/85) issued on 13 October 1987, not adopted.
EC v. Japan: *Japan – Trade in Semi-Conductors,* report of the panel (L/6309 *BISD* 35S/116) adopted on 4 May 1988.

EC v. United States: *United States Tax Legislation (DISC)* (L/4422 *BISD* 23S/113) adopted on 7-8 December 1981.
EC v. United States: *United States – Definition of Industry Concerning Wine and Grape Products,* report by the Panel (SCM/71 *BISD* 39S/436) issued on 24 March 1986 and adopted by the Committee on Subsidies and Countervailing Measures on 28 April 1992.
EC v. United States: *United States – Restrictions on the Importation of Sugar and Sugar-Containing Products Applied under the 1955 Waiver and under the Headnote to the Schedule of Tariff Concessions,* report of the panel (L6631 *BISD* 37S/228) adopted on 7 November 1990.
EC v. United States: *United States – Section 337 of the Tariff Act of 1930,* report of the panel (L/6439 *BISD* 36S/345) adopted on 7 November 1989.
Hong Kong v. EC: *EEC – Quantitative Restrictions Against Imports of Certain Products from Hong Kong*, report of the panel (L/5511 *BISD* 30S/129) adopted on 12 July 1983.
Japan v. EC: *EEC - Regulation on Imports of Parts and Components*, report of the panel (L/6657 *BISD* 37S/132) adopted on 16 May 1990.
Mexico, Canada and the EC v. United States: *United States – Taxes on Petroleum and Certain Imported Substances,* report of the panel (L/6175 *BISD* 34S/136) adopted on 17 June 1987.
Norway v. Germany: *Treatment by Germany of Imports of Sardines*, report of the panel (G/26 *BISD* 1S/53) adopted on 31 October 1952.
United States v. Canada: *Canada – Import Restrictions on Ice Cream and Yoghurt* report of the panel (L/6568 *BISD* 36S/68) adopted on 5 December 1989.
United States v. Canada: *Canadian Countervailing Duties on Grain Corn from the United States,* report of the panel (SCM/140 and Corr.1, *BISD* 39S/411) adopted by the Committee on Subsidies and Countervailing Measures on 26 March 1992.
United States v. EC: *European Economic Community – Restrictions on Imports of Apples – Complaint by the United States,* report of the panel (L/6513 *BISD* 36S/135) adopted on 22 June 1989.
United States v. EC: *European Communities – Programme of Minimum Import Prices, Licences, and Surety Deposits for Certain Processed Fruits and Vegetable,* report of the panel (L/4687 *BISD* 25S/68) adopted on 18 October 1978.
United States v. EC: *European Economic Community - Subsidies on Export of Wheat Flour* report of the panel (SCM/42) issued on 21 March 1983 (not adopted).
United States v. EC: *European Economic Community – Payments and Subsidies Paid to Processors and Producers of Oilseeds and Related Animal-Feed Proteins,* report of the panel (L/6627 *BISD* 37S/86) adopted on 25 January 1990.
United States v. EC: *European Economic Community – Production Aids Granted on Canned Peaches, Canned Pears, Canned Fruit Cocktail and Dried Grapes,* report of the panel (L/5778) circulated to the contracting parties on 20 February 1985 (not adopted).
United States v. EC: *European Economic Community – Restrictions on Imports of Apples: Complaint by the United States,* report of the panel (L/6513 *BISD* 36S/135) adopted on 22 June 1989

United States v. EC: *European Economic Community – Subsidies on Export of Pasta Products* report of the panel (SCM/43) issued 19 May 1983 (not adopted).

United States v. EC: *Follow-up on the Panel Report "European Economic Community – Payments and Subsidies Paid to Processors and Producers of Oilseeds and Related Animal-Feed Proteins", Report of the Members of the Original Oilseeds Panel* (DS28/R 39S/91) issued on 31 March 1992 (not adopted).

United States v. Japan: *Japan – Restrictions on Imports of Certain Agricultural Products*, report of the panel (L/6253 *BISD* 35S/163) adopted on 22 March 1988.

United States v. Japan: *Japanese Measures on Imports of Leather*, report of the panel (L/5623 *BISD* 31S/94) adopted on 15/16 May 1984.

United States v. Korea: *Republic of Korea – Restrictions on Imports of Beef – Complaint by the United States,* report of panel (L/6503 *BISD* 36S/268) adopted on 7 Nov. 1989.

United States v. Norway: *Norway – Restrictions on Imports of Apples and Pears,* report of the panel (L/6474 *BISD* 36S/306) adopted on 22 June 1989.

United States v. Thailand: *Thailand – Restrictions on Importation of and Internal Taxes on Cigarettes,* report of the panel (DS10/R *BISD* 37S/200) adopted on Nov. 1990.

Uruguay v. Austria, Belgium, Canada, Czechoslovakia, Denmark, Finland, France, Federal Republic of Germany, Italy, Japan, The Netherlands, Norway, Sweden, Switzerland and the United States of America: *Uruguayan Recourse to Article XXIII,* report of the panel (L/1923 *BISD* 11S/95) adopted on 16 Nov. 1962.

WTO Cases

Australia and New Zealand v. United States, *United States – Safeguard Measures on Imports of Fresh, Chilled or Frozen Lamb Meat from New Zealand and Australia,* Report of the Panel (WT/DS177/R WT/DS178/R) 21 December 2000.

Brazil v. Canada: *Canada – Measures Affecting the Export of Civilian Aircraft*, report of the Appellate Body (WT/DS/70/AB/R) 2 August 1999.

Brazil v. Canada: *Canada – Measures Affecting the Export of Civilian Aircraft*, report of the panel (WT/DS70/R) 14 April 1999.

Brazil v. EC: *European Communities – Measures Affecting the Importation of Certain Poultry Products*, report of the Appellate Body (WT/DS69/AB/R) 13 July 1998.

Brazil v. EC: *European Communities - Measures Affecting the Importation of Certain Poultry Products*, report of the panel (WT/DS69/R) 12 March 1998.

Canada v. Brazil: *Brazil – Export Financing Programme for Aircraft,* report of the panel (WT/DS46/R) 14 April 1999.

Canada v. Brazil: *Brazil – Export Financing Programme for Aircraft,* report of the Appellate Body (WT/DS46/AB/R) 2 August 1999.

Canada, EC and the United States v. Japan: *Japan – Taxes on Alcoholic Beverages*, report of the panel (WT/DS8/AB/R, WT/DS10/AB/R, WT/DS11/AB/R) 4 October 1996.

EC and Japan v. Canada: *Canada – Certain Measures Affecting the Automotive Industry,* report of the panel (WT/DS139/R, WT/DS142/R) 11 February 2000.

EC and Japan v. Canada: *Canada – Certain Measures Affecting the Automotive Industry,* report of the Appellate Body (WT/DS139/AB/R WT/DS142/AB/R) 31 May 2000.

EC v. Korea, *Korea – Definitive Safeguard Measure on Imports of Certain Dairy Products,* report of the Appellate Body (WT/DS98/AB/R) adopted on 12 January 2000.

EC v. Korea, *Korea – Definitive Safeguard Measure on Imports of Certain Dairy Products,* report of thc pancl (WT/DS98/R) 21 June 1999.

EC v. United States: *United States – Imposition of Countervailing Duties on Certain Hot-Rolled Lead and Bismuth Carbon Steel Products Originating in the United Kingdom*, report of the panel (WT/DS138/R) 23 December 1999.

EC v. United States: *United States – Imposition of Countervailing Duties on Certain Hot-Rolled Lead and Bismuth Carbon Steel Products Originating in the United Kingdom*, report of the panel (WT/DS138/AB/R) 10 May 2000.

EC v. United States: *United States – Tax Treatment for "Foreign Sales Corporations"* report of the panel (WT/DS108/R) 8 October 1999.

EC v. United States: *United States – Tax Treatment for "Foreign Sales Corporations"* report of the Appellate Body (WT/DS108/AB/R) 24 February 2000.

EC, Japan, and the United States v. Indonesia: *Indonesia – Certain Measures Affecting the Automobile Industry,* report of the panel (WT/DS54/R, WT/DS55/R, WT/DS59/R, WT/DS64/R) 2 July 1998.

Ecuador, Guatemala, Honduras, Mexico and the United States v. EC: *European Communities – Regime for the Importation, Sale and Distribution of Bananas,* report of the panel (WT/DS27/R/ECU; WT/DS27/R/GTM, WT/DS27/R/HND; WT/DS27/R/MEX; WT/DS27/R/USA) 22 May 1997.

Ecuador, Guatemala, Honduras, Mexico and the United States v. EC: *European Communities – Regime for the Importation, Sale and Distribution of Bananas,* report of the Appellate Body (WT/DS27/AB/R) 9 September 1997.

India v. United States: *United States – Measures Affecting Imports of Shirts and Blouses from India: Complaint by India*, report of the Appellate Body (WT/DS33/AB/R) 25 April 1997.

India, Malaysia, Pakistan and Thailand v. United States: *United States – Import Prohibition of Certain Shrimp and Shrimp Products:* report of the Appellate Body, (WT/DS58/AB/R, 12 October 1998).

Korea v. United States: *United States – Anti-Dumping Duty on Dynamic Random Access Semiconductors (DRAMs) of One Megabit or Above from Korea*, report of the panel (WT/DS99/R) 19 March 1999.

Mexico v. Guatemala: *Guatemala – Anti-Dumping Investigation Regarding Portland Cement From Mexico,* report of the Appellate Body (WT/DS60/AB/R) 2 Nov. 1998.

New Zealand and United States v. Canada: *Canada – Measures Affecting the Importation of Milk and the Exportation of Dairy Products,* report of the Appellate Body (WT/DS103/AB/R, WT/DS113/AB/R) 13 October 1999.

New Zealand and United States v. Canada: *Canada – Measures Affecting the Importation of Milk and the Exportation of Dairy Products,* report of the panel (WT/DS103/R, WT/DS113/R) 17 May 1999.

Philippines v. Brazil: *Brazil – Measures Affecting Desiccated Coconut,* report of the panel (WT/DS22/R) 17 October 1996.

Philippines v. Brazil: *Brazil – Measures Affecting Desiccated Coconut,* report of the Appellate Body (WT/DS22/AB/R) 21 February 1997.

United States and Australia v. Korea, *Korea – Measures Affecting Imports Of Fresh, Chilled And Frozen Beef,* report of the panel (WT/DS161/R, WT/DS169/R, 31 July 2000).

United States v. Australia: *Australia – Subsidies Provided to Producers and Exporters of Automotive Leather,* report of the panel (WT/DS126/R) 25 May 1999.

United States v. Canada: *Canada – Certain Measures Concerning Periodicals*, report of the Appellate Body (WT/DS31/AB/R) 30 June 1997.

United States v. India: *India – Quantitative Restrictions on Imports of Agricultural, Textile and Industrial Products,* report of the panel (WT/DS90/R) 6 April, 1999.

United States and Australia v. Korea, *Korea – Measures Affecting Imports of Fresh, Chilled and Frozen Beef,* report of the panel, (WT/DS161/R, WT/DS169/R) 31 July 2000.

Venezuela and Brazil v. United States: *United States – Standards for Reformulated and Conventional Gasoline*, report of the Appellate Body (WT/DS2/AB/R) 20 May 1996.

Official Documents

GATT Committee on Agriculture, *Progress Report to the Council of Representatives Presented to the CONTRACTING PARTIES at their Thirty-Ninth Session* (L/5563 *BISD* 30S/101).

GATT, *Agricultural Protection: Second Report of Committee II* (L/1192 *BISD* 9S/110) adopted on 20 May 1960.

GATT, *Agricultural Protection: Third Report of Committee II* (L/1461 *BISD* 10S/135) adopted on 15 November 1961.

GATT, *Draft Final Act Embodying the Results of the Uruguay Round of Multilateral Trade Negotiations* (MTN.TNC/W/FA) 20 December 1991.

GATT, *First Report of Committee II* (COM.II/5 *BISD* 8S/125) adopted on 29 May 1959.

GATT, *Framework Agreement on Agriculture Reform Programme: Draft Text by the Chairman* (GATT Doc. MTN.GNG/NG5/W/170).

GATT, *Guiding Principles to Be Followed in Considering Applications for Waivers,* (L/532 *BISD* 5S/25) adopted on 1 November 1956.

GATT, *Improvements to the GATT Dispute Settlement Rules and Procedures* (*BISD* 36S/61) adopted on 12 April 1989.

GATT, *Mid-Term Meeting*, GATT Doc. MTN.TNC/11 (Special Distribution) 21 April 1989.

GATT, *Ministerial Declaration on the Uruguay Round* (MIN.DEC). adopted in Punta del Este, Uruguay, on 20 September 1986, reproduced in, *GATT Focus Newsletter*, No. 41, (October 1986).

GATT, *Modalities for the Establishment of Specific Binding Commitments under the Reform Programme* (MTN.GNG/MA/W/24 20) Dec. 1993.

GATT, *Opening Statement Made by Dr. Julio Maria Sanguinetti, President of the Oriental Republic of Uruguay, at the GATT Ministerial Meeting in Punta del Este* (MIN(86)/1) 15 September 1986.

GATT, *Operation of the Provisions of Article XVI,* Report of the GATT Panel on Subsidies (L/1442 & Add. 1-2, *BISD* 10S/201) adopted on 21 November 1961.

GATT, *Other Barriers to Trade,* Working Party Report (L/334, and Addendum, *BISD* 3S/222) adopted on 3 March 1955.

GATT, *Report of the Group on Quantitative Restrictions and other Non-Tariff Barriers* (L/5713 *BISD* 31S/212) adopted on 30 November 1984.

GATT, *Report of the Working Party on United States Import Restrictions on Agricultural Products,* (L/5569 *BISD* 30S/222) adopted on 9 March 1983.

GATT, *Report on the Review Pursuant to Article XVI:5* (L/1160, *BISD* 9S/188) adopted on 24 May 1960.

GATT, *Second Report of the Group of Experts on Anti-Dumping and Countervailing Duties* (L/1141 *BISD* 9S/194) adopted on 27 May 1960.

GATT, *Statement by Mr. A. Dunkel, Director-General, to the Punta del Este Ministerial Conference* (MIN(86)/5) 15 September 1986.

GATT, Sub-Committee on Institutional, Procedural and Legal Matters of the Preparatory Committee for the World Trade Organization, *Terms of Reference for the WTO Committee on Agriculture as Agreed by the Sub-Committee at Its Meeting on 7 October 1994* (PC/IPL/1) 14 October 1994.

GATT, *The Mid-Term Review Agreement* (MTN.TNC/11) 21 April 1989.

GATT, *Thirty-Eighth Session at Ministerial Level: Ministerial Declaration* (L/5424 *BISD* 29S/9-22) adopted on 29 November 1982.

GATT, *Waiver Granted to the United States in Connection with Import Restrictions Imposed under Section 22 of the United States Agriculture Adjustment Act (of 1993) as Amended, Decision of 5 March 1955, BISD* 3S/32.

International Law Commission, *Yearbook of the International Law Commission* Vol. II (A/CN.4/SER.A/1966/Add.1) (1966).

Ricupero, R. *Report of the Secretary-General of UNCTAD to UNCTAD X* (TD/390), Bangkok, 12-19 February, 2000.

UN World Food Council, *The Consequences for Food Security of the Multilateral Trade Negotiations in the Uruguay Round: Report by the Secretariat* (WFC/1991/4) April 1991.

UNCTAD, *Identification of New Trading Opportunities Arising from the Implementation of the Uruguay Round Agreements in Selected Sectors and Markets: Report by the UNCTAD Secretariat* (Distr. General TD/B/WG.8/2) 19 June 1995.

United States, *Submission of the United States on Comprehensive Long-Term Agricultural Reform* (GATT Doc. No. MTN.GNG/NG5/W/118) 25 October 1989.

Vienna Convention on the Law of Treaties (done at Vienna, 23 May 1969, 1155 U.N.T.S. 33)

WTO Committee on Agriculture, *Annual Monitoring Exercise in Respect of the Follow-Up to the Ministerial Decision on Measures Concerning the Possible Negative Effects of the Reform Programme on Least-Developed and Net Food-Importing Developing Countries* (G/AG/GEN/40) 19 November 1999.

WTO Committee on Agriculture, *Annual Monitoring Exercise in Respect of the Follow-Up to the Ministerial Decision on Measures Concerning the Possible Negative Effects of the Reform Programme on Least-Developed and Net Food-Importing Developing Countries* (G/AG/GEN/15) December 1997.

WTO Committee on Agriculture, *Communication from the Executive Director of the International Grains Council Presented to the 19-20 March 1998 Meeting of the Committee on Agriculture* (G/AG/GEN/20) 24 March 1998.

WTO Committee on Agriculture, *Compliance With Notification Obligations "Overdue Notifications": Discussion Paper by the United States* (G/AG/W/33) 11 June 1998.

WTO Committee on Agriculture, *Decision by the Committee on Agriculture at Its Meeting on 21 November 1995 Relating to the Establishment of a List of WTO Net Food-Importing Developing Countries for the Purposes of the Marrakesh Ministerial Decision on Measures Concerning the Possible Negative Effects of the Reform Programme on the Least Developed and Net Food-Importing Developing Countries ("The Decision")* (G/AG/3) 24 November 1995.

WTO Committee on Agriculture, *Implementation of the Decision on Measures Concerning the Possible Negative Effects of the Reform Programme on Least-Developed and Net Food-Importing Developing Countries* (G/AG/W/42) 10 February 1999.

WTO Committee on Agriculture, *Issues Regarding Export Subsidy Notifications: Discussion Paper By Australia* (G/AG/W/37) 12 November 1998.

WTO Committee on Agriculture, *List of "Significant Exporters" for the Purposes of the Notification Requirements in Respect of Export Subsidy Commitments: Addendum* (G/AG/2/Add.1) 16 October 1995.

WTO Committee on Agriculture, *Notification Requirements and Formats* (G/AG/2) 30 June, 1995.

WTO Committee on Agriculture, *Organization of Work and Working Procedures of the Committee on Agriculture* (G/AG/1) 28 March 1995.

WTO Committee on Agriculture, *Preparatory Work Programme in Respect of Paragraph 3(i) and 3(ii) of the Marrakesh Ministerial Decision on Measures Concerning the Possible Negative Effects of the Reform Programme on Least-Developed and Net Food-Importing Developing Countries* (G/AG/W/20) 14 March 1996.

WTO Committee on Agriculture, *Report by the Committee on Agriculture on the Marrakesh Ministerial Decision on Measures Concerning the Possible Negative Effects of the Reform Programme on Least-Developed and Net Food-Importing Developing Countries: Report for the Singapore Ministerial Conference* (G/L/125) 24 October 1996.

WTO Committee on Agriculture, *Special Agricultural Safeguard: Background Paper by the Secretariat* (G/AG/NG/S/9) 6 June 2000.

WTO Committee on Agriculture, *Statement by the Observer from the Food and Agriculture Organization Presented to the 25–26 March 1999 Meeting of the Committee on Agriculture* (G/AG/GEN/36) 31 March 1999.

WTO Committee on Agriculture, *Statement by the Representative of the FAO to a*

Meeting of the Committee on Agriculture on 20-21 November 1997 (WTO G/AG/GEN/15).

WTO Committee on Agriculture, *Statement by the Representative of the OECD* (G/AG/GEN/40) 19 November 1999.

WTO Committee on Agriculture, *Statement by the Representative of the World Food Programme (WFP) to a Meeting of the Committee on Agriculture on 20–21 November 1997* (G/AG/GEN/15).

WTO Committee on Agriculture, *Summary of the Statement by the Representative of the Food and Agriculture Organization to the Meeting of the Committee on Agriculture on 20–21 November 1997* (G/AG/GEN/15) 18 December 1997.

WTO Committee on Agriculture, *Summary Report of the Meeting Held on 27–28 March 1995* (G/AG/R/1).

WTO Committee on Agriculture, *Summary Report of the Meeting Held on 28–29 September 1995* (G/AG/R/3).

WTO Committee on Agriculture, *Summary Report of the Meeting Held on 20–21 November 1995* (G/AG/R/4).

WTO Committee on Agriculture, *Summary Report of the Meeting Held on 26-27 June 1997* (G/AG/R/11).

WTO Committee on Agriculture, *Summary Report of the Meeting Held on 20-21 Nov., 1997* (G/AG/R/13).

WTO Committee on Agriculture, *Summary Report of the Meeting Held on 25–26 Sept. 1997* (G/AG/R/12).

WTO Committee on Agriculture, *Summary Report of the Meeting Held on 24–25 Sept. 1996* (G/AG/R/6).

WTO Committee on Agriculture, *Summary Report of the Meeting Held on 28 Nov. 1996* (G/AG/R/9).

WTO Committee on Agriculture, *Summary Report of the Meeting Held on 25–26 March 1999* (G/AG/R/18) 7 May 1999

WTO Committee on Agriculture, *Summary Report of the Meeting Held on 19–20 March 1998* (G/AG/R/14) 30 April 1998.

WTO Committee on Agriculture, *Summary Report of the Meeting Held on 17-18 November 1998* (G/AG/R/17) 25 January 1999

WTO Committee on Agriculture, *Summary Report of the Meeting Held on 25–26 June 1998: Note by the Secretariat* (G/AG/R/15).

WTO Committee on Agriculture, *WTO List of Net Food-Importing Developing Countries for the Purposes of the Marrakesh Ministerial Decision on Measures Concerning the Possible Negative Effects of the Reform Programme on Least-Developed and Net Food-Importing Developing Countries* (G/AG/5) 3 April 1996.

WTO Committee on Agriculture, *WTO Room Document, Compliance with Notification Obligations*, 19–20 March 1998.

WTO Council for Trade in Goods, *Hungary – Agricultural Export Subsidies* (G/L/183) 6 October 1997.

WTO Dispute Settlement Body, *Hungary – Export Subsidies in Respect of Agricultural Products: Request for Consultations by Argentina, Australia, Canada, New Zealand, Thailand and the United States* (WT/DS35/1, G/L/70, G/AG/W/23) 2 April 1996.

WTO General Council, *Decision-Making Procedures Under Articles IX and XII of the WTO Agreement as Agreed by the General Council on 15 November 1995* (WT/L/93).

WTO General Council, *Hungary – Agreement On Agriculture: Decision Of 22 October 1997* (WT/L/238) 29 October 1997.

WTO General Council, *Hungary – Report of the Government of Hungary under the Decision of 22 October 1997* (WT/L/290) 27 November 1998.

WTO General Council, *Hungary – Report of the Government of Hungary under the Decision of 22 October 1997: Addendum* (WT/L/290/Add.1) 17 February 1999.

WTO, *Agriculture Negotiations, 23–24 March 2000 Talks Reach Swift Agreement On "Phase 1"* (Press/172, 27 March 2000).

WTO, *The results of the Uruguay Round of Multilateral Trade Negotiations: the Legal Texts* (1995).

WTO, *WTO Services and Agriculture Negotiations: Meetings Set for February and March* (Press/167) 7 February 2000.

INDEX